4e

Introduction to
BUSINESS

FLORIDA ATLANTIC UNIVERSITY

THOMSON
—— ✳ ——
SOUTH-WESTERN

Australia · Brazil · Canada · Mexico · Singapore · Spain · United Kingdom · United States

THOMSON

SOUTH-WESTERN

Introduction to Business, Fourth Edition
Jeff Madura

VP/Editorial Director:
Jack W. Calhoun

Sr. Publisher:
Melissa S. Acuña

Developmental Editor:
Rebecca von Gillern

Marketing Manager:
Nicole C. Moore

Production Project Manager:
Amy McGuire

Manager of Technology, Editorial:
Vicky True

Technology Project Editor:
Kristen Meere

Web Coordinator:
Karen Schaffer

Sr. Manufacturing Coordinator:
Diane Lohman

Production House:
G & S Typesetters

Printer:
Transcontinental Interglobe
Beauceville, QC

Art Director:
Stacy Jenkins Shirley

Internal Designer:
Knapke Design
Mason, OH

Cover Designer:
Knapke Design
Mason, OH

Cover Images:
© Getty Image

Photography Manager:
Deanna Ettinger

Photo Researcher:
Charlotte Goldman

Cartoonist:
Bob Burchett

Student Edition ISBN 0-324-40711-4
Instructor's Edition ISBN 0-324-36080-0

Library of Congress Control Number:
2005937623

For more information about our products,
contact us at:

Thomson Learning Academic
Resource Center
1-800-423-0563

Thomson Higher Education
5191 Natorp Boulevard
Mason, OH 45040
USA

To Mary

Brief Contents

Contents

Chapter 2 Business Ethics and Social Responsibility   36

Chapter 3 Assessing Economic Conditions   72

Part II
Starting a New Business   157

Chapter 5 Selecting a Form of Business Ownership   158

Chapter 6 Entrepreneurship and Business Planning   190

Part III
Management   239

Chapter 7 Managing Effectively   240

Chapter 8 Organizational Structure   276

Part IV
Managing Employees   361

Chapter 10 Motivating Employees   362

Chapter 11 Hiring, Training, and Evaluating Employees 396

Part V
Marketing   447

Chapter 12 Creating and Pricing Products   448

Chapter 14 Promoting Products   526

Part VI
Financial Management   565

Chapter 15 Accounting and Financial Analysis   566

Chapter 16 Financing   598

Chapter 17 Expanding the Business   640

Preface

Welcome to this Introduction to Business course! This course can have a major impact on your career direction and future success regardless of whether you major in business, the sciences, or the liberal arts. Whatever your major may be, you are likely to end up pursuing a career in a business setting. For example, if you major in science, you may work for a biotechnology firm and can benefit from an understanding of business concepts such as managing an organization, working with employees, and managing employees. If you select journalism as a major, you may work for a media or publishing firm and, therefore, can benefit from an understanding of business concepts such as providing a product desired by consumers. Business concepts such as creating ideas, leadership, teamwork, and quality control are relevant to almost everyone, no matter what career is chosen.

An Introduction to Business course provides the foundation of business knowledge that can enable you to utilize your talents in the business world. It also provides you with an overview of many different business topics, allowing you to determine the specific field of business (management, marketing, etc.) you would like to pursue.

What Makes This Text Unique?

Approach and Focus

▶ Focus on a business plan and decision making

▶ Focus on key concepts

New and Enhanced Content

▶ All updated content

▶ Expanded coverage of topics

▶ New *Decision Making* feature

Engaging Pedagogy

▶ Value-added student tutorials

▶ Small business applications

▶ Valuation emphasis

▶ Practical applications and team-building exercises

▶ Focus on learning skills endorsed by AACSB and SCANS

▶ Reinforcement of key concepts

Students Supplements Package

▶ Xtra!

▶ Website

Approach and Focus

Focus on a Business Plan and Decision Making

This new edition focuses on the managerial perspective of running a business so that you are constantly put in the position of experiencing the dilemmas and tradeoffs involved with decision making. The first chapter provides a brief overview of business planning for all functions of a business. This overview serves as an outline for the text. In each chapter, the key concepts are applied to a business so that you will recognize how the concepts are used to make business decisions.

Each part of the text represents a key component of the business plan. Part I explains the key functions of a business, the ethical and social responsibilities of a business, and its exposure to the economic and global environment. Part II describes how the business determines its form of organization and its business plan. Parts III and IV focus on the management of a business, while Part V focuses on marketing, and Part VI explains the financial management of the business.

Focus on Key Concepts

This textbook will prepare you for the business world by focusing on business concepts, without dwelling on definitions. Its application of business concepts to decision making allows you to appreciate the dilemmas faced by businesses. Some of the key business concepts include the following:

▶ How the objectives of a firm's managers may conflict with those of its stockholders.

▶ How a firm's executives frequently face ethical dilemmas.

▶ How a firm's decision to expand may be dependent on economic conditions.

▶ How a firm's decision to expand overseas may depend on the foreign competition.

▶ How compensation schemes to motivate managers sometimes backfire.

▶ How a firm's product quality can be measured through feedback from customers.

▶ How a firm can use the Internet to improve its marketing.

▶ How a firm's financing decisions can affect its risk.

▶ How the decisions made within the various departments of a business are integrated.

New and Enhanced Content

All Updated Content

The text has been completely revised and designed to emphasize events and technology changes that have had a major impact on businesses over the past year. More attention is given to business ethics as a result of the Enron and WorldCom scandals and reports that some executives have mis-led employees and stockholders about the financial condition of their firms. This text covers the responsibilities of firms to their employees and stockholders and emphasizes the recent conflicts between executives and the stockholders of some firms. It also explains the controls that firms should establish to ensure that executives behave in a manner that serves the firm's employees and stockholders rather than themselves.

Expanded Coverage of Topics

The following business concepts have become more crucial to the success of a business over time and, therefore, are given extra attention in this new edition:

▶ E-commerce

▶ E-marketing

▶ Conflicts of interest between managers and subordinates and strategies to resolve those conflicts

▶ Entrepreneurship

▶ Supply chain management

▶ The merging of Internet businesses with traditional businesses

▶ The euro

This edition provides comprehensive treatment of key business topics while also addressing exciting, current topics. Every effort has been made to create a balance by providing enough coverage of important concepts without overburdening you with information that is covered in subsequent business courses.

New *Decision Making* Feature

This edition includes a new feature called *Decision Making*. Each chapter introduces a specific firm that must make decisions related to the material in the chapter. Then at the end of each section of the chapter, the *Decision Making* feature illustrates how that firm makes decisions related to the key concept described in that section. At the end of the chapter, the firm's decisions regarding the key concepts in the chapter are summarized to illustrate how they are related.

Engaging Pedagogy

This new edition of the text includes many features designed specifically to help you retain the information you will be learning. Studies show that learning new concepts in different ways is the best way to retain what you have learned. With this in mind, the following elements have been included in every chapter of the text to help every student retain the concepts covered.

Value-Added Student Tutorials

In-Text Study Guide
The *In-Text Study Guide* serves as a study guide *without the additional cost.* Segments focus on test preparation, with at least 10 true/false and 25 multiple-choice questions per chapter. Answers to these questions, along with references to the pages where the answers can be found, are provided in Appendix C of the text.

Self-Scoring Exercises
Self-Scoring Exercises are provided throughout the text to prepare students for the business world. These exercises allow students to discover their own strengths and weaknesses when making business decisions.

Small Business Applications

Continuing Example of College Health Club
College Health Club presents dilemmas faced by the owner, Sue Kramer, a young entrepreneur. Students can put themselves in Sue's position and figure out how they would resolve the various dilemmas she encounters when managing her small business. Students' problem-solving skills and critical thinking abilities are strengthened as they learn some of the challenges and potential rewards of owning a small business. *College Health Club* also increases the relevance of chapter material by demonstrating how concepts discussed in each chapter are applied to making real-world business decisions.

It's Your Decision
This end-of-chapter exercise gives students an opportunity to provide their opinions and advice on how the small business, College Health Club (discussed in every chapter), should be managed. Questions prompt the students to make managerial decisions for College Health Club involving issues discussed in the chapter.

Small Business Survey

Small Business Survey provides a reality-based picture of small business decision making. The surveys cover various topics, including the typical background of board members and how CEOs of small businesses use their time to manage employees.

Campus.com

Students are put in the position of owners of a small business called *Campus.com,* which sells information about college campuses to prospective students over the Internet. They are asked to make decisions about how to apply business concepts covered within each part of the text. By the end of the semester, they will have completed a business plan for this small business. Students can utilize the *Business Plan* templates found in *Xtra!* to build their business plan. This project offers students the opportunity to work in teams and to develop their communication skills by sharing their ideas with their team or with the class.

Running Your Own Business

An alternative business plan project is the *Running Your Own Business* project. Students are allowed to create their own business idea. At the end of each part of the text, students are guided step-by-step through issues and decisions they would face in running their own business. They develop a business plan as they go through the chapters of the text. At the end of the school term, students can convert their accumulated answers into a formal business plan. Students can utilize the accompanying *Business Plan* found in *Xtra!* to build their business plan. This exercise also enables students to improve their writing and speaking skills as they learn to communicate their ideas.

Business Plan

Business Plan templates both the *Campus.com* and *Running Your Own Business* end-of-part projects can be found in *Xtra!*. These templates provide pre-designed documents that students can fill in as they complete their business plans for these projects.

Cases

Short cases present real-world scenarios for students to analyze and make decisions about the direction of a business. The cases cover businesses such as Ben & Jerry's and Yahoo!

End-of-Chapter Video Cases

Video cases at the end of each chapter bring a real business into the classroom. Students can discuss the situation faced by the business and analyze the results of the action the business decided to take.

End-of-Part Integrative Video Cases

Two *end-of-part integrative video case* illustrates how key concepts of chapters within each part are integrated. The end-of-part exercises that accompany these videos help students "pull it all together." These video cases are also available digitized *Xtra!* so that students can view them in or out of class.

Valuation Emphasis

Dell's Secret to Success

Dell's Secret to Success at the end of each chapter enables students to recognize how a real firm's business decisions affect its value, and therefore affect the return to its shareholders. Specific questions challenge students to learn firsthand how Dell relies on key business concepts covered in this text.

The Stock Market Game

This end-of-part feature puts students in the position of shareholders. Each student selects a stock in which he or she would like to invest, tracks the firm's stock price throughout the school term, and investigates how that firm manages its business operations. Students learn how to retrieve the annual report of their firm and find news stories about it. This exercise can be done individually or in teams. It allows students to

▶ witness how a firm's value is affected by its decisions;

▶ monitor the change in the stock's price over the school term so that they can determine which stock performs the best over the term; and

▶ develop analytical and communication skills by explaining the relationship between the firm's decisions and the stock's value over the semester.

See page 30 at the end of Chapter 1 for an introduction to the Stock Market Game and instructions to get started.

Investing in a Business

This end-of-chapter feature sends students to the websites of real companies to research and answer questions about how the chapter concepts can affect the firm's business. This exercise shows students how they can learn more about a firm by exploring its website. *Xtra!* includes a flash presentation, which guides students through this exercise by using Krispy Kreme as an example and demonstrating where information can be found on that company's website.

Practical, Real-World Applications and Team-Building Exercises

Your Career in Business

Each part of the text concludes with a section that helps students better understand various business majors and professions and think about the career they might pursue. Through these sections, students will learn about various business majors offered by colleges and universities that relate directly to each part. They will also become familiar with the primary emphasis of the courses that are required for each business major. Students will also learn about the various careers that they can pursue depending on their particular major, including a job description and the salary range.

In addition, a new *Careers Prologue* offers practical advice to help students get the most our of their college courses, choose a career, and apply for a job. It includes information on where to look for jobs, tips on how to create a résumé, and advice on how to prepare for a job interview.

Cross Functional Teamwork

Cross Functional Teamwork boxes explain the need for managers of different functional areas to make decisions as a team in order to increase a firm's value. These features illustrate to students how and why various areas need to work together.

Global Business

Global Business boxes in each chapter show how global realities affect every area of business. The features emphasize how decisions to pursue international opportunities can enhance a firm's value.

Focus on Learning Skills Endorsed by AACSB and SCANS

This text offers several features and exercises that allow students to build the learning skills that are endorsed by the American Association of Collegiate Schools of Business (AACSB) and by the Secretary's Commission on Achieving Necessary Skills (SCANS). In particular, this text emphasizes the development of four skills:

▶ Decision making and planning

▶ Teamwork

▶ Technology

▶ Communication

Decision making is emphasized in every chapter and is the focus of the new *Decision Making* feature. Teamwork is emphasized in the *Cross Functional Teamwork* feature. The role of technology in business is discussed in every chapter, and an updated technology appendix describes new technological developments and their impact on business.

All four of the skills are emphasized in the exercises. For example, students are challenged to be creative by forming their own business idea. The cases and other end-of-chapter exercises frequently put students in positions where they must make business decisions. Various exercises allow teams so that students can work together to resolve business dilemmas. Some of the exercises require students to communicate their views through a written report or a presentation.

Reinforcement of Key Concepts

Many of the features just described reinforce the key concepts in each chapter. This leads to better understanding on the part of the student. In turn, instructors have more flexibility to focus on current events and class discussions.

To illustrate how this text can ensure a clear understanding through reinforcement, consider the concept of making a decision on how to promote a product, which is discussed in Chapter 14. The *Small Business Survey* feature in that chapter discusses the opinions of small business owners about the skills that are necessary to be successful in sales. The *Global Business* feature in that chapter examines the decisions the health club owner must make as she considers various strategies to promote its services. The *Investing in a Business* exercise in that chapter asks students to determine how the firm that they decided to invest in at the beginning of the term promotes its products. The *Case* in that chapter illustrates the decisions involved in promoting a product on a website. The *Video Case* illustrates promotion strategies for Oxygen. The *Dell's Secret to Success* feature in that chapter explains Dell's promotion strategy. Finally, the *In-Text Study Guide* in that chapter allows students to test their understanding of promotion strategies. Students are consistently empowered to make decisions as if they were managers of a firm.

Every key concept in the text can be reinforced with one or more of the text features just described. Thus, instructors have a variety of features available to them and may choose to emphasize different features to reinforce each concept.

Student Supplements Package

Xtra!

Designed as an electronic student tutorial, *Xtra!* include the digitized Video Cases, self-assessment quiz questions. Flashcards with key terms from each chapter, a PowerPoint® presentation, Business Company and Resource Center infomarks and questions, and the *Business Plan* templates tied to both the *Campus.com* and *Running Your Own Business* in as they complete their business plans for these projects.

Website

A text support website at **http://madura.swlearning.com** offers many resources for both instructors and students. Instructors can access downloadable supplement materials, while students can access interactive quizzes, chapter links, career-related links, and updated information for the Dell Annual Report Project.

Acknowledgments

The author and the entire Thomson publishing team are grateful to the reviewers whose feedback was so important to the success of this current edition. They are:

Kenneth Armstrong
Anderson University

David Oliver
Edison College

Marvin Recht
Butler University

Charlane Held
Onondaga Community College

Jude Rathburn
University of Wisconsin, River Falls

Dennis Shannon
Southwestern Illinois College

Ralph Jagodka
Mt. San Antonio College

We also are very grateful to the supplement preparers listed below:

Ralph Jagodka
Mt. San Antonio College

Andrea McKeon
Florida Community College

Finally, the author wishes to express his gratitude to the publishing team at South-Western who helped to ensure a quality final product:

Melissa Acuña
Senior Publisher

Nicole Moore
Marketing Manager

Stacy Shirley
Art Director

Rebecca von Gillern
Developmental Editor

Amy McGuire
Production Project Manager

And a special thanks to Kimberly Gleason, Julia Knispel, and Diana Murphy for their excellent contribution to the text and supplements package.

About the Author

Jeff Madura is the SunTrust Professor of Finance at Florida Atlantic University. Among his many publications are several other textbooks, including *International Financial Management* and *Financial Markets and Institutions*. His articles on business have appeared in numerous journals, including *Journal of Financial and Quantitative Analysis, Journal of Banking and Finance, Journal of Business Research, Financial Review, Journal of Financial Research, Columbia Journal of World Business, Journal of International Money and Finance,* and *Journal of Business Strategies*. He has received awards for teaching and research and has served as a consultant for many businesses. He has served as Director for the Southern Finance Association and the Eastern Finance Association and has also served as President of the Southern Finance Association.

Part I

Business Environment

A business is created to provide products or services to customers. If it can conduct its operations effectively, its owners earn a reasonable return on their investment in the firm. In addition, it creates jobs for employees. Thus, businesses can be beneficial to society in various ways. The first step in understanding how businesses operate is to recognize their most important functions and the environment in which they operate. Part I, which contains Chapters 1 through 4, provides this background. A business must understand the environment in which it operates in order to be successful.

Chapter 1 describes the motives of people to create a business, identifies the stakeholders (participants) involved in a business, and explains the most important functions of a business. Chapter 2 describes the responsibility of a business toward all of its stakeholders and to its social environment. It also explains how the firm can improve its performance by acting responsibly toward its stakeholders. Chapter 3 explains how a business is exposed to economic conditions and how it adapts its operations in response to these conditions. Chapter 4 explains how a business is exposed to global conditions and how it adapts its operations in response to these conditions. In general, businesses are exposed to the business environment. But some businesses are more successful than others because they make better decisions in response to changes in the business environment.

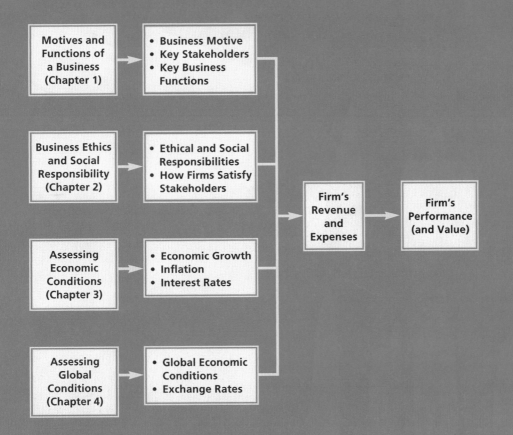

Chapter

1

GETTY IMAGES

DVD rental shops like this one have been established by entrepreneurs to satisfy customers and generate profits.

Motives and Functions of a Business

A business (or firm) is an enterprise that provides products or services desired by customers. According to the U.S. Labor Department, more than 800,000 businesses are created in the United States every year. Along with large, well-known businesses such as The Coca-Cola Company and IBM, there are many smaller businesses that provide employment opportunities and produce products or services that satisfy customers. What do Alicia Keys, a casino, a DVD rental firm, your local dentist, the New York Yankees organization, your plumber, and your favorite restaurant have in common? They are all businesses that provide products or services desired by customers.

Consider a business called 4 Eyes DVD that is being created as an outlet for DVD rentals desired by customers. Some of the more important decisions are:

- Is it is worthwhile to create this business?
- What resources does this business need to provide its services?
- What types of stakeholders must this business attempt to satisfy?
- What are the key functions that managers must perform to manage this business?
- What characteristics in the business environment must the managers monitor?

All businesses must make these types of decisions, whether they provide DVD rentals, produce computers, offer dentistry services, or build houses.

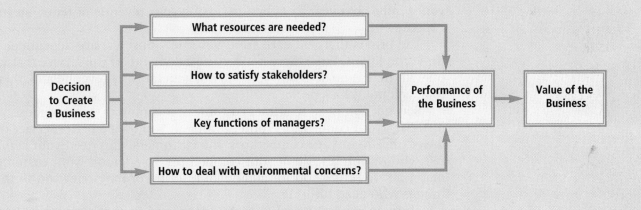

The Goal of a Business

1

Explain the goal of a business.

What is the goal of a business? Businesses are established to serve the needs of consumers by owners who seek to make profits. The people who create a business may see an opportunity to produce a product or service that is not already being offered by other firms. Alternatively, they may believe that they can produce a product or service that they can sell for a lower price than existing firms. By providing a product that is desired by customers, they may be able to make profits for their business.

Where the Profits Come From

Businesses such as Dell, Gap, Ford Motor Company, and Motorola were created to provide products to customers. Businesses such as Southwest Airlines and Hilton Hotels were created to provide services to customers. Other service firms include dentists, hairstylists, travel agencies, insurance companies, tax services, and law firms. Some firms, such as AT&T, Microsoft, and IBM, provide both products and services to customers. Managing a service business can be just as challenging and rewarding as managing a business that produces products.

A business receives revenue when it sells its products or services. It incurs expenses from paying its employees and when it purchases machinery or facilities. The difference between the revenue and the expenses is the profit (or earnings) generated by the business. The profits go to the owners of the business. Thus, owners who create a business have a strong incentive to ensure that it is successful, as they are directly rewarded for their efforts.

For example, assume that you have decided to offer to tutor other students in the basics of developing a website because you know that many students would be willing to pay for this service. During this year, you receive $5,000 from students for tutoring, and you pay a total of $1,000 in expenses to advertise your service in the college newspaper. Your profit is shown below:

$$\begin{array}{ll} \text{Revenue} & \$5{,}000 \\ -\ \underline{\text{Expenses}} & -\ \underline{\$1{,}000} \\ =\ \text{Profit} & =\ \$4{,}000 \end{array}$$

Since you are the only owner of this business, all the profits go to you, although you may be taxed on the profits that you earn. You can increase your profits next year by either increasing your revenue or reducing your expenses.

The profits that you earn from your new business are dependent on three conditions. First, there needs to be a demand for the service that you offer. If there is no demand, you will not generate any revenue and, therefore, will not earn a profit.

Second, you need to attract customers, meaning that they choose you instead of your competitors (other tutors). If you offer a better service or a lower price than your competitors, the customers who need your service may choose you instead of your competitors. In addition, your customers may want to rehire you for additional tutoring or may refer you to their friends who need tutoring.

Third, to earn high profits, you need to keep your expenses low. If you can run your business efficiently, your expenses should be relatively low, and you will be rewarded with higher profits. Although most businesses are more complicated than the business just described, their performance is also dependent on these three conditions.

Profit as a Motive to Understand Business

If you develop a good understanding of business, you may be more capable of creating and running a successful business, and you will be directly rewarded with higher profits. Yet, even if you never plan to run your own business, you may profit from understanding how a business operates.

First, if you develop strong business skills, you may be able to obtain a better job. Second, you are likely to find your job more enjoyable if you understand how job tasks are related to the firm and its industry. Third, you should be able to perform better, which could result in a more satisfying career path. Fourth, if you ever invest in businesses, you may be better able to identify the types of businesses that are likely to perform well. As a result, you may invest your money wisely and enjoy higher returns on your investments. Thus, you can still profit from understanding business even if you do not own a business.

How the Profit Motive Is Influenced by the Government

In the United States and most other countries, people are free to start businesses and profit from them. Countries such as the United States, in which people can create their own businesses to serve the preferences and needs of consumers, have a free-market economy. Governments of free-market economies recognize the advantages of allowing business ownership. Not only do businesses serve consumers, but by creating work for the business owners and employees, they also reduce the country's unemployment.

In socialistic countries such as the former Soviet Union, businesses were typically owned by the government and were not profit oriented. Without the prospect of earning a profit, most people could not afford to create a business and had to find some alternative form of work to earn an income. Furthermore, without a profit motive, businesses had no incentive to produce products that satisfy consumers' needs. Consequently, consumers were not able to obtain some products that they desired. In the last several years, many governments in these countries have sold the former government businesses to private owners and also are allowing people to start new businesses. In most countries, individuals are now allowed to own businesses, although some governments provide more incentives than others to encourage individuals to create new businesses.

Many hospitals are nonprofit but must still manage their resources properly to provide good customer service and to use their funds properly.

nonprofit organization
an organization that serves a specific cause and is not intended to make profits

GETTY IMAGES

Nonprofit Businesses

Not all business are created to make a profit. A **nonprofit organization** is an organization that serves a specific cause and is not intended to make profits. When its revenue exceeds its expenses in a particular period, the profits are reinvested in the organization. In the United States, a nonprofit organization is not taxed as long as it qualifies by meeting specific requirements established by the Internal Revenue Service. Common examples of nonprofit organizations include some hospitals, schools, charitable organizations, and churches.

Although a nonprofit organization is not totally focused on

Decision Making

Decisions to Create a Business

Consider the situation of 4 Eyes DVD, which was introduced at the beginning of the chapter. Juan Gomez initially created this business because he knew that customers in his town wanted to rent DVDs. Second, he believed that he could offer a much wider selection of DVDs and at a lower price than the only other DVD rental outlet in town. Third, he believed that he could keep his expenses low by renting space in a busy strip mall that is centrally located and easily accessible. The competitor's DVD rental outlet is in a very exclusive shopping mall at the north end of town. Consequently, its rent is very high, and its location is convenient only for the wealthy people who live in that area.

1. Explain how 4 Eyes DVD could generate more profits as a result of having an easily accessible central location rather than being in the exclusive shopping mall at one end of town.

2. Last month, 4 Eyes DVD generated revenue of $15,000 and had total expenses of $9,000. Determine its profit level for last month.

ANSWERS: 1. It should be able to generate a large volume of rentals in a busy, easily accessible section of town, which results in high revenue. It also has a lower rent expense than if it were in the mall. 2. Its profits are based on revenue minus expenses, or $15,000 − $9,000 = $6,000.

making profits, it is still run like a business. For example, consider the business of a nonprofit hospital. It charges prices for its services just like a for-profit hospital. The hospital will still bill the patient's insurance for services rendered and bill the patient for any amounts not paid by the insurance company. If the hospital provided all of its services for free, it would quickly use up all the funds that were donated to finance it as well as any accumulated profits it had generated. Its employees earn salaries just like the employees of for-profit hospitals. If the hospital does not pay competitive salaries, its doctors, nurses, and other staff will seek employment elsewhere. Thus, it must provide its health-care services in an efficient manner, or it will not have adequate funding to stay in business and continue to serve the community. Like for-profit hospitals, if it wants to expand and needs more money than it has received from donations or accumulated over time, the hospital may even obtain financing from creditors.

Resources Used to Produce Products or Services

Identify the resources a business uses to produce a product or service.

To produce a product or service, firms rely on the following factors of production:

▶ Natural resources

▶ Human resources

▶ Capital

▶ Entrepreneurship

Natural Resources

natural resources
any resources that can be used in their natural form

Natural resources include any resources that can be used in their natural form. The most obvious natural resource that is commonly used by businesses to produce products or services is land. Agricultural businesses rely on land to grow crops. Other businesses rely on land to establish a site for their production.

Human Resources

human resources
people who are able to perform work for a business

Human resources are the people who are able to perform work for a business. They may contribute to production by using their physical abilities, such as working in a factory to construct a product. Alternatively, they may contribute by using their mental abilities, such as proposing a change in the existing production process or motivating other workers.

Capital

capital
machinery, equipment, tools, and physical facilities used by a business

Capital includes machinery, equipment, tools, and physical facilities. All of these types of capital are commonly used by human resources to produce products. Physical facilities are typically necessary to produce many services as well as products. Especially in recent years, technology has enabled businesses to use their capital more effectively.

technology
knowledge or tools used to produce products and services

How Technology Has Helped Businesses Improve Their Capital   **Technology** can be defined as knowledge or tools used to produce products or services. The Internet is an obvious example of technology. By using technology to improve their capital, many businesses are able to produce products and services more quickly and at a higher quality. Thus, they are better able to meet the needs of consumers.

information technology
technology that enables information to be used to produce products and services

An important subset of technology, **information technology,** involves the use of information to produce products and services. It includes the use of computers to transfer information among departments within a firm and the use of the Internet to provide customers with information. Information technology accounts for only about 8 percent of the total output produced in the United States, but it represents more than one-third of the growth in the U.S. output produced. A recent study by the U.S. Commerce Department estimates that about half of all U.S. workers will soon be employed in industries that produce information technology. It also found that information technology has reduced the cost of producing products and resulted in lower prices of products. Furthermore, workers in the technology industries earn about $53,000 per year on average versus $30,000 for workers in other industries.

electronic business (e-business) or electronic commerce (e-commerce)
use of electronic communications, such as the Internet, to produce or sell products and services

A related type of technology is **electronic business (e-business),** also referred to as **electronic commerce (e-commerce),** which is the use of electronic communications to produce or sell products and services.

Amazon receives its orders online and commonly uses its distribution center to accommodate the orders.

CORBIS, CHICAGO

E-business includes both business transactions, such as sales of products over the Internet, and interactions between a firm and its suppliers over the Internet. In fact, many people use the terms *information technology* and *e-commerce* interchangeably.

An example of a successful e-business idea is Amazon.com, which enables customers to purchase books and other products online. Amazon .com's creativity is not the product (books) but an alternative method of reaching customers. Its customers use the Internet to have their book orders delivered to them rather than having to go to a retail bookstore. Several other firms have applied the same idea to their own businesses. Computer firms now sell computers over the Internet, toy manufacturers sell toys over the Internet, and automobile manufacturers sell automobiles over the Internet. Hotels, airlines, and cruiselines allow customers to make reservations over the Internet.

Exhibit 1.1 describes some of the successful firms that have been created to capitalize on e-business. Notice that these businesses started

Exhibit 1.1

Successful Internet Businesses

Business Name	Business Description	How the Business Was Created
1. Amazon.com	This online bookseller is frequently cited as an Internet success story. Customers can purchase books and music and participate in auctions at its website. Amazon's innovative bookselling idea allows the company to offer popular titles at deeply discounted prices due to low overhead costs.	Jeff Bezos founded the company in 1994. Bezos quit his job as vice president of a Wall Street firm, moved to Seattle, and started the business in his garage. When Amazon.com opened for business in July 1995, Bezos himself frequently dropped off the packages at the post office. Bezos's estimated net worth (value of his house and other assets after paying off any debts) is now $10 billion.
2. Yahoo!	This Internet search engine is the most visited site on the Web. It has evolved to offer a wide variety of other products to attract users. Free e-mail, Web page hosting, and custom-designed start-up pages are just a few of the options available. Revenues are generated through advertising sales.	David Filo and Jerry Yang were Ph.D. students at Stanford who had put together an electronic directory of their favorite websites. It was essentially a list of their bookmarks that they titled Yahoo! (which stands for Yet Another Hierarchical Officious Oracle). The site was generating so much traffic that the students dropped out of school and launched their company in 1995. Each of the founders now has a net worth of nearly $4 billion.
3. eBay	eBay is an online auction service that enables users to sell goods to each other. The person-to-person services attract a wide variety of goods, most of them used. Sellers develop a reputation, which creates some level of trust and excuses eBay from any responsibility. The company profits by charging fees based on the sale price.	The company evolved out of a method that Pierre Omidyar devised to help his girlfriend collect Pez candy dispensers. By 1996, the volume of goods traded forced Omidyar to quit his job at General Magic and devote all his time to the company. The company has been profitable since 1996.
4. Google	Google became very popular as a search engine because of its ability to effectively accommodate requests by users who wanted to search the Internet. This substantial reliance on Google meant that Google could sell advertising on its website or charge websites that want to have "sponsored links" displayed by Google in response to specific search terms.	In 1996, Sergey Brin and Larry Page were graduate students in Stanford's computer science department. They were interested in tracking the success of various websites. They then attempted to create a search engine that would account for the popularity of websites when identifying websites that fit search terms. The value in this search engine is that it screened out websites that were less likely to satisfy the search. This led to the creation of Google. On August 18, 2004, Google went public. At that time, Brin and Page still retained ownership of some shares, making their net worth more than $3 billion each.

out very small and were created to offer a product or service that was not being provided by other firms. Thus, these new businesses were created to accommodate the needs or preferences of customers. As these e-businesses were created, many existing firms recognized that they should develop their own e-business to satisfy their customers. Thus, the innovations of some e-businesses transformed the way that all firms conduct business.

Many firms applied e-business to facilitate their existing operations. The Internet allows for easier communication from the firm to the consumer, from the firm to another firm, and from the consumer to the firm. Information flows freely between firms and consumers, avoiding the delays and disrupted business transactions that used to occur when the two parties were not available at the same time to communicate. Firms are also using e-business to complement rather than replace their traditional operations. Consumers who want to use traditional channels to make orders can still do so, while other consumers can communicate their orders electronically. Thus, even if a firm is not classified as an Internet company, it can still use e-business to enhance its value.

Although the use of the Internet to serve consumers has attracted considerable attention, the Internet is also having an important impact on the way businesses serve other businesses (referred to as "business-to-business e-commerce" or "B2B e-commerce"). Business-to-business e-commerce might be used, for example, when a firm needs construction work to repair its facilities, wants an outside firm to conduct seminars to improve relationships among employees, or requires specific supplies for its production process. The firm can request bids online from several businesses that may meet its needs and then select the firm that submits the best bid. This process is much easier and faster than calling various firms and waiting for return phone calls. Furthermore, having to send a message online forces the bidders to specify their bids in writing.

Business-to-business e-commerce has already reduced the expenses associated with transactions between firms and is expected to reduce them even further once all firms take full advantage of the technology. In particular, firms that rely on other businesses for supplies, transportation services, or delivery services can reduce their expenses substantially by using business-to-business e-commerce.

Entrepreneurship

entrepreneurship
the creation of business ideas and the willingness to take risk; the act of creating, organizing, and managing a business

entrepreneurs
people who organize, manage, and assume the risk of starting a business

Entrepreneurship involves the creation of business ideas and the willingness to accept risk. **Entrepreneurs** attempt to identify business opportunities. When they find one, they invest some of their own money to create a business with the expectation that they will earn adequate profits as a reward for their efforts. However, they face the risk that the profits of the business may not be as high as expected. In fact, if expenses exceed revenue, the profits may be negative and the business could fail. In a free-market economy, many businesses may be created within the same industry, which results in intense competition. In this situation, a firm that charges too high a price for its product may fail because customers will switch to its competitors. Similarly, a firm that is not well managed may fail because its expenses are too high. This risk of failure can reduce the motive to create a business.

Entrepreneurs realize that if they overestimate the potential profitability of a business or manage the business poorly, they will lose the money

Out of
Business

Decision Making

How to Use the Factors of Production

Different businesses use the factors of production in different ways. First, 4 Eyes DVD (introduced at the beginning of the chapter) uses natural resources (land) for its business. The decision about natural resources determined the location of the DVD rental outlet. The location decision has an impact on the profits of the business because customers want convenience.

Second, human resources (employees) are needed to decide which DVDs to purchase each week for the purpose of renting them out. The human resources also serve the customers who wish to rent DVDs. The specific human resources who are hired can affect the degree of customer service and therefore the performance of 4 Eyes DVD. If the employees order the proper DVDs, they can enhance the revenue earned from DVD rentals. Therefore, the decision regarding human resources affects the profits of the business.

Third, 4 Eyes DVD needs capital (physical facilities) so that customers can review the selection of DVDs and choose the DVDs they wish to rent. 4 Eyes DVD's decisions about its physical facilities will influence the desirability of its DVD outlet. Those decisions will also affect its cost and, therefore, its profits.

Fourth, the creation of the DVD rental business was due to entrepreneurship. The owner, Juan Gomez, recognized an opportunity to create a business that would serve customers and invested his own money in the business. He may earn a large income from 4 Eyes DVD if it is successful, but he could also lose his entire investment if the business fails. The manner in which this entrepreneur uses the factors of production will determine whether the business will be a success.

1. How will the profits of 4 Eyes DVD be affected if it hires either too many human resources? What if it hires too few human resources (such that customers receive poor service)?

2. How will the profits of 4 Eyes DVD be affected if its physical facilities are too small (such that it does not have room for its selection of DVDs to rent)? What if its physical facilities are much larger than is necessary?

ANSWERS: 1. If it hires too many human resources, its profits will be reduced because its expenses will be excessive. If it does not hire enough human resources, its profits will be reduced because its revenue will be lower. 2. If its facilities are too small, its profits will be reduced because its revenue will be lower. If its facilities are too large, its profits will be lower because its expenses from leasing space will be excessive.

that they invested. Thus, they will incur a direct penalty if they make a bad decision. To limit their risk, entrepreneurs should be cautious and realistic before deciding to invest their money to create a new business. However, those entrepreneurs who develop good business ideas that serve consumer needs and who manage their business efficiently may be rewarded with large profits.

Identify the key stakeholders that are involved in a business.

stakeholders
people who have an interest in a business; the business's owners, creditors, employees, suppliers, and customers

Key Stakeholders in a Business

Every business involves transactions with people. Those people are affected by the business and therefore have a stake in it. They are referred to as **stakeholders,** or people who have an interest (or stake) in the business. Five types of stakeholders are involved in a business:

▶ Owners

▶ Creditors

▶ Employees

▶ Suppliers

▶ Customers

Each type of stakeholder plays a critical role for firms, as explained next.

Owners

Every business begins as a result of ideas about a product or service by one or more entrepreneurs. As explained earlier, entrepreneurship is the act of creating, organizing, and managing a business. Today, more than 8 million people in the United States are entrepreneurs. Entrepreneurs are critical to the development of new business because they create new products (or improve existing products) desired by consumers.

People will be willing to create a business only if they expect to be rewarded for their efforts. The rewards of owning a business come in various forms. Some people are motivated by the chance to earn a large income. Others desire to be their own boss rather than work for someone else. Many people enjoy the challenge or the prestige associated with owning a business. Most business owners would agree that *all* of these characteristics motivated them to start their own business.

A recent survey by the Center for Entrepreneurial Leadership found that 69 percent of high school students were interested in starting their own business. Yet, about 86 percent of the students rated their business knowledge as very poor to fair. People need to learn how a business operates before they set out to create a business.

How Ownership Spreads   An entrepreneur who creates a business initially serves as the sole owner. Yet, in order to expand, the business may need more funding than the entrepreneur can provide. Consequently, the entrepreneur may allow other people to invest in the firm and become co-owners.

When the ownership of the firm is shared, the proportion of the firm owned by the existing owners is reduced. Consider a bakery that two people created with a $100,000 investment each. Each person owns one-half of the firm. They can obtain more funds by allowing a third person to invest in the firm. If the third person invests $100,000, each of the three

SMALL BUSINESS SURVEY

Background of Owners

In a recent National Small Business poll conducted for the NFIB Research Foundation, small business owners were asked how many years they worked for another firm before they began their own business. Their responses are shown here:

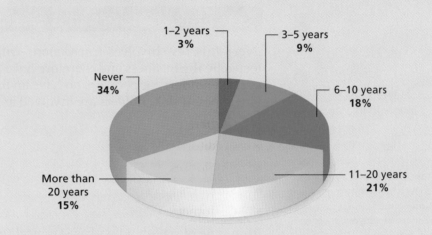

Notice the large proportion of owners who never worked for any other business before starting their own business.

Those business owners who previously worked for another business were asked what type of firm they worked for before starting their own business. Their responses are shown here:

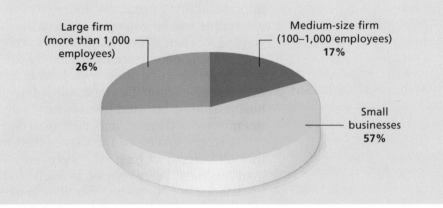

---

stock
certificates of ownership of a business

stockholders (shareholders)
investors who become partial owners of firms by purchasing the firm's stock

people will own one-third of the firm. Any profits (or earnings) of the firm that are distributed to the owners will be shared among three owners. By accepting investment from more owners, however, the firm may be able to expand its business so that the original owners benefit despite their decreased share of ownership.

Many firms have grown by issuing stock to other investors; that is, they essentially sell a portion of the ownership to these investors. The **stock** received by investors is a certificate representing ownership of the specific business. The investors who purchase stock are called **stockholders** (or **shareholders**) of those firms. The funds received by a firm that issues stock

SMALL BUSINESS SURVEY (Continued)

Business owners were also asked how many years of experience they had (working for other firms) in producing, distributing, or selling the same products or services as those that they sell now. Their responses are shown here:

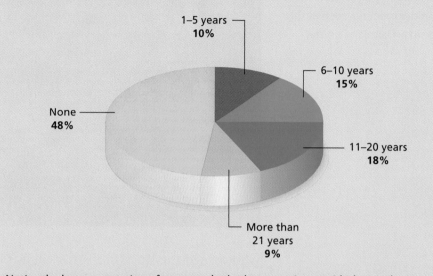

Notice the large proportion of owners who had no experience with the products that their business sells before they became the owner. This suggests that they were able to adapt their business skills to the product.

The owners were also asked to describe their educational background. Their responses are shown here:

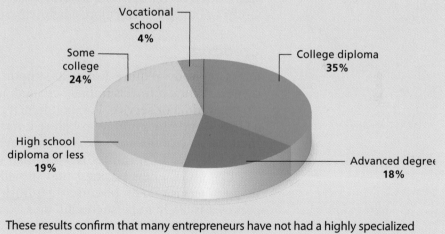

These results confirm that many entrepreneurs have not had a highly specialized education.

can be used to expand the business. Large firms such as Cisco Systems, IBM, and General Motors now have millions of stockholders, but when they were created, they were small businesses.

When a firm's performance improves, its value may increase as well, as reflected in a higher stock price for those who own the stock. Stockholders can sell their stock to other investors whenever they want. They benefit when a firm performs well because they will be able to sell the stock at a higher price than they paid for it if the firm's value rises. As an extreme example, stockholders of Dell, Inc., have doubled their investment in some years because Dell performed so well. At the other extreme, stockholders

The executives of public companies communicate to their shareholders not only through financial reports but also during the annual shareholder meeting, such as this one by Daimler-Chrysler.

who owned the stock of firms such as Enron and Global Crossing at the time these firms went bankrupt lost their entire investment.

A firm has a responsibility to the stockholders who have invested funds. It is expected to invest those funds in a manner that will increase its performance and value. Consequently, it should be able to provide the stockholders with a decent return on their investment. Some firms perform much better than others, however, so investors must carefully assess a firm's potential performance before investing in its stock.

Creditors

Firms typically require financial support beyond that provided by their owners. When a firm is initially created, it incurs expenses before it sells a single product or service. For example, it may have to buy machinery, rent a facility, and hire employees before it has any revenue. In the first several months, its expenses may exceed its revenue even if it is well managed. Therefore, the firm cannot rely on cash from sales to cover its expenses. The owners of a new business may initially have to rely on friends or family members for credit because their business does not have a history that proves it is likely to be successful and therefore able to pay off its credit in a timely manner.

Even firms that have existed for a long time, such as Little Caesars Pizza, Disney, and Nike, need financial support as they attempt to expand. A fast-growing business such as Little Caesars Pizza would not generate sufficient earnings to cover new investment in equipment or buildings.

creditors
financial institutions or individuals who provide loans

Many firms that need funds borrow from financial institutions or individuals called **creditors,** who provide loans. Bank of America, SunTrust Bank, and thousands of other commercial banks commonly serve as creditors for firms. Firms that borrow from creditors pay interest on their loans. The amount borrowed represents the debt of the firm, which must be paid back to the creditors along with interest payments over time. Large firms such as General Motors and DuPont have billions of dollars in debt.

Creditors will lend funds to a firm only if they believe the firm will perform well enough to pay the interest on the loans and the principal

One reason for the success of Southwest Airlines is its attention to satisfying its customers.

LANDOV LLC

(amount borrowed) in the future. The firm must convince the creditors that it will be sufficiently profitable to make the interest and principal payments.

Employees

Firms hire employees to conduct their business operations. Some firms have only a few employees; others, such as General Motors and IBM, have more than 200,000 employees. Many firms attribute their success to their employees. Consider the following statements that firms made about their employees in recent annual reports:

"Sara Lee is determined to be an employer of choice for highly talented people, retaining and attracting world-class individuals who have a passion to excel, strong ethical values and a driving entrepreneurial character."

—Sara Lee

"We continually invest in our people—the source of our innovation and competitiveness—who strive each day to find new products and technologies that will significantly improve everyday living."

—The Dow Chemical Company

managers
employees who are responsible for managing job assignments of other employees and making key business decisions

Those employees who are responsible for managing job assignments of other employees and making key business decisions are called **managers.** The performance of a firm is highly dependent on the decisions of its managers. Although managers' good decisions can help a firm succeed, their bad decisions may cause a firm to fail.

Goals of Managers   The goal of a firm's managers is to maximize the firm's value and, therefore, to maximize the value of the firm's stock. Maximizing firm value is an obvious goal for many small businesses since the owner and manager are often the same. In contrast, most stockholders of a publicly traded firm do not work for the firm. They rely on the firm's managers to maximize the value of the stock held by stockholders. The following statements from recent annual reports illustrate the emphasis firms place on maximizing shareholder value:

"We are not promising miracles, just hard work with a total focus on why we're in business: to enhance stockholder value."

—Zenith Electronics

"We believe that a fundamental measure of our success will be the share-holder value we create over the long term."

—Amazon.com

"Everything we do is designed to build shareholder value over the long haul."

—Wal-Mart

"We create value for our share owners, and that remains our true bottom line."

—The Coca-Cola Company

Maximizing the firm's value encourages prospective investors to become shareholders of the firm.

To illustrate how managers can enhance a firm's value, consider the case of Dell, Inc., which created an efficient system for producing computers. This resulted in low costs and allowed Dell to provide high-quality computers at low prices. Over time, Dell's sales increased substantially, as did its profits. The ability of Dell's managers to control costs and sell computers at low prices satisfied not only its customers but also its owners (shareholders).

Suppliers

Firms commonly use materials to produce their products. For example, automobile manufacturers use steel to make automobiles, while home builders need cement, wood siding, and many other materials. Firms cannot complete the production process if they cannot obtain the materials. Therefore, their performance is partially dependent on the ability of their suppliers to deliver the materials on schedule.

Customers

Firms cannot survive without customers. To attract customers, a firm must provide a desired product or service at a reasonable price. It must also ensure that the products or services produced are of adequate quality so that

Gap has created a very successful business as a retail clothing store that targets young customers.

GETTY IMAGES

customers are satisfied. If a firm cannot provide a product or service at the quality and price that customers desire, customers will switch to the firm's competitors. Motorola and Saturn (a division of General Motors) attribute some of their recent success to recognizing the types of products that consumers want. These firms also are committed to quality and to pricing their products in a manner that is acceptable to customers.

Summary of Key Stakeholders

Firms rely on entrepreneurs (owners) to create business ideas and possibly to provide some financial support. They rely on other owners and creditors to provide additional financial support. They rely on employees (including managers) to produce and sell their products or services. They rely on suppliers to provide the materials needed for production. They rely on customers to purchase the products or services they produce. The president of Goodyear Tire and Rubber Company summarized the relationship between a firm and its stakeholders in a recent annual report: "Last year I reaffirmed our values—protecting our good name, focusing on customers, respecting and developing our people [employees], and rewarding investors."

To illustrate the roles of stakeholders, reconsider the example of the DVD rental business. The owner who created the business makes decisions about its location, the types of DVDs to offer for rent, whether to sell other products (such as video games), and the prices to charge for DVD rentals and other products. The business needs creditors to support it with funding so that it has sufficient funds to cover its expenses. It needs employees to receive deliveries of new DVDs, organize them, and serve customers. It needs suppliers to supply the DVDs. Finally, the business needs customers to generate revenue.

Interaction among Stakeholders   The interaction among a firm's owners, employees, customers, suppliers, and creditors is illustrated in Exhibit 1.2. Managers decide how the funds obtained from owners, creditors, or sales to customers should be utilized. They use funds to pay for the resources (including employees, supplies, and machinery) needed to produce and promote their products. They also use funds to repay creditors. The money left over is profit. Some of the profit (or earnings) is retained and reinvested by the firm. Any remaining profit is distributed as **dividends,** or income that the firm provides to its owners.

dividends
income that the firm provides to its owners

Exhibit 1.2

Interaction among Owners, Employees, Customers, Suppliers, and Creditors

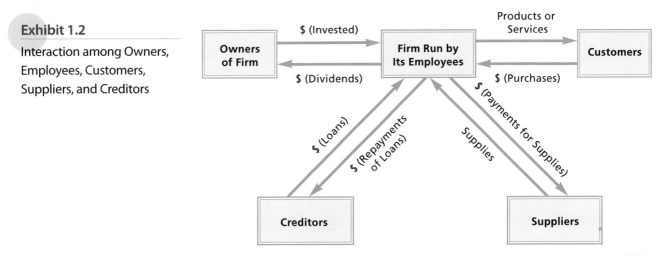

Decision Making

How Business Decisions Affect Stakeholders

The decisions of a business affect its performance, which in turn affects all of its stakeholders. Consider 4 Eyes DVD introduced earlier. If it makes good business decisions, its profits will be higher, and the entrepreneur who owns the business will receive higher profits. It will have sufficient revenue to pay any interest expenses on loans from creditors. It can afford to pay reasonable compensation to its employees and may even want to hire more employees if it expands over time. It can afford to continue to pay its suppliers (the firms that sell it DVDs) and will be able to order more supplies in the future.

1. Explain how the decision to borrow too much money might prevent 4 Eyes DVD from satisfying its stakeholders.

2. If the owner of 4 Eyes DVD hires his sons as employees and pays them excessive salaries, how would this affect the other stakeholders?

ANSWERS: 1. It may be unable to pay its interest expenses on the loan each month. The business would fail, and any payments to employees, suppliers, or even the entrepreneur (as income) would be discontinued. 2. Because of overpaying those employees, 4 Eyes DVD may not have sufficient funds for its other stakeholders.

Describe the business environment to which a firm is exposed.

The Business Environment

The success of a business is generally dependent on the business environment. Even after a business is created, its entrepreneurs and managers must continually monitor the environment so that they can anticipate how the demand for its products or its cost of producing products may change. The business environment can be segmented into the following parts:

▶ Social environment

▶ Industry environment

▶ Economic environment

▶ Global environment

Social Environment

The social environment, which includes demographics and consumer preferences, represents the social tendencies to which a business is exposed. The **demographics,** or characteristics of the population, change over time. As the proportions of children, teenagers, middle-aged consumers, and senior citizens in a population change, so does the demand for a firm's products. Thus, the demand for the products produced by a specific business may increase or decrease in response to a change in demographics. For example, an increase in the elderly population has led to an increased demand for many prescription drugs.

Changes in consumer preferences over time can also affect the demand for the products produced. Tastes are highly influenced by technology. For example, the availability of pay-per-view television channels may cause some consumers to stop renting DVDs. The ability of consumers to download music may cause them to discontinue their purchases of CDs in retail stores. As technology develops, demand for some products increases, while demand for other products decreases. Many businesses closely monitor changes in consumer preferences so that they can accom-

demographics
characteristics of the human population or specific segments of the population

modate the changing needs of consumers and increase their profitability as a result.

Industry Environment

The industry environment represents the conditions within the firm's industry to which the firm is exposed. The conditions in each industry vary according to the demand and the competition. Firms benefit from being in an industry that experiences a high consumer demand for its products. For example, the demand for cell phones is very high. However, industries that have a high demand for their products also tend to have substantial competition because many firms enter the industry. Intense competition is good for consumers because it forces firms to keep their prices relatively low in order to compete. For firms, however, competition may result in lower revenue and, therefore, lower profits.

Economic Environment

Economic conditions have a strong impact on the performance of each business. When the economy is strong, employment is high, and compensation paid to employees is also high. Since people have relatively good income under these conditions, they purchase a large amount of products. The firms that produce these products benefit from the large demand. They hire many employees to ensure that they can produce a sufficient amount of products to satisfy the demand. They can also afford to pay high wages to their employees.

When the economy is weak, firms tend to lay off some of their employees and cannot afford to pay high wages. Since people have relatively low income under these conditions, they purchase a relatively small amount of products. The firms that produce these products are adversely affected because they can not sell all the products that they produce. Consequently, they may need to lay off some employees. Under these circumstances, some firms fail, and all of their employees lose their jobs. The unemployment rate rises as a result. The economic environment is more fully described in Chapter 3.

Global Environment

The global environment may affect all firms directly or indirectly. Some firms rely on foreign countries for some of their supplies or sell their products in various countries. They may even establish subsidiaries in foreign countries where they can produce products and sell them. Even if a firm is not planning to sell its products in foreign countries, it must be aware of the global environment because it may face foreign competition when it sells its products locally.

Furthermore, global economic conditions can affect local economic conditions. If economic conditions weaken in foreign countries, the foreign demand for U.S. products will decrease. Consequently, sales by U.S. firms will decrease, and this may result in some layoffs. The general income level in the United States will decline, and U.S. consumers will have less money to spend. The demand for all products will decline, even those that are sold only in the United States. Thus, even firms that have no international business can be affected by the global environment. The global environment is described more fully in Chapter 4.

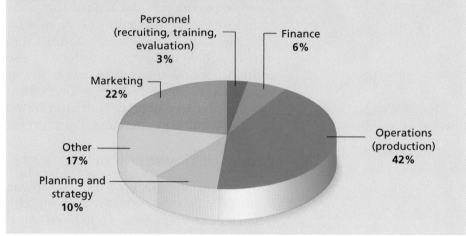

SMALL BUSINESS SURVEY

How Business Owners Use Their Time

In a recent National Small Business poll conducted for the NFIB Research Foundation, owners of small businesses were asked how they allocate their time toward a variety of business tasks. Their responses are shown here:

Personnel (recruiting, training, evaluation) 3%

Finance 6%

Marketing 22%

Operations (production) 42%

Other 17%

Planning and strategy 10%

Decision Making

Responding to the Business Environment

Recall that 4 Eyes DVD was created because there was very limited competition for DVD rentals in the town. The business environment can change over time, however, and firms will have to respond to those changes in order to survive.

1. Suppose that the social environment changes such that consumers prefer pay-per-view television to renting DVDs. How will the profits of 4 Eyes DVD be affected?

2. Suppose that a new DVD rental outlet opens in the center of town. How will the profits of 4 Eyes DVD be affected?

3. What can 4 Eyes DVD do to counter a new competitor?

ANSWERS: 1. The change in the social environment will reduce consumer demand for DVD rentals, which will reduce the revenue and therefore the profits of 4 Eyes DVD. 2. The opening of a new DVD rental outlet will reduce the revenue and profits of 4 Eyes DVD. 3. 4 Eyes DVD can counter a new competitor by reducing its prices on its DVD rentals and by offering other products such as DVDs for sale. However, the effectiveness of these strategies may depend on the prices charged by the new competitor.

Key Types of Business Decisions

Describe the key types of business decisions.

management
means by which employees and other resources (such as machinery) are used by the firm

The key types of decisions involved in running a business can be classified as management, marketing, and finance decisions. **Management** is the means by which employees and other resources (such as machinery) are used by the firm. **Marketing** is the means by which products (or services) are developed, priced, distributed, and promoted to customers. **Finance** is the means by which firms obtain and use funds for their business operations.

A firm's decisions are commonly based on data and information, which are provided by its accounting and information systems. **Accounting** is the summary and analysis of the firm's financial condition and is used to make

marketing
means by which products (or services) are developed, priced, distributed, and promoted to customers

finance
means by which firms obtain and use funds for their business operations

accounting
summary and analysis of the firm's financial condition

information systems
include information technology, people, and procedures that work together to provide appropriate information to the firm's employees so they can make business decisions

various business decisions. **Information systems** include information technology, people, and procedures that provide appropriate information so that the firm's employees can make business decisions. Business majors take courses in management, marketing, and finance so that they can understand the key decisions made by a business and how to make these decisions. They take courses in accounting and information systems so that they can understand how to analyze data and use their analysis to make decisions.

How Business Decisions Affect Performance

Examples of management, marketing, and finance decisions are provided in Exhibit 1.3. Notice from this exhibit that management decisions focus on the use of resources, marketing decisions focus on the products, and finance decisions focus on obtaining or using funds.

As mentioned earlier, a firm's performance is commonly measured by its earnings (or profits). The effect that each type of business decision has on a firm's earnings is illustrated in Exhibit 1.4. Since management decisions focus on the utilization of employees and other resources, they affect the amount of production expenses incurred. Since marketing decisions focus on strategies that will make the product appealing to customers, they affect the firm's revenue. Marketing decisions also influence the amount of expenses incurred in distributing and promoting products. Since finance decisions focus on how funds are obtained (borrowing money versus issuing stock), they influence the amount of interest expense incurred. As the management, marketing, and finance decisions affect either a firm's revenue or expenses, they affect the earnings and therefore the performance of the firm.

Although some decisions focus on only one function, many decisions require interaction among management, marketing, and finance. For example, production managers of a cell phone manufacturer receive sales projections from the marketing managers to determine how much of the product to produce. The finance managers must receive the planned

Exhibit 1.3

Common Business Decisions

Management Decisions

1. What equipment is needed to produce the product?

2. How many employees should be hired to produce the product?

3. How can employees be motivated to perform well?

Marketing Decisions

1. What price should be charged for the product?

2. Should the product be changed to be more appealing to customers?

3. Should the firm use advertising or some other strategy to promote its product?

Finance Decisions

1. Should financial support come from the sale of stock or from borrowing money? Or a combination of both?

2. Should the firm attempt to obtain borrowed funds for a short-term period (such as one year) or a long-term period?

3. Should the firm invest funds in a new business project that has recently been proposed (such as expansion of its existing business or development of a new product), or should it use these funds to repay debt?

Exhibit 1.4

How Business Decisions
Affect a Firm's Earnings

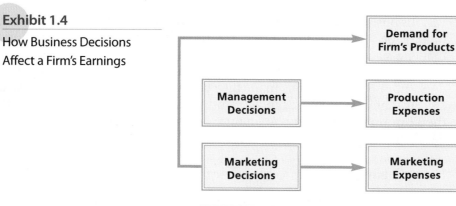

production volume from the production managers to determine how much funding is needed.

How Some Business Functions Enhance Decision Making

Proper business decisions rely on accounting and information systems.

Accounting   Managers of firms use accounting to monitor their operations and to report their financial condition to their owners or employees. They can also assess the performance of previous production, marketing, and finance decisions. They may even rely on accounting to detect inefficient uses of business resources that can be eliminated. Consequently, a firm's accounting function can be used to eliminate waste, thereby generating higher earnings.

Information Systems   Firms use information systems to continually update and analyze information about their operations. This information can be used by the firm's managers to make business decisions. In addition, the information can be used by any employee within the firm who has access to a personal computer. For example, FedEx uses information on its computer system to track deliveries and determine when packages will arrive at their destination.

Applying the Key Types of Decisions to a Single Business

To illustrate the key types of business decisions, reconsider the example of the DVD rental business. The management decisions of this business determine how its employees and other resources should be used. The typical management decisions of this firm are:

▶   How many employees should it hire?

▶   What salary should it pay each employee?

▶   What should be the job description of each employee?

▶   To whom should each employee report within the business?

▶   How should the business motivate its employees to perform well?

▶   How should it use the space in its store?

▶   Should it charge a late fee?

The marketing decisions of the DVD rental business determine how the DVD rentals should be priced, distributed, and promoted. The typical marketing decisions of this firm are:

▶ What is the profile of the typical customer who will rent its DVDs?

▶ Should it charge a membership fee to rent DVDs?

▶ What price should it charge per rental?

▶ Should it allow a discount for frequent customers?

▶ Should it consider distributing DVD rentals by delivery or through the Internet?

▶ Should it advertise its business? If so, where should it advertise?

The finance decisions of the DVD rental business determine how it obtains funds and uses the funds it obtains. The typical finance decisions of this firm are:

▶ How much money should it borrow?

▶ Where should it apply to obtain a loan?

▶ Should it use some of the borrowed funds to expand?

▶ How can it expand its business so that its value will increase?

The DVD rental business relies on accounting and information systems to report its financial condition on a periodic basis. This information would be used to help make some of the decisions described above. For example, by monitoring how its revenue changes in response to a change in the membership fee, the business can decide what fee is most appropriate. Its decision about how much money to borrow is based on how much money it has (as reported by the accounting function) versus what it needs to meet its business objectives.

Results of Bad Business Decisions

When firms make bad decisions, their performance suffers. Exhibit 1.5 provides examples of how bad management, marketing, or finance decisions can result in poor performance. In each example, the bad decision

Decision Making

Integrating Business Functions

Many business functions are integrated, meaning that one function is dependent on other functions. Consider the case of 4 Eyes DVD. The management decision about how much space to rent will influence the finance decision about of how much money the business needs to borrow, because renting a larger store will be more costly and require more financing. Its marketing decision regarding pricing and advertising may affect the demand for its DVD rentals. If the demand is high, the store will require more employees to provide customer service. Thus, the marketing decision influences the management decision of how many employees to hire.

1. Explain whether the management decisions of 4 Eyes DVD affect its revenue or its expenses, or both.

2. Explain whether the firm's marketing decisions affect its revenue or its expenses, or both.

ANSWERS: 1. Most management decisions affect the firm's level of expenses, but they can also have an impact on the service to customers and therefore may affect the revenue as well. 2. Most marketing decisions affect the firm's level of expenses, but they can also affect revenue because they are typically intended to increase sales volume and therefore revenue.

Exhibit 1.5

How Bad Business Decisions
Affect the Profits Earned
by the Owners

leads to either a reduction in revenue or higher-than-necessary expenses
and, therefore, results in lower profits.

Preview of This Text

The focus of this text is on decision making by a business, and the chapters
are organized with this focus in mind. A broad overview of the text is provided in Exhibit 1.6. A firm needs to understand its environment before it

Exhibit 1.6

Overview of the Text

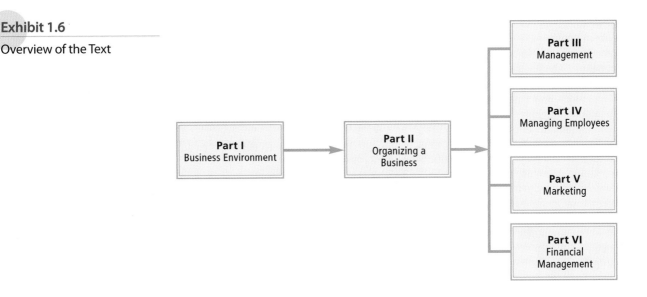

can make business decisions. Accordingly, Part I contains chapters on business ethics, the firm's social responsibility to its environment (Chapter 2), the economic environment (Chapter 3), and the global environment (Chapter 4).

Part II is focused on creating a business. It contains chapters on selecting a form of business organization (Chapter 5) and entrepreneurship (Chapter 6). These chapters explain how a business is created and discuss the initial planning decisions that are necessary to guide the business toward profitability.

Part III describes how to manage business operations, with chapters on effective management (Chapter 7), the organizational structure of a business (Chapter 8), and improving productivity and quality (Chapter 9). These chapters explain the organization of jobs within the firm, the sequence of production tasks, and the methods of improving quality.

Part IV describes how to manage employees, with chapters on motivating employees (Chapter 10) and hiring, training, and performance evaluation (Chapter 11). A firm is only as strong as its employees, and these chapters discuss how a firm's treatment of its employees can improve its performance.

Part V is focused on marketing, with chapters on creating and pricing products (Chapter 12), distributing products (Chapter 13), and promoting products (Chapter 14). These chapters cover all the major decisions that are intended to make products and services attractive and accessible to customers.

Part VI is focused on financial management, with chapters on accounting (Chapter 15), financing (Chapter 16), and expanding the business, (Chapter 17). These chapters explain how a firm's financial condition is reported, how firms obtain funds, and how firms decide to use funds.

To illustrate how these parts fit together, consider how the DVD rental business mentioned earlier could apply the parts of this text:

▶ Apply Part I concepts to:

  ▶ Determine if the DVD rental service faces much competition.

  ▶ Decide whether the economic environment is favorable (whether customers can afford to rent DVDs).

▶ Apply Part II concepts to:

  ▶ Help the owner decide whether to own the business by himself or invite other partners to share ownership.

  ▶ Develop long-term business goals regarding the DVD rental business and a broad plan to achieve those goals.

▶ Apply Part III concepts to:

  ▶ Recognize the skills needed to organize the DVD rental operations.

  ▶ Decide on the different job descriptions of the employees hired and to whom each position reports.

  ▶ Decide how to improve the DVD rental process over time.

▶ Apply Part IV concepts to:

  ▶ Determine how to motivate employees so that they perform their duties properly.

  ▶ Use proper screening to hire employees, and effectively train and evaluate the employees hired.

▶ Apply Part V concepts to:

  ▶ Use the firm's reputation to offer additional services.

  ▶ Consider alternative ways of making the DVD rental service accessible to customers.

  ▶ Promote the DVD rental service to attract more customers.

▶ Apply Part VI concepts to:

  ▶ Measure the recent performance and financial condition of the DVD rental business.

  ▶ Decide how to obtain funds to finance business expansion.

  ▶ Consider various ways of restructuring the DVD rental business to improve its performance.

COLLEGE HEALTH CLUB: BUSINESS DECISIONS AT COLLEGE HEALTH CLUB

Many of the key concepts in this text are applied to one small business (a health club) in a feature that appears in every chapter. The applications demonstrate how business decisions are made and how they are related. They also show that even the smallest business must make decisions about all types of business functions.

Sue Kramer recently graduated with a degree in business from Texas College in Dallas, Texas. She has always wanted to own and manage a business. Throughout her college years, she belonged to Energy Health Club, a 20-minute drive from the college campus. She noticed that many other students from Texas College were members of this club. She also knew other students who wanted to join a health club, but lived on campus and did not have a car. There was a health club called Magnum Club in the shopping mall just across the street from the college, but it was very expensive and focused on personal training. Magnum Club recently closed those facilities and moved to a downtown location far from Texas College.

For some time, Sue has considered opening a health club next to the Texas College campus that would cater to students. Shortly after graduation, Sue distributed a survey to hundreds of students at the college to determine whether they would be interested in joining a health club and what types of facilities and equipment they would desire. Now that Magnum Club has moved, there are no health clubs very close to campus. The shopping center where Magnum Club was located is a perfect location for a health club catering to students because students frequently go to stores in that center.

Sue is motivated to start the health club business because she believes that she satisfies all three conditions necessary to make the business successful. First, there is a demand for the service. Second, her business could attract customers because there is not much competition nearby. Third, she has the business skills that would allow her to run the business efficiently and keep expenses low.

Sue must consider how the business environment could affect her health club. She believes that the social environment is favorable because students are conscious about fitness. She also believes that industry conditions are favorable because there is no longer any competition near the college campus.

Near the end of each chapter, the key concepts of the chapter will be applied to develop the health club business. As a preview, Sue will establish ethical guidelines for her business (Chapter 2) and consider the economic (Chapter 3) and global environment (Chapter 4) surrounding her business. Next, she will select a form of business organization (Chapter 5) and use her entrepreneurial skills to develop goals and a broad plan for her business (Chapter 6). Then she will make decisions about the management of the firm's operations (Chapters 7–9), managing employees (Chapters 10–11), marketing (Chapters 12–14), and financial management (Chapters 15–17). By the end of the text, Sue will have covered all the major decisions regarding how to run her health club.

Summary

1 Businesses are established to serve the needs of consumers. Entrepreneurs are encouraged to start a business because they can earn income (profits) if their business is successful. They are motivated to make decisions that will increase business revenue and keep expenses low so that they can earn high profits. The creation of successful businesses can be beneficial to the entrepreneurs and other owners who earn profits, the employees who are paid income, and the consumers whose needs are satisfied. You can profit from an understanding of business even if you do not plan to run a business because the knowledge may help you succeed in your job position, in your career path, or even from investing in a business.

2 Businesses use factors of production such as natural resources (land), human resources, capital (including technology), and entrepreneurship. They use land to establish a location for producing or selling products; they use human resources to perform the production and make other business decisions. They rely on capital to produce their products. They rely on entrepreneurship for guidance at the time they are created and as they evolve.

3 The key stakeholders in a business are owners, creditors, employees, suppliers, and customers. The owners invest in the firm, while creditors lend money to the firm. Employees are hired to conduct the firm's business operations efficiently in order to satisfy the owners. Suppliers provide the materials that the firm needs to produce its product.

4 Businesses are exposed to the social, industry, economic, and global environments. They monitor the social environment to anticipate changes in the demand for their products in response to changing demographics and changing preferences of consumers. They monitor the industry environment to assess the level of competition. They monitor the economic and global environments to anticipate how the local global economies may affect the demand for their products.

5 The key types of business decisions are management, marketing, and finance decisions. Management decisions determine how the firm's resources are allocated. Marketing decisions determine the product to be sold, along with the pricing, distribution, and promotion of that product. Finance decisions determine how the firm obtains and invests funds. Business decisions are improved as a result of accounting and information systems. Accounting is used to monitor performance and detect inefficient uses of resources in order to improve business decisions. Information systems provide the firm's employees with information that enables them to improve business decisions.

Key Terms

accounting 21
capital 7
creditors 14
demographics 18
dividends 17
electronic business (e-business) 7
electronic commerce (e-commerce) 7

entrepreneurs 9
entrepreneurship 9
finance 21
human resources 7
information systems 21
information technology 7
management 20
managers 15
marketing 21

natural resources 6
nonprofit organization 5
stakeholders 11
stock 12
stockholders (shareholders) 12
technology 7

Review & Critical Thinking Questions

1. Describe the roles of the five key stakeholders in a business.

2. Explain how and why the ownership of a business may spread.

3. What is information technology? Why has information technology recently received so much attention in business?

In-Text Study Guide

Answers are in Appendix C at the back of book.

27. _____ summarize(s) the firm's financial condition for use in making various business decisions.
    a) Accounting
    b) Information systems
    c) Production
    d) Marketing
    e) Management

28. Business decisions involving how to obtain the necessary funds to be used by the firm are _____ decisions.
    a) finance
    b) marketing
    c) accounting
    d) information systems
    e) management

29. Managers rely on _____ to detect the inefficient use of resources.
    a) owners
    b) creditors
    c) marketing research
    d) marketing mix studies
    e) accounting data

30. The purpose of an industry business environmental assessment is to determine the:
    a) degree of competition.
    b) inflation rate.
    c) unemployment rate.
    d) population growth.
    e) economic growth.

31. The key types of business decisions can be classified as management, marketing, and:
    a) accounting.
    b) production.
    c) inventory.
    d) finance.
    e) information systems.

32. The uncertainty of future earnings is:
    a) capitalization.
    b) incentive.
    c) risk.
    d) hazard.
    e) venture finance.

33. The _____ environment includes changes in consumer preferences over time.
    a) industry
    b) social
    c) economic
    d) global
    e) retail

34. Stakeholders who provide materials to produce products are:
    a) owners.
    b) creditors.
    c) employees.
    d) suppliers.
    e) customers.

35. The profit motive is influenced by the government because:
    a) governments of free-market economies encourage the profit motive.
    b) businesses are owned by the government.
    c) governments of free-market economies discourage the profit motive.
    d) governments are shareholders of the firm.
    e) governments buy businesses from individuals.

Chapter

2

PHOTOEDIT, INC.

Businesses like this one need to balance their obligations to customers, employees, investors, and creditors.

Business Ethics and Social Responsibility

A firm's employees should practice business ethics, which involves following a set of principles when conducting business. Each firm has a social responsibility, which is the firm's recognition of how its business decisions can affect society. The term *social responsibility* is sometimes used to describe the firm's responsibility to its community and to the environment. However, it may also be used more broadly to include the firm's responsibility to its customers, employees, stockholders, and creditors. Although the business decisions a firm makes are intended to increase its value, the decisions must not violate its ethics and social responsibilities.

Cool Jewel Company produces and sells costume jewelry for children and teenagers. Much of its jewelry is made in Asian and Latin American countries, where wages are very low. It relies on funding from large investors and from loans by commercial banks.

Cool Jewel Company is reassessing its corporate responsibilities, in light of recent media attention focused on businesses that have not fulfilled their corporate responsibilities. Some firms were recently criticized for (1) using misleading advertising to attract customers, (2) mistreating their employees, and (3) failing to repay their debts. To ensure that it meets its corporate responsibilities, Cool Jewel decides to develop a formal code of ethics. Specifically, it must decide:

▶ What is its responsibility to customers?

▶ What is its responsibility to employees?

▶ What is its responsibility to its investors?

▶ What is its responsibility to creditors?

▶ What is its responsibility to the environment and community?

Cool Jewel's responsibility to its customers influences customer loyalty and, therefore, affects the revenue that it generates. Its relationship with employees influences the effort they will exert on various tasks, which can also affect the revenue generated.

All businesses must recognize their responsibilities to their stakeholders and make decisions that reflect these responsibilities. This chapter explains how decisions about ethical and social responsibilities by Cool Jewel Company or any other firm can be made in a manner that maximizes the firm's value.

Business Ethics and Social Responsibility → Business Decisions → Firm's Earnings → Value of Firm

Out of
Business

OUR CUSTOMERS ARE NOT SATISFIED WITH OUR PRODUCTS.
OUR INVESTORS ARE NOT SATISFIED WITH OUR PERFORMACE.
SO THERE IS ONLY ONE SOLUTION…GO FIND NEW CUSTOMERS
AND INVESTORS WHO DO NOT KNOW US VERY WELL

CEO

SOCIAL RESPONSIBILITY MEETING IN PROGRESS

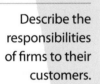

Describe the
responsibilities
of firms to their
customers.

social responsibility
a firm's recognition of how its
business decisions can affect
society

Responsibility to Customers

A firm's responsibility to customers goes beyond the provision of products
or services. Firms have a **social responsibility** when producing and selling
their products, as discussed next.

Responsible Production Practices

Products should be produced in a way that ensures customer safety. Products should carry proper warning labels to prevent accidents that could result from misuse. For some products, information on possible side effects
should be provided. For example, Tylenol gelcaps, Nyquil cough syrup,
and Coors beer all have warning labels about possible adverse effects.

Responsible Sales Practices

Consider the following sales practices that are commonly used. An employee of a car dealership tries to sell a car at the sticker price to any customers who are not aware that the usual selling price is at least $2,000
below the sticker price. The employee earns a higher commission from
selling the car at a higher price. A salesperson at a health food store sells
supplements, claiming that they will build muscle, even though he knows
the they could have dangerous side effects. A phone company salesperson
sells a customer a specific plan that appears cheap, but will typically result
in very high fees because of some requirements that are not disclosed during the sale.

When employees may benefit from commissions, they may be
tempted to hide the truth in order to sell products or services. Therefore, firms need guidelines that discourage employees from using overly
aggressive sales strategies or deceptive advertising. They may also use
customer satisfaction surveys to ensure that customers were treated

A sampling of warnings used on prescriptions.

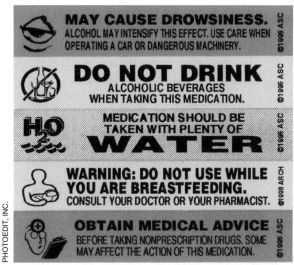

PHOTOEDIT, INC.

properly by salespeople. The surveys should be conducted after customers make a purchase to determine whether the product worked as the salesperson said that it would.

How Firms Ensure Responsibility toward Customers

A firm can ensure responsibility toward its customers by following these steps:

business responsibilities
a set of obligations and duties regarding product quality and treatment of customers, employees, and owners that a firm should fulfill when conducting business

1. **Establish a Code of Responsibilities**   Firms can establish a code of **business responsibilities** that sets guidelines for product quality, as well as guidelines for how employees, customers, and owners should be treated. The pledge (from an annual report) by Bristol-Myers Squibb Company in Exhibit 2.1 is an example of a code of ethics and responsibilities. Many firms distribute a booklet on ethics and responsibilities to all their employees.

Exhibit 2.1

Excerpts from a Pledge of Ethics and Responsibility by Bristol-Myers Squibb Company

The Bristol-Myers Squibb Pledge
TO THOSE WHO USE OUR PRODUCTS . . .
We affirm Bristol-Myers Squibb's commitment to the highest standards of excellence, safety and reliability in everything we make. We pledge to offer products of the highest quality and to work diligently to keep improving them.
TO OUR EMPLOYEES AND THOSE WHO MAY JOIN US . . .
We pledge personal respect, fair competition and equal treatment. We acknowledge our obligation to provide able and humane leadership throughout the organization, within a clean and safe working environment. To all who qualify for advancement, we will make every effort to provide opportunity.
TO OUR SUPPLIERS AND CUSTOMERS. . .
We pledge an open door, courteous, efficient and ethical dealing, and appreciation of their right to a fair profit.
TO OUR SHAREHOLDERS . . .
We pledge a companywide dedication to continued profitable growth, sustained by strong finances, a high level of research and development, and facilities second to none.
TO THE COMMUNITIES WHERE WE HAVE PLANTS AND OFFICES . . .
We pledge conscientious citizenship, a helping hand for worthwhile causes, and constructive action in support of civic and environmental progress.
TO THE COUNTRIES WHERE WE DO BUSINESS . . .
We pledge ourselves to be a good citizen and to show full consideration for the rights of others while reserving the right to stand up for our own.
ABOVE ALL, TO THE WORLD WE LIVE IN . . .
We pledge Bristol-Myers Squibb to policies and practices which fully embody the responsibility, integrity and decency required of free enterprise if it is to merit and maintain the confidence of our society.

The code of responsibilities is not intended to cover every possible action by a firm that would be unfair to customers. Nevertheless, it serves as a guide for the firm to consider when expanding its business. For example, consider a firm that implements a code that emphasizes safety for customers. Whatever the firm may produce in the future, it should always ensure that the products are not harmful. Thus, this code does not force the firm to produce any particular product but simply ensures that any product will be tested to ensure that it is safe for customers. If another provision of the code is honest communication with customers, then the advertising of all of the firm's products should conform to these guidelines. Although some government laws prohibit blatantly false advertising, this type of provision within a code of ethics and responsibilities would prevent advertising that is deceptive. To the extent that the code can enhance a firm's image and credibility, it may enhance the firm's value.

2. **Monitor Complaints**   Firms should make sure that customers have a phone number that they can call if they have any complaints about the quality of the product or about how they were treated by employees. The firm can attempt to determine the source of the complaint and ensure that the problem does not occur again. Many firms have a department that receives complaints and attempts to resolve them. This step may involve assessing different parts of the production process to ensure that the product is produced properly. Or it may require an assessment of particular employees who may be violating the firm's code of responsibilities to its customers.

3. **Obtain and Utilize Customer Feedback**   Firms can ask customers for feedback on the products or services they recently purchased, even if the customers do not call to complain. This process may detect some other problems with the product's quality or with the way customers were treated. For example, automobile dealers such as Saturn send a questionnaire to customers to determine how they were treated by salespeople. Customers may also be asked whether they have any complaints about the automobile they recently purchased. Once the firm is informed of problems with either production defects or customer treatment, it should take action to correct these problems.

Role of Consumerism

consumerism
the collective demand by consumers that businesses satisfy their needs

Specific groups of consumers are also calling for firms to fulfill their responsibilities toward customers. **Consumerism** is the collective demand by consumers that businesses satisfy their needs. Consumer groups became popular in the 1960s and have become increasingly effective as they have grown.

Role of the Government

In addition to the codes of responsibility established by firms and the wave of consumerism, the government attempts to ensure that firms fulfill their responsibility to customers through various laws on product safety, advertising, and industry competition.

Government Regulation of Product Safety   The government protects consumers by regulating the quality of some products produced by firms. For ex-

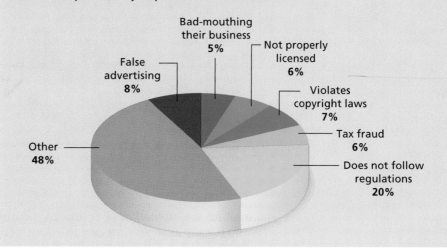

SMALL BUSINESS SURVEY

Illegal or Unethical Activities of Firms

Based on a recent National Small Business poll conducted for the NFIB Research Foundation, 21 percent of small businesses believe that a competitor is competing illegally or unethically. When asked to describe the main illegal or unethical activity of their competitor, they responded as shown below:

Bad-mouthing their business 5%
Not properly licensed 6%
False advertising 8%
Violates copyright laws 7%
Tax fraud 6%
Other 48%
Does not follow regulations 20%

ample, the Food and Drug Administration (FDA) is responsible for testing food products to determine whether they meet specific requirements. The FDA also examines new drugs that firms have recently developed. Because potential side effects may not be known immediately, the FDA tests some drugs continually over several years.

Government Regulation of Advertising   The federal government has also established laws against deceptive advertising. Nevertheless, it may not be able to prevent all unethical business practices. Numerous examples of advertising could be called deceptive. It is difficult to know if a product is "new and improved." In addition, a term such as *lowest price* may have different meanings or interpretations.

Government Regulation of Industry Competition   Another way the government ensures that consumers are treated properly is to promote competition in most industries. Competition between firms is beneficial to consumers, because firms that charge excessive prices or produce goods of unacceptable quality will not survive in a competitive environment. Because of competition, consumers can avoid a firm that is using deceptive sales tactics.

monopoly
a firm that is the sole provider of goods or services

A firm has a **monopoly** if it is the sole provider of goods or services. It can set prices without concern about competition. However, the government regulates firms that have a monopoly. For example, it regulates utility firms that have monopolies in specific locations and can control the pricing policies of these firms.

In some industries, firms negotiated various agreements to set prices and avoid competing with each other. The federal government has attempted to prevent such activity by enforcing antitrust laws. Some of the more well-known antitrust acts are summarized in Exhibit 2.2. All of these

Exhibit 2.2

Key Antitrust Laws

▶ **Sherman Antitrust Act (1890)** Encouraged competition and prevented monopolies.

▶ **Clayton Act (1914)** Reinforced the rules of the Sherman Antitrust Act and specifically prohibited the following activities because they reduced competition:

   ▶ *Tying agreements* Forced firms to purchase additional products as a condition of purchasing the desired products.

   ▶ *Binding contracts* Prevented firms from purchasing products from a supplier's competitors.

   ▶ *Interlocking directorates* The situation in which the same person serves on the board of directors of two competing firms.

▶ **Federal Trade Commission Act (1914)** Prohibited unfair methods of competition; also provided for the establishment of the Federal Trade Commission (FTC) to enforce antitrust laws.

▶ **Robinson-Patman Act (1936)** Prohibited price policies or promotional allowances that reduce competition within an industry.

▶ **Celler-Kefauver Act (1950)** Prohibited mergers between firms that reduce competition within an industry.

acts share the objective of promoting competition, with each act focusing on particular aspects that can influence the degree of competition within an industry.

The trucking, railroad, airline, and telecommunications industries have been deregulated, allowing more firms to enter each industry. In addition, banks and other financial institutions have been deregulated since 1980 and now have more flexibility on the types of deposits and interest rates they can offer. They also have more freedom to expand across state lines. In general, deregulation results in lower prices for consumers.

Decision Making

Ensuring Responsibility toward Customers

Recall that Cool Jewel Company (introduced in the beginning of the chapter) sells costume jewelry. Most of its jewelry is imitation gold or silver. Cool Jewel does not pretend that it uses real gold or silver and specifically states that its jewelry is imitation. Its salespeople receive a commission based on the amount of products that they sell, but it warns the salespeople that they must tell customers that the jewelry is imitation and is not as durable as gold or silver jewelry.

1. How can honest sales practices by Cool Jewel Company result in higher sales over time?

2. How can Cool Jewel Company ensure that its salespeople are honest in describing the jewelry to customers?

ANSWERS:1. Honest sales practices may inspire more trust in customers, and the customers may respond by coming back to buy more jewelry over time. 2. It can post a sign in the store explaining that the jewelry is imitation so that its salespeople are not tempted to tell customers that the jewelry is real. It can also discipline any salespeople who are found to be dishonest to customers.

Describe the responsibilities of firms to their employees.

Responsibility to Employees

Firms also have a responsibility to their employees to ensure their safety, proper treatment by other employees, and equal opportunity.

Employee Safety

Firms ensure that the workplace is safe for employees by closely monitoring the production process. Some obvious safety precautions are to check machinery and equipment for proper working conditions, require safety glasses or any other equipment that can prevent injury, and emphasize any special safety precautions in training seminars.

Firms that create a safe working environment prevent injuries and improve the morale of their employees. Many firms now identify workplace safety as one of their main goals. Dow Chemical Company has adopted a pledge of no accidents and no injuries to its employees. Levi Strauss & Co. imposes safety guidelines not only on its U.S. facilities but also on the Asian factories where some of its clothes are made. Starbucks Coffee Company has developed a code of conduct in an attempt to improve the quality of life of its employees in coffee-producing countries.

Owners of a firm recognize that the firm will incur costs in meeting responsibilities such as employee safety. The firm's efforts to provide a safe working environment represent a necessary cost of doing business.

Proper Treatment by Other Employees

Firms are responsible for ensuring that employees are treated properly by other employees. Two key issues concerning the treatment of employees are diversity and the prevention of sexual harassment, which are discussed next.

Starbucks has established a code of conduct for its employees.

GETTY IMAGES

Exhibit 2.3

Proportion of Women and Minorities in Various Occupations

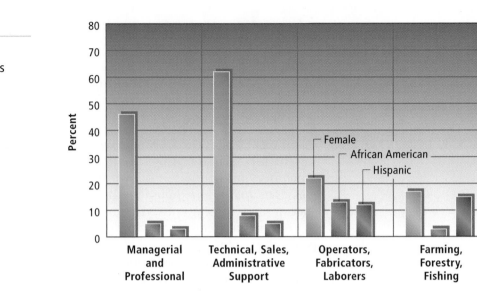

Diversity   In recent years, the workforce has become much more diverse. More women have entered the job market, and more minorities now have the necessary skills and education to qualify for high-level jobs. Exhibit 2.3 shows the proportions of various job categories held by women, African Americans, and Hispanics.

Diversity issues are not restricted to gender and race. Employees may come from completely different backgrounds and have different beliefs, which could lead to conflict in the workplace. For example, some employees may have strong political beliefs, which could cause friction with others who do not share those beliefs, even if their work assignments are unrelated to politics. In addition, some employees may be much older than others, which may lead to opposing views about issues in or outside the workplace. Many firms attempt to integrate employees with various backgrounds so that they learn to work with each other toward common goals of the firm even if they have differing views on issues outside the workplace.

Many firms have responded to the increased diversity among employees by offering diversity seminars, which inform employees about cultural diversity. Such information can help employees recognize that certain statements or behavior may be offensive to other employees.

Based on a recent survey by the Society for Human Resource Management, 73 percent of firms integrate diversity initiatives into key business practices for employees in substantially different groups. In addition, 85 percent of all firms integrate diversity initiatives into key business practices for employees of various racial backgrounds.

The following statement from a recent annual report of General Motors reflects the efforts that have been made by many firms to encourage diversity:

"Internally, we are working to create an environment where diversity thrives. We are trying to remove barriers that separate people and find new ways to engage teams to maximize productivity and profitability. This is being done through communication, teamwork, mutual support, and pulling together to achieve common objectives. Our challenge is to seek a diverse

population in leadership roles with a wide range of backgrounds, views, and experiences to ensure we capture diverse perspectives to meet and exceed customer expectations."

Johnson & Johnson, The Coca-Cola Company, IBM, Merrill Lynch, Sara Lee Corporation, and many other firms have made major efforts to promote diversity. Rockwell International has a diversity task team that developed guidelines for workforce diversity planning in each of its businesses. Xerox has improved its workplace diversity in recent years.

sexual harassment
unwelcome comments or actions of a sexual nature

Prevention of Sexual Harassment Another workplace issue is **sexual harassment,** which involves unwelcome comments or actions of a sexual nature. For example, one employee might make unwelcome sexual advances toward another and use personal power within the firm to threaten the other employee's job status. Firms attempt to prevent sexual harassment by offering seminars on the subject. Like diversity seminars, these seminars can help employees recognize that some statements or behavior may be offensive to other employees. These seminars are not only an act of responsibility to employees but also can improve a firm's productivity by helping employees get along.

Equal Opportunity

Employees who apply for a position at a firm should not be subjected to discrimination because of their national origin, race, gender, or religion. The Civil Rights Act of 1964 prohibits such forms of discrimination. The act is enforced by a federal agency known as the Equal Employment Opportunity Commission (EEOC). Beyond the federal guidelines, many firms attempt to ensure equal treatment among applicants for a position by assigning someone to monitor the hiring process. The concept of equal treatment applies not only to the initial hiring of an employee but also to annual raises and promotions within the firm.

affirmative action
a set of activities intended to increase opportunities for minorities and women

Many firms and government agencies implement **affirmative action** programs, which represent a set of activities intended to increase opportunities for minorities and women. Denny's (a restaurant business) was charged with racial discrimination in 1993. That same year, it began implementing a program to promote diversity. In recent years, Denny's has increased both its minority management and the number of franchises owned by African Americans.

How Firms Ensure Responsibility toward Employees

Firms can ensure that their responsibility toward employees will be fulfilled by taking the following steps.

Code of Responsibility A firm's responsibility toward its employees should be disclosed in its code of responsibilities. As with the responsibilities toward customers, the code will not attempt to spell out the recommended behavior in every situation, but it can offer some guidance for the decisions made by the firm. For example, the code may state that hiring decisions should be made without any form of bias. The firm should establish a hiring procedure that satisfies this provision. The procedure may specify that an ad describing the main duties of the job position be placed in the local newspaper for two weeks before anyone is hired. Doing this will help to ensure that the most qualified person is hired for the job. Thus, the procedure is implemented in a manner that is consistent with the firm's responsibility of hiring without any form of bias.

Grievance Policy   To ensure that employees receive proper treatment, many firms establish a grievance policy for employees who believe they are not being given equal opportunity. A specific person or department is normally assigned to resolve such complaints. This procedure is similar to that used to address customer complaints. By recognizing the complaints, the firm attempts both to resolve them and to revise its procedures to prevent further complaints.

A good example of a firm that has made an effort to resolve employee complaints is Marriott, which has implemented three strategies. First, it has set up a mediation process, in which a neutral person outside the firm (called a *mediator*) assesses the employee complaint and suggests a solution. The mediator does not have the power to enforce a final judgment but may help the employee and the firm resolve the conflict.

Second, Marriott offers a toll-free number for employees to call if they believe they were subjected to discrimination, harassment, or improper firing. Marriott begins to investigate the complaint within three days of the call. Third, Marriott allows the employee to voice complaints in front of a panel of other employees who determine whether the employee's complaints are valid, based on Marriott's existing guidelines.

Marriott's procedure for resolving employee complaints has shown positive results. EEOC investigations of employee complaints against Marriott declined by 50 percent in the year after the procedure was implemented and by 83 percent in the next year. Since more employee complaints are resolved within the firm, employees are more satisfied with their jobs and focus on satisfying customers.

The cost of attempting to listen to every employee complaint can be substantial for a firm, however. Furthermore, some of the complaints may not be valid. Firms must attempt to distinguish between complaints that are valid and those that are not and then focus on resolving the valid complaints.

Conflict with Employee Layoffs

Some business decisions are controversial because although they improve the firm's performance, they may adversely affect employees and the local community. Consider the following example, which reflects a common dilemma that many firms face. As your firm's business grew, you hired more employees. Unfortunately, demand for your product has declined recently, and you no longer need 20 of the employees that you hired over the last two years. If you lay off 20 employees, you will reduce your expenses substantially and satisfy your stockholders. However, you may be criticized for not serving employees' interests. This situation is unpleasant because the layoffs may be necessary (to cut expenses) for your firm to survive. If your firm fails, all your other employees will be out of work as well.

This dilemma has no perfect solution. Many firms may do what's best for the business, while attempting to reduce the adverse effects on their employees. For example, they may help laid-off employees find employment elsewhere or may even attempt to retrain them for other jobs within the firm.

Global Business

Global Ethics

U.S. firms typically have a code of ethics that provides guidelines for their employees. However, these guidelines may be much more restrictive than those generally used in some foreign countries. Consider a U.S. firm that sells supplies to foreign manufacturers. Both its code of ethics and the U.S. Foreign Corrupt Practices Act prevent the firm from offering payoffs ("kickbacks") to any employees of the manufacturing companies that order its supplies. Competitors based in other countries, however, may offer payoffs to employees of the manufacturing companies. In some countries, this type of behavior is acceptable. Thus, the U.S. supplier is at a disadvantage because its employees are required to follow a stricter code of ethics. This is a common ethical dilemma that U.S. firms face in a global environment. The employees of U.S. firms must either ignore their ethical guidelines or be at a disadvantage in certain foreign countries.

Another ethical dilemma that U.S. firms may face involves their relationship with certain foreign governments. Firms that conduct business in foreign countries are subject to numerous rules imposed by the local government. Officials of some foreign governments commonly accept bribes from firms that need approval for various business activities. For example, a firm may need to have its products approved for safety purposes, or its local manufacturing plant may need to be approved for environmental purposes. The process of approving even minor activities could take months and prevent the firm from conducting business. Those firms that pay off government officials may receive prompt attention from the local governments. Employees of Lockheed Martin were charged with bribing Egyptian government officials to win a contract to build new aircraft. Executives of IBM's Argentina subsidiary were charged with bribing Argentine government officials to generate business from the government.

A recent assessment of foreign countries by the U.S. Commerce Department and intelligence agencies detected numerous deals in which foreign firms used bribes to win business contracts over U.S. competitors. Many of these foreign firms are located in France, Germany, and Japan, as well as in some less-developed countries.

Many U.S. firms attempt to follow a worldwide code of ethics that is consistent across countries. This type of policy reduces the confusion that could result from using different ethical standards in different countries. Although a worldwide code of ethics may place a U.S. firm at a disadvantage in some countries, it may also enhance the firm's credibility.

Satisfying Employees

Some firms go beyond the responsibility of ensuring safety, proper treatment, and equal opportunity. These firms have taken initiatives to ensure that employees enjoy their jobs. This can increase the job satisfaction level of employees and reduce employee turnover. These firms realize that satisfied employees will do a better job for customers and that the customers, in turn, will be more satisfied. Here are some examples of initiatives by firms that were recently rated as the best for employees.

▶ Wegman's Food Market (in New York) has provided college scholarships for more than 17,000 of its full-time and part-time employees over the last 20 years. It also provides extensive training to ensure that its employees have the knowledge they need to perform their specific jobs. Its employee turnover is substantially lower than that of other grocery stores.

▶ Station Casinos (in Nevada) offers full-service on-site dentistry and 24-hour child care for employees.

▶ General Mills (in Minnesota) reimburses tuition up to $6,000 per year for its new employees.

- ▶ CarlMax (in Virginia) holds frequent meetings with employees to ask their opinions about what the company should change.
- ▶ Publix Super Markets (in Florida) provides health benefits for some part-time employees and an annual bonus of up to a week's salary plus an extra week of vacation time.
- ▶ J.M. Smucker (in Ohio) offers complimentary bagels and muffins to its employees every day.
- ▶ SAS Institute (in North Carolina) has a gym, a pool, ping-pong tables, and tennis courts for its employees.

General Mills allows its employees access to its fitness center, as a way of ensuring that the employees enjoy their work environment.

AP/WIDE WORLD PHOTOS

Decision Making

Ensuring Responsibility toward Employees

Cool Jewel Company has established guidelines to ensure fair treatment toward employees. First, it provides safety training for the employees who make the jewelry. Second, it communicates to all employees that sexual harassment will not be tolerated and has established a procedure so that any employees who feel that they have been harassed can file a complaint. Third, the hiring process focuses on finding the best person for each position and emphasizes equal opportunity for all races and genders. As a result of its excellent treatment of its employees, Cool Jewel has very little employee turnover, which is one of the main reasons for its success.

1. Why can Cool Jewel's responsibility toward employees result in better business performance?
2. Should Cool Jewel's hiring policy allow family members of existing employees to be hired?

ANSWERS: 1. Responsibility toward employees can increase the level of employee satisfaction and thereby encourage employees to perform well. 2. The hiring policy should allow the hiring of family members only if the business needs to hire and if those family members are the best qualified for the job positions.

Describe the
responsibilities of firms
to their stockholders.

Responsibility to Stockholders

Firms are responsible for satisfying their owners (or stockholders). Employees may be tempted to make decisions that satisfy their own interests rather than those of the owners. For example, some employees may use the firm's money to purchase computers for their personal use rather than for the firm.

How Firms Ensure Responsibility

Managers of a firm monitor employee decisions to ensure that they are made in the best interests of the owners. Employee compensation may be directly tied to the firm's performance. For example, a firm may provide its top managers with some of the firm's stock as partial compensation. If the managers make decisions that lead to a high level of performance, the value of the firm's stock should increase, and therefore the value of the stock held by the managers should increase. In this way, employees benefit directly when they make decisions that maximize the value of the firm.

Conflicts in the Efforts to Ensure Responsibility   Tying employee compensation to the firm's performance can resolve some conflicts of interest but create others. Some top managers who have received stock have later reported an artificially high performance level for the firm in a period when they wanted to sell their stock holdings. This allowed them to sell their stock at a relatively high price. Rather than improving the firm's performance, these managers manipulated the financial reporting to exaggerate the firm's performance. When investors decide whether to buy stock, they commonly rely on information disclosed by the firm to determine whether its stock would be a good investment.

There are many cases of firms misleading existing and prospective investors by neglecting to mention relevant information that would have made their stock less desirable. In addition, there are many cases of firms issuing exaggerated estimates of their revenue or earnings. When a firm misleads investors by creating an overly optimistic view of its potential performance, it can cause investors to pay too much for its stock. The stock's price will likely decline once the firm's true financial condition becomes apparent.

In January 2001, the chief executive officer (CEO) of Oracle Corporation sold 29 million shares of his holdings of Oracle stock. During the next few months, the firm disclosed that its earnings for the first quarter of 2001 would be lower than expected, and the stock price declined in response. Oracle's stockholders alleged that the CEO knew this information and sold his stock holdings before disclosing the bad news. That is, the investors who purchased the shares that were sold by the CEO claimed that they paid a much higher price than they should have paid for the stock and consequently incurred large losses on their investment.

One of the most blatant examples of a firm's managers misleading its existing and prospective stockholders is the case of Enron, Inc. Enron was one of the fastest-growing firms in the 1990s. Nevertheless, it created misleading financial statements, which led investors to believe that it was performing better than it really was. Consequently, some investors were fooled into paying much more for the stock than they should have during the 1999–2000 period. While Enron was creating such an optimistic

Enron CEO Ken Lay is led away in handcuffs by FBI agents after Enron was charged with providing misleading information to its investors.

view of its financial condition, some of its top managers were selling their holdings of Enron stock. Thus, they were dumping their shares while the price was high—before investors recognized that Enron's financial condition was much weaker than reported. While Enron's top managers earned large gains on their stock holdings, the investors who purchased Enron stock at this time lost most or all of their investment. In November 2001, Enron filed for bankruptcy, and the stock essentially became worthless. Thus, the top managers of Enron who were able to sell their stock at a high price (before the bad news was disclosed) benefited at the expense of other stockholders.

In recent years, executives at other firms including WorldCom have also been accused of attempting to sell their holdings of their firm's stock before unfavorable information about the firm was disclosed to the public. The initial intent of tying employee compensation to the firm's value was to ensure that employees would serve the interests of stockholders, but the practice has enabled some managers to benefit at the expense of stockholders.

Investors have become much more suspicious of firms' financial reports now that they are aware that some firms may engage in unethical reporting. Some firms have taken the initiative to reduce suspicion by providing more complete financial statements that are also more understandable and more readily interpreted.

In 2002, Congress passed the Public Company Accounting Reform and Investor Protection Act, also known as the Sarbanes-Oxley Act after the politicians who created it. This law was intended to encourage publicly traded firms to behave more responsibly toward their stockholders. First, the law attempts to ensure that publicly traded firms clarify the information that they provide to stockholders. Second, firms are required to establish methods to ensure that they can detect errors in their financial reporting systems. Third, top executives and board members are held more accountable for errors in financial reporting. Despite these measures, the act does not necessarily prevent managers from serving their own interests rather than stockholders' interests. For example, an executive could still hire family members or friends or make bad decisions about investing in projects. Thus, the act does not correct bad performance, but only attempts to ensure that firms accurately report their performance and document the processes and information that they use to make decisions.

How Stockholders Ensure Responsibility

shareholder activism
active efforts by stockholders to influence a firm's management policies

institutional investors
financial institutions that purchase large amounts of stock

In recent years, there has been much **shareholder activism,** or active efforts by stockholders to influence a firm's management policies. Stockholders have been especially active when they are dissatisfied with the firm's executive salaries or other policies.

The stockholders who have been most active are **institutional investors,** or financial institutions that purchase large amounts of stock. For example, insurance companies invest a large portion of the insurance premiums that they receive in stocks. If institutional investors invest a large amount of money in a particular stock, the return on their investment is highly dependent on how that firm performs. Since many institutional investors commonly invest $10 million or more in a single firm's stock, they pay close attention to the performance of any firm in which they invest.

If an institutional investor believes the firm is poorly managed, it may attempt to meet with the firm's executives and express its dissatisfaction. It may even attempt to team up with other institutional investors who also own a large proportion of the firm's stock. This gives them more negotiating power because the firm's executives are more likely to listen to institutional investors who collectively hold a large proportion of the firm's stock. The institutional investors do not attempt to dictate how the firm should be managed. Instead, they attempt to ensure that the firm's managers make decisions that are in the best interests of all stockholders.

Conflict with Excessive Executive Compensation

A firm's managers can attempt to satisfy its stockholders by ensuring that funds invested by the stockholders are put to good use. If these funds are used to cover unnecessary expenses, the firm's profits are reduced, which reduces the return that stockholders receive on their investment. Stockholders are often particularly concerned about the salaries paid to the firm's CEO and other executives. The following example illustrates the potential effect that excessive executive salaries can have on a firm's performance (and therefore on the returns to stockholders).

Consider two firms called Firm C and Firm D, which are in the same industry and have similar revenue and expenses, as shown in Exhibit 2.4. Assume that the only difference is that Firm C pays its top five executives a total of $30 million in annual salary, while Firm D pays its top five executives a total of $5 million. As shown in Exhibit 2.4, the annual profits of Firm D are $25 million higher than those of Firm C. This difference can be attributed to Firm C's higher executive salary expenses. Thus, the stockholders of Firm C receive a smaller return than the stockholders of Firm D.

Exhibit 2.4

Impact of Executive Salaries on a Firm's Performance

	Firm C	Firm D
Revenue	$200,000,000	$200,000,000
−Expenses (except executive salaries)	−150,000,000	−150,000,000
−Executive salaries expense	−30,000,000	−5,000,000
=Profits	=$20,000,000	=$45,000,000

CEO compensation has increased substantially over recent decades. In 1980, the average compensation of CEOs was about 42 times the average compensation of employees. In 1990, it was about 85 times the average salary of employees. In 2000, it was more than 500 times the average salary of employees.

Some customers and stockholders may argue that firms paying executives such high salaries are not meeting their social responsibilities. These firms may be serving the interests of the executives and not the stockholders who own the firm. Although it may be possible to justify very high compensation for CEOs who have been successful, it is difficult to justify such compensation for CEOs whose companies have performed poorly. In some recent years, the compensation of many CEOs increased even though the earnings or stock price of their firm declined. The compensation paid to CEOs is partially influenced by the size of the firm. CEOs of larger firms tend to earn higher salaries, even when their firm performs poorly.

Decision Making

Responsibility toward Investors

The board of directors of Cool Jewel Company has developed a compensation policy for its top executives that is also intended to satisfy its investors (stockholders). The executives receive a salary and 5,000 shares of the firm's stock each year. Thus, they have an incentive to make decisions that will increase the stock's price (and therefore satisfy stockholders) because this increases the value of the stock that they are given. To ensure that the executives do not manipulate the level of reported profits upward just to increase the stock price temporarily so they can sell their stock, the board of directors requires the executives to hold the stock for a minimum of five years. This encourages the executives to make business decisions that will increase the company's long-term performance.

1. Explain why Cool Jewel's executives would not be tempted to manipulate the stock price.
2. Explain how Cool Jewel's board of directors could adjust the mixture of salary and stock if they wanted to give executives more incentive to make decisions to increase the stock's value (and thus serve stockholders).

ANSWERS: 1. Cool Jewel's executives are required to hold their stock for five years, so during that period, they are not able to benefit from temporarily manipulating the earnings level. 2. The board could use a compensation formula that contains a lower salary and more stock to give executives more incentive to make decisions that result in a higher stock price.

Responsibility to Creditors

4

Describe the responsibilities of firms to their creditors.

Firms are responsible for meeting their financial obligations to their creditors. If a firm is experiencing financial problems and is unable to meet its obligations, it should inform its creditors. Sometimes creditors are willing to extend payment deadlines and may even offer advice on how the firm can improve its financial condition. A firm has a strong incentive to satisfy its responsibility to creditors. If the firm does not pay what it owes to creditors, it may be forced into bankruptcy.

How Firms Violate Their Responsibility

Some firms violate their responsibility to creditors by providing misleading financial information that exaggerates their financial condition. For example, Enron's financial reporting misled its creditors as well as its stockholders. Enron received some loans from creditors that it would not have received if the creditors had known of its weaknesses. Specifically, Enron did not disclose some of its debt. Creditors would have been concerned about extending more credit if they had fully understood how much debt Enron already had. By hiding some debt, Enron was able to more easily borrow funds. Ultimately, however, it went bankrupt because it could not cover the payments on all of its debt. Many creditors lost hundreds of millions of dollars because of the large amount of credit they provided to Enron that would never be paid back. Although creditors recognize the possible risk that a business will fail and be unable to repay its loans, they were angry that Enron used unethical financial reporting methods to obtain loans. While some firms have received bad publicity for distorting their financial condition, others have taken the initiative to give creditors more detailed and clear financial information.

Decision Making

Tradeoffs from Satisfying All Stakeholders

To illustrate the tradeoffs involved in trying to satisfy all stakeholders, consider the case of Cool Jewel Company. Last year, the demand for Cool Jewel's products increased substantially, so it hired several additional employees. This year, however, the demand for its products has declined, and its revenue has declined as a result. The managers of Cool Jewel face a dilemma. If they retain all the employees, their expenses will be excessive, and they may not be able to make the debt payments they owe to creditors. If the company continues to incur high expenses, it will likely fail. This would adversely affect the owners and creditors and would ultimately result in the elimination of all employees. Thus, the desire to completely satisfy the existing employees will not satisfy the owners or the creditors or even the employees in the long run.

Cool Jewel managers decide to lay off some employees. They lay off those employees who were most recently hired and inform them that the company would like to rehire them as soon as the demand for its products increases again. This decision was intended to best serve all of Cool Jewel's stakeholders over the long term.

1. In the future, how might Cool Jewel avoid situations in which it has too many full-time employees and has to lay off some of them?

2. Why must Cool Jewel fulfill its obligations toward its creditors before its other stakeholders?

ANSWERS: 1. Cool Jewel could hire some part-time employees in periods when demand for its products is abnormally high, and it could avoid hiring additional full-time employees until it is confident that it will always need them. 2. The creditors provide credit, and if they do not receive the debt payments owed to them, the firm will likely fail. Thus, Cool Jewel needs to cover its obligations to its creditors first.

5

Describe the
responsibilities of
firms to the environment.

Responsibility to the Environment

The production processes that firms use, as well as the products they produce, can be harmful to the environment. The most common abuses to the environment are discussed next, along with recent actions that firms have taken to improve the environment.

Air Pollution

Some production processes cause air pollution, which is harmful to society because it inhibits breathing. For example, the production of fuel and steel, as well as automobile use, increases the amount of carbon dioxide in the air.

How Firms Prevent Air Pollution   Automobile and steel firms have reduced air pollution by changing their production processes so that less carbon dioxide escapes into the air. For example, firms such as Honeywell and Inland Steel spend substantial funds to reduce pollution. Ford Motor Company has formulated an environmental pledge, which states that it is dedicated to developing environmental solutions and intends to preserve the environment in the future.

How the Government Prevents Air Pollution   The federal government has also become involved by enforcing specific guidelines that call for firms to limit the amount of carbon dioxide caused by the production process. In 1970, the Environmental Protection Agency (EPA) was created to develop and enforce pollution standards. In recent years, pollution control laws have become more stringent.

Businesses sometimes cause pollution in the production or transportation of their products. In this picture, workers clean up an oil spill off Malibu Beach, California.

PHOTOEDIT, INC.

Land Pollution

Land has been polluted by toxic waste resulting from some production processes. A related form of land pollution is solid waste, which does not deteriorate over time. As a result of waste, land not only looks less attractive but also may no longer be useful for other purposes, such as farming.

How Firms Prevent Land Pollution   Firms have revised their production and packaging processes to reduce the amount of waste. They now store toxic waste and deliver it to specified toxic waste storage sites. They also recycle plastic and limit their use of materials that would ultimately become solid waste. Many firms have environmental programs that are designed to reduce damage to the environment. For example, Homestake Mining Company recognizes that its mining operations disturb the land, so it spends money to minimize any effect on the environment. PPG Industries restructured its production processes to generate about 6,000 fewer tons of waste in a single year. Kodak recycles more than a half-billion pounds of material a year and also supports a World Wildlife Fund environmental education program. IBM typically spends more than $30 million a year for environmental assessments and cleanup. ChevronTexaco and DuPont spend hundreds of millions of dollars every year to comply with environmental regulations. Rockwell International has reduced its hazardous waste by more than 50 percent in recent years.

Conflict with Environmental Responsibility

Although most firms agree that a clean environment is desirable, they may disagree on how much responsibility they have for improving the environment. Consider two firms called Firm A and Firm B, which have similar revenue and expenses. Firm A, however, makes a much greater effort to clean up the environment; it spends $10 million, while Firm B spends $2 million. The profit of each firm is shown in Exhibit 2.5. Firm A has an annual profit of zero, while Firm B has an annual profit of $8 million. If you could invest in the stock of either Firm A or Firm B, where would you invest your money? Most investors desire to earn a high return on their money. Although they recognize that a firm may have some environmental cleanup expenses, they do not want those expenses to be excessive. Therefore, most investors would prefer to invest in Firm B rather than Firm A.

Firm A could attempt to recapture its high environmental cleanup expenses by charging a higher price for its product. In this way, it may be able to spend heavily on the environment, while still generating a reasonable return for its stockholders. This strategy makes the customers pay for its extra environmental cleanup. A problem, however, is that if Firm A charges a higher price than Firm B, many customers will switch to Firm B so that they can pay the lower price.

As this example illustrates, there is a limit to how much firms can spend on improving the environment. Firms have a responsibility to avoid damaging the environment, but if they spend excessively on environmental improvement, they will not satisfy most of their customers or owners.

Although firms have increased their efforts to clean up the environment, they do not necessarily agree with the guidelines imposed by the government. Oil refineries that are losing money remain open to avoid the cleanup that the EPA would require if they closed down. Some refineries would pay about $1 billion for cleanup costs because of the EPA's strict guidelines. Firms have questioned many other environmental guidelines imposed by the EPA.

Exhibit 2.5

Effect of Environmental Expenses on Business Performance

	Firm A	Firm B
Revenue	$90,000,000	$90,000,000
Total operating expenses	−80,000,000	−80,000,000
Environmental cleanup expenses	−10,000,000	−2,000,000
Profit	0	$8,000,000

Decision Making

Ensuring Responsibility toward the Environment

Cool Jewel Company ensures that its manufacturing process does not harm the environment. Its executives would like to demonstrate their commitment to improving the environment, but they recognize that using company funds to improve the environment may reduce the amount of funds available to pay stakeholders such as creditors and employees. Therefore, the managers decide to produce some small inexpensive pins with the inscription "save the environment." Every customer who spends more than $20 in Cool Jewel's retail stores will receive this piece of jewelry. Cool Jewel's business name is also inscribed on the pin. Thus, the jewelry not only serves as a gesture toward a clean environment but also provides the firm with some name recognition.

1. How might Cool Jewel Company benefit from its concern for the environment?
2. Should Cool Jewel allocate a substantial amount of funds for environmental cleanup, even though it did not harm the environment?

ANSWERS: 1. Its customers may appreciate its concern and be more willing to buy jewelry there. 2. It should not spend excessively on the environment because it may not have sufficient funds to meet its commitments to its other stakeholders.

Describe the responsibilities of firms to their communities.

Responsibility to the Community

When firms establish a base in a community, they become part of that community and rely on it for customers and employees. Firms demonstrate their concern for the community by sponsoring local events or donating to local charities. For example, SunTrust Bank, IBM, and many other firms have donated funds to universities. Bank of America has provided loans to low-income neighborhoods and minority communities. The Cheesecake Factory, a famous restaurant chain, established a foundation that not only raises funds for charities but also demonstrates the company's concern for its customers and community. In 2003, total cash donations by 500 large U.S. firms amounted to $3.26 billion. Wal-Mart was the top donor, with donations of $176 million. Ford Motor Company donated $120 million, while Johnson & Johnson donated $99 million and Exxon-Mobil donated $97 million.

For a multinational corporation, the community is its international environment. Many of the firms that engage in substantial international business have increased their international donations. Nike's donations to foreign countries now represent 39 percent of its total donations, while IBM's foreign donations represent about 30 percent of its total. When the tsunami disaster struck Indonesia and other Southeast Asian nations in December 2004, many U.S. firms quickly responded with contributions. FedEx made some of its planes available to help move 230 tons of medical supplies to the devastated areas. Coca-Cola, Dow Chemical, ExxonMobil, Microsoft, and Wal-Mart each contributed millions of dollars. Coca-Cola also delivered 500,000 bottles of water.

Conflict with Maximizing Social Responsibility

The decisions of a firm's managers that maximize social responsibility could conflict with maximizing firm value. The costs involved in achieving such a goal will have to be passed on to consumers. Thus, the attempt to maximize responsibility to the community may reduce the firm's ability to provide products at a reasonable price to consumers.

FedEx volunteered its transportation to deliver medical supplies in response to the 2005 tsunami disaster.

AP/WIDE WORLD PHOTOS

Many companies support charitable organizations that promote nutrition, education, performing and visual arts, or amateur athletics. Even though this social support requires a considerable financial commitment, the firm can gain from an enhanced image in the eyes of the consumers to whom it sells its products. In a sense, the charitable support not only can help society but also can be a valuable marketing tool to improve the firm's image. People expect firms to give something back to society. In a recent Corporate Citizenship Study, 78 percent of all respondents said that firms have a responsibility to support causes, while 84 percent said that they want the firms serving their communities to be committed to social issues. Consequently, both society and stockholders can benefit from the charitable donations. If a company identifies a charitable cause that is closely related to its business, it may be able to simultaneously contribute to society and maximize the firm's value. For example, a running shoe manufacturer may sponsor a race, or a tennis racket manufacturer may sponsor a tennis tournament.

Apple and IBM invest substantial funds in local education programs. Not only is this investment helpful to the communities, but it also results in computer sales to schools. Home Depot donates to community programs that use much of the money for housing projects. Many Checkers restaurants have been located in inner-city areas. They not only provide jobs to many minorities but also have been profitable.

One of the best examples of a firm that has demonstrated its social responsibility in a manner that has also enhanced its performance is The Coca-Cola Company. It initiated a 10-year, $60 million sponsorship of Boys & Girls Clubs of America—the largest donation of funds by a firm to a specific cause. The sponsorship involves several events, such as basketball and golf tournaments and after-school reading sessions. Coca-Cola's name will be promoted at the events, which can help attract new young customers to its products.

Dow Chemical Company has created a Community Advisory Panel, which identifies community needs and ensures that Dow gives to its communities. Its recent community acts include funding education programs in South America where it conducts some of its business, supporting a Habitat for Humanity homebuilding project in Korea, and funding a new art center in West Virginia.

Decision Making

Ensuring Responsibility toward the Community

Cool Jewel Company has its headquarters in Los Angeles, California, but has retail outlets scattered throughout the United States. It wanted to demonstrate its responsibility toward its community and felt that its community included not just its headquarters location, but all locations where it has retail outlets. Cool Jewel's managers wanted to provide community service in a manner that would be recognized by the communities, so they decided to produce additional imitation gold wristwatches to be awarded as gifts for accomplishments by local people. For example, Cool Jewel worked with a local school system to give the wristwatches to the top students at each school. It also awarded the watches to numerous volunteers who contributed to their local communities. The watches also served as a form of public relations because they were inscribed with Cool Jewel's name and logo. Thus, Cool Jewel was able to contribute to its community while increasing its name recognition.

1. Cool Jewel considered giving cash awards for accomplishments by local people. Why would giving wristwatches be a more suitable way to increase its name recognition?

2. Why would Cool Jewel attract more demand for its products by serving the local communities where its retail stores are located rather than the community surrounding its headquarters?

ANSWERS: 1. Its wristwatches may become a conversation piece, and they also serve as a sample of the product that it sells. 2. It is important to appeal to the communities that may potentially buy products at the retail stores, so Cool Jewel should attempt to serve those communities.

Summary of Business Responsibilities

Firms have many responsibilities to employees, stockholders, creditors, the environment, and the community that must be recognized when doing business. The following quotations from recent annual reports illustrate firms' general concern about ethics and social responsibility:

"A comprehensive annual ethics training program heightens the awareness of our employees and provides guidelines to resolve issues responsibly."

—Rockwell International

"Boise Cascade is committed to protecting the health and safety of our employees, being a responsible corporate citizen in the communities in which we operate, and providing active stewardship of the timberlands under our management."

—Boise Cascade

Self-Scoring Exercise

Assessing the Ethical Standards of the Firm Where You Work

Think about the organization you currently work for or one you know something about and complete the following Ethical Climate Questionnaire. Use the scale below and write the number that best represents your answer in the space next to each item.

To what extent are the following statements true about your company?

Completely false	Mostly false	Somewhat false	Somewhat true	Mostly true	Completely true
0	1	2	3	4	5

_____ 1. In this company, people are expected to follow their own personal and moral beliefs.

_____ 2. People are expected to do anything to further the company's interests.

_____ 3. In this company, people look out for each other's good.

_____ 4. It is very important to follow the company's rules and procedures strictly.

_____ 5. In this company, people protect their own interests above other considerations.

_____ 6. The first consideration is whether a decision violates any law.

_____ 7. Everyone is expected to stick by company rules and procedures.

_____ 8. The most efficient way is always the right way in this company.

_____ 9. Our major consideration is what is best for everyone in the company.

_____ 10. In this company, the law or ethical code of the profession is the major consideration.

_____ 11. It is expected at this company that employees will always do what is right for the consumer and the public.

To score the questionnaire, first add up your responses to questions 1, 3, 6, 9, 10, and 11. This is subtotal number 1. Next, reverse the scores on questions 2, 4, 5, 7, and 8 (5 = 0, 4 = 1, 3 = 2, 2 = 3, 1 = 4, 0 = 5). Add the reverse scores to form subtotal number 2. Add subtotal number 1 to subtotal number 2 for an overall score.

Subtotal 1 _____ + Subtotal 2 _____ = Overall Score _____.

Overall scores can range from 0 to 55. The higher the score, the more the organization's culture encourages ethical behavior.

> "We . . . believe that to create long term value for shareholders, we must also create value in our relationships with customers, employees, suppliers and the communities in which we operate."
>
> —Briggs & Stratton

Most firms have procedures in place to ensure that their social responsibilities are satisfied. They also enforce codes that specify their responsibilities. Prudential Securities has created a position called "Corporate Values Officer" to ensure that its social responsibilities are fulfilled.

Some firms may make more of an effort to follow ethical standards than others. The first Self-Scoring Exercise allows you to assess the ethical standards of the firm where you work. Employees may vary in their perception of what behavior is ethical. The second Self-Scoring Exercise provides a variety of situations that would probably be perceived as unethical by some people but as acceptable by others.

Business Responsibilities in an International Environment

When firms compete in an international environment, they must be aware of cultural differences. Firms from some countries do not necessarily view certain business practices such as payoffs to large customers or to suppliers as unethical. This makes it difficult for other firms to compete for international business. Nevertheless, firms typically attempt to apply their ethical guidelines and corporate responsibilities in an international setting. By doing so, they establish a global reputation for running their business in an ethical manner.

Protestors stand in front of a Gap store, protesting Gap's purchases of some of its clothing from Asian factories that allegedly mistreat their employees.

GETTY IMAGES

In 2004, Gap, Inc., took a major step toward social responsibility in the international environment that may serve as a model for other firms in the future. It conducted a major assessment of the 3,000 factories in Africa, China, India, South America, and other locations that produce the clothing it sells. The workers in these factories are not employees of Gap, but since Gap relies on these factories for its clothing, it felt responsible for ensuring that the workers have reasonable working conditions. In its 40-page social responsibility report, the company reported that many of these factories do not follow reasonable labor standards. This was a bold move by Gap, because it acknowledged that it was unaware that some workers who produce its clothing did not have adequate working conditions. As a result of its assessment, Gap stopped using some factories where conditions were inadequate. This is Gap's way of protesting against bad working conditions and indicating that it does not want to do business with any factory that does not treat its employees properly.

The Cost of Fulfilling Social Responsibilities

A summary of possible expenses incurred as a result of social responsibilities is provided in Exhibit 2.6. Some firms incur large expenses in all areas of social responsibility. For example, automobile manufacturers such as Ford Motor Company and General Motors must ensure that their production of automobiles does not harm the environment. Second, they must ensure that all employees in their massive workforces are treated properly. Third, they must ensure that they deliver a safe and reliable product to their customers.

In recent years, many new government regulations have been imposed to create a cleaner environment and ensure that firms do not neglect other social responsibilities. Normally, all the firms in an industry will raise their prices to cover the expenses associated with following new government regulations. For example, restrictions on cutting down trees resulted in higher expenses for paper companies. These companies raised their prices

Self-Scoring Exercise

Assessing Whether Specific Situations Are Ethical

The purpose of this exercise is to explore your opinions about ethical issues faced in organizations. The class should be divided into 12 groups. Each group will randomly be assigned one of the following issues:

1. Is it ethical to take office supplies from work for home use? Make personal long-distance calls from the office? Use company time for personal business? Or do these behaviors constitute stealing?

2. If you exaggerate your credentials in an interview, is it lying? Is lying to protect a co-worker acceptable?

3. If you pretend to be more successful than you are to impress your boss, are you being deceitful?

4. How do you differentiate between a bribe and a gift?

5. If there are slight defects in a product you are selling, are you obligated to tell the buyer? If an advertised "sale" price is really the everyday price, should you divulge the information to the customer?

6. Suppose you have a friend who works at the ticket office for the convention center where Shania Twain will be appearing. Is it cheating if you ask the friend to get you tickets so that you won't have to fight the crowd to get them? Is buying merchandise for your family at your company's cost cheating?

7. Is it immoral to do less than your best in work performance? Is it immoral to accept workers' compensation when you are fully capable of working?

8. What behaviors constitute emotional abuse at work? What would you consider an abuse of one's position of power?

9. Are high-stress jobs a breach of ethics? What about transfers that break up families?

10. Are all rule violations equally important? Do employees have an ethical obligation to follow company rules?

11. To what extent are you responsible for the ethical behavior of your co-workers? If you witness unethical behavior and don't report it, are you an accessory?

12. Is it ethical to help one work group at the expense of another group? For instance, suppose one group has excellent performance and you want to reward its members with an afternoon off. The other work group will have to pick up the slack and work harder if you do this. Is this ethical?

Once your group has been assigned its issue, you have two tasks:

1. First, formulate your group's answer to the ethical dilemmas.

2. After you have formulated your group's position, discuss the individual differences that may have contributed to your position. You will want to discuss the individual differences presented in this chapter as well as any others that you believe affected your position on the ethical dilemma.

Your instructor will lead the class in a discussion of how individual differences may have influenced your positions on these ethical dilemmas.

to cover these higher expenses. Maintaining social responsibilities is necessary but costly, and customers indirectly pay the expenses incurred.

Cost of Complaints

When assessing the expense involved in dealing with customer or employee complaints, firms normally consider the cost of hiring people to resolve the complaints. However, they must also consider the cost of defending against possible lawsuits by customers and employees. Customers suing firms for product defects or deceptive advertising and employees suing their firms for discrimination are common practices today.

A number of expenses can be associated with a lawsuit. First, the court may fine a firm that is found guilty. Some court-imposed fines have amounted to several million dollars. Second, some lawsuits are settled out of court, but the settlement may require the firm to make some payment to customers or employees. Third, a firm may incur substantial expenses when hiring an attorney. Many lawsuits continue for several years, and the expenses of the attorney (or a law firm) for a single case may exceed $1 million. Fourth, an indirect cost of a lawsuit is the decline in demand for a firm's product because of bad publicity associated with the lawsuit. This results in less revenue to the firm.

The high cost of customer complaints is a reason by itself for firms to be ethical and socially responsible. Yet, even when firms establish and enforce a comprehensive code of social responsibility, they do not necessarily avoid complaints and lawsuits. They must recognize this when estimating the expenses involved in social responsibility.

Exhibit 2.6

Possible Expenses Incurred as a Result of Social Responsibilities

Responsibility to:	Expenses Incurred as a Result:
Customers	Establishing program to receive and resolve complaints Conducting surveys to assess customer satisfaction Lawsuits by customers (product liability)
Employees	Establishing program to receive and resolve complaints Conducting surveys to assess employee satisfaction Lawsuits by employees based on allegations of discrimination
Stockholders	Disclosing financial information periodically Lawsuits by stockholders based on allegations that the firm's managers are not fulfilling their obligations to stockholders
Environment	Complying with governmental regulations on environment Complying with self-imposed environmental guidelines
Community	Sponsoring community activities

Cross Functional Teamwork

Ethical Responsibilities across Business Functions

The perception of a firm's ethical standards is dependent on its team of managers. The ethical responsibilities of a firm's managers vary with their specific job assignments. Production managers are responsible for producing a product that is safe. They should also ensure that the production process satisfies environmental standards.

Marketing managers are responsible for marketing a product in a manner that neither misrepresents the product's characteristics nor misleads consumers or investors. Marketing managers must communicate with production managers to ensure that product marketing is consistent with the production. Any promotion efforts by marketing managers that make statements about product quality should be assessed by production managers to ensure accuracy.

Financial managers are responsible for providing accurate financial reports to creditors or investors who may provide financial support to the firm. They rely on information from production and marketing managers when preparing their financial reports.

A firm earns a reputation for being ethical by ensuring that ethical standards are maintained in all business functions. If some members of its team of managers are unethical, the entire firm will be viewed as unethical.

COLLEGE HEALTH CLUB: SOCIAL RESPONSIBILITY DECISIONS AT CHC

As a college student, Sue Kramer always had an interest in the social responsibility of businesses. Now that she is establishing the College Health Club (CHC), she can apply her beliefs about social responsibility to her own business. Sue recognizes that being socially responsible may reduce her firm's earnings or result in higher prices to her customers because attending to many social responsibilities can increase expenses. Sue's goal is to develop strategies for satisfying CHC's social responsibilities in a manner that can still maximize the firm's value.

Sue identifies the following specific responsibilities of CHC to her customers, employees, environment, and community:

▶ **Responsibility to Customers** Sue plans to spend some of her time talking with customers at the health club to determine whether the customers (members) are satisfied with the facilities that CHC offers. She also plans to send out a survey to all the members to obtain more feedback. Furthermore, she offers a money-back guarantee if the customers are not satisfied after a two-week trial period.

Sue's efforts are intended not only to fulfill a moral responsibility but also to increase the firm's memberships over time. In the health club business, the firm's reputation for satisfying the customer is important. Many customers choose a health club because of referrals by other customers. Therefore, Sue hopes that her efforts will identify ways in which she can make CHC more appealing to potential members. She also wants to show her interest in satisfying the existing members.

▶ **Responsibility to Employees** Sue started the business with herself as the only full-time employee. However, she has one part-time employee (Lisa Lane) and expects to hire more employees over time as the number of memberships increases. Sue plans to pay employee wages that are consistent with those of other health clubs in the area. She also plans to have employees who are diverse in gender and race. Her goal is not just to demonstrate her willingness to seek diversity but also to attract diversity among customers as well. For example, she wants her health club to have a somewhat even mix of males and females and believes that an even mix of employees over time might attract an even mix of customers.

▶ **Responsibility to the Environment** Since the health club is a service, no production process is involved that could damage the environment. However, Sue will establish recycling containers for cans of soft drinks consumed at CHC.

▶ **Responsibility to the Community** Sue feels a special allegiance to Texas College, which she has attended over the last four years. She has volunteered to offer a free seminar on health issues for the college students. She believes that this service will not only fulfill her moral responsibility but also allow her to promote her new health club located next to the college campus. Therefore, her community service could ultimately enhance the value of CHC.

▶ **Summary of CHC's Social Responsibilities** In general, Sue is developing strategies that will not only satisfy social responsibilities but also retain existing customers and attract new customers. She has created the following pledge, which she will use as a guideline when making various business decisions:

Pledge of Social Responsibilities at CHC

Sue Kramer, owner of CHC, recognizes her firm's responsibility to its customers, its employees, its owners, its creditors, and the environment. CHC intends to offer its customers excellent service at reasonable prices. It will consider feedback from customers and attempt to continually improve its services to satisfy customers. It will offer its employees a safe working environment and equal opportunities without bias. The firm will be managed in a manner that will maximize the value of the business for any owners who are invited to invest in the firm over time. CHC recognizes its responsibility to make timely payments on debt owed to creditors. It also pledges to conduct its business in a manner that will not harm the environment. By satisfying customers, employees, and creditors, CHC should establish a good reputation and attract more customers in the future.

Summary

1 The behavior of firms is molded by their business ethics, or set of moral values. Firms have a responsibility to produce safe products and to sell their products without misleading the customers. They ensure social responsibility toward customers by establishing a code of ethics, monitoring customer complaints, and asking customers for feedback on products that they recently purchased.

2 Firms have a responsibility to provide safe working conditions, proper treatment, and equal opportunity for employees. They can satisfy their responsibility toward employees by enforcing safety guidelines, offering seminars on diversity, and establishing a grievance procedure that allows employees to report any complaints.

3 Firms have a responsibility to satisfy the owners (or stockholders) who provided funds. They attempt to ensure that managers make decisions that are in the best interests of stockholders.

4 Firms have a responsibility to meet their financial obligations to their creditors. This responsibility includes not only paying their debts but also not supplying creditors with misleading information about their financial condition.

5 Firms have a responsibility to maintain a clean environment when operating their businesses. However, they incur expenses when attempting to fulfill their environmental responsibility.

6 Firms have a social responsibility to the local communities where they attract customers and employees. They provide donations and other benefits to these communities.

How the Chapter Concepts Affect Business Performance

A firm's decisions regarding the ethics and social responsibility concepts summarized above can enhance its business performance. By following ethical practices, a firm can gain the trust of its customers who will return to buy more products. By treating its employees well, it motivates them to work harder. By making its debt payments to its creditors on time, it gains the trust of creditors for when it needs more funding. All of the firm's decisions are intended to enhance its performance and the value of its stock, which satisfies its shareholders.

Key Terms

affirmative action   45
business responsibilities   39
consumerism   40

institutional investors   51
monopoly   41
sexual harassment   45

shareholder activism   51
social responsibility   38

Review & Critical Thinking Questions

1. Define business ethics and describe an ethical situation in which you had to distinguish between right and wrong.

2. Identify the entities to which firms have a social responsibility. Briefly describe the social responsibility a firm has to each entity.

3. How can tying employee compensation to a firm's performance resolve some conflicts of interest? How can tying employee compensation to a firm's performance create other conflicts of interest?

4. Identify the actions a firm can take to ensure that if fulfills its social responsibility to its customers.

5. What is the purpose of a code of responsibilities?

6. How can a business fulfill its social responsibility to its customers and still earn a profit?

7. Explain the role the government plays in ensuring that firms become socially responsible to customers.

8. What is the purpose of a grievance policy?

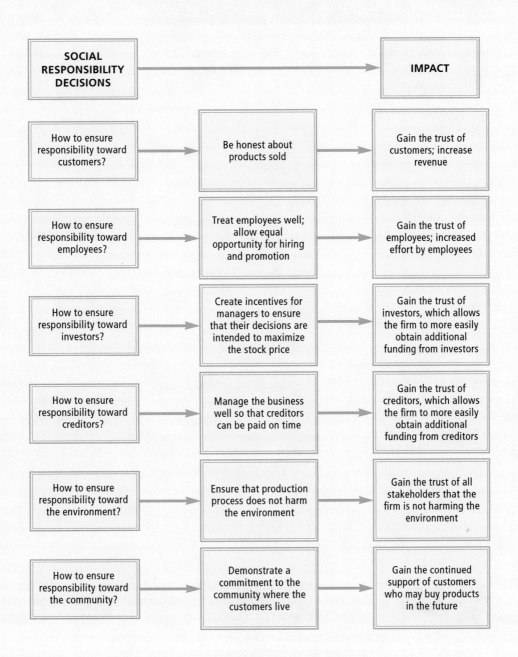

9. Briefly describe a firm's social responsibility to its community and the environment.

10. Describe the most common abuses of the environment and explain how businesses can prevent them.

11. How does a business's responsibility to its community affect product prices? Are firms that maximize their social responsibility to the community able to maximize shareholder value? Why or why not?

12. Identify and explain the conflicting objectives that often challenge a manager's responsibility.

13. Identify expenses that a firm may incur when assuming social responsibility for customers and employees.

Discussion Questions

1. Assume that you are a manager. Broadly speaking, how would your firm's business ethics and social responsibility affect your decision making? What effect would these issues have on the organization's bottom line (earnings)?

2. Assume that you are a manager. What are your ethical responsibilities to the following: (a) employees, (b) stockholders, (c) customers, and (d) suppliers?

3. You are an employee at XYZ Corporation. You just discovered that a manager deliberately neglected to include a large expense in the company's last annual report. The manager also told you that he plans to sell some of the stock he owns in the firm soon. How does this manager benefit at the expense of other employees? What are the ethical implications of his actions?

4. How could a firm use the Internet to promote the business ethics and social responsibility it practices?

5. Discuss the pros and cons of affirmative action programs and how they affect business recruiting and selection efforts. Do you think they constrain or aid businesses?

6. You are the manager of a clothing manufacturer with operations in several developing countries. You discover that employees are not being treated according to your company's ethical standards. What options are available to you to change the way employees are treated?

7. You are a manager of a company that manufactures phosphates; during the manufacturing process, these chemicals contaminate the environment and harm the ecosystem of birds that nest in the area. Cleaning up the chemicals would be too costly for your firm to continue to be profitable. What alternatives are available for you to engage in and still maintain your responsibility to the community?

8. As an employee of a large multinational firm, you are attempting to negotiate with a high-level political official to purchase a large piece of land for a factory in a developing country. The political official asks you for a substantial "gift" to his political campaign. What is an ethical solution to his request?

9. You are a small business owner in a small town. You are approached by a local school's football team about sponsoring a fundraising event to raise money for a trip out of state for a national football game. How can you maintain your responsibilities to creditors and still fund the community project?

IT'S YOUR DECISION: ETHICS AT CHC

1. Sue was recently asked if she wants to sell aerobics clothing in her health club. A clothing firm has the clothing produced in Asia and would sell it to her customers at a reasonable price and still earn a profit. Sue has heard that this firm hires children to make the clothing under poor working conditions. Should Sue sell this clothing at CHC?

2. Based on the information in the previous question, what is Sue's social responsibility (if any) to prevent improper treatment of employees in other countries?

3. Sue has several friends at Texas College who would like a part-time job at the health club. However, she knows that CHC would perform better if she hires part-time students who are majors in exercise science. Does Sue have a social responsibility to hire her friends?

4. Do you think a services firm like a health club has different social responsibilities than a manufacturing firm has?

5. Sue finds out that some trainers at CHC are encouraging customers to use certain herbal supplements. Sue learns that the supplements may cause physical harm to the customers. Should she fire the trainers?

Investing in a Business

Using the annual report of the firm in which you would like to invest, complete the following:

1 Many firms disclose their policies on ethics and social responsibilities within their annual reports. Does your firm mention any specific policies that encourage employees' ethical behavior? Does the firm give any specific examples of how it accomplishes these goals?

2 Describe your firm's policies on its social responsibility toward its community and the environment. Does the firm give any specific examples of how it accomplishes these goals?

3 Explain how the business uses technology to enhance its business ethics and social responsibility. For example, does it use the Internet to provide information regarding its business practices? Does it provide a place for customer complaints on the Internet?

4 Go to http://hoovers.com and locate the NEWS SEARCH. Type in the name of the firm in the space provided, and review the recent news stories about the firm. Summarize any (at least one) recent news story about the firm that applies to one or more of the key concepts in this chapter.

Case: Social Responsibility at Ben & Jerry's Ice Cream

Ben & Jerry's Ice Cream began as a small business and has grown into an international corporation. Its mission statement includes provisions about (1) producing a good product for its customers, (2) providing an economic reward (profits) to its shareholders, and (3) fulfilling its social responsibility. These three goals have no particular order. Ben & Jerry's believes that it should not focus on any one goal but should achieve all three goals.

Ben & Jerry's directs 7.5 percent of its pretax profits to a foundation, which donates money to specific charitable organizations. In another effort to fulfill its social responsibility, Ben & Jerry's works with small businesses, as its owners remember that it was once a small business. It relies on small businesses for some of the materials used in its production process.

Ben & Jerry's has proved that it can achieve its economic mission while fulfilling its social mission. Its social commitment has enhanced Ben & Jerry's reputation, increased its name recognition, and stimulated demand for its ice cream. Thus, the company's social mission has enhanced its profits and therefore is aligned with its economic mission.

Questions

1 Why do you think Ben & Jerry's has a social mission?

2 Does the firm's social mission conflict with its economic mission?

3 Do you think the shareholders disapprove of Ben & Jerry's social mission?

Video Case: Social Responsibility at Timberland

Timberland Corporation is a manufacturer of outdoor clothing and accessories, including weatherproof jackets, shoes, and boots. Its motto is "make it better," and its management says it is committed to improving the environment. On Earth Day (April 22), Timberland organizes projects to encourage schools around the United States to teach children about protecting the environment and to refurbish schools and children's camps. Timberland also sponsors an event called Servapolooza, in which many of its employees take part. To encourage employees to participate, Timberland allows each employee some time off to engage in community service

and measures its success by the number of awards it wins for community service. Timberland's website also provides a clearinghouse of volunteer activities for community service, ranging from food drives to marsh restoration. You can get more information about Timberland at http://www.timberland.com.

Questions

1 What kind of marketing benefits might Timberland obtain from its community service efforts?

2 Which stakeholders benefit from Timberland's efforts to be a good corporate citizen? Why might the

customers of Timberland be supportive of the firm's efforts to help the environment?

3　How might Timberland's community service efforts help it to perform better? Should Timberland's stockholders be enthusiastic about the firm's expenditures for the environment and time off for workers?

4　How might Timberland's focus on children-centered projects generate new customers for Timberland?

5　Should Timberland expect to get better performance from its employees by allowing them time off for community service? How?

Internet Applications

1.　http://www.issproxy.com/index.jsp

Look at some of the news items on this website. What kinds of conflicts can you identify between stockholders of businesses? Do managers always act in the interest of their stockholders, or do they sometimes pursue their own interests?

2.　http://www.transparency.org

Transparency International is an organization that rates countries by the likelihood of bribery and corruption there. Look at the Bribe Payer's Survey. In which countries were businesses least likely to be expected to pay a

bribe? Which countries received the best rankings? What can businesses to do avoid paying bribes?

3.　http://www.hummingbird.com/about/governance/index.html?cks5y

Look at Hummingbird, Ltd.'s code of corporate ethics. What does "conflict of interest" mean? What does Hummingbird define as ethical behavior? Why might Hummingbird inform the public of its code of ethics? How might Hummingbird benefit from the code of ethics?

Dell's Secret to Success

Go to http://www.reportgallery.com and review Dell's most recent annual report. Also, go to Dell's website (http://www.dell.com) and in the section "about Dell," review the background material about Dell that relates to this chapter.

Questions

1　Describe Dell's goals with respect to the communities where it works.

2　Dell's website describes the various charities and community programs the company has initiated. Briefly summarize a few of Dell's programs. Describe Dell's efforts to improve the environment.

3　Dell's website describes its code of conduct, which contains terms such as *trust, integrity, honesty, respect,* and *responsibility.* Review Dell's code of conduct. What is Dell attempting to accomplish with its code of conduct?

In-Text Study Guide

Answers are in Appendix C at the back of book.

True or False

1. The responsibility of firms toward customers can be enforced by specific groups of consumers.
2. The government protects consumers by regulating the quality of some products that firms produce.
3. Deregulation results in lower prices for consumers.
4. The Clayton Act is intended to restrict competition.
5. U.S. firms that conduct business in foreign countries are not subject to the rules enforced by the local government.
6. In recent years, stockholders have been active in trying to influence a firm's management practices.
7. An attempt by a firm to maximize social responsibility to the community may reduce the firm's ability to provide products at a reasonable price to consumers.
8. In recent years, pollution laws have become less stringent.
9. Employees commonly sue firms for product defects or deceptive advertising.
10. Marketing managers are primarily responsible for providing accurate financial information to creditors and investors.

Multiple Choice

11. The recognition of how a firm's business decisions can affect society is its:
    a) moral code.
    b) social responsibility.
    c) conservation policies.
    d) recycling program.
    e) consumer bill of rights.
12. A firm's _____ is measured by its stock price, which can be negatively affected by unethical business practices:
    a) value
    b) revenue
    c) bond rating
    d) risk
    e) return on equity
13. Many U.S. firms provide guidelines of behavior to employees through a code of:
    a) reciprocity.
    b) cartel arrangements.
    c) kickback arrangements.
    d) technical production manuals.
    e) responsibilities and ethics.
14. Firms can ensure responsibility to customers by:
    a) safe manufacturing techniques.
    b) proper disposal of toxic waste.
    c) employee diversity programs.
    d) soliciting feedback about products.
    e) full financial disclosure.
15. _____ represents the collective consumer demand that businesses satisfy their needs.
    a) Conservationism
    b) Consumerism
    c) Social responsibility
    d) Business ethics
    e) Recycling
16. The act that prohibits unfair methods of competition is the:
    a) Humphrey Act.
    b) Civil Rights Act of 1964.
    c) Federal Trade Commission Act.
    d) Garn Act.
    e) Reagan Antitrust Act.
17. Tying agreements, binding contracts, and interlocking directorates are prohibited by the:
    a) Clayton Act.
    b) Sherman Antitrust Act.
    c) Robinson-Patman Act.
    d) Celler-Kefauver Act.
    e) Federal Trade Commission Act.

In-Text Study Guide

18. The act that prohibits mergers between firms that reduce competition within an industry is the:
    a) Robinson-Patman Act.
    b) Celler-Kefauver Act.
    c) Federal Trade Commission Act.
    d) Clayton Act.
    e) Sherman Antitrust Act.

19. Which of the following represents legislation passed to prevent firms from entering into agreements to set prices and avoid competition?
    a) affirmative action laws
    b) deregulation codes
    c) antitrust laws
    d) consumerism laws
    e) Food and Drug Administration Act

20. If a firm is the sole provider of a good or service, it is a(n):
    a) unsuccessful organization.
    b) sole proprietorship.
    c) deregulated firm.
    d) institutional investor.
    e) monopoly.

21. The following industries have been deregulated, allowing more firms to enter the industry, except for:
    a) trucking.
    b) railroads.
    c) airlines.
    d) boating.
    e) telecommunications.

22. The act that prohibits price differences on promotional allowances that reduce competition within an industry is the:
    a) Celler-Kefauver Act.
    b) Robinson-Patman Act.
    c) Clayton Act.
    d) Sherman Antitrust Act.
    e) Federal Trade Commission Act.

23. The act that encourages competition and prevents monopolies is the:
    a) Deregulation Act.
    b) Federal Trade Commission Act.
    c) Robinson-Patman Act.
    d) Celler-Kefauver Act.
    e) Sherman Antitrust Act.

24. Unwelcome comments or actions of a sexual nature are examples of:
    a) business as usual.
    b) sexual harassment.
    c) equal employment opportunities.
    d) workplace diversity.
    e) deregulation.

25. Which of the following terms describes a set of activities intended to increase opportunities for minorities and women?
    a) affirmative action
    b) Americans with Disabilities Act
    c) minimum wage law
    d) antitrust action
    e) consumerism

26. The act that prohibits discrimination due to national origin, race, gender, or religion is the:
    a) Clayton Act.
    b) Sherman Antitrust Act.
    c) Federal Trade Commission Act.
    d) Civil Rights Act of 1964.
    e) Robinson-Patman Act.

27. One example of a firm's attempt to ensure the proper and equal treatment of all employees is the establishment of a:
    a) labor contract.
    b) strike.
    c) grievance procedure.
    d) walkout.
    e) lockout.

28. The firm's management is responsible for satisfying its:
    a) union demands.
    b) owners or stockholders.

In-Text Study Guide

Answers are in Appendix C at the back of book.

   c) business agents.

   d) competition.

   e) friends.

29. If a firm exaggerates its estimates of revenues or earnings:
    a) investors pay too much for the stock.
    b) stock value initially declines.
    c) equity is diluted.
    d) insider trading is occurring.
    e) the stock is illiquid.

30. Tying employee compensation to firm performance can lead to:
    a) lack of employee motivation.
    b) resolution of all conflicts of interest within the firm.
    c) enhanced ethical behavior by employees.
    d) excessive turnover.
    e) manipulation of financial reporting.

31. An active role by stockholders in influencing a firm's management policies is called:
    a) empowerment.
    b) reengineering.
    c) self-managed teams.
    d) quality circles.
    e) shareholder activism.

32. Shareholder activism is most commonly practiced by:
    a) customers.
    b) chief executive officers.
    c) institutional investors.
    d) managers.
    e) the government.

33. Assuming everything else is the same, a firm that pays higher executive salaries will experience a _____ rate of return on the stockholders' investment than a firm that pays lower executive salaries.
    a) more stable
    b) lower
    c) higher

   d) steadier

   e) more erratic

34. Firms are responsible to their creditors by meeting their:
    a) dividend payments.
    b) financial obligations.
    c) retained earnings.
    d) stockholders' equity.
    e) treasury stock.

35. If a firm fails to meet its responsibilities to _____, it may be forced into bankruptcy.
    a) its employees
    b) the environment
    c) the government
    d) its creditors
    e) its owners

36. Enron's main ethical breach was:
    a) improper disposal of toxic waste
    b) sex discrimination
    c) misleading financial reporting
    d) unsafe products
    e) violation of antitrust laws

37. A firm's decision to maximize its social responsibilities may conflict with its responsibility to:
    a) monopolize the marketplace.
    b) provide safe products for customers.
    c) maximize the opportunities for women and minorities.
    d) maximize the firm's value for stockholders.
    e) follow government regulations.

38. Most firms have procedures in place as well as codes to ensure individual employee accountability. This is a part of their:
    a) program network.
    b) division of work.
    c) local area network.
    d) social responsibility.
    e) recycling program.

INDEX STOCK IMAGERY

Chapter
3

Like most businesses, the performance of a tile business is highly dependent on the economic conditions.

Assessing Economic Conditions

Economic conditions reflect the level of production and consumption for a particular country, area, or industry. Macroeconomic conditions reflect the overall U.S. economy; microeconomic conditions are more focused on the business or industry of concern. This chapter focuses on U.S. macroeconomic conditions, and the following chapter focuses on how global conditions affect business decisions made by a firm.

Economic conditions can affect the revenue or expenses of a business and therefore can affect the value of that business. Consider the case of Prestige Tile Company, which installs fancy tile in hotels, restaurants, and other businesses. Although the demand for its service has grown substantially over time, the demand tends to be stronger when the economy is strong and its clients' businesses are performing well.

Prestige Tile Company must forecast the demand for its service so that it can make sure it has enough tile and enough employees to satisfy that demand. Since the demand is dependent on economic conditions, the amount of tile that Prestige Tile will produce is dependent on economic conditions. In addition, government policies can affect economic conditions and must be considered as well. Thus, Prestige Tile Company must determine:

▶ How will economic growth affect the revenue and expenses associated with its service?

▶ How will inflation affect the revenue and expenses associated with its service?

▶ How will interest rates affect the revenue and expenses associated with its service?

▶ How will prevailing government policies affect the revenue and expenses associated with its service?

These types of assessments are necessary for all businesses. Although every business is not affected in the same manner by changing economic conditions, most businesses are affected to some degree. This chapter explains how the assessment of the economic environment by Prestige Tile Company or any other firm can be conducted in a manner that maximizes the firm's value.

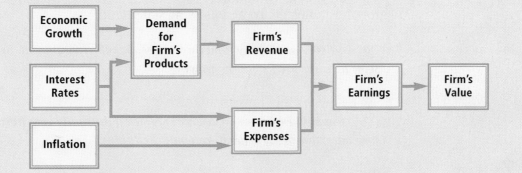

1

Explain how economic
growth affects business
performance.

economic growth
the change in the general level of
economic activity

Economic growth represents the change in the general level of economic activity. Sometimes economic growth is strong, and other times it is relatively weak.

Strong Economic Growth

When U.S. economic growth is stronger than normal, the total income level of all U.S. workers is relatively high, so there is a higher volume of spending on products and services. Since the demand for products and services is high, firms that sell products and services should generate higher revenue.

How the Impact of a Strong Economy Spreads across Firms   The impact of a stronger economy can spread quickly across all businesses. Once consumers begin to increase their spending, firms experience a stronger demand for their products and may begin to hire more employees to accommodate that increased demand. They may also need to expand their operations, which results in increased demand for supplies, construction services, and materials. Then, the construction firms may have to hire more workers to accommodate the increased demand for construction. As more jobs are created, the general income level of consumers rises, allowing them to spend more money. In addition, investors who invested in businesses tend to earn a higher return on their investment when the economy is strong, and they may spend much or all of that return on products and services. Thus, the extra income causes a favorable ripple effect throughout the economy.

Weak Economic Growth

Whereas strong economic growth enhances a firm's revenue, slow economic growth results in low demand for products and services, which can reduce a firm's revenue. Even firms that provide basic products or services are adversely affected by a weak economy because customers tend to reduce their demand. For example, the demand for coffee at Starbucks is affected by general economic conditions. Since specialty coffee is not really a necessity, demand for it is stronger when consumers are earning a relatively high income and can afford it. The demand for soft drinks and bottled water is also affected, as some people rely more on tap water under weak economic conditions. The potential impact of slower economic growth is reflected in the following statements:

"Our caution stems largely from the macroeconomic environment, in which some forecasts are for slower growth."

—Hewlett-Packard

"[The company] expects to experience significant fluctuations in future [performance] due to . . . general economic conditions."

—Amazon.com

recession
two consecutive quarters of negative economic growth

When economic growth is negative for two consecutive quarters, the period is referred to as a **recession**.

Businesses tend to impose layoffs when economic conditions weaken, because they no longer need all of their employees once the demand for their products or services is reduced.

GETTY IMAGES

When the U.S. economy is weak, some U.S. workers are laid off by firms and therefore have less money that they can use to buy products or services. Other U.S. workers fear that they may be laid off and try to save more of their income in case they lose their jobs in the future. They only spend money on necessities. Thus, the demand for many products and services is reduced. This results in reduced revenue (and profits) for many firms. Since the firms are not able to sell all the products or services they can produce, they may attempt to reduce their expenses by laying off even more workers. Because a recession causes a reduction in income and demand, it has a major adverse impact on the performance of firms.

How the Impact of a Weak Economy Spreads across Firms   The impact of weak economic conditions can spread quickly across all businesses. For example, the demand for new cars sold by automakers such as Ford Motor Company and General Motors declines, leaving them with more cars produced than they can sell. They may respond by closing production plants and laying off workers. Those workers have less income, so they reduce their demand for various products. Then, the firms that produce those products experience a decline in sales because of the reduced demand. Because they cannot sell all the products that they produce, they may need to reduce production and lay off workers. So the effect ripples through the economy. In addition, when the automakers reduce their production, their need for materials such as steel declines. Thus, the firms that produce steel may experience a decline in demand and may need to lay off workers.

Even when firms are not laying off workers, they tend to cut back on any plans for expansion during a weak economy. Thus, their demand for construction services and materials declines. Even if people are not laid off, they recognize that the economy is weak and are less willing to spend money because they could be laid off in the future. This also results in a reduction in the demand for products.

When conditions are weak, some businesses are affected more than others. Nevertheless, most businesses are adversely affected by economic conditions because the demand for products in almost all industries declines.

Indicators of Economic Growth

Two common measures of economic growth are the level of total production of products and services in the economy and the total amount of expenditures (also called **aggregate expenditures**). The total production level and total aggregate expenditures in the United States are closely related, because a high level of consumer spending reflects a large demand for products and services. The total production level is dependent on the total demand for products and services.

aggregate expenditures
the total amount of expenditures in the economy

Businesses can monitor the U.S. total production level by keeping track of the **gross domestic product (GDP)**, which is the total market value of all final products and services produced in the United States. The GDP is reported quarterly in the United States. The trend of GDP growth is shown in Exhibit 3.1. Notice that GDP growth is typically between 4 and 7 percent on an annualized basis. In the 1990–1991 period and in 2001, the U.S. economy was very weak, which led to recessions in those periods (see the shaded area in Exhibit 3.1). Economic growth is commonly interpreted as the percentage of change in the GDP from one period (such as a quarter) to another. Businesses tend to monitor changes in economic growth, which may signal a change in the demand for their products or services.

gross domestic product (GDP)
the total market value of all final products and services produced in the United States

An alternative indicator of economic growth is the unemployment level. Businesses may monitor various unemployment indicators because they can indicate whether economic conditions are improving. The four different types of unemployment are as follows:

frictional unemployment
people who are between jobs

▶ **Frictional unemployment** (also referred to as *natural unemployment*) represents people who are between jobs. That is, their unemployment status is temporary, as they are likely to find employment soon. For example, a person with marketable job skills might quit her job before finding a new one because she believes she will find a new job before long.

seasonal unemployment
people whose services are not needed during some seasons

▶ **Seasonal unemployment** represents people whose services are not needed during some seasons. For example, ski instructors may be unemployed in the summer.

cyclical unemployment
people who are unemployed because of poor economic conditions

▶ **Cyclical unemployment** represents people who are unemployed because of poor economic conditions. When the level of economic activity declines, the demand for products and services declines, which reduces the need for workers. For example, a firm may lay off factory workers if the demand for its product declines.

structural unemployment
people who are unemployed because they do not have adequate skills

▶ **Structural unemployment** represents people who are unemployed because they do not have adequate skills. For example, people who have limited education may be structurally unemployed.

Of the four types of unemployment, the cyclical unemployment level is probably the best indicator of economic conditions. When economic growth improves, businesses hire more people and the unemployment rate declines. Unfortunately, determining how much of the unemployment level is cyclical can be difficult. Some people assume that when the unemployment rate changes, the change is primarily due to economic cycles. A lower unemployment rate may be interpreted as an indicator of increased economic growth. Conversely, a higher unemployment rate is commonly interpreted as a sign of reduced economic growth. From 2000

Exhibit 3.1

Trend of Gross Domestic
Product (GDP)

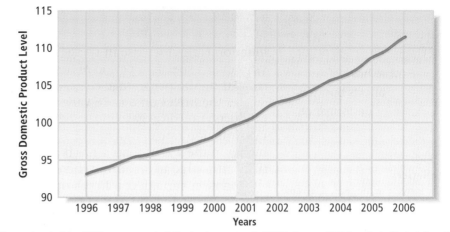

The numbers in this exhibit are measured relative to a base amount of 100 in the year 2000, in order to illustrate how the
level has grown since the year 2000.

to 2002, as the economy weakened, the unemployment level increased. In
the 2003–2004 period, however, the economy improved, and the unemployment level declined.

Many other indicators of economic growth, such as the industrial production index, new housing starts, and the personal income level, are
compiled by divisions of the federal government and reported in business
magazines and newspapers.

Variation in the Sensitivity to Economic Growth   Some firms are more sensitive
than others to economic conditions because the demand for their product
is more sensitive to such conditions. For example, the demand for the
product (food) provided by McDonald's is not very sensitive to economic
conditions because people still purchase McDonald's food even when the
economy is weak. In contrast, the demand for new automobiles is more
sensitive to economic conditions. When the economy is weak, the demand
for new automobiles declines. Therefore, the performance of car manufacturers is very sensitive to economic conditions.

Decision Making

Responding to Economic Growth

Prestige Tile Company (described in the chapter introduction) specializes in the production of fancy tile that it installs in the lobbies of hotels, banks, restaurants, and other
companies. The economy has been strong, so its customers have been experiencing high
profits and have been able to afford the services of Prestige Tile. Therefore, Prestige Tile
Company has received a large number of orders for its tile installation. Now however, its
production plant is at full capacity, so it cannot increase its business this year unless it en-
larges its production plant, which will be costly.

1.   Explain how Prestige Tile's decision to expand its production plant is dependent on its
     expectations of economic growth.

2.   Prestige Tile is considering hiring four more full-time workers because of the recent
     strong demand for its tile installation service. Explain how its decision to hire more em-
     ployees is dependent on its expectations of economic growth.

ANSWERS: 1. If the economy weakens, the demand for its tile will likely decline, and it will not need extra capacity. Therefore,
Prestige Tile will expand only if it believes that economic growth will be strong and result in an increase in the demand for its
services. 2. If the economy weakens, the demand for its tile will likely decline, and it will not need the extra workers. Therefore, it should hire the workers only if it believes that economic growth will be strong and result in an increase in the demand
for its services.

Explain how inflation affects business performance.

inflation
the increase in the general level of prices of products and services over a specified period of time

cost-push inflation
the situation when higher prices charged by firms are caused by higher costs

Impact of Inflation

Inflation is the increase in the general level of prices of products and services over a specified period of time. The inflation rate can be estimated by measuring the percentage change in the consumer price index, which indicates the prices on a wide variety of consumer products such as grocery products, housing, gasoline, medical services, and electricity. The annual U.S. inflation rate is shown in Exhibit 3.2. The inflation rate was generally higher in the 1970s than it has been in more recent years, which was partially attributed to an abrupt increase in oil prices then.

Inflation can affect a firm's operating expenses from producing products by increasing the cost of supplies and materials. Wages can also be affected by inflation. A higher level of inflation will cause a larger increase in a firm's operating expenses. A firm's revenue may also be high during periods of high inflation because many firms charge higher prices to compensate for their higher expenses.

Types of Inflation

Inflation may result from a particular event that increases the costs of production. When the price of aluminum rises, for example, firms such as PepsiCo and Coca-Cola incur higher costs and may increase the prices of their soft drinks. If the cost of steel increases, firms such as General Motors and Ford Motor Company that use steel to produce vehicles may increase the prices of their vehicles. When firms charge higher prices due to higher costs, **cost-push inflation** occurs. To illustrate the potential impact of cost-push inflation, consider how all the manufacturers of products must deliver their products to stores across the country. The transportation cost includes the price of gasoline. When oil prices increase, the cost of producing gasoline increases as well. Suppliers of gasoline tend to pass the high cost on by raising their gasoline prices. Consequently, the manufacturers of products incur higher costs for transporting their products. If they do not increase the prices of their products to reflect the higher costs, their profits will decline.

Sometimes, though, firms do increase the prices of their products to reflect their higher costs. In this case, the consumers pay higher prices for products because of the higher price of oil. Also, consider that the higher

Exhibit 3.2

U.S. Inflation Rates over Time

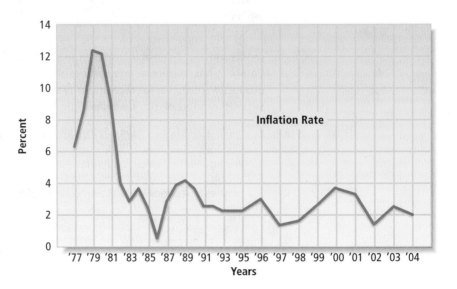

The business expense of transporting products increases when gasoline prices rise, and businesses commonly pass the increased expenses on to consumers.

AP/WIDE WORLD PHOTOS

gasoline prices increase airlines' cost of providing travel services. If airlines increase airfares to reflect the higher costs, all the businesses that rely on air travel incur higher costs. In addition, consumers using airlines will be forced to pay higher prices.

When consumers pay higher prices for products as a result of inflation, they have less money available to buy other products. They struggle to stay within their spending budget and may need to borrow money. Alternatively, they may be forced to reduce their spending on other products, which causes the demand for those products to decline. Consequently, firms will experience a lower level of revenue.

Inflation can also be caused by strong consumer demand. Consider a situation in which consumers increase their demand for most products and services. Some firms may respond by increasing their prices. When prices of products and services are pulled up because of strong consumer demand, **demand-pull inflation** occurs. In periods of strong economic growth, strong consumer demand can cause shortages in the production of some products. Firms that anticipate shortages may raise prices because they are confident they can sell the products anyway.

demand-pull inflation
the situation when prices of products and services are pulled up because of strong consumer demand

Strong economic growth may place pressure on wages as well as prices. Strong economic growth may mean fewer unemployed people, so workers may negotiate for higher wages. Firms may be more willing to pay higher wages to retain their workers when no other qualified workers are available. As firms pay higher wages, production costs rise, and firms may attempt to increase their prices to recover the higher expenses.

Variation in the Sensitivity to Inflation   Some firms are much more exposed to inflation than others because of the types of expenses they incur in their production process. For example, delivery service firms such as FedEx and UPS are very exposed to the cost of oil because they need to purchase so much gasoline for their delivery trucks every day. Travel agencies are also very exposed because people may travel less when the cost of driving or flying is high due to high gasoline prices. Conversely, service firms (such as a dental or doctor's office) may not be affected by the increased cost of oil.

Decision Making

Responding to a Change in Inflation

Prestige Tile Company relies on materials for its production of tile. Recently, inflation has increased, and all its suppliers raised their prices for those materials by 10 percent. If Prestige Tile decides to maintain its existing prices, its profits will decline because of the increased cost of materials. If it attempts to raise its prices to cover the higher cost of materials, the demand for its tile may decline and so will its revenue. Thus the profits of Prestige Tile Company will likely decline as a result of the higher cost of materials.

1. Explain how Prestige Tile's decision to expand its production plant is dependent on inflation.
2. What other types of expenses incurred by Prestige Tile Company could be affected by inflation?

ANSWERS: 1. If inflation increases and Prestige Tile raises its price, the demand for its product may decline, so it would not need to expand its production plant. 2. If inflation increases, the cost of any machinery could increase. The expense of renting facilities could increase. Employees may demand larger raises to keep up with inflation.

3

Explain how interest rates affect business performance.

Impact of Interest Rates

Interest rates determine the cost of borrowing money. They can affect a firm's performance by having an impact on its expenses or on its revenue, as explained next.

Impact on a Firm's Expenses

Firms closely monitor interest rates because they determine the amount of expense a business will incur if it borrows money. If a business borrows $100,000 for one year at an interest rate of 8 percent, the interest expense is $8,000 (computed as $.08 \times \$100,000$). At an interest rate of 15 percent, however, the interest expense would be $15,000 (computed as $.15 \times \$100,000$). Imagine how the interest rate level can affect some large firms that have borrowed more than $1 billion. An interest rate increase of just 1 percent on $1 billion of borrowed funds results in an extra annual interest expense of $10 million.

Changes in market interest rates can influence a firm's interest expense because the loan rates that commercial banks and other creditors charge on loans to firms are based on market interest rates. Even when a firm obtains a loan from a commercial bank over several years, the loan rate is typically adjusted periodically (every six months or year) based on the prevailing market interest rate at that time.

Exhibit 3.3 illustrates the annual interest expense for a reputable U.S. firm that borrows $1 million from a bank each year and earns $100,000 in annual profits before paying its interest expense. The interest expenses are adjusted each year according to the market interest rates prevailing in the United States during that year. As this exhibit shows, interest rates can significantly influence a firm's profit. Firms incurred much higher interest expenses in the early 1980s because interest rates were so high then.

Exhibit 3.3

Effect of Interest Rates on Interest Expenses and Profits

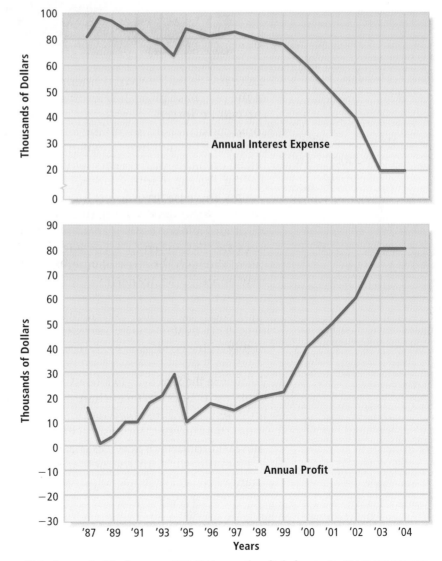

Note: Assume that the firm earns $100,000 in annual profits before paying its interest expense.

When interest rates rise, it affects the monthly payment on car loans and may reduce the demand by consumers for new cars.

PHOTOEDIT, INC.

Since interest rates affect the cost of financing, some possible projects considered by the firm that would be feasible during periods of low interest rates may not be feasible during periods of high interest rates. That is, the project may not generate an adequate return to cover financing costs. Consequently, firms tend to reduce their degree of expansion when interest rates are high.

Impact on a Firm's Revenue

Some products that are sold by firms are commonly purchased with credit. When consumers buy new cars, they may make just a small down payment and obtain a loan to cover the remainder of the purchase price. If interest rates increase, consumers who buy a new car will be forced to make higher monthly payments. This may prevent some consumers from buying a new car because they are unwilling or unable to make such high payments. Thus, high interest rates can lead to reduced demand for new cars, which results in lower sales at car dealerships and for the car manufacturers.

An increase in interest rates can also reduce the demand for new homes for the same reason. Consumers typically rely on a small down payment and a loan to cover most of the purchase price of a home. If interest rates are high when they consider buying a home, they may not be able to afford the high monthly payments on the loan. Therefore, the demand for new homes typically declines, and firms that build homes experience a decline in business. Firms such as Caterpillar and Weyerhaeuser that produce equipment and construction products also experience a decline in business. This explains why firms involved in the construction industry are highly influenced by interest rate movements.

Variation in the Sensitivity to Interest Rates   Some firms are more sensitive to changes in interest rates than others. For example, firms that have very little debt may be somewhat insulated from changes in interest rates because their interest expenses will not change very much. In addition, firms that sell products or services that are paid for with cash should not experience major shifts in the demand for their products when interest rates change.

Global Business

Capitalizing on Global Economic Conditions

The demand for a firm's products is dependent on the economic growth where the products are sold. Given the mature economy of the United States, its potential for economic growth is limited. Less-developed countries, however, have much greater potential for economic growth because they have not yet taken full advantage of existing technology. Furthermore, the governments of many less-developed countries are trying to accelerate their economic growth by encouraging more business development by entrepreneurs. Many of these governments have also allowed U.S. firms to enter their markets. These U.S. firms are attempting to capitalize on the changing economic and political conditions in less-developed countries by selling their products there.

The Coca-Cola Company is among many U.S. firms that have targeted countries with high potential for economic growth. Its sales have increased substantially in Brazil, Chile, East Central Europe, North Africa, and China. The Coca-Cola Company's increased sales in these countries can be attributed in part to economic growth, which increases the amount of consumer spending. It can also be attributed to reductions in government restrictions imposed on U.S. firms that desire to conduct business in these countries.

Other U.S. firms are planning major expansion in less-developed countries to capitalize on the changes in economic and political conditions. General Motors plans to expand in various Asian markets, including China, India, and Indonesia, where the potential for economic growth is strong.

U.S. firms that attempt to capitalize on economic growth in foreign countries can be adversely affected if these countries experience a recession. If a U.S. firm diversifies its business among several different countries, however, a recession in any single foreign country should not have a major effect on the firm's worldwide sales.

Decision Making

Responding to a Change in Interest Rates

Prestige Tile Company relies on borrowed funds to support its operations. Thus, if interest rates rise, its interest expenses will increase, and its profits will decline. In addition, many of its customers borrow funds to finance the cost of having tile installed at their businesses. These customers are less willing to order new tile when the cost of borrowing is high, which means that the demand for Prestige Tile's installation services will decline, and so will its revenue.

1. Explain how lower interest rates should affect the profits of Prestige Tile Company
2. If Prestige Tile is already at full production capacity, why might its decision of whether to expand its production plant depend on its expectations of future interest rates?

ANSWERS: 1. Lower interest rates will result in lower interest expenses and an increase in the demand for its services (higher revenue if it has the capacity to accommodate the higher demand). Both effects can result in higher profits. 2. It may need to expand only if it believes that lower interest rates will occur and cause an increase in its demand. In addition, its expansion will be less costly to finance if interest rates are lower.

Explain how market prices are determined.

How Market Prices Are Determined

The performance of firms is affected by changes in the prices they charge for products (which influence their revenue) and the prices they pay for supplies and materials (which influence their operating expenses). The prices of products and supplies are influenced by demand and supply conditions.

The following framework uses demand and supply conditions to explain how prices of products change over time. The market price of a product is influenced by the total demand for that product by all customers. It is also affected by the supply of that product produced by firms. The interaction between demand and supply determines the price, as explained in detail next.

Demand Schedule for a Product

demand schedule
a schedule that indicates the quantity of a product that would be demanded at each possible price

The demand for a product can be shown with a **demand schedule**, or a schedule that indicates the quantity of the product that would be demanded at each possible price. Consider personal computers as an example. Assume that the demand schedule for a particular type of personal computer is as shown in the first and second columns in Exhibit 3.4 for a given point in time. If the price is relatively high, the quantity demanded by consumers is relatively low. For example, if the price is $3,000, only 8,000 of these computers will be demanded (purchased) by consumers. At the other extreme, if the price is $1,000, a total of 25,000 of these computers will be demanded by customers. The quantity of personal computers demanded is higher when the price is lower.

The graph in Exhibit 3.4, which is based on the table, shows the relationship between the price of a computer and the quantity of computers demanded by consumers. The demand curve (labeled D_1) shows that as the price decreases, the quantity demanded increases.

Supply Schedule for a Product

supply schedule
a schedule that indicates the quantity of a product that would be supplied (produced) by firms at each possible price

The supply of a product can be shown with a **supply schedule**, or a schedule that indicates the quantity of the product that would be supplied (produced) by firms at each possible price. Assume that the supply schedule for the type of personal computer already discussed is as shown in the first and

Exhibit 3.4

How the Equilibrium Price Is Determined by Demand and Supply

If the Price of a Particular Computer Is:	The Quantity of These Computers Demanded by Consumers Will Be:	The Quantity of These Computers Supplied (Produced) by Firms Will Be:
$3,000	8,000	30,000
2,500	14,000	24,000
2,000	18,000	18,000
1,500	22,000	16,000
1,000	25,000	10,000

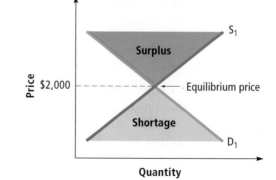

third columns of Exhibit 3.4 for a given point in time. When the price at which the personal computer can be sold is relatively high, firms will produce a large supply of this computer. For example, if the price is $3,000, 30,000 of these computers will be produced. Firms are willing to produce the computers at this price because they will earn a high profit if they can sell the computers at such a high price.

At the other extreme, if the price of computers is only $1,000, only 10,000 of these computers will be produced. The quantity supplied is much smaller at a low price because some firms will be unwilling to produce the computers if they can sell them for only $1,000. If some firms' actual cost of producing the computers is above this price of $1,000, these firms will be unwilling to produce the computers.

The graph accompanying Exhibit 3.4, which is based on the table, shows the relationship between the price of a computer and the quantity of computers supplied (produced) by firms. The supply curve (labeled S1) shows that as price increases, the quantity of computers supplied increases.

Interaction of Demand and Supply

The interaction of the demand schedule and supply schedule determines the price. Notice from Exhibit 3.4 that at relatively high prices of computers (such as $3,000), the quantity supplied by firms exceeds the quantity demanded by customers, resulting in a so-called **surplus** of computers. For example, at the price of $3,000 the quantity supplied is 30,000 units and the quantity demanded is 8,000 units, resulting in a surplus of 22,000 units. This surplus occurs because consumers are unwilling to purchase computers when the price is excessive.

When the price of a computer is relatively low, the quantity supplied by firms will be less than the quantity demanded by customers, resulting in a so-called **shortage** of computers. For example, at a price of $1,000, the quantity demanded by customers is 25,000 units, while the quantity supplied by firms is only 10,000 units, causing a shortage of 15,000 units.

Notice from Exhibit 3.4 that at a price of $2,000, the quantity of computers supplied by firms is 18,000 units, and the quantity demanded by customers is also 18,000 units. At this price, there is no surplus and no shortage. The price at which the quantity of a product supplied by firms equals the quantity of the product demanded by customers is called the **equilibrium price**. This is the price at which firms normally attempt to sell their products.

At any price above the equilibrium price, the firms will be unable to sell all the computers they produce, resulting in a surplus. Therefore, they would need to reduce their prices to eliminate the surplus. At any price below the equilibrium price, the firms will not produce a sufficient quantity of computers to satisfy all the customers willing to pay that price (resulting in a shortage). The firms could raise their price to correct the shortage.

The demand and supply concepts just applied to a particular type of computer can also be applied to every product or service that firms produce. Each product or service has its own demand schedule and supply schedule, which will determine its own equilibrium price.

Effect of a Change in the Demand Schedule

As time passes, changing conditions can cause a demand schedule or a supply schedule for a specific product to change. Consequently, the equilibrium price of that product will also change. Reconsider the previous

surplus
the situation when the quantity supplied by firms exceeds the quantity demanded by customers

shortage
the situation when the quantity supplied by firms is less than the quantity demanded by customers

equilibrium price
the price at which the quantity of a product supplied by firms equals the quantity of the product demanded by customers

Exhibit 3.5

How the Equilibrium Price
Is Affected by a Change
in Demand

If the Price of a Particular Computer Is:	The Quantity of These Computers Demanded by Consumers Was:	But the Quantity of These Computers Demanded by Consumers Will Now Be:
$3,000	8,000	18,000
2,500	14,000	24,000
2,000	18,000	28,000
1,500	22,000	32,000
1,000	25,000	35,000

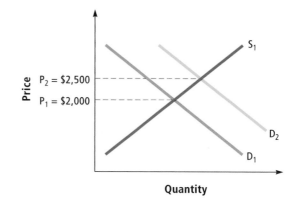

example and assume that computers become more desirable to potential consumers. Assume that the demand schedule for the computer changes as shown at the top of Exhibit 3.5. At any given price, the quantity demanded is now 10,000 units higher than it was before the computer became more popular. The graph accompanying Exhibit 3.5 shows how the demand curve shifts outward from D_1 to D_2.

Now consider the effect of this change in the demand schedule on the equilibrium price of computers. Assuming that the supply schedule remains unchanged, the effect of the change in the demand schedule on the equilibrium price is shown in Exhibit 3.5. At the original equilibrium price of $2,000, the quantity of computers demanded is now 28,000, while the quantity of computers supplied is still 18,000. A shortage of computers occurs at that price. At a price of $2,500, however, the quantity of computers supplied by firms equals the quantity of computers demanded by customers. Therefore, the new equilibrium price is $2,500. The graph at the bottom of Exhibit 3.5 confirms that the shift in the demand schedule from D_1 to D_2 causes the new equilibrium price of computers to be $2,500.

The graph illustrating the effect of a shift in the demand schedule on the equilibrium price of a product can be supplemented with simple logic. When a product becomes more popular, consumers' demand for that product increases, resulting in a shortage. Under these conditions, firms recognize that they can sell whatever amount they produce at a higher price. Once the price is raised to the level at which the quantity supplied is equal to the quantity demanded, the shortage is corrected.

Effect of a Change in the Supply Schedule

Just as the demand for a product may change, so may the supply. A change in the supply can also affect the equilibrium price of the product. To illus-

Exhibit 3.6

How the Equilibrium Price Is Affected by a Change in Supply

If the Price of a Particular Computer Is:	The Quantity of These Computers Supplied by Firms Was:	But the Quantity of These Computers Supplied by Firms Will Now Be:
$3,000	30,000	36,000
2,500	24,000	30,000
2,000	18,000	24,000
1,500	16,000	22,000
1,000	10,000	16,000

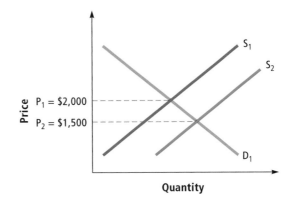

trate this effect, reconsider the original example in which the equilibrium price of computers was $2,000. Now assume that improved technology allows firms to produce the computer at a lower cost. In this case, firms will be willing to produce a larger supply of computers at any given price, which reflects a change in the supply schedule.

Assume that as a result of the improved technology (lower production costs), the supply schedule changes as shown in Exhibit 3.6. At any given price, the quantity supplied is now 6,000 units higher than it was before the improved technology. The graph accompanying Exhibit 3.6 shows how the supply schedule shifts outward from S_1 to S_2.

Now consider the effect of this change in the supply schedule on the equilibrium price of computers. Assuming that the demand schedule remains unchanged, the effect of the change in the supply schedule on the equilibrium price is shown in Exhibit 3.6. At the original equilibrium price of $2,000, the quantity of computers demanded is 18,000, while the quantity of computers supplied (produced) is now 24,000. A surplus of computers occurs at that price. At a price of $1,500, however, the quantity of computers supplied by firms equals the quantity of computers demanded by consumers. Therefore, the new equilibrium price is $1,500. The graph at the bottom of Exhibit 3.6 confirms that the shift in the supply schedule from S_1 to S_2 causes the new equilibrium price of computers to be $1,500.

The graph illustrating the effect of a shift in the supply schedule on the equilibrium price of a product can be supplemented with simple logic. When improved technology allows firms to produce a product at a lower cost, more firms will be willing to produce the product. This results in a larger supply produced, which causes a surplus. Firms recognize that the only way they will be able to sell all that is supplied (produced) is to lower the price of the product. Once the price is lowered to the level at which the quantity supplied is once again equal to the quantity demanded, the surplus is eliminated.

Effect of Demand and Supply on the General Price Level

So far the discussion of demand and supply has focused on one product to show how the equilibrium price of that product might change. Now consider how the general price level for all products might change. The general price level is an average of prices of all existing products and services. If the total (aggregate) demand by consumers for all or most products suddenly increases (perhaps because of an increase in the income level of most consumers), the general level of prices could rise. The general price level may also be affected by shifts in the supply schedules for all goods and services. If the supply schedule of all or most products suddenly decreases (perhaps because of increasing expenses when producing the products), the general level of prices should rise.

Decision Making

Using Supply and Demand to Monitor Market Prices

Prestige Tile Company can use supply and demand analysis to explain the prices it faces. When the cost of materials used to produce tile increases, the tile firms are less willing to provide tile at a particular price. The result is an inward shift in the supply curve for the industry, which leads to a higher equilibrium price for tile in the industry. Prestige Tile Company will likely increase its price under these conditions.

1. Explain how the equilibrium quantity of tile changes as a result of the increased cost of production described earlier.
2. Explain how the equilibrium price level of tile would likely change if there is a sudden decline in the cost of materials.

ANSWERS: 1. An increase in the cost of production results in an inward shift in the supply curve, which causes the new equilibrium quantity to be lower. 2. A sudden decline in the cost of materials would result in an outward shift in the supply schedule for tile because firms would be willing to supply tile at a lower price. Thus, the equilibrium price would increase.

Factors That Influence Market Prices

Thus far, examples have illustrated how the demand by customers or the supply produced by firms can change, causing a new market price. Shifts in the demand schedule or the supply schedule can be caused by several factors, some of which are identified next.

Consumer Income

Consumer income determines the amount of products and services that individuals can purchase. A high level of economic growth results in more income for consumers. When consumers' income rises, they may demand a larger quantity of specific products and services. That is, the demand schedules for various products and services may shift out in response to higher income, which could result in higher prices.

When economic conditions are strong, income levels are high, and the demand by consumers for new homes increases.

AP/WIDE WORLD PHOTOS

Conversely, when consumers' income level declines, they may demand a smaller quantity of specific products. For example, in the early 1990s, the average income level in the United States declined substantially in specific areas where firms relied on government contracts (such as for building missiles and the like). The federal government's cutbacks on such expenditures resulted in less work for firms in specific regions of the country. As income declined, the demand for new homes in these areas declined, causing a surplus of new homes. The firms that were building new homes were forced to lower their prices because of the surplus.

Consumer Preferences

As consumer preferences (or tastes) for a particular product change, the quantity of that product demanded by consumers may change. There are numerous examples of products whose prices rose in response to increased demand. For example, the price of a scalped ticket at a sold-out event such as a concert, the World Series, or the Super Bowl may easily exceed $500.

When a product becomes less popular, the demand for the product declines. The resulting surplus may force firms to lower their prices to sell what they produce. For example, when specific clothes become unpopular, clothing manufacturers sell these clothes at discounted prices just to eliminate the surplus.

Production Expenses

Another factor that can affect equilibrium prices is a change in production expenses. When firms experience lower expenses, they are willing to supply (produce) more at any given price (as explained earlier). This results in a surplus of the product, forcing firms to lower their price to sell all that they have produced. For example, the prices of musical compact discs have declined every year since they were first introduced.

When expenses of firms increase, the opposite result occurs. For example, insurance companies that had insured South Florida homes in the early 1990s incurred high expenses in the aftermath of Hurricane Andrew. Some of these companies decided that they would no longer supply this insurance service in South Florida. Those companies that were still willing to provide insurance were able to raise their prices.

As production of CDs and DVDs became more efficient, their prices declined.

PHOTOEDIT, INC.

Decision Making

Assessing the Potential Change in Market Prices

Prestige Tile Company has noticed that the market price of tile in the industry recently increased as a result of the higher cost of materials. Now its managers are trying to determine whether the price may change further as a result of other factors. If consumer income continues to rise, this may result in a strong demand for tile. Consumer preferences for the tile have also changed as this type of tile has become extremely popular. Both factors may lead to a general increase in the price of tile in the industry.

1. If the general price level of tile in the industry increases as Prestige Tile expects, will the firms that sell tile generate higher profits?
2. If the general price level of tile increases, but Prestige Tile's main competitor does not raise its prices, should Prestige Tile increase its prices?

ANSWERS: 1. Although the general price level has increased, so has the cost of production; therefore, the firms that sell tile will generate higher profits only if their revenue increased by a greater degree than their expenses. 2. Prestige Tile Company may be forced to maintain its existing price if it does not want to lose any of its business to its main competitor.

Explain how the government influences economic conditions.

money supply
demand deposits (checking accounts), currency held by the public, and traveler's checks

Government Influence on Economic Conditions

The federal government can influence the performance of businesses by imposing regulations, such as the environmental regulations discussed in the preceding chapter, or by enacting policies that affect economic conditions. To influence economic conditions, the federal government implements monetary and fiscal policies, which are discussed next.

Monetary Policy

In the United States, the term **money supply** normally refers to demand deposits (checking accounts), currency held by the public, and traveler's checks. This is a narrow definition, as there are broader measures of the money supply that count other types of deposits as well. Regardless of the precise definition, any measure of money represents funds that financial institutions can lend to borrowers.

The U.S. money supply is controlled by the **Federal Reserve System** ("the Fed"), which is the central bank of the United States. The Fed sets the **monetary policy**, which represents decisions on the money supply level in the United States. The Fed can easily adjust the U.S. money supply by billions of dollars in a single day. Because the Fed's monetary policy affects the money supply level, it affects interest rates. When the Fed affects interest rates with its monetary policy, it directly affects a firm's interest expenses. Second, it can affect the demand for the firm's products if those products are commonly purchased with borrowed funds.

A Typical FOMC Meeting   The Fed's monetary policy is decided by the Federal Open Market Committee (FOMC), which has 12 voting members. This committee meets about every six weeks to determine whether interest rates should be adjusted. Each FOMC meeting begins with an assessment of several measures of aggregate production levels, inventory levels, and price levels in the United States. The objective of this assessment is to predict U.S. economic growth and inflation, assuming that the Fed does not adjust its monetary policy. The minutes of the meetings show that the committee members carefully consider any economic indicators that can be used to anticipate future economic growth or inflation. For example, a recent reduction in business inventories may suggest that economic growth is increasing and that firms will need to boost production to replenish their inventories. Conversely, an increase in inventories may indicate that firms will have to lower production and possibly reduce their workforces.

The committee also pays close attention to any factors that can affect inflation. Oil prices are closely monitored because they affect the cost of producing and transporting many products. A reduction in business inventories when production is near full capacity may indicate an excessive

Federal Reserve System
the central bank of the United States

monetary policy
decisions on the money supply level in the United States

Businesses closely monitor the Fed's monetary policy because they realize how a change in interest rates can affect the demand for their products.

demand for products that will pull prices up. The Fed becomes concerned when several indicators suggest that higher inflation is likely.

How the Fed Can Reduce Interest Rates   The Fed maintains some funds outside the banking system, which are not loanable funds. These funds are not available to firms or individuals who need to borrow. The Fed can use these funds to purchase Treasury securities held by individuals and firms. These purchases provide individuals and firms with new funds, which they deposit in their commercial banks. Consequently, the money supply increases because the commercial banks and other financial institutions can loan out these funds. In other words, the Fed's action increases the supply of loanable funds. Assuming that the demand for loanable funds remains unchanged, the increase in the supply of loanable funds should cause interest rates to decrease. The impact of the supply of loanable funds on interest rates is discussed in more detail in the Chapter 16 appendix. By reducing interest rates, the Fed may be able to stimulate economic growth. The lower borrowing rates may entice some consumers and firms to borrow more funds and spend more money, which can result in higher revenue and earnings for businesses.

How the Fed Can Increase Interest Rates   When the Fed reduces the U.S. money supply, it pulls funds out of commercial banks and other financial institutions. This reduces the supply of funds that these financial institutions can lend to borrowers. Assuming that the demand for loanable funds remains unchanged, the decline in the supply of loanable funds should cause interest rates to rise. The higher interest rates increase the cost of borrowing and thus tend to discourage consumers and firms from borrowing. The Fed raises interest rates when it wants to reduce the degree of spending in the United States. The Fed might do this because an excessive amount of spending can cause a higher degree of inflation. Therefore, when the Fed raises interest rates in an effort to reduce spending, it is actually trying to reduce the level of inflation.

Though the Fed may succeed in reducing inflation by increasing interest rates, the higher interest rates can adversely affect the performance of businesses in the short term. As already mentioned, higher interest rates increase the cost of borrowing and may reduce total spending in the United States. Higher interest rates force firms to incur higher interest expenses when they borrow, which can reduce their profits. In addition, when there is less total spending in the United States, the total demand for products and services is reduced, and the demand for each firm's products or services may be reduced. This results in less revenue and therefore lower profits for firms.

Fiscal Policy

fiscal policy
decisions on how the federal government should set tax rates and spend money

Fiscal policy involves decisions on how the federal government should set tax rates and spend money. These decisions are relevant to businesses because they affect economic growth and therefore can affect the demand for a firm's products or services.

Revision of Personal Income Tax Rates   Consider a fiscal policy that reduces personal income taxes. With this policy, people would have higher after-tax incomes, which might encourage them to spend more money. Such behavior reflects an increase in the aggregate demand for products and services produced by businesses, which would improve the performance of businesses.

Revision of Corporate Taxes   Fiscal policy can also affect a firm's after-tax earnings directly. For example, assume the corporate tax rate is reduced from 30 percent to 25 percent. If a specific corporation's before-tax earnings are $10 million, its taxes would have been $3 million (computed as 30% × $10,000,000) at the old tax rate. Now, however, at a corporate tax rate of 25 percent, its taxes are $2.5 million (computed as 25% × $10,000,000). Therefore, the corporation's after-tax earnings are now $500,000 higher, simply because the corporate taxes are $500,000 lower.

Revision in Excise Taxes   **Excise taxes** are taxes imposed by the federal government on particular products. These taxes raise the cost of producing these goods. Consequently, manufacturers tend to incorporate the tax into the price they charge for the products. Thus, consumers indirectly incur the tax. The tax may also discourage consumption of these goods by indirectly affecting the price. Excise taxes are imposed on various products, including alcohol and tobacco.

excise taxes
taxes imposed by the federal government on particular products

Revision in the Budget Deficit   The fiscal policy set by the federal government dictates the amount of tax revenue generated by the federal government and the amount of federal spending. If federal government spending exceeds the amount of federal taxes, a **federal budget deficit** results.

When the federal government receives less revenue than it spends, it must borrow the difference. For example, if the federal government plans to spend $900 billion but receives only $700 billion in taxes (or other revenue), it has $200 billion less than it desires to spend. It must borrow $200 billion to have sufficient funds for making its expenditures (as shown in Exhibit 3.7). If the federal government needs to borrow additional funds, it creates a high demand for loanable funds, which may result in higher interest rates (for reasons explained earlier).

In the 1998–2000 period, the federal government spent less funds than it received, which resulted in a small surplus. Under these conditions, the government's budget policy does not place upward pressure on interest rates. In 2001, the tax revenue received by the U.S. government declined because income levels declined as the economy weakened. In addition, the U.S. government spent more money in 2001 due to expenses associated with the September 11 tragedy and the subsequent war. Therefore, the U.S. government experienced a budget deficit in 2001. The increase in government spending in the 2001–2002 period was offset by a reduction in spending by consumers and businesses, however, so demand for loanable funds remained relatively low, as did interest rates.

federal budget deficit
the situation when the amount of federal government spending exceeds the amount of federal taxes and other revenue received by the federal government

Exhibit 3.7

Example of How a Budget Deficit Occurs

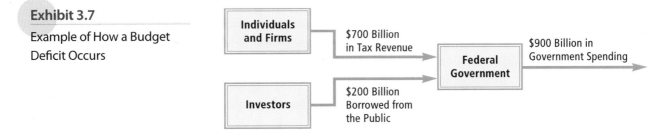

Summary of Government Influence on Economic Factors

Exhibit 3.8 provides a summary of how the federal government can affect the performance of firms. Fiscal policy can affect personal tax rates and therefore influence consumer spending behavior. It can also affect corporate tax rates, which influence the earnings of firms. Monetary policy can affect interest rates, which may influence the demand for a firm's product (if the purchases are sometimes paid for with borrowed funds). By influencing interest rates, monetary policy also affects the interest expenses that firms incur.

Dilemma of the Federal Government

The federal government faces a dilemma when attempting to influence economic growth. If it can maintain a low rate of economic growth, it can prevent inflationary pressure caused by an excessive demand for products. A restrictive monetary or fiscal policy may be used for this purpose. A restrictive monetary policy leads to low growth in the money supply over time, which tends to place upward pressure on interest rates. This discourages borrowing and therefore can reduce total spending in the economy. A restrictive fiscal policy results in high taxes and low government spending.

Although restrictive monetary and fiscal policies may keep inflation low, a critical tradeoff is involved. The unemployment rate may be higher when the economy is stagnant. The federal government can use a more stimulative policy (such as low tax rates or a monetary policy designed to reduce interest rates) to boost economic growth. Although these policies increase economic growth, they may also cause higher inflation.

Exhibit 3.8

How Government Policies Affect Business Performance

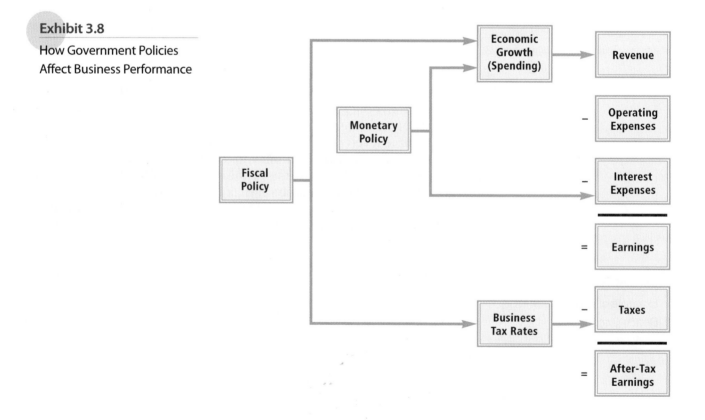

Cross Functional Teamwork

Economic Effects across Business Functions

Since managers of a firm have different responsibilities, they assess different aspects of the economic environment. Managers who focus on production monitor the changes in economic conditions that could affect the firm's production costs. They tend to monitor inflationary trends, or changes in the price levels of specific supplies or equipment that they purchase.

Marketing managers attempt to forecast sales of their products and assess economic conditions that affect the demand for the products, such as economic growth. They may also monitor interest rates if the products are commonly purchased with borrowed funds because the demand for these products may increase in response to a reduction in interest rates. Since the firm's production volume is dependent on the forecasted demand for the product, it is influenced by economic conditions.

Marketing managers assess economic conditions because their marketing decisions can be affected by the strength of the economy. Some of a firm's products (such as necessities and relatively inexpensive products) may be marketed more heavily when economic conditions are weak because these products may be more popular at that time. Conversely, the firm may market its expensive products more heavily when economic conditions are more favorable.

The firm's financial managers monitor the economic conditions that affect the cost of financing. They tend to focus on interest rates because the firm's financing expenses are directly affected by changes in interest rates.

When different types of managers forecast economic conditions so that they can make business decisions, they should work as a team. Otherwise, some forecasts of some economic conditions may vary across managers, which may cause their business decisions to be different. For example, if the marketing managers of an automobile manufacturer forecast low interest rates, they will expect a high sales volume, which will require a large production of automobiles. However, if the production managers forecast high interest rates, they will expect a lower level of sales and will be concerned that a large production volume could cause excessive inventories.

Some firms assign one person or department to develop the forecasts of all economic conditions, which the managers use in all business functions. In this way, all managers make decisions according to the same forecasts of economic conditions.

Rarely is a consensus reached on whether the government should use a stimulative or restrictive policy at a given point in time. During the late 1990s, the federal government used stimulative monetary policies because inflation was very low and was not expected to be a serious problem. This monetary policy helped to increase economic growth during that period. As the economy weakened, in the early 2000s, stimulative monetary policies were used in an effort to increase economic growth.

Managers of firms commonly attempt to forecast how future fiscal and monetary policies will affect economic conditions. Then they use this information to predict the demand for the firm's product, its labor and material costs, and its interest expenses. To illustrate, assume an automobile manufacturer forecasts that next year's interest rate on consumer loans will decrease by 2 percent. This forecast of interest rates will be used to forecast the demand for the firm's automobiles. Lower interest rates will probably lead to higher demand, because more consumers will be willing to finance their purchases of new automobiles. Assume that the firm believes that for every 1 percent decrease in interest rates, demand for its automobiles will increase by 3 percent. Thus, it anticipates a 6 percent increase in sales volume in one year.

Decision Making

Responding to Changes in Monetary Policy

Prestige Tile Company is considering whether to expand its production plant and hire more workers. These decisions are dependent on its expectations of economic growth and interest rates. Its managers believe that the Federal Reserve will increase interest rates in the near future in order to reduce inflation in the United States. The higher interest rates will likely make it more expensive for consumers to borrow and, therefore, will reduce the amount of spending that is financed with borrowed funds. In addition, the higher interest rates will increase the cost of borrowing to Prestige Tile if it borrows funds to finance its expansion. Given the conditions that will result from the Fed's monetary policy, Prestige Tile Company decides that it should not expand its production plant.

1. If other industries are affected in the same manner as Prestige Tile, explain how the Fed's monetary policy will affect economic conditions.

2. Explain how the Fed's monetary policy may affect the prices for tile charged by Prestige Tile Company and its competitors.

ANSWERS: 1. The Fed's monetary policy will reduce economic growth.   2. The Fed's monetary policy could result in a reduced consumer demand for tile, which would lead to lower prices.

COLLEGE HEALTH CLUB: IMPACT OF ECONOMIC CONDITIONS ON CHC

As Sue Kramer develops her business plan for College Health Club (CHC), she needs to recognize the exposure of her business to economic conditions. Based on expected economic conditions, she anticipates that she will have 300 memberships over the first year. If economic conditions weaken, however, some students will probably lose their part-time jobs in the local community and will not be able to afford a health club membership. If the economy weakens, Sue expects that there will be only 260 memberships. Conversely, if the economy strengthens, she expects that there will be 340 memberships in the first year. She therefore determines CHC's revenue for each of these three scenarios as shown in row 3 of the following table. Assuming that CHC's expenses would not be affected, CHC's earnings would be as shown in row 6.

	Present Economic Conditions	If the Economy Weakens	If the Economy Strengthens
(1) Price per membership	$500	$500	$500
(2) Number of members in first year	300	260	340
(3) Revenue in first year = (1) × (2)	$150,000	$130,000	$170,000
(4) Operating expenses	$138,000	$138,000	$138,000
(5) Interest expenses	$4,000	$4,000	$4,000
(6) Earnings before taxes = (3) − (4) − (5)	$8,000	−$12,000	$28,000

As the table shows, CHC's revenue will be lower when economic conditions are weaker. Since most of CHC's expenses (such as rent) are fixed, any change in revenue has a direct effect on earnings. Thus, if a weaker economy causes CHC's revenue to be lower, CHC's earnings will also be lower. A weaker economy could even force Sue to lower the membership price, which could also reduce revenue.

Summary

1 Economic growth affects a firm's performance because it can affect the income levels of consumers and therefore affect the demand for a firm's products. When the economy is strong, the demand for a firm's products is strong, and its profits are relatively high. When the economy is weak, the demand for a firm's products is low, and its profits are relatively low.

2 Inflation affects a firm's performance because it can affect the revenue or expenses of a firm. When inflation is high, firms incur higher costs of production. If they pass on the higher cost to consumers by raising prices, the consumers may reduce their demand for the products, and revenue (and profits) will decline. If the firms do not pass on the higher cost, their revenue may not be affected. However, since their expenses are higher, their profits will decline.

3 Interest rates affect a firm's performance because they can affect the revenue or expenses of a firm. When interest rates increase, the firm's cost of borrowing increases. Therefore, its expenses increase, and

its profits may decline. In addition, high interest rates can discourage consumers from buying particular products (such as new cars or homes) that they normally purchase with credit, because the loan payments would be too high. The firms that offer these products experience a decline in demand and therefore a decline in revenue when interest rates are high. Therefore, they tend to experience lower profits under these conditions.

4 Market prices are determined by demand and supply conditions. The demand for a product is influenced by consumer income and preferences. Higher consumer income generally results in a higher demand for products. The amount of a product produced is influenced by production expenses. Firms will supply products to the market only if the market price is high enough to more than cover expenses.

5 The federal government influences macroeconomic conditions by enacting monetary or fiscal policies. Its monetary policy affects the amount of funds available at commercial banks and other financial institutions and therefore affects

interest rates. Its fiscal policy affects the taxes imposed on consumers, which can influence the amount of spending by consumers and therefore affect the performance of firms. Fiscal policy is also used to tax the earnings of firms.

How the Chapter Concepts Affect Business Performance

A firm's decisions must take into account the economic conditions summarized earlier. Firms attempt to anticipate changes in economic conditions so that they can ensure that they have enough production to satisfy demand. A firm's forecast of demand influences its decisions regarding the quantity of materials to order, whether to expand production space, and whether to hire more employees. Firms also attempt to assess how their costs may change in response to possible changes in economic conditions so that they can anticipate how much money they will need to cover expenses in the future. Overall, firms that can anticipate how economic conditions will change are better prepared to deal with changes in demand or in production costs.

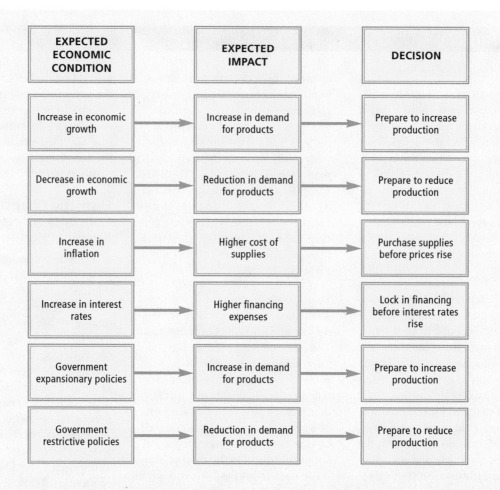

EXPECTED ECONOMIC CONDITION	EXPECTED IMPACT	DECISION
Increase in economic growth	Increase in demand for products	Prepare to increase production
Decrease in economic growth	Reduction in demand for products	Prepare to reduce production
Increase in inflation	Higher cost of supplies	Purchase supplies before prices rise
Increase in interest rates	Higher financing expenses	Lock in financing before interest rates rise
Government expansionary policies	Increase in demand for products	Prepare to increase production
Government restrictive policies	Reduction in demand for products	Prepare to reduce production

Key Terms

aggregate expenditures 76
cost-push inflation 78
cyclical unemployment 76
demand schedule 84
demand-pull inflation 79
economic growth 74
equilibrium price 85
excise taxes 93

federal budget deficit 93
Federal Reserve System 91
fiscal policy 92
frictional unemployment 76
gross domestic product (GDP) 76
inflation 78
monetary policy 91
money supply 90

recession 74
seasonal unemployment 76
shortage 85
structural unemployment 76
supply schedule 84
surplus 85

Review & Critical Thinking Questions

1. List and briefly describe macro-economics factors that affect business performance.

2. Describe the four different types of unemployment and explain which type a college graduate would face upon entering the job market.

3. Why should firms be concerned with changes in interest rates?

4. What are the two basic determinants of market prices? How are shortages and surpluses corrected in the marketplace?

5. Define and explain price equilibrium for businesses and con-

sumers. What is the effect on the equilibrium price when there is a surplus or shortage?

6. Briefly describe three factors that influence market prices.

7. Explain the effect of demand and supply on the general price level in the economy.

8. Define monetary policy. Who is responsible for regulating monetary growth in the United States?

9. Describe how the Fed can reduce interest rates. How can the Fed increase interest rates?

10. Distinguish between macroeconomics and microeconomics. Are fiscal policy decisions of a macroeconomic or microeconomic nature?

11. Discuss the two primary responsibilities of the federal government in establishing economic policies. What does it mean to have a budget deficit?

Discussion Questions

1. In your community, do businesses and housing show signs of economic growth or of weak economic conditions? What effect do these conditions have on inflation and interest rates?

2. Discuss the current interest rate environment. Do you think interest rates are likely to increase or decrease in the near future?

3. How could a firm use the Internet to assess the current level of some macroeconomic factors that may affect business performance, such as economic growth and inflation? How could a firm use the Internet to determine the demand for its products?

4. Assume that you are a manager in a plant that produces rollerblades. What factors would you consider in determining the price for this product?

5. When college students are given federal grants (such as Pell Grants) that cover some education expenses, does this reflect a form of fiscal policy or monetary policy? Explain your answer.

6. Discuss the effects of a federal government budget deficit. How could a budget deficit affect borrowing by firms and households?

7. If you were considering buying a house or car, how would interest rates affect your decision?

8. Does the ability to use information technology to transfer information throughout a large company at a lower cost affect the supply or demand curve?

9. Imagine that you plan to rent an apartment. If rent control policies are in place that keep rent below the market price determined by supply and demand, will there be a shortage or a surplus of apartments?

10. If you had to forecast future economic performance, what factors would you consider in your forecast? Rank your factors in order of importance.

IT'S YOUR DECISION: ECONOMIC EXPOSURE AT CHC

1. Would the business performance of CHC be more exposed to economic growth in the United States as a whole or to economic growth in the local area? Why?

2. Assume that the federal government is expected to raise income taxes for all people, regardless of income level. How could this change in tax policy affect the performance of CHC?

3. Would CHC's business performance be more exposed to inflation in the United States as a whole or in the local area? How could CHC's future expenses be affected by inflation?

4. Explain how marketing at CHC could be affected by economic conditions. Then explain how the amount of aerobics classes and other health club services produced could be affected by economic conditions.

5. A health club differs from manufacturing firms in that it produces a service rather than products. Consider Local Video, Inc., which manufactures video games that are primarily sold to the students at Texas College. Is this manufacturing firm more exposed than CHC to the overall economic conditions in the United States? Now consider Tex, Inc., which produces video games for adults throughout the United States. Is Tex, Inc., more exposed to the overall economic conditions in the United States than CHC is? Explain.

Investing in a Business

Using the annual report of the firm in which you would like to invest, complete the following:

1 Was your firm's performance affected by economic growth last year? If so, how? Are these trends expected to continue? What does your firm plan to do about the economic conditions it faces?

2 Was your firm's performance affected by inflation or interest rates last year? If so, how?

3 Explain how the firm uses technology to assess its economic environment. For example, does it use the Internet to assess the economic environment?

Case: Impact of Economic Conditions

Gold Autoparts, Inc., produces automobile parts that are purchased by various automobile manufacturers that are building new cars. Gold has had some success in selling its parts to automobile manufacturers because they do not have to produce those parts if they can rely on Gold to do so.

Gold has recently created a website that lists all of its parts and the prices charged for them. The automobile manufacturers can order parts online, and Gold tries to fill these orders quickly.

Gold attempts to anticipate when orders will increase so that it can produce enough parts to fill orders. It realizes that the demand for its auto parts is dependent on economic conditions that affect the demand for new cars. When demand for new cars increases, more new cars are produced, and there is greater demand for Gold's parts.

Tom Gold, president of Gold Autoparts, expects that economic growth will increase this year. He expects that interest rates will be relatively low over the next year. He also expects that foreign car manufacturers will introduce many new types of cars into the U.S. market. At this time, Gold Autoparts focuses its business on U.S. automobile manufacturers.

Questions

1 How will Gold Autoparts, Inc., be affected if economic growth increases as expected?

2 How will Gold Autoparts be affected if interest rates decline as expected?

3 How might the introduction of many new cars by foreign car manufacturers affect Gold's business?

4 Overall, do you think conditions will cause an increase or decrease in the demand for Gold's auto parts?

Video Case: Exposure of Ben & Jerry's to Economic Conditions

Ben & Jerry's, which makes ice cream, was founded in 1978 in Burlington, Vermont, by Ben Cohen and Jerry Greenfield with a $12,000 investment, a $5 correspondence course in ice cream making, and a rock salt ice cream maker. They converted an abandoned gas station into their first Ben & Jerry's store. Today, Ben & Jerry's is a large, well-known maker of high-quality ice cream, frozen yogurt, and sorbet. Ben & Jerry's emphasizes its strong commitment to the global community and to the environment. It also has an image of being socially conscious, standing for "we do good by doing good," which resonates with consumers. Still, the company is exposed to many uncontrollable external factors. It must respond to a younger market. It must also satisfy legal requirements regarding disclosure of nutritional content on its label. It is also exposed to competition from premium brands such as Häagen-Dazs.

Ben & Jerry's could be exposed to economic conditions such as inflation or a recession. For example, most companies experience a decline in the demand for their products when the economy weakens because people cannot afford to buy as many products and services. However, Ben and Jerry's is not highly sensitive to adverse economic conditions because its product is an "affordable luxury" that consumers can buy as a treat even during bad economic conditions. Thus, it is less sensitive to economic changes such as recession and inflation. For more information on Ben & Jerry's, go to the company's website at http://www.benjerry.com.

Questions

1. Explain why high inflation could adversely affect companies like Ben & Jerry's.

2. Explain why a recession could adversely affect companies like Ben & Jerry's.

3. Explain in your own words why Ben & Jerry's is not highly sensitive to economic conditions.

4. How does its social responsibility agenda make Ben and Jerry's less exposed to economic shocks?

Internet Applications

1. http://www.stlouisfed.org

What is the St. Louis Fed, and what kinds of activities does it engage in? Look at the FOMC information about the Federal Open Market Committee (FOMC). Has the FOMC taken any type of action recently? What kinds of data does the St. Louis Fed provide? Look at "About the Fed." What cities are part of the Federal Reserve System?

2. http://research.stlouisfed.org/fred2

Look at the different kinds of macroeconomic data available on this website. Which data would you use if you were attempting to forecast a recession in the U.S. economy? Click on "Interest Rates." What kinds of interest rates are listed? Why do interest rates differ on different kinds of instruments?

Dell's Secret to Success

Go to http://www.reportgallery.com and review Dell's most recent annual report. Also, go to Dell's website (http://www.dell.com) and in the section "about Dell," review the background material about Dell that relates to this chapter.

Questions

1. Describe how Dell's business performance was affected by recent economic conditions. Does it appear that Dell's business performance was sensitive to the economy? Explain.

2. During a weak economy, the demand for some of Dell's products may decline. Which products would likely experience a decline in demand?

3. If interest rates increase, why might the demand for Dell's products be affected?

In-Text Study Guide

Answers are in Appendix C at the back of book.

True or False

1. Macroeconomics is focused on a specific business or industry of concern.

2. When U.S. economic growth is lower than normal, the total income level of all U.S. workers is relatively high.

3. Economic growth represents the change in the general level of economic activity.

4. The total amount of expenditures in the economy is known as aggregate expenditures.

5. Structural unemployment refers to workers who lose their jobs due to a decline in economic conditions.

6. A higher level of inflation will cause a larger decrease in a firm's operating expenses.

7. Inflation is usually measured as the percentage change in gross domestic product.

8. The demand for a product can be shown with a demand schedule, which indicates the quantity of the product that would be demanded at each possible price.

9. The Federal Reserve System sets the monetary policy that determines the money supply in the United States.

10. The Fed affects interest rates by changing the supply of funds banks can loan.

Multiple Choice

11. _____ conditions reflect the overall performance of the nation's economy.
    a) Microeconomic
    b) Multi-economic
    c) Macroeconomic
    d) Proto-economic
    e) Supraeconomic

12. All of the following are examples of macroeconomic concerns except:
    a) a drop in the nation's gross domestic product.
    b) an increase in the rate of inflation.
    c) a strike by workers at a local bakery.
    d) an increase in the amount of cyclical unemployment.
    e) an increase in the rate of interest charged on bank loans.

13. The total market value of all final goods and services produced in the United States is known as:
    a) gross domestic product.
    b) aggregate expenditures.
    c) fiscal output.
    d) the production quota.
    e) aggregate supply.

14. Jan is currently between jobs, but she has marketable job skills and is confident she will find work in the near future. Jan's current situation would be an example of _____ unemployment.
    a) seasonal
    b) structural
    c) functional
    d) frictional
    e) cyclical

15. The type of unemployment that represents people who are unemployed because of poor economic conditions is:
    a) functional unemployment.
    b) cyclical unemployment.
    c) seasonal unemployment.
    d) structural unemployment.
    e) general unemployment.

In-Text Study Guide

Answers are in Appendix C at the back of book.

16. The type of inflation that requires firms to increase their prices to cover increased costs is referred to as:
    a) demand-pull inflation.
    b) stagflation.
    c) cost-push inflation.
    d) disequilibrium.
    e) unemployment.

17. The prices firms pay for supplies or materials directly influence their:
    a) operating expenses.
    b) operating revenue.
    c) dividends.
    d) stockholders' equity.
    e) economic assets.

18. An increase in the general level of prices of products and services over a specified period of time is called:
    a) inflation.
    b) stagflation.
    c) unemployment.
    d) disinflation.
    e) equilibrium.

19. _____ represent the cost of borrowing money.
    a) Discount factors
    b) Depreciation rates
    c) Inflation premiums
    d) Dividends
    e) Interest rates

20. Over the next several years, economic growth in less-developed nations is:
    a) unlikely to occur due to lack of natural resources in most of these countries.
    b) likely to occur, but at a much slower rate than growth in the United States.
    c) likely to be greater than the growth in the United States, thus providing U.S. firms with important market opportunities.
    d) unlikely to occur because of the anti-growth attitudes of their governments.
    e) likely to be quite rapid, but U.S. firms are unlikely to benefit since they view the opportunities in less-developed countries as being too risky.

21. A typical demand schedule shows that:
    a) as price decreases, quantity demanded will also decrease.
    b) as price decreases, quantity demanded will increase.
    c) quantity supplied can never be less than quantity demanded.
    d) the total quantity of goods consumers want to buy will fall during periods of inflation.
    e) a firm can always increase its revenue by increasing the prices it charges for its products.

22. A supply schedule shows:
    a) the relationship between quantity supplied and quantity demanded.
    b) how the quantity firms supply in the market affects their total profits.
    c) the quantity firms are willing to supply at each possible price.
    d) the average cost of supplying various quantities of a good.
    e) the relationship between the amount of labor and other inputs the firm employs and the quantity of output the firm can produce.

23. At the equilibrium price for a product, the:
    a) firms in the market are maximizing their total revenue.
    b) consumers in the market have spent all of their income.
    c) firms in the market are maximizing their total output.
    d) firms in the market are just breaking even.
    e) quantity demanded by consumers equals the quantity supplied by firms.

In-Text Study Guide

Answers are in Appendix C at the back of book.

24. If the market price of a good is above the equilibrium price:
    a) a surplus will exist, which will put downward pressure on prices.
    b) the supply curve will shift to the right as firms rush to take advantage of the high price.
    c) the demand curve will shift to the left as consumers decrease the quantity they buy.
    d) the government will intervene to force the price downward.
    e) a shortage will exist, which will force the price even higher.

25. If the market price is below the equilibrium price:
    a) quantity demanded will exceed quantity supplied, resulting in a shortage.
    b) quantity demanded will exceed quantity supplied, resulting in a surplus.
    c) quantity supplied will exceed quantity demanded, resulting in a shortage.
    d) quantity supplied will exceed quantity demanded, resulting in a surplus.
    e) the supply curve will shift to the left and the demand curve will shift to the right.

26. An increase in the demand for a product is likely to cause:
    a) a matching decrease in supply.
    b) an increase in the equilibrium price.
    c) the supply curve to shift to the right.
    d) a decrease in the equilibrium price.
    e) the government to attempt to increase production quotas.

27. If consumer incomes increase, the effect on consumer decisions about how much they want to buy can be shown by:
    a) shifting the demand curve outward (to the right).
    b) shifting the supply curve outward.
    c) shifting the demand curve inward (to the left).
    d) moving downward to the right along the demand curve.
    e) shifting the supply curve inward.

28. The _____ of the United States is defined as the total amount of demand deposits, currency held by the public, and traveler's checks.
    a) financial wealth
    b) financial reserves
    c) money supply
    d) total banking assets
    e) gross domestic product

29. The central bank of the United States, where the money supply is controlled and regulated, is the:
    a) Federal Reserve System.
    b) Senate.
    c) Department of Congress.
    d) Council of Economic Advisers.
    e) Board of Directors.

30. A major effect of the Federal Reserve's monetary policies is to bring about changes in the:
    a) stock of gold held by the government to back the money supply.
    b) income tax rates paid by households and businesses.
    c) size of the federal budget deficit.
    d) amount the government spends to finance social programs.
    e) interest rates banks charge when they make loans.

31. Which of the following is the best example of the federal government's use of fiscal policy?
    a) The Federal Reserve places new regulations on the nation's banks that require them to make more loans to minorities and women.
    b) The U.S. Treasury announces that it has redesigned the nation's paper money to make the bills more difficult to counterfeit.

In-Text Study Guide

Answers are in Appendix C at the back of book.

c) The government cuts taxes during an economic downturn.

d) The president appoints a new commission to look into concerns about how pollution is damaging the environment.

e) The Federal Reserve gives banks more funds to enable them to make more loans.

32. Taxes that the federal government imposes on particular products are called:
   a) excise taxes.
   b) import taxes.
   c) export taxes.
   d) quotas.
   e) embargoes.

33. When the amount of federal government spending exceeds the amount of federal taxes, the result is called a:
   a) trade deficit.
   b) federal budget deficit.
   c) balance of payments.
   d) price equilibrium.
   e) opportunity cost.

34. Restrictive monetary and fiscal policies may keep inflation low, but the critical tradeoff is that they may also cause:
   a) disinflation.
   b) environmental problems.
   c) massive crime.
   d) unemployment.
   e) higher inflation.

35. The government can prevent inflationary pressure caused by an excessive demand for products by maintaining a low rate of:
   a) fiscal policies.
   b) economic growth.
   c) monetary policies.
   d) unemployment.
   e) savings.

LANDOV LLC

The Learning Goals
of this chapter are to:

Explain the motives for U.S. firms to
engage in international business. *1*

Describe how firms conduct
international business. *2*

Explain how barriers to international
business have been reduced and
describe the barriers that remain. *3*

Explain how foreign characteristics
can influence a firm's
international business. *4*

Explain how exchange rate movements
can affect a firm's performance. *5*

Businesses like this one commonly
produce products that they sell
to many different countries.

Assessing Global Conditions

Many U.S. firms have capitalized on opportunities in foreign countries by engaging in international business. The amount of international business has grown in response to the removal of various international barriers. Even small U.S. firms are now engaging in international business by purchasing foreign supplies or by selling their products in foreign countries.

International economic conditions affect a firm's revenue and expenses and therefore affect its value. To illustrate how the international environment can affect the value of a business, consider the case of Victory Company, which produces computer games and wants to expand its business internationally. Since expansion of business into foreign countries can be very expensive, Victory Company wants to carefully assess whether to expand and where to expand. The performance of Victory's business in a foreign country is dependent on the country's cultural and financial characteristics. In addition, the performance is affected by economic conditions in the country because the demand for computer games is influenced by the income level of the local people.

Specifically, Victory Company must determine:

▶ How could international business enhance its performance?

▶ What methods might it use to engage in international business?

▶ What foreign characteristics will influence its level of business in foreign countries?

▶ How will its international business be affected by exchange rates?

All firms that conduct international business must address these types of questions. These firms commonly strive to increase their international business because an increase in the foreign demand for their products results in higher revenue and earnings. By understanding the foreign characteristics that influence its level of international business, Victory Company can attempt to offer its product to foreign customers. This chapter explains how the assessment of the global environment by Victory Company or any other firm can be conducted in a manner that maximizes the firm's value.

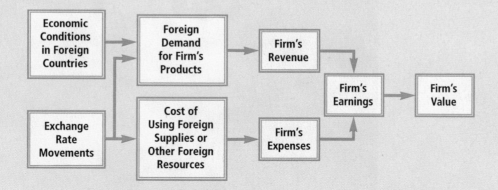

107

How International Business Can Enhance Performance

International business can enhance a firm's performance by increasing its revenue or reducing its expenses. Either result leads to higher profits for the firm. There are various motives for international business, and each of them allows the firm to benefit in a manner that can enhance its performance. Some of the more common motives to conduct international business are:

▶ Attract foreign demand

▶ Capitalize on technology

▶ Use inexpensive resources

▶ Diversify internationally

Firms that engage in international business are commonly referred to as multinational corporations. Some multinational corporations such as Amazon.com, The Gap, IBM, and Starbucks are large well-known firms, but many small U.S. firms also conduct international business so that they can enhance their performance.

Attract Foreign Demand

Some firms are unable to increase their market share in the United States because of intense competition within their industry. Alternatively, the U.S. demand for the firm's product may decrease because of changes in consumer tastes. Under either of these conditions, a firm might consider foreign markets where potential demand may exist. Many firms, including DuPont, IBM, and PepsiCo, have successfully entered new foreign markets to attract new sources of demand. Wal-Mart Stores has recently opened stores in numerous countries, including Mexico and Hong Kong. Boeing (a U.S. producer of aircraft) recently received orders for jets from China Xinjiang Airlines and Kenya Airways.

eBay has created a service to many foreign markets that was not available in the past.

LANDOV LLC

Procter & Gamble has foreign subsidiaries in many different countries so that it can produce and sell products around the world.

LANDOV LLC

Avon Products has opened branches in many countries, including Brazil, China, and Poland. McDonald's is now in more than 80 different countries and generates more than half of its total revenue from foreign countries. Hertz has expanded its agencies in Europe and in other foreign markets. Amazon.com has expanded its business by offering its services in many foreign countries.

Blockbuster has more than 3,000 stores located in 27 markets outside the United States. It is focusing its efforts for future growth in those markets because it already has business there and therefore has some name recognition. General Electric's philosophy is that economic growth will be uneven across countries, so it must position its businesses in those markets where demand will increase. It believes that as globalization continues, only the most competitive companies will be able to effectively serve their employees and stockholders. In 1999, Autozone established its first retail store for auto parts in Mexico because many older vehicles are still in use in that country, so demand for auto parts is high. Today, Autozone has 49 stores in Mexico. eBay has provided some foreign markets with a service that was not previously available in those areas. It has served hundreds of millions of requests to buy or sell products from consumers in more than 150 countries.

The Coca-Cola Company's business has also expanded globally over time. Now the company has a significant presence in almost every country. It expanded throughout Latin America, western Europe, Australia, and most of Africa before 1984. Since then, it has expanded into eastern Europe and most of Asia.

The motivation of firms to attract foreign demand is summarized in a recent annual report of Procter & Gamble (P&G):

"More than 80 percent of P&G's sales come from the top 10 markets. We need to keep driving P&G growth in these countries, which are some of the biggest and strongest economies in the world. P&G's business in the top 10 countries taken together is growing at a rate of 11% per year. P&G is a leader in these markets. . . . Yet, despite this strength in P&G's 10 largest countries, we still have significant opportunities to grow."

—Procter & Gamble

SMALL BUSINESS SURVEY

International Business

In a recent National Small Business poll conducted for the NFIB Research Foundation, the owners of small businesses that conduct international business were asked about their strategy for generating sales in foreign countries. Their responses are shown below:

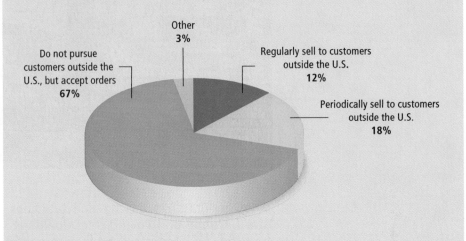

They were also asked where they generated most of their international sales in the last three years. Their responses are shown below:

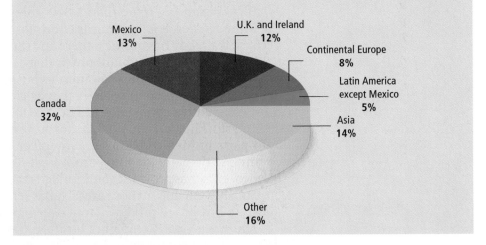

Capitalize on Technology

Many U.S. firms have established new businesses in the so-called developing countries (such as those in Latin America), which have relatively low levels of technology. AT&T and other firms have established new telecommunications systems in developing countries. Other U.S. firms that create power generation, road systems, and other forms of infrastructure have extensive business in these countries. Ford Motor Company and General Motors have attempted to capitalize on their technological advantages by establishing plants in developing countries throughout Asia, Latin America, and eastern Europe. IBM is doing business with the Chinese government to capitalize on its technology. Amazon.com can capitalize on its

SMALL BUSINESS SURVEY

When asked about the profitability of their sales to customers outside the United States as compared to their profitability of their sales to U.S. customers, they responded as shown below:

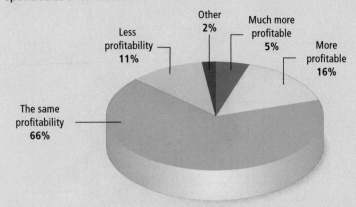

- Other 2%
- Much more profitable 5%
- More profitable 16%
- Less profitability 11%
- The same profitability 66%

The small business owners were also asked whether the majority of their orders from outside the United States were placed on their website. Their responses here are classified according to the size of the business:

	Businesses with 1 to 9 Employees	Businesses with 10 to 19 Employees	Businesses with 20 to 249 Employees
Yes	29%	20%	10%
No	65%	77%	89%
Not applicable	6%	3%	1%

Notice that the website was most important for the smallest businesses and less important for the larger small businesses, which may have employees who can contact foreign customers directly.

These small business owners were also asked whether barriers imposed by foreign governments limit their ability to increase sales outside the United States. Their responses are shown here for various types of government barriers:

	Tariffs	Excessive Red Tape and Regulations
Severely limits	10%	18%
Somewhat limits	27%	22%
Does not limit	59%	58%
Other	4%	2%

technology advantage by expanding in foreign countries where technology is not as advanced.

Use Inexpensive Resources

Labor and land costs can vary significantly among countries. Firms often attempt to set up production at a location where land and labor are inexpensive. Exhibit 4.1 illustrates how hourly compensation (labor) costs can vary among countries. The costs are much higher in the developed countries (such as the United States and Germany) than in other countries (such as Mexico and Taiwan). Numerous U.S. firms have established subsidiaries in countries where labor costs are low. For example, Converse has

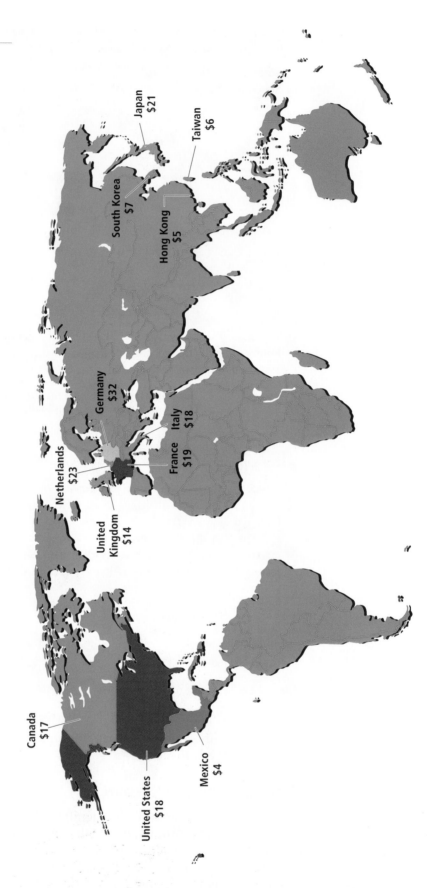

Exhibit 4.1

Approximate Hourly
Compensation Costs for
Manufacturing across
Countries

Japan
$21

Taiwan
$6

South Korea
$7

Hong Kong
$5

Germany
$32

Italy
$18

France
$19

Netherlands
$23

United
Kingdom
$14

Canada
$17

United States
$18

Mexico
$4

shoes manufactured in Mexico. Dell, Inc., has disk drives and monitors produced in Asia. General Electric, Motorola, Texas Instruments, Dow Chemical, and Corning have established production plants in Singapore and Taiwan to take advantage of lower labor costs. Many firms from the United States and western Europe have also established plants in Hungary, Poland, and other eastern Europe countries, where labor costs are lower. General Motors pays its assembly-line workers in Mexico about $10 per day (including benefits) versus about $220 per day for its assembly-line workers in the United States.

Diversify Internationally

When all the assets of a firm are designed to generate sales of a specific product in one country, the profits of the firm are normally unstable. This instability is due to the firm's exposure to changes within its industry or within the economy. The firm's performance is dependent on the demand for this one product and on the conditions of the one economy in which it conducts business. The firm can reduce such risk by selling its product in various countries.

Because economic conditions can vary among countries, U.S. firms that conduct international business are affected less by U.S. economic conditions. A U.S. firm's overall performance may be more stable if it sells its product in various countries so that its business is not influenced solely by the economic conditions in a single country. For example, the demand for PepsiCo's products in Mexico might decline if the Mexican economy is weak, but at the same time economic growth in Brazil, the Netherlands, and Spain might result in a higher overall demand for PepsiCo's products.

Exhibit 4.2 shows how DuPont has diversified its business across countries. Because DuPont has achieved geographic diversification, it is not as exposed to the economic conditions in the United States. Of course, it is somewhat exposed to economic conditions in the foreign countries where it conducts its business.

The amount of products imported through harbors is higher when international trade restrictions are reduced or eliminated.

GETTY IMAGES

Combination of Motives

Many U.S. firms engage in international business because of a combination of the motives just described. For example, when 3M Company engages in international business, it attracts new demand from customers in foreign countries. Second, it is able to capitalize on its technology, which is often more advanced than the technology available to local

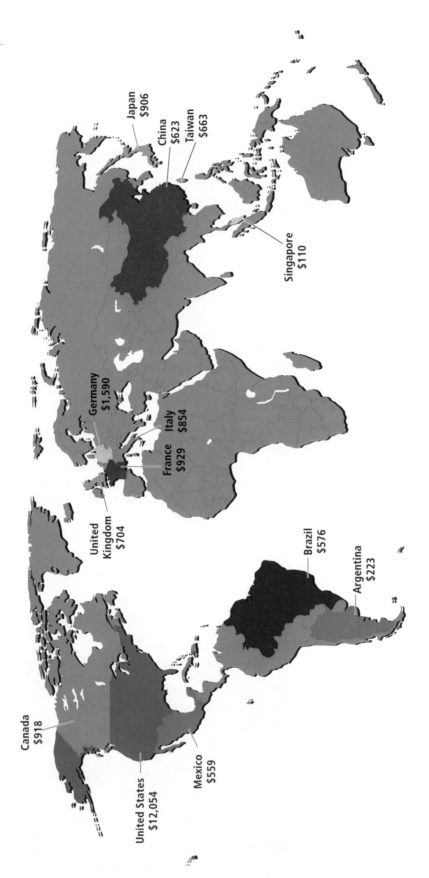

Exhibit 4.2

DuPont's Geographic
Diversification (measured
by annual sales in millions
of dollars)
Source: 2001 annual report.

Japan
$906

China
$623

Taiwan
$663

Singapore
$110

Germany
$1,590

Italy
$854

France
$929

United
Kingdom
$704

Brazil
$576

Argentina
$223

Canada
$918

United States
$12,054

Mexico
$559

firms in these countries. Third, it is able to use low-cost land and labor in some countries. Finally, it is able to diversify its business among countries. It has also reduced its exposure to U.S. economic conditions by increasing its international business over time.

General Electric is another example of a major firm that has expanded internationally in recent years. It has substantial business in Europe. Its sales have also increased in Latin America and the Pacific Basin. Wal-Mart is another firm that has been motivated by the reasons just described to expand into foreign countries.

Decision Making

Using International Business to Reduce Expenses

Victory Company (introduced at the beginning of this chapter) produces computer games and sells them in the United States. Its major concern is the high cost of producing the computer chips that it uses in the computer games. None of the U.S. chip manufacturers can produce the chips at a lower cost, so Victory Company contacts a supplier in China and describes the types of computer chips that it needs. The supplier offers to produce and transport computer chips to Victory Company for a price that is 30 percent below Victory's prevailing cost of producing its own chips. By shifting its production of chips to China, Victory Company is able to reduce its production expenses and compete more effectively in the computer game industry.

1. Explain why Victory Company can obtain the chips from the supplier in China at a lower price than a U.S. supplier would charge.

2. Explain how a tax on the computer chips imported from China could affect Victory's profits.

ANSWERS: 1. The cost of labor in China is very low, which results in a lower cost of producing many types of products and supplies. 2. A tariff on chips from China would raise the price that Victory Company would have to pay for the chips. Thus, Victory's cost of obtaining the chips would increase and its profits would decrease.

How to Conduct International Business

2

Describe how firms conduct international business.

A firm may use various methods to conduct international business. The more common methods of conducting international business that a firm should consider are:

▶ Importing

▶ Exporting

▶ Direct foreign investment (DFI)

▶ Outsourcing

▶ Strategic alliances

Importing

importing
the purchase of foreign products or services

Importing involves the purchase of foreign products or services. For example, some U.S. consumers purchase foreign automobiles, clothing, cameras, and other products from firms in foreign countries. Many U.S. firms import materials or supplies that are used to produce products. Even if these firms sell the products locally, they can benefit from international

The large balance of trade deficit has attracted much attention and concern from U.S. politicians.

business. They import foreign supplies that are less expensive or of a higher quality than alternative U.S. supplies.

Factors That Influence the Degree of Importing The degree to which a firm imports supplies is influenced by government trade barriers. Governments may impose a **tariff** (or tax) on imported products. The tax is normally paid directly by the importer, who typically passes the tax on to consumers by charging a higher price for the product. Thus, the product may be overpriced compared with products produced by firms based in that country. When governments impose tariffs, the ability of foreign firms to compete in those countries is restricted.

tariff
a tax on imported products

Governments can also impose a **quota** on imported products, thereby limiting the amounts of specific products that can be imported. This type of trade barrier may be even more restrictive than a tariff because it places an explicit limit on the amount of a specific product that can be imported.

quota
a limit on the amounts of specific products that can be imported

In general, trade barriers tend to both discourage trade and protect specific industries from foreign competition. However, many trade barriers have been removed in Europe and in many Asian countries. In addition, since 1993 when the North American Free Trade Agreement (NAFTA) removed many restrictions on trade among Canada, Mexico, and the United States, U.S. firms have had more opportunities to expand their businesses in Canada and Mexico. At the same time, however, they are also more exposed to competition from foreign firms within the United States.

Exporting

exporting
the sale of products or services (called exports) to purchasers residing in other countries

Exporting is the sale of products or services (called exports) to purchasers residing in other countries. Many firms, such as DuPont, Intel, and Zenith, use exporting as a means of selling products in foreign markets. Many smaller firms in the United States also export to foreign countries.

Trend of U.S. Exports and Imports The trend of U.S. exports and imports is shown in Exhibit 4.3. Notice that the amount of U.S. exports and imports

Exhibit 4.3

Trend of U.S. Exports and Imports

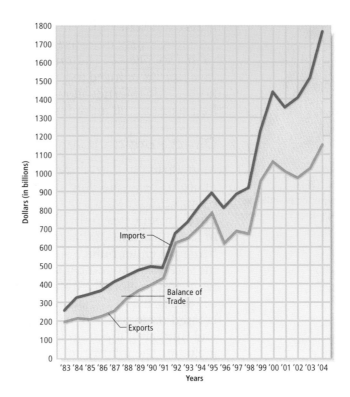

more than quadrupled between 1980 and the 2004, reflecting the increased importance of international trade.

The U.S. **balance of trade,** which is also shown in Exhibit 4.3, is equal to the level of U.S. exports minus the level of U.S. imports. A negative balance of trade is referred to as a **trade deficit** and means that the United States is importing (purchasing) more products and services from foreign countries than it is selling to foreign countries. The United States has consistently had a trade deficit since 1980, and it has become even more negative (larger deficit) in recent years.

When a country has a trade deficit, its consumers may be benefiting from imported products that are less expensive than locally produced products. At the same time, however, the purchase of imported products implies less reliance on domestic production in favor of foreign production. Thus, it may be argued that a large trade deficit causes a transfer of jobs to some foreign countries.

How the Internet Facilitates Exporting   Many firms use their websites to identify the products that they sell, along with the price for each product. This allows them to easily advertise their products to potential importers anywhere in the world without mailing brochures to various countries. In addition, they can add to their product line and change prices by simply revising the website. Thus, importers can keep abreast of an exporter's product information by monitoring the exporter's website.

Firms can also use their websites to accept orders online. Some products such as software can be delivered from the exporter to the importer directly over the Internet in the form of a file that lands in the importer's computer. Other products must be shipped, but the Internet makes it easier to track the shipping process. The importer can transmit its order for products via e-mail to the exporter. The exporter's warehouse then fills the order. When the products are shipped from the warehouse, an e-mail

balance of trade
the level of exports minus the level of imports

trade deficit
the amount by which imports exceed exports

message is sent to the importer and to the exporter's headquarters. The warehouse may even use technology to monitor its inventory of products so that suppliers are automatically notified to send more supplies when the inventory is reduced to a specific level. If the exporter uses multiple warehouses, the Internet allows them to work as a network so that if one warehouse cannot fill an order, another warehouse will.

Direct Foreign Investment (DFI)

direct foreign investment (DFI)
a means of acquiring or building subsidiaries in one or more foreign countries

Many firms engage in **direct foreign investment (DFI),** which is a means of acquiring or building subsidiaries in one or more foreign countries. For example, Ford Motor Company has facilities in various countries that produce automobiles and sell them in those locations. Blockbuster has stores in various countries that rent DVDs to customers in those countries. A U.S. firm may either build a subsidiary in a foreign country or acquire an existing foreign firm and convert that into its subsidiary. Many U.S. firms expand internationally by acquiring foreign firms. They most commonly acquire firms in Canada and the United Kingdom but have recently increased their acquisitions in countries such as Brazil, the Czech Republic, and Hungary. Direct foreign investment is feasible in a variety of situations, including the following:

1. A firm that has successfully exported to a foreign country desires to reduce its transportation costs. It establishes a subsidiary in the foreign country to manufacture the product and sell it in that country. Kellogg Company uses this strategy and has production plants in 19 different countries, including China and India. Nike initially subcontracted with factories in Taiwan and Korea to produce athletic shoes to be sold in Asian countries. It then expanded its production facilities in foreign countries so that they could produce shoes to be sold in Europe and South America.

2. A firm that has been exporting products is informed that the foreign government will impose trade barriers. Therefore, the firm establishes a subsidiary that can manufacture and sell products in that country. In this way, it avoids the trade barriers.

3. A foreign country is desperately in need of advanced technology and offers a U.S. firm incentives, such as free use of land, to establish a subsidiary in that country. The foreign country also expects that the firm will employ some local workers.

4. A U.S. firm believes that it can substantially reduce its labor costs by shifting its production facilities to a developing country where labor and land are less expensive.

Although DFI can often be feasible, firms should conduct a thorough analysis of the costs and benefits before investing. Once funds are spent on DFI, the decision cannot easily be reversed because the foreign facilities would have to be sold at a loss in most cases.

Foreign Expansion in the United States   Just as U.S. firms have expanded into foreign countries, foreign firms have expanded into the United States. In some industries, such as the automobile, camera, and clothing industries, many foreign firms offer their products in the United States. Some foreign firms have established new subsidiaries in the United States, such as Toyota (expanded its Kentucky plant), Mitsubishi Materials (built a silicon plant in Oregon), and Honda (expanded its Ohio plant). Other foreign firms such as Sony have acquired firms in the United States. Many foreign

Out of
Business

AND SO Mr. JOHNSON, UPON YOUR ADVICE THAT OUTSOURCING SHOULD BE USED FOR ALL BASIC JOB POSITIONS THAT CAN BE DONE CHEAPER IN OTHER COUNTRIES, WE HAVE DECIDED TO OUTSOURCE YOUR CEO POSITION.

BOARD MEMBERS

firms have spent hundreds of millions of dollars to develop or expand their U.S. businesses. Since foreign firms have expanded into the United States, even those U.S. firms that only sell their products domestically are subject to foreign competition.

Outsourcing

Firms commonly outsource some of their services to foreign countries as a means of using cheaper labor. For example, a U.S. manufacturing firm

Many U.S. businesses outsource some of their production to companies such as this one in New Delhi, India.

GETTY IMAGES

may outsource its technology support staff to Bulgaria, China, or another country where labor costs are low. A U.S. computer company may outsource its computer help desk to India. Some U.S. firms use outsourcing as a means of reducing their expenses.

When a U.S. firm outsources, the employees whose jobs are transferred from the United States to other countries, and especially those people who lose their jobs due to the outsourcing, are highly critical of the firm. However, the firm might counter that it needs to outsource in order to compete with other firms that also rely on cheaper foreign labor in some manner. In addition, it may suggest that its use of outsourcing is no different than the actions of other U.S. firms that import supplies or engage in direct foreign investment in low-wage countries. All of these actions are motivated by the desire to benefit from the use of cheap foreign labor.

Strategic Alliances

strategic alliance
a business agreement between firms whereby resources are shared to pursue mutual interests

joint venture
an agreement between two firms about a specific project

U.S. and foreign firms commonly engage in **strategic alliances,** which are business agreements that are in the best interests of the firms involved. Various types of international alliances between U.S. firms and foreign firms can be made. One type is a **joint venture,** which involves an agreement between two firms about a specific project. Joint ventures between U.S. and non-U.S. firms are common. The U.S. firm may produce a product and send it to a non-U.S. firm, which sells the product in that country. The non-U.S. firm is involved because it knows the culture of that country and is more capable of selling the product there.

In another type of joint venture, two firms participate in the production of a product. This type of joint venture is common in the automobile industry. The automakers in the United States are involved in a variety of ventures with foreign manufacturers. General Motors dealerships and Ford Motor Company dealerships sell cars manufactured by firms in France, Japan, and South Korea. RJR Nabisco has engaged in joint ventures with some food producers in some of the former Soviet republics. This gives Nabisco access to local production facilities and skilled workers. These joint ventures reflect the improved commercial relations with the former Soviet republics that have led to a major change in attitude by U.S. companies about doing business in those areas.

international licensing agreement
a type of alliance in which a firm allows a foreign company (called the "licensee") to produce its products according to specific instructions

Another type of alliance is an **international licensing agreement,** in which a firm allows a foreign company (called the "licensee") to produce its products according to specific instructions. Many U.S. beer producers engage in licensing agreements with foreign firms. The foreign firm is given the technology to produce the products. As the foreign firm sells the products, it channels a portion of revenue to the licensing firm. The advantage of licensing is that the firm is able to sell its product in foreign markets without the costs involved in exporting or direct foreign investment. One disadvantage, however, is that the foreign firm shares the profits from products sold in the foreign country.

How the Internet Facilitates Licensing   Some firms with international reputations use their brand name to advertise products over the Internet. They then license manufacturers in foreign countries to produce some of their products subject to their specifications. For example, Mesa Company set up a licensing agreement with a manufacturer in Indonesia to produce its product, which Mesa advertises over the Internet. When Mesa receives orders for its product from customers in Asia, it relies on this manufacturer to produce and deliver the products ordered. This expedites the delivery process and may even enable Mesa to have the products manufactured at a lower cost than if it produced them itself.

Decision Making

Choosing a Strategy to Expand Overseas

Victory Company sells its computer games only in the United States, but it believes it could also serve the Canadian market. It must decide on the best strategy for entering that market. One possibility is to establish a subsidiary in Canada, which would produce the computer games there and sell them locally. However, Victory does not want to incur the cost of establishing another production plant. It has the capacity to increase production in its existing plant, so it decides to use that plant to produce more computer games and will export them to some retail stores in Canada. If the Canadian demand for computer games at these retail stores is very strong, Victory will consider establishing a Canadian subsidiary in the future. Overall, Victory's decision to export its product to Canada will increase its revenue. It will incur some expenses to advertise its computer games in the Canadian market. If its revenue from exporting exceeds the cost of producing these exports and the advertising expenses in Canada, Victory's profits will increase as a result of exporting its computer games to Canada.

1. Another strategy for Victory would be to establish a joint venture with a U.S. firm that would transport the computer games to Canada and sell them to the retail stores there. This firm would receive a commission of 15 percent on all sales of the computer games. What would be the advantage of this joint venture for Victory Company?

2. What would be a disadvantage of the joint venture described above for Victory Company?

ANSWERS: 1. The advantage is that the joint venture would save Victory in advertising and shipping expenses. 2. The disadvantage is that Victory would have to pay the firm 15 percent on all the sales, so it would receives only 85 percent of the sales proceeds.

Explain how barriers to international business have been reduced and describe the barriers that remain.

Barriers to International Business

In recent decades, an important factor contributing to the increase in international business has been the reduction in trade barriers. Nevertheless, firms that consider conducting international business must be aware that barriers still exist.

Reduction in Barriers

The barriers to international business have been reduced over time through various free trade agreements and the formation of free trade zones such as the European Union. The following are some examples of how barriers have been reduced.

NAFTA   As a result of the North American Free Trade Agreement (NAFTA) of 1993, trade barriers between the United States, Mexico, and Canada were eliminated. Consequently, firms in the United States now have more freedom to export their products to the other countries, while firms in Mexico have more freedom to export their products to the United States.

GATT   Following NAFTA, the General Agreement on Tariffs and Trade (GATT) called for the reduction or elimination of trade restrictions on specified imported products across 117 countries. It also led to the creation of the World Trade Organization (WTO), which now has 140 member countries. This accord has enabled firms to more easily export their products to other countries.

Latin America   In June 2003, the United States and Chile signed a free trade agreement to remove tariffs on more than 90 percent of the products that are sent between the two countries. Many other trade agreements are in the process of being negotiated between the United States and Latin American countries.

European Union   During the 1980s and 1990s, the countries in the European Union agreed to eliminate many trade barriers. By 2002, most of these countries had also adopted the euro as their currency. This has made it easier for firms in one European country to export their products to firms in other European countries because the importers and exporters now use the same currency and thus no longer face the costs and risks associated with exchanging currencies.

In 2004, the European Union accepted the following new members, most of which are in eastern Europe: Cyprus, the Czech Republic, Estonia, Hungary, Latvia, Lithuania, Malta, Poland, Slovakia, and Slovenia. Consequently, the restrictions on the new members' trade with western Europe were reduced. Since these countries have substantially lower wages than those in western Europe, firms from the United States and elsewhere can establish manufacturing plants in these countries to produce products and export them to western Europe.

Reduced Barriers on Direct Foreign Investment   In recent years, many Asian, European, and Latin American countries have reduced their barriers on direct foreign investment. Consequently, firms now have more freedom to establish subsidiaries or to acquire existing companies there. In some countries, the governments have even offered firms incentives to encourage them to establish facilities there. These governments recognize that foreign ownership of local facilities could benefit the economy by creating jobs.

Remaining Barriers

Firms should recognize, however, that even though barriers to international business have been reduced, some governments continue to impose barriers in order to protect their local firms or to punish certain countries for their actions. These barriers may prevent a firm from pursuing international business in a specific country. Alternatively, they may increase the cost of pursuing international business. In some cases, the potential advantages of pursuing international business are outweighed by the costs of circumventing the barriers. Common barriers include trade barriers such as the tariffs and quotas described earlier, as well as barriers aimed at preventing a firm from establishing a subsidiary (direct foreign investment) in another country.

Barriers Used to Protect Local Firms   Any government may be tempted to impose barriers to protect its own firms. For example, the U.S. government may impose trade barriers such as tariffs on imported steel, even though such barriers are in conflict with previous trade agreements with other countries. The government may argue that such action is appropriate because the foreign steel firms receive subsidies from their government that enable them to be more competitive and therefore can afford to sell their steel at a price that is lower than their expenses (referred to as **dumping**). The foreign government, in turn, may claim that it does not provide subsidies, and the dispute may take years to resolve. Meanwhile, the foreign government

dumping
selling products in a foreign country at a price below the cost of producing those products

may retaliate by imposing tariffs on products that its consumers import from the United States, such as chemicals. Any such intervention by a government to protect its local firms disrupts the spirit of global competition between firms.

Barriers Used to Punish Countries   Trade barriers are sometimes used to punish countries for various actions. For example, trade restrictions may be imposed on countries that do not enforce environmental laws or child labor laws, or initiate war against another country, or are unwilling to participate in a war against an unlawful dictator of another country.

Disagreements about International Trade Policy

Disagreements on international trade policy will always exist. People whose job prospects are affected either positively or negatively by international trade tend to have very strong opinions about international trade policy. Most people agree that free trade can encourage more intense competition among firms, which can be beneficial because it gives consumers the opportunity to obtain products where the quality is highest and the prices are low. Free trade should cause production to move to those countries where it can be done most efficiently. Each country's government wants to increase its exports because a rise in exports results in a higher level of production and income and may create jobs. A job created in one country, however, may be lost in another. Therefore, any workers who might lose their jobs because of free trade will likely argue against free trade policies and call for the imposition of trade barriers.

People also disagree on the type of strategies a government should be allowed to use to increase its respective country's share of the global market. They may agree that a tariff or quota on imported goods prevents free trade and gives local firms an unfair advantage in their own market. At the same time, however, they may disagree on whether governments should be allowed to use other more subtle trade restrictions against foreign firms or provide incentives that give their local firms an advantage. Consider the following situations that commonly occur:

1. Firms based in one country are not subject to environmental restrictions and therefore can produce at a lower cost than firms in other countries.

2. Firms based in one country are not subject to labor laws and are able to produce products at a lower cost than firms in other countries by relying mostly on children to produce the products.

3. Firms based in one country are allowed by their government to offer bribes to large customers when pursuing business deals in a particular industry. These firms have a competitive advantage over firms in other countries that are not allowed to offer bribes.

4. Firms in one country receive tax breaks if they are in specific industries. Such breaks are not necessarily subsidies, but they are still a form of government financial support.

In each of these situations, firms in one country may have an advantage over firms in other countries. Every government uses some strategies of this sort that may give its local firms an advantage.

Every meeting held to discuss international trade attracts a large number of protesters. These protesters tend to have their own agendas, which are not always closely related to each other. International trade may not even be the focus of each protest, but it is often regarded as the ultimate cause of the problem (at least in the mind of that protester). Although the protesters are generally dissatisfied with existing trade policies, they do not agree on how trade policies should be changed. These disagreements are similar to those that occur between government representatives when they are negotiating international trade policy.

A firm is not responsible for resolving the conflicts over international trade policy. Nevertheless, it should be aware that such conflicts exist. It should also recognize how international trade policy affects its competitive position in the industry and how changes in policy could affect its position in the future.

Decision Making

Responding to Potential Trade Barriers

Recall that Victory Company has capitalized on the cheap labor in China by importing the computer chips it needs to produce its computer games. Victory Company recognizes that its international business with China could be subject to trade barriers in the future. The U.S. government is under pressure from various groups to impose sanctions on China because of accusations that it allows children to work and does not enforce safe working conditions for its people. Therefore, it is possible that future imports from China could be restricted or subject to a tariff by the U.S. government. Victory Company wants to make sure that it can continue operating efficiently even if its imports from China are restricted. Because of the high cost, it would prefer not to obtain the computer chips from other U.S. suppliers. Therefore, it decides to contact a computer chip manufacturer in Mexico and negotiates a deal that will enable it to periodically purchase some computer chips from this manufacturer. If imports from China are restricted in the future, Victory will increase its orders from the Mexican manufacturer. In this way, it has an alternative supplier that can provide computer chips at a lower cost than it would have to pay a U.S. supplier.

1. Do you think Victory Company would consider solving its dilemma by negotiating a deal with a second computer chip manufacturer in China?

2. Is it possible that trade barriers may be imposed on the imports from Mexico?

ANSWERS: 1. No. If trade barriers are imposed on Victory's original supplier in China, they will likely be imposed on other suppliers in China. 2. The U.S. government could also impose trade barriers on imports from Mexico. However, it is unlikely that the government would impose new trade barriers on both China and Mexico.

4

Explain how foreign characteristics can influence a firm's international business.

How Foreign Characteristics Influence International Business

When a firm engages in international business, it must consider the following characteristics of foreign countries:

▶ Culture

▶ Economic system

▶ Economic conditions

▶ Exchange rates

▶ Political risk and regulations

Culture

Because cultures vary, a firm must learn a foreign country's culture before engaging in business there. Poor decisions can result from an improper assessment of a country's tastes, habits, and customs. Many U.S. firms know that cultures vary and adjust their products to fit the culture. For example, McDonald's sells vegetable burgers instead of beef hamburgers in India. PepsiCo (owner of Frito Lay snack foods) sells Cheetos without cheese in China because Chinese consumers dislike cheese, and it has developed a shrimp-chip to satisfy consumers in Korea. Beer producers sell nonalcoholic beer in Saudi Arabia, where alcohol is not allowed.

Wal-Mart is still learning from its experience in many countries. When it established stores in Argentina, it initially used the same store layout as in the United States, but it quickly learned that the local people preferred a different layout. In addition, it conducted meetings with suppliers in English, even though the primary language of the suppliers was Spanish. Wal-Mart's expansion into Mexico was more effective because it acquired a large Mexican retail firm and was able to rely on it for information about the local culture.

Economic System

A firm must recognize the type of economic system used in any country where it considers doing business. A country's economic system reflects the degree of government ownership of businesses and intervention in business. A U.S. firm will normally prefer countries that do not have excessive government intervention.

Although each country's government has its own unique policy on the ownership of businesses, most policies can be classified as capitalism, communism, or socialism.

Capitalism   **Capitalism** allows for private ownership of businesses. Entrepreneurs have the freedom to create businesses that they believe will serve the people's needs. The United States is perceived as a capitalist society

capitalism
an economic system that allows for private ownership of businesses

Wal-Mart's stores in Mexico (like this one in Mexico City) have benefited from suggestions by local retail managers of a store that it acquired.

CORBIS, CHICAGO

Global Business

Nonverbal Communications in Different Cultures

Nonverbal behavior can only be interpreted within a specific cultural context. Here are five common nonverbal behaviors and how they are interpreted in different countries or geographic areas. Caution is always the better part of valor in using nonverbal behaviors outside your native land.

▶ *Withholding eye contact:*
  ▶ In the United States, it indicates shyness or deception.
  ▶ In Libya, it is a compliment to a woman.
  ▶ In Japan, it is done in deference to authority.
▶ *Crossing legs when seated:*
  ▶ In the United States, it is done for comfort.
  ▶ In Arab countries, it is an insult to show the soles of the feet.

▶ *Displaying the palm of the hand:*
  ▶ In the United States, it is a form of greeting, such as a wave or handshake.
  ▶ In Greece, it is an insult.
▶ *Joining the index finger and thumb to make an O:*
  ▶ In the United States, it means "okay."
  ▶ In Mediterranean countries, it means "zero" or "the pits."
  ▶ In Japan, it means money.
  ▶ In Tunisia, it means "I'll kill you."
  ▶ In Latin America, it is an obscene gesture.
▶ *Standing close to a person while talking:*
  ▶ In the United States, it is an intrusion, and the speaker is viewed as pushy.
  ▶ In Latin America and southern Europe, it is the normal spatial distance for conversations.

---

because entrepreneurs are allowed to create businesses and compete against each other. In a capitalist society, entrepreneurs' desire to earn profits motivates them to produce products and services that satisfy customers. Competition allows efficient firms to increase their share of the market and forces inefficient firms out of the market.

U.S. firms can normally enter capitalist countries without any excessive restrictions by the governments. Typically, though, the level of competition in those countries is high.

communism
an economic system that involves public ownership of businesses

Communism **Communism** is an economic system that involves public ownership of businesses. In a purely communist system, entrepreneurs are restricted from capitalizing on the perceived needs of the people. The government decides what products will be produced and in what quantity. It may even assign jobs to people, regardless of their interests, and sets the wages to be paid to each worker. Wages may be somewhat similar, regardless of individual abilities or effort. Thus, workers do not have much incentive to excel because they will not be rewarded for abnormally high performance.

In a communist society, the government serves as a central planner. It may decide to produce more of some type of agricultural product if it observes a shortage. Since the government is not concerned about earning profits, it does not focus on satisfying consumers (determining what they want to purchase). Consequently, people are unable to obtain many types of products even if they can afford to buy them. In addition, most people do not have much money to spend because the government pays low wages.

Countries in eastern Europe, such as Bulgaria, Poland, and Romania, had communist systems before 1990. During the 1990s, however, government intervention in these countries declined. Prior to the 1990s, communist countries restricted most U.S. firms from entering, but as they began to allow more private ownership of firms, they also allowed foreign firms to enter.

socialism

an economic system that contains some features of both capitalism and communism

Socialism   **Socialism** is an economic system that contains some features of both capitalism and communism. For example, governments in some so-called socialist countries allow people to own businesses and property and to select their own jobs. However, these governments are highly involved in the provision of various services. Health-care services are run by many governments and are provided at a low cost. Also, the governments of socialist countries tend to offer high levels of benefits to unemployed people. Such services are indirectly paid for by the businesses and the workers who earn income. Socialist governments impose high tax rates on income so that they have sufficient funds to provide all their services.

Socialist countries face a tradeoff when setting their tax policies, though. To provide a high level of services to the poor and unemployed, the government must impose high tax rates. Many businesses and workers in socialist countries, however, would argue that the tax rates are excessive. They claim that entrepreneurs may be discouraged from establishing businesses when the government taxes most of the income to be earned by the business. Entrepreneurs thus have incentive to establish businesses in other countries where taxes are lower. But if the government lowers the tax rate, it may not generate enough tax revenue to provide the services.

A socialist society may discourage not only the establishment of new businesses but also the desire to work. If the compensation provided by the government to unemployed workers is almost as high as the wages earned by employed workers, unemployed people have little incentive to look for work. The high tax rates typically imposed on employed people in socialist countries also discourage people from looking for work.

Comparison of Socialism and Capitalism   In socialist countries, the government has more influence because it imposes higher taxes and can spend that tax revenue as it chooses. In capitalist countries, the government has less influence because it imposes lower taxes and therefore has less funds to spend on the people. Businesses and highly skilled workers generally prefer capitalist countries because there is less government interference.

Even if a capitalist country is preferred, people may disagree on how much influence the government should have. For example, some people in the United States believe that the government should provide fewer services to the unemployed and the poor, which would allow for lower taxes. Other people believe that taxes should be increased so that the government can allocate more services to the poor.

Many countries exhibit some combination of capitalism and socialism. For example, the governments of many developed countries in Europe (such as Sweden and Switzerland) allow firms to be privately owned but provide various services (such as health care) for the people. Germany's government provides child-care allowances, health care, and retirement pensions. The French government commonly intervenes when firms experience financial problems.

European countries have recently attempted to reduce their budget deficits as part of a treaty supporting closer European relations. This may result in less government control because the governments will not be able to spend as much money.

Privatization   Historically, the governments of many countries in eastern Europe, Latin America, and the Soviet Bloc owned most businesses, but in recent years they have allowed for private business ownership. Many government-owned businesses have been sold to private investors. As a result of this so-called **privatization,** many governments are reducing their influence and allowing firms to compete in each industry. Privatization allows firms to focus on providing the products and services that people desire and forces the firms to be more efficient to ensure their survival. Thousands of businesses in the former Soviet Bloc have been privatized. Some U.S. firms have acquired businesses sold by the governments of the former Soviet republics and other countries. Privatization has provided an easy way for U.S. firms to acquire businesses in many foreign countries.

privatization
the sale of government-owned businesses to private investors

Privatization in many countries, such as Brazil, Hungary, and the countries of the former Soviet Bloc, is an abrupt shift from tradition. Most people in these countries have not had experience in owning and managing a business. Even those people who managed government-owned businesses are not used to competition because the government typically controlled each industry. Therefore, many people who want to own their own businesses have been given some training by business professors and professionals from capitalist countries such as the United States. In particular, the MBA Enterprise Corps, headquartered at the University of North Carolina, has sent thousands of business students to less-developed countries.

Even the industrialized countries have initiated privatization programs for some businesses that were previously owned by the government. The telephone company in Germany has been privatized, as have numerous large government-owned businesses in France.

Economic Conditions

To predict demand for its product in a foreign country, a firm must attempt to forecast the economic conditions in that country. The firm's overall performance is dependent on the foreign country's economic growth and on the firm's sensitivity to conditions in that country, as explained next.

Economic Growth   Many U.S. firms have recently expanded into smaller foreign markets because they expect that economic growth in these countries will be strong, resulting in a strong demand for their products. For example, Heinz has expanded its business throughout Asia. General Motors, Procter & Gamble, AT&T, Ford Motor Company, and Anheuser-Busch plan new direct foreign investment in Brazil. The Coca-Cola Company has expanded in China, India, and eastern Europe.

The primary factor influencing the decision by many firms to expand in a particular foreign country is the country's expected economic growth, which affects the potential demand for their products. If firms overestimate the country's economic growth, they will normally overestimate the demand for their products in that country. Consequently, their revenue may not be sufficient to cover the expenses associated with the expansion.

Domino's Pizza, a U. S. firm, is one of many companies that have been expanding into smaller foreign markets. The expectation is that these targeted smaller markets will have strong economic growth and demand for their products will grow.

GETTY IMAGES

In addition, foreign countries may experience weak economies in some periods, which can adversely affect firms that serve those countries. For example, during the Asian crisis of 1997–1998, Asian economies were weak, and U.S. firms with business in Asia, such as Nike and Hewlett-Packard, experienced a decline in the demand for their products. In 2001–2002, worldwide economic conditions were generally weak, and many U.S. companies that served foreign countries were adversely affected. Economic conditions in the United States were also weak. Consequently, firms with business diversified across different countries were not insulated from the weak economic conditions because these conditions existed in most countries during this period. For example, DuPont, Nike, 3M, and Hewlett-Packard experienced lower-than-expected revenue because of weak European economies in the 2001–2002 period. To illustrate the impact of global economic conditions, consider the comments made by Dell, Inc., in a recent annual report:

"During 2002, worldwide economic conditions negatively affected demand for the Company's products and resulted in declining revenue and earnings. . . . The Company believes that worldwide economic conditions will improve. However, if economic conditions continue to worsen, or if economic conditions do not improve as rapidly as expected, the Company's revenue and earnings could be negatively affected."

Sensitivity to Foreign Economic Conditions   A U.S. firm's exposure to a foreign country's economy is dependent on the proportion of the firm's business conducted in that country. To illustrate, compare the influence of Canada's economy on two U.S. firms (Firm X and Firm Y), as shown in Exhibit 4.4. Assume that Firm X typically generates 20 percent of its total revenue from selling its products in Canada and 80 percent of its total revenue from the

Exhibit 4.4

Comparing the Influence of the Canadian Economy on Two U.S. Firms

U.S. Firm	Total Annual Revenue	Proportion of Canadian Business	Proportion of U.S. Business	Annual Revenue from Canadian Business	Annual Revenue from U.S. Business
Firm X	$100,000,000	20%	80%	$20,000,000	$80,000,000
Firm Y	10,000,000	60%	40%	6,000,000	4,000,000

United States. Firm Y typically generates 60 percent of its total revenue from Canada and 40 percent of its total revenue from the United States. A weak economy in Canada will likely have a more negative effect on Firm Y because it relies more on its Canadian business.

Some U.S. firms, such as The Coca-Cola Company, Dow Chemical, and ExxonMobil, generate more than half of their total revenue from foreign countries. Nevertheless, they are not heavily influenced by any single foreign country's economy because their international business is scattered across many countries. The Coca-Cola Company, for example, conducts business in more than 200 foreign countries. The demand for Coca-Cola's soft drink products may decline in some countries where the weather is cooler than normal, but this unfavorable effect can be offset by a higher demand for the company's products in other countries where the weather is warmer than normal.

Exchange Rates

Countries generally have their own currency. The United States uses dollars ($), the United Kingdom uses British pounds (£), Canada uses Canadian dollars (C$), and Japan uses Japanese yen (¥). As mentioned earlier, 12 European countries recently adopted the euro (€) as their currency. Exchange rates between the U.S. dollar and any currency fluctuate over time. Consequently, the number of dollars a U.S. firm needs to purchase foreign supplies may change even if the actual price charged for the supplies by the foreign producer does not. When the dollar weakens, foreign currencies strengthen; thus, U.S. firms need more dollars to purchase a given amount of foreign supplies. Exchange rate fluctuations can also affect the foreign demand for a U.S. firm's product because they affect the actual price paid by the foreign customers (even if the price in dollars remains unchanged).

Political Risk and Regulations

political risk
the risk that a country's political actions can adversely affect a business

A firm must also consider the political risk and regulatory climate of a country before deciding to do business there. **Political risk** is the risk that a country's political actions may adversely affect a business. Political crises have occurred in many countries throughout eastern Europe, Latin America, and the Middle East. U.S. firms are subject to policies imposed by the governments of the foreign countries where they do business. Firms are also vulnerable to the possibility that political problems between two governments may cause consumers to react negatively against the firms because of their country of origin. During the war in Iraq in 2003, anti-American protests against the war in the Middle East and other countries forced some U.S.-based multinational corporations to temporarily shut

SMALL BUSINESS SURVEY

Do Small Firms Conduct International Business?

A recent survey asked 384 Entrepreneur of the Year award winners whether they conducted international business. About one-third of the firms had annual sales of less than $15 million. Results of the survey are disclosed in the following pie chart:

Firms Whose International Sales:

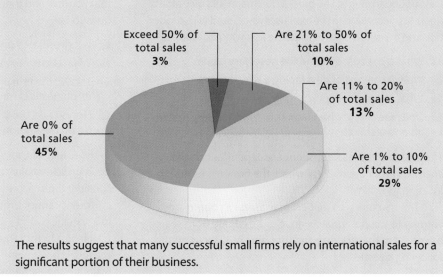

Exceed 50% of total sales **3%**

Are 21% to 50% of total sales **10%**

Are 11% to 20% of total sales **13%**

Are 0% of total sales **45%**

Are 1% to 10% of total sales **29%**

The results suggest that many successful small firms rely on international sales for a significant portion of their business.

down their operations in some countries. In addition, the protests led to a decline in the demand for the products of some U.S.-based firms.

As an extreme form of political risk, a foreign government may take over a U.S. firm's foreign subsidiary without compensating the U.S. firm in any way. A more common form of political risk is that the foreign government imposes higher corporate tax rates on foreign subsidiaries. Some governments impose a tax on funds sent by a subsidiary to the parent firm (headquarters) in the home country. They may even prevent the funds from being sent for a certain period of time. The exposure of multinational companies to political risks is clearly emphasized in a recent annual report of Dell, Inc.:

"The Company's future growth rates and success are dependent on continued growth and success in international markets. . . . The success and profitability of the Company's international operations are subject to numerous risks and uncertainties, including local economic and labor conditions, political instability, unexpected changes in the regulatory environment, trade protection measures, tax laws, and foreign currency exchange rates."

Corruption   Corruption is a form of political risk that can have a major impact on firms attempting to do business in a country. For example, a firm that wants to establish a business in a specific country may obtain a quick approval only if it provides payoffs to some government officials. Thus, corruption increases the cost of doing business. It may also be viewed as illegal. Firms may therefore be discouraged from doing business in those countries that have more corruption. Transparency International

Cross Functional Teamwork

Managing International Business across Business Functions

When a firm plans to conduct business in a foreign country, it should request input from its managers across various departments. The production managers may assess a country according to the expenses associated with production and therefore may focus on the following questions:

1 What is the cost of hiring the necessary labor?
2 What is the cost of developing a new facility?
3 What is the cost of purchasing an existing facility?
4 Does the country have access to the necessary materials and technology?

The answers to these questions are dependent on the specific part of the country where the firm is considering locating its facility.

The marketing managers may assess a country according to the potential revenue to be earned from selling a product in that country and therefore may focus on the following questions:

1 What is the foreign demand for the firm's product?
2 What changes need to be made in the product to satisfy local consumers?
3 What types of marketing strategies would be effective in that country?
4 What is the cost of marketing the product in that country?

The financial managers may assess a country according to the costs of financing any business conducted in that country and therefore may focus on the following questions:

1 Is it possible to obtain a local loan in that country?
2 What is the interest rate charged on local loans?
3 Should the firm use some of its retained earnings from its domestic business to support any foreign business?
4 How would the firm's earnings increase as a result of doing business in the foreign country?

Because of these cross functional relationships, the decision to establish a business in a foreign country must consider input across departments. The production department cannot properly estimate the production costs in a specific country until the marketing department determines whether the product must be revised to satisfy the local consumers. Also, the financial managers cannot estimate the earnings from this business until they receive estimates of revenue (from the marketing department), production expenses (from the production department), and marketing expenses (from the marketing department).

(see http://www.transparency.org) calculates a corruption index for most countries. The ratings for selected countries are shown in Exhibit 4.5. Countries with relatively high ratings have less corruption.

Regulatory Climate   Government regulations such as environmental laws vary among countries. By increasing costs, these laws can affect the feasibility of establishing a subsidiary in a foreign country. Stringent building codes, restrictions on the disposal of production waste materials, and pollution controls are examples of regulations that may force subsidiaries to incur additional costs. Many European countries have recently imposed tougher anti-pollution laws as a result of severe pollution problems.

Another type of regulatory problem occurs when countries do not enforce their laws. Some countries do not enforce regulations that protect copyrights laws. Thus, a firm that produces products such as books or music CDs may not benefit from establishing a business in these countries because the product may be easily copied by local firms without any penalty for violating copyright laws.

Exhibit 4.5

Corruption Index Ratings for Selected Countries (Maximum rating = 10. High ratings represent low corruption.)

Country	Index Rating	Country	Index Rating
Finland	9.7	Chile	7.4
Denmark	9.6	France	6.9
New Zealand	9.5	Spain	6.9
Singapore	9.4	Taiwan	5.7
Sweden	9.3	Uruguay	5.5
Netherlands	8.9	Italy	5.3
Switzerland	8.8	Malaysia	5.2
Canada	8.7	Hungary	4.8
United Kingdom	8.7	Greece	4.3
Austria	8.0	Brazil	3.9
Hong Kong	8.0	Czech Republic	3.9
Germany	7.7	Mexico	3.6
Belgium	7.6	China	3.4
Ireland	7.6	India	2.8
United States	7.5	Russia	2.7

Source: Transparency International, 2003.

U.S. businesses have some difficulty exporting to countries that do not enforce laws against counterfeiting. In this picture, counterfeit DVDs of U.S. films are for sale at a shop in Shenzehn, China.

AP/WIDE WORLD PHOTOS

Some countries also do not enforce bribery laws. As a result of the Foreign Corrupt Practices Act, U.S. firms are not allowed to offer bribes to government officials or political candidates. Some U.S. firms argue that they are at a disadvantage because they are unable to offer bribes to government officials in a foreign country, when some other firms can.

Countries also differ in the penalties they may impose on businesses for producing defective products or discriminating against employees. The U.S. court system has a worldwide reputation for imposing excessive penalties on businesses. In numerous cases, a person who was injured because of poor judgment blamed the injury on the product and won a lawsuit against a business in a U.S. court. Even if a business can prove that it was not at fault, defending against a lawsuit can be very expensive. Non-U.S. firms may be discouraged from establishing businesses in the United States for this reason.

Given the major differences in regulations among countries, a firm must understand the rules of any country where it is considering conducting business. Firms should pursue only those international business opportunities where the potential benefits are not offset by costs associated with regulations.

Decision Making

Assessing Foreign Characteristics

Recall that Victory Company recently planned to export computer games to Canada. It considers the characteristics of Canada that could affect the demand for its computer games. First, Canadian culture in the English-speaking provinces is somewhat similar to U.S. culture, but the computer games would have to be translated into French for the French-speaking provinces. Second, the Canadian government will not impose barriers against the games. Third, Canadian regulations do not prohibit these types of imports. Victory Company decides that it will attempt to sell its computer games to retail stores in the English-speaking provinces of Canada. If the games become popular in these provinces, it may consider creating computer games in the French language and exporting them to the French provinces.

1. Explain how Canada's culture may change over time in a manner that could affect Victory's performance.

2. Explain how Canada's political risk could affect Victory's performance.

ANSWERS: 1. Canada's consumers may change their preferences over time, such that they may not want computer games. This would result in a reduction in the demand for Victory's computer games and therefore a reduction in Victory's performance. 2. Canada could change its treatment toward firms that are based outside Canada but sell products in Canada. It might impose taxes on Victory Company, which would increase the cost of selling products in Canada and would reduce Victory's performance.

How Exchange Rate Movements Can Affect Performance

Explain how exchange rate movements can affect a firm's performance.

International trade transactions typically require the exchange of one currency for another. For example, if a U.S. firm periodically purchases supplies from a British supplier, it will need to exchange U.S. dollars for the British currency (pounds) to make the purchase. This process is shown in Exhibit 4.6.

Generally, the exchange rate between a given currency and the U.S. dollar fluctuates daily. When the exchange rate changes, U.S. firms involved in international trade are affected. The impact of exchange rate movements on a U.S. firm can be favorable or unfavorable, depending on the characteristics of the firm, as illustrated by the following examples.

Exhibit 4.6

Example of Importing
by a U.S. Firm

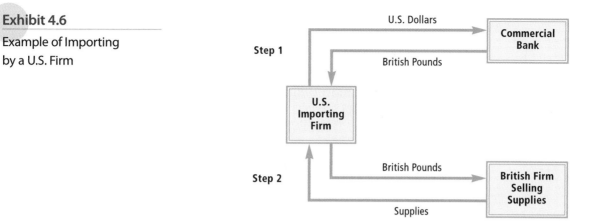

Impact of a Weak Dollar on U.S. Importers

Assume that the value of the pound (£), the British currency, at a given point in time is $2.00. That is, each dollar is worth one-half of a British pound. If a U.S. firm needs £1,000,000 to purchase supplies from a British supplier, it will need $2,000,000 to obtain those pounds, as shown:

$$\text{Amount of \$ Needed} = (\text{Amount of £ Needed} \times \text{Value of £})$$
$$= £1,000,000 \times \$2.00$$
$$= 2,000,000$$

appreciates
strengthens in value

Now assume that the pound **appreciates** (or strengthens in value) against the dollar. This also means that the dollar weakens (is worth less) against the pound. For example, assume the pound is now equal to $2.02 instead of $2.00. Now the U.S. firm needs $20,000 more to obtain the pounds than it needed before the pound appreciated. Thus, the cost of the supplies has increased for the U.S. firm as a result of the appreciation in the British pound (a weaker dollar). This illustrates why a weak dollar adversely affects U.S. firms that frequently import supplies.

Impact of a Strong Dollar on U.S. Importers

depreciates
weakens in value

Now consider a situation in which the pound **depreciates,** or weakens in value against the dollar. This also means that the dollar strengthens against the pound. For example, assume the pound's value was $2.00 but has declined to $1.90 over the last month. If the U.S. firm needs to obtain £1,000,000, it will be able to purchase the pounds for $100,000 less than was needed before the pound depreciated. The firm's payment has declined by 5 percent because the pound's value has declined by 5 percent.

This example shows how the depreciation of a foreign currency against the dollar (a stronger dollar) reduces the expenses of a U.S. firm that is purchasing foreign supplies. This explains why a strong dollar favorably affects U.S. firms that frequently import supplies.

Actual Effects of Exchange Rate Movements on U.S. Importers

To illustrate the impact of a change in a currency's value on U.S. importers, consider how many dollars you would pay for a pair of jeans that are sold in the United Kingdom at two different points in time. Assume that the jeans are priced at 50 British pounds. In January 2002, the value of a British pound (£) was about $1.43, so you would have paid:

$$\text{Payment in Dollars} = (\text{Payment in £}) \times (\text{Exchange Rate})$$
$$= £50 \times \$1.42$$
$$= \$71.00$$

In August 2005, the value of a British pound was about $1.76, so you would have paid:

$$\text{Payment in Dollars} = (\text{Payment in £}) \times (\text{Exchange Rate})$$
$$= £50 \times \$1.76$$
$$= \$88.00$$

Your cost increased by $17, or by about 24 percent, because the value of pound increased by about 24 percent over this period.

Now consider the impact on U.S. firms that import a large amount of products from the United Kingdom. If the U.K. exporter charges the same price in August 2005 as in January 2002, the cost to the importers would rise by 24 percent over this period because of the change in the exchange rate. The pound depreciated substantially in some periods, such as 1981–1984, 1991–1993, and 2001. In other periods, such as 1985–1987 and 2002–2004, the pound appreciated. When the pound appreciated, the amount of dollars needed to buy British imports increased. Conversely, when the pound depreciated, the amount of dollars needed to buy British imports declined. The expenses of a U.S. importing firm are highly sensitive to changes in the value of the pound.

The exchange rates of currencies of less-developed countries fluctuate more than those of developed countries. For example, some currencies have depreciated by more than 20 percent in a single month. Consequently, U.S. firms that do business in less-developed countries are exposed to wide swings in exchange rates.

Impact of a Weak Dollar on U.S. Exporters

Just as exchange rate movements can affect U.S. importing firms, they can also affect U.S. firms that export products to other countries. The effect of a weak dollar will be examined first, followed by the effect of a strong dollar.

Consider how a U.S. firm that exports equipment to a British firm is affected by a weak dollar. The exporting process is shown in Exhibit 4.7. If the U.S. exporter wants to receive U.S. dollars for its equipment, the British firm must first exchange its currency (pounds) into dollars at a commercial bank (Step 1 in Exhibit 4.7). Then the British firm uses these dollars to purchase the equipment of the U.S. exporting firm (Step 2).

If the dollar weakens, the British firm can obtain the dollars it needs with fewer pounds. Therefore, it may be willing to purchase more equipment from the U.S. exporting firm. The U.S. firm's revenue will rise in response to a higher demand for the equipment it produces. Therefore, its profits should increase as well.

As this example shows, a weak dollar can result in higher revenue and profits for U.S. firms that frequently export their products. U.S. exporting

Exhibit 4.7

Example of Exporting by a U.S. Firm

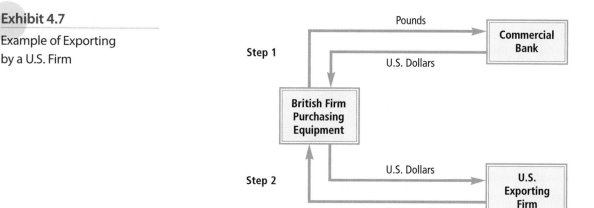

firms tend to benefit from a weak dollar because their prices are perceived as inexpensive by foreign customers who must convert their currencies into dollars. A weak dollar favorably affects U.S. firms that export heavily because foreign demand for the products they export increases substantially when the dollar is weak.

Impact of a Strong Dollar on U.S. Exporters

Now consider a situation in which the value of the pound depreciates against the dollar. As the pound's value declines, the British firm must exchange more British pounds to obtain the same amount of dollars as before. That is, it needs more pounds to purchase equipment from the U.S. firm. Consequently, it may reduce its purchases from the U.S. firm and perhaps will search for a British producer of the equipment to avoid having to obtain dollars.

As this example shows, a strong dollar can result in lower revenue for U.S. firms that frequently export their products. A strong dollar adversely affects U.S. exporting firms because the prices of their exports appear expensive to foreign customers who must convert their currencies into dollars. When the dollar strengthens, U.S. exporting firms such as Procter & Gamble and Boeing are adversely affected.

Hedging against Exchange Rate Movements

hedge
action taken to protect a firm against exchange rate movements

U.S. firms commonly attempt to **hedge,** or protect against exchange rate movements. They can hedge most effectively when they know how much of a specific foreign currency they will need or will receive on a specific date in the future.

forward contract
provides that an exchange of currencies will occur at a specified exchange rate at a future point in time

forward rate
the exchange rate that a bank will be willing to offer at a future point in time

Hedging Future Payments in Foreign Currencies   Consider a firm that plans to purchase British supplies and will need £1,000,000 in 90 days to pay for those supplies. It can call a large commercial bank that exchanges foreign currencies and request a so-called **forward contract,** which provides that an exchange of currencies will occur for a specified exchange rate at a future point in time. In this case, the forward contract will specify an exchange of dollars for £1,000,000 in 90 days. In other words, the firm wants to purchase pounds 90 days forward.

The bank will quote the **forward rate,** or the exchange rate that the bank will be willing to offer at a future point in time. The forward rate is

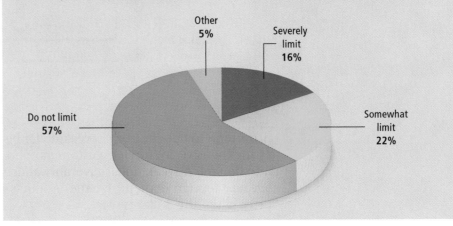

spot exchange rate
the exchange rate quoted for immediate transactions

normally close to the **spot exchange rate,** which is the exchange rate quoted for immediate transactions. Assume that the bank quotes a 90-day forward rate of $1.80 for the British pound. If the firm agrees to this quote, it has agreed to a forward contract. It will lock in the purchase of £1,000,000 in 90 days for $1.80 per pound, or $1,800,000 for the £1,000,000. Once the firm hedges its position, it has locked in the rate at which it will exchange currencies on that future date, regardless of the actual spot exchange rate that occurs on that date. In this way, the U.S. firm hedges against the possibility that the pound will appreciate over that period.

Hedging Future Receivables in Foreign Currencies   U.S. firms can also hedge when they expect to receive a foreign currency in the future. For example, consider a U.S. firm that knows it will receive £1,000,000 in 90 days. It can call a commercial bank and negotiate a forward contract in which it will provide the £1,000,000 to the bank in exchange for dollars. Assuming that the 90-day forward rate is $1.80 (as in the previous example), the firm will receive $1,800,000 in 90 days (computed as $1.80 × £1,000,000). By using a forward contract, this firm locks in the rate at which it can exchange its pounds for dollars, regardless of the spot exchange rate that occurs on that date. In this way, the U.S. firm hedges against the possibility that the pound will depreciate over the period of concern.

Limitations of Hedging   A major limitation of hedging is that it prevents favorable exchange rate effects as well as unfavorable effects. For example, reconsider the initial example in which the firm locks in the purchase of pounds 90 days ahead at a forward rate of $1.80. If the actual spot exchange rate in 90 days is $1.70, the firm would have been better off without the hedge. Nevertheless, it is obligated to fulfill its forward contract by exchanging dollars for pounds at the forward exchange rate of $1.80. This example illustrates why many U.S. firms hedge only when they expect that their future international business transactions will be adversely affected by exchange rate movements.

How Exchange Rates Affect Foreign Competition

Many U.S. firms compete with foreign firms in the U.S. market. Exhibit 4.8 shows a common situation in the United States. RCA is a U.S. firm that sells televisions in the U.S. market. It competes with many foreign competitors that export televisions to the United States. Retail stores purchase televisions from RCA as well as other firms.

Assume that the stores mark up the price of each television by 20 percent. When these stores purchase Japanese televisions, they convert dollars to Japanese yen (the Japanese currency). If the value of the yen depreciates against the dollar, the store needs fewer dollars to purchase the Japanese televisions. If it applies the same markup, it can reduce its price on the Japanese televisions. Therefore, increased foreign competition (due to depreciation of one or more foreign currencies) may cause RCA to lose some U.S. business.

If the foreign currency appreciates against the dollar, the foreign competitors may be unable to compete in the United States because the prices of imported products will rise. Using our example, if the Japanese yen appreciates, the retail store will need more dollars to purchase the Japanese televisions. When applying its markup, it will need to increase its price on the Japanese televisions. Therefore, U.S. firms such as RCA may gain more U.S. business.

Exhibit 4.8

How Exchange Rates Affect the Degree of Foreign Competition

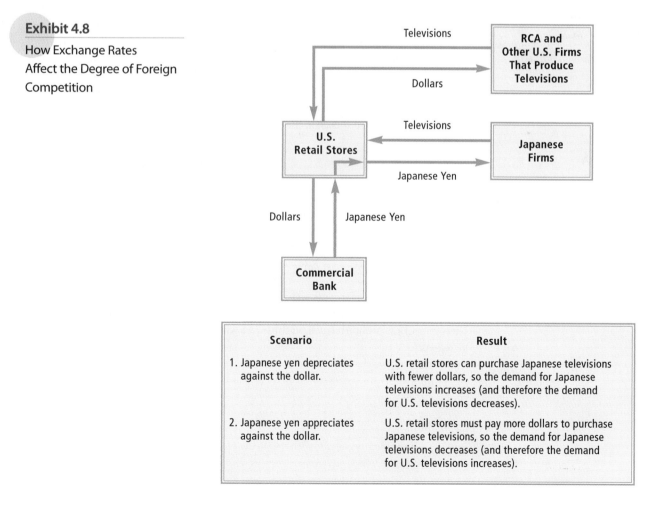

Scenario	Result
1. Japanese yen depreciates against the dollar.	U.S. retail stores can purchase Japanese televisions with fewer dollars, so the demand for Japanese televisions increases (and therefore the demand for U.S. televisions decreases).
2. Japanese yen appreciates against the dollar.	U.S. retail stores must pay more dollars to purchase Japanese televisions, so the demand for Japanese televisions decreases (and therefore the demand for U.S. televisions increases).

Decision Making

The Decision to Hedge Exchange Rate Risk

Victory Company has decided to sell its computer games to retail stores in Canada. It will bill the stores upon delivery and give them 30 days to pay the bill. It will accept payment in Canadian dollars and then convert the proceeds into U.S. dollars. If Victory delivers a large order, it may become concerned that the value of the Canadian dollar will depreciate against the U.S. dollar by the time it converts the Canadian dollars into U.S. dollars. Therefore, it plans to obtain a 30-day forward contract so that it can lock in the amount of U.S. dollars it will receive from the order.

1. If the Canadian dollar depreciates during the 30-day period after the order is delivered, will Victory Company benefit from its forward hedge? Explain.

2. If the Canadian dollar appreciates during the 30-day period after the order is delivered, will Victory benefit from its forward hedge? Explain.

ANSWERS: 1. Yes. Victory Company would receive more U.S. dollars from converting the Canadian dollar payment at the forward rate it established earlier than if it converted the Canadian dollar payment at the prevailing spot rate. 2. No. Victory Company would receive less U.S. dollars from converting the Canadian dollar payment at the forward rate it established earlier than if it converted the Canadian dollar payment at the prevailing spot rate.

COLLEGE HEALTH CLUB: CHC'S EXPOSURE TO GLOBAL CONDITIONS

College Health Club (CHC) sells its services locally, and its competitors are local. Therefore, global conditions do not have a direct effect on its business. However, Sue Kramer, the president of CHC, plans to purchase vitamin supplements from Mexico and sell them at the club. The price she is charged is 100 Mexican pesos per jar. She plans to order just one case containing 200 jars initially and will order more after these jars are sold. The present exchange rate of the peso is $.08, but Sue wants to know how a change in the exchange rate will affect the price that she will pay in dollars. Her calculations of the potential exchange rate effects are shown in the following table.

	If the Exchange Rate Is $.08	If the Exchange Rate Is $.09
(1) Number of jars ordered	200	200
(2) Purchase price per jar in Mexican pesos	100 pesos	100 pesos
(3) Exchange rate	$.08	$.09
(4) Purchase price per jar in dollars	$8.00	$9.00
(5) Total purchase price = (1) × (4)	$1,600.00	$1,800.00

A case of vitamin supplements will cost $200 more if the value of the peso increases by $.01 by the time the bill is paid. Sue plans to sell the jars to CHC's members for $12 per jar. Therefore, CHC's profit from selling these jars will be reduced if the value of the peso increases.

Summary

1 The main reasons U.S. firms engage in international business are to

▶ attract foreign demand,

▶ capitalize on technology,

▶ use inexpensive resources, or

▶ diversify internationally.

The first two reasons reflect higher revenue, while the third reason reflects lower expenses. The fourth reason reflects less risk by reducing exposure to a single economy.

2 The primary ways in which firms conduct international business are:

▶ importing,

▶ exporting,

▶ direct foreign investment,

▶ outsourcing, and

▶ strategic alliances.

Many U.S. firms have used all of these strategies.

3 Even though barriers to international business have been reduced over time, some barriers to international business still exist. Some governments continue to impose barriers in order to protect their local firms or to punish countries for their actions. Barriers can either prevent firms from entering foreign markets or make it more expensive for them to do so. The status of barriers can change over time. Firms need to recognize the existing barriers so that they can decide whether entering a specific foreign market is worthwhile.

4 When firms sell their products in international markets, they assess the cultures, economic systems and conditions, exchange rate risk, and political risk and regulations in those markets. A country's economic conditions affect the demand by its citizens for the firm's product. The larger the proportion of the firm's total sales generated in a specific foreign country, the more sensitive is the firm's revenue to that country's economic conditions.

5 Exchange rate movements can affect U.S. firms in various ways, depending on their characteristics. U.S. importers benefit from a strong dollar. U.S. exporters benefit from a weak dollar but are adversely affected by a strong dollar. U.S. firms competing with foreign firms that export to the U.S. market are adversely affected by a strong dollar, because the products exported by foreign firms appear inexpensive to U.S. consumers when the dollar is strong.

How the Chapter Concepts Affect Business Performance

A firm's decisions regarding the international business concepts summarized above affect its performance. Its decision regarding the countries where its products are produced affects its cost of production. Its decision regarding where its products are sold affects its revenue. Economic conditions in foreign countries influence the demand for the firm's products and its cost of producing the products. The strategy (such as exporting, direct foreign investment, etc.) a firm uses in an attempt to capitalize on international business opportunities can affect its cost of production and the demand for its products. The firm's decision to hedge its exposure to exchange rate movements affects the amount of revenue it receives from its international business.

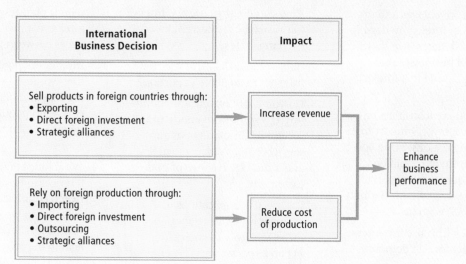

Key Terms

appreciates 135
balance of trade 117
capitalism 125
communism 126
depreciates 135
direct foreign investment
   (DFI) 118
dumping 122

exporting 116
forward contract 137
forward rate 137
hedge 137
importing 115
international licensing
   agreement 120
joint venture 120

political risk 130
privatization 128
quota 116
socialism 127
spot exchange rate 138
strategic alliance 120
tariff 116
trade deficit 117

Review & Critical Thinking Questions

1. Explain why a business may want to sell its product or service in a foreign country.

2. Why might foreign competitors have an advantage over U.S. firms in some cases?

3. In which areas of the world have changes in economic and political conditions created opportunities for U.S. firms to more easily pursue international business? Provide specific examples.

4. What are tariffs and quotas? Explain how tariffs and quotas affect the price of imports.

5. Distinguish exporting from importing. Can a business such as DuPont be involved in both exporting and importing? How?

6. What is direct foreign investment (DFI)? Why should a company be particularly careful when engaging in DFI?

7. Identify and explain the various types of international alliances between U.S. firms and foreign firms.

8. Explain the difference between a direct foreign investment and a strategic alliance undertaken by an international business.

9. Identify and briefly describe the foreign characteristics that can influence international business investments.

10. Explain the differences between capitalism, communism, and socialism.

11. Why must a firm assess economic conditions before entering a foreign market? What determines a U.S. firm's exposure to a foreign country's economy?

12. Explain why many U.S. firms may increase their foreign acquisitions in response to exchange rate movements.

Discussion Questions

1. Discuss the advantages and disadvantages of foreign ownership in the United States. Are there any types of businesses that should not be sold to a foreign investor?

2. Assume you are a business entrepreneur. Do you support free trade among nations, or do you believe that there should be tariffs and quotas on imported goods? How would each position affect the U.S. economy?

3. How could a firm use the Internet to attract foreign demand?

How could a firm use the Internet to access the current level of exchange rates?

4. How could a U.S. firm use the Internet to facilitate exporting?

5. Do you think Americans should buy U.S.-produced goods and services or foreign goods and services? Does either practice affect the U.S. balance of trade? Comment.

6. Discuss the implications of a stronger dollar in relation to other foreign currencies for (1) an exporter and (2) someone

who is planning to travel to a foreign country. Are there differences between the two parties?

7. Discuss the potential problems that would arise from exporting CDs and books to countries with high political risk. What might happen to sales in these countries?

8. What kinds of cross-cultural differences in business practices between countries could lead to mistakes in business practices? Which foreign entry mode would lead to the fewest mistakes?

9. What kinds of barriers around the world inhibit the expansion of U.S. firms into foreign markets? What impacts do these barriers have on local customers?

10. Do you support trade boycotts against countries with poor human rights records? Why or why not? If a trade boycott prevents cheap imports from entering the United States, what will be the impact on the local economy and on consumers?

It's Your Decision: Global Exposure at CHC

1. CHC may purchase exercise machines that are produced in Chile. How will the cost of the machines be affected by the value of the Chilean peso?

2. Why is CHC's business performance somewhat insulated from global conditions?

Investing in a Business

Using the annual report of the firm in which you would like to invest, complete the following:

1. Describe the means (if any) by which the firm engages in global business. Does it export? Does it import? Does the firm have foreign subsidiaries overseas? Joint ventures?

2. In what foreign countries does the firm do business? Is the firm seeking to expand into new foreign markets? How does its overseas sales growth compare with its domestic sales growth?

3. Does the firm's annual report specifically mention foreign firms as a source of competition?

4. Was the firm's performance affected by exchange rate movements last year? If so, how?

5. Explain how the business uses technology to assess the global environment in which it operates. For example, does it use certain websites to determine its exchange rate risk? Does it use the Internet to determine its global competition?

6. Go to http://hoovers.com and locate the NEWS SEARCH. Type in the name of the firm in the space provided, and review the recent news stories about the firm. Summarize any (at least one) recent news story about the firm that applies to one or more of the key concepts in this chapter.

Case: Global Expansion by Linton Records

Linton Records is a U.S. producer of recordings of soul music, which are sold in the United States and exported to Europe. A year ago, the company entered into a joint venture with a distributor in London to retail its records. It is planning to import British rock into the United States, as it has just entered into a strategic alliance with this distributorship. Sales are expected to increase 20 percent a year over first-year sales of £12.5 million. Linton receives payment for its exports in British pounds. The dollar has been weakening against the British pound.

Linton Records has learned that its product line will be subject to a tariff on goods imported into Europe. The tariff is related to the European Union, the common market alliance that includes many European countries. The company has expressed concern because it believes that political intervention disrupts the free flow of trade as it exists in the United States.

Management is developing a strategic alliance with a French manufacturer to produce compact discs for the entire operation. The company expects to cut production costs by 25 percent because of the French firm's advanced technology. In this strategic alliance, the French manufacturer will buy all its raw materials from a company in Bonn, Germany. In addition to the distributorship in London, Linton Records plans to open new markets in six different countries in western Europe in the future.

Questions

1 Discuss the primary reasons why Linton Records may benefit from its international business.

2 How will Linton Records be affected if the dollar weakens further?

3 Should music imported by U.S. firms from England be subjected to a tariff?

Video Case: Global Business at Lonely Planet

Lonely Planet provides resource guidebooks covering 230 countries, as well as an online forum where travelers can post their traveling experiences. People with a passion for travel are the target market for the guidebooks. Lonely Planet's goal is to produce books that show readers the "whole picture," including that the world is multidimensional and not all happy. Because Lonely Planet has offices in many different countries, it has to develop an Internet marketing strategy that is customized for each country.

Lonely Planet manager Howard Riley says that branding, or having a distinction that resonates with the target market, is extremely important and is a way for the company to talk to the customer. For example, the book on China is available in Chinese as well as English. Riley maintains that the best way to handle global marketing is to allow travelers to see the same image of Lonely Planet no matter where they are in the world. Though he says that the term *global* no longer exists, he argues that there is a layer of "globalness" with an audience that shares a passion for travel. Hence, the objective of the marketing campaign is to "present the world"

to readers around the world through the guidebooks. Riley observes that working for a global company makes you reassess all the assumptions about management you have formed in your home country. He says that managers have to be brave and take risks with marketing and that firms have to have a clear global message.

Questions

1 How does Lonely Planet differentiate its brand from its competitors in global markets?

2 How can Lonely Planet use technology to advance its brand image around the world?

3 Why is branding critical for a firm like Lonely Planet?

4 What kinds of management challenges does Howard Riley face as a global manager?

5 How does being the manager of a global business differ from being a manager of a domestic business in terms of establishing a brand image?

Internet Applications

1. http://www.countryreports.org

In the drop-down screen, choose a country. What kinds of data are available? What can you learn about culture, economic conditions, and other characteristics that would help you do business in that country?

2. http://www.trading-safely.com

Look at the countries listed for which analysis is provided. What is the risk of Burundi? What is the risk of

Finland? In which countries is the risk so high that you would be reluctant to do business there?

3. http://www.cia.gov/cia/publications/factbook

Look at the information provided by the U.S. Central Intelligence Agency. Select a country. How does the information provided help you make business decisions about that country?

Dell's Secret to Success

Go to http://www.reportgallery.com and review Dell's most recent annual report. Also, go to Dell's website (http://www.dell.com) and in the section "about Dell," review the background material about Dell that relates to this chapter.

Questions

1 Describe Dell's growth in international markets. Does it appear that Dell's international business is growing?

2 Dell's website explains that it established a manufacturing facility in Ireland in 1990 (just six years after the company was created) in order to serve Europe and Africa. What do you think motivated Dell to enter these new markets?

3 Dell's website explains that in 1996 it established a manufacturing facility in Malaysia to serve the Asia-Pacific region. Why do you think it decided not to use its Ireland facility to serve the Asia-Pacific region?

In-Text Study Guide

Answers are in Appendix C at the back of book.

True or False

1. An important reason U.S. firms establish new businesses in less-developed countries is to capitalize on technological advantages.

2. The best way for a firm to stabilize its profits over time is to focus its efforts on producing and selling one specific product in one specific country.

3. Land and labor costs can vary significantly among countries.

4. U.S. firms that provide services are more likely to face strong foreign competition than firms that produce manufactured goods.

5. A tax placed on imported goods is called a tariff.

6. Competition among firms is usually more intense in communist economies than it is in capitalist economies.

7. A key advantage of socialist economies is the emphasis on keeping tax rates as low as possible.

8. A firm's performance in a foreign country is dependent on that country's economic growth.

9. If firms overestimate the economic growth in a particular country, they will normally overestimate the demand for their products in that country.

10. The values of most currencies are not allowed to change relative to the dollar.

Multiple Choice

11. A country that has relatively low technology is termed a(n):
    a) least-favored nation.
    b) post-communist country.
    c) pre-industrial nation.
    d) backward nation.
    e) developing country.

12. All of the following are important reasons why U.S. firms engage in international business except to:
    a) attract foreign demand.
    b) capitalize on technology.
    c) take advantage of lower taxes in socialist economies.
    d) use inexpensive labor and natural resources available in less-developed countries.
    e) diversify internationally.

13. A major reason U.S. firms want to achieve international diversification is that it:
    a) exposes them to cultural diversity.
    b) enables them to take big tax write-offs.
    c) helps them stabilize profits, thus reducing their risk.
    d) allows them to acquire more advanced technology.
    e) allows them to offer stock to foreign investors, thus increasing their financial base.

14. With the implementation of NAFTA in 1993:
    a) most trade restrictions between the United States, Canada, and Mexico were removed.
    b) European nations began using a common currency.
    c) U.S. firms were encouraged to invest in the less-developed nations of Asia, Central America, and Africa.
    d) the World Bank was given the authority to set interest rates on international business loans.
    e) countries were no longer allowed to have trade deficits continue for more than three years.

15. A number of European nations recently agreed to share a common currency known as the:
    a) gifspen.
    b) francmarc.
    c) European pound.
    d) euro.
    e) NAFTA.

In-Text Study Guide

Answers are in Appendix C at the back of book.

16. The purchase of foreign supplies by IBM is an example of:
    a) direct foreign investment.
    b) exporting.
    c) importing.
    d) international licensing.
    e) a joint venture.

17. The U.S. government just imposed a numerical limit on the amount of widgets that may be imported, which is called a:
    a) quota.
    b) tariff.
    c) call rate.
    d) exchange factor.
    e) limit order.

18. A negative balance of trade is referred to as a:
    a) trade deficit.
    b) trade surplus.
    c) favorable balance of payments.
    d) direct investment.
    e) hedge.

19. The sale of film produced by Kodak in the United States to Chinese firms is an example of:
    a) direct foreign investment.
    b) exporting.
    c) importing.
    d) international licensing.
    e) a joint venture.

20. When a firm in one country acquires or builds a subsidiary in another country, it is engaging in:
    a) arbitrage.
    b) a joint venture.
    c) foreign aid.
    d) a forward contract.
    e) direct foreign investment.

21. A(n) _____ is a strategic alliance in which a firm allows a foreign company to produce its products according to specific instructions.
    a) international cartel
    b) international licensing agreement
    c) joint venture
    d) international limited partnership
    e) limited liability contract

22. Under _____ the government owns most businesses and decides what products to produce and in what quantity.
    a) socialism
    b) capitalism
    c) communism
    d) dualism
    e) pluralism

23. In a _____ economy, businesses are privately owned and profit-seeking entrepreneurs are free to start businesses they believe will serve the people's needs.
    a) capitalist
    b) communist
    c) feudalist
    d) mercantilist
    e) pluralist

24. _____ is an economic system that allows some private ownership of businesses and property but also has an active government sector and high tax rates to support the government's programs.
    a) Socialism
    b) Capitalism
    c) Feudalism
    d) Mercantilism
    e) Dualism

In-Text Study Guide

25. In recent years, governments of many nations have sold government-owned and -operated businesses to private investors. This process is known as:
    a) public disinvestment.
    b) privatization.
    c) repatriation.
    d) democratization.
    e) public capitalization.

26. The political and regulatory risks to a U.S. firm operating in a foreign country include all of the following, except:
    a) inflation of the currency.
    b) higher tax rates for foreign subsidiaries.
    c) taking over U.S. companies without compensation.
    d) strict pollution controls.
    e) eviction from property.

27. The dollar weakens against the British pound if the value of the pound:
    a) depreciates.
    b) sells off.
    c) softens.
    d) appreciates.
    e) declines.

28. If the dollar depreciates relative to the Japanese yen:
    a) Japanese goods will seem cheaper to American importers.
    b) gold will flow from the United States to Japan.
    c) American goods will seem less expensive to Japanese consumers.
    d) the dollar must appreciate relative to some other Asian currency.
    e) the U.S. government will have to intervene to increase the value of the dollar.

29. One disadvantage of hedging is that it:
    a) is illegal in many foreign countries.
    b) requires businesses to pay additional taxes on their earnings.
    c) is considered unethical behavior by some investors.
    d) prevents not only unfavorable, but also favorable, changes in exchange rates.
    e) greatly increases the risk of doing business in foreign countries.

30. A _____ states an exchange of currencies that will occur at a specified exchange rate at some future point in time.
    a) reserve clause
    b) forward contract
    c) limit order
    d) market order
    e) fixed time exchange contract

31. When businesses take action to lock in a specific exchange rate for a future international transaction in order to reduce risk, their strategy is referred to as:
    a) rate fixing.
    b) trading on reserve.
    c) selling short.
    d) hedging.
    e) trading on margin.

32. If you plan to convert dollars to obtain Japanese yen today, you would pay the:
    a) spot rate.
    b) open market rate.
    c) discount rate.
    d) hedge rate.
    e) forward rate.

Summary/Part I

Business Environment

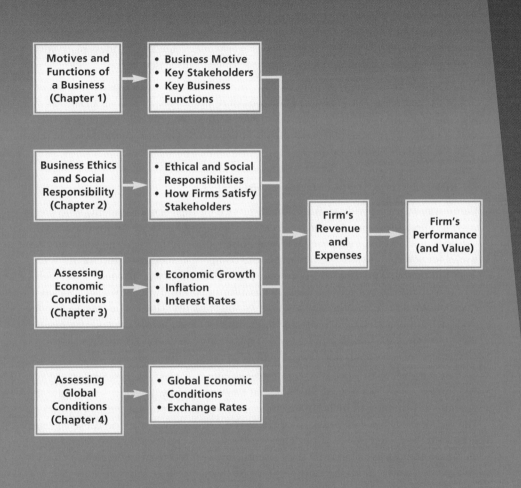

Motives and Functions of a Business (Chapter 1)	→	• Business Motive • Key Stakeholders • Key Business Functions
Business Ethics and Social Responsibility (Chapter 2)	→	• Ethical and Social Responsibilities • How Firms Satisfy Stakeholders
Assessing Economic Conditions (Chapter 3)	→	• Economic Growth • Inflation • Interest Rates
Assessing Global Conditions (Chapter 4)	→	• Global Economic Conditions • Exchange Rates

Firm's Revenue and Expenses → Firm's Performance (and Value)

Developing a Business Plan for Campus.com

Following is a business idea called Campus.com that has been created for you. It is your job to develop a plan for the business during the school term, applying many of the key concepts discussed in each chapter. At the end of each part, questions will guide your development of the business. By the end of the school term, you will have developed a complete business plan for Campus.com. This exercise will not only enhance your understanding of business concepts but will also demonstrate how the concepts are integrated; it can also enhance your teamwork and communication skills.

Your instructor will tell you whether you will be developing the business plan by yourself or as part of a team. There is no single perfect method for developing the business, so your (or your team's) business plan may vary from the plans created by other students (or student teams). However you develop the business plan, your method should be based on logical business concepts discussed in the chapters.

As you (or your team) answer the questions at the end of each part, you can insert your answers in the Business Plan booklet or on the Business Plan CD-ROM that are supplied with the text. Once you (or your team) complete the questions at the end of each part, you will have completed the business plan for Campus.com and will be ready to implement your plan.

Business Idea (related to Chapter 1)

Campus.com will provide an information service for high school students who are assessing different colleges to which they may apply. It will provide information on the lifestyles at any college that they select. High school students might find this service useful for several reasons. First, many books compare academic requirements at colleges but provide very limited information on student lifestyles. Second, some high school students do not rely on the lifestyle information in these books because they question whether the authors really understand students. Third, students do not necessarily want to purchase an entire volume on all colleges across the country just to obtain information on the few colleges to which they may apply. Fourth, students recognize that the material in these books can become outdated.

For these reasons, the business of Campus.com can satisfy high school students. The business does not require any physical facilities initially. It requires a website that provides information to high school students who wish to purchase the information. The website will show an index of all colleges. Customers will click on those colleges for which they want information. They must submit a credit card number and will be charged $1 for each college that they select. They will receive immediate information on their computer about the campus lifestyles of each college selected.

The main expenses for Campus.com are the creation of the website and gathering information about every college campus from reliable sources. Initially, this information will be gathered by ordering back issues of campus newspapers for the last year and then summarizing the campus activities for each college. In addition, the plan is to send a brief survey to about 30 students at each school (offering $20 to each respondent who fills out the survey), asking them to answer general questions about the activities and to rate the campus in terms of its sports activities, entertainment on campus, and nightlife. You hope to receive responses from at least 20 students before you summarize the information for each college. The information will be updated every three months by paying some of the same students who completed the first survey to fill out an updated survey. Thus, the information that you provide to customers is frequently updated, which is an advantage over any books they could buy in stores.

Main Sources of Revenue and Expenses

The success of this business is highly dependent on your revenue and expenses. What will be the main source of your revenue? What will be the main source of your expenses? Should you pay yourself a salary, or will you reinvest any earnings in the firm? Summarize your comments in your business plan for Campus.com.

Responsibility to Customers, Employees, and Owners (related to Chapter 2)

Describe the how the business will fulfull its responsibilities to its customers, its employees, and its owners.

Exposure to Economic Conditions (related to Chapter 3)

In your business plan for Campus.com, explain whether and how the firm's performance may be affected if economic conditions change. For example, would the demand for Campus.com's services be affected if economic conditions deteriorate? Why?

Global Conditions (related to Chapter 4)

Describe in the business plan how Campus.com could expand outside the United States. In this part of the plan, identify the logical choice of a foreign country that Campus.com could target.

Communication and Teamwork

Your instructor may ask you (or your team) to hand in and/or present the sections of your business plan that relate to this part of the text. As you build the plan at the end of each part of the text, you can continue to use the Business Plan booklet or CD-ROM.

Integrative Video Case: Establishing a Business and Its Corporate Responsibility

Founded by Robert Redford with money obtained from his salary for the movie *Butch Cassidy and the Sundance Kid* and other investors, Sundance Catalog became a mail-order business before mail-order businesses gained popularity. Larry Rosenthal, the CEO of Sundance Catalog, which is based in Utah, initially helped to write the business plan and obtain funding for the company. Sundance Catalog is associated with name recognition; Robert Redford is associated with environmental support and support of the arts. Sundance Catalog stands for environmental responsibility, support of the arts, creativity, and responsible business.

Questions

1 How can Sundance's corporate responsibility affect its profitability?

2 Explain how Sundance's form of corporate responsibility might change if it became a large corporation and spread its business throughout the United States.

3 How can Sundance's corporate responsibility affect its financing?

The Stock Market Game

Determine how the stock you selected is performing.

Check Your Performance

1 What is the value of your stock investment today?

2 What is your return on your investment?

3 How does your return compare to those of other students? (This comparison tells you whether your stock's performance is relatively high or low.)

Explaining Your Stock Performance

Stock prices are frequently influenced by the economic environment, including economic, industry, and global conditions. Review the latest news about your stock.

1 Determine whether your stock's price was affected (since you purchased it) as a result of the business environment (the main topic in this part of the text).

2 Identify the specific changes in the business environment (interest rate movements, industry competition, etc.) that may have caused the stock price to change.

3 Did your stock's price increase or decrease in response to changes in the business environment?

Running Your Own Business

The following exercise allows you to apply the key concepts covered in each chapter to a business that you would like to create for yourself. Applying these concepts to a business in which you are interested enables you to recognize how these concepts are used in the business world. Since this part focused on the business environment, you will be asked specific questions about the business environment that affects your business. Chapter 1 focused on the creation of a business idea, so the first questions will ask you to create your own business idea. Give this some serious thought because you will be developing specific details about your business idea at the end of each part. In Chapter 1, you learned how a college student developed a health club business. One could develop numerous types of small businesses without necessarily being a business expert. If you do not have any ideas initially, consider the types of businesses that are in a shopping mall. Or consider the firms that produce and sell products to those businesses. You might look through the Yellow Pages to find other types of small businesses.

The "Running Your Own Business" exercise at the end of each part will apply the key concepts in the chapters in that part to the business that you create. You can record good business ideas in the Business Plan booklet or on the Business Plan CD-ROM that are supplied with the text. By developing a business idea, you may actually implement it someday. Alternatively, you may realize from developing your idea why such a business could fail, which may lead you to alternative business ideas.

When developing your business idea, try to create a business that will require you to hire at least a few employees in the future. By doing this, you will find it easier to apply the concepts related to managing employees in later chapters.

1 Describe in general terms the type of business that you would like to create.

2 Explain in general terms how your business would offer some advantage over competing firms.

3 Describe the risk of your business. That is, explain what conditions could result in lower revenue or higher expenses than you expect.

4 Describe the ethical dilemmas (if any) that you might face in your business. How do you plan to handle these situations?

5 What types of social responsibilities would your business have toward your employees, customers, or community? What, if any, special policies would you establish to take better care of your employees, customers, or community?

6 Explain how your business would use the Internet to provide relevant information to its customers, employees, and shareholders. Would it use the Internet to fulfill some of its social responsibilities? How?

7 How would the performance of your business be affected by economic conditions in the local area? How would it be affected by economic conditions across the United States? How would your company be affected by global economic events?

8 How would the performance of your business be affected by an increase in interest rates?

9 Explain whether your business would benefit from importing any supplies from foreign countries.

10 Will your business attempt to export any products to foreign countries? Identify which countries could be targeted. Will your business compete against foreign competitors?

11 Explain how the performance of your business would be affected in any way by exchange rate movements.

Your Career in Business: *Pursuing a Major and a Career in Economics*

If you are very interested in the topics covered in this section, you may want to consider a major in economics. Some of the more common courses taken by economics majors are summarized here.

Common Courses for Economics Majors

▶ *Principles of Macroeconomics* Focuses on the economy as a whole, inflation, and the impact of government policies on economic conditions.

▶ *Principles of Microeconomics* Focuses on how firms set prices and determine how much to produce.

▶ *Intermediate Macroeconomics* Analyzes the tradeoffs resulting from government policies.

▶ *Intermediate Microeconomics* Focuses on profits, wages, and the market structure.

▶ *International Economics* Focuses on the comparison of different economies, international trade and capital flows, and the development of emerging economies.

▶ *Labor Economics* Focuses on the relationships between firms and their employees, including the role of labor unions.

▶ *Mathematical Economics* Explains how mathematics can be used to solve economics problems.

▶ *Econometrics* Applies statistical models to assess economic relationships.

▶ *Urban Economics* Emphasizes economic development and the environment within urban areas.

▶ *Managerial Economics* Examines how economic theories can be used in making managerial decisions related to production and pricing.

▶ *Money and Banking* Focuses on money, the banking system, and credit, as well as the impact of monetary policy on economic conditions.

▶ *Industrial Economics* Focuses on economic concepts related to industry, including pricing, competition, and market share.

Careers in Economics

The following websites provide information about common job positions, salaries, and careers for students who major in economics:

▶ Job position websites:

http://jobsearch.monster.com	Information on jobs in Finance, Economics, Government, or Policy.
http://careers.yahoo.com	Information on jobs in Banking, Mortgage Loans, or Government.
http://collegejournal.com/salarydata	Information on jobs in Banking or Financial Services.

Some of the job positions described in these websites may require work experience or a graduate degree.

Part II
Starting a New Business

Part II explains the general functions involved in organizing a business. Chapter 5 describes the alternative forms of business ownership that entrepreneurs can select when they create a new business. Since no single type of ownership is perfect for all firms, the advantages and disadvantages of each form are considered. Entrepreneurs must consider the characteristics of their new business when deciding which form of ownership would be most appropriate. Chapter 6 explains how entrepreneurship can be used to create or improve a business. A successful business requires not only a good business idea, but also effective planning to ensure that the idea is properly implemented. Chapter 6 also explains the key components of a business plan.

Selecting a Form of Business Ownership (Chapter 5)	→	• **The Possible Forms of Business Ownership** • **Risks of Owning a Business**	→	**Firm's Performance (and Value)**
Entrepreneurship and Business Planning (Chapter 6)	→	• **Assessment of Market Conditions** • **The Key Business Functions** • **Developing a Business Plan**		

Chapter

5

Entrepreneurs like the owner of this bike shop must decide on the type of ownership that will offer the greatest benefits.

The Learning Goals
of this chapter are to:

Describe the advantages and disadvantages of a sole proprietorship.

1

Describe the advantages and disadvantages of a partnership.

2

Describe the advantages and disadvantages of a corporation.

3

Explain how the potential return and risk of a business are affected by its form of ownership.

4

Describe methods of owning existing businesses.

5

Selecting a Form of Business Ownership

When entrepreneurs establish a business, they must decide on the form of business ownership. There are three basic forms of business ownership: sole proprietorship, partnership, and corporation. The form that is chosen can affect the profitability, risk, and value of the firm.

Consider the case of the Rugged Bike Shop, which was recently created by three entrepreneurs. The entrepreneurs want to use a form of business ownership that gives each of them equal ownership. They want to limit their liability and would like easy access to funding if they need it. They also want to consider how they might obtain the ownership of other bike businesses if they decide to expand in other locations.

The entrepreneurs creating the Rugged Bike Shop must decide:

▶ What are the advantages and disadvantages of a proprietorship, a partnership, and a corporation?

▶ How will the form of business ownership they choose affect their risk?

▶ What methods can they use to obtain ownership of existing businesses?

The business ownership decision determines how the earnings of a business are distributed among the owners of the business, the degree of liability of each owner, the degree of control that each owner has in running the business, the potential return of the business, and the risk of the business. These types of decisions are necessary for all businesses. This chapter explains how the business ownership decisions of the Rugged Bike Shop or any other firm can be made in a manner that maximizes the firm's value.

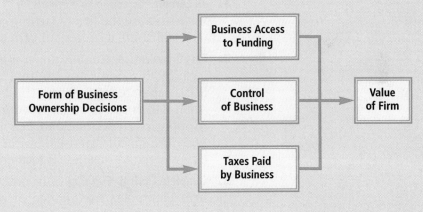

Sole Proprietorship

A business owned by a single owner is referred to as a **sole proprietorship.** The owner of a sole proprietorship is called a **sole proprietor.** A sole proprietor may obtain loans from creditors to help finance the firm's operations, but these loans do not represent ownership. The sole proprietor is obligated to cover any payments resulting from the loans but does not need to share the business profits with creditors.

sole proprietorship
a business owned by a single owner

sole proprietor
the owner of a sole proprietorship

Typical examples of sole proprietorships include a local restaurant, a local construction firm, a barber shop, a laundry service, and a local clothing store. About 70 percent of all firms in the United States are sole proprietorships. But because these firms are relatively small, they generate less than 10 percent of all business revenue. The earnings generated by a sole proprietorship are considered to be personal income received by the proprietor and are subject to personal income taxes collected by the Internal Revenue Service (IRS).

Characteristics of Successful Sole Proprietors

Sole proprietors must be willing to accept full responsibility for the firm's performance. The pressure of this responsibility can be much greater than any employee's responsibility. Sole proprietors must also be willing to work flexible hours. They are on call at all times and may even have to substitute for a sick employee. Their responsibility for the success of the business encourages them to continually monitor business operations. They must exhibit strong leadership skills, be well organized, and communicate well with employees.

Many successful sole proprietors had previous work experience in the market in which they are competing, perhaps as an employee in a competitor's firm. For example, restaurant managers commonly establish their own restaurants. Experience is critical to understanding the competition and the behavior of customers in a particular market.

Advantages of a Sole Proprietorship

The sole proprietor form of ownership has the following advantages over other forms of business ownership:

1. **All Earnings Go to the Sole Proprietor** The sole proprietor (owner) does not have to share the firm's earnings with other owners. Thus, the rewards of establishing a successful firm come back to the owner.

2. **Easy Organization** Establishing a sole proprietorship is relatively easy. The legal requirements are minimal. A sole proprietorship need not establish a separate legal entity. The owner must register the firm with the state, which can normally be done by mail. The owner may also need to apply for an occupational license to conduct a particular type of business. The specific license requirements vary with the state and even the city where the business is located.

3. **Complete Control** Having only one owner with complete control of the firm eliminates the chance of conflicts during the decision-making process. For example, an owner of a restaurant can decide on the menu, the prices, and the salaries paid to employees.

4. **Lower Taxes** Because the earnings in a proprietorship are considered to be personal income, they may be subject to lower taxes than those imposed on some other forms of business ownership, as will be explained later in this chapter.

Disadvantages of a Sole Proprietorship

Along with its advantages, the sole proprietorship has the following disadvantages:

unlimited liability
no limit on the debts for which the owner is liable

1. **The Sole Proprietor Incurs All Losses** Just as sole proprietors do not have to share the profits, they are unable to share any losses that the firm incurs. For example, assume you invest $10,000 of your funds in a lawn service and borrow an additional $8,000 that you invest in the business. Unfortunately, the revenue is barely sufficient to pay salaries to your employees, and you terminate the firm. You have not only lost all of your $10,000 investment in the firm but also are liable for the $8,000 that you borrowed. Since you are the sole proprietor, no other owners are available to help cover the losses.

2. **Unlimited Liability** A sole proprietor is subject to **unlimited liability,** which means there is no limit on the debts for which the owner is liable. If a sole proprietorship is sued, the sole proprietor is personally liable for any judgment against that firm.

3. **Limited Funds** A sole proprietor may have limited funds available to invest in the firm. Thus, sole proprietors have difficulty engaging in airplane manufacturing, shipbuilding, computer manufacturing, and other businesses that require substantial funds. Sole proprietors have limited funds to support the firm's expansion or to absorb temporary losses. A poorly performing firm may improve if given sufficient time. But if this firm cannot obtain additional funds to make up for its losses, it may not be able to continue in business long enough to recover.

4. **Limited Skills** A sole proprietor has limited skills and may be unable to control all parts of the business. For example, a sole proprietor may have difficulty running a large medical practice because different types of expertise may be needed.

Decision Making

Deciding on the Sole Proprietor Form of Business

Recall that the Rugged Bike Shop (introduced at the beginning of the chapter) was created by three people. They considered an arrangement in which only one of them (Mia Adams) would serve as sole proprietor. In that case, her two friends would be full-time employees, rather than owners, and would receive regular salaries. However, her friends already had other jobs and wanted partial ownership in the business. Therefore, they decided that a sole proprietorship would not be an appropriate form of business ownership.

1. Explain how the income that Mia's two friends would earn from the Rugged Bike Shop would differ if they were employees of a sole proprietorship rather than owners.

2. Explain how the amount of funding provided by the owners would be different if Mia had created a sole proprietorship, instead of having all three people be owners in the business.

ANSWERS: 1. The income of Mia's friends would be more certain if they were employees. It is uncertain if it is in the form of profits because the profits are uncertain. 2. The amount of funding provided by the owners would be smaller if Mia had created a sole proprietorship; the funding will be larger if Mia's friends are owners as well.

Describe the advantages and disadvantages of a partnership.

partnership
a business that is co-owned by two or more people

partners
co-owners of a business

general partnership
a partnership in which all partners have unlimited liability

limited partnership
a firm that has some limited partners

limited partners
partners whose liability is limited to the cash or property they contributed to the partnership

general partners
partners who manage the business, receive a salary, share the profits or losses of the business, and have unlimited liability

Partnership

A business that is co-owned by two or more people is referred to as a **partnership.** The co-owners of the business are called **partners.** The co-owners must register the partnership with the state and may need to apply for an occupational license. About 10 percent of all firms are partnerships.

In a **general partnership,** all partners have unlimited liability. That is, the partners are personally liable for all obligations of the firm. Conversely, in a **limited partnership,** the firm has some **limited partners,** or partners whose liability is limited to the cash or property they contributed to the partnership. Limited partners are only investors in the partnership and do not participate in its management, but because they have invested in the business, they share its profits or losses. A limited partnership has one or more **general partners,** or partners who manage the business, receive a salary, share the profits or losses of the business, and have unlimited liability. The earnings distributed to each partner represent personal income and are subject to personal income taxes collected by the IRS.

Advantages of a Partnership

The partnership form of ownership has three main advantages:

1. Additional Funding An obvious advantage of a partnership over a sole proprietorship is the additional funding that the partner or partners can provide. Therefore, more money may be available to finance the business operations. Some partnerships have thousands of partners, who are all required to invest some of their own money in the business. This type of partnership has much potential for growth because of its access to substantial funds.

The firm Look-Look.com of Hollywood, California, which conducts online research on trends of people between ages 14 and 30, is a partnership managed by the two partners shown here.

2. **Losses Are Shared** Any business losses that the partnership incurs are spread across all of the partners. Thus, a single person does not have to absorb the entire loss. Each owner will absorb only a portion of the loss.

3. **More Specialization** With a partnership, partners can focus on their respective specializations and serve a wide variety of customers. For example, an accounting firm may have one accountant who specializes in personal taxes for individuals and another who specializes in business taxes for firms. A medical practice partnership may have doctors with various types of expertise.

Disadvantages of a Partnership

Along with its advantages, the partnership has the following disadvantages:

1. **Control Is Shared** The decision making in a partnership must be shared. If the partners disagree about how the business should be run, business and personal relationships may be destroyed. Some owners of firms do not have the skills to manage a business.

2. **Unlimited Liability** General partners in a partnership are subject to unlimited liability, just like sole proprietors.

3. **Profits Are Shared** Any profits that the partnership generates must be shared among all partners. The more partners there are, the smaller the amount of a given level of profits that will be distributed to any individual partner.

S-Corporations

S-corporation
a firm that has 100 or fewer owners and satisfies other criteria. The earnings are distributed to the owners and taxed at the respective personal income tax rate of each owner.

A firm that has 100 or fewer owners and satisfies other criteria may choose to be a so-called **S-corporation.** The owners of an S-corporation have limited liability (like owners of corporations), but they are taxed as if the firm were a partnership. Thus, the earnings are distributed to the owners and taxed at the respective personal income tax rate of each owner. Some state governments also impose a corporate tax on S-corporations. Many accounting firms and small businesses select the S-corporation as a form of ownership.

Limited Liability Company (LLC)

limited liability company (LLC)
a firm that has all the favorable features of a typical general partnership but also offers limited liability for the partners

A type of general partnership called a **limited liability company (LLC)** has become popular in recent years. An LLC has all the favorable features of a typical general partnership but also offers limited liability for the partners. It typically protects a partner's personal assets from the negligence of other partners in the firm. This type of protection is highly desirable for partners, given the high frequency of liability lawsuits. The assets of the company (such as the property or machinery owned by the company) are not protected. Although S-corporations may also provide liability protection, various rules may restrict the limited liability of some owners of S-corporations. An LLC is not subject to such stringent rules.

An LLC must be created according to the laws of the state where the business is located. The precise rules on liability protection vary among the states. Numerous general partnerships (including many accounting firms) have converted to LLCs to capitalize on the advantages of a partnership, while limiting liability for their owners.

Decision Making

Deciding on the Partnership Form of Business

Reconsider the case of the Rugged Bike Shop. The three entrepreneurs all want ownership of the business. They are all willing to accept liability, but they would prefer that their personal assets be protected from the possible negligence of the other partners. They decide that a limited liability company would be the ideal type of general partnership to form.

1. If the owners of the Rugged Bike Shop form a partnership, how can the business obtain funding if it does not want to borrow funds?
2. If the owners of the Rugged Bike Shop form a partnership, why might the business have insufficient funds to open additional bike shops in the future?

ANSWERS: 1. It can obtain funding if the partners increase their equity investment in the business. 2. It would have limited access to equity because there are only three owners who can provide equity funding.

Describe the advantages and disadvantages of a corporation.

corporation
a state-chartered entity that pays taxes and is legally distinct from its owners

charter
a document used to incorporate a business. The charter describes important aspects of the corporation.

bylaws
general guidelines for managing a firm

Corporation

A third form of business is a **corporation,** which is a state-chartered entity that pays taxes and is legally distinct from its owners. Although only about 20 percent of all firms are corporations, corporations generate almost 90 percent of all business revenue. Exhibit 5.1 compares the relative contributions to business revenue made by sole proprietorships, partnerships, and corporations.

To form a corporation, an individual or group must adopt a corporate **charter,** or a document used to incorporate a business, and file it with the state government. The charter describes important aspects of the corporation, such as the name of the firm, the stock issued, and the firm's operations. The people who organize the corporation must also establish **bylaws,** which are general guidelines for managing the firm.

Since the shareholders of the corporation are legally separated from the entity, they have limited liability, meaning that they are not held personally responsible for the firm's actions. The most that the stockholders of a corporation can lose is the amount of money they invested.

The stockholders of a corporation elect the members of the board of directors, who are responsible for establishing the general policies of the

Exhibit 5.1

Relative Contributions to Business Revenue of Sole Proprietorships, Partnerships, and Corporations

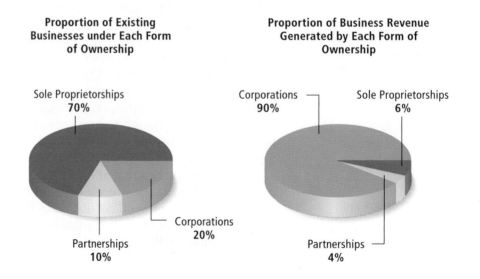

Out of Business

I THINK WE ARE READY TO BECOME A CORPORATION, AS WE HAVE ALREADY USED ALL THE MONEY INVESTED BY THE PARTNERS.

firm. One of the board's responsibilities is to elect the president and other key officers (such as vice-presidents), who are then given the responsibility of running the business on a day-to-day basis.

If the board of directors becomes displeased with the performance of the key officers, the board has the power to replace them. Similarly, if the stockholders become displeased with the performance of members of the board, the stockholders can replace the directors in the next scheduled election. In some corporations, one or a few individuals may serve as a stockholder, as a member of the board of directors, and as a key officer of the firm. The chief executive officer of a business commonly serves as the chair of the board.

How Stockholders Earn a Return

Stockholders can earn a return on their investment in a firm in two different ways. First, they may receive dividends from the firm, which are a portion of the firm's recent earnings over the last three months that are distributed to stockholders. Second, the stock they hold may increase in value. When the firm becomes more profitable, the value of its stock tends to rise, meaning that the value of stock held by owners has increased. Thus, they can benefit by selling that stock for a much higher price than they paid for it.

In the late 1990s, stock prices of many firms more than doubled. When stockholders invest in a stock, however, they also face the risk that the stock price may decline. In the 2000–2002 period, the performance of firms was generally weak, and stock prices of many firms declined by more than 50 percent. Some firms failed, causing investors in the firms' stock to lose 100 percent of their investment.

Private versus Public Corporations

privately held
ownership is restricted to a small group of investors

People become owners of a corporation by purchasing shares of stock. Many small corporations are **privately held,** meaning that ownership is restricted to a small group of investors. Some well-known privately held

Enterprise Rent-A-Car agency is one of many large companies that remains privately held.

LANDOV LLC

publicly held
shares can be easily purchased or sold by investors

going public
the act of initially issuing stock to the public

firms include L. L. Bean, Enterprise Rent-A-Car, and Rand McNally & Co. Most large corporations are **publicly held,** meaning that shares can be easily purchased or sold by investors.

Stockholders of publicly held corporations can sell their shares of stock when they need money, are disappointed with the performance of the corporation, or simply expect that the stock price will not rise in the future. Their stock can be sold (with the help of a stockbroker) to some other investor who wants to invest in that corporation.

Although virtually all firms (even Ford Motor Company) were privately held when they were created, some of these firms became publicly held when they needed funds to support large expansion. The act of initially issuing stock to the public is called **going public.** Recently, well-known firms such as Barnesandnoble.com, United Parcel Service (UPS), and Google have gone public to raise funds.

Publicly held corporations can obtain additional funds by issuing new common stock. This means that either their existing stockholders can purchase more stock, or other investors can become stockholders by purchasing the corporation's stock. By issuing new stock, corporations may obtain whatever funds are needed to support any business expansion. Corporations that wish to issue new stock must be able to convince investors that the funds will be utilized properly, resulting in a reasonable return for the investors.

Advantages of a Corporation

The corporate form of ownership offers the following advantages:

1. **Limited Liability** Owners of a corporation have limited liability (as explained earlier), whereas sole proprietors and general partners typically have unlimited liability.

2. **Access to Funds** A corporation can easily obtain funds by issuing new stock (as explained earlier). This allows corporations the flexibility to

grow and to engage in new business ventures. Sole proprietorships and partnerships have less access to funding when they wish to finance expansion. To obtain more funds, they may have to rely on their existing owners or on loans from creditors.

3. **Transfer of Ownership** Investors in large, publicly traded companies can normally sell their stock in minutes by calling their stockbrokers or by selling it online over the Internet. Conversely, owners of sole proprietorships or partnerships may have some difficulty in selling their share of ownership in the business.

Disadvantages of a Corporation

Along with its advantages, the corporate form of ownership has the following disadvantages:

1. **High Organizational Expense** Organizing a corporation is normally more expensive than creating the other forms of business because of the necessity to create a corporate charter and file it with the state. Some expense may also be incurred in establishing bylaws. Issuing stock to investors also entails substantial expenses.

2. **Financial Disclosure** When the stock of a corporation is traded publicly, the investing public has the right to inspect the company's financial data, within certain limits. As a result, firms may be obligated to publicly disclose more about their business operations and employee salaries than they would like. Privately held firms are not forced to disclose financial information to the public.

3. **Agency Problems** Publicly held corporations are normally run by managers who are responsible for making decisions for the business that will serve the interests of the owners. Managers may not always act in the best interests of stockholders, however. For example, managers may attempt to take expensive business trips that are not necessary to manage the business. Such actions may increase the expenses of running a business, reduce business profits, and therefore reduce the returns to stockholders. When managers do not act as responsible agents for the shareholders who own the business, a so-called **agency problem** results. There are many examples of high-level managers who made decisions that were in their best interests, at the expense of shareholders. One of the most blatant examples occurred at Enron, Inc., which went bankrupt in 2001. Agency problems are less likely in proprietorships because the sole owner may also serve as the sole manager and make most or all business decisions.

agency problem
when managers do not act as responsible agents for the shareholders who own the business

4. **High Taxes** Since the corporation is a separate entity, it is taxed separately from its owners. The annual taxes paid by a corporation are determined by applying the corporate tax rate to the firm's annual earnings. The corporate tax rate is different from the personal tax rate. Consider a corporation that earns $10 million this year. Assume that the corporate tax rate applied to earnings of corporations is 30 percent this year (the corporate tax rates can be changed by law over time). Thus, the taxes and after-tax earnings of the corporation are as follows:

Earnings before Tax = $10,000,000
Corporate Tax = 3,000,000   (computed as 30% × $10,000,000)
Earnings after Tax = $7,000,000

One of the main reasons why Enron went bankrupt is because some of its high-level managers made decisions that benefited themselves at the expense of shareholders.

If any of the after-tax earnings are paid to the owners as dividends, the dividends represent personal income to the stockholders. Thus, the stockholders will pay personal income taxes on the dividends. Continuing with our example, assume that all of the $7 million in after-tax earnings is distributed to the stockholders as dividends. Assume that the personal tax rate is 10 percent for all owners who will receive dividends (personal tax rates depend on the person's income level and can be changed by law over time). The actual dividend income received by the stockholders after paying income taxes is as follows:

$$\begin{aligned}
\text{Dividends Received} &= \$7,000,000 \\
\text{Taxes Paid on Dividends} &= \underline{\$700,000}\quad (\text{computed as } 10\% \times \$7,000,000) \\
\text{Income after Tax} &= \underline{\underline{\$6,300,000}}
\end{aligned}$$

Since the corporate tax was $3,000,000 and the personal tax was $700,000, the total tax paid as a result of the corporation's profits was $3,700,000, which represents 37 percent of the $10,000,000 profit that the corporation earned.

As this example shows, owners of corporations are subject to double taxation. First, the corporation's entire profits from their investment are subject to corporate taxes. Then, any profits distributed as dividends to individual owners are subject to personal income taxes. Exhibit 5.2 shows the flow of funds between owners and the corporation to illustrate how owners are subject to double taxation.

To recognize the disadvantage of double taxation, consider what the taxes would have been for this business if it were a sole proprietorship or partnership rather than a corporation. The $10,000,000 profit would have been personal income to a sole proprietor or to partners and would

Exhibit 5.2

Illustration of Double
Taxation

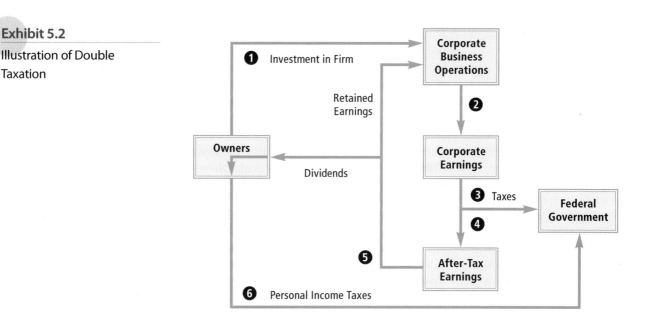

have been subject to personal taxes. Assuming a personal tax rate of
20 percent, the total tax would be $2,000,000 (computed as 20 percent ×
$10,000,000), which is less than the total amount that a corporation that
earned the same profit and its stockholders together would pay. Even if the
personal income tax rate of a sole proprietor or a partner was higher than
20 percent, the taxes paid by a corporation and its stockholders would
probably still be higher. A comparison of the tax effects on corporations
and sole proprietorships is provided in Exhibit 5.3.

One way that a corporation may reduce the taxes paid by its owners is
to reinvest its earnings (called "retained earnings") rather than pay the

Exhibit 5.3

Comparison of Tax Effects on Corporations and Sole Proprietorships

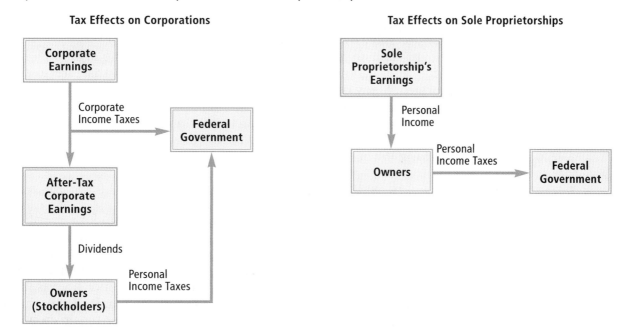

earnings out as dividends. If owners do not receive dividends from a corporation, they will not be subject to personal taxes on the profits earned by the corporation. This strategy makes sense only if the corporation can put the retained earnings to good use.

When stockholders of a corporation sell their shares of stock for more than they paid for them, they earn a **capital gain,** which is equal to the price received from the sale of stock minus the price they paid for the stock. The stockholders must pay a capital gains tax on the capital gain, however. Thus, whether stockholders receive income from selling the stock at a gain or from receiving dividend payments, they are subject to taxes.

capital gain
the price received from the sale of stock minus the price paid for the stock

Comparing Forms of Business Ownership

No single form of business ownership is ideal for all business owners. An individual setting up a small business may choose a sole proprietorship. Some people who decide to co-own a small business may choose a partnership. If they wish to limit their liability, however, they may decide to establish a privately held corporation. If this corporation grows substantially over time and needs millions of dollars to support additional business expansion, it may convert to a publicly held corporation so that it can obtain funds from stockholders.

Using the Internet to Compare Forms of Business Ownership

Many excellent sources of information on forms of business ownership are available on the Internet. A one starting point is the Small Business Administration (SBA). Among the resources offered at the SBA's home page (http://www.sbaonline.sba.gov) are the following:

▶ Information on local SBA offices.

▶ Access to the Service Corps of Retired Executives (SCORE), consisting of over 10,000 retired business people who have volunteered to help small businesses for free.

▶ SBA publications. The range of topics covered by the publications is enormous, and each can be copied directly to the entrepreneur's computer at no charge.

All of these services are available through local SBA offices, as well as being accessible over the Internet.

In addition to government agencies, many private organizations provide information and services to small businesses that are just being formed. Many of these organizations, such as The Company Corporation, allow corporations and other forms of businesses to be set up entirely over the Internet. A particularly attractive feature of these services is their low cost. Nevertheless, some entrepreneurs may still prefer to hire an attorney to form the business, especially if their ownership situation is complicated.

How Business Ownership Can Change

As an example of how the optimal form of ownership for a specific business can change over time, consider the history of PC Repair Company, which specializes in repairing personal computers. The owner, Ed Everhart, started his business in Columbus, Ohio, in 1983. He initially used his garage as work space to fix customers' computers. Since he was the sole owner at that time, his business was a proprietorship. By 1989, the business had grown, and Ed wanted to open a computer repair shop downtown. He needed more funds to purchase a shop and hire employees. He asked a friend, Maria Rosas, if she wanted to become a partner by investing funds in the firm and working for the business. She agreed, so the business was converted from a proprietorship to a partnership. From Ed's point of view, the main benefit was that Maria could invest money that would help the business grow. In addition, she had good computer repair skills. The main disadvantage was that he was no longer the sole decision maker, but he and Maria usually agreed on how to run the business.

By 2000, the business had grown even more. Ed and Maria wanted to establish three more computer repair shops in Columbus, so they obtained funds from eight friends who served as limited partners. These limited partners invested in the business because they expected that it would flourish and provide them with a good return on their investment. In 2006, Ed and Maria wanted to expand their business throughout Ohio, but they needed a substantial amount of funds to do so. They decided to issue stock to the public, with the help of a financial institution. Their stock offering raised $20 million, although about $1.5 million of the proceeds went to pay expenses associated with the stock offering. At this time, the ownership of the business was converted from a partnership to a corporation. The corporate form of ownership allowed the business to expand. With the establishment of several repair shops throughout Ohio, the firm now had the potential to generate large earnings. The organization was also much more complex than when the business was a proprietorship. Ed and Maria still made the business decisions, but they were now accountable to hundreds of other investors who were part-owners of the business. Thus, by 2006 PC Repair Company had changed considerably since its beginnings in a garage 23 years earlier.

Decision Making

Deciding on the Corporation Form of Business

Recall that the Rugged Bike Shop was organized as a partnership. Now the three partners are considering long-term plans for setting up similar bike shops around the country. First, their original bike shop will need to be successful. If it is, they will expand throughout their city, and if these businesses are successful, they would like to create hundreds of new bike shops across the country. To support expansion across the country, however, they will need millions of dollars and will be able to obtain such a large amount of funds only if they become a corporation and go public.

1. Explain why it may be difficult for the Rugged Bike Shop to go public in the future.
2. How will the proportion of the business owned by each of the three entrepreneurs (now one-third) change if the Rugged Bike Shop goes public?

ANSWERS: 1. It would have to demonstrate to potential investors that it could successfully expand across the country and show that hundreds of new bike shops are needed. 2. The proportion would be reduced because other owners would own much of the business if it goes public someday.

4

Explain how the potential return and risk of a business are affected by its form of ownership.

How Ownership Can Affect Return and Risk

When business owners assess a possible investment in any business, they consider both the potential return and the risk from that type of investment. The potential return and the risk from investing in a business are influenced by its form of ownership. Thus, entrepreneurs should consider how the form of ownership affects the potential return and the risk when deciding on the optimal form of ownership for their business.

Impact of Ownership on the Return on Investment

The return on investment in a firm is derived from the firm's profits (also called "earnings" or "income"). As described earlier, when a firm generates earnings, it pays a portion to the IRS as income taxes. The remaining (after-tax) earnings represent the return (in dollars) to the business owners. However, the dollar value of a firm's after-tax earnings is not necessarily a useful measure of the firm's performance unless it is adjusted for the amount of the firm's **equity,** which is the total investment by the firm's stockholders. For this reason, business owners prefer to measure a firm's profitability by computing its **return on equity (ROE),** which is the earnings as a proportion of the equity:

equity
the total investment by the firm's stockholders

return on equity (ROE)
earnings as a proportion of the firm's equity

$$ROE = \frac{\text{Earnings after Tax}}{\text{Equity}}$$

For example, if the stockholders invested \$1 million in a firm and its after-tax earnings last year were \$150,000, its return on equity last year was:

$$ROE = \frac{\$150,000}{\$1,000,000}$$

$$= .15, \text{ or } 15\%$$

Thus, the firm generated a return equal to 15 percent of the owners' investment in the firm.

The return on equity for Zemax Company is shown in Exhibit 5.4. Notice that Zemax generated earnings before taxes of \$100 million. Of this amount, \$30 million (30 percent) was used to pay corporate taxes. The remaining \$70 million represents after-tax earnings. Given the total investment (equity) in Zemax Company of about \$350 million, the after-tax earnings represent a return of 20 percent (computed as \$70 million divided by \$350 million).

The large amount of equity that Zemax Company obtained as a result of choosing the corporate form of ownership has enabled it to grow and generate a large amount of sales and earnings. If Zemax had chosen the partnership form of ownership, its growth would have been limited.

However, access to a large amount of equity is beneficial only if the firm can put the equity to good use. If a firm has more equity than it can use, its performance will be weak. Consider the situations of Firms A and B. Firm A is a partnership and Firm B is a corporation.

	Firm A (Partnership)	Firm B (Corporation)
Earnings after taxes last year	\$15 million	\$15 million
Owners' equity	\$100 million	\$300 million
Return on equity	15%	5%

Exhibit 5.4

Return on Equity for
Zemax Company

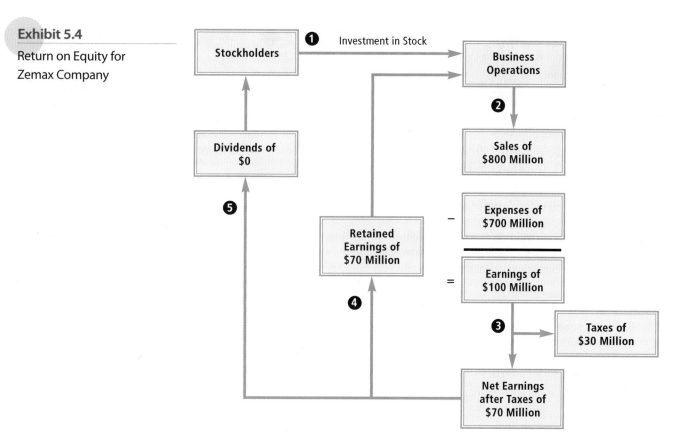

Return of Equity (ROE)
Given that the equity of Zemax was about $350 million, its ROE was:

$$ROE = \frac{\text{Earnings after Taxes}}{\text{Equity}}$$

$$= \frac{\$70\ \text{million}}{\$350\ \text{million}}$$

$$= 20\%$$

Notice that the firms had the same dollar value of earnings after taxes. However, the corporation has three times the equity investment of the partnership. The return on equity is much higher for the partnership than for the corporation because the partnership achieved the same level of earnings with a smaller equity investment.

Impact of Ownership on Risk

risk
the degree of uncertainty about a
firm's future earnings

The **risk** of a firm represents the degree of uncertainty about the firm's future earnings, which reflects an uncertain return to the owners. A firm's future earnings are dependent on its future revenue and its expenses. Firms can experience losses if the revenue is less than expected or if the expenses are more than expected. Some firms that experience severe losses ultimately fail. In these cases, the owners may lose most or all of the funds they invested in the firms.

Since sole proprietorships tend to be small businesses with very limited funds, they are generally riskier than larger businesses such as partnerships and corporations. Consider a sole proprietorship that has revenue of

Cross Functional Teamwork

Sources of Risk across Business Functions

A firm relies on the management of resources (including human resources and other resources such as machinery), marketing, and finance functions to perform well. Poor performance can normally be attributed to poor management of resources, poor marketing, or poor financing, as explained next.

If resources are not properly managed, the firm will incur excessive expenses. The following are typical mistakes that can cause excessive production expenses:

1. Hiring more employees than necessary, which results in high operating expenses.
2. Hiring fewer employees than necessary, which prevents the firm from achieving the desired volume or quality of products.
3. Hiring employees who lack proper skills or training.
4. Investing in more equipment or machinery than necessary, which results in high operating expenses.
5. Investing in less equipment or machinery than necessary, which prevents the firm from achieving the desired volume or quality of products.

The following are typical marketing mistakes that can cause poor performance:

1. Excessive spending on marketing programs.
2. Ineffective marketing programs, which do not enhance the firm's revenue.

The following are typical finance mistakes that can cause poor performance:

1. Borrowing too much money, which results in a high level of interest expenses incurred per year.
2. Not borrowing enough money, which prevents a firm from investing the necessary amount of funds to be successful.

Since business decisions are related, a poor decision in one department can affect other departments. For example, a computer manufacturer's production volume is based on the forecasted demand for computers by the marketing department. When the marketing department underestimates the demand, the manufacturer experiences shortages.

$200,000 and expenses of $300,000 this year. It needs $100,000 of equity to cover its loss. If it has only $60,000, it cannot cover the loss. If the business had another owner, it would have more equity and might be able to cover its loss.

The limited funding of sole proprietorships also means that they are not able to diversify their business. If their single line of business experiences problems, they are highly susceptible to failure. An event such as a workers' strike in a supplier firm or reduced demand for the type of products they produce can result in failure. In contrast, a larger firm that sells a diversified product line may not be severely affected by events that adversely affect only one of its products. The death or retirement of a key manager can also have a great impact on a sole proprietorship. Larger businesses typically have several employees in high-level positions who can make key decisions, so no one person is irreplaceable.

When deciding on ownership, the following tradeoff should be obvious. The greater the number of owners, the larger the amount of funds that can be accessed, but the larger the number of people who share in the performance of the business. Thus, a sole proprietorship can reduce its risk by converting to a partnership so that it can access more funds. A partnership can reduce its risk by converting to a corporation so that it can access more funds.

Decision Making

Deciding Whether to Add Partners to Reduce Risk

Recall that the Rugged Bike Shop has three partners. The partners recognize that if the business suffers losses, they will each incur one-third of the losses. They could reduce their risk by inviting more partners to invest in the firm. In that way, any losses would be shared by more partners. If they invite more partners and the business is profitable, however, they would each receive a smaller share of the profits. Since they believe that the business has sufficient funding, they decide not to invite any more partners into the business at this time.

1. How would the decision-making process of the Rugged Bike Shop change if the three partners had invited other partners to invest in the business?
2. Why might their decision have been different if they needed funding to expand and could not easily borrow funds?

ANSWERS: 1. The decision-making process would be more complicated because more partners would be involved in the decisions. 2. They might have decided to add partners if they needed funds and could not borrow because additional partners would have provided more equity for the business.

Obtaining Ownership of an Existing Business

5

Describe methods of owning existing businesses.

Some people become the sole owners without starting the business. The following are common methods by which people become owners of existing businesses:

▶ Assuming ownership of a family business

▶ Purchasing an existing business

▶ Franchising

Assuming Ownership of a Family Business

Many people work in a family business and after a period of time assume the ownership of it. This can be an ideal way to own a business because its performance may be somewhat predictable as long as the key employees continue to work there. Major decisions regarding the production process and other operations of the firm have been predetermined. If the business has historically been successful, a new owner's main function may be to ensure that the existing operations continue to run efficiently. Alternatively, if the business is experiencing poor performance, the new owner may have to revise management, marketing, and financing policies.

Purchasing an Existing Business

Businesses are for sale on any given day in any city. They are often advertised in the classified ads section of local newspapers. Businesses are sold for various reasons, including financial difficulties and the death or retirement of an owner.

People considering the purchase of an existing business must determine whether they have the expertise to run the business or at least properly monitor the managers. Then they must compare the expected benefits of the business with the initial outlay required to purchase it. The seller of the business may provide historical sales volume, which can be used to estimate the future sales volume. However, the prospective buyer must be cautious when using these figures. In some businesses such as dentistry and hairstyling, personal relationships between the owner and customers are critical. Many customers may switch to competitors if the ownership changes. For these types of businesses, the historical sales volume may substantially overestimate future sales. For other, less personalized businesses such as grocery stores, a change of ownership is not likely to have a significant effect on customer preferences (and therefore on sales volume).

Franchising

franchise
an arrangement whereby a business owner allows others to use its trademark, trade name, or copyright, under specific conditions

A **franchise** is an arrangement whereby a business owner (called a **franchisor**) allows another (the **franchisee**) to use its trademark, trade name, or copyright, under specified conditions. Each individual franchise operates as an independent business and is typically owned by a sole proprietor. Thus, a new business is created using the trademark and name of the existing franchisor.

franchisor
a firm that allows others to use its trade name or copyright, under specified conditions

Franchises in the United States number over 500,000, and they generate more than $800 billion in annual revenue. Some well-known franchises include McDonald's, Thrifty Rent-a-Car System, Dairy Queen, Super 8 Motels, Inc., TGI Fridays, Pearle Vision, Inc., and Baskin-Robbins. The costs of purchasing a franchise can vary significantly, depending on the specific trademarks, technology, and services provided to the franchisees.

franchisee
a firm that is allowed to use the trade name or copyright of a franchise

Types of Franchises Most franchises can be classified as a distributorship, a chain-style business, or a manufacturing arrangement.

distributorship
a type of franchise in which a dealer is allowed to sell a product produced by a manufacturer

In a **distributorship,** a dealer is allowed to sell a product produced by a manufacturer. For example, Chrysler and Ford dealers are distributorships.

chain-style business
a type of franchise in which a firm is allowed to use the trade name of a company and follows guidelines related to the pricing and sale of the product

In a **chain-style business,** a firm is allowed to use the trade name of a company and follows guidelines related to the pricing and sale of the product. Some examples are McDonald's, CD Warehouse, Holiday Inn, Subway, and Pizza Hut.

Dunkin Donuts is one of many franchises that has grown throughout the United States and even in foreign countries.

AP/WIDE WORLD PHOTOS

Self-Scoring Exercise

In a **manufacturing arrangement,** a firm is allowed to manufacture a product using the formula provided by another company. For example, Microsoft might allow a foreign company to produce its software, as long as the software is sold only in that country. Microsoft would receive a portion of the revenue generated by that firm.

Advantages of a Franchise   The typical advantages of a franchise are as follows:

1. **Proven Management Style** Franchisees look to the franchisors for guidance in production and management. McDonald's provides extensive training to its franchisees. The management style of a franchise is already a proven success. A franchise's main goal is to duplicate a proven business in a particular location. Thus, the franchise is a less risky venture than a new type of business, as verified by a much higher failure rate for new businesses.

2. **Name Recognition** Many franchises are nationally known because of advertising by the franchisor. This provides the franchisee with name recognition, which can significantly increase the demand for the product. Therefore, owners of Holiday Inn, Pizza Hut, and other franchises may not need to spend money on advertising because the franchises are already popular with consumers.

3. **Financial Support** Some franchisees receive some financial support from the franchisor, which can ensure sufficient start-up funds for the franchisee. For example, some McDonald's franchisees receive funding from McDonald's. Alternatively, franchisees can purchase materials and supplies from the franchisor on credit, which represents a form of short-term financing.

manufacturing arrangement
a type of franchise in which a firm is allowed to manufacture a product using the formula provided by another company

Disadvantages of a Franchise   Two common disadvantages of franchising are as follows:

1. **Sharing Profits**   In return for services provided by the franchisor, the franchisee must share profits with the franchisor. Annual fees paid by the franchisee may be 8 percent or more of the annual revenue generated by the franchise.

2. **Less Control**   The franchisee must abide by guidelines regarding product production and pricing, and possibly other guidelines as well. Consequently, the franchisee's performance is dependent on these guidelines. Owners are not allowed to revise some of the guidelines.

Though decision making is limited, owners of a franchise still make some critical decisions. They must decide whether a particular franchise can be successful in a particular location. In addition, even though the production and marketing policies are somewhat predetermined, the owners are responsible for managing their employees. They must provide leadership and motivation to maximize production efficiency. Thus, a franchise's performance is partially dependent on its owners and managers.

The Popularity of Business-to-Business Franchises   Franchises that serve other businesses (called business-to-business or B2B franchises) have grown substantially in the last few years. In particular, many franchises focus on providing hiring services, consulting services, and training services for firms. These types of franchises are popular because they normally require a smaller initial investment than many other franchises such as hotels and restaurants. Many B2B franchises can be operated by computer from a home office and therefore can be started with an investment of between $30,000 and $100,000. In contrast, restaurant franchises may require an investment of $150,000 or more. In addition, a B2B franchise can use computer technology instead of employees to do some of the work, such as sorting résumés and offering training with animated computer files. Furthermore, since a B2B franchise interacts with other businesses, less weekend work may be required than with restaurant franchises, which commonly operate seven days a week.

McDonald's provides training to its franchisees to ensure that the operations are properly organized.

Global Business

Ownership of Foreign Businesses

Opportunities in foreign countries have encouraged many entrepreneurs in the United States to establish foreign businesses in recent years. A common way for an entrepreneur to establish a foreign business is to purchase a franchise created by a U.S. firm in a foreign country. For example, McDonald's, Pizza Hut, and KFC have franchises in numerous foreign countries. The potential return on these franchises may be higher than in the United States if there is less competition.

Another popular way for U.S. entrepreneurs to own a foreign business is to purchase a business that is being sold by the foreign government. During the 1990s, many governments in eastern Europe and Latin America sold a large number of businesses that they had owned. They also encouraged more competition among firms in each industry. Entrepreneurs recognized that many businesses previously owned by the government were not efficiently managed. Consequently, many businesses were perceived as having relatively low values, thus enabling some entrepreneurs to purchase the businesses at low prices. However, these businesses were subject to a high degree of risk because the foreign environment was unstable. Since most of the

businesses in these countries had been managed by their respective governments, the rules for privately owned businesses were not completely established. The tax rates that would be imposed on private businesses were uncertain. The degree of competition was also uncertain, as firms were now free to enter most industries.

Given the uncertainties faced by new businesses in these foreign countries, some entrepreneurs made agreements with existing foreign firms rather than establishing their own business. For example, suppose that an entrepreneur recognizes that various household products will be popular in some Latin American countries but prefers not to establish a firm there because of uncertainty about tax rates and other government policies. The entrepreneur may make an agreement with an existing firm that distributes related products to retail stores throughout Latin America. This firm will earn a fee for selling the household products produced by the entrepreneur. This example is just one of many possible arrangements that allow U.S. entrepreneurs to capitalize on opportunities in a foreign country without owning a business there.

Decision Making

Deciding Whether to Establish Franchises

A well-known bicycle company in town has asked the three partners of the Rugged Bike Shop if they want to convert their new bike shop business into a chain-style franchise. The franchisor would provide them with guidance in running the bike shop business, but they would have to allocate a portion of their profits to the franchisor. The partners believe that they can manage the bike shop business on their own and do not want to share the profits of their business. Therefore, they decline the franchisor's offer.

1. Do you think the partners of the Rugged Bike Shop should have accepted the franchisor's offer?

2. Do you think the Rugged Bike Shop can serve as a franchisor for other investors who want to run a bike shop business?

ANSWERS: 1. The answer depends on whether the franchisor would truly offer some name recognition or better guidance for the Rugged Bike Shop. The partners would have to weigh these benefits against the cost of being a franchisee, which is the portion of profits paid by the franchisee to the franchisor. 2. The Rugged Bike Shop cannot serve as a franchisor at this point because it does not have any name recognition and has not yet proved that its management style is successful. No other bike shop owners would believe that they would benefit from having the Rugged Bike Shop as a franchisor.

COLLEGE HEALTH CLUB: BUSINESS OWNERSHIP AT CHC

One of the decisions that Sue Kramer needs to make as part of her business plan is the appropriate form of business ownership for College Health Club (CHC). Diane Burke, a relative of Sue's, has offered a loan of $40,000 if she believes that the business plan is feasible. Diane is willing to provide the funds as a 10-year loan and will charge an interest rate of 10 percent. If Sue accepts the funds as a loan, then she will be the sole owner of CHC. However, she will have to pay Diane interest of $4,000 at the end of each year (computed as $40,000 × 10%).

Alternatively, Diane is willing to provide the funds as an equity investment. This would make her an owner of the firm. In this case, Diane's investment would be two-thirds of the total investment in the firm, and she would receive two-thirds of the proceeds when the business is sold, perhaps several years from now.

Sue realizes that CHC's earnings would be $4,000 higher each year if she accepts the funds as an equity investment rather than a loan, because she would avoid the interest expense. This is the advantage of the partnership form of ownership. In addition, any losses incurred by CHC would be shared if she allows Diane to be a partner.

If Sue uses the partnership form, however, she would receive only one-third of the proceeds when the business is sold, and Diane would receive the remainder. In addition, Sue would have to share the decision making with Diane. With the proprietorship form of ownership, Sue would receive the entire proceeds if she sells the business someday. Furthermore, she would have complete control. She believes that she can run CHC better by herself than if other partners are involved in the business decisions.

After weighing the advantages and disadvantages of a sole proprietorship versus a partnership, Sue decides that the proprietorship is the more desirable form of ownership. She risks losing more of her own money as the sole proprietor, but she is willing to take that risk because she is confident that her business will be successful.

Sue does not even consider the corporation form of ownership at this point because she is just starting a very small business. If she ever decides to expand the business by allowing for additional owners, the partnership form would be more appropriate than the corporation form. She would consider forming a corporation only if she plans to expand her health clubs throughout Texas.

Summary

1 A sole proprietorship is owned by a single person who often manages the firm as well. Its advantages are that all earnings go to the sole owner, it is easy to organize, the owner has complete control, and taxes may be lower. Its disadvantages are that the sole owner incurs all losses (if there are any), has unlimited liability, has limited funds, and may have limited skills to run the entire business.

2 A partnership has two or more co-owners who may manage the firm as well. It can allow for more financial support by owners than a sole proprietorship, but it also requires that control and profits of the firm be shared among owners. In addition, its owners have unlimited liability.

3 A corporation is an entity that is viewed as separate from its owners. Owners of a corporation have limited liability, while owners of sole proprietorships and partnerships have unlimited liability.

4 The return and the risk from investing in a business are dependent on the form of business ownership. The return on equity is higher if a business can use a limited amount of equity. Sole proprietorships have the potential to generate a high return to the owners because there is only one owner. However, they are generally more risky because of their limited funding, among other reasons. A business can reduce its risk by allowing additional owners, but the tradeoff is that its profitability is spread among all the owners.

5 The common methods by which people can obtain ownership of existing businesses are as follows:

▶ Assuming ownership of a family business

▶ Purchasing an existing business

▶ Franchising

Assuming the ownership of a family business is desirable because a person can normally learn much about that business before assuming ownership. Many people are not in a position to assume a family business, however. Before purchasing an existing business, one must estimate future sales and expenses to determine whether making the investment is feasible. Franchising may be desirable for people who will need some guidance in running the firm. However, the franchisee must pay annual fees to the franchisor.

How the Chapter Concepts Affect Business Performance

A firm's decisions regarding the business ownership concepts summarized here can affect the performance of a business. The partnership allows greater access to funding than the sole proprietorship. It also allows more people who can make business decisions, but that may also result in more conflicts about decisions. The corporation allows greater access to funding than either the partnership or the sole proprietorship. A larger number of investors can spread the risk, as business losses are shared. However, when more investors invest in a business, the business profits are spread to a greater degree among investors.

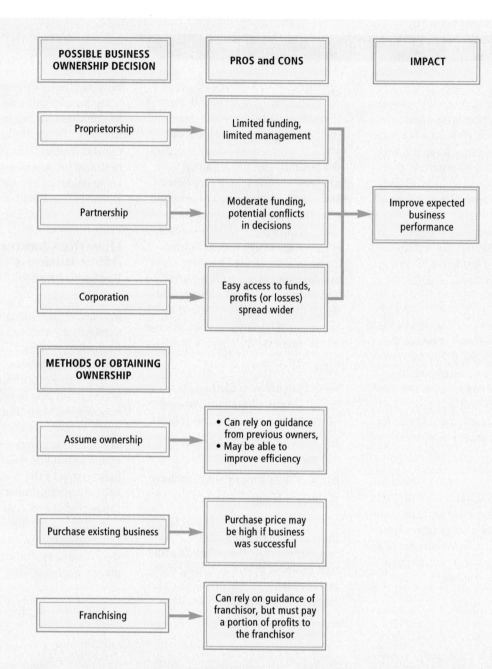

POSSIBLE BUSINESS OWNERSHIP DECISION	PROS and CONS	IMPACT

Proprietorship → Limited funding, limited management

Partnership → Moderate funding, potential conflicts in decisions → Improve expected business performance

Corporation → Easy access to funds, profits (or losses) spread wider

METHODS OF OBTAINING OWNERSHIP

Assume ownership → • Can rely on guidance from previous owners, • May be able to improve efficiency

Purchase existing business → Purchase price may be high if business was successful

Franchising → Can rely on guidance of franchisor, but must pay a portion of profits to the franchisor

Key Terms

agency problem   167
bylaws   164
capital gain   170
chain-style business   176
charter   164
corporation   164
distributorship   176
equity   172
franchise   176
franchisee   176

franchisor   176
general partners   162
general partnership   162
going public   166
limited liability company
    (LLC)   163
limited partners   162
limited partnership   162
manufacturing arrangement   177
partners   162

partnership   162
privately held   165
publicly held   166
return on equity (ROE)   172
risk   173
S-corporation   163
sole proprietor   160
sole proprietorship   160
unlimited liability   161

Review & Critical Thinking Questions

1. What are the key differences among a sole proprietorship, a partnership, and a corporation?

2. List and briefly describe the advantages and disadvantages of a sole proprietorship.

3. Distinguish between a general partnership and a limited partnership.

4. What is an S-corporation? What are the advantages of an S-corporation?

5. What is a limited liability company (LLC)? What are the differences between an S-corporation and a limited liability company?

6. How can stockholders earn a return on their investment?

7. Identify and explain the differences between privately held and publicly held corporations.

8. List and briefly describe the advantages and disadvantages of a corporation.

9. Explain why stockholders are concerned that managers may not always act in their best interests.

10. Explain the difference between the corporate tax rate and the personal tax rate.

11. Describe a franchise and identify its advantages and disadvantages.

12. What are B2B franchises? Provide some examples of B2B franchises. Why are B2B franchises popular?

Discussion Questions

1. Assume you are a management consultant. For each of the following situations, recommend an appropriate form of business ownership:

   a. Four physicians wish to start a practice together, and each wants to have limited liability.

   b. A friend wants to open her own convenience store.

   c. An entrepreneur wants to acquire a large steel business in the United States.

   d. Five friends want to build an apartment complex and are not concerned about limited liability.

2. What basic steps must be undertaken to organize a corporation in your state?

3. Discuss and give examples of what you believe is the most common form of business ownership in your hometown.

4. Assume you are starting your own business. What decisions do you have to make concerning the type of ownership and control of your business?

5. Discuss the advantages and disadvantages of starting your own business compared to buying a franchise.

6. You are operating a sole proprietorship with a single product line, men's hair shampoo. Explain how a recession would affect your business versus a business with a more diversified product line.

7. Discuss the benefits and costs of taking on other equity owners in your business.

8. Discuss the advantages of a corporation. What aspects of control are given up when the firm uses the corporate ownership form?

9. What are the disadvantages of unlimited liability in a sole proprietorship. What happens to the personal wealth of the owner if he or she is sued? Would this discourage you from starting up a sole proprietorship?

10. Discuss the characteristics of an S-corporation and a corporation. What benefits apply to the owners of an S-corporation that are not available for other forms of business ownership?

It's Your Decision: Ownership at CHC

1. One advantage of a partnership is that it allows partners to focus on their respective specializations. Should this advantage cause Sue Kramer to search for a partner for her health club business?

2. How will CHC be taxed, given that Sue plans to be the sole owner?

3. What is an advantage for Sue of starting her own health club instead of operating a franchise health club?

4.   Explain how Sue's decision to be the sole owner will affect her marketing and production plans. How might the marketing and production plans be different if she had invited several investors to invest substantial amounts of equity in her business?

5.   A health club differs from manufacturing firms in that it produces a service rather than products. Why might Sue need other partners if she had established a manufacturing firm instead of a health club?

Investing in a Business

Using the annual report of the firm in which you would like to invest, complete the following:

1   Each annual report contains an income statement, which discloses the firm's earnings before taxes, its taxes, and its earnings after taxes over the most recent year. Search for the table called "Income Statement" and determine your firm's earnings before taxes, taxes paid, and earnings after taxes last year. What proportion of your firm's earnings were eventually paid as taxes?

2   Is your firm involved in franchising? If so, describe its franchises. Check its website to obtain franchise information.

3   Describe any conditions mentioned in the annual report that expose the firm to risk.

4   Explain how the business uses technology to provide information about its form of business ownership. For example, does it use the Internet to disclose the form of business ownership it uses?

5   Go to http://hoovers.com and locate the NEWS SEARCH. Type in the name of the firm in the space provided, and review the recent news stories about the firm. Summarize one recent news story about the firm that applies to one or more of the key concepts in this chapter.

Case: Deciding the Type of Business Ownership

Paul Bazzano and Mary Ann Boone are lifelong friends and have decided to go into business. They are not sure what form of business ownership and control to use. Paul would like to invest his savings of $25,000, but he does not want to take an active role in managing the day-to-day operations of the business. Mary Ann is a self-starter, enjoys cooking and baking, and has a vast number of pizza recipes. An existing pizza business is for sale for $50,000. Paul and Mary Ann both like the idea of investing in a business. Mary Ann has $5,000 she would like to contribute and believes that buying an existing business has certain advantages. She likes the idea that Paul will not be an active owner and that she will have full control of the pizza operation.

The existing business has sales of $150,000 and generates earnings after taxes of $32,500. Mary Ann believes the business can be expanded and foresees future growth by expanding into different locations throughout the Boston area. She projects two more stores in the next five years.

Questions

1   What form of business ownership would you recommend for this business?

2   Would Mary Ann's form of ownership be any different from Paul's?

3   How could Paul and Mary Ann determine the return on their investment after their first year of business? Assume that Paul and Mary Ann can borrow the remaining $20,000 needed to finance the purchase when answering this question.

4   Describe the risk of this business.

Video Case: Organization of Annie's Homegrown Business

When Ann Whithey realized that consumers did not like the orange color of popcorn, she started a business to produce and sell white popcorn. She later decided to expand into other "smart foods" and obtained the necessary financing from external investors, called venture capitalists. In 1989, Ann decided to sell her firm and start another business that would focus on natural, organic foods.

Ann initially established her business as a sole proprietorship. She focuses her time on being creative rather than on the day-to-day operations of the business and does not go to sales meetings. The small size of Annie's Homegrown allows for considerable flexibility and enabled the company to get new products to market quickly. At the same time, because of the company's small size, creditors ask Ann herself to personally guarantee repayment of the loans when the company obtains financing.

Because of the popularity of the products, Annie's Homegrown expanded substantially. It went public in 1996, allowing individual investors to invest in the firm, and providing Annie's with funds to support its growth.

Questions

1. What are the costs and benefits if Ann Whithey decided to keep her business small rather than expand into a very large business?

2. What kinds of conditions might lead Ann to expand her business by raising equity capital?

3. Why might Ann prefer to obtain funds by borrowing rather than than through issuing stock?

4. When Ann needed funding in the earlier years of her business, she relied heavily on borrowed funds. In 1996, her firm raised funds through the issuance of stock to the public. Why do you think that Ann was able to more easily raise funds through her stock offering in 1996 than if she attempted that financing strategy in the earlier years of her business?

5. Do you think Ann would benefit from franchising her business?

Internet Applications

1. http://www.alllaw.com/articles/business_and
_corporate/article3.asp

Examine this website. What differences are presented here between S-corporations and corporations? What similarities are presented? What are the costs and benefits of both forms of business ownership?

2. http://smallbusiness.yahoo.com/resources/
bizFilings.php?mcid=1&scid=60

Examine the information on different business forms of business ownership. Click on "Detailed State Incorporation" information. How do different states handle incorporation laws? What basic facts of incorporating can you identify under the Incorporation FAQ? What are the basic steps of forming a nonprofit corporation?

Dell's Secret to Success

Go to http://www.reportgallery.com and review Dell's most recent annual report. Also, go to Dell's website (http://www.dell.com) and in the section "about Dell," review the background material about Dell that relates to this chapter.

Questions

1. Could Dell have achieved its existing level of business if it had been organized as a partnership instead of a corporation? Explain.

2. When Michael Dell created the company in 1984, do you think Dell was a corporation?

3. What do you think caused Dell to become a corporation?

In-Text Study Guide

Answers are in Appendix C at the back of book.

True or False

1. The legal requirements for establishing a sole proprietorship are very difficult.

2. One advantage of sole proprietorships is that this form of ownership provides easy access to additional funds.

3. Limited partners are investors in the partnership and participate in the management of the business.

4. The limited liability feature is an advantage of owning a sole proprietorship.

5. When a corporation distributes some of its recent earnings to stockholders, the payments are referred to as capital gains.

6. If the board of directors becomes displeased with the performance of the key officers, the board has the power to replace them.

7. Publicly held corporations can obtain additional funds by issuing new common stock.

8. Publicly held corporations are required to disclose financial information to the investing public.

9. To incorporate a business, one must adopt a corporate charter and file it with the state government where the business is to be located.

10. The form of ownership of a firm should not be changed unless there are major tax advantages.

11. Distributorships, chain-style businesses, and manufacturing arrangements are all common types of franchises.

Multiple Choice

12. When entrepreneurs establish a business, they must first decide on the form of:
    a) divestiture.
    b) global expansion.
    c) joint venture.
    d) ownership.

13. The following are possible forms of business ownership except for a:
    a) sole proprietorship.
    b) partnership.
    c) bureaucracy.
    d) corporation.

14. Joe wants to form his own business. He wants to get started as quickly and inexpensively as possible and has a strong desire to control the business himself. He is confident he will be successful and wants to keep all the profits himself. Joe's goals indicate he would probably choose to operate his business as a(n):
    a) limited partnership.
    b) limited liability company.
    c) S-corporation.
    d) franchise.
    e) sole proprietorship.

15. A business owned by a single owner is referred to as a:
    a) partnership.
    b) sole proprietorship.
    c) limited partnership.
    d) corporation.
    e) subchapter S-corporation.

In-Text Study Guide

Answers are in Appendix C at the back of book.

16. A disadvantage of a sole proprietorship is that:
    a) sole proprietors have very little control over the operations of the business.
    b) sole proprietors have unlimited liability.
    c) it is more difficult and expensive to establish than other forms of business.
    d) its earnings are subject to higher tax rates than other forms of business.
    e) sole proprietors are required to share the firm's profits with employees.

17. Partners have unlimited liability in a:
    a) general partnership.
    b) corporation.
    c) limited partnership.
    d) cooperative.

18. In a limited partnership:
    a) all partners have limited liability.
    b) the partnership exists only for a limited time period, or until a specific task is accomplished.
    c) the limited partners do not participate in management of the company.
    d) the partners agree to operate in a limited geographic area.
    e) no more than 100 partners may invest in the company at any one time.

19. When two or more people, having complementary skills, agree to co-own a business, this agreement is referred to as a:
    a) partnership.
    b) sole proprietorship.
    c) cooperative.
    d) corporation.
    e) joint venture.

20. A firm that has 100 owners or less and also meets other criteria may choose to be a so-called:
    a) cooperative.
    b) proprietorship.
    c) joint venture.
    d) S-corporation.
    e) bureaucracy.

21. A general partnership that protects a partner's personal assets from the negligence of other partners is called a:
    a) limited liability company.
    b) cooperative.
    c) private corporation.
    d) master limited partnership.
    e) protected partnership.

22. A corporation is:
    a) easier to form than other types of businesses.
    b) a state-chartered entity that is legally distinct from its owners.
    c) a business that is owned and operated by a government agency.
    d) a form of business that is legally exempt from paying taxes on earnings.
    e) simply another term for a large sole proprietorship.

23. The ___ has the most potential for raising a large amount of funds:
    a) proprietorship.
    b) corporation.
    c) limited partnership.
    d) unlimited partnership.
    e) S-corporation.

In-Text Study Guide

Answers are in Appendix C at the back of book.

24. Important aspects of a corporation, such as the name of the firm, information about the stock issued, and a description of the firm's operations, are contained in a:
    a) mission.
    b) policy.
    c) charter.
    d) plan.
    e) venture.

25. The members of the board of directors of a corporation are chosen by the corporation's:
    a) president and chief executive officer.
    b) creditors.
    c) general partners.
    d) stockholders.
    e) charter members.

26. When ownership of a small corporation is restricted to a small group of investors, it is:
    a) publicly held.
    b) government owned.
    c) bureaucratic.
    d) privately held.
    e) perfectly competitive.

27. When a corporation's shares can be easily purchased or sold by investors, it is:
    a) publicly held.
    b) privately held.
    c) institutionalized.
    d) monopolized.
    e) franchised.

28. People become owners of a corporation by purchasing:
    a) shares of stock.
    b) corporate bonds.
    c) retained earnings.
    d) inventory.
    e) accounts receivable.

29. Agency problems are least likely in:
    a) sole proprietorships.
    b) limited liability companies.
    c) general partnerships.
    d) publicly held corporations.
    e) privately held corporations.

30. When stockholders of a corporation sell shares of stock for more than they paid for them, they receive a:
    a) dividend.
    b) premium.
    c) capital gain.
    d) discount.
    e) stock option.

31. The return on investment in a firm is derived from the firm's ability to earn:
    a) assets.
    b) liabilities.
    c) profits.
    d) expenses.

32. The total amount invested in a company by its owners is called:
    a) the corporate margin.
    b) equity.
    c) working capital.
    d) the stock premium.
    e) treasury stock.

33. The degree of uncertainty about future earnings, which reflects an uncertain return to the owners, is known as:
    a) certainty.
    b) profits.
    c) risk.
    d) equity.
    e) dividends.

In-Text Study Guide

Answers are in Appendix C at the back of book.

34. An arrangement whereby business owners allow others to use their trademark, trade name, or copyright under specified conditions is a:
    a) franchise.
    b) labor union.
    c) bureau.
    d) joint venture.
    e) cartel.

35. A business that is allowed to use the trade name of a company and follows guidelines related to the pricing and sales of the products is a:
    a) joint venture.
    b) monopoly.
    c) chain-style business.
    d) sole proprietorship.

36. All of the following are common types of franchise arrangements except:
    a) business agencies.
    b) chain-style businesses.
    c) manufacturing arrangements.
    d) distributorships.

37. Sharing profits and less control of the business ownership are two common disadvantages of:
    a) sole proprietorships.
    b) downsizing.
    c) divestiture.
    d) franchising.

38. Advantages of business-to-business franchises include all of the following except:
    a) tax advantages.
    b) smaller initial investment.
    c) ability for home-based work.
    d) substitution of computer technology for employees.

Chapter

6

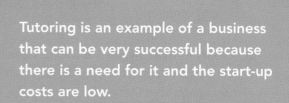

INDEX STOCK IMAGERY

Tutoring is an example of a business that can be very successful because there is a need for it and the start-up costs are low.

The Learning Goals of this chapter are to:

Identify the advantages and disadvantages of being an entrepreneur and creating a business.

1

Identify the market conditions that should be assessed before entering a market.

2

Explain how a new business can develop a competitive advantage.

3

Explain how to develop a business plan.

4

Identify the risks to which a business is exposed, and explain how they can be managed.

5

Entrepreneurship and Business Planning

Entrepreneurs seek to create a business that will generate profits for themselves. They search for opportunities where they may be able to offer consumers a product or service that is either priced lower or of better quality than what is offered by existing firms. In this way, they may be able to satisfy customers and generate revenue. They also hope to produce the product at a relatively low cost so that their revenue exceeds their cost, resulting in profits.

People do not need to be geniuses to establish their own business ideas. They simply need to recognize the market's need for a particular product or service that they could provide. Consider the case of Rob Mason, who just graduated from college and is considering creating his own business. While in college, he frequently worked as a tutor for students to earn money. He believes that there may be a need for a full-time tutoring business.

Rob needs to make several decisions that will influence the success of his business. Specifically, Rob must:

▶ Determine whether his personality fits the entrepreneurial profile.

▶ Determine how to capitalize on market conditions.

▶ Develop a competitive advantage.

▶ Develop a business plan.

▶ Determine how to manage the risk of his business.

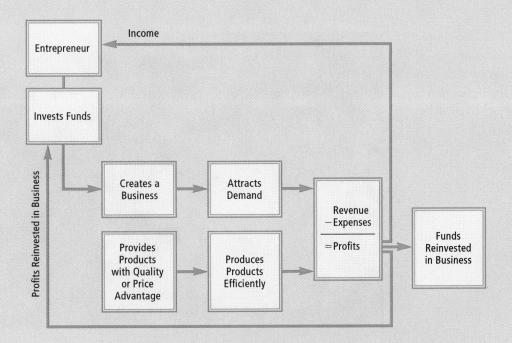

1

Identify the advantages and disadvantages of being an entrepreneur and creating a business.

Creating a New Business

Each year, hundreds of thousands of small businesses are created. Though the largest businesses receive the most publicity, small businesses are vital to the economy. More than 99 percent of all firms have fewer than 500 employees. Small businesses are created by entrepreneurs who have a business idea and are willing to invest their own money to back the idea. Many new businesses are created with a very small amount of money, which limits the amount of funds that the entrepreneur might lose. Here is a brief summary of how three successful small business were created:

▶ Domino's Pizza (of Ann Arbor, Michigan) is a classic example of a business that started with little funding. It was established when Tom Monaghan (a college dropout) and his brother bought a bankrupt pizza parlor in 1960. Tom had to borrow the $500 that he needed to invest in the firm. Later, he bought his brother's interest in the business. Domino's Pizza now generates sales of about $1 billion per year.

▶ Jeremy's MicroBatch Ice Cream (of Philadelphia, Pennsylvania) applied the microbrewery concept to ice cream. It makes ice cream in small quantities and sells it in limited editions. The owner, Jerry Kraus, created the business idea for a class project when he was a student at the University of Pennsylvania.

▶ Glow Dog, Inc. (of Concord, Massachusetts), sells light-reflective clothing for pets. The owner, Beth Marcus, thought of this business idea when she was walking her dog at night and realized that the dog was not visible to passing motorists. After just two years in business, her firm averaged annual sales of more than $1 million.

The point of these examples is that business ideas are not restricted to unusual inventions, as many simple ideas have led to successful businesses. Many business ideas are revisions of a previous business idea that failed.

Domino's Pizza recognized that many consumers wanted their pizza delivered to them, and it provided this service before many of its competitors.

GETTY IMAGES

For example, many restaurant businesses have failed in one location, but succeeded when they were moved to a different location.

Online Resources for Creating a Business

Starting a small business can be a difficult process. Business publications and the Small Business Administration (SBA) have been the usual sources for advice. Financing has primarily been available through local financial institutions and has been relatively difficult to obtain.

The Internet has made this process much easier. A variety of sites provide advice about starting a business. Information on government grants, advice about specific industries, business plan templates, and discussions of legal issues are readily available.

Yahoo!'s Small Business site (http://smallbusiness.yahoo.com) is a good place to find links to more specific information. American Express (http://americanexpress.com/smallbusiness) provides information about building a business. The SBA (http://www.sbaonline.sba.gov) offers information about government programs and other relevant information for small businesses.

Obtaining financing is crucial to beginning any business, and there are sites to facilitate this process, too. Quicken Small Business (http://www.quicken.com/small_business) matches entrepreneurs with lenders. Once a questionnaire has been completed, the site offers advice on the most appropriate financing. It also provides a list of interested banks and the appropriate applications. Garage.com (http://www.garage.com) targets start-up companies in the high-tech sector and matches the companies with investors. The Elevator (http://www.thelevator.com) also matches entrepreneurs with investors and does not restrict itself to high-tech firms. The Internet is always changing, so the sites listed here may become obsolete. Nevertheless, a simple search for small business resources will find numerous sites with much information.

Some of the more useful websites on starting a small business are:

▶ *Yahoo!'s Small Business site (http://smallbusiness .yahoo.com)*

▶ *American Express (http://americanexpress .com/smallbusiness)*

▶ *Small Business Administration (http://www .sbaonline.sba.gov)*

▶ *Quicken Small Business (http://www.quicken .com/small_business)*

Pros and Cons of Being an Entrepreneur

People are not born entrepreneurs. They choose to be entrepreneurs, rather than working as employees for a business. Some of the more important advantages of being an entrepreneur are:

▶ As an entrepreneur, you may possibly earn large profits on your business, and therefore earn a much higher income than if you worked for another business.

▶ You can be your own boss and run the business the way that you want.

▶ Because you are in control, you do not need to fear being mistreated by a boss or being fired.

▶ You have the satisfaction of working in a business that you created, and you will likely be more willing to work because you are directly rewarded for your work in the form of higher business profits.

Being an entrepreneur also has some disadvantages that should be considered:

▶ You may possibly incur large losses and could even lose your entire investment in the business.

The singer Beyonce is an entrepreneur. She has created music that appeals to customers around the world.

AP/WIDE WORLD PHOTOS

▶ Though you may be in control of the business, you have to ensure that the business functions properly. Being in control does not necessarily mean that you can skip work whenever you desire; the income you earn is tied to how well the business is managed on a daily basis.

▶ Though, as the owner of a business, you will not be fired, you could still lose your source of income if the business fails.

Entrepreneurial Profile

Entrepreneurs tend to have specific characteristics that distinguish them from other people. While entrepreneurs may have numerous characteristics, most fit the following profile. Consider whether you fit the entrepreneurial profile.

▶ **Risk Tolerance** Entrepreneurs must be willing to accept the risk of losing their business investment.

▶ **Creativity** Entrepreneurs recognize ways to increase customer satisfaction. They may detect a need by customers for a product or service that does not exist, and then attempt to satisfy that need. Or they may recognize that an existing product or service has deficiencies and attempt to improve on it.

▶ **Initiative** Entrepreneurs must be willing to take the initiative to make their ideas happen. They are able to recognize challenges and deal with them directly. To take the initiative, entrepreneurs need to have ambition and be persistent.

All of these characteristics are needed. Risk tolerance is necessary to invest in a new business. Creativity is needed not just to create a business idea, but to make the idea work. It may be used to detect customers' preferences for a new product, to design a new product that will satisfy customers, to ensure efficient production of that product, and to advertise the product. The business idea is just a part of the overall process necessary to have a successful business, however. Creativity is also required to expand the business's product line and to compete against other firms that produce related products. Initiative and ambition are necessary to obtain information before making decisions about where to produce, how much to produce, how to advertise, and how to obtain financing.

There are creative people who do not have the initiative, ambition, or risk tolerance to capitalize on their creativity. They may believe that a specific new product would be popular, but they lack the initiative, risk tolerance, or ambition to pursue the business idea. Conversely, there are people who have initiative, but lack creativity. They may not be able to recognize the need for a new product or an improved product.

Decision Making

Deciding Whether to Create a New Business

Now that Rob Mason has graduated from college, he wants to establish a business of tutoring business students on a full-time basis (as mentioned at the beginning of the chapter). Rob considers whether his personality traits fit the entrepreneurial profile. He is willing to take the risk that a business he creates might fail. He is very creative and has always had ideas about how businesses could more effectively serve customers. Finally, he has the initiative to implement his business ideas. Rob can start the tutoring business with very limited funds because he can attempt to attract customers (students who need tutoring in business courses) with ads on bulletin boards around the campus. He will also rely on referrals for business. He will not need an office as he can tutor students in a quiet place on campus.

1. What is the service that Rob's business produces?
2. Why does the success of this business depend on customer satisfaction?

ANSWERS: 1. Rob produces knowledge and a learning process. 2. The demand for his business is dependent on referrals, and there will be more referrals if customers are satisfied.

Assessing Market Conditions

Identify the market conditions that should be assessed before entering a market.

Before creating a new business for a particular market, the following conditions in that market should be considered:

▶ Demand

▶ Competition

▶ Labor conditions

▶ Regulatory conditions

Demand

Every product has its own market, where there are consumers who purchase the product and businesses that sell the product. In the market for personal computers (PCs), there is demand by millions of people for PCs, and there are many businesses (such as Dell and Hewlett-Packard) that produce PCs to accommodate that demand. There is also a market for services such as those provided by hairstylists, dentists, and mechanics. Since these services cannot be shipped, the demand for services within an area is accommodated by firms within that area. For example, the entire demand for auto mechanic services in a specific small town may be accommodated by a total of three auto mechanic businesses. Thus, there are many markets for a single service, with each market representing a specific area.

Over a given time period, firms in a specific market can perform much better than others because the total demand for the products in that market is high. The demand for most products is partially influenced by general economic conditions because consumers tend to buy more products and services when the economy is strong and they have a good income. The demand is also influenced by conditions within the specific market of concern. The demand for baby clothes is highly dependent on the number of children that are born. The demand for hotels in Florida during the winter is partially dependent on the weather in the northern states. In cold winters, more tourists travel to Florida.

The demand within a particular market changes over time. When it increases, the businesses within that market tend to benefit because their sales increase. Entrepreneurs tend to develop new businesses in markets where there is a strong demand so that they can benefit from that demand.

Just as an increase in demand is beneficial to firms in that market, a decline in demand has adverse effects. Consider the case of Bell Sports Corporation, which was once the largest producer of motorcycle helmets. It experienced a decline in business because the demand for these helmets

Bell Sports Corporation shifted from its initial product of motorcycle helmets toward bicycle helmets and is always attempting to refine its helmets to serve the preferences of its customers.

leveled off. As the demand for bicycles increased, Bell switched its production process to make bicycle helmets instead. It also began to produce other bicycle accessories, such as child seats, safety lights, and car racks. In this way, it diversified its product line so that it was not completely reliant on its bicycle helmet business.

Competition

market share
a firm's sales as a proportion of the total market

Each business has a **market share,** which represents its sales volume as a percentage of the total sales in a specific market. If the total sales in the market for a particular product are $10 million this year, a firm that experienced sales of $2 million has a market share of 20 percent (computed as $2 million divided by $10 million). That is, the firm has 20 percent of the market.

If the competition within a particular market is limited, firms can more easily increase their market share and therefore increase their revenue. In addition, they may also be able to increase their price without losing their customers. Therefore, entrepreneurs prefer to pursue markets where competition is limited.

When competition in a particular market increases, it can reduce each firm's market share, thereby reducing the quantity of units sold by each firm in the market. Second, a high degree of competition may force each firm in the market to lower its price to prevent competitors from taking away its business. Consider the intense competition recently in the market for long-distance phone services.

Firms that compete within a market for a particular product or service typically want to increase their market share. However, all firms cannot increase their share simultaneously. One firm's increase in market share occurs at the expense of another firm's decline in market share. For example, suppose that in a particular market (such as a small town), there will be a total of 6,000 visits to dentists this year. That is, the total demand for dentistry services in one year is 6,000. At this time, there are two dentists in the market. If a new dentistry business enters the market, any customers that it attracts will represent a reduction in business for the other two dentists. As a new business penetrates (enters) a market, it takes a portion of the market from other firms. Thus, it gains market share, while other firms may lose market share. Since its competitors prefer not to give up any of their market share, they may use various business strategies to counter the entrance of a new business into the market. It is difficult for a new business to continually increase its market share, especially when additional new businesses enter the market.

segments
subsets of a market that reflect a specific type of business and the perceived quality

Competition within Segments   Each market has **segments,** or subsets that reflect a specific type of business and the perceived quality. Thus, a market can be narrowly defined by type of business and quality. Segmenting the market in this way allows a firm to identify its main competitors so that they can be assessed.

A market can be segmented by specific types of customers. For example, in the car rental market, some firms (such as Hertz) focus heavily on business customers, while others (such as Dollar and Payless) focus more on individuals who are on vacation. Thus, an entrepreneur who plans to create a new car rental business must decide which segment to enter. This decision will affect the types of customers that it targets for its business.

SMALL BUSINESS SURVEY

Competition

Based on a recent National Small Business poll conducted for the NFIB Research Foundation, small businesses see their main competition as shown below:

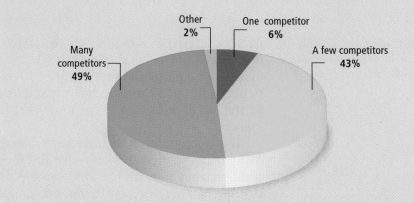

In general, most small businesses are concerned about more than one competitor. When asked how the number of competitors has changed in the last three years, the small businesses responded as follows:

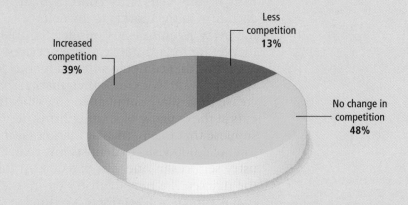

When asked where their main competition is located, the small businesses responded as follows:

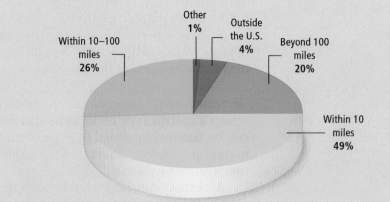

When asked about exposure to competition from Internet and mail-order companies, 9 percent of small businesses stated that they faced significant competition from this type of company, while 16 percent stated that they faced marginal competition from this type of company.

Global Business

Assessing a Market from a Global Perspective

When U.S. firms engage in international business, they must consider the segments within the foreign countries of concern. A specific product that is classified in a specific segment in the United States may be classified in a different segment in other countries. A product that is perceived as an inexpensive necessity in the United States may be perceived as an expensive luxury product in less-developed countries. U.S. firms may revise the quality and price of their products to satisfy a particular market segment. For example, household products that U.S. consumers view as basic necessities may not be affordable to consumers in some less-developed countries, so entrepreneurs considering producing such products would need to revise their strategies for competing in those markets. They may need to price their products low enough in those countries to attract demand.

Exhibit 6.1

Identifying Market Segments

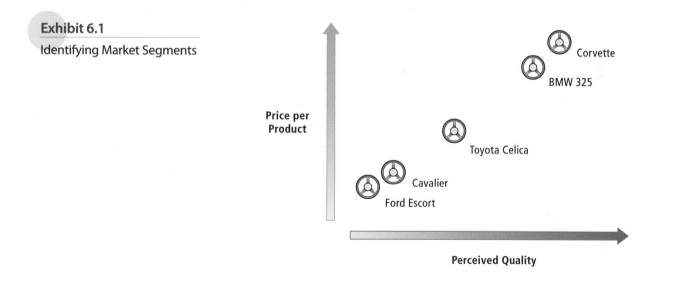

A market may also be segmented by quality. Exhibit 6.1 shows different quality segments (based on customer perceptions) in the market for small cars. Each type of car in this market is represented by a point. Some cars, such as the BMW and the Corvette, are perceived to have high quality (measured according to engine size and other features that customers desire) and a relatively high price. Other cars have a moderate quality level and a lower price, such as the Toyota Celica. The Ford Escort and the Chevy Cavalier represent cars in a lower quality and price segment. Because each consumer focuses only on one particular market segment, the key competitors are within that same segment. For example, the Escort and Cavalier are competitors within the low-priced segment. The Escort is not viewed as a competitor to the higher-priced cars. If a car company wants to produce a new small car, it assesses the competition according to the segment that it plans to target.

Unionized businesses are commonly subjected to strikes by their workers.

GETTY IMAGES

Labor Conditions

Some markets have specific labor characteristics. The cost of labor is much higher in industries such as health care that require specialized skills. Unions may also affect the cost of labor. Some manufacturing industries, particularly those in the northern states, have labor unions, and labor costs in these industries are relatively high. Industries that have labor unions may also experience labor strikes. Understanding the labor environment within an industry can help an entrepreneur estimate labor expenses and decide whether a new business could produce products at lower costs than existing firms.

Regulatory Conditions

The federal government may enforce environmental rules or may prevent a firm from operating in particular locations or from engaging in particular types of business. For example, Blockbuster is affected by state and federal regulations regarding advertising, consumer protection, provision of credit, franchising, zoning, land use, health and safety, and working conditions.

Although all industries are subject to some form of government regulation, some industries face especially restrictive regulations. Automobile and oil firms have been subject to increased environmental regulations. Firms in the banking, insurance, and utility industries have been subject to regulations on the types of services they can provide. Companies such as Amazon.com that rely heavily on the Internet for their business are exposed to some additional regulations governing the Internet and e-commerce. For example, they could be affected by laws regarding the protection of consumer data. If more regulations are implemented to ensure greater protection, the costs to Amazon.com of running its business could increase. Entrepreneurs who wish to enter any industry must recognize all the regulations that are imposed on that industry.

Firms that are already operating in an industry must also monitor industry regulations because they may change over time. For example, recent reductions of regulations in the banking industry have allowed banks more freedom to engage in other types of business. Some banks have attempted to capitalize on the change in regulations by offering new services.

SMALL BUSINESS SURVEY

Impact of Regulations on Small Businesses

In a recent National Small Business poll conducted for the NFIB Research Foundation, small business owners were asked if government regulations are a problem. Their responses are shown here:

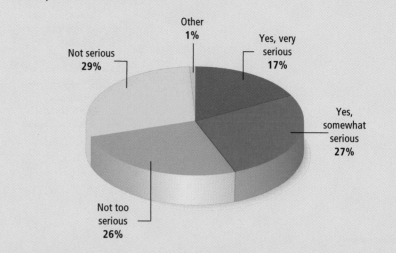

They were also asked the single greatest problem they face as a result of government regulation. Their responses are shown here:

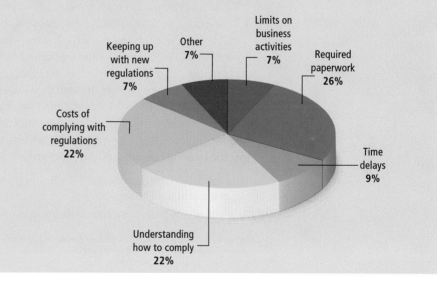

Summary of Market Conditions

An entrepreneur must consider all of the market conditions identified here before deciding to create a new business. The means by which these conditions affect the potential performance of the business are shown in Exhibit 6.2. Demand and competition affect the demand for a firm's products and therefore affect its revenue. Since these conditions also influence the quantity of products that a new business would produce, they also affect operating costs, such as manufacturing and administrative expenses. Any changes in the labor and regulatory environments typically affect the expenses of a new business.

Exhibit 6.2

Effects of Market Conditions
on a Firm's Performance

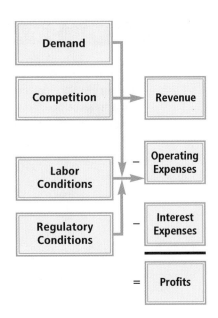

Decision Making

How to Capitalize on Market Conditions

Recall that Rob Mason plans to establish a tutoring business on campus. He has reviewed the market conditions that could affect the success of his business. First, the demand for tutoring services on campus is high. Many students are willing to hire a tutor, especially before exams. The business would face competition, mainly from students who are tutoring part time, just as Rob did when he was in school. However, many of these tutors are not very effective at tutoring, even though they understand the material. Rob has more experience as a tutor and has established a good reputation among business students for his tutoring. The university has no regulations that would prevent Rob from establishing a tutoring business. Based on his overall assessment of the market conditions, he decides that the tutoring business could be successful.

1.   Explain why the demand for Rob's tutoring service may be much greater at some times of the year than others.
2.   Explain why Rob might have difficulty charging a very high price for his tutoring.

ANSWERS: 1. The demand may be high during midterm exams and at the end of a semester but not at other times.   2. Rob's competitors are student tutors who normally do not charge a high price for tutoring, so if he charges a high price, he may lose some business to his competitors.

Developing a Competitive Advantage

3

Explain how a new business can develop a competitive advantage.

Once entrepreneurs have identified and assessed their key competitors, they can search for ways to increase or at least maintain their market share. They must assess their specific market segment to determine whether they have a competitive advantage.

Key Advantages

While businesses use numerous strategies to develop a competitive advantage, most strategies are intended to produce products more efficiently or to produce a higher quality.

Produce Products Efficiently   If a new business can produce a product of similar quality at a lower cost, it can price the product lower than its competitors. This should enable the new firm to take away some of its competitors' market share. The low production cost may result from efficient management of the firm's employees (human resources) and its production process.

Some entrepreneurs attempt to achieve a price advantage even when they do not have a cost advantage. For example, an entrepreneur may notice that the only gas station in a populated area is charging high prices for its gasoline. The entrepreneur may consider establishing a new gas station in the area, with lower prices as its competitive advantage. However, the existing gas station may lower its prices in response to the new competitor. In this example, the entrepreneur's competitive advantage may be eliminated unless it has a cost advantage.

New airlines commonly attempt to achieve a price advantage over their competitors by advertising special fares on various routes over a particular period. The objective is to attract a higher demand by pulling customers away from other airlines. In many cases, the other airlines respond by lowering their airfares by the same amount. If some of the airlines are less efficient, however, they may not be able to continue the low fares for a long period of time (because their costs may exceed the fares charged). Thus, the new firms may drive the inefficient competitors out of the industry.

Produce Higher-Quality Products   If a new business can produce a product of higher quality without incurring excessive costs, it has a competitive advantage over other competitors in the same price range. Various characteristics may cause a product to be of better quality. It may be easier to use,

Some new businesses, like JetBlue, owe part of their success to their ability to provide their services more efficiently than their competition.

LANDOV LLC

SMALL BUSINESS SURVEY

Quality as a Competitive Advantage

In a recent National Small Business poll conducted for the NFIB Research Foundation, small business owners were asked whether achieving the highest quality for their existing products or services is part of their strategy to develop a competitive advantage. Their responses are shown here:

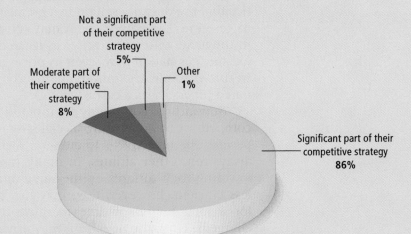

The small business owners were also asked whether better service is part of their strategy to develop a competitive advantage. Their responses are shown here:

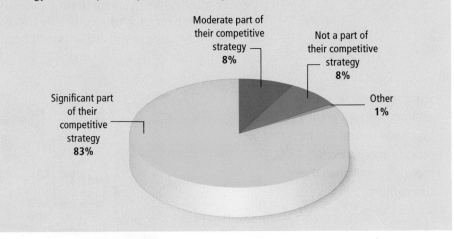

last longer, or provide better service. The specific characteristics that determine perceived quality vary among products. For soft drinks, quality may be measured by taste. For outdoor furniture, quality may be measured by durability. For computers, quality may be measured by ease of use, the service provided, and processing speed. By achieving higher quality, a firm can satisfy customers to a greater degree.

Using the Internet to Create a Competitive Advantage

Many firms rely on the Internet to create a competitive advantage. They establish a website, where they advertise their products. Web-based businesses can accept credit card payments online for their products and then ship the products to customers. Some Web-based businesses rely completely on their website for all of their business, while other Web-based businesses rely on their website to complement their existing operations.

Advantages of a Web-Based Business   One of the most important advantages of a website is that it may be able to replace a store. Amazon.com's website serves as a great example of how a website can provide personalized service to customers. The site allows customers to use a search term to browse existing books for sale and to access information and opinions by previous purchasers about any book. The site can also inform customers about other books that are related to the book they are viewing. It can even remind them about other books that they have purchased recently. In many ways, the site provides personalized service beyond what you would normally expect to receive in a bookstore.

A business website can be especially effective in reducing expenses when it provides services in the form of information. Many travel services such as flights, hotel rooms, and car rentals can be easily booked online. Some travel agencies do all of their work through their website, while others use the website to complement their existing shops. Hotels, airlines, and car rental agencies rely on some travel agencies to book reservations. In addition, they have established their own websites so that customers can make reservations there.

Consider a business website that can fulfill orders by customers online. If the website is used instead of a physical store, the business avoids the high cost of renting store space. Consequently, a website creates opportunities for many entrepreneurs who cannot afford to rent space. It may also avoid the cost of employees who would be needed to accept payments in the store or serve customers.

Another benefit of a Web-based business is that it can reach additional customers and therefore increase the revenue that the business generates. Some websites focus on providing information about what the business sells. Car dealers offer information about their latest models. Restaurants provide updates on their menus. Many retail stores do not view the Internet as a perfect substitute for the store, however, because some shoppers

Some businesses, such as DeliveryWine.com have used the Internet to take orders and deliver products. This allows consumers to shop from their computers.

still prefer to shop at a store. Nevertheless, by establishing a website, stores can appeal to other shoppers who have no interest in going to a store. Furthermore, they can advertise their products and attract more customers to the store.

Expenses of a Web-Based Business

Along with the competitive advantages, some expenses are associated with a Web-based business. First, there is the cost of developing a website and installing a shopping cart system on the site to accept orders. A Web design firm may charge as little as $500 to develop a basic website for a business, but a very comprehensive website can cost more than $20,000.

Second, a firm is needed to screen the credit card payments and ensure that the customers are using legitimate credit cards. This firm will accept payment and deposit the funds received into a bank account established by the business. It will charge a monthly fee for its services. In addition, the business will have to pay fees to credit card sponsors (MasterCard, Visa, etc.), such as 3 percent of the payments.

Third, businesses commonly pay a website firm a small monthly fee to host the site and ensure that the site is constantly accessible to potential clients.

Fourth, a business may need to pay marketing expenses to increase its visibility to customers. A business may rely on search engines (such as Google or Yahoo!) to direct customers to its site, but many other competitive websites may offer similar products. Furthermore, many websites that are not trying to sell products may receive higher priority from search engines. Consequently, a search online by a customer for a particular product may result in a list of more than 1,000 websites. Few customers are likely to search beyond the first 10 sites on the list. Thus, a business may need to hire a Web marketing firm to help it receive higher priority on search engines. Consider how many more customers would visit a website if it is the very first site, rather than the fiftieth site, shown by a search engine in response to a specific search term.

Using SWOT Analysis to Develop a Competitive Advantage

Entrepreneurs commonly use *SWOT analysis* to develop a competitive advantage. The acronym *SWOT* stands for *s*trengths, *w*eaknesses, *o*pportunities, and *t*hreats. Thus, a new business can use SWOT analysis to assess its own strengths (such as a lower price or higher quality) and weaknesses, as well as the external opportunities and threats it faces.

For example, when Amazon.com was created, its strengths included the creativity of its employees and its ability to apply technology. A possible weakness was the lack of traditional retail outlets to sell books (although that is also its strength because Amazon.com can avoid intermediaries). Its opportunities were the potential markets for other related products online and the potential growth in the demand for online services in foreign countries. Its threats included competitors that could create similar online book businesses to provide the same type of services for consumers.

SWOT analysis is useful for existing businesses as well as for new businesses. It can help direct a firm's future business by using the firm's strengths to capitalize on opportunities, while reducing its exposure to threats.

SMALL BUSINESS SURVEY

Technology as a Competitive Advantage

In a recent National Small Business poll conducted for the NFIB Research Foundation, small business owners were asked whether they rely on technology as part of their strategy to develop a competitive advantage. Their responses are shown here:

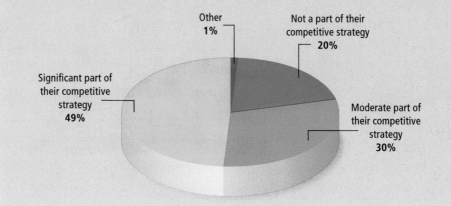

Other
1%

Not a part of their competitive strategy
20%

Significant part of their competitive strategy
49%

Moderate part of their competitive strategy
30%

Decision Making

Developing a Competitive Advantage

As Rob Mason planned his tutoring business, he realized that he would need to provide his service in an efficient manner. He is able to use quiet areas on campus for his tutoring and therefore does not have any business expenses associated with renting an office or facility for his business. He also needs a competitive advantage over other tutors. For each business course in which he can serve as a tutor, he has developed a large number of practice questions. This distinguishes him from other tutors, who typically just try to explain difficult concepts to the students. Rob believes that by helping students work on practice questions, they will be better prepared for exams. He asks them to take his practice exam before he begins tutoring them so that he can focus on the areas where they are weakest. At the end of the sessions, he has them take a practice exam again to demonstrate how much they have learned from his tutoring. Rob's tutoring process is very organized, and he uses this process as his competitive advantage.

1.   How can Rob make students aware of his competitive advantage?
2.   How can Rob determine whether he is providing a quality service for his customers?

ANSWERS: 1. He could advertise the tutoring process that he uses on his website.   2. He could assess their improvement on his practice exams, or on their actual exams, or he could ask each student to rate his tutoring performance after the sessions have been completed.

Developing the Business Plan

Explain how to develop a business plan.

After entrepreneurs assess markets and consider their competitive advantages, they may decide to create a particular business. They will need to develop a **business plan,** which is a detailed description of the proposed business, including a description of the product or service, the resources needed for production, the marketing needed to sell the product or service, and the financing required.

Out of Business

DO YOU HAVE A BUSINESS PLAN THAT SHOWS HOW YOU WILL USE THE FUNDS OUR BANK LENDS YOUR COMPANY?

WHY, SURE! OUR PLAN IS TO BORROW FROM ANOTHER BANK JUST IN TIME TO PAY OFF YOUR LOAN.

LOAN OFFICER

CEO

business plan

a detailed description of the proposed business, including a description of the product or service, the types of customers it would attract, the competition, and the facilities needed for production

The business plan forces the entrepreneurs to think through the details of how they would run the business. Thus, it serves as a checklist to ensure that they have considered all the key functions of the business. Second, the entrepreneurs can provide the business plan to investors who may be willing to serve as partial owners or to various creditors (such as commercial banks) that may be willing to provide business loans. Thus, the business plan should be clear and must convince others that the business will be profitable. If investors do not believe in the business plan, they will be unwilling to invest funds in the business. If creditors do not believe in the plan, they will not supply any loans. In that case, the entrepreneurs will have to rely only on their own funds, which may not be sufficient to support the business.

The business plan's usefulness is not limited to helping the entrepreneurs raise funds to support the opening of the business. The plan will be used as a guide for making business decisions throughout the life of the business. It provides a sense of direction for the business's future development. The success or failure of any firm is partially dependent on its business plan. Many business planning packages and software are available and can be used to develop the business plan. However, the key contents of the business plan require the vision and insight of the entrepreneur. A complete business plan normally includes an assessment of the business environment, a management plan, a marketing plan, and a financial plan, as explained in detail next.

Assessment of the Business Environment

The business environment surrounding the business includes the economic environment, the industry environment, and the global environment.

Economic Environment The economic environment is assessed to determine how demand for the product may change in response to future economic conditions. The demand for a product can be highly sensitive to the

The foreign demand for a particular product sold by a U.S. business is partially dependent on the prevailing values of foreign currencies relative to the dollar.

strength of the economy. Therefore, the feasibility of a new business may be influenced by the economic environment.

Industry Environment The industry environment is assessed to determine the degree of competition. If a market for a specific product is served by only one or a few firms, a new firm may be able to capture a significant portion of the market. One must also ask whether a similar product could be produced and sold at a lower price, while still providing reasonable earnings. A related question is whether the new business would be able to produce a higher-quality product than its competitors. A new business idea is more likely to be successful if it has either a price or a quality advantage over its competitors.

Global Environment   The global environment is assessed to determine how the demand for the product may change in response to future global conditions. The global demand for a product can be highly sensitive to changes in foreign economies, the number of foreign competitors, exchange rates, and international trade regulations.

Management Plan

A management plan, which includes an operations plan, focuses on the firm's proposed organizational structure, production, and human resources.

Organizational Structure   An organizational structure identifies the roles and responsibilities of the employees hired by the firm. The organizational structure of a new factory is more complicated than that of a pizza delivery shop. If the owner plans to manage most of the operations, the organizational structure is simple. Some businesses begin with the owner assuming most responsibilities, but growth requires the hiring of managers. Even if the owners initially run the business, they should develop plans for the future organizational structure. A job description for each employee should be included, along with the estimated salary to be paid to each employee.

Production   Various decisions must be made about the production process, such as the site (location) of the production facilities and the design and layout of the facilities. The location decision can have a major effect on a firm's performance because it influences both the cost of renting space in a building and the revenue generated by the business. The proposed design and layout of the facilities should maximize the efficiency of the space available. This proposal should include cost estimates for any machinery or equipment to be purchased. The cost estimates for factories are normally more complicated than those for retail stores.

The business plan should also include the owners' plans for the business's future growth. As a business grows, it needs more space to allow for more production or to accommodate more customers. Its size will need to be sufficient to allow it to meet its production goals or accommodate all of its customers. It could easily meet these goals by selecting a site with extra space. The more space it obtains, however, the higher will be the cost of leasing the space. The entrepreneurs do not want to pay for space that they will not use. The business's future production is based on demand for its product, which is uncertain. Since the entrepreneurs do not know how much production will be necessary, they face a tradeoff. If they select a site with too much space, the business will not use all of its space. Alternatively, if they select a site that is too small, the business may not be able to produce a sufficient volume to accommodate demand.

Those businesses that require a large investment in facilities to produce their product can survive only if they attract substantial demand for their product. For example, a book publisher needs a printing press. If it prints and sells just a few copies of a book, it will not generate enough revenue to pay for producing the book. Therefore, it needs to sell a large number of the books that it produces so that it can recover the cost of its printing press. In this type of business, there are **economies of scale,** which means that the average cost per unit produced declines as the firm produces more units. Firms that have expensive machinery can benefit from economies of scale. However, they must be able to sell a large volume of their product in order to benefit from economies of scale.

economics of scale
as the quantity produced increases, the cost per unit decreases

Many firms that provide services also have economies of scale. A dental office may spend $30,000 or more on X-ray machines and drills. If the dentist uses the drills only a few times, the cost for each use will be very high. However, if the dentist uses the drills frequently, the cost for each use will be low. To use the drills frequently, the dentist needs many customers. In this way, the dental office can generate enough revenue to recover the cost of the drills.

Human Resources   Many businesses begin with just a single owner who works without any employees. The owner is focused on making the business successful because the owner has invested his or her own funds in the business and is entitled to the profits of the business. As a business grows, it tends to hire more employees. In general, employees are not as concerned about a business as its owners because they have not invested their own money in the firm. Thus, they may not be motivated to ensure that the business is successful.

Managers of a business are supposed to ensure that employees are doing their job. However, if managers have to oversee a large number of employees, they may not be able to adequately monitor the employees. A firm could become inefficient if it has many employees and their job descriptions are not clear. In addition, some managers may decide to hire additional employees to make their own job easier, but these extra employees may not be necessary.

A business must set up a work environment that will motivate the employees. It must also have a plan for monitoring and evaluating employees.

By monitoring and compensating employees properly, the business can ensure that the employees are striving to maximize its performance.

Marketing Plan

A marketing plan focuses on the target market, product characteristics, pricing, distribution, and promotion.

Target Market   A new business may be unknown to its target market and will need to gain the trust of customers. If its owners believe their product is better than other products, they will need to prove that their product is better. Customers are not necessarily going to switch to a new product, especially if they are satisfied with existing products with which they are familiar. New businesses rely on various marketing strategies to attract customers, such as advertising their product, offering a special discount, or even providing free samples to the customers.

Once a new business establishes a base of initial customers, it may benefit from repeat business or referrals. Many new small businesses generate much of their revenue from repeat customers. Businesses that produce services such as hairstyling, maid service, and dentistry can benefit from repeat customers because the service is needed frequently. If the first customers are satisfied, they may not only be repeat customers, but may refer the business to their family members or friends. Then those referrals may purchase the product or service, and if satisfied, they may refer the business to others. The customer base of the business can expand as the referrals continue to spread.

In many cases, a firm will find that it cannot rely only on referrals to achieve the volume of business it desires. It will likely need to spend money on advertising or on other marketing strategies to increase its customer base.

Businesses commonly provide free samples to make consumers more aware of their products. A stormtrooper, one of the Star Wars characters, provides free samples of the Star Wars-themed M&M candies.

LANDOV LLC

Product Characteristics   The business plan should describe the characteristics of the product, with an emphasis on what makes the product more desirable than similar products offered by competitors. A product may be desirable because it is easier to use, is more effective, or lasts longer. Any competitive advantage of this product over similar products should be identified.

Pricing   The proposed price of the product should be included. Prices of similar products sold by competitors should also be mentioned. The price will influence the demand for the product.

Distribution   The business plan should describe the means by which the product will be distributed to the customers. Some products are sold to customers directly, while others are distributed through retail outlets.

Promotion   The business plan should also describe the means by which the product will be promoted. The promotion strategy should be consistent with the customer profile. For example, products that appeal to college students may be advertised in student newspapers.

Financial Plan

The financial plan determines the means by which the business is financed. It also attempts to demonstrate that the creation of the business is feasible.

Financing   The creation of a business requires funds to purchase machinery and materials, rent space, hire employees, and conduct marketing. Most firms rely heavily on funding from the entrepreneurs who established them.

Creditors typically prefer that a business demonstrate that it is capable of covering its loan payments before they will provide a loan. Because a new business does not have a history, creditors may be willing to provide a loan only if it is backed by collateral, such as a building or computers owned by the owner. The creditors will claim the collateral if their loan is not repaid. They may limit the size of the loan to the market value of the owner's collateral.

In addition, creditors will want to look closely at the financial condition of the owners. In some cases, they may require personal financial information that the owners may prefer not to disclose. Creditors may also require that the owners back the loan with their own assets (such as a home). Given the restrictions imposed by many creditors, entrepreneurs may initially attempt to borrow funds from family members or friends who are more willing to provide loans.

Even after a business is established, it may need financing as it grows. The funds may be used to invest in a larger production site or to hire more employees. As time passes, the business's growth should result in higher revenue, and part of that revenue can be used to cover the interest expenses on a loan or to pay off the loan.

Once a business grows and establishes a track record of good performance, it may be able to borrow funds from financial institutions. To obtain a loan from a financial institution (such as a commercial bank), the firm will need to present a detailed business plan. The lending institution assesses the business plan to determine whether the business is likely to be successful and therefore deserves a loan. A business might consider issuing stock only after demonstrating adequate performance for several years.

Funding by the SBA   As mentioned earlier, the Small Business Administration (SBA) has been a key source of funding for new businesses. It is a federal agency that was created in 1953 to assist and protect the interests of small businesses. The SBA relies on financial institutions (such as banks) to provide loans to applicants who qualify, but it sets the financial requirements for obtaining the loans. It backs the loans by guaranteeing a portion of each loan. The lenders are more willing to provide the loans because the SBA promises partial repayment of the loans. Since 1964, the SBA has had a program under which it backs loans to small business owners below the poverty level who do not meet the standard credit and collateral requirements but have promising business ideas. Over time, the SBA has added numerous programs, including one that provides management assistance for small businesses owned by women, minorities, and armed forces veterans.

The SBA also offers the SBA Express program, which is tailored to start-up retail firms that have revenue of $6 million or less and manufacturing firms with less than 500 employees. This program provides a fast response to requests for loans by entrepreneurs. In 2003, about 37,000 loans—about half of all SBA loans—were provided through the SBA Express program. Recently, the volume of micro-business loans (less than $100,000) to small businesses has increased substantially.

Feasibility   Another benefit of developing a business plan is that it forces entrepreneurs to assess the feasibility of their potential business before they invest their money and time in creating it. As briefly described in an earlier chapter, a business's feasibility can be measured by calculating its expected earnings (profits). Earnings are measured as revenue minus expenses, as shown in Exhibit 6.3. The expected revenue to be generated by the business is based on the sales volume (number of units sold) times the price per unit. A firm's revenue is influenced by its marketing. Expenses can be categorized as operating expenses or interest expenses. Operating

Exhibit 6.3

How a Firm's Earnings Are Measured

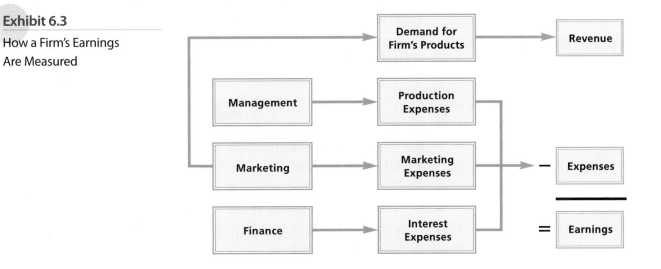

expenses can be broadly defined as the expenses associated with business operations, such as production and marketing expenses. Therefore, operating expenses are dependent on the firm's production and marketing. Interest expenses are the interest payments made to creditors from which funds were borrowed. The interest expenses are dependent on how much money the firm borrows.

When revenue exceeds total expenses, earnings are positive. Entrepreneurs will seriously consider establishing a business only if it is expected to generate positive earnings over time, as those earnings will provide the return on their investment. Entrepreneurs should also consider the risk of a business, which can be measured as the uncertainty of the future earnings. The less uncertainty surrounding the future earnings, the more desirable is the business.

Online Resources for Developing a Business Plan

In the past, putting a business plan together was both time-consuming and expensive. Today, business plan software can make the process much easier. Most of the software packages contain a collection of options, which can be used to create a thorough business plan. The best packages incorporate many of the following capabilities:

▶ **Business Plan Outlines** Packages normally offer one or more outlines of business plans that can be altered to fit most businesses. Some packages take entrepreneurs through a series of questions in order to create a tailor-made plan.

▶ **Text Generation** Much of the information that goes into a business plan is standardized. Business plan software can insert such text directly into the plan, making the appropriate substitutions for company names and products. Once in place, the text can be edited as needed.

▶ **Forecasting** Any business plan software packages should include the ability to create consistent projections. The software package should be able to predict sales and costs in various ways (for example, using percentage growth models, market share models, or values that are individually specified by the planner) and should ensure that interrelated data are consistent. For example, when the planner changes values in a table of projected market shares, forecasted sales in other parts of the document should automatically be updated.

▶ **Graphics** Business plan software offers the ability to create charts of several different types (bar charts, pie charts, line charts) and should also allow users to draw other common charts, such as organizational charts.

▶ **Supplementary Documents** A number of business plan packages offer supplementary documents, such as disclosure agreements, which are often used in conjunction with business plans, although not necessarily as part of the document.

Summary of a Business Plan

The key parts of a business plan are summarized in Exhibit 6.4. Exhibit 6.5 shows the typical sequence of business decisions that are made in

Exhibit 6.4

Contents of a Typical
Business Plan

I.   DESCRIPTION AND OWNERSHIP OF PROPOSED BUSINESS

▶ Describe the product (or service) provided by the proposed business.

II. ASSESSMENT OF THE BUSINESS ENVIRONMENT

▶ *Economic Environment:* Describe the prevailing economic conditions and the exposure of the firm to those conditions.

▶ *Industry Environment:* Describe the competition in the industry and the general demand for the product in the industry.

▶ *Global Environment:* Describe the prevailing global conditions that relate to the business, such as foreign markets where the business may sell products in the future or obtain supplies.

III. MANAGEMENT PLAN

▶ *Organizational Structure:* Describe the organizational structure and show the relationships among the employee positions. This structure should also identify the responsibilities of each position in overseeing other positions and describe the specific tasks and salaries of managers and other employees.

▶ *Production Process:* Describe the production process, including the site, design, and layout of the facilities needed to produce a product. Also, describe the planned amount of production per month or year.

IV. MANAGING EMPLOYEES

▶ Describe the work environment used to motivate employees and the plans for training, evaluating, and compensating employees.

V.   MARKETING PLAN

▶ *Target Market:* Describe the profile (such as the typical age and income level) of the customers who will purchase the product and therefore make up the target market. (Who will buy the product?)

▶ *Product Characteristics:* Explain desirable features of the product. (Why will customers buy the product?)

▶ *Pricing:* Describe how the product will be priced relative to competitors' products. (How much will customers pay for the product?)

▶ *Distribution:* Describe how the product will be distributed to customers. (How will customers have access to the product?)

▶ *Promotion:* Describe how the product will be promoted to potential customers. (How will customers be informed about the product?)

VI. FINANCIAL PLAN

▶ *Funds Needed:* Estimate the amount of funds needed to establish the business and to support operations over a five-year period.

▶ *Feasibility:* Estimate the revenue, expenses, and earnings of the proposed business over the next five years. Consider how the estimates of revenue, expenses, and earnings of the proposed business may change under various possible economic or industry conditions.

Exhibit 6.5

Common Sequence of
Business Decisions Made in
Developing a Business Plan

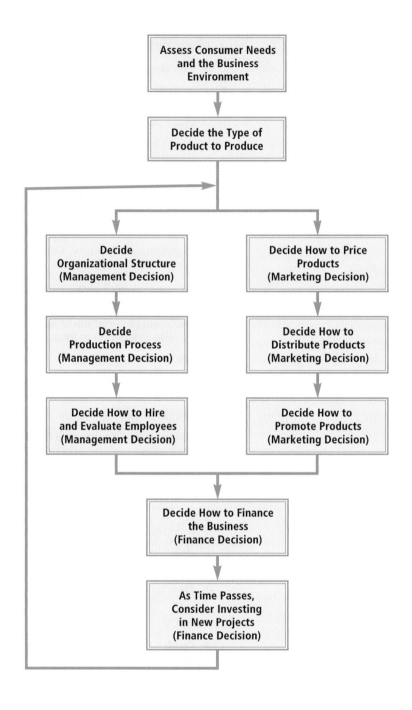

developing a business plan. Many decisions can be made only after the entrepreneur has decided on the type of product or service that will be produced and sold. The management and marketing decisions can be made after identifying the product (or product line). Once all management and marketing decisions are made, the amount of funds needed to support the business can be determined. The financing decision of how to finance the firm is dependent on how much funding is needed. All of these key business decisions must be reassessed periodically as the firm's business grows and its product line expands.

The remaining chapters in this text are organized so that each part of the text represents a part of the business plan. The management plan is dis-

Cross Functional Teamwork

Industry Effects across Business Functions

When a new business is considered, the assessment of a market will vary with the perspective. Entrepreneurs must consider different perspectives. For the purpose of managing production, the focus is on labor costs in the industry of concern. Production costs will also be influenced by the level of technology and regulatory changes in the industry that could require revisions to the production process.

A marketing perspective assesses the competitors in the industry to become aware of the features of competing products. This information is used when developing strategies to make a new product superior to those sold by competitors. The marketing perspective must consider the insight from the production perspective on the expenses that would result from making the product superior.

A financial perspective focuses on determining the amount of funding that will be needed to support the new business, and the possible ways to obtain the funds. It relies on the production perspective for estimates on the amount of funds needed to support the production process. It relies on the marketing perspective for estimates on the amount of revenue that will be generated by the new business and for estimates on the expenses associated with advertising the business. Overall, the entrepreneurs must consolidate the production, marketing, and finance perspectives before they can decide whether it is worthwhile to create a new business.

cussed in Part III, and managing employees is described in Part IV. The marketing plan is discussed in Part V. The financial plan is covered in Part VI. Thus, the key concepts discussed in each part of the text can be applied to develop a specific part of the business plan.

Assessing a Business Plan

Many business ideas that seem reasonable at first may not be undertaken because the entrepreneur has various concerns after developing the business plan. For example, the plan may reveal that the revenue will not be sufficient or the expenses will be too high to make the business worthwhile. Under these conditions, the business idea should be completely discarded. Perhaps one or more aspects of the proposed business need to be changed, and then a new assessment of the revenue and expenses should be conducted to determine whether the business is feasible. Even after a business is created, it must have long-term plans for its production, management of employees, marketing, and financing. Therefore, business planning is not confined to the creation of the business, but must be continued as the business evolves.

SMALL BUSINESS SURVEY

What Are the Major Concerns of Small Businesses?

A survey of small businesses was conducted to determine their major concerns. The businesses were segmented into two groups: those with annual sales of less than $3 million and those with annual sales of more than $3 million. The following table shows the percentage of firms in each group that identified various problems as a serious concern:

Problem	Firms with Less Than $3 Million in Sales	Firms with More Than $3 Million in Sales
Inadequate planning	58%	33%
Inadequate financing	48%	21%
Inadequate managerial skills of some employees in key positions	46%	23%
Not prepared for economic downturns	37%	26%
Inability to respond to market changes	30%	31%
Environmental regulations	29%	38%
Nonenvironmental regulations	18%	22%
Litigation (such as defending against lawsuits)	15%	21%
Employee theft or fraud	13%	11%
Foreign competition	11%	24%

Many of the major concerns detected by this survey have already been discussed in this text; others will be discussed in later chapters. Some of the concerns reflect exposure to economic conditions (economic downturns), industry conditions (regulations), and global conditions (foreign competition). Other concerns focus on the firm's management (planning), marketing (response to market changes), and financing.

Decision Making

Deciding on a Business Plan

Now that Rob Mason has decided to create a tutoring business, he wants to develop a business plan. Because Rob will work full-time at this business, he wants it to grow. He develops a business plan that will satisfy his goals.

Rob will call the business A+ Tutoring. He will not need an office or any other employees initially. He will initially focus on basic business courses, but if the business is successful, he wants to expand into other subjects in which students commonly need tutoring, such as math and science. Rob is not qualified to tutor in these subjects, but he could hire employees who are qualified and train them to apply his tutoring methods with practice exams.

To advertise his tutorial services, Rob will develop a website that will describe his services in detail. He will also post ads on bulletin boards around campus. In addition, he will pay to advertise his tutoring business in the school newspaper on a daily basis. This will be his main method of attracting students.

Rob recognizes that the demand for his services will be higher during midterm and final exams. Therefore, he will offer a price discount for tutorial services at other times during the school year to ensure that he will always have students to tutor.

Eventually, Rob hopes to expand the business beyond tutoring for specific courses. He would also like to tutor high school students who are preparing to take the ACT exams and college business students who are preparing for the GRE or GMAT exams. He would likely need to hire a few employees who have more experience in preparing students for these types of exams. He ultimately hopes to have an office where the employees could tutor the students. If he is successful in achieving this goal, Rob would then like to open A+ Tutoring businesses near other college campuses. Alternatively, he would like to establish a Web-based A+ Tutoring business where students could subscribe to his service and receive practice tests and self-learning tutorials. The Web-based business would not be as personal as his tutoring service, but Rob believes that it could provide effective tutorials and would attract students who can access the Internet. Rob recognizes that he cannot achieve all of his goals immediately, so he decides to achieve them in phases. His first goal is simply to focus on tutoring business students on one campus.

1. What would be the danger if Rob established his A+ Tutoring service on multiple college campuses immediately?
2. A great deal of free information is available to college students about any subject. How might the availability of this free information affect the demand for A+ Tutoring services?

ANSWERS: 1. The danger is that Rob would implement some business ideas without having tested them on a smaller scale. He would need to finance this expansion with borrowed funds without knowing if his business ideas will work. If these ideas fail, his business will fail, and he will be unable to repay the loans. He should experiment with his business ideas on a smaller scale before he expands. 2. Students may prefer to access the free information rather than hire a tutoring service, so the demand for tutoring could decline.

5

Identify the risks to which a business is exposed, and explain how they can be managed.

business risk the possibility that a firm's performance will be lower than expected because of its exposure to specific conditions

Risk Management by Entrepreneurs

As entrepreneurs plan their new business, they recognize that they are exposed to **business risk,** or the uncertainty of the future performance of a business. The future profits of a business are uncertain because of uncertainty surrounding the expected revenue and expected expenses. Some businesses have much more risk than others. For example, a business of tutoring on a college campus has business risk, but the investment of funds to create the business is minimal, so the potential losses are limited. Conversely, consider a business that wants to produce a drug that will cure a particular disease. It must invest substantial funds in laboratories and highly skilled employees to try to develop the drug. This business will perform very well if a cure is found. But if its drug is not effective, the business will have no revenue, will have incurred large expenses, and will likely fail. It is subject to a very high degree of business risk because there is much uncertainty about its future performance.

As part of the business planning process, entrepreneurs must consider the sources of business risk that could cause their business to perform poorly. Some sources of risk such as economic conditions are beyond their control. But many other sources of risk are within their control. Such sources of risk are said to result from firm-specific characteristics. Exhibit 6.6 lists some of the more common firm-specific sources of business risk. Several of these are discussed here, along with strategies that entrepreneurs can use to reduce their exposure. One way that entrepreneurs may reduce their risk exposure is by purchasing insurance; Exhibit 6.7 lists some types of insurance that a firm might purchase.

It may seem that entrepreneurs are being pessimistic if they anticipate conditions that could adversely affect their business. However, any entrepreneurs who ignore possible adverse conditions when planning their

Businesses commonly incur large expenses when attempting to develop new products, especially in the chemical and biotechnology industries.

GETTY IMAGES

business are not being realistic. Proper business planning includes preparing for the possibility of adverse conditions so that the business can survive even if such conditions occur.

Reliance on One Customer

Firms that rely on a single customer for most of their business have a high degree of business risk because their performance will decline substantially if the customer switches to a competitor. For example, a firm may rely on selling some of the products it produces to the federal government. If the federal government reduces its spending, it will order fewer products from the firm. Firms can reduce their reliance on a single customer by attempting to spread the sales of their products across various customers.

Reliance on One Supplier

Firms that rely on a single supplier for most of their supplies may be severely affected if that supplier does not fulfill its obligations. If that supplier suddenly goes out of business, the firm may experience a major shortage of supplies. Firms that use several suppliers are less exposed to the possibility of a single supplier going out of business, because they will still receive their supply orders from the other suppliers.

Reliance on a Key Employee

When a firm relies on a key employee for its business decisions, the death or resignation of that employee could have a severe impact on the firm's performance. Consider a computer repair business that has only one employee who can perform the repairs. If the employee dies or leaves the firm, other employees may not be able to perform this job. Until the employee can be replaced, business performance may decline. Since a business cannot be managed as well following the loss of a key employee, it may be less capable of covering its expenses.

Exhibit 6.6

Exposure to Firm-Specific
Characteristics

Characteristic	How Firm Is Exposed
Limited funding	Limited ability to cover expenses.
Reliance on one product	Revenue will be reduced substantially if there is a large decline in the demand for a single product.
Reliance on one customer	Revenue will decline substantially if the customer no longer purchases the firm's product.
Reliance on one supplier	Potential shortages of supplies if supplier experiences problems.
Reliance on a key employee	Performance will decline if the employee dies, becomes ill, or leaves the firm.
Property losses	Expenses incurred from covering damage to property.
Liability losses	Expenses incurred from covering liability for damage to others or their property.
Employee compensation claims	Expenses incurred from covering compensation claims.

Exhibit 6.7

Some Types of Insurance
a Firm Might Purchase

Type of Insurance	Coverage Provided
Business interruption insurance	Covers against losses due to a temporary closing of the business.
Credit line insurance	Covers debt payments owed to a creditor if a borrower dies.
Fidelity bond	Covers against losses due to dishonesty by employees.
Marine insurance	Covers against losses due to damage during transport.
Malpractice insurance	Covers professionals from losses due to lawsuits by dissatisfied customers.
Surety bond	Covers losses due to a contract not being fulfilled.
Umbrella liability insurance	Provides additional coverage beyond that provided by other existing insurance policies.
Employment liability insurance	Covers claims against wrongful termination and sexual harassment.

Hedging against Losses Resulting from a Key Employee's Death Firms can hedge against losses resulting from a key employee's death by purchasing life insurance for their key employees. The policy identifies the firm as the beneficiary in the event that a key employee dies. Thus, when a key employee dies, this type of insurance provides the firm with compensation, which the firm can use to offset the possible losses or reduced performance. The firm is cushioned from the loss of a key employee and may be able to survive while it attempts to hire a person to fulfill the key employee's responsibilities. Consider an individual who runs a small business and applies for a business loan at a local bank. If the individual is killed in an accident, the business may deteriorate and the loan would not be paid off. A life insurance policy could designate creditors (such as a bank) as the beneficiaries to protect them against such a risk. Using this strategy, the business is more likely to be approved for a loan.

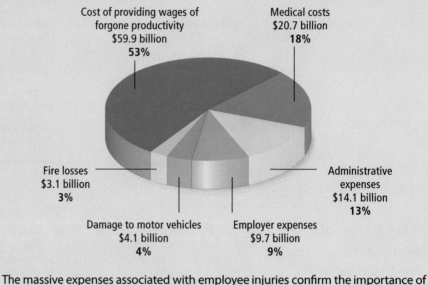

SMALL BUSINESS SURVEY

What Is the Cost of Employee Injuries?

A survey found that employee injuries cost firms about $111.6 billion annually. The following chart shows a breakdown of the expenses incurred by firms:

Cost of providing wages of
forgone productivity
$59.9 billion
53%

Medical costs
$20.7 billion
18%

Fire losses
$3.1 billion
3%

Administrative
expenses
$14.1 billion
13%

Damage to motor vehicles
$4.1 billion
4%

Employer expenses
$9.7 billion
9%

The massive expenses associated with employee injuries confirm the importance of proper risk management to ensure that the work environment is safe.

Hedging against the Illness or Loss of a Key Employee   The illness or resignation of a key employee may also adversely affect the performance of a firm. To try to prevent employees from becoming ill, many firms offer a program that enables their employees to obtain health insurance from health insurance companies. The insurance is generally cheaper when purchased through the firm. Even if a firm provides a health insurance plan for its employees, it may still be affected by the temporary absence of an employee. Firms can reduce the potential adverse effect of an employee's illness by ensuring that more than one employee can perform each task. To attempt to prevent key employee from resigning, firms can offer good compensation and benefits.

Exposure to E-risk

Information technology has created new risks and increased the complexity of risk management. For example, there is the risk that electronic data may be stolen and used in a manner that adversely affects the business. Online banking and securities trading have created large exposures to risk. These services are vulnerable to potential losses from security breaches through network hacking, viruses, and electronic thefts. New businesses can hire firms to establish a computer system that is protected from this exposure. Alternatively, a business may attempt to purchase insurance to cover against loss of business income, damage to reputation, loss of intellectual property, interruption of service liability, and liabilities incurred as a result of electronically published information.

Businesses engaging in e-commerce are exposed to e-risk, which includes the possibility of receiving viruses through the Internet that can destroy computer information.

Scan Result   **Virus W32.*Sircam. Worm@mm* found. File NOT cleaned.**

This file contains a computer worm, a program that spreads very quickly over the Internet to many computers and can delete files, steal sensitive information, or render your machine unusable.

> This attachment has a virus that may infect your computer. It cannot be cleaned.
> We recommend that you DO NOT download this attachment.

Decision Making

How to Manage Risk

As Rob Mason creates his A+ Tutoring business, he considers the key sources of risk that make the future performance of his business uncertain. One of his main concerns is that the performance of his business is completely dependent on his health. If he is unable to work for any reason, his business will not generate any revenue. Rob decides that he will not attempt to hedge this risk as he is young and single and is not supporting a family at this time. He is also concerned about his exposure to e-risk. Any information that he places on his website (such as samples of practice tests) might be stolen and used by other tutors who are trying to increase their tutoring business. Rob decides that he can protect against this risk by limiting the number of sample practice questions that he posts on his website. He decides to use his website primarily to explain his credentials and his tutoring style. If he ever attempts to create a Web-based tutorial business, however, it would be highly exposed to e-risk because competitors might steal the contents and use the material for their own tutorial businesses.

1. How will the revenue of A+ Tutoring be affected in a period when Rob goes on vacation?
2. If Rob has a family in a few years, should he protect against the risk of being out of work due to illness?

ANSWERS: 1. The revenue of the business will be zero in a period when Rob is not working. 2. Rob should reconsider purchasing insurance that would provide financial benefits to his family in the event of his death, and he should also consider purchasing insurance to cover the business against a key employee (himself) being ill and unable to work.

COLLEGE HEALTH CLUB: DEVELOPING A BUSINESS PLAN

Now that Sue Kramer has assessed the environment (from Chapters 1–4) and selected the proprietorship form of business organization (Chapter 5), she needs to develop a business plan for College Health Club (CHC). She can lease space where Magnum Club was located (across the street from the college campus) before it relocated to downtown. Since Magnum purchased new equipment when it moved, it is willing to lease the equipment and weight machines that are still in its previous location for $600 per month or $7,200 per year.

Sue has accumulated savings of $20,000 over the years. Her husband's income will cover their normal household expenses, so she can use the $20,000 to invest in her business. She develops her business plan, which is summarized next.

Business Idea

The business is a health club called College Health Club (CHC) that will be located in a shopping mall just across from the Texas College campus. It will sell memberships on an annual basis. The health club should appeal to the students because it is convenient and would be affordable to them.

Management Plan

▶ *Production Process:* The business will provide its members with health club services, such as access to exercise machines, weight machines, and aerobics classes. It will rent the exercise and weight machines that were previously owned by Magnum Club for $7,200 per year. It will rent the space in the shopping mall across from the Texas College where Magnum Club was located. The rent expense for the facilities will be $5,000 per month, or $60,000 per year. Utility expenses are estimated to be $700 per month, or $8,400 for the first year.

▶ *Organizational Structure:* Sue Kramer will be the president of CHC and will also manage CHC. She will not require a salary as manager of the business, as she wants to limit the salary expenses in the first few years.

Managing Employees

Sue will hire some part-time employees who are majoring in exercise science at Texas College. Typically, one or two employees will be working whenever the health club is open. Sue will train the employees. The total salary expense of CHC is estimated to be $4,000 per month, or $48,000 during the first year.

Marketing Plan

▶ *Target Market:* CHC will primarily target students at Texas College, but will also attempt to attract nonstudents who live nearby. The main competitor is Energy Club, but it is a 20-minute drive from the campus. Based on her survey of students about their interest in joining a health club, Sue is very confident that a minimum of 200 students will become members in CHC's first year of business. Her best guess is that 300 students will become members in CHC's first year. She expects that the membership will grow each year.

▶ *Pricing:* The price for an annual membership will be $500, which is less than the prices of most health clubs in the area.

▶ *Promotion:* CHC will advertise in the Texas College newspaper and use other promotion methods such as posters throughout the campus. Sue estimates that the cost of promoting CHC will be $300 per month, or $3,600 for the first year.

Financial Plan

▶ *Funding:* Sue will invest $20,000 in the business. She expects that she will need an additional $40,000 to run the business. Diane Burke, a relative of Sue's, has offered to lend the business $40,000 if she believes that the business plan is feasible. She will charge an interest rate of 10 percent on the loan. If Sue accepts the funds as a loan, she will have to pay Diane interest of $4,000 at the end of each year (computed as $40,000 × 10%).

▶ *Revenue:* CHC's main source of revenue will be the annual membership fees. Sue estimates that there will be 300 paid memberships over the first year. Since the membership fee is $500, CHC should receive a total of $150,000 in revenue (estimated as $500 × 300 members). The revenue is expected to increase yearly as the number of members increases.

▶ *Expenses:* The monthly expenses expected to be incurred by CHC are summarized in Exhibit 6.8. The expenses are segmented into operating expenses, which result from operating the business, and interest expenses, which are incurred as a result of financing the business. CHC's main operating expenses will be the cost of renting the facilities, salaries, utility expenses, the cost of renting the exercise and weight machines, marketing expenses, and the cost of insuring the business. The total expenses in the first year are expected to be $142,000. The annual expenses are expected to be stable over time.

▶ *Earnings:* CHC's earnings (before taxes) in the first year are derived by subtracting the annual expenses from the annual revenue, as shown in Exhibit 6.9. Since the total revenue should increase over time (due to an increase in memberships) while the expenses remain stable, the earnings should increase over time. The earnings generated by CHC will be reinvested to support future expansion of the existing club or the possible establishment of an additional health club near a different college campus.

Exhibit 6.8

Expected Monthly Expenses of CHC

	Monthly Expenses	Total Expenses in First Year
Operating Expenses		
Rent facilities	$5,000	$60,000
Salaries	4,000	48,000
Utilities	700	8,400
Rent exercise and weight machines	600	7,200
Marketing expenses	300	3,600
Liability insurance	800	9,600
Miscellaneous	100	1,200
Total Operating Expenses		**$138,000**
Interest expenses		4,000
Total Expenses		**$142,000**

Exhibit 6.9

Expected Performance of CHC in the First Year

Revenue	**$150,000**
Total operating expenses	−138,000
Interest expenses	−4,000
Earnings before Taxes	**$8,000**

Summary

1 Entrepreneurs are responsible for creating thousands of new businesses every year. The advantages of starting your own business include being directly rewarded if the business performs well and being your own boss. Being an entrepreneur also has some disadvantages that should be considered; these include the possible loss of your investment in the new business and the heavy responsibility of ensuring that the business functions properly on a daily basis.

To be an entrepreneur, you must

▶ be willing to accept the risk of losing your investment in a new business,

▶ be creative so that you can develop a good business idea, and

▶ be willing to take the initiative to make your business ideas happen.

2 The main market characteristics that an entrepreneur should assess before entering the market are

▶ demand,

▶ competition,

▶ labor conditions, and

▶ regulatory conditions.

The overall demand in the market and the degree of competition affect the demand for a firm's products or services and therefore affect the firm's revenue. The labor and regulatory environments typically affect the firm's expenses. Therefore, the firm's profits resulting from new business are influenced by these market factors.

3 A new business can develop a competitive advantage within its market segment through efficient production (which allows it to charge a lower price) or by offering a product of better quality.

4 A business plan forces an owner of a proposed business to specify all the key plans for the business. The business plan normally consists of (1) an assessment of the business environment; (2) a management plan that explains how the firm's resources are to be used; (3) a marketing plan that explains the product pricing, distribution, and promotion plans; and (4) a financial plan that demonstrates the feasibility of the business and explains how the business will be financed.

Even after the business is established, the business plan is continually revised in response to changes in market conditions, competition, and economic conditions. The parts of this text are organized so that each part represents a part of the business plan. The chapters in each part will cover the concepts that are necessary to develop that part of the business plan.

5 An entrepreneur who creates a business must consider its exposure to various forms of risk, along with methods to protect against those forms of risk. Some of the common forms of risk include heavy reliance of the business on one customer, or one supplier, or one employee. In addition, a business may be exposed to e-risk.

How the Chapter Concepts Affect Business Performance

A firm's decisions regarding both entrepreneurship and planning affect its performance. When entrepreneurs create a business idea, they must make many related decisions that affect the business performance as much as the business idea itself. They need to determine how to implement their business in a manner that can capitalize on market conditions. To attract demand for their products or services, they need to develop a competitive advantage. They also need an effective business plan that guides their business decisions, and they must also determine how they will manage the risk of the business.

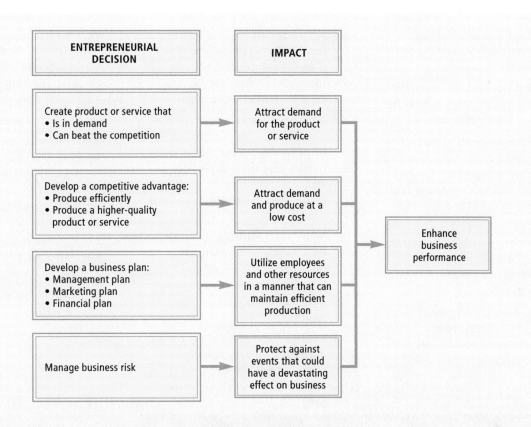

Key Terms

business plan   208
business risk   219

economics of scale   210
market share   197

segments   197

Review & Critical Thinking Questions

1. Apply this chapter to the automobile industry. Identify and explain the main characteristics of the automobile industry that can influence business performance.

2. Explain why the cost of labor in some industries, such as the health-care industry, is so high.

3. Why is government regulation more restrictive in some industries than in others? Provide specific examples.

4. How do you think a firm might monitor the industry in which it operates?

5. Discuss what happens to a firm that has a large market share in a market in which demand suddenly increases.

6. Why is a firm facing less competition in its market more profitable?

7. Identify the steps a firm should take before deciding to compete in a specific market.

8. How are existing firms in a market affected when a new firm with a competitive advantage enters the market?

9. List some characteristics that could create a competitive advantage for a firm.

10. What are the basic market characteristics that influence business performance?

11. Distinguish between the responsibilities of a marketing manager and a financial manager in monitoring a particular industry.

12. How can the government play a role in entrepreneurship?

13. Why do you think that such a large proportion of businesses are small rather than large?

What kinds of small businesses do you see on your way to school?

14. What advice would you give someone starting a new entrepreneurial venture?

15. Where do funds to start a new business come from? What are the advantages and disadvantages of financing a new business with debt?

16. What are the pros and cons of entrepreneurship? Do you think you have the skills required, including risk tolerance, to be an entrepreneur?

17. What are the characteristics of a good entrepreneur? Which of the characteristics are your strengths and weaknesses?

18. Why is it difficult to maintain market share permanently? How does the competitive environment affect a firm's ability to keep its market share high?

19. How does a firm develop a competitive advantage? How can firms establish a reputation for quality, and what impact does such a reputation have on a firm's ability to capture market share?

20. What are the advantages and disadvantages of a Web-based business? What would you consider important elements of a SWOT analysis for a Web-based business?

21. Explain some of the concerns an entrepreneur may have when starting a new business.

22. What is a business plan? Why should a business plan be very clear and precise? Explain what is included in a business plan.

23. What are the three major plans within a business plan?

24. Explain why business plans are closely reviewed by creditors or investors. Are business plans only needed when raising support for the opening of the business? Explain.

25. Describe the components included in a marketing plan.

26. Give a brief description of a typical financial plan for starting a new business.

Discussion Questions

1. Do you believe business enterprise should be regulated by the federal government or that the marketplace should determine prices? Discuss.

2. A group is discussing how competitive forces can be preserved within the marketplace of a free enterprise system. What are your views on the issue?

3. How can a firm use the Internet to determine how its competitors are performing and how they are affected by market conditions?

4. Assume that you are a production manager in the automobile industry. Do you think your operation should be labor-intensive or capital- (machinery) intensive? Discuss.

5. Consider a car that has typically been classified in the low-price segment, but has been unable to compete there because it is priced higher than the other cars in that segment. What alternative strategies are possible for the car as it is redesigned for the next year?

6. How might businesses be affected by labor laws and regulations?

7. When planning a business, what kinds of stakeholders should an entrepreneur consider? How can the entrepreneur meet the needs of the stakeholders and still make a profit?

8. How can entrepreneurs hedge against the loss of a key employee to another company?

9. How might a U.S. firm with no foreign sales or assets be exposed to changes in the global competitive market?

10. How might a Web-based firm attract potential customers? What kinds of challenges might it face in terms of product, price, promotion, and distribution?

11. You have just opened a small pizzeria in your hometown. Since you put up all the funds yourself, you did not develop a business plan for the pizzeria. Discuss the possible disadvantages of this action.

12. How could a potential firm use the Internet to plan its business? How could a firm use the Internet to promote its business once it is established?

13. Wal-Mart is planning to open a new store in your local area. Since Wal-Mart is nationally known, is it necessary for this store to have a marketing plan designed for this particular location?

14. Why would anyone consider life insurance for a business partner? After all, it is simply an expense. Defend your answer.

15. Assume you are an entrepreneur and that your business has only one customer, the federal government. What are the various types of business risks to which your firm is exposed?

IT'S YOUR DECISION: INDUSTRY EXPOSURE AND BUSINESS PLANNING AT CHC

1. Explain how the increased popularity of exercise videos and portable weight machines will affect the number of CHC's memberships, its revenue, and its earnings.

2. How could Sue differentiate her services to maintain her customers (mostly students) even if a new competitor enters the market?

3. How might the degree of competition affect the amount of marketing CHC requires? How might the degree of competition affect the amount of aerobics classes and other health club services produced at CHC?

4. Assuming that the estimated expenses in the first year are $142,000, determine how CHC's estimated earnings before taxes are affected by the following possible industry scenarios:

If a Competing Health Club Is Established within _____ Miles of CHC	Expected Membership at CHC in the First Year	Earnings before Taxes at CHC in the First Year
4	280	_____
7	290	_____
10	294	_____

Explain the relationship between the proximity of the competitor and CHC's expected earnings.

5. A health club differs from manufacturing firms in that it produces a service rather than products. As with most service firms, CHC's main competition would come from competitors based in the same area. Explain why manufacturing firms may be more exposed to competitors that are located far away.

6. How does Sue's marketing plan affect CHC's expenses and revenue?

7. How does Sue's production plan affect CHC's expenses and revenue?

8. Explain how the production plan is dependent on the marketing plan. That is, explain why the decisions as to how much equipment to have and how much space to rent are dependent on the decision regarding the degree to which the health club is marketed.

Investing in a Business

Using the annual report of the firm in which you would like to invest, complete the following:

Questions

1. Describe the competition within your firm's industry. If the annual report does not contain information, try to find a magazine or newspaper article that discusses the competitive environment within your firm's industry. How successful is your firm compared with its competitors?

2. Was your firm's performance affected by industry conditions last year? If so, how?

3. Explain how the business uses technology to assess its industry environment. For example, does it use the Internet to assess the industry environment? Does it use the Internet to assess the performance of its competitors?

4. Go to http://hoovers.com and locate the NEWS SEARCH. Type in the name of the firm in the space provided, and review the recent news stories about the firm. Summarize any (at least one) recent news story about the firm that applies to one or more of the key concepts in this chapter.

Case: Planning a Business

Yahoo!'s original owners were students who created informational websites as a hobby. They realized how valuable this service was to people and turned their hobby into a business. Yahoo! has become a very successful business over a short period of time. It has expanded the information it provides on its website to include stock quotations, sports, weather, Yellow Pages, and business news. Its popularity has generated revenue from firms that pay Yahoo! to advertise their products on its website. Yahoo! is continually changing its website to provide additional information. It attempts to offer whatever information customers want so that it will become even more popular and attract even more advertising revenue. It relies on customer feedback to determine what customers like about its website. It receives a substantial amount of immediate feedback every day in the form of e-mail from its customers.

Questions

1 What do you think Yahoo!'s business plan is regarding its production of a service and how it generates revenue?

2 Given that Yahoo!'s business plan seems to be working, why is it still necessary for Yahoo! to focus on continual improvement based on feedback from its customers?

3 Why might Yahoo!'s business plan change over time?

Video Case: Caribou Coffee

Caribou Coffee operates coffee shops and distributes coffee by partnering with grocery stores and employers and through licensing agreements. It is a leading coffee shop in Minneapolis and is growing in popularity in Atlanta, Washington, D.C., and Chicago. Caribou argues that profits come from two sources—cutting costs and increasing sales. A Caribou manager points out that competent people increase sales in retail shops; thus, if the firm focuses only on profits and ignores its employees, it will not increase its sales. Thus, Caribou recognizes the importance of its employees for its success. Caribou also realizes that it needs to stay focused, and though it monitors competitors such as Starbucks to get ideas, it worries more about making a quality product and improving relationships with customers. Caribou must carefully assess new markets before expanding because there are inefficiencies in creating a new market. The assessment includes evaluating the size of the market, the quality of the market, and the demand for coffee, and determining whether other lucrative locations could lead to expansions in close regional markets. For more information on Caribou Coffee, go to http://www.cariboucoffee.com.

Questions

1 How does Caribou Coffee turn its commitment to its employees into a competitive advantage?

2 What marketing techniques does Caribou use?

3 What problems does Caribou face when entering new markets?

4 What problems did Caribou confront in its Chicago market?

5 What role does brand awareness play in Caribou's success?

Internet Applications

1. http://www.osha.gov

Click on "Small Business" on the left-hand side. What kinds of regulations are imposed by the Occupational Safety and Health Administration? How might these regulations affect labor expenses for firms?

2. http://www.sba.gov/starting_business/planning/basic.html

What services are offered by the Small Business Administration to help entrepreneurs? Click on "Finding a Niche." How can firms use this information to identify a potential market for their products?

3. http://www.bplans.com/dp

Click on "Sample Plans" and then on the business plan of your choice. How do firms describe their business to potential creditors? What keys to success can you identify for the firm you selected?

4. http://www.miracles4fun.com

This is a small entrepreneurial business. What kinds of products does this company produce? What are the strengths, weaknesses, opportunities, and threats (SWOT) that this business faces? How does technology play a role in the success of this business? How can this firm use global business to increase its profits?

Dell's Secret to Success

Go to http://www.reportgallery.com and review Dell's most recent annual report. Also, go to Dell's website (http://www.dell.com) and in the section "about Dell," review the background material about Dell that relates to this chapter.

Questions

1 What is Dell's competitive advantage over its competitors?

2 Explain how Dell benefits from selling products directly to customers rather than relying on retail stores for much of its sales.

3 Explain how Dell's reputation can create a competitive advantage.

In-Text Study Guide

Answers are in Appendix C at the back of book.

True or False

1. A firm can safely conclude that it will perform well over the next year if there are favorable economic conditions in the United States.

2. Total revenue is dependent on the quantity of units sold and the expenses of producing those units.

3. A firm that faces a high degree of competition can sell a low-quality product at a high price and thereby generate a high level of profit.

4. The cost of labor is high in industries that require specialized skills.

5. All industries are subject to some form of government regulation.

6. Market share refers to an individual firm's sales expressed as a proportion of the total market sales.

7. All firms in an industry commonly increase their market share at the same time.

8. The risk to business owners with a firm is limited, because they are guaranteed to receive their initial investment back.

9. Diversification can reduce a firm's exposure to poor performance in a particular market.

10. Improved product quality can create a competitive advantage for a firm.

11. A business plan is intended to provide information for potential investors or creditors of a proposed business.

12. A marketing plan focuses on various decisions that must be made about the production process, such as site location and design and layout of the facilities.

Multiple Choice

13. A market characteristic that influences business performance is:
    a) social responsibility.
    b) competition.
    c) machinery.
    d) inflation throughout the United States.
    e) gross domestic product.

14. As market demand changes, so does the _____ of firms in the industry.
    a) performance.
    b) business ethics.
    c) consumerism.
    d) conservationism.
    e) regulatory environment.

15. Over a given time period, firms in a specific market where the product is desired by consumers can perform better than firms in other markets. This performance difference is due to differences in:
    a) market supply.
    b) market share.
    c) equilibrium price.
    d) market demand.
    e) industry conditions.

16. Total revenue is the result of multiplying the selling price of the product times the:
    a) quantity of units sold.
    b) quantity of units produced.
    c) quantity of labor hours used.
    d) quality demanded by consumers.
    e) quantity of government regulations.

17. A firm can charge a higher price without losing its customers if it does not have much:
    a) production.
    b) competition.
    c) marketing.
    d) advertising.
    e) industry demand.

In-Text Study Guide

Answers are in Appendix C at the back of book.

18. Labor costs are often higher in industries that have:
    a) labor unions.
    b) unemployment.
    c) savings.
    d) demand schedules.
    e) interest expense.

19. According to the text, industry regulations have recently been reduced in the:
    a) automobile industry.
    b) chemical industry.
    c) oil industry.
    d) banking industry.
    e) steel industry.

20. Managers will monitor changes in labor costs in order to control:
    a) marketing costs.
    b) macro economics.
    c) production costs.
    d) social responsibility.
    e) industry demand.

21. The performance of a firm can be highly dependent on the following market conditions except for:
    a) regulatory conditions.
    b) labor conditions.
    c) competition.
    d) demand.
    e) taxes.

22. Changes in demand and competition affect both the demand for a firm's products and the firm's:
    a) location.
    b) customer service.
    c) revenue.
    d) recycling.
    e) segmentation.

23. A firm's share of total sales in the market is called its:
    a) market demand.
    b) regulatory environment.
    c) market share.
    d) economic segment.
    e) competitive advantage.

24. Another name for subsets in a market that reflect a specific type of business and the perceived quality is:
    a) demographics.
    b) marketing.
    c) sales.
    d) segments.
    e) economics.

25. A firm must assess its specific market segment to determine whether it has a(n):
    a) forecast.
    b) competitive advantage.
    c) industry condition.
    d) cost differential.
    e) shift in supply.

26. After a firm identifies a specific market, it can segment that market by:
    a) level of employees.
    b) scrap reworked.
    c) labor environment.
    d) conservationism.
    e) quality segments.

27. Once a firm has identified and assessed its key competitors, it must search for ways to increase or at least maintain its:
    a) labor environment.
    b) regulatory environment.
    c) market share.
    d) competition.
    e) social costs.

In-Text Study Guide

28. Even if a firm does not have a cost advantage, it may still create a(n):
    a) inflation advantage.
    b) condition advantage.
    c) monopoly advantage.
    d) price advantage.
    e) ethics advantage.

29. Firms commonly use a _____ analysis to develop a competitive advantage.
    a) SWOT
    b) SPUR
    c) SNAP
    d) STEP
    e) SPOT

30. Entrepreneurs need to find a product or service that has a(n):
    a) market edge.
    b) competitive advantage.
    c) structural incentive.
    d) economic niche.
    e) consumer linkage.

31. The management plan that identifies the roles and responsibilities of the employees hired by the firm is the:
    a) unity of command.
    b) division of work.
    c) degree of specialization.
    d) organizational structure.
    e) standardization concept.

32. A marketing plan focuses on all the following except:
    a) financing the business.
    b) a profile of typical customers.
    c) product characteristics.
    d) pricing of the product.
    e) distribution of the product.

33. A plan that demonstrates why the business is feasible and proposes how the business should be financed is the:
    a) production report.
    b) marketing plan.
    c) financial plan.
    d) human resource plan.
    e) bottom-up plan.

34. A business plan is a detailed description of the proposed business that includes all of the following except:
    a) description of the business.
    b) types of customers it would attract.
    c) competition.
    d) facilities needed for production.
    e) monetary and fiscal policy.

Summary/Part II

Starting a New Business

Selecting a Form of Business Ownership (Chapter 5)	→	• The Possible Forms of Business Ownership • Risks of Owning a Business		Firm's Performance (and Value)
Entrepreneurship and Business Planning (Chapter 6)	→	• Assessment of Market Conditions • The Key Business Functions • Developing a Business Plan		

Business Organization for Campus.com

Industry Segments (related to Chapter 5)

In your business plan, identify the various segments of the industry that Campus.com could target. The business was initially created to serve high school students who are about to graduate. Could the business offer different levels of service to its main market (high school students) and charge higher prices for some types of services?

Ownership (related to Chapter 5)

Decide what is the optimal form of business ownership for this firm, and indicate that form in your business plan for Campus.com. To answer this question, consider whether you would prefer to be the sole owner of Campus.com or to invite other individuals into the firm to form a partnership. If you are working with a team of students, you already have a partnership. In your business plan, explain why you selected the form of ownership you chose for Campus.com. What are the advantages of forming a partnership for this firm? What are the disadvantages of forming a partnership?

Competition (related to Chapter 6)

In your business plan for Campus.com, describe any existing competition for its product, including services that provide general information about colleges throughout the United States.

Communication and Teamwork

You (or your team) may be asked by your instructor to hand in and/or present the section of your business plan that relates to this part of the text.

Integrative Video Case: Growing a Small Business

When small businesses attempt to grow, they are limited in terms of how they can raise capital. They may be limited to family, friends, and credit cards, often with high interest rates. How can a firm obtain financing? The owners of Jagged Edge, a small business that manufactures mountain climbing gear, had a difficult time obtaining a bank loan. The financials of the firm could not prove to banks that it was credible. After watching the business grow and being presented with an outstanding business plan, however, the bank became convinced that the firm could go through the Small Business Administration to obtain lower-cost funding. The bank ended up being a customer of the company. When another small business owner, Lori Davis, opened a clothing store and attempted to obtain a bank loan, she found that her background in the industry helped her obtain funds.

Questions

1 What challenges do small businesses face when they try to raise growth capital?

2 Why is funding a business on credit cards a bad idea?

3 What does a small business need to provide to the bank when it seeks loans?

The Stock Market Game

Determine how the stock you selected is performing.

Check Your Performance

1 What is the value of your stock investment today?

2 What is your return on your investment?

3 How does your return compare to those of other students? (This comparison tells you whether your stock portfolio's performance is relatively high or low.)

Running Your Own Business

1 Explain whether your business will be a sole proprietorship, a partnership, or a corporation. Why did you make this decision?

2 Describe the main competitors that would be competing against your business. Would it be easy for additional competitors to enter your market? Could you effectively expand your business?

3 How would the performance of your business be affected by market conditions? Explain.

4 What competitive advantage of your business can be affected by market conditions? Explain.

Your Career in Business: *Pursuing a Major and a Career in Entrepreneurship*

If you are interested in the topics covered in this section, you may want to consider a major in entrepreneurship. Some of the more common courses taken by entrepreneurship majors are summarized here

Common Courses for Entrepreneurship Majors

▶ *Financial Management* Explains the different types of business organizations, along with the advantages and disadvantages of each, financing decisions by firms, and investment decisions by firms.

▶ *Management* Explains the basics of a business organization, the skills necessary to be a manager, and the resources needed by a business.

▶ *Marketing* Focuses on how to price a product, advertise a product, and distribute a product to the market.

▶ *Financing for Small Businesses* Explores how small businesses can finance their growth, the types of institutions that may facilitate the financing, and the phases of financing that may ultimately lead to an initial public offering of stock once the firm has grown substantially.

▶ *Entrepreneurship* Focuses on developing product ideas, testing the product, surveying the market, and using creativity to expand the product line.

Part III

Management

The chapters in Part III describe some of the key components of effective management. These components are (1) recognition of the skills necessary to be effective managers (Chapter 7), (2) proper assignments of job responsibilities (Chapter 8), (3) efficient allocation of resources for production (Chapter 9), and (4) proper monitoring and improvement of product quality (Chapter 9).

Effective management requires that job responsibilities be properly assigned within the organizational structure. Ideally, the organizational structure allows some control over each job assignment so that all types of tasks can be monitored. The organizational structure may also at-tempt to ensure employee input on various tasks by assigning extra responsibilities to employees.

Effective management also requires an efficient production process, which involves the selection of a plant site and the design and layout of the production facilities.

Effective management also requires an effort to continuously improve the quality of each product that is produced. Quality management forces employees to specify the desired quality level, to consider how the production process can be revised to achieve that quality level, and to continuously monitor the quality level by using various quality control methods.

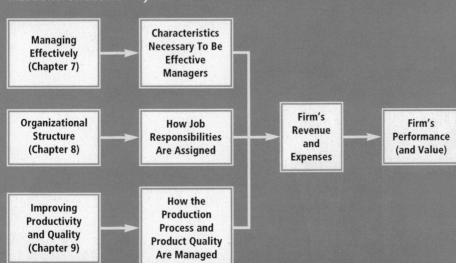

Chapter

7

CORBIS, CHICAGO

Decisions by Zycles Company regarding management levels, functions, and skills it needs for its production of motorcycles will influence its future performance and value.

The Learning Goals of this chapter are to:

1 Identify the levels of management.

2 Identify the key functions of managers.

3 Describe the skills that managers need.

4 Describe methods that managers can use to utilize their time effectively.

240

Managing Effectively

Management involves the utilization of human and other resources (such as machinery) in a manner that best achieves the firm's plans and objectives. According to a recent survey by Shareholder Surveys, shareholders rank good management and long-term vision as the two most important characteristics of a firm. Consider the situation of Zycles Company, which produces and sells motorcycles, Zycles Company must decide:

▶ What levels of management does it need to manage its business?

▶ What functions are required of the managers who manage the business?

▶ What skills do the managers need?

▶ How can Zycles Company ensure that the managers use their time efficiently?

The decision about the levels of management needed affects the expense of running the business. The decision about the functions is necessary to ensure that the managers can complete all the required tasks. The decision about the managers' skills is needed to ensure that the managers are capable of completing all the necessary tasks. The decision about how the managers should use their time is necessary to get the most work out of the managers so that the firm does not need to hire too many managers.

The types of decisions described above are necessary for all businesses. This chapter explains how Zycles Company or any other firm can determine the necessary levels, functions, skills, and efficiency for its managers that will maximize its value.

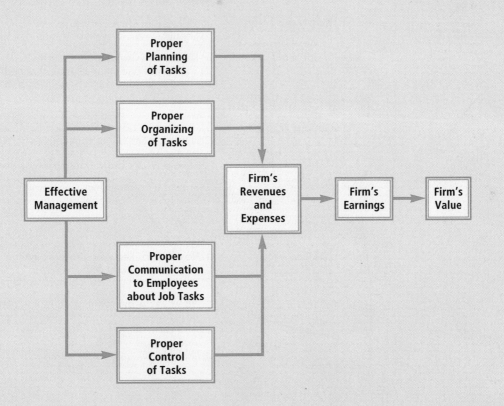

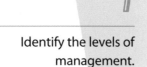

top (high-level) management
managers in positions such as president, chief executive officer, chief financial officer, and vice-president who make decisions regarding the firm's long-run objectives

middle management
managers who are often responsible for the firm's short-term decisions

supervisory (first-line) management
managers who are usually highly involved with the employees who engage in the day-to-day production process

Levels of Management

Employees who are responsible for managing other employees or other resources serve as managers, even if their official title is different. The functions of managers vary with their respective levels within the firm. **Top (high-level) management** includes positions such as president, chief executive officer (who commonly also serves as president), chief financial officer, and vice-president. These managers make decisions regarding the firm's long-run objectives (such as three to five years ahead).

Middle management is often responsible for the firm's short-term decisions, as these managers are closer to the production process. Middle managers resolve problems and devise new methods to improve performance. Middle management includes positions such as regional manager and plant manager.

Supervisory (first-line) management is usually highly involved with the employees who engage in the day-to-day production process. Supervisors deal with problems such as worker absenteeism and customer complaints. Supervisory management includes positions such as account manager and office manager. The types of functions that each level of management conducts are summarized in Exhibit 7.1.

The relationships among top, middle, and supervisory managers can be more fully understood by considering a simple example. Exhibit 7.2 shows the responsibilities of all managers in light of a firm's new plans to expand production and increase sales. The middle and top managers must

Exhibit 7.1

Comparison of Different Levels of Management

Title	Types of Decisions
Top Management	
President	1) Should we create new products? 2) Should we expand? 3) How can we expand? Through acquisitions?
Chief Financial Officer	1) Should more funds be borrowed? 2) Should we invest available funds in proposed projects?
Vice-President of Marketing	1) Should an existing product be revised? 2) Should our pricing policies be changed? 3) Should our advertising strategies be changed?
Middle Management	
Regional Sales Manager	1) How can we boost sales in a particular city? 2) How can complaints from one of our largest customers be resolved? 3) Should an additional salesperson be hired?
Plant Manager	1) Should the structure of the assembly line be revised? 2) Should new equipment be installed throughout the plant?
Supervisory Management	
Account Manager	1) How can workers who process payments from various accounts be motivated? 2) How can conflicts between two workers be resolved?
Supervisor	1) How can the quality of work by assembly-line workers be assessed? 2) How can assembly-line tasks be assigned across workers? 3) How can customer complaints be handled?

make production, marketing, and finance decisions that will achieve the new plans. The supervisory managers provide specific instructions to the new employees who are hired to achieve the higher production level.

Exhibit 7.2

Comparison of Responsibilities among Managers

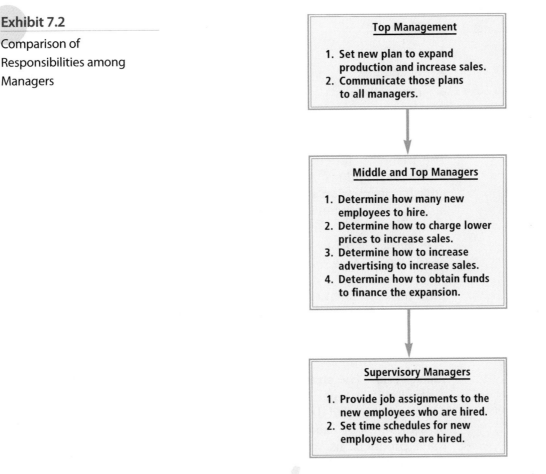

Top Management

1. **Set new plan to expand production and increase sales.**
2. **Communicate those plans to all managers.**

Middle and Top Managers

1. **Determine how many new employees to hire.**
2. **Determine how to charge lower prices to increase sales.**
3. **Determine how to increase advertising to increase sales.**
4. **Determine how to obtain funds to finance the expansion.**

Supervisory Managers

1. **Provide job assignments to the new employees who are hired.**
2. **Set time schedules for new employees who are hired.**

Decision Making

Interaction among Management Layers

Zycles Company (introduced at the beginning of the chapter) relies on three levels of managers to manage its business of producing and selling motorcycles. Its supervisory managers monitor the assembly-line operations and interact with the assembly-line workers on a daily basis. The middle managers are heavily involved with selling the motorcycles to various dealerships. They determine what types of motorcycles the dealerships want to buy, and they also respond to any complaints from the dealerships about previous orders. The middle managers interact with the supervisory managers when problems occur with the assembly-line production. The high-level managers determine the future design of the motorcycles, how to finance future operations, and how to advertise the company's products. The high-level managers consider any information provided by the middle managers before making key decisions.

1. Explain why the feedback from the middle managers to the supervisory managers may affect the assembly-line process.

2. Explain why the feedback from the middle managers to the high-level managers may affect key decisions such as the creation of a new motorcycle design.

ANSWERS: 1. The middle managers may pass along complaints that dealerships have received from customers about a problem that is caused by the production process, and this information may lead to a change in the assembly-line process that could correct the problem. 2. The middle managers can relay information from the dealerships about the styles of motorcycles that customers would like to buy if they were available.

2

Identify the key functions of managers.

Functions of Managers

Most managerial functions can be classified into one of the following categories:

▶ Planning
▶ Organizing
▶ Leading
▶ Controlling

Planning

planning
the preparation of a firm for future business conditions

mission statement
a description of a firm's primary goal

The **planning** function represents the preparation of a firm for future business conditions. As the first step in the planning process, the firm establishes its **mission statement,** which describes its primary goal. For example, here is the mission statement of Bristol-Myers Squibb:

> *"The mission of Bristol-Myers Squibb is to extend and enhance human life by providing the highest quality health and personal care products."*

Most mission statements are general, like that of Bristol-Myers Squibb. The mission of General Motors is to be the world's leader in transportation products, and the mission of Ford Motor Company is to be the world's leading consumer company providing automotive products and services.

strategic plan
identifies a firm's main business focus over a long-term period, perhaps three to five years

Strategic Plan   The **strategic plan** identifies the firm's main business focus over a long-term period. The strategic plan is more detailed than the mission statement and describes in general terms how the firm's mission is to be achieved. For example, if a firm's mission is to produce quality computer products, its strategic plan might specify the particular computer products to be produced and the manner in which they will be sold (retail outlets, Internet, etc.).

The strategic plan typically includes goals and strategies that can be used to satisfy the firm's mission. For example, a recent annual report of Bristol-Myers Squibb listed the following among its main goals and strategies:

Goals:

"Leadership in each product category and in each geographic market in which we compete. We aim to achieve number one or number two position with increasing market shares."

"Superior customer satisfaction by providing the highest quality products and services to our customers. We will strive to be rated number one or two with continuous improvement as rated by our customers."

"Superior steady shareholder returns, as measured by a number one or two competitive position in economic performance within our industry."

"An organization which is committed to winning through teamwork, empowerment, customer focus, and open communications."

Out of Business

Strategies:

"Our mission and goals will be achieved by adhering to the following core strategies:

▶ *Achieve unit growth fueled internally by new products, geographic expansion, and marketing innovation, and externally through acquisition, joint venture and licensing agreements.*

▶ *Dedicate ourselves to being recognized as the best in research and development across our businesses . . .*

▶ *Achieve continuous improvement in our cost structure . . .*

▶ *Attract, develop, motivate, and retain people of the highest caliber. The company's reporting, reward and recognition systems will be built around attainment of the goals identified above."*

Once a firm specifies its mission, it can develop plans to achieve that mission.

A firm's mission can change over time. When eBay was created, its mission was to create an online auction system that would allow buyers and sellers to interact to purchase and sell products. As eBay became increasingly popular, it expanded its system to include several foreign countries, and it established a more ambitious mission—to serve buyers and sellers anywhere who wish to buy or sell practically anything.

tactical planning
smaller-scale plans (over one or two years) that are consistent with the firm's strategic (long-term) plan

Tactical Planning   High-level and middle managers also engage in **tactical planning,** or smaller-scale plans (over one or two years) that are consistent with the firm's strategic (long-term) plan. Tactical planning normally focuses on a short-term period, such as the next year or so. To develop their tactical plan, managers of AT&T and other firms assess economic conditions, the general demand for various products, the level of competition among firms producing those products, and changes in technology. They use their vision to capitalize on opportunities in which they have some

Cross Functional Teamwork

Interaction of Functions to Achieve the Strategic Plan

The development of a strategic plan requires interaction among the firm's managers who are responsible for different business functions. Recall that the strategic plan of Bristol-Myers Squibb mentioned earlier includes goals of increased market share, customer satisfaction, and continuous improvement. The firm's strategies to achieve those goals include the creation of new products, continuous improvement in cost structure (high production efficiency), and retaining good employees.

The management function of Bristol-Myers Squibb can help achieve the firm's goals by assessing the needs of consumers so that the firm can create new products. It can also attempt to assess customers' satisfaction with existing products and use marketing strategies to increase the market share of these products. The financing function of Bristol-Myers Squibb can help achieve the firm's goals by determining the level of borrowing that will be sufficient to support the firm's operations.

Since the business functions are related, a strategic plan can be implemented only when the interaction among business functions is recognized. A strategic plan that focuses on increased sales will likely require more production and financing. The table below shows some common ways that the goals of a strategic plan can be achieved by each function.

How Various Business Functions Are Used to Achieve the Strategic Plan

Function	Typical Goals or Strategies That Can Be Achieved by This Function
Management	High production efficiency
	High production quality
	Customer satisfaction
	Employee satisfaction
Marketing	Innovation (new products)
	Increase market share of existing products
	Customer satisfaction
Finance	Reduce financing costs
	Efficient use of funds

advantages over other firms in the industry. If a firm's strategic plan is to increase its market share by 20 percent, its tactical plans may focus on increasing sales in specific regions that have less competition. As time passes, additional tactical planning will be conducted in accordance with the strategic plan.

operational planning
establishes the methods to be used in the near future (such as the next year) to achieve the tactical plans

Operational Planning Another form of planning, called **operational planning,** establishes the methods to be used in the near future (such as the next year) to achieve the tactical plans. Continuing our example of a firm whose tactical plan is to increase sales, the operational plan may specify the means by which the firm can increase sales. That is, the operational plan may specify an increase in the amount of funds allocated to advertising and the hiring of additional salespeople.

eBay has expanded its business around the world. Here it is hosting an event in Germany.

GETTY IMAGES

The goals of operational planning are somewhat dependent on the firm's long-term goals. For example, a firm's top managers may establish a goal of 12 percent annual growth in sales over the next several years. The firm's salespeople may be asked to strive for a 1 percent increase in total sales per month during the upcoming year. Their month-to-month goals are structured from the long-term goals established by top management.

policies
guidelines for how tasks should be completed

When firms engage in operational planning, they must abide by their **policies,** or guidelines for how tasks should be completed. For example, a policy on the hiring of employees may require that a specific process be followed. Policies enforced by firms ensure that all employees conduct specific tasks in a similar manner. The policies are intended to prevent employees from conducting tasks in a manner that is inefficient, dangerous, or illegal.

procedures
steps necessary to implement a policy

Most policies contain **procedures,** or steps necessary to implement a policy. For example, a policy for hiring may specify that an ad is to be placed in the local newspaper for so many days and that the criteria for the job must be disclosed in the ad. These procedures are intended to prevent abuses, such as a manager hiring a friend or relative who is not really qualified for the job. Without procedures, managers could make decisions that conflict with the company's goals.

As another example, a firm may implement procedures for air travel to ensure that employees use airlines that have relatively low prices and that they fly second class. These procedures are intended to prevent managers from incurring excessive travel expenses.

contingency planning
alternative plans developed for various possible business conditions

Contingency Planning Some of a firm's plans may not be finalized until specific business conditions are known. For this reason, firms use **contingency planning;** that is, they develop alternative plans for various possible business conditions. The plan to be implemented is contingent on the business conditions that occur. For example, a firm that produces sports equipment may plan to boost its production of rollerblades in response to recent demand. At the same time, however, it may develop an alternative plan for using its resources to produce other equipment instead of rollerblades if demand declines. It may also develop a plan for increasing its production if the demand for its rollerblades is much higher than expected.

A manager discusses plans for production with factory workers.

GETTY IMAGES

Some contingency planning is conducted to prepare for possible crises that may occur. For example, airlines may establish contingency plans in the event that various problems arise, as illustrated in Exhibit 7.3.

The September 11 crisis prompted many firms to develop a contingency plan in the event of a future crisis. Some firms established backup production plans in case their normal facilities are not functioning properly. Other firms have identified backup office space that can be used if their normal offices are destroyed or otherwise are unusable. Many firms have also attempted to back up their information files and store them at an alternative location.

Relationships among Planning Functions The relationships among the planning functions are shown in Exhibit 7.4. Notice how the tactical plan is dependent on the strategic plan and the operational plan is based on the tactical plan. The contingency plan offers alternatives to consider instead of the operational plan in specific situations (such as higher or lower demand for the product than anticipated).

To fully understand how these plans fit together, assume that your firm produces men's shirts and that your strategic plan specifies goals of expanding into related products. In this case, your tactical plan may focus on producing one other product along with men's shirts, such as women's shirts. The operational plan will specify the changes in the firm's operations that are necessary to produce and sell women's shirts. Specifically, the plan will determine how much more fabric must be purchased each month, how the women's shirts will be priced, and where they will be sold. A contingency plan can also be prepared in the event that excessive competition develops in the market for women's shirts. If this occurs, the contingency plan may be to expand into different products, such as men's pants.

Organizing

organizing
the organization of employees and other resources in a manner that is consistent with the firm's goals

The **organizing** function involves the organization of employees and other resources in a manner that is consistent with the firm's goals. Once a firm's goals are established (from the planning function), resources are obtained

Exhibit 7.3

Illustration of Contingency
Planning

Situation	Contingency Plan
Overbooked reservations	To reduce the number of customers who need that flight, offer customers who are willing to be bumped (wait for next flight) a free round-trip ticket to the destination of their choice in the future.
Minor airplane repair needed	Have airline mechanics available at each major airport in the event that a minor repair is needed.
Major airplane repair needed	If the airplane is not suitable for flying, attempt to reroute the passengers who were supposed to be on that plane by reserving seats for them on other flights.

Exhibit 7.4

How Planning Functions
Are Related

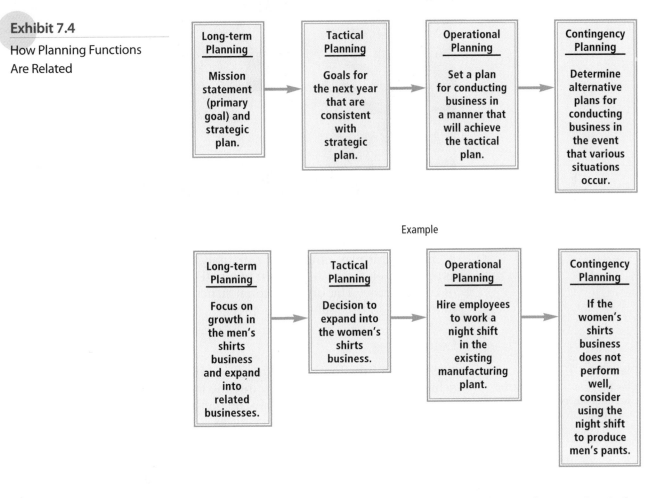

and organized to achieve those goals. For example, employees of Daimler-Chrysler are organized among assembly lines to produce cars or trucks in a manner consistent with the company's goals.

The organizing function occurs continuously throughout the life of the firm. This function is especially important for firms that frequently restructure their operations. Organizational changes such as the creation of a new position or the promotion of an employee occur frequently. These changes may even necessitate revisions of job assignments of employees whose job positions have not changed.

To illustrate the importance of the organizing function, consider a construction company that builds homes. The general contractor assigns tasks to the employees. From the laying of the foundation to painting, most tasks

A general contractor reviews the building plans of a home to ensure that the home is built as planned.

CORBIS, CHICAGO

must be completed in a particular order. Since all tasks cannot be completed simultaneously, the contractor has workers working on different homes. In this way, employees can apply their respective specialties (such as painting, electrical, and so on) to whatever homes are at the proper stage of construction. The organizational structure of a business is discussed in more detail in the following chapter.

Leading

leading
the process of influencing the habits of others to achieve a common goal

The **leading** function is the process of influencing the habits of others to achieve a common goal. It may include the communication of job assignments to employees and possibly the methods of completing those assignments. It may also include serving as a role model for employees. The leading should be conducted in a manner that is consistent with the firm's strategic plan.

The leading function involves not only instructions on how to complete a task but also incentives to complete it correctly and quickly. Some forms of leading may help motivate employees. One method is to delegate authority by assigning employees more responsibility. Increased responsibility can encourage employees to take more pride in their jobs and raise their self-esteem. If employees are more actively involved in the production process and allowed to express their concerns, problems can be resolved more easily. Managers who allow much employee feedback may prevent conflicts between management and employees, or even conflicts among employees. To the extent that the leading function can enhance the performance of employees, it will enhance the performance of the firm.

initiative
the willingness to take action

For managers to be effective leaders, they need to have **initiative,** which is the willingness to take action. Managers who have all other skills but lack initiative may not be very effective. Some managers who recognize the need to make changes are unwilling to take action because making changes takes more effort than leaving the situation as is, and change may upset some employees. For example, consider a manager who recognizes that the firm's expenses could be reduced, without any adverse effect on the firm, by eliminating a particular department. Nevertheless, this manager may refrain from suggesting any action because it might upset some employees. Managers are more likely to initiate change if they are directly rewarded for suggesting any changes that enhance the firm's value.

Leadership Styles   Although all managers have their own leadership styles, styles can be classified generally as autocratic, free-rein, or participative. Managers who use an **autocratic** leadership style retain full authority for decision making; employees have little or no input. For example, if managers believe that one of their manufacturing plants will continue to incur losses, they may decide to close the plant without asking for input from the plant's workers. Autocratic managers may believe that employees cannot offer input that would contribute to a given decision. Employees are instructed to carry out tasks as ordered by autocratic leaders and are discouraged from being creative. In general, employees who desire responsibility are likely to become dissatisfied with such a management style.

Managers who use a **free-rein** (also called "laissez-faire") management style delegate much authority to employees. This style is the opposite extreme from the autocratic style. Free-rein managers communicate goals to employees but allow the employees to choose how to complete the objectives. For example, managers may inform workers in a manufacturing plant that the plant's performance must be improved and then allow the workers to implement an improvement strategy. Employees working under a free-rein management style are expected to manage and motivate themselves daily.

In the **participative** (also called democratic) leadership style, the leaders accept some employee input but usually use their authority to make decisions. This style requires frequent communication between managers and employees. Managers who use a participative management style allow employees to express their opinions but do not pressure employees to make major decisions. For example, managers of a General Motors plant may consider the ideas of assembly-line workers on how to improve the plant's performance, but the managers will make the final decisions.

A comparison of leadership styles is provided in Exhibit 7.5. The optimal leadership style varies with the situation and with employees'

autocratic
a leadership style in which the leader retains full authority for decision making

free-rein
a leadership style in which the leader delegates much authority to employees

participative
a leadership style in which the leaders accept some employee input but usually use their authority to make decisions

Exhibit 7.5

How Leadership Style Affects Employee Influence on Management Decisions

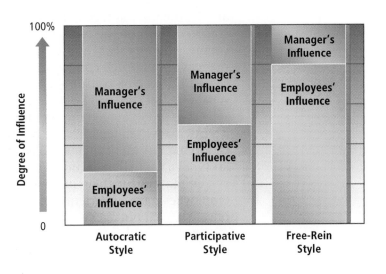

Global Business

Conflicts with the Goal of a Multinational Corporation

As part of their role as leaders, managers should influence other employees to focus on maximizing the firm's value. Sometimes, however, managers are tempted to make decisions that conflict with this goal. For example, a decision to establish a foreign subsidiary (a subsidiary in a foreign country) in one country versus another may be based on the country's appeal to a particular manager rather than on its potential benefits to shareholders. Decisions to expand may be determined by the desires of managers to make their respective divisions grow in order to receive more responsibility and compensation.

The costs of ensuring that managers maximize shareholder wealth (referred to as *agency costs*) are normally larger for multinational corporations than for purely domestic firms, for several reasons. First, multinational corporations that have subsidiaries scattered around the world may experience larger agency problems because monitoring managers of distant subsidiaries is more difficult. Second, managers of foreign subsidiaries who have been raised in different cultures may not follow uniform goals. Third, the sheer size of the larger multinational corporations can also create large agency problems.

Managers of foreign subsidiaries may be tempted to make decisions that maximize the values of their respective subsidiaries. This objective will not necessarily coincide with maximizing the value of the overall firm. Consider the case of Texen, Inc., which produces and sells wallets in the United States. It established a subsidiary in Mexico to produce and sell wallets in South America. Instead, the subsidiary exported the wallets to the United States, thereby taking away some of Texen's U.S. business. The managers of the subsidiary focused on a strategy that would enhance the subsidiary's value without realizing that this strategy could adversely affect Texen, the parent company.

If the U.S. managers of the parent company conduct their function of leading properly, they will communicate the goals that the subsidiary managers should follow. The U.S. managers should ensure that the subsidiary managers understand that a decision that maximizes the value of a subsidiary may be detrimental to the firm overall. Thus, in making decisions, the managers of a subsidiary should always consider the potential impact on other subsidiaries and on the parent.

experience and personalities. The free-rein style may be appropriate if employees are highly independent, creative, and motivated. An autocratic style may be most effective for managing employees with low skill levels or high turnover rates. Participative management is effective when employees can offer a different perspective because of their closer attention to daily tasks.

Within a given firm, all three leadership styles may be used. For example, the top management of General Motors may use autocratic leadership to determine the types of automobiles (large versus small cars, luxury versus economy cars, and so on) to design in the future. These plans are made without much employee input because the top managers can rely on recent surveys of consumer preferences along with their own vision of what types of cars will be in demand in the future.

Once top management identifies the types of automobiles to produce, a participative leadership style may be used to design each type of car. That is, top management may establish general design guidelines for a particular type of car to be produced (such as specifying a small economy car) and ask employees for their suggestions on developing this type of car. These employees have experience on specific assembly-line operations and can offer useful input based on various production or quality problems they experienced with other cars. The top managers will make the final deci-

Managers must continually work together to make decisions related to production, marketing, and finance in order to achieve the business's strategic plan.

GETTY IMAGES

sions after receiving the engineers' proposed designs, which are based on input from numerous employees. This example reflects a participative style because managers use their authority to decide on the particular type of product to be produced but solicit input from many employees.

After the design of a specific car is completed, managers use a free-rein style for some parts of the production process. For example, a group of employees may be assigned to a set of assembly-line tasks. They may be allowed to assign the specific tasks among themselves. They may also be allowed to rotate their specific jobs to avoid boredom. This example reflects the free-rein style because the employees are allowed to choose how to achieve the firm's objectives.

Controlling

controlling
the monitoring and evaluation of tasks

The **controlling** function involves the monitoring and evaluation of tasks. To evaluate tasks, managers should measure performance in comparison with the standards and expectations they set. That is, the controlling function assesses whether the plans set within the planning function are achieved. Standards can be applied to production volume and cost, sales volume, profits, and several other variables used to measure a firm's performance. The controlling function allows for continual evaluation so that the firm can ensure that it is following the course intended to achieve its strategic plan.

The strategic plan of Bristol-Myers Squibb (presented earlier) states that its reward systems will be based on standards set by the goals identified within that plan. An example of how the controlling function can be used to assess a firm's operations is shown in Exhibit 7.6.

Exhibit 7.6

Example of the Controlling Function

	Actual Level Last Week	Standards (Expected Level)	Assessment
Sales volume	300 units	280 units	OK
Production volume	350 units	350 units	OK
Labor expenses	$10,000	$9,000	Too high
Administrative expenses	$14,500	$15,000	OK
Equipment repair	$3,000	$1,000	Too high

Global Business

Leadership Styles for Global Business

When U.S. firms establish subsidiaries in foreign countries, they must determine the type of leadership style to use in those subsidiaries. The firms do not automatically apply the style they use in the United States because conditions in foreign countries may be different. In some countries that have only recently encouraged private ownership of businesses (such as Hungary, Ukraine, and China), people are not accustomed to making decisions that will maximize the value of the business. Many people have had experience only in managing government-owned businesses. In those businesses, management decisions tended to focus on satisfying government goals rather than on maximizing the value of the business. Furthermore, the businesses had little or no competition, so managers could make decisions without concern about losing market share. Now, when U.S. firms establish subsidiaries in such countries, the firms may use a more autocratic leadership style for their subsidiaries. Instructions come from the U.S. headquarters, and the managers of the foreign subsidiaries are responsible for carrying out those instructions. When the managers have problems, they contact U.S. headquarters for advice.

Although many U.S. firms have recently adopted free-rein and participative styles in the United States, they may nevertheless be reluctant to give too much power to managers of some of their foreign subsidiaries. As the managers of the subsidiaries gain experience working for the firm and in a competitive environment, they may be given more power to make decisions.

When a U.S. firm has foreign subsidiaries in several different countries, its choice of a leadership style may vary with the characteristics of the foreign country. For example, it may allow a participative style in industrialized countries where managers are experienced in making business decisions aimed at maximizing the firm's value. The same firm may impose an autocratic style in a country where most business managers are not accustomed to making business decisions in this manner. No one particular leadership style is always appropriate for all countries. The firm must consider the country's characteristics before deciding which leadership style to use. Furthermore, the proper leadership style for any particular country may change over time in response to changes in the country's conditions.

Some standards such as profits are general and apply to all departments of a firm. Thus, no single department is likely to be entirely accountable if the firm's profits are not sufficient. Other standards focus on a particular operation of the firm. For example, production volume, production cost per unit, and inventory level standards can be used to monitor production. A specified volume of sales can be used as a standard to monitor the effectiveness of marketing strategies.

The main reason for setting standards is to detect and correct deficiencies. When deficiencies are detected, managers must take corrective action. For example, if labor and equipment repair expenses are too high, the firm will attempt to identify the reason for the high costs so that it can prevent them in the future. If a firm finds that its sales volume is below standards, its managers will determine whether to revise the existing marketing strategies or penalize those employees who are responsible for the deficiency. Deficiencies that are detected early may be more easily corrected. By identifying deficiencies that must be corrected, the controlling function can help to improve a firm's performance.

In some cases, the standards rather than the strategies need to be corrected. For example, a particular advertising strategy to boost automobile sales may fail when interest rates are high because consumers are unwilling to borrow money to purchase automobiles at those interest rates. The failure to reach a specified sales level may be due to the high interest rates rather than a poor advertising strategy.

Control by Investors   Corporate governance involves the oversight or governance of corporate management. High-level managers are indirectly controlled by the corporate governance process. Investors of publicly traded firms try to ensure that the managers make effective decisions that will maximize the firm's performance and value. Investors have some influence over management because they can complain to the board of directors or to executives if the managers are making poor decisions. The board and executives are especially concerned about satisfying institutional investors that hold large amounts of the firm's shares because if those investors sell all their holdings of the firm's shares, a pronounced decline in the stock's price could occur.

In some cases, the institutional investors form a group so that they will have greater influence on the firm's management. Institutional Shareholder Services (ISS), Inc., is a firm that organizes institutional shareholders to push for a common cause. When ISS receives feedback from institutional investors about a particular firm, it organizes a conference call with high-ranking executives of the firm and allows investors to listen in on the call. Unlike earnings conference calls, which are controlled by the firm, the conference call is run by ISS, which asks questions that focus on the institutional shareholders' concerns about the firm's management. Typical questions asked by ISS include:

▶ Why is your chief executive officer (CEO) also the chairman of the board?

▶ Why is your executive compensation much higher than the industry norm?

▶ What is your process for nominating new board members?

Transcripts of the conference call are available within 48 hours after the call.

Control of Reporting   Another objective of the controlling process is to ensure accurate reporting within the firm. Investors of publicly traded firms attempt to have some control over a firm's management by reviewing the financial statements that the firm releases on a quarterly basis. In recent years, some publicly traded firms used reporting procedures that intentionally exaggerated the firm's revenue or profit over a particular time period. Such inaccurate reporting may mislead investors who are trying to monitor a firm's management by causing the management to look better than it actually is. Consequently, investors may overestimate the value of the firm and therefore pay too much for its stock. In addition, executives who hold the firm's stock may be able to sell it for a high price to investors who were misinformed about the firm's profits.

The Sarbanes-Oxley Act (SOX) was enacted in 2002 in an effort to prevent such reporting abuses. It requires firms to implement a system that allows their level of productivity and profitability to easily be monitored. The system must be designed to detect reporting discrepancies so that a firm's reported financial performance can easily be checked on a periodic basis. In general, the financial performance is based on the firm's revenue and expenses. Most firms use software programs that can verify their information about revenue and expenses and determine whether the financial

Exhibit 7.7

Integration of Management
Functions

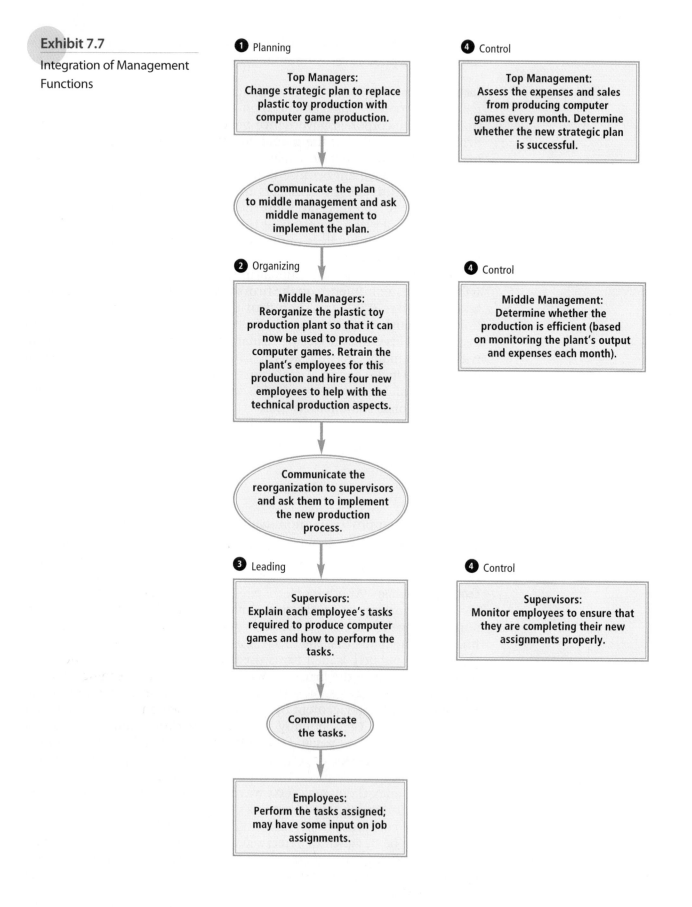

❶ Planning

Top Managers:
Change strategic plan to replace plastic toy production with computer game production.

Communicate the plan to middle management and ask middle management to implement the plan.

❷ Organizing

Middle Managers:
Reorganize the plastic toy production plant so that it can now be used to produce computer games. Retrain the plant's employees for this production and hire four new employees to help with the technical production aspects.

Communicate the reorganization to supervisors and ask them to implement the new production process.

❸ Leading

Supervisors:
Explain each employee's tasks required to produce computer games and how to perform the tasks.

Communicate the tasks.

Employees:
Perform the tasks assigned; may have some input on job assignments.

❹ Control

Top Management:
Assess the expenses and sales from producing computer games every month. Determine whether the new strategic plan is successful.

❹ Control

Middle Management:
Determine whether the production is efficient (based on monitoring the plant's output and expenses each month).

❹ Control

Supervisors:
Monitor employees to ensure that they are completing their new assignments properly.

reporting is consistent with the information provided by various departments within the firm.

Integration of Management Functions

To illustrate how the four different functions of management are integrated, consider a firm that makes children's toys and decides to restructure its operations. Because of low sales, the top managers create a new strategic plan to discontinue production of plastic toys and to begin producing computer games. This planning function will require the use of the other management functions, as shown in Exhibit 7.7. The organizing function is needed to reorganize the firm's production process so that it can produce computer games. The leading function is needed to provide employees with instructions on how to produce the computer games. The controlling function is needed to determine whether the production process established to produce computer games is efficient and whether the sales of computer games are as high as forecasted.

In a small business, the owner may frequently perform all the management functions. For example, an owner of a small business may revise the strategic plan (planning function), reorganize the firm's production facility (organizing function), assign new tasks to the employees (leading function), and then assess whether all these revisions lead to acceptable results (controlling function).

Use of Technology and Software to Improve Management Functions

Technology facilitates the integration of management functions. The planning function may easily involve input from various managers

Employees gather around a desk to listen in on a video conference.

CORBIS, CHICAGO

through an online network. Once specific plans are set, they can be immediately communicated to managers at all offices or plants. Next, the managers decide how to achieve the plans that have been established. Then they perform the leading function by offering instructions to their employees. They may provide some general instructions online and other instructions on a more personal level. Finally, an online network can be used to conduct the controlling function. As employees perform their duties, their managers are informed of the amount of output produced, and they relay the information to the top managers who initially established the plans. If the operations are not working according to the plan, this will be detected within the controlling function. Under these circumstances, either the operations or the plan can be modified.

Software to Improve Management Functions

Recently, computer software packages have been developed to help managers conduct their functions more effectively. This software supports a wide range of activities, including the following:

▶ **Personnel Hiring** Software for screening job applicants, based upon psychological principles, can be used to assess attitudes and potential fit with the company. Software of this type has long been used at a number of well-known companies, such as Mrs. Field's Cookies.

▶ **Personnel Evaluation** Reviewing and evaluating personnel has long been a sensitive task that is dreaded by many managers. Software is available that helps managers in constructing and writing reviews, as well as recording employee progress toward goals. Such software can help managers get through the review process and can be extremely valuable in documenting poor performance leading to an employee termination. Such documentation can be extremely valuable if the terminated employee sues his or her former employer.

▶ **General Management** A wide range of software is available to assist managers in day-to-day management activities. Calendar and scheduling software can be used for appointments and for time management. Personnel software can form the basis of a personnel system, keeping track of assorted information such as vacation usage, medical benefits, pension contributions, and so forth. In addition, some versions of personnel software provide managers with templates for creating complete personnel manuals. Contact management software can help sales personnel keep track of customer calls. Financial software can aid managers in making reasonable projections of future business. A wide range of software supports specific activities, such as creating presentations and business planning.

▶ **Negotiating** A number of software packages have been developed that employ psychological models to help managers devise negotiating strategies for various situations. The software design is based on the principle that different negotiating styles should be employed when dealing with different types of individuals.

▶ **Decision Making** A growing number of software packages are designed to help managers make decisions more rationally. Using tested decision-making techniques, they force managers to identify and prioritize alternatives in such a way that they can be ranked in an internally consistent fashion.

▶ **Creativity** Some software is designed to stimulate managerial creativity. Such packages employ techniques drawn from brainstorming research and may also employ question-and-answer sessions designed to inspire managers with new ideas.

Although it is unlikely that software will ever substitute for managerial experience, managers are increasingly using software to supplement their own management techniques.

In-Text Study Guide

Answers are in Appendix C at the back of book.

34. All of the following guidelines should be followed when using time management except:
    a) setting proper priorities.
    b) centralizing responsibility.
    c) scheduling long intervals of time for large tasks.
    d) minimizing interruptions.
    e) delegating some tasks to employees.

35. A manager faced with a large task that will take more than one day to complete should:
    a) demand help from other employees.
    b) take frequent breaks to refresh his/her concentration.
    c) retain sole responsibility for the project.
    d) set short-term goals.
    e) automatically assign the project top priority.

GETTY IMAGES

The decisions by Mars Technology regarding its organizational structure will influence its future performance and therefore its value.

The Learning Goals of this chapter are to:

Explain the purpose of an organizational structure and how organizational structure varies among firms. *1*

Explain how accountability can be achieved in an organizational structure. *2*

Describe how centralized and decentralized organizational structures differ. *3*

Discuss methods firms can use to obtain employee input. *4*

Identify methods that can be used to departmentalize tasks. *5*

Organizational Structure

Each firm should have a strategic plan that identifies the future direction of its business. The responsibilities of its managers should be organized to achieve the strategic plan. Each firm establishes an organizational structure that identifies responsibilities for each job position and the relationships among those positions. The organizational structure also indicates how all the job responsibilities fit together. The organizational structure affects the efficiency with which a firm produces its product and therefore affects the firm's value.

Consider the situation of Mars Technology Company, which has production plants in four different cities that produce high-technology products including digital cameras and miniature computers. Mars Technology must determine:

▶ What is the ideal organizational structure for its business?

▶ Should it decentralize its decision making?

▶ How can it develop an effective informal structure?

▶ How should its tasks be departmentalized?

The organizational structure decision determines how many different layers of management the firm will have. Mars Technology can reduce expenses by having fewer layers of management, but it also wants to ensure that it has enough employees to cover all necessary tasks. The way it decides to departmentalize will affect the number of employees needed to complete all tasks and therefore will also affect its expenses. Since these decisions affect the level of Mars Technology's expenses, they also affect the level of its earnings and therefore influence its value.

All business must make the types of decisions described above. This chapter explains how Mars Technology or any other firm can establish an organizational structure and departmentalize in a manner that maximizes the firm's value.

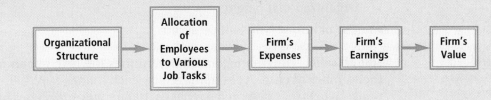

Purpose and Types of Organizational Structure

1

Explain the purpose of an organizational structure and how organizational structure varies among firms.

An **organizational structure** identifies responsibilities for each job position and the relationships among those positions. In general, a firm wants to establish an organizational structure that ensures that all employees are in positions where they can be properly guided and monitored by someone above them to do their jobs efficiently. If some job positions are not under the supervision of any other position, those positions may not contribute much to production because the employees will lack the guidance that

organizational structure
identifies responsibilities for each job position and the relationships among those positions

they need. Alternatively, if job positions report to two or more higher-level positions, they may not contribute much to production because the employees may receive conflicting guidance from multiple bosses. Thus, a proper organizational structure can allow the firm to utilize its employees efficiently, which will enable it to produce its product or service at a relatively low cost.

A firm's organizational structure can be illustrated with an organization chart, which shows the interaction among job positions. This chart indicates the **chain of command,** which identifies the job positions to which all types of employees must report. The chain of command also indicates who is responsible for various activities. Since employees often encounter problems that require communication with other divisions, it helps to know who is responsible for each type of task.

chain of command
identifies the job position to which each type of employee must report

The president (who also typically holds the position of chief executive officer, or CEO) has the ultimate responsibility for the firm's success. The president normally attempts to coordinate all divisions and provide direction for the firm's business. In most firms, many managerial duties are delegated to other managers. Vice-presidents normally oversee specific divisions or broad functions of the firm and report to the president.

The chain of command can be used to ensure that managers make decisions that maximize the firm's value rather than serve their own interests. For example, some managers may be tempted to hire friends for specific job positions. To the extent that their actions are monitored within the chain of command, they are more likely to make decisions that serve the firm rather than their self-interests. If managers at each level report their key decisions to other managers, the decisions are subject to scrutiny. This monitoring process is not intended to take away a manager's power, but to ensure that the power is used to serve the goals of the firm.

How Organizational Structure Varies among Firms

Different firms use different organizational structures. The specific organizational structure used by a firm may be influenced by the specific characteristics of its business and can affect the firm's performance. Organizational structure can vary among firms according to:

▶ Span of control

▶ Organizational height

▶ Use of line versus staff positions

span of control
the number of employees managed by each manager

Span of Control   Top management determines the firm's **span of control,** or the number of employees managed by each manager. When an organizational structure is designed so that each manager supervises just a few employees, it has a narrow span of control. Conversely, when it is designed so that each manager supervises numerous employees, it has a wide span of control. When numerous employees perform similar tasks, a firm uses a wide span of control because these employees can be easily managed by one or a few managers. A firm with highly diverse tasks may need more managers with various skills to manage the different tasks, resulting in a narrow span of control.

Exhibit 8.1 illustrates how the span of control can vary among firms. The organizational structure at the top of the exhibit reflects a narrow span of control. Each employee oversees only one other employee. The nature of the business may require highly specialized skills in each position so that employees may focus on their own tasks and not have to monitor a large

Exhibit 8.1

Distinguishing between
a Narrow and a Wide
Span of Control

Narrow Span of Control

Wide Span of Control

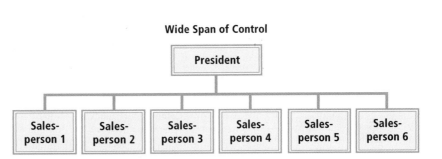

set of employees. The organizational structure at the bottom of the exhibit reflects a wide span of control. The president directly oversees all the other employees. Such a wide span of control is more typical of firms in which many employees have similar positions that can easily be monitored by a single person.

Organizational Height   The organizational structure can also be described by its height. A tall organizational structure implies that there are many layers from the bottom of the structure to the top. Conversely, a short (or flat) organizational structure implies that there is not much distance from the bottom of the structure to the top because there are not many layers of employees between the bottom and top. Many firms that are able to use a wide span of control tend to have a flat organizational structure because they do not require many layers. Conversely, firms that need to use a narrow span of control tend to have a tall organizational structure with many layers. Notice that in Exhibit 8.1, the organizational structure with the narrow span of control is tall, while the organizational structure with the wide span of control is flat.

Line versus Staff Positions   The job positions in an organizational structure can be classified as line positions or staff positions. **Line positions** are established to make decisions that achieve specific business goals. **Staff positions** are established to support the efforts of line positions, rather than to achieve specific goals of the firm. For example, managers at Black & Decker who are involved in the production of power tools are in line positions. Employees in staff positions at Black & Decker offer support to the managers who are in line positions. Thus, the staff positions provide

line positions

job positions established to make decisions that achieve specific business goals

staff positions

job positions established to support the efforts of line positions

Exhibit 8.2

Comparison of a Line
Organization with a
Line-and-Staff Organization

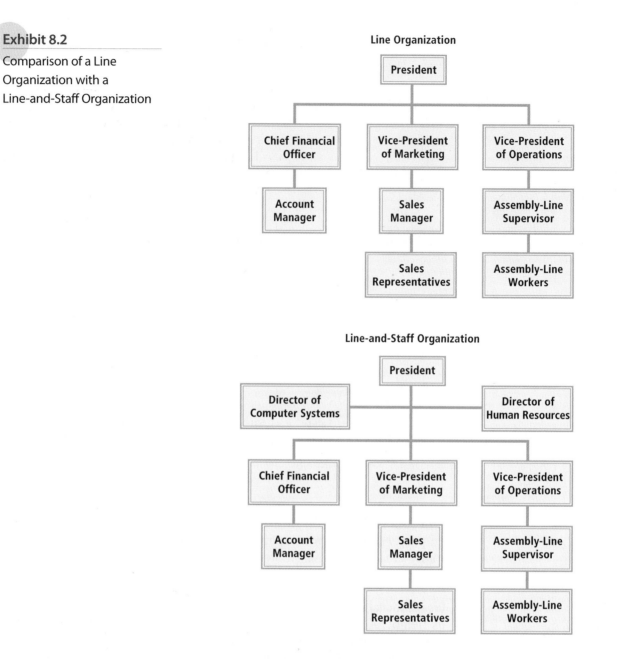

assistance to the line positions, and the authority to make decisions is assigned to the line positions.

An organizational structure that contains only line positions and no staff positions is referred to as a **line organization.** This type of organizational structure may be appropriate for a business that cannot afford to hire staff for support, such as a small manufacturing firm.

Most firms need some staff positions to provide support to the line positions. An organizational structure that includes both line and staff positions and assigns authority from higher-level management to employees is referred to as a **line-and-staff organization.**

Exhibit 8.2 depicts a line organization and a line-and-staff organization. The line-and-staff organization in this exhibit includes a director of computer systems, who oversees the computer system, and a director of human resources, who is involved with hiring and training employees. These two positions are staff positions because they can assist the finance, marketing, and production departments but do not have the authority to make decisions that achieve specific business goals.

line organization
an organizational structure that
contains only line positions and
no staff positions

line-and-staff organization
an organizational structure that
includes both line and staff positions and assigns authority from
higher-level management to
employees

Impact of Information Technology on Organizational Structure

Whatever type of organizational structure a firm uses, technology facilitates communication among the job positions throughout the organizational structure. All parts of a firm use technology, and a wide variety of departments include technology experts among their employees. Technology and the professionals working in the field must support and connect every area of the organization.

The integration of information technology (IT) requires communication among employees. A conscious effort must be made to maintain relationships with the groups each participant represents. IT representatives must communicate the options under consideration and solicit expertise when needed. Other members of the project team or department should inform the ultimate end users about the key issues under consideration and request feedback. These relationships are often overlooked and lost as the immediate challenge of the design overwhelms everything else. Therefore, relationships with other future participants should be maintained through planned communication as the project progresses.

Technology and the knowledge-based economy are not constrained by the physical objects and materials of a firm. Information is flexible and can be structured and organized in a number of different ways. For example, videoconferencing and telecommuting allow members of project teams from different departments to work together regardless of their location or their department. Thus, technology enables departments within a firm to communicate more easily.

Decision Making ▶ Selecting an Organizational Structure

The decision regarding a firm's organizational structure is dependent on the characteristics of the firm. Recall that Mars Technology Company owns production plants in four different cities that produce high-technology products such as digital cameras and miniature computers. The firm has four divisions, each of which includes a production plant served by factory workers, who report to supervisors. The supervisors in turn report to a top-line manager. Every division also has three vice-presidents—one for finance, one for marketing, and one for production. Mars Technology is failing and a new CEO, Dennis Berrett, was recently hired to improve the firm's performance. He closely reviews the job descriptions of all job positions and quickly realizes that some of the higher-level job positions are not necessary. Most of the actual work is being done at the factory level, and all the other positions are simply pushing paperwork up the organizational structure. The CEO considers what the optimal organizational structure would be if the firm had just been created. He decides that vice-presidents are needed only at the main production plant. By eliminating vice-presidents at the other divisions, the firm will be able to reduce expenses by more than $1 million per year.

1. At all levels above the supervisor, the original organizational structure at Mars Technology Company represented a narrow span of control. What is a disadvantage of this structure?

2. In the past, all the vice-presidents at Mars Technology Company spent much of their time arguing that their respective divisions needed more money. Why might such turf battles be reduced in the future as a result of the revised organizational structure?

ANSWERS: 1. The disadvantage is that it is expensive to have many job positions that oversee only a few other positions. Such a structure results in too many salaries to be paid.   2. With the revised organizational structure, there will only be vice-presidents at the main division. They can make decisions that benefit the firm, as they are less likely to allocate funds to any specific division unless the division deserves funding.

Explain how accountability can be achieved in an organizational structure.

Accountability in an Organizational Structure

While the organizational structure indicates job descriptions and the responsibilities of employees and managers, the firm also needs to ensure that its employees and managers are accountable. One of the important duties of the firm's managers is to evaluate the employees and make them accountable for fulfilling their responsibilities. The job descriptions provide direction for the job positions, but the managers above the positions must determine whether the employees performed according to their job descriptions.

The high-level managers of the firm, including the CEO and the vice-presidents, are accountable for the general performance of the firm. If they enforce a proper system of monitoring and accountability down through each layer of employees, they can ensure that the firm's employees are doing their jobs. These high-level managers also make many of the key decisions regarding the firm's product line, production process, compensation system, marketing, and financing. They tend to be well rewarded when the firm performs well, but they must also be held accountable if the firm has major problems. The board of directors, an internal auditor, and an internal control process can ensure that firms achieve accountability in the organizational structure.

Role of the Board of Directors

board of directors
a set of executives who are responsible for monitoring the activities of the firm's president and other high-level managers

Each firm has a **board of directors,** or a set of executives who are responsible for monitoring the activities of the firm's president and other high-level managers. Even the top managers of a firm may be tempted to make decisions that serve their own interests rather than those of the firm's owners. For example, the top managers may decide to use company funds to purchase private jets to use when they travel on business. This decision may be driven by their own self-interests. It may result in high ex-

Board meetings are necessary to discuss major issues or dilemmas faced by the business.

GETTY IMAGES

SMALL BUSINESS SURVEY

Who Are the Board Members of Small Firms?

A recent survey asked the CEOs of small firms (with less than $50 million in annual sales) about the background of their outside board members. The results of the survey follow.

Background	Percentage of Firms Whose Board Members Have That Background
Executives of other firms	69%
Major investors in the firm	36%
Retired business executives	30%
Attorneys	29%
Accountants	22%
Bankers	18%
Business consultants	13%
Customers	2%
Others	3%

The results suggest that these firms rely heavily on executives and major investors to serve as their outside board members. The attorneys, accountants, and business consultants who are hired as outside board members typically also perform other duties (such as legal or banking duties) for the firm.

penses, reduce the firm's value, and therefore be detrimental to the firm's owners.

The board of directors is also responsible for supervising the business and affairs of the firm. In addition to attempting to ensure that the business is managed with the intent of serving its shareholders, the directors are also responsible for monitoring operations and ensuring that the firm complies with the law. They cannot oversee every workplace decision, but they can force the firm to have a process that guides some decisions about moral and ethical conduct. The directors can also ensure that the firm has a system for internal control and reporting. The directors are selected by the shareholders and serve as their representatives, as confirmed by a quotation from Sears' annual report:

"The board of directors regularly reviews the corporation's structure to determine whether it supports optimal performance and thus serves the best interests of shareholders by delivering shareholder value."

The 1,000 largest U.S. firms have 12 directors on their boards on average. Board members who are also managers of the same firm (such as the CEO) are referred to as **inside board members.** Board members who are not managers of the firm are referred to as **outside board members.** Some firms, including General Electric and PepsiCo, provide directors with stock as partial compensation. This type of compensation may motivate the directors to serve the interests of the firm's shareholders because the board members will benefit if the firm's stock price rises.

inside board members
board members who are also managers of the same firm

outside board members
board members who are not managers of the firm

In general, the board focuses on major issues and normally is not involved in the day-to-day activities of the firm. Key business proposals, made by a firm's managers, such as acquisitions or layoffs, must be approved by the board. For example, America Online's decision to merge with Time Warner required board approval. Directors may also initiate changes in a firm. For example, the board may decide that the firm's CEO needs to be replaced or that the firm's businesses should be restructured. Board meetings generally are scheduled every few months or are called when the directors' input is needed on an important issue. Board members of numerous firms have become more active in recent years.

Conflicts of Interest within the Board   A board of directors is expected to ensure that top managers serve the interests of the firm rather than their own self-interests, but some directors also face conflicts of interest. As mentioned above, the board normally includes some insiders (employees) of the firm such as the CEO and some vice-presidents. These insiders will not be effective monitors of their own actions. For example, the insiders are not going to complain if the firm's managerial compensation is excessive, because they benefit directly as managers of the firm. In addition, some insider board members are not going to question the decisions of the CEO, because the CEO determines their compensation.

A board of directors may be more willing to take action if most of its members are outside directors (and therefore are not employees of the firm). The outside board members may suggest policies that will benefit shareholders, even if the policies are not supported by the firm's top managers. Therefore, shareholders tend to prefer that the board contain more outside directors.

Nevertheless, even outside directors may be subject to a conflict of interests that may inhibit their ability or willingness to make tough decisions for the firm. To illustrate these conflicts, consider the information about the board of directors of Gonzaga Company, shown in Exhibit 8.3. Notice from the exhibit that five of the eight board members are not employees of Gonzaga Company and therefore are outside directors. Yet, those five outside directors have conflicts of interest that may prevent them from making tough decisions about the top management. One of the outside directors is related to the CEO, while the other four outside directors receive money from Gonzaga Company in some form. Therefore, these outside directors will not be effective at representing the interests of Gonzaga's shareholders.

Recall the case of Enron, which distorted its financial statements to make its financial condition look better than it was. A committee from Enron's board was responsible for ensuring that the financial statements were properly checked. Of the six members on that committee, one received $72,000 per year from a consulting contract with Enron. Two other members were employed by universities that received large donations from Enron. Thus, three of the committee members were subject to a conflict of interest and should not have been on this committee. Such conflicts of interest explain why many of the actions of Enron's top managers were not questioned.

Resolving Conflicts of Interest   The recent publicity about conflicts of interest within boards of directors has caused many firms to restructure their

Exhibit 8.3

Example of How Some Board Members Are Subject to a Conflict of Interest

Name of Board Member	Job Position	Classified as Inside or Outside Director	Potential Conflict of Interest
Ed Martin	CEO of Gonzaga Co.	Inside	Since the CEO is a key decision maker of Gonzaga Co., he has a potential conflict of interest. A CEO is not an effective monitor of the decisions made by top management.
Lisa Kelly	Vice-President of Finance for Gonzaga Co.	Inside	Since the VP is a key decision maker of Gonzaga Co., she has a potential conflict of interest. A VP is not an effective monitor of the decisions made by top management.
Jerry Coldwell	Vice-President of Operations for Gonzaga Co.	Inside	Since the VP is a key decision maker of Gonzaga Co., he has a potential conflict of interest. A VP is not an effective monitor of the decisions made by top management.
Dave Jensen	Owner of a firm that is the key supplier of parts to Gonzaga Co.	Outside	Dave's company benefits directly from decisions of Gonzaga's top management to buy supplies from his firm. Thus, he is not likely to keep Gonzaga's top managers in line.
Sharon Martin (daughter-in-law of Ed Martin)	Vice-president of a real estate firm that does no business with Gonzaga Co.	Outside	Since Sharon is related to the CEO of Gonzaga, she is not likely to keep Gonzaga's top managers in line.
Karen Chandler	Independent consultant, who does a substantial amount of work for Gonzaga Co.	Outside	Karen relies on Gonzaga Co. for a large portion of her income, and therefore she is not likely to keep Gonzaga's top managers in line.
Terry Olden	Previous CEO of Gonzaga Co., now retired.	Outside	Terry no longer works at Gonzaga Co., but he is close to the top managers. Therefore, he is not likely to keep Gonzaga's top managers in line.
Mary Burke	CEO of a nonprofit health firm that receives large annual donations from Gonzaga Co.	Outside	Since Mary's firm receives donations from Gonzaga Co., she is not likely to keep Gonzaga's top managers in line.

boards to ensure that the board is composed in a manner that effectively serves the shareholders. For example, eBay's corporate governance guidelines include the following:

"The Board should be composed of directors who are chosen based on integrity, judgment, and experience. The directors should have high-level managerial experience to deal with complex problems. They should represent the best interests of the stockholders."

EBay usually attempts to have one or more former managers on its board. At the end of each board meeting, the outside board members have the option to meet separately without the inside directors. This gives the outside directors a chance to voice any concerns that the inside directors are making decisions to benefit themselves rather than the shareholders.

Similarly, Disney states in a recent annual report:

"We have established governance as a high priority at Disney for one simple reason—it's the right thing to do. By investing in Disney, shareholders are placing their trust in the board to help shape the overall course of the company's business and to hold management accountable for its performance."

Intel Corporation has clearly defined the role of its board of directors:

"The board is the company's governing body; responsible for hiring, overseeing and evaluating management, particularly the chief executive officer (CEO); and management runs the company's day-to-day operations. The end result is intended to be a well-run, efficient company that identifies and deals with its problems in a timely manner, creates value for its stockholders, and meets its legal and ethical responsibilities.

"We take our corporate governance seriously, expecting to achieve the same continuous improvement as in all of our business operations. Eight of our 11 directors are independent from the company except for their service to the board. They are not employees and do not have other business or consulting engagements with the company . . . . We expect that our directors will be engaged with us both inside and outside of board and committee meetings. Our directors meet with senior management on an individual basis, and attend and participate in employee forums. Unaccompanied by senior management, individual directors visit Intel sites around the world— an excellent opportunity for them to assess local site issues directly. These activities help to keep the board better informed, and make the board's oversight and input more valuable . . . . Separating the roles of chairman (of the board) and CEO is an important step toward better corporate governance . . . . My job as chairman is to ensure it is organized to fulfill its responsibilities. I preside at the board meetings, make sure that the board receives the right information, set board meeting agendas, and ensure that the directors have sufficient time for discussion."

— Andrew S. Grove, Chairman of the Board at Intel Corporation

Many firms that explain how they prevent conflicts of interest do not practice what they preach. For example, Disney recently experienced significant management problems and conflicts of interest even while its annual reports suggested that governance was a high priority.

Board Committees   In recent years, committees made up of members of the board of directors have been given specific assignments to ensure proper oversight of the firm. Though every publicly traded firm has its own set of committees, the following committees are commonly formed:

▶ **Compensation Committee.** Reviews existing salaries and compensation formulas for high-level managers, including the CEO.

▶ **Nominating Committee.** Assesses whether the existing board members have the knowledge and skills necessary to be effective; makes recommendations to the board of directors about the size and composition of the board.

▶ **Audit Committee.** Oversees the hiring and work of an external auditor that audits the firm's financial statements.

All three types of committees commonly consist of only independent board members to ensure that there will be no conflicts of interest. For example, J.C. Penney's policy is that its compensation committee will include only outside directors who are not employees or managers of the firm. Consequently, the committee can set the firm's compensation policy without being subjected to conflicts of interest.

Oversight of the Internal Auditor

internal auditor
responsible for ensuring that all departments follow the firm's guidelines and procedures

As another way to achieve accountability, many firms employ an **internal auditor,** who is responsible for ensuring that all departments follow the firm's guidelines and procedures. For example, an internal auditor may assess whether employees followed the firm's hiring procedures when filling job positions recently. The internal auditor is not attempting to interfere with managerial decisions, but is simply attempting to ensure that the procedures used to make those decisions are consistent with the firm's guidelines. Although the specific emphasis of an internal auditor varies among firms, some attention is commonly given to ensuring that employees' actions are consistent with the recommended procedures for hiring new employees, evaluating employees, maintaining safety, and responding to customer complaints.

Internal Control Process

As a result of the Sarbanes-Oxley Act, publicly traded firms were required to establish processes for internal control that enable them to more accurately monitor their financial performance over time. An internal control process complements the work of the internal and external auditors. It is a system that generates timely and accurate reporting of financial information and establishes controls over that information. Thus, it allows a firm's managers to more easily monitor the firm's financial condition. It also allows the firm to provide more accurate and timely disclosure of information to the public. Shareholders benefit from the firm's internal control process, because they want to be informed about the firm's recent performance and financial condition. The Sarbanes-Oxley Act caused firms to improve their internal control process by doing the following:

▶ Establishing a centralized database of information.

▶ Ensuring that all data reported by each division are reviewed for accuracy.

▶ Implementing a system that detects possible errors in the data.

▶ Acknowledging the risk associated with specific business operations.

▶ Ensuring that all departments are using consistent data.

▶ Speeding the process by which data are transferred among departments.

▶ Having their executives sign off (that is, take personal responsibility for) on specific financial statements to verify their accuracy.

The specific internal control process implemented varies among firms, but all of the systems use computer software that facilitates the reporting of financial information. All of them also require the work of employees to input data and evaluate the financial information.

One criticism of the Sarbanes-Oxley Act is that establishing an internal control process was a major expense for many firms. Some firms incurred a cost of $1 million or more to implement their system. Nevertheless, the internal control process may provide additional benefits because it not only allows for a better flow of information to the public, but also ensures that managers have up-to-date and reliable information when making decisions. Since many decisions are dependent on information, the improvement in the internal flow of information may allow managers to make better decisions.

Decision Making

Oversight of an Organizational Structure

As Mars Technology Company revises its organizational structure, it also decides to provide for proper oversight to ensure that its managers are accountable for their assignments. Until recently, its board of directors was mostly made up of the firm's managers. The new CEO proposes that most of the managers on the board be replaced by outside directors (who do not work at Mars). In addition, he proposes that an outside member should serve as the chair of the board rather than himself. These changes would give more power to outsiders and possibly prevent conflicts of interest that may occur when managers have too much power on the board. Mars also established some internal controls to measure the productivity at each production facility on a weekly basis. This will allow Mars to more easily assess the performance of the managers at each facility.

1. Is there any possible disadvantage of having a board that is mostly made up of outsiders?

2. Is there any possible disadvantage of having a substantial amount of internal controls? In other words, is it possible that internal controls can ever be excessive and adversely affect the firm?

ANSWERS: 1. One possible disadvantage is that outsiders may not understand the business well enough to oversee it properly and to guide management. 2. Some internal controls are expensive and may not be worth their expense.

3

Describe how centralized and decentralized organizational structures differ.

Distributing Authority among the Job Positions

A firm must determine how to distribute authority to make decisions among the job positions. Two firms may have the same organization chart, but the middle managers at one firm may be given much more authority than those at the other firm. The distribution of authority is often described by whether the firm is centralized or decentralized.

Centralization

centralized
most authority is held by the high-level managers

Some firms are **centralized;** that is, most authority is held by the high-level managers. In centralized firms, middle and supervisory managers are responsible for day-to-day tasks and for reporting to the top managers, but they are not allowed to make many decisions.

Decentralization

decentralized
authority is spread among several divisions or managers

autonomy
divisions can make their own decisions and act independently

In recent years, many firms have **decentralized,** meaning that authority is spread among several divisions or managers. An extreme form of decentralization is **autonomy,** in which divisions are permitted to make their own decisions and act independently. The trend toward decentralization is due to its potential advantages.

Advantages   A decentralized organizational structure can improve a firm's performance in several ways. First, decentralization reduces operating expenses because salaries of some employees who are no longer needed are eliminated.

Second, decentralization can shorten the decision-making process because lower-level employees are assigned more power. Decisions are made more quickly if the decision makers do not have to wait for approval from top managers. Many firms, including IBM, have decentralized to accelerate their decision making.

Third, delegation of authority can improve the morale of employees, who may be more enthusiastic about their work if they have more responsibilities. In addition, these managers become more experienced in decision making. Therefore, they will be better qualified for high-level management positions in the future. Decentralization has contributed to innovation at many technology firms, where many managers have become more creative. In addition, decentralization allows those employees who are closely involved in the production of a particular product to offer their input.

Johnson & Johnson is a prime example of a firm that has benefited from decentralization. It has numerous operating divisions scattered among more than 50 countries, and most of the decision making is done by the managers at those divisions. As a result, each unit can make quick decisions in response to local market conditions.

Disadvantages   A decentralized organizational structure can also have disadvantages. It could force some managers to make major decisions even

Employees of IBM are involved in a management training seminar. The management of IBM has been decentralized, allowing employees more power to make decisions.

CORBIS, CHICAGO

Self-Scoring Exercise

How Decentralized Is Your Company?

Decentralization is one of the key design dimensions in an organization. It is closely related to several behavioral dimensions of an organization, such as leadership style, degree of participative decision making, teamwork, and the nature of power and politics within the organization.

The following questionnaire allows you to get an idea of how decentralized your organization is. (If you do not have a job, have a friend who works complete the questionnaire to see how decentralized his or her organization is.) Which level in your organization has the authority to make each of the following decisions? Answer the questionnaire by circling one of the following:

0 = The board of directors makes the decision.
1 = The CEO makes the decision.
2 = The division/functional manager makes the decision.
3 = A sub-department head makes the decision.
4 = The first-level supervisor makes the decision.
5 = Operators on the shop floor make the decision.

Decision Concerning:	Circle Appropriate Level
a. The number of workers required.	0 1 2 3 4 5
b. Whether to employ a worker.	0 1 2 3 4 5
c. Internal labor disputes.	0 1 2 3 4 5
d. Overtime worked at shop level.	0 1 2 3 4 5
e. Delivery dates and order priority.	0 1 2 3 4 5
f. Production planning.	0 1 2 3 4 5
g. Dismissal of a worker.	0 1 2 3 4 5
h. Methods of personnel selection.	0 1 2 3 4 5
i. Method of work to be used.	0 1 2 3 4 5
j. Machinery or equipment to be used.	0 1 2 3 4 5
k. Allocation of work among workers.	0 1 2 3 4 5

Add up all your circled numbers. Total = _____. The higher your number (for example, 45 or more), the more decentralized your organization. The lower your number (for example, 25 or less), the more centralized your organization.

though they lack the experience to make such decisions or prefer not to do so. Also, if middle and supervisory managers are assigned an excessive amount of responsibilities, they may be unable to complete all of their tasks.

Proper Degree of Decentralization The proper degree of decentralization for any firm is dependent on the skills of the managers who could be assigned more responsibilities. Decentralization can be beneficial when the managers who are given more power are capable of handling their additional responsibilities. For example, assume that a firm's top managers have previously determined annual raises for all assembly-line workers but now decide to delegate this responsibility to the supervisors who monitor those workers. The supervisors are closer to the assembly line and are possibly in a better position to assess worker performance. Therefore, decentralization may be appropriate. The top managers may still have final approval of the raises that the supervisors propose for their workers.

As a second example, assume that top managers allow assembly-line supervisors to decide what price the firm will bid for a specific business that is for sale. Assembly-line supervisors normally are not trained for this type of task and should not be assigned to it. Determining the proper price to bid for a business requires a strong financial background and should not be delegated to managers without the proper skills.

As these examples demonstrate, high-level managers should retain authority for tasks that require their specialized skills but should delegate authority when the tasks can be handled by other managers. Routine decisions should be made by the employees who are closely involved with the tasks of concern. Decision making may improve because these employees are closer to the routine tasks and may have greater insight than top managers on these matters.

Some degree of centralization is necessary when determining how funds should be allocated to support various divisions of a firm. If managers of each division are given the authority to make this decision, they may request additional funds even though their division does not need to expand. Centralized management of funds can prevent division man-

Global Business

How Organizational Structure Affects the Control of Foreign Operations

A firm that has subsidiaries scattered around the world will find it more difficult to ensure that its managers serve the shareholders' interests rather than their own self-interests. In other words, the firm will experience more pronounced agency problems. First, it is difficult for the parent's top managers to monitor operations in foreign countries because of the distance from headquarters. Second, managers of foreign subsidiaries who have been raised in different cultures may not follow uniform goals. Third, the sheer size of the larger multinational corporations can also create large agency problems.

The magnitude of agency costs can vary with the management style of the multinational corporation. A centralized management style can reduce agency costs because it allows managers of the parent to control foreign subsidiaries and therefore reduces the power of subsidiary managers. However, the parent's managers may make poor decisions for the subsidiary because they are less familiar with its financial characteristics.

A decentralized management style is likely to result in higher agency costs because subsidiary managers may make decisions that do not focus on maximizing the value of the entire multinational corporation. Nevertheless, this style gives more control to the managers who are closer to the subsidiary's operations and environment. To the extent that subsidiary managers recognize the goal of maximizing the value of the overall firm and are compensated in accordance with that goal, the decentralized management style may be more effective.

Given the obvious tradeoff between centralized and decentralized management styles, some multinational corporations attempt to achieve the advantages of both styles. They allow subsidiary managers to make the key decisions about their respective operations, but the parent's management monitors the decisions to ensure that they are in the best interests of the entire firm.

The Internet makes it easier for the parent to monitor the actions and performance of foreign subsidiaries. Since the subsidiaries may be in different time zones, it is inconvenient and expensive to require frequent phone conversations. In addition, financial reports and designs of new products or plant sites cannot be easily communicated over the phone. The Internet allows the foreign subsidiaries to e-mail updated information in a standardized format to avoid language problems and to send images of financial reports and product designs. The parent can easily track inventory, sales, expenses, and earnings of each subsidiary on a weekly or monthly basis.

---

agers from making decisions that conflict with the goal of maximizing the firm's value.

downsizing
an attempt by a firm to cut expenses by eliminating job positions

Effect of Downsizing on Decentralization   As firms expanded during the 1980s, additional management layers were created, resulting in taller organization charts. In the 1990s and early 2000s, however, many firms have attempted to cut expenses by eliminating job positions. This so-called **downsizing** has resulted in flatter organization charts with fewer layers of managers. Continental Airlines, IBM, General Motors, Sears, and many other firms have downsized in recent years.

As some management positions are eliminated, many of those responsibilities are delegated to employees who previously reported to the managers whose positions have been eliminated. For example, Amoco (now part of BP Amoco) eliminated a middle layer of its organizational structure. When managers in the middle of the organization chart are removed, other employees must be assigned more power to make decisions. Thus, downsizing has resulted in a greater degree of decentralization.

Downsizing has also affected each manager's span of control. When many middle managers are eliminated, the remaining managers have more diverse responsibilities. Consequently, the organizational structure of many firms now reflects a wider span of control, as illustrated in Exhibit 8.4.

Out of Business

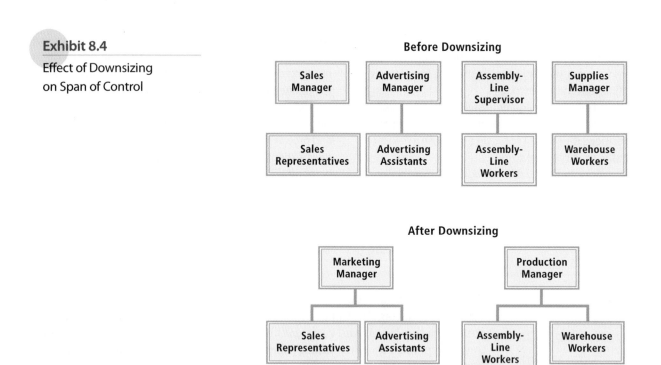

Effect of Downsizing on Span of Control

In addition to removing some management layers and creating a wider span of control, downsizing has also led to the combination of various job responsibilities within the organizational structure. Whereas job assignments traditionally focused on production tasks, more attention is now given to customer satisfaction. Many firms recognize that they must rely on their current customers for additional business in the future and have revised their strategic plan to focus on achieving repeat business from their customers. In many cases, customers would prefer to deal with a single employee rather than several different employees. Consequently, employees are less specialized because they must have diverse skills to accommodate the customers.

Decision Making

Whether to Decentralize?

The decision to decentralize is dependent on the specific characteristics of the firm. To illustrate, consider Mars Technology Company, which has executives at its headquarters. The company has four divisions; each division has a top-line manager and some supervisors who oversee the assembly-line production by the employees. Mars Technology wants to delegate the authority for various decisions to the proper managers. It decides to delegate the authority for assessing the performance of the assembly-line workers and the supervisory managers. The supervisory managers are given the authority to evaluate the assembly-line workers because they interact with these workers and closely monitor their work. The top-line manager at each division is given the authority to evaluate the supervisors at that plant because this manager commonly interacts with the supervisors and can monitor their performance. The executives are not based at the divisions and therefore do not closely interact with assembly-line workers or supervisory managers. Therefore, the tasks of evaluating employees should be decentralized.

In contrast, the major decisions about the long-term expansion at each division are centralized. The executives closely monitor the overall performance at each production plant. They decide whether each plant should expand, based on the existing demand for the products of that division. Thus, the executives are responsible for strategic planning that serves as a guide for the firm. The decentralized decisions focus more on day-to-day operations of the production at each division, while the centralized decisions focus on the future growth of each division.

1. Would there be any disadvantage to Mars Technology of relying on the managers at the divisions for decisions about production, beyond the heavy burden of responsibility on the managers?

2. Would the factory workers at Mars Technology be more satisfied if the day-to-day production decisions were centralized or decentralized?

ANSWERS: 1. A possible disadvantage is that the managers may not have the skills to make the decisions or even to make reasonable recommendations, but Dennis Berrett (the CEO) can review their recommendations before he uses them. 2. Decentralized decision making is more likely to account for the views of the factory workers, which could be beneficial to them.

Structures That Allow More Employee Input

Discuss methods firms can use to obtain employee input.

Firms commonly rely on the input of employees from various divisions for special situations. For this reason, they may need to temporarily adjust their formal organizational structure so that some extra responsibilities may be assigned. A firm may obtain employee input by using the following to complement its formal organizational structure:

▶ Matrix organization

▶ Intrapreneurship

▶ Informal organizational structure

Each of these methods is discussed in turn.

Matrix Organization

matrix organization
an organizational structure that enables various parts of the firm to interact to focus on specific projects

Firms are often confronted with special circumstances that require input from their employees. In a **matrix organization,** various parts of the firm interact to focus on specific projects. Because the projects may take up only a portion of the normal workweek, participants can continue to perform their normal tasks and are still accountable to the same boss for those tasks.

For example, a firm that plans to install a new computer system may need input from each division on the specific functions that division will require from the system. This example is illustrated in Exhibit 8.5. As the exhibit shows, the finance, marketing, and production divisions each have one representative on the team; each representative can offer insight from the perspective of his or her respective division. The team of employees will periodically work on the assigned project until it is completed. Some employees may be assigned to two or more projects during the specific period. The lower horizontal line in Exhibit 8.5 shows the interaction among the representatives from different divisions. The manager of this project is a computer systems employee, who will report the recommendations of the matrix organization to the president or to some other top manager.

An advantage of the matrix approach is that it brings together employees who can offer insight from different perspectives. Each participant who is assigned to a specific group (or team) has particular skills that can contribute to the project. By involving all participants in decision making, this teamwork may provide more employee satisfaction than typical day-to-day assignments. Firms such as Intel, IBM, and Boeing commonly use teams of employees to complete specific projects.

One possible disadvantage of a matrix organization is that no employee may feel responsible because responsibilities are assigned to teams of several employees. Therefore, a firm that uses teams to complete various tasks may designate one job position to have the responsibility of organizing the team and ensuring that the team's assignment is completed before the deadline. The person designated as project manager (or team leader) of a specific project does not necessarily have authority over the other participants for any other tasks.

Another disadvantage of the matrix organization is that any time used to participate in projects reduces the time allocated for normal tasks. In some cases, ultimate responsibility is not clear, causing confusion. Many firms eliminated their matrix structure for this reason.

Intrapreneurship

Some firms not only seek input from employees on specific issues but also encourage employees to offer ideas for operational changes that will enhance the firm's value. These firms may even create a special subsidiary

Exhibit 8.5

A Matrix Organization for a Special Project to Design a New Computer System

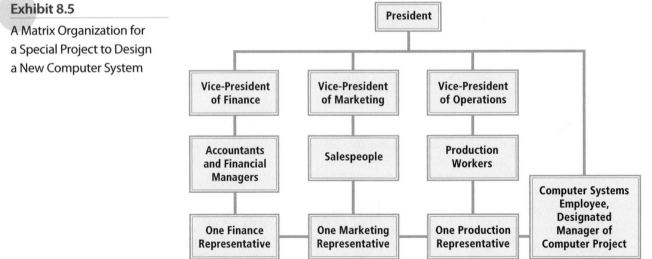

3M Company encourages its employees to be creative, which has led to the creation of products such as its Post-it notes.

LANDOV LLC

within their organizational structure in which particular employees are given the responsibility to innovate. In this way, the costs and benefits of innovation can be estimated separately from the rest of the business operations.

Particular employees of a firm can be assigned to generate ideas, as if they were entrepreneurs running their own firms. This process is referred to as **intrapreneurship,** as employees are encouraged to think like entrepreneurs within the firm. They differ from entrepreneurs, however, in that they are employees rather than owners of the firm. Some employees may even be assigned the responsibility of developing new products or ideas for improving existing products. A potential disadvantage of intrapreneurship is that it can pull employees away from normal, day-to-day production tasks. Nevertheless, it can also allow firms to be more innovative because employees are encouraged to search for new ideas. Many firms, including Apple Computer and 3M Company, have used intrapreneurship to encourage new ideas.

Intrapreneurship is likely to be more successful if employees are rewarded with some type of bonus for innovations that are ultimately applied by the firm. The firm should also attempt to ensure that any ideas that employees develop are seriously considered. If managers shoot down ideas for the wrong reasons (jealousy, for instance), employees may consider leaving the firm to implement their ideas (by starting their own business).

intrapreneurship
the assignment of particular employees of a firm to generate ideas, as if they were entrepreneurs running their own firms

Informal Organizational Structure

All firms have both a formal and an informal organizational structure. The **informal organizational structure** is the informal communications network that exists among a firm's employees. This network (sometimes called the "grapevine") develops as a result of employee interaction over time. Some employees interact because they work on similar tasks. Employees at different levels may interact in a common lunch area or at social events.

informal organizational structure
an informal communications network among a firm's employees

Communication   A firm may take steps to develop an informal organizational structure to encourage communication between managers and employees in a less formal environment. For example, the firm may organize social events within the firm. This does not affect the formal organizational structure, but it does create a complementary network to ensure more social interaction between employees at different levels. Consequently, the employees should have a better understanding of the managers who monitor them, and the managers should have a better understanding of their employees. In addition, the managers may receive more informal feedback from their employees that they would not receive from the formal organizational structure. The feedback will be more informative than if a manager sends out a formal survey once a year asking employees for any concerns or suggestions that they may have. The employees may think that the manager was forced to send out the survey and is not really interested in their concerns. Assuming that it is just a formality and that their responses will be ignored, they will not make much of an effort to provide their opinions.

If a manager asks for feedback in an informal environment, however, the employees may be more willing to provide it because they realize that the manager is truly interested in their opinions. They may make suggestions about improving relations with employees, work conditions, salaries, or even product innovations. These types of suggestions could allow the firm to improve the level of employee job satisfaction, or improve the production process, and therefore could motivate employees to work more efficiently. Without an informal organizational structure, the firm might never receive these suggestions. Furthermore, with an informal structure information can travel quickly from the bottom to the top of the organization, so the higher-level managers will be tuned in to the morale of the employees.

Another advantage of an informal organizational structure is that employees who need help in performing a task may benefit from others. If employees had to seek help through the formal structure, they would have to go to the person to whom they report. If that particular person is not available, the production process could be slowed. An informal structure may also allow employees to substitute for one another, thereby ensuring that a task will be completed on time. In addition, an informal structure can reduce the amount of manager involvement.

An informal structure may also encourage friendships among employees, which may lead to employees being more satisfied with their jobs. On-the-job friendships could be the major factor that discourages them from looking for a new job. This is especially true of lower-level jobs that pay low wages. Because friendship can strongly influence employee satisfaction, firms commonly encourage social interaction by organizing social functions.

Disadvantages   Along with the advantages just described, an informal structure also has some disadvantages. Perhaps the main disadvantage is that employees may obtain incorrect or unfavorable information about the firm through the informal structure. Even if the information is untrue or is a gross exaggeration, it can have a major impact on employee morale. For example, when a boss meets with some employees on an informal basis, other employees who were left out of the meeting may become jealous or believe that they are not receiving as much attention. They may even start rumors about how the boss gives some employees more favorable treatment than others. Unfavorable information that has an adverse impact tends to travel faster and further throughout an informal structure than favorable information does.

Decision Making

Creating an Effective Informal Structure

Recall that the task of Dennis Berrett, the new CEO of Mars Technology Company, is to revise the firm's organizational structure. He also needs to establish an informal structure to improve the morale among workers at one of the company's production plants. A few unhappy employees have spread rumors that the plant is going to close down or that most employees at the plant will be fired in the near future. Dennis has sent out messages denying that changes are planned, but the employees tend to believe the rumors because they are closer to the employees who spread the rumors than to the managers.

Dennis needs an informal structure that will allow for more interaction between the employees and the managers at the plant. However, he does not want to use up excessive work time because he needs to ensure that workers are fulfilling their production jobs during work hours. So he decides to sponsor a lunch session every Friday at a local restaurant for the plant's employees. A manager will be present to discuss any topics of concern to the employees. In addition, Dennis himself plans to attend the lunch session one Friday a month to meet with employees and hear their concerns. As a result of the lunch sessions, managers will have a better understanding of the employees' concerns, and employees will better trust the managers. This informal structure should improve the morale of the employees, the productivity of the firm, and its performance.

1. Is there any disadvantage to the informal structure established for the employees at Mars Technology Company?

2. Would Mars Technology's informal structure be effective if the lunch sessions included only the factory workers?

ANSWERS: 1. The disadvantage is that the informal structure could cause the employees to be disappointed when they receive some informal information from the managers, but the informal structure should generally have favorable effects. 2. The informal structure would not be effective if the lunch sessions included only the factory workers because they would not have access to a higher-level manager who could prevent the spreading of rumors

Identify methods that can be used to departmentalize tasks.

departmentalize
assign tasks and responsibilities to different departments

Methods of Departmentalizing Tasks

When developing or revising an organizational structure, high-level management must first identify all the different job assignments, tasks, and responsibilities. The next step is to **departmentalize** those tasks and responsibilities, which means to assign the tasks and responsibilities to different departments. The best way of departmentalizing depends on the characteristics of the business. By using an efficient method of departmentalizing tasks and responsibilities, a firm can minimize its expenses and maximize its value. The following are four of the more popular methods of departmentalizing:

▶ By function
▶ By product
▶ By location
▶ By customer

Departmentalize by Function

When firms departmentalize by function, they allocate their tasks and responsibilities according to employee functions. The organization chart shown in Exhibit 8.6 is departmentalized by function. The finance, marketing, and production divisions are separated. This system works well for firms that produce just one or a few products, especially if the managers communicate across the functions.

Departmentalize by Product

In larger firms with many products, departmentalizing by product is common. Tasks and responsibilities are separated according to the type of product produced. The organization chart shown in Exhibit 8.7 is departmentalized by product (soft drink, food, and restaurant). This type of organizational structure is used by General Motors, which has created divisions such as Buick, Cadillac, and Chevrolet.

Many large firms departmentalize by both product and function, as shown in Exhibit 8.8. The specific divisions are separated by product, and

Exhibit 8.6

Departmentalizing by Function

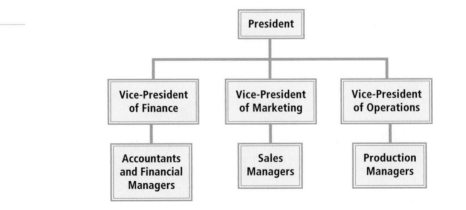

Cross Functional Teamwork

Relationship between Organizational Structure and Production

To illustrate how the organizational structure is affected by a firm's management, marketing, and finance decisions, consider a firm that produces office desks and distributes them to various retail office furniture outlets. The organizational structure will be partially dependent on the product mix (a marketing decision). If the firm diversifies its product line to include office lamps, file cabinets, and bookcases, its organizational structure will have to specify who is assigned to produce and manage these other products. The plant site selected must be large enough, and the firm's design and layout must be flexible enough, to allow for the production of these other products.

Exhibit 8.7

Departmentalizing by Product

Exhibit 8.8

Departmentalizing by Product and Function

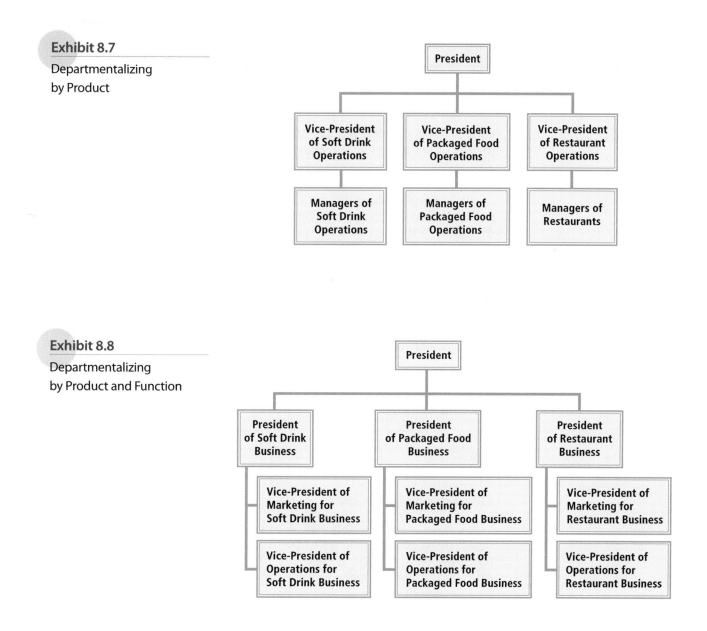

General Motors departmentalizes by product when managing its production.

GETTY IMAGES

each product division is departmentalized by function. Thus, each product division may have its own marketing, finance, and production divisions. This system may appear to be inefficient because it requires several divisions. Yet, if the firm is large enough, a single division would need to hire as many employees as are needed for the several divisions. Separation by product allows employees to become familiar with a single product rather than having to keep track of several different products.

Departmentalizing by product enables a firm to more easily estimate the expenses involved in the production of each product. The firm can be viewed as a set of separate business divisions (separated by product), and each division's profits can be determined over time. This allows the firm to determine the contribution of each business division to its total profits, which is useful when the firm is deciding which divisions should be expanded.

For a small or medium-sized firm with just a few products, departmentalizing by product would lead to an inefficient use of employees, resulting in excessive expenses. A single financial manager should be capable of handling all financial responsibilities, and a single marketing manager should be capable of handling all marketing responsibilities. Thus, there is no reason to departmentalize by product.

Departmentalize by Location

Tasks and responsibilities can also be departmentalized by location by establishing regional offices to cover specific geographic regions. This system may be appealing if corporate customers in particular locations frequently purchase a variety of the firm's products. Such customers would be able to contact the same regional office to place all of their orders. Large

Global Business

Organizational Structure of a Multinational Corporation

The organizational structure of a multinational corporation is complex because responsibilities must be assigned not only to U.S. operations but also to all foreign operations. To illustrate, consider General Motors, which has facilities in Europe, Canada, Asia, Latin America, Africa, and the Middle East. It has departmentalized by location, so either a president or a vice-president is in charge of each foreign region. Specifically, a president is assigned to GM of Mexico, a president to GM of Brazil, a vice-president to Asian and Pacific operations, a president to GM of Canada Limited, and a vice-president to Latin American, African, and Middle East operations. In Europe, one vice-president is assigned to sales and marketing, and a second vice-president is assigned to Europe's manufacturing plants. Thus, the European operations are also departmentalized by function.

Even when firms departmentalize their U.S. operations by product or by function, they commonly departmentalize their foreign operations by location. Since some foreign operations are distant from the firm's headquarters, departmentalizing operations in a foreign country by product or function would be difficult. If the foreign operations were departmentalized by product, an executive at the U.S. headquarters would have to oversee each product produced in the foreign country. If the operations were departmentalized by function, an executive at the U.S. headquarters would have to oversee each function conducted at the foreign facility. Normally, executives at the U.S. headquarters cannot easily monitor the foreign operations because they are not there on a daily or even a weekly basis. Consequently, it is more appropriate to assign an executive at the foreign facility the responsibility of overseeing a wide variety of products and functions at that facility.

In recent years, some multinational corporations have begun to select people who have international business experience for their boards of directors. Such directors are better able to monitor the firm's foreign operations. Furthermore, some multinational corporations have become more willing to promote managers within the firm who have substantial experience in international business. Sometimes a corporation will assign employees to its foreign facilities so that they can gain that experience.

---

accounting firms departmentalize by location in order to be close to their customers.

When a firm is departmentalized by location, it can more easily estimate the expenses incurred at each location. The firm can be viewed as a set of divisions separated by location, with each location generating its own profits. This allows the firm to identify the locations that have been performing well, which may help it determine which locations should attempt to expand their business.

Departmentalize by Customer

Some firms establish separate divisions based on the type of customer. For example, some airlines have a separate reservations division that focuses exclusively on group trips. Computer firms such as Dell have designated some salespeople to focus exclusively on selling computers to school systems. They also have some divisions that focus on online sales to individuals, while others focus on large corporate customers.

Cross Functional Teamwork

Interaction among Departments

Although the organizational structure formally indicates to whom each employee reports, it still allows interaction among different departments. For example, a firm may departmentalize by function so that one executive is responsible for the management of operations, a second executive is responsible for the marketing function, and a third executive is responsible for the financing function.

Though each function appears independent of the others on the organization chart, executives in charge of their respective functions must interact with the other departments. Exhibit 8.9 shows how the marketing, production, and finance departments rely on each other for information before making decisions. The marketing department needs to be aware of any changes in the production of a product and the volume of the product that will be available before it finalizes its marketing strategies. The production department needs customer satisfaction information as it considers redesigning products. It also needs to receive forecasts of expected sales from the marketing department, which affect the decision of how much to produce. The marketing and production departments provide the finance department with their forecasts of funds needed to cover their expenses. The finance department uses this information along with other information to determine whether it needs to obtain additional financing for the firm.

Exhibit 8.9

Flow of Information
across Departments

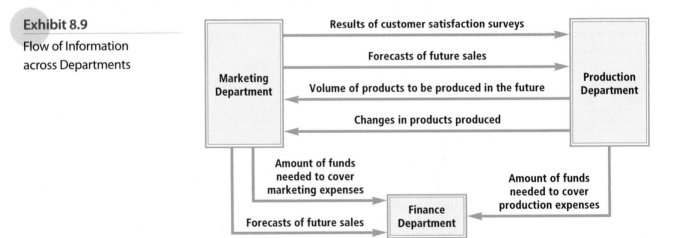

Decision Making

How to Departmentalize

Mars Technology Company produces four types of products. It wants to determine whether to departmentalize by product or by location. If it departmentalizes by product, it will need to hire managers who specialize in each of the four products that are produced at each of the four locations (Boston, Chicago, Denver, and Los Angeles). These managers would have to travel to each of the four cities periodically to monitor the production and conditions at each division. These managers would focus on the production of the specific product to which they were assigned and would not make marketing or finance decisions. Mars Technology Company decides that the existing top-line manager at each division can adequately monitor the production at the division. Therefore, it decides to continue departmentalizing by location. This avoids the expenses that would be incurred if the new managers were hired, as well as the expenses of having the managers travel frequently to all four locations.

1. Why might Mars Technology Company more seriously consider departmentalizing by product if all of its divisions were located in one city?
2. If Mars Technology Company's products required specialized managers who knew the details of each product, how might this complicate the decision to departmentalize?

ANSWERS: 1. If all the divisions were in one city, Mars Technology Company could more easily departmentalize by product, and the managers could easily oversee all the production centers. But since the locations are widely separated, the decision to departmentalize by location is more efficient. 2. The company would need to have managers for each product, and that would be costly because these managers would have to travel across cities to monitor each of the divisions.

COLLEGE HEALTH CLUB: DEPARTMENTALIZING TASKS AT CHC

Another decision that Sue Kramer needs to make as part of her business plan is how to departmentalize tasks at College Health Club (CHC). She first considers the main functions of CHC and who will perform these functions. She will decide on the marketing plan that will be implemented to attract new customers. The health club services will be provided by Sue and her part-time employees. Sue will make any future financing decisions for CHC. All services will be provided at one location. Sue needs to departmentalize tasks at CHC so that aerobics classes can be held in one part of the club while members can use exercise and weight machines in another area. She decides that she will establish a weekly aerobics schedule and assign a specific employee (or herself) to lead each class. When employees are not leading an aerobics class, they will be assigned to help members use the exercise and weight machines.

Although all health club services are currently provided at one location, Sue may open additional health clubs in the future. She then will departmentalize by location because any part-time employees will be assigned to only one of the health club locations.

Summary

1 The organizational structure of a firm identifies responsibilities for each job position within the firm and the relationships among those positions. The structure enables employees to recognize which job positions are responsible for the work performed by other positions.

The organizational structure can vary among firms according to the

▶ span of control, which determines the number of employees managed by each manager;

▶ organizational height, which determines the number of layers from the top to the bottom of the structure; and

▶ use of line positions (established to make decisions) versus staff positions (established to support the line positions).

2 An organizational structure needs to ensure accountability at all levels including high-level managers. A firm's board of directors is responsible for overseeing the decisions made by the CEO and other high-level managers. Boards that include many members who are managers of the firm may be unwilling to discipline a CEO because those directors' compensation levels may be dictated by the CEO. Therefore, boards tend to be more effective when they include more outside directors who are independent (are not employees of the firm).

Firms also have internal control processes that ensure accountability by requiring frequent and accurate reporting of financial data; this information can be used to monitor the activities and performance of various divisions within the firm. The internal control not only allows for a better flow of information to the public, but also ensures that managers have up-to-date and reliable information when making decisions.

3 Firms vary in the degree to which they distribute authority. Centralized firms assign most of the authority to the high-level managers. Decentralized firms spread the authority among several divisions or managers. Decentralization is desirable because it can speed the decision-making process and give employees more power and job satisfaction. However, firms must be careful to ensure that the managers who are given substantial authority are capable of handling the responsibilities that they are assigned.

4 A firm can benefit from receiving frequent feedback from its employees regarding work conditions, salaries, or even product innovations; the firm can use the suggestions to increase employee job satisfaction or improve the production process. However, its organizational structure may not necessarily encourage much employee feedback. To obtain employee feedback, firms may implement the following to complement their organizational structure:

▶ matrix organization, which allows employees from different divisions of the firm to interact;

▶ intrapreneurship, which encourages employees to think like entrepreneurs by giving them some responsibility for offering suggestions about improving a specific product or part of the production process; and

▶ informal organizational structure, which forces interaction between employees and managers at different levels so that employees have the opportunity to offer feedback to managers on an informal basis.

5 The main methods of departmentalizing are by

▶ function, in which tasks are separated according to employee functions;

▶ product, in which tasks are separated according to the product produced;

▶ location, in which tasks are concentrated in a particular division to serve a specific area; and

▶ customer, in which tasks are separated according to the type of customer that purchases the firm's products.

How the Chapter Concepts Affect Business Performance

A firm's decisions regarding the organizational structure concepts summarized here affect its performance. Its organizational structure determines the job positions and layers of managers used to run the business and therefore determines the amount of money that will be needed to compensate all these job positions. Its decision to decentralize can reduce the layers of management and therefore the expenses associated with management. An effective informal structure can improve employee morale. The decision on how to departmentalize affects the efficiency with which managers can manage the business.

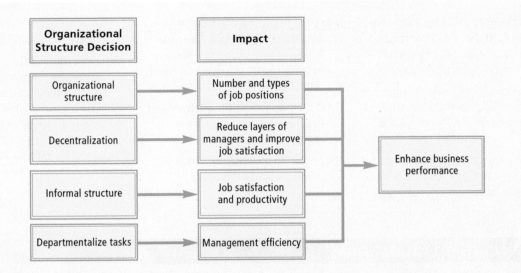

Key Terms

autonomy 289
board of directors 282
centralized 288
chain of command 278
decentralized 289
departmentalize 298
downsizing 291

informal organizational
  structure 296
inside board members 283
internal auditor 287
intrapreneurship 295
line organization 280
line positions 279

line-and-staff organization 280
matrix organization 293
organizational structure 278
outside board members 283
span of control 278
staff positions 279

Review & Critical Thinking Questions

1. Define organizational structure. Explain how a firm's organizational structure can affect its value.

2. Explain the following statement: "Generally speaking, no one specific organizational structure is optimal for all firms."

3. Define inside board members and outside board members. What type of compensation may motivate these directors to serve the interests of the firm's shareholders?

4. Why may shareholders prefer that the board of directors contain more outside directors than inside directors? Can there still be conflicts of interest within the board if it is composed primarily of outside directors?

5. Describe the role of an internal auditor.

6. How would the span of control differ for a firm with numerous employees who perform similar tasks and for a firm with highly diverse tasks?

7. What is decentralization? Explain the advantages and disadvantages of decentralization.

8. Explain the difference between line positions and staff positions within an organization. Provide examples of each.

9. Assume that you are creating a new organizational structure for your firm that allows more employee input. Identify and explain three methods you could use to revise the organizational structure.

10. What is an informal organizational structure? Explain the advantages and disadvantages of an informal organizational structure.

11. Explain why the organizational structure of a multinational corporation that operates a global business is so complex. What methods of departmentalizing are commonly used by multinational corporations?

12. Explain the phase "cross functional teamwork" and how it relates to interaction among departments.

13. If you were going to invest in a company, how could you get information about the board of directors? What kinds of conflicts of interest would you look for?

14. Is it possible that a very informal organizational structure might engender a lack of respect for authority? Why or why not?

15. How can a multinational firm successfully decentralize without losing control of its operations and business functions?

16. What aspects of intrapreneurship can lead to value maximization for the firm?

17. Why might a firm utilize a matrix organization? Can you think of any situations where a matrix organization might be important?

18. What do you think are the most important provisions of the Sarbanes-Oxley Act?

19. What are the three main committees of the board of

directors? How can they interact to discipline management?

20. How might a firm's managers structure the board of directors so that the board will not exercise a great deal of oversight over the managers? In other words, what types of boards could be detrimental to monitoring?

Discussion Questions

1. You work at a software company that does not have a clearly identifiable chain of command. Over lunch, another manager informs you that he is going to hire his cousin, a software engineer, for a position at your company. "I already know she can do the job. Why should I bother interviewing other employees?" What is wrong with the manager's actions?

2. Assume that you are a high-level manager and are revising the organizational structure of your firm. Identify and explain the main methods for departmentalizing the tasks and responsibilities to the different departments.

3. Assume that you have just been named the project manager for

a firm. The project involves employees from various parts of the firm. What type of temporary organizational structure would you recommend and why?

4. Explain the following statement: "Departmentalization is the building block for organizational structure."

5. How could a firm use the Internet to provide information about its organizational structure?

6. Express your opinion of the informal organization. Is it the same as the "grapevine"? Should a manager ever participate in the "grapevine" with employees?

7. For what kinds of businesses might a narrow span of control work best? When might a wide span of control work best?

8. Consider a company like Home Depot. Who are its line workers? Who are its staff workers?

9. Consider the internal control process required by the Sarbanes-Oxley Act. Do you think the expenses of implementing better internal controls are offset by the benefits of having the controls?

10. How can an informal organizational structure prevent rumors and gossip from spreading throughout the organization? What might be a drawback to an informal organizational structure?

It's Your Decision: Organizational Structure at CHC

1. One alternative span of control Sue could have is to assign the part-time employees to different levels. For example, the employee who has been employed at CHC the longest would have the most seniority and could be put in charge of the others. Would this span of control be more effective at CHC than the wide span of control in which all of the employees will report to Sue? Is any disadvantage associated with giving one of the employees power over the others?

2. Sue may consider hiring a college student majoring in exercise science for an intrapreneurship position during the summer. How could this student help CHC besides as a typical employee?

3. CHC's organizational structure is set up so that each part-time employee will lead aerobics classes, which is essentially a part of production (producing a service). In addition,

each part-time employee will show prospective members around the club, which is a marketing function. Explain why assigning integrated tasks to employees may be more effective than assigning each employee just one type of task.

4. Assuming that CHC's total non-salary expenses are expected to be $94,000 and that the membership fee is $500, determine how the club's estimated earnings are affected by the following possible closing times:

If CHC Closes at _____ Each Night	Estimated Annual Salary Expenses Incurred in the First Year	Expected Memberships in the First Year	CHC's Expected Earnings before Taxes in the First Year
11 P.M.	$48,000	300	_____
10 P.M.	$44,000	290	_____
9 P.M.	$40,000	280	_____

Based on this analysis, what time do you think CHC should close each night?

5. A health club differs from manufacturing firms in that it produces a service rather than products. Should manufacturing firms have a narrower span of control than service firms like CHC?

Investing in a Business

Using the annual report of the firm in which you would like to invest, complete the following:

Questions

1. Describe the organizational structure of the firm.

2. Does the firm appear to have many high-level managers?

3. Has the firm downsized in recent years by removing middle managers from its organizational structure?

4. Explain how the business uses technology to promote its organizational structure. For example, does it use the Internet to provide information about its organizational structure? Does it provide information regarding the methods of departmentalizing tasks?

5. Go to http://hoovers.com and locate the NEWS SEARCH. Type in the name of the firm in the space provided, and review the recent news stories about the firm. Summarize any (at least one) recent news story about the firm that applies to one or more of the key concepts in this chapter.

Case: Creating an Organizational Structure

Janet Shugarts is the president of a barbecue sauce manufacturer in Austin, Texas. A manager in production has come up with a new barbecue recipe that he claims will be the best on the market because it's hot and spicy and has a flavor that the competition cannot match.

Janet has recently received new marketing research information. The research indicates that most Europeans prefer a hot and spicy barbecue sauce. The marketing manager is excited about this new product and believes it can be exported to Europe.

Janet has just come out of a meeting with her four managers from production, marketing, finance, and human resources. They have decided to establish a sales office for the barbeque sauce in Paris, France. The plan is to create a project team to set up a production facility within a year in France. The marketing manager will head this project team. He has requested that this subsidiary be decentralized to provide him with an opportunity to make timely decisions in this local market.

Because of this expansion, Janet is planning to increase her existing workforce of 120 employees by 20 percent. She has recently hired a human resource manager to take charge of the recruiting and selection function. A rumor circulating around the plant through the "grapevine" hints that employees may attempt to bring in a union. The human resource manager is alarmed because of his position on the organization chart. His position is listed as a support position; thus, he can only advise and make recommendations to a line manager concerning issues related to recruiting and selection.

Questions

1 Has Janet created an organizational structure? If so, how?

2 Why would the marketing manager request decentralization of authority in Paris, France?

3 Does this organization reflect a line-and-staff organizational structure? If so, explain.

4 What possible disadvantage could result from the decentralization of the marketing function of the foreign sales office?

Video Case: Student Advantage

Student Advantage offers meal and debit cards that are used on many university campuses. Its core competency is forging partnerships with universities and corporations to create products and services that help students buy the things they need at a discount from stores such as Barnes & Noble and Champs Sporting Goods. Student Advantage recognizes job strengths and relationships. It attempts to create structure that builds shareholder value, makes employees accountable, and sustains a chain of command and communication.

Student Advantage had to quickly learn the technological capabilities at different universities so that it would know how to sell its products. It uses contingency planning and makes cautious technology investments to reduce risk. A challenge for Student Advantage is that the students who are the market for its products are very technologically sophisticated, so Student Advantage must work to stay ahead of the technology curve. For more information on Student Advantage, go to http://www.studentadvantage.com/discountcard.

Questions

1 How does Student Advantage use technology to market its products and to provide internal controls?

2 How does the emphasis on e-business allow Student Advantage to expand into new markets?

Internet Applications

1. Go to the website of a company that provides an annual report. Many companies describe their organizational structure in their annual reports. Describe the organizational structure based on the information that you find. Does the structure appear to have many layers? Do tasks appear to be departmentalized? Explain. Alternatively, is the company departmentalized by product, or location, or by customer?

2. http://www.epa.gov/epahome/organization.htm

Examine the Web page of the Environmental Protection Agency. Describe the organization of the agency. Why do nonprofit or government organizations need to have a sound organizational structure? Click on the Administrator/Deputy Administrator home page and organizational chart. What are some of the offices under the Administrator?

3. http://www2.coca-cola.com

Click on "Leadership." Examine the information on this website. Describe the composition of the board of directors and the executive committees. Does the structure appear to have many layers? Do the tasks seem departmentalized? Explain.

4. http://www.pg.com/company/who_we_are/index.jhtml

Click on "History." Who were the founders of Procter and Gamble? How has the organizational structure of P&G changed over time from a partnership to a global corporation? Now click on "Global Operations." How do you think the organizational structure of P&G differs from that of a purely domestic firm? Does P&G appear to have a centralized or a decentralized structure?

Dell's Secret to Success

Go to http://www.reportgallery.com and review Dell's most recent annual report. Also, go to Dell's website (http://www.dell.com) and in the section "about Dell," review the background material about Dell that relates to this chapter.

Questions

1 Describe Dell's organizational structure based on the position titles of its senior officers. Do you think the structure is fragmented according to function or location?

2 What is the role of Dell's board of directors?

3 What is the general role of Dell's top-level management?

In-Text Study Guide

Answers are in Appendix C at the back of book.

True or False

1. An organization chart shows the interaction among employee responsibilities.

2. An organizational structure identifies the responsibilities of each job position and the relationships among those positions.

3. A company's board of directors normally takes an active role in managing the firm's day-to-day activities.

4. Inside board members are more likely than outside members to support changes that will benefit the firm's stockholders, especially if the firm's top managers do not support the changes.

5. An organizational structure that is designed to have each manager supervise just a few employees has a narrow span of control.

6. In recent years, most firms have attempted to centralize authority in the hands of a few key executives.

7. Firms will have either a formal organizational structure or an informal organizational structure, but can never have both types of organizational structures at the same time.

8. An advantage of a firm's informal organizational structure is that it encourages the formation of friendships, which can improve morale and job satisfaction.

9. Organizing a firm by both product and function is not effective for companies that operate in only one location.

10. When a firm is departmentalized by location, its expenses involved in each location can be more easily estimated.

11. Most firms departmentalize their foreign operations by function.

Multiple Choice

12. The responsibilities of a firm's managers should be organized to achieve the:
    a) grapevine.
    b) formal contingency.
    c) strategic plan.
    d) chain of command.
    e) bureaucratic organization.

13. The president of a company:
    a) determines which members of the board of directors will be reappointed.
    b) coordinates the actions of all divisions and provides direction for the firm.
    c) directly supervises the actions of all other employees.
    d) seldom delegates managerial duties to other managers.
    e) operates independently of the board of directors.

14. The _____ for a firm identifies the job position to which each type of employee must report.
    a) chain of command
    b) job matrix
    c) staffing chart
    d) flow chart
    e) informal structure

15. The ultimate responsibility for the success of a firm lies with the:
    a) president.
    b) internal auditor.
    c) customer.
    d) competition.
    e) labor union.

In-Text Study Guide

16. The outside members of the board of directors of a company are those directors who:
    a) live outside the state in which the corporation received its charter.
    b) are not managers of the firm.
    c) are not stockholders in the firm.
    d) serve on the board without direct compensation.
    e) were appointed by the president of the firm rather than selected by the firm's stockholders.

17. The board of directors has the responsibility of representing the interests of the firm's:
    a) top management.
    b) employees.
    c) customers.
    d) creditors.
    e) shareholders.

18. Members of a firm's board of directors are selected by the firm's:
    a) top management.
    b) management council.
    c) shareholders.
    d) creditors.
    e) employees.

19. Members of the board of directors who are also managers of the same firm are known as:
    a) ex-officio board members.
    b) primary board members.
    c) unelected board members.
    d) inside board members.
    e) organizational board members.

20. Which member of the board of directors would be least likely to have a conflict of interest?
    a) outside director with consulting ties to company
    b) inside director with vice presidential position
    c) the CEO
    d) outside director retired from company
    e) outside director, CEO of another firm

21. The _____ refers to the number of employees managed by each manager.
    a) scope of authority
    b) management ratio
    c) employee limit
    d) span of control
    e) manager-employee multiplier

22. Span of control is determined by:
    a) consultants.
    b) staff.
    c) top management.
    d) employees.
    e) customers.

23. The _____ ensures that all departments follow the firm's guidelines and procedures.
    a) CEO
    b) internal auditor
    c) board of directors
    d) project manager
    e) inside director

24. A firm in which managers have narrow spans of control tends to have:
    a) a tall organizational structure.
    b) very decentralized decision making.
    c) a small number of employees.
    d) very few layers of management.
    e) a very large number of people serving on its board of directors.

25. The strategy of spreading authority among several divisions or managers is called:
    a) centralization.
    b) decentralization.
    c) decision rationing.
    d) abdication of authority.
    e) adjudication of authority.

In-Text Study Guide

Answers are in Appendix C at the back of book.

26. An extreme form of decentralization in which divisions can make their own decisions and act independently is called:
    a) centralization.
    b) autonomy.
    c) span of control.
    d) span of management.
    e) departmentalization.

27. A possible disadvantage of decentralization is that it:
    a) may require inexperienced managers to make major decisions they are not qualified to make.
    b) usually increases the firm's operating expenses.
    c) slows down the decision-making process.
    d) harms employee motivation by forcing them to take on more responsibilities.
    e) prevents employees from making creative decisions.

28. Which of the following is not an advantage of decentralization?
    a) shortens the decision-making process
    b) reduces salary expenses
    c) delegates specialized decisions to low-level employees
    d) delegation of authority may improve employee morale
    e) improves employee qualifications for promotion

29. One outcome of the recent downsizing by many corporations during the 1990s and early 2000s was:
    a) an increase in the layers of management.
    b) a narrower span of control for most managers.
    c) decentralization of authority.
    d) increased costs of production.
    e) a big reduction in the importance of the informal organizational structure.

30. Employees who serve in _____ positions provide assistance and support to employees who serve in line positions.
    a) secondary
    b) nominal
    c) reserve
    d) nonlinear
    e) staff

31. Jobs that are established to make decisions that achieve specific business goals are:
    a) staff positions.
    b) line positions.
    c) line-and-staff functions.
    d) temporary jobs.
    e) job placement.

32. Firms use a(n) _____ organization to allow the various parts of a firm to interact as they focus on a particular project.
    a) matrix
    b) quasi-linear
    c) tabular
    d) extracurricular
    e) cellular

33. One possible disadvantage of a matrix organization is that it:
    a) makes it difficult for different departments to communicate with each other.
    b) reduces employee satisfaction by requiring workers to perform monotonous tasks.
    c) reduces the time employees have to perform their normal duties.
    d) puts too much power in the hands of a small number of top managers.
    e) allows top management to make decisions without input from the board.

In-Text Study Guide

34. A process whereby particular employees of a firm can be assigned to create ideas as if they were entrepreneurs is referred to as:
    a) staff organization.
    b) intrapreneurship.
    c) co-ownership.
    d) leadership.
    e) line organization.

35. All of the following are common ways of departmentalizing a firm except by:
    a) function.
    b) product.
    c) customer.
    d) time period.
    e) location.

Chapter

9

GETTY IMAGES

Decisions by Cell One regarding its use of human resources, its site, and its quality control will influence its future performance and its value.

The Learning Goals of this chapter are to:

Identify the key resources used for production.   *1*

Identify the factors that affect the plant site decision.   *2*

Describe how various factors affect the design and layout decision.   *3*

Describe the key tasks that are involved in production control.   *4*

Describe the key factors that affect production efficiency.   *5*

Improving Productivity and Quality

Firms are created to produce products or services. Production management (also called operations management) is the management of the process in which resources are used to produce products or services. The specific process chosen by a firm to produce its products or services can affect its value. Consider the situation of Cell One Company, which produces and sells cell phones. Cell One Company must decide:

▶ What human resources and other resources are needed to produce its cell phones?

▶ At what site should it produce its cell phones?

▶ What can it do to control the quality of its production?

▶ How can it produce its cell phones more efficiently?

The decisions about the human resources and other resources needed affect Cell One's cost of production. Its ability to control its production will affect the quality of the cell phones produced and, therefore, will affect the demand for its cell phones. If Cell One Company can improve its efficiency, it can reduce its expenses and, therefore, improve its performance.

All businesses must make the types of decisions described above. This chapter explains how Cell One Company or any other firm can make production management decisions in a manner that maximizes the firm's value.

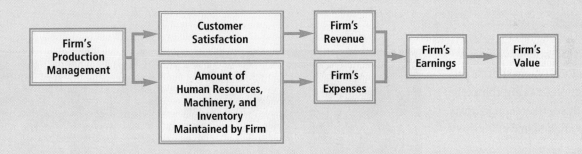

Resources Used for the Production Process

1

Identify the key resources used for production.

Whether a firm produces products or services, it needs a **production process** (also called **conversion process**), or a series of tasks in which resources are used to produce a product or service. A process identifies the mixture of resources allocated for production, the assignment of tasks, and the sequence of tasks.

Many possible production processes can achieve the production of a specific product. Thus, effective **production management** (or **operations management**) aims at developing an efficient (relatively low-cost) and

**production process
(conversion process)**
a series of tasks in which resources
are used to produce a product
or service

**production management
(operations management)**
the management of a process in
which resources (such as employees and machinery) are used to
produce products and services

high-quality production process for producing specific products and
services. Specifically, production management can achieve efficiency by
determining the proper amount of materials to use, the proper mix of resources to use, the proper assignments of the tasks, and the proper sequence of the tasks. Production management can contribute to the success
of both manufacturing firms and service-oriented firms. For example, the
success of Southwest Airlines, a service-oriented firm, is attributed to its
low-cost production of air transportation for customers. Thus, the profits
and value of each firm are influenced by its production management.

The main resources that firms use for the production process are human resources (employees), materials, and other resources (such as buildings, machinery, and equipment). Firms that produce products tend to use
more materials and equipment in their production process. Firms that produce services (such as Internet firms) use more employees and information technology.

Human Resources

Firms must identify the type of employees needed for production. Skilled
labor is necessary for some forms of production, but unskilled labor can be
used for other forms. Some forms of production are labor-intensive in that
they require more labor than materials. The operating expenses involved
in hiring human resources are dependent both on the number of employees and on their skill levels. Because of the employee skill level required,
an Internet firm incurs much larger salary expenses than a grocery store.

Materials

The materials used in the production process are normally transformed by
the firm's human resources into a final product. Tire manufacturers rely
on rubber, automobile manufacturers rely on steel, and book publishers

This factory has various work-
stations, where specific production tasks are completed.
At this workstation, employees engage in welding.

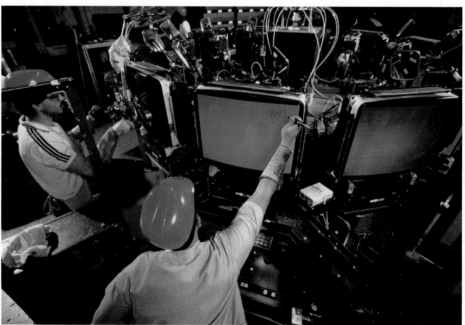

GETTY IMAGES

rely on paper. Service firms such as travel agencies and investment advisers do not rely as much on materials because they do not engage in manufacturing.

Other Resources

A building is needed for most forms of production. Manufacturers use factories and offices. Service firms use offices. The site may be owned or rented by the firm. Since purchasing a building can be expensive, some firms simply rent the buildings they use. Renting also allows the firm to move at the end of the lease period without having to sell the building. Machinery and equipment are also needed by many manufacturing firms. Technology may also be a necessary resource for manufacturing and service firms.

Combining the Resources for Production

work station
an area in which one or more employees are assigned a specific task

assembly line
a sequence of work stations in which each work station is designed to cover specific phases of the production process

Managers attempt to utilize the resources just described in a manner that achieves production at a low cost. They combine the various resources with the use of work stations and assembly lines. A **work station** is an area in which one or more employees are assigned a specific task. A work station may require machinery and equipment as well as employees.

An **assembly line** consists of a sequence of work stations in which each work station is designed to cover specific phases of the production process. The production of a single product may require several work stations, with each station using employees, machinery, and materials. Since the cost of all these resources along with the building can be substantial, efficient management of the production process can reduce expenses, which can convert into higher profits.

An example of a typical production process is shown in Exhibit 9.1. Employees use buildings, machinery, and equipment to convert materials into a product or service. For example, employees of printing firms use machines for typesetting, printing, and binding to produce books. Employees of General Nutrition Centers (GNC) use its manufacturing plant (which is the size of four football fields) to produce more than 150,000 bottles of vitamins per day.

Most production processes are more efficient when different employees are assigned different tasks. In this way, employees can utilize their unique types of expertise to specialize in what they do best.

Exhibit 9.1

Resources Used
in Production

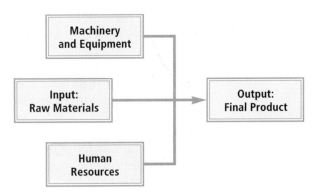

Decision Making

Determining the Resources Needed

When Cell One Company (introduced earlier) developed its business, it needed to decide on the proper combination of resources to use for its production. It initially used human resources for most of its production process. Now, however, it relies more heavily on machinery for various phases of the production process in order to reduce its operating expenses. Advances in technology allow some parts to be produced and assembled by machines. Cell One's human resources have been reassigned to jobs that require other types of skills and cannot be done by machines.

1. Is there a disadvantage to Cell One's relying on machinery for its production?
2. Some employees suggest that Cell One should hire more people to show its support for workers. Do you think Cell One should hire more employees for this reason?

ANSWERS: 1. One possible disadvantage is a lack of quality control under some circumstances, but some machines can monitor quality better than people can.   2. If Cell One hires more people just to show its support for employees, it may incur excessive expenses and could possibly fail as a result.

Selecting a Site

Identify the factors that affect the plant site decision.

A critical decision in production management is the selection of a site (location) for the factory or office. Location can significantly affect the cost of production and therefore the firm's ability to compete against other firms. This is especially true for industrial firms such as Bethlehem Steel and Daimler-Chrysler, which require a large investment in plant and equipment.

Factors Affecting the Site Decision

Several factors must be considered when determining the optimal site. The most relevant factors are identified here.

Cost of Workplace Space   The cost of purchasing or renting workplace space (such as buildings or offices) can vary significantly among locations. Costs are likely to be high near the center of any business district where land costs are high. Costs also tend to be higher in certain regions. For example, office rental rates are generally higher in the northeastern states than in other areas. This is one major reason why companies located in northern cities have relocated to the South during the last 10 years.

Cost of Labor   The cost of hiring employees varies significantly among locations. Salaries within a city tend to be higher than salaries outside the city for a given occupation. Salaries are also generally higher in the North than the South for a given occupation. This is another reason why many companies have relocated to the South.

Tax Incentives   Some local governments may be willing to grant tax credits to attract companies to their area. The governments offer this incentive to increase the employment level and improve economic conditions in the area.

Source of Demand   If a firm plans to sell its product in a specific location, it may establish its plant there. The costs of transporting and servicing the product can be minimized by producing at a site near the source of demand.

Access to Transportation   When companies sell products across the nation, they may choose a site near their main source of transportation. They also need to be accessible so that materials can be delivered to them. Some factories and offices are established near interstate highways, rivers, or airports for this reason.

Supply of Labor   Firms that plan to hire specialized workers must be able to attract the labor needed. They may choose a location where a large supply of workers with that particular specialization exists. For instance, high-tech companies tend to locate near universities where there is an abundance of educated labor.

Evaluating Possible Sites

When a firm evaluates various sites, it must consider any factors that may affect the desirability of each site. The choice of the location within a city is also critical. A retail store may attract many customers simply because they are driving by and notice the store. Therefore, a retail store in an area without much traffic will need other ways (such as advertising) to attract customers. If the firm intends to rent space, it is important to meet with the landlord before deciding on a specific location. In some locations, leases are very restrictive and may require a large deposit that will be lost if the business decides to move.

When the firm has identified all of the factors that it should consider, it can assign a weight to each factor that reflects that factor's importance. Labor-intensive firms would likely place a high weight on the cost of human resources while other firms may be less concerned about this factor. Firms that sell products or services at the site will assign a high weight to the amount of traffic. Starbucks retail stores are commonly located in places where many people walk, such as downtown areas, suburban retail centers, office buildings, and university campuses. When Blockbuster opens new stores, it looks for areas with a high concentration of people but attempts to avoid areas already served by other Blockbuster stores so that it will not pull customers away from those stores.

Once the firm determines the weight assigned to each factor, it evaluates each possible site on all relevant factors to determine a weighted rating for each factor. Then, the ratings are combined to determine the overall rating for each possible site.

Starbucks commonly establishes its sites in locations where many people (potential customers) walk.

CORBIS, CHICAGO

SMALL BUSINESS SURVEY

Location as a Competitive Advantage

In a recent National Small Business poll conducted for the NFIB Research Foundation, small businesses were asked whether they rely on their choice of business location as part of their strategy to develop a competitive advantage. Their responses are shown here:

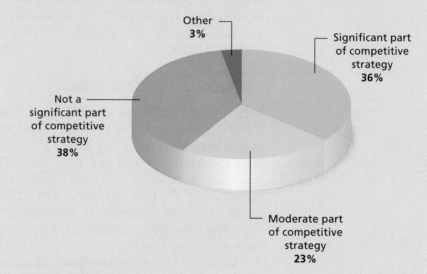

Other
3%

Significant part
of competitive
strategy
36%

Not a
significant part
of competitive
strategy
38%

Moderate part
of competitive
strategy
23%

The small businesses were also asked whether they focus on having minimal investment overhead (facilities and employees) as part of their strategy to develop a competitive advantage. Their responses are shown here:

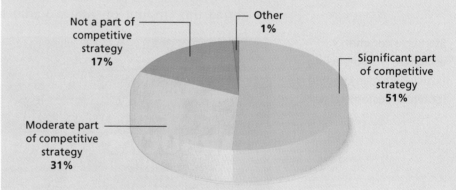

Not a part of
competitive
strategy
17%

Other
1%

Significant part
of competitive
strategy
51%

Moderate part
of competitive
strategy
31%

Global Business

Selecting a Foreign Production Site

The selection of a foreign production site by a U.S. firm is critical because location affects the firm's operating expenses and therefore its earnings. Consider the case of Pfizer, a U.S. firm that produces pharmaceutical and consumer products, including Listerine, Halls cough drops, Clorets mints, Certs mints, and Trident gum. Pfizer has operations in more than 100 countries. Its extensive development of foreign operations was motivated by global demand for its products. Pfizer attempts to offer "every product, everywhere." Consequently, it established production sites that were convenient to the foreign markets where it planned to sell products.

The selection of a production site by any multinational corporation is crucial because costs vary substantially among countries. Annual office rental rates per square foot are more than five times higher in Paris than in Mexico City and more than twice as high in Tokyo as in Paris. The cost of human resources is generally much lower in less-developed countries, but the supply of skilled labor in those countries may be inadequate. Furthermore, consumer demand for products in those countries may be low, so the products would have to be transported to other countries with much higher demand. Multinational corporations must assess the tradeoffs involved. If the products are light in weight (and therefore involve low transportation expenses), a multinational corporation might be willing to use facilities in less-developed countries and transport the products to areas where demand is higher.

Decision Making ▶ Choosing the Optimal Site

The ideal way to select a site is dependent on the characteristics of the firm. To illustrate, consider Cell One Company (introduced in the introduction to the chapter), which specializes in the production of cell phones. It has a production facility in New York City, but wants to consider four alternative sites for its production plant. It develops a site evaluation matrix, as shown in Exhibit 9.2. Possible sites are listed at the left. The columns identify the factors that need to be evaluated. These factors are rated from 1 (outstanding) to 5 (poor). The overall rating assigned to any potential site can be determined by averaging the ratings for that site. If some factors are more important than others, however, they deserve to have a relatively higher influence on the overall ratings.

The site evaluation matrix in Exhibit 9.2 is simplified in that it focuses on only two factors for each city. The land cost is presumed to be the more important factor and has an 80 percent weight. The supply of labor receives the remaining 20 percent weight. The weighted rating shown in Exhibit 9.2 is equal to the rating times the weight of the rating. The weighted ratings for each factor are combined to determine the total rating for each city. For example, the Austin, Texas, site received a land cost rating of 3, which converts to a weighted rating of 2.4 (computed as $3 \times .8$). It also received a supply of labor rating of 1, which converts to a rating of .2 (computed as $1 \times .2$). Its total rating is 2.6 (computed as $2.4 + .2$).

Once Cell One Company determines a rating for each factor, it can derive the total rating for each site considered. Based on the ratings for the four sites in Exhibit 9.2, the Omaha site had the best rating and thus would be selected as the site.

Exhibit 9.2

Example of a Site
Evaluation Matrix

Possible Sites	Land Cost		Supply of Labor		Total Rating
	Rating	Weighted Rating (80% of Weight)	Rating	Weighted Rating (20% Weight)	
Austin, TX	3	2.4	1	.2	2.6
Chicago, IL	4	3.2	2	.4	3.6
Los Angeles, CA	5	4.0	3	.6	4.6
Omaha, NE	1	.8	3	.6	1.4

If another firm assessed the same four sites in Exhibit 9.2, it might come to a different conclusion for two reasons. First, it might use different factors in its matrix. Second, it might rate the factors differently. For example, one city may have an abundance of people with computer development skills, but have fewer people with the skills to manage a bank.

Once a particular area (such as a city or county) has been chosen, the precise location must be decided. Some of the factors already mentioned will influence this decision. In addition, factors such as traffic, crime rate, and worker access to public transportation may influence the decision.

1. Why will the site that Cell One Company selects affect is degree of reliance on specific resources?

2. Why would Cell One's site selection decision be different if it needs a large space, versus a small space, for its business?

ANSWERS: 1. The expenses of using various resources vary with the location. If the site is in a location where workers can be hired at a low cost, then Cell One may hire more employees. If wages are high in this location, then Cell One may use more machinery so that it can minimize the number of workers it hires.   2. If Cell One needs a large space, it will likely prefer a site where the cost of renting space is low.

Describe how various
factors affect the design
and layout decision.

design
the size and structure of a plant
or office

layout
the arrangement of machinery
and equipment within a factory
or office

Selecting the Design and Layout

Once a site for a manufacturing plant or office is chosen, the design and layout must be determined. The **design** indicates the size and structure of the plant or office. The **layout** is the arrangement of the machinery and equipment within the factory or office.

The design and layout decisions directly affect operating expenses because they determine the costs of rent, machinery, and equipment. They may even affect the firm's interest expenses because they influence the amount of money that must be borrowed to purchase property or machinery.

Factors Affecting Design and Layout

Design and layout decisions are influenced by the following characteristics.

Site Characteristics   Design and layout decisions are dependent on some characteristics of the site selected. For example, if the site is in an area with high land costs, a high-rise building may be designed so that less land will be needed. The layout of the plant will then be affected by the design.

product layout
a layout in which tasks are positioned in the sequence that they are assigned

fixed-position layout
a layout in which employees go to the position of the product, rather than waiting for the product to come to them

flexible manufacturing
a production process that can be easily adjusted to accommodate future revisions

Production Process   Design and layout are also dependent on the production process to be used. If an assembly-line operation is to be used, all tasks included in this operation should be in the same general area. A **product layout** positions the tasks in the sequence that they are assigned. For example, one person may specialize in creating components, while the next person assembles the components, and the next person packages the product. A product layout is commonly used for assembly-line production.

Alternatively, some products (such as airplanes, ships, or homes) are completely produced in one fixed position, which requires a **fixed-position layout.** The employees go to the product, rather than having the product come to them.

Many firms now use **flexible manufacturing,** a production process that can be easily adjusted to accommodate future revisions. This enables the firm to restructure its layout as needed when it changes its products to accommodate customer demand. Many auto plants use flexible manufacturing so that they can produce whatever cars or trucks are in demand. A flexible layout normally requires that employees have flexible skills.

Product Line   Most firms produce more than one product or service at their site. Firms with a narrow product line focus on the production of one or a few products, which allows them to specialize. Firms with a broad product line offer a wide range of products.

As market preferences change, demand for products changes. The layout must be revised to accompany these changes. For example, the popularity of sport utility vehicles has caused many automobile manufacturers to allocate more of their layout for the production of these vehicles. The allocation of more space for one product normally takes space away from others, unless the initial design and layout allowed extra space for expansion.

Desired Production Capacity   When planning both design and layout, the firm's desired production capacity (maximum production level possible) must be considered. Most firms attempt to plan for growth by allowing flexibility to increase the production capacity over time. The design of the building may allow for additional levels to be added. The proper layout can open up more space to be used for increased production.

If firms do not plan for growth, they will be forced to search for a new site when demand for their product exceeds their production capacity. When a firm maintains its existing site and develops a second site to expand, it must duplicate the machinery and job positions assigned at the original site. Consequently, production efficiency tends to decrease. To avoid this problem, the firm may relocate to a site with a larger capacity.

Although having a layout that allows for growth is desirable, it is also expensive. A firm must invest additional funds to obtain additional land or floor space. This investment ties up funds that might be better used by the firm for other purposes. Furthermore, if growth does not occur, the layout will be inefficient because some of the space will continue to be unused.

A firm may achieve greater production capacity without changing its design and layout if employees can do some or all of their work at home. Given the improvements in telecommunications (computer networks, e-mail, and fax machines), employees of some businesses no longer need to be on site. When the employees who work at home need to come in to work, they use work spaces that are not permanently assigned to anyone. For example, a firm may keep an office available with a desk, a computer, and a telephone for any employee who normally works at home but needs to use temporary work space at the firm. This practice is referred to as **hotelling** (or **just-in-time office**). For example, hotelling may be appropriate for salespeople who travel frequently and generally work from a home office.

**hotelling
(just-in-time office)**
providing an office with a desk, a computer, and a telephone for any employee who normally works at home but needs to use work space at the firm

A worker shovels freshly made butter into the processing line at the Cabot Creamery plant in Cabot, Vermont.

Decision Making

Determining the Optimal Design and Layout

The ideal design and layout of a firm are dependent on its specific characteristics. To illustrate, recall that Cell One Company had a production plant in New York, and recently decided to establish a new plant in Omaha, Nebraska. Now Cell One has decided to close the New York plant because of the high rent at that location, which pushes up its cost of production. Instead, it will produce all of its cell phones at the Omaha plant.

Cell One has been creating advertising brochures for its cell phones from an office in New York City, but it wants to reduce its office space there because of the high cost of rent. The office has five employees who use computer software to create and print the brochures and mail them to lists of prospective customers. Cell One decides to stop renting office space. Instead, will give each of the employees a computer and let them work at home. The employees can correspond with each other by e-mail. Once their files for a brochure are complete, they will now send the files to a printing company, which will print the brochures and send them to the addresses on the mailing list. Cell One will have to pay the printing company for the printing and mailing, but it will avoid the high cost of rent because it no longer needs to rent office space in New York City. Thus, by devising a design and layout that reduce its expenses associated with production and marketing, Cell One Company will be able to increase its profits.

1. Is there a disadvantage to Cell One of changing the design and layout of the office so that the employees work from home?
2. Why can't the design and layout of Cell One's production facility be eliminated in the same manner as the advertising office?

ANSWERS: 1. The employees will not be working in the same location, which could result in some inconvenience if they need to discuss any issues as a group. But most communication can occur by e-mail or by phone. 2. The production facility requires physical space where products can be produced, whereas the production of brochures can be done simply with computers and does not require any other facilities.

Describe the key tasks that are involved in production control.

production control
involves purchasing materials, inventory control, routing, scheduling, and quality control

Production Control

Once the plant and design have been selected, the firm can engage in **production control,** which involves the following:

▶ Purchasing materials

▶ Inventory control

▶ Routing

▶ Scheduling

▶ Quality control

Purchasing Materials

Managers perform the following tasks when purchasing supplies. First, they must select a supplier. Second, they attempt to obtain volume discounts. Third, they determine whether to delegate some production tasks to suppliers. These tasks are discussed next.

Selecting a Supplier of Materials   In selecting among various suppliers, firms consider characteristics such as price, speed, quality, servicing, and credit availability. A typical approach to evaluating suppliers is to first obtain prices from each supplier. Next, a sample is obtained from each supplier

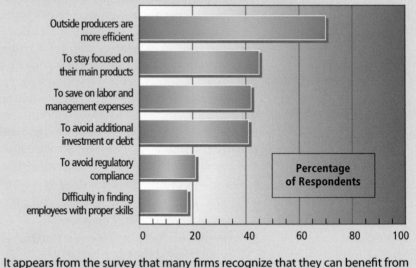

and inspected for quality. Then, these suppliers are asked to provide further information on their speed of delivery and their service warranties in case any delivery problems occur. The firm may then try out a single supplier and evaluate its reliability over time.

Alternatively, a firm may initially use a few suppliers and later select the supplier that has provided the best service. Some firms avoid depending on a single supplier so that if any problems occur with one supplier, they will not have a major impact on the firm.

Another consideration in selecting a supplier may be its ability to interact with an Internet-based order system. Many firms now rely on *e-procurement,* or the use of the Internet to purchase some of their materials. This reduces the time that employees must devote to orders and can reduce expenses. A basic system detects the existing level of supplies and automatically orders additional supplies once the quantity on hand falls to a specific level. Some systems are more sophisticated and can handle additional tasks.

Obtaining Volume Discounts   Firms that purchase a large volume of materials from suppliers may obtain a discounted price on supplies while maintaining quality. This practice has enabled firms such as AT&T and General Motors to reduce their production expenses in recent years.

Delegating Production to Suppliers   Manufacturers commonly use **outsourcing;** that is, they purchase parts from suppliers rather than producing the parts.

outsourcing
purchasing parts from a supplier rather than producing the parts

Outsourcing can reduce a firm's expenses if suppliers can produce the parts at a lower cost than the firm itself. Some manufacturers have even begun delegating some parts of the production process to suppliers. Consider a manufacturing firm located in a city where wages are generally high. This firm has been ordering several components from a supplier and assembling them at its own plant. It may be better to have the supplier partially assemble the components before shipping them to the manufacturer. Some of the assembly task would thereby be shifted to the supplier. Partial assembly by the supplier may cost less than paying high-wage employees at the manufacturing plant.

Although outsourcing can be beneficial, it places much responsibility on other manufacturing companies. Thus, when a firm outsources, its ability to meet its production schedule depends on these other companies. For this reason, a firm that outsources must be very careful when selecting the suppliers on which it will rely.

Lockheed Martin not only relies heavily on suppliers, but has used online technology to link them up with its engineers so that they can work together to build a new stealth fighter plane. The project involves 80 major suppliers of engines, landing gear, and other components. By linking to the suppliers, the company expects to save about $250 million over the 10-year period necessary to design the plane. British Petroleum uses online technology to link its suppliers with the architects who are renovating its gas stations. It has more than 10,000 gas stations in the United States. By allowing collaboration between the architects and suppliers, it can do the renovation work in half the expected time.

deintegration
the strategy of delegating some production tasks to suppliers

The strategy of delegating some production tasks to suppliers is referred to as **deintegration** and is illustrated in Exhibit 9.3. The production process within the plant is no longer as integrated, because part of the production is completed by the supplier before the supplies or components are delivered to the manufacturing plant. Automobile manufacturers have deintegrated their production processes by delegating some production tasks to suppliers or other firms. For example, Ford Motor Company purchases fully assembled automobile seats from Lear Seating. By doing so, it saves hundreds of dollars per automobile because the supplier's cost of labor is lower than Ford's cost.

Exhibit 9.3

Effects of Deintegration

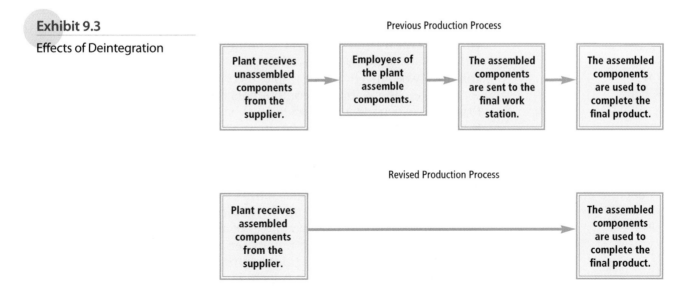

Electronic Payments for Supplies Firms are increasingly paying for their supplies electronically instead of paying by check. This allows for a more efficient production system. To use electronic payments, a firm maintains a sufficient balance in its account. After receiving an order of supplies, it instructs its bank to transfer a payment from its account to the account of the supplier. Recent technology allows even small businesses to efficiently send payments in this manner rather than writing checks.

Inventory Control

inventory control
the process of managing inventory at a level that minimizes costs

Inventory control is the process of managing inventory at a level that minimizes costs. It requires the management of materials inventories, work-in-process inventories, and finished goods inventories, as explained next.

carrying costs
costs of maintaining (carrying) inventories

Control of Materials Inventories When firms carry excessive inventories of materials, they may need to borrow more funds to finance these inventories. This increases their **carrying costs,** or their costs of maintaining (carrying) inventories. Carrying costs include financing costs as well as costs associated with storing or insuring inventories. Although firms can attempt to reduce their carrying costs by frequently ordering small amounts of materials, this strategy increases the costs involved in placing orders (called **order costs**). Any adjustment in the materials purchasing strategy will normally reduce carrying costs at the expense of increasing order costs, or vice versa.

order costs
costs involved in placing orders for materials

just-in-time (JIT)
a system that attempts to reduce materials inventories to a bare minimum by frequently ordering small amounts of materials

A popular method for reducing carrying costs is the **just-in-time (JIT)** system originated by Japanese companies. This system attempts to reduce materials inventories to a bare minimum by frequently ordering small amounts of materials. It can reduce the costs of maintaining inventories. However, it also entails a cost of managerial time required for frequent ordering and a cost of frequent deliveries. In addition, the JIT system could result in a shortage if applied improperly. Nevertheless, U.S. firms such as Applied Magnetics Corporation and Black & Decker Corporation have improved their productivity by effectively using JIT inventory management.

materials requirements planning (MRP)
a process for ensuring that materials are available when needed

Materials requirements planning (MRP) is a process for ensuring that the materials are available when needed. Normally requiring the use of a computer, MRP helps managers determine the amount of specific materials that should be purchased at any given time. The first step in MRP is to work backward from the finished product toward the beginning and determine how long in advance materials are needed before products are completely produced. For example, if computers are to be assembled by a specific date, the computer components must arrive by a specific date before then, which means that they must be ordered even earlier. As the firm forecasts the demand for its product in the future, it can determine the time at which the materials need to arrive to achieve a production level that will accommodate the forecasted demand.

work-in-process inventories
inventories of partially completed products

Control of Work-in-Process Inventories Firms must also manage their **work-in-process inventories,** which are inventories of partially completed products. Firms attempt to avoid shortages of all types of inventories. The direct consequence of a shortage in raw materials inventory or work-in-process inventory is an interruption in production. This can cause a shortage of the final product, and therefore results in forgone sales.

Employees fill orders in an Amazon.com warehouse.

CORBIS, CHICAGO

Control of Finished Goods Inventories   As demand for a firm's product changes over time, managers need to monitor the anticipated supply-demand differential. Consider the case of Amazon.com. It must maintain a sufficient stock of whatever books, DVDs, and other products may be ordered by customers. Maintaining an inventory of products uses up space, however. Therefore, Amazon.com attempts to accurately forecast the demand for its products so that its inventory is sufficient to accommodate demand without being excessive.

Blockbuster partially attributes its success to its efficient management of inventory. It effectively anticipates the demand for DVD rentals and therefore has a sufficient supply for customers. Autozone also attempts to manage its inventory of auto parts at all of its retail stores efficiently. Recently, it increased the size of its inventory to ensure that the stores will be able to accommodate the demand for any particular parts. This decision was based on the tradeoff of having to invest more funds to provide the inventory versus the lost sales that result when parts are not available.

Inventory decisions may adjust during the year due to seasonal demand. For example, stores that sell swimsuits experience their strongest demand during the summer. They need to maintain higher inventory levels in those months to ensure that they can accommodate demand.

If an excess supply of a product is anticipated, a firm can avoid excessive inventories by redirecting its resources toward the production of other products. For example, Ford Motor Company redirects resources away from the production of cars that are not selling as well as expected. Alternatively, a firm that experiences an excess supply of products can continue its normal production schedule and implement marketing strategies (such as advertising or reducing the price) that will increase demand.

If an increase in demand is anticipated, firms become concerned about possible shortages and must develop a strategy to boost production volume. They may schedule overtime for workers or hire new workers to achieve higher levels of production.

Impact of Technology on Inventory Control   Firms can use the Internet to improve their inventory control. Krispy Kreme has created online networks of shops that are close to each other so that a shop that experiences a surplus or shortage can get help from another shop nearby. Consequently, Krispy Kreme shops rarely experience major shortages now. General Motors uses electronic auctions on the Internet to sell off leased cars at the end of their leases. It now sells hundreds of thousands of cars each year through these auctions for an estimated savings of about $200 million per year.

Routing

Routing is the sequence (or route) of tasks necessary to complete the production of a product. Raw materials are commonly sent to various work stations so that they can be used as specified in the production process. A specific part of the production process is completed at each work station. For example, the production of a bicycle may require (1) using materials to produce a bike frame at one work station, (2) assembling wheels at a second work station, and (3) packaging the frames and wheels that have been assembled at a third work station.

The routing process is periodically evaluated to determine whether it can be improved to allow a faster or less expensive production process. General Motors, DaimlerChrysler, and United Parcel Service have streamlined their routing process to improve production efficiency.

Scheduling

Scheduling is the act of setting time periods for each task in the production process. A **production schedule** is a plan for the timing and volume of production tasks. For example, the production schedule for a bicycle may set a time of two hours for each frame to be assembled and one hour for each wheel to be assembled. Scheduling is useful because it establishes the expected amount of production that should be achieved at each work station over a given day or week. Therefore, each employee understands what is expected. Furthermore, scheduling allows managers to forecast how much will be produced by the end of the day, week, or month. If a firm does not meet its production schedule, it will not be able to accommodate customer orders in a timely fashion and will lose some of its customers.

Impact of Technology on Production Scheduling   Many firms have used technology to improve their production scheduling. For example, Weyerhaeuser (a manufacturer of doors) allows customers to access its website where they can specify the features of the door they desire and receive instant pricing on a door with those features. Consequently, orders are now placed more quickly. In addition, there is less chance of error because the customers specify the desired features themselves rather than communicating the information to someone who would then have to communicate the information to the manufacturing department. Deliveries are now almost always on schedule.

Production scheduling is also being improved by the use of computer-based systems called *enterprise resource planning (ERP)* systems. These complex software packages can connect the computer systems from different departments. The goal is to automate accounting, production, order taking, and the other basic processes of the business. ERP achieves this by recording every transaction, from taking an order to delivering a finished product, and updating the entire system. The practical application allows the customer to place an order (either through traditional sales channels or electronically) that automatically schedules the items in the production line, adjusts raw materials inventories, and schedules the delivery. At the same time, the appropriate accounting entries are made and invoices sent. This high degree of integration allows every user at the firm to be better informed about its resources and commitments.

Integration is the key difference between ERP systems and the mainframe systems that have been used by many large production companies.

Firms such as U.S. Steel use technology to set and monitor the production schedule.

LANDOV LLC

Mainframe systems offered little flexibility and resulted in firms becoming departmentalized. For instance, different production facilities would each have their own departments for obtaining supplies. Each production facility would order materials according to its own needs, even though all facilities used the same material. The different systems made it difficult to have consolidated knowledge of how much material was purchased, who it was purchased from, and the costs involved. An ERP system puts all of the production facilities on the same platform so that the overall process can be consolidated and costs are reduced.

A firm can extend its ERP system to the Internet where customers can access a website to learn which products are available and which have been committed to other customers. The firm may also demand that its suppliers offer the same ability so that supplies can be ordered quickly. This coordination allows the firm to eliminate inventory, improve connections with suppliers, and decrease overall costs.

ERP systems can be expensive, however. The price depends on the complexity of the system and the number of users that will access it. Installation requires data to be reformatted and network systems to be overhauled.

Scheduling for Special Projects   Scheduling is especially important for special long-term projects that must be completed by a specific deadline. If many related tasks must be completed in a specific sequence, scheduling can indicate when each task should be completed.

Gantt chart
a chart illustrating the expected timing for each task in the production process

One method of scheduling tasks for a special project is to use a **Gantt chart** (named after its creator, Henry Gantt), which illustrates the expected timing for each task within the production process. As an example of how a Gantt chart can be applied, assume that a chemical firm must produce 500 one-gallon containers of Chemical Z for a manufacturer. The production process involves creating large amounts of Chemicals X and Y, which are then mixed in a tank to produce Chemical Z. Next, Chemical Z must be poured into gallon containers and then packaged in cases to be delivered. Notice that while the first two tasks can be completed at the same time, each remaining task cannot begin until the previous task is completed.

The Gantt chart is shown in Exhibit 9.4. The bars can be marked when the respective tasks are completed to keep track of the production status.

Another method of scheduling tasks for a special project is the **program evaluation and review technique (PERT),** which schedules tasks in a manner that will minimize delays in the production process. PERT involves the following steps:

program evaluation and review technique (PERT)
a method of scheduling tasks to minimize delays in the production process

1. The various tasks involved in the production process are identified.

2. The tasks are arranged in the order in which they must take place; this sequence may be represented on a chart with arrows illustrating the path or sequence of the production process.

3. The time needed for each activity is estimated.

An example of PERT as applied to the firm's production of Chemical Z is shown in Exhibit 9.5. The production of Chemical X (Task 1) and Chemical Y (Task 2) can be conducted simultaneously. The mixing of Chemicals X and Y (Task 3) cannot begin until Tasks 1 and 2 are completed.

Exhibit 9.4

Example of a Gantt Chart

Production Tasks	Week 1	Week 2	Week 3	Week 4	Week 5
1. Produce Chemical X.	▨				
2. Produce Chemical Y.	▨				
3. Mix Chemicals X and Y in a tank to produce Chemical Z.			▨		
4. Pour Chemical Z into 500 one-gallon containers.				▨	
5. Package the one-gallon containers into cases.					▨

Exhibit 9.5

Determining the Critical Path Based on a Sequence of Production Tasks

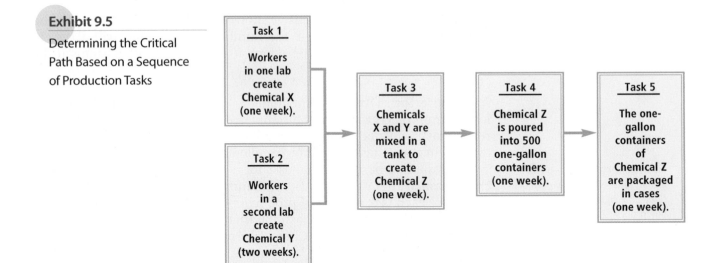

Each sequence of tasks is referred to as a path. For example, the sequence of Tasks 1, 3, 4, and 5 represents one path. A second path is the sequence of Tasks 2, 3, 4, and 5. The accumulated time for this path is five weeks. The **critical path** is the path that takes the longest time to complete. In our example, the critical path is the sequence of Tasks 2, 3, 4, and 5; that path takes five weeks. It is important to determine the time necessary to complete the steps within the critical path, since the production process will take that long.

critical path
the path that takes the longest time to complete

Identifying the critical path and calculating the time it requires allows managers to estimate the slack time (extra time) on the other paths and reduce any inefficiencies that can be caused by that slack time. The five-week period has no slack time for the workers involved in the critical path. Since the other path in Exhibit 9.5 has a completion time of four weeks, it has slack time of one week over a five-week period. Therefore, some of the workers assigned to Task 1 may be assigned to help with the second task of the critical path sequence. This may reduce the time necessary to complete the critical path.

The tasks that are part of the critical path should be reviewed to avoid delays or increase production speed. Tasks estimated to take a long time are closely monitored because any delays in these tasks are more likely to cause a severe delay in the entire production process. Furthermore, firms attempt to determine whether these tasks can be performed more quickly so that the critical path is completed in less time.

Quality Control

Quality can be defined as the degree to which a product or service satisfies a customer's requirements or expectations. Quality relates to customer satisfaction, which can have an effect on future sales and therefore on the future performance of the firm. Customers are more likely to purchase additional products from the same firm if they are satisfied with the quality. Firms now realize that it is easier to retain existing customers than it is to attract new customers who are unfamiliar with their products or services. Thus, firms are increasingly recognizing the impact that the quality of their products or services can have on their overall performance.

quality
the degree to which a product or service satisfies a customer's requirements or expectations

Quality control is a process of determining whether the quality of a product or a service meets the desired quality level and identifying improvements (if any) that need to be made in the production process. Quality can be measured by assessing the various characteristics (such as how long the product lasts) that enhance customer satisfaction. The quality of a computer may be defined by how well it works and how long it lasts. Quality may also be measured by how easy the computer is to use or by how quickly the manufacturer repairs a computer that experiences problems. All of these characteristics can affect customer satisfaction and therefore should be considered as indicators of quality.

quality control
a process of determining whether the quality of a product meets the desired quality level

The quality of services sold to customers must also be assessed. For example, Amazon.com produces a service of fulfilling orders of books, CDs, and other products ordered over the Internet by customers. Its customers assess the quality of the service in terms of the ease with which they can send an order over the Internet, whether they receive the proper order, and how quickly the products are delivered.

The act of monitoring and improving the quality of products and services produced is commonly referred to as **total quality management (TQM),** which was developed by W. Edwards Deming. Among TQM's key

total quality management (TQM)
the act of monitoring and improving the quality of products and services provided

Cross Functional Teamwork

Interaction of Functions Involved in Total Quality Management

Total quality management requires an ongoing product assessment, beginning from the time product materials are ordered and continuing until the customer has purchased and used the product. Consequently, TQM requires an interaction of business functions. The key management functions involved in TQM are ordering the proper types and amounts of supplies, achieving efficient (low-cost) production of the product, and ensuring that the product satisfies the firm's production standards.

The key marketing functions involved in TQM are achieving efficient use of marketing strategies, ensuring customer satisfaction, and obtaining feedback from customers on how to improve the product. When marketing managers receive a similar criticism about a product from many customers, they should contact the production managers, who may redesign the product. This interaction between management and marketing functions is shown in Exhibit 9.6.

The financing function is indirectly affected, as changes in expenses or revenue resulting from TQM may alter the amount of new financing that the firm needs.

Exhibit 9.6

Interaction between Management and Marketing Functions When Implementing Total Quality Management

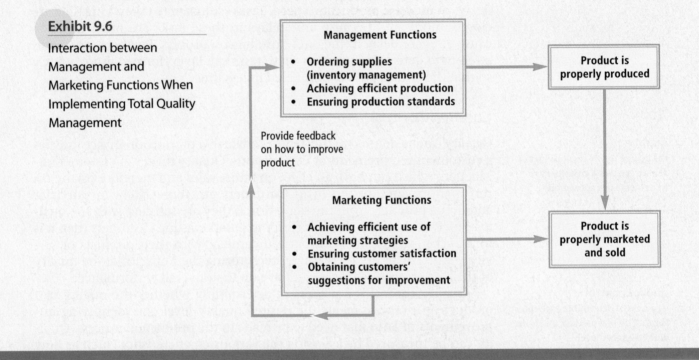

guidelines for improving quality are the following: (1) provide managers and other employees with the education and training they need to excel in their jobs, (2) encourage employees to take responsibility and to provide leadership, and (3) encourage all employees to search for ways to improve the production process. Production quotas are discouraged so that employees can allocate more of their time to leadership and the improvement of the production process. Many firms use teams of employees to assess quality and offer suggestions for continuous improvement.

To ensure that quality is maintained, firms periodically evaluate the methods used to measure product or service quality. They rely on various techniques to assess quality, as described next.

Control by Technology Motorola and many other firms use computers to assess quality. The computers can determine whether each component of a

Global Business

Global Quality Standards

Firms that conduct international business may attempt to satisfy a set of global quality standards. These standards have been established by the International Standards Organization (ISO), which includes representatives from numerous countries. Firms are not required to meet these standards. By voluntarily meeting them, however, a firm can become certified, which may boost its credibility when selling products to foreign customers, who may be more comfortable if the firm has met the standards.

The certification process commonly costs at least $20,000 and takes at least one year. The standards focus on the design, manufacturing process, installation, and service of a product. Independent auditors review the firm's operations and decide whether to certify the firm. A publication called ISO 9000 specifies the standards for production quality. Another set of standards (called ISO 14000) applies to the environmental effects of the production process.

Firms may also have to meet other standards to sell their products in specific foreign countries. For example, the Japanese government assesses any products that are sold in Japan to ensure that they are safe. Japan's safety standards have discouraged firms based in the United States and other countries from attempting to sell products in Japan. Thus, the standards may serve as a barrier that protects local firms in Japan from foreign competitors.

The quality of services is also dependent on the manner by which a business combines its human resources with its other resources. The successful production of a concert by the singer Usher depends not only on his ability but also other human resources who are involved with planning, scheduling, and operating equipment.

GETTY IMAGES

product meets specific quality standards. Computer-controlled machinery has electronic sensors that can screen out defective parts.

Dell, Inc., uses custom configurations to ensure a high level of product quality and thereby fulfill its responsibility to its customers. It relies on its computer network to track its products from the point of initial sales contact to the time the product is sent to the customer, and beyond. Specifically, for a given order, Dell knows the date of the initial query by the customer, the date the order was placed, the date the order was delivered, the dates technical support was requested, and the types of support that were provided. This tracking system offers several benefits. First, Dell can determine the speed at which it fills an order. Second, it has a history of its communications with the customer in case any dispute arises. Third, from the technical support communications, Dell can determine the type of support that was needed. When Dell redesigns its computers in the future, it can take these requests for support into consideration.

quality control circle
a group of employees who assess the quality of a product and offer suggestions for improvement

Control by Employees   Firms also use their employees to assess quality. Many firms such as IBM and DaimlerChrysler use a **quality control circle,** which is a group of employees who assess the quality of a product and offer suggestions for improvement. Quality control circles usually allow for more interaction among workers and managers and provide workers with a sense of responsibility.

sampling
randomly selecting some of the products produced and testing them to determine whether they satisfy the quality standards

Control by Sampling   Firms also assess quality by **sampling,** or randomly selecting some of the products produced and testing them to determine whether they satisfy the quality standards. Firms may check one unit per 100 units produced and concentrate specifically on possible flaws that have been detected in previous checks.

Control by Monitoring Complaints   Quality should be assessed not only when the product is produced but also after it is sold. Some quality deficiencies may not become evident until after customers use the products. The quality of products that have been sold can be assessed by monitoring the proportion of products returned or by tracking customer complaints. Additional customer feedback can be obtained by conducting surveys. Firms can obtain customers' opinions on product quality by sending them a survey months after the sale.

Correcting Deficiencies   The purpose of the quality control process is not only to detect quality deficiencies but also to correct them. If quality is deficient, the problem was likely caused by one of the following factors: inadequate materials provided by suppliers, inadequate quality of work by employees, or malfunctioning machinery or equipment.

If inadequate materials caused the quality deficiency, the firm may require the existing supplier to improve the quality or may obtain materials from a different supplier in the future. If the cause is the work of employees, the firm may need to retrain or reprimand those employees. If the cause of quality deficiency is the machinery, the firm may need to to replace the machinery or make repairs.

While most production deficiencies cause a reduction in customer satisfaction, some deficiencies are worse than others. When a firm's product deficiency causes harm to a customer, the customer may bring a lawsuit against the firm claiming that it is liable for the harm caused by its product. The firm may incur major expenses if it must pay compensation to a customer as a result of a lawsuit. In addition, the firm may develop a bad reputation if there is publicity about its products causing harm to customers, and it may experience a loss in sales as a result. Quality control may ensure that products will not cause harm to customers. However, even the best quality control cannot prevent some liability lawsuits. Unfortunately, the court system does not severely penalize frivolous lawsuits, so some people file frivolous lawsuits against firms, hoping to win large monetary rewards. For example, some people put needles in a can of Pepsi and tried to claim that the needles were due to Pepsi's production process. In 2005, a woman claimed that she found a cutoff finger in a bowl of Wendy's chili that was caused by Wendy's production process. In these

SMALL BUSINESS SURVEY

Exposure to Liability Lawsuits

In a recent National Small Business poll conducted for the NFIB Research Foundation, owners of small businesses were asked whether they believe liability laws favor those who file liability lawsuits or those who must defend against liability. Their responses are shown here:

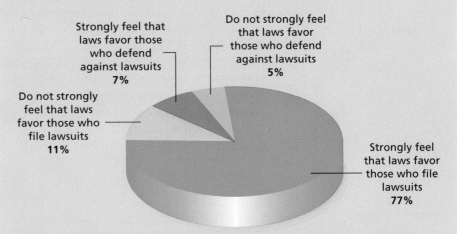

Strongly feel that laws favor those who defend against lawsuits
7%

Do not strongly feel that laws favor those who defend against lawsuits
5%

Do not strongly feel that laws favor those who file lawsuits
11%

Strongly feel that laws favor those who file lawsuits
77%

The small business owners were also asked if they were concerned about being subjected to a liability lawsuit. Their responses are shown here:

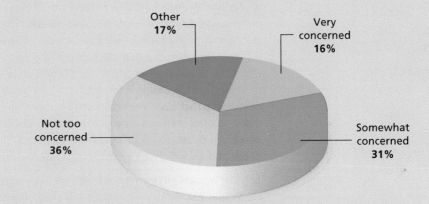

Other
17%

Very concerned
16%

Not too concerned
36%

Somewhat concerned
31%

The owners of small businesses who participated in the survey and had been sued cited the following reason for the liability lawsuit:

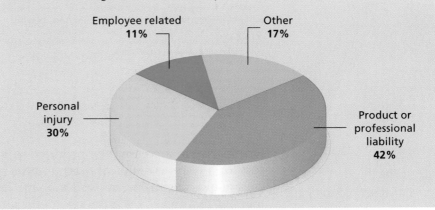

Employee related
11%

Other
17%

Personal injury
30%

Product or professional liability
42%

cases, the firms were able to prove that the claims were false. Yet, even if a firm does do not have to pay compensation, it will incur major expenses defending against liability lawsuits, whether legitimate or frivolous.

Winners of the Malcolm Baldrige National Quality Awards   Firms that have recently won National Quality Awards used innovation to improve their quality. Cat Financial is a business that finances large orders of equipment from Caterpillar. Its services are available online, allowing customers to apply for financing and obtain information from the website without having to call a customer service representative. Stoner is the smallest business to ever win a Baldrige Quality Award. It has only 48 employees. Stoner created a software system to integrate its production, inventory, and distribution. Thus, its distribution decisions can be made with up-to-date information about production and inventory. Its decisions about future production can account for the latest inventory level. Though larger firms have used such technology, it is unusual for such a small company to have such an efficient system for integrating its production and distribution.

Decision Making ▸ Deciding on Quality Control

The optimal method for quality control is dependent on the firm's specific characteristics. To illustrate, recall the case of Cell One Company, which specializes in producing cell phones. The manufacturing process involves mostly machinery. To ensure that the cell phones are made properly, Cell One uses the following quality control techniques. First, it uses machines that test to make sure that the length and weight of each cell phone fall within the production specifications. Second, an employee briefly checks each cell phone to ensure that the design is correct. Third, Cell One inscribes its e-mail address on all of its products so that customer's can e-mail complaints and suggestions. When any of these quality control methods detects a deficiency, Cell One revises its production to correct the deficiency. By ensuring quality control, Cell One Company has attracted a large demand for its cell phones, which has increased revenue and therefore increased profits.

1.   Why would Cell One rely on feedback from customers for quality control? Shouldn't it be able to catch production defects without relying on customer feedback?

2.   Why would Cell One's decisions regarding quality control possibly affect its decisions about design and layout?

ANSWERS: 1. A product may not satisfy customers even if it has no defects. Quality control is needed to ensure that the product has quality from the customer's perspective and therefore will be desired by customers. 2. Quality control may require machinery or employees on the production site and therefore may affect the design and layout of production. For example, the machinery for quality control may be inserted at various places within the assembly operation so that quality can be assessed at various phases of production.

Methods to Improve Production Efficiency

Describe the key factors that affect production efficiency.

Firms strive to increase their **production efficiency,** which reflects a lower cost for a given amount of output and a given level of quality. Managers continually search for ways to manage human and other resources in a manner that improves production efficiency. Firms recognize the need to continually improve because other competitors may become more efficient and take their business away.

production efficiency
the ability to produce products at a low cost

benchmarking
a method of evaluating performance by comparison to some specified (benchmark) level, typically a level achieved by another company

stretch targets
production efficiency targets (or goals) that cannot be achieved under present conditions

automated
tasks are completed by machines without the use of employees

Production efficiency is important to service firms as well as manufacturing firms. For example, airlines need to be efficient in their service of flying passengers from one location to another so that they can achieve low expenses.

Many firms that set production efficiency goals use **benchmarking,** which is a method of evaluating performance by comparison to some specified (benchmark) level—typically, a level achieved by another company. For example, a firm may set a goal of producing baseball caps at a cost of $3 per cap, which is the average cost incurred by the most successful producer of baseball caps.

The top managers of some firms set production efficiency targets (or goals) that cannot be achieved under present conditions. These targets are referred to as **stretch targets** because they are stretched beyond the ordinary. Stretch targets may be established in response to a decline in the firm's market share or performance. For example, 3M Company created a stretch target that 30 percent of its sales should be derived from sales of products created in the last four years. This target was intended to encourage more development of new products so that 3M did not rely on its innovations from several years ago.

Firms can improve production efficiency through the following methods:

▶ Technology
▶ Economies of scale
▶ Restructuring

Each of these methods is discussed in turn.

Technology

Firms may improve their production efficiency by adopting new technology. New machinery that incorporates improved technology can perform tasks more quickly.

Many production processes have become **automated;** that is, tasks are completed by machines without the use of employees. Since machinery can be less costly than human resources, automation may improve production efficiency. Guidelines for effective automation are summarized in Exhibit 9.7.

Many firms such as Albertson's (a grocery chain) and Home Depot have improved production efficiency with the use of computer technology.

Exhibit 9.7

Guidelines for Effective Automation

To effectively capitalize on the potential benefits from automation, the following guidelines should be considered:

1. *Plan.* Automation normally does not simply speed up work; instead, it may require the elimination of some production steps. Planning is necessary to decide what type of automation will be most appropriate (computers versus other machinery).

2. *Use Automation Where the Benefits Are Greatest.* It may not be efficient to evenly allocate automation among all parts of the production process. Some workers will not be able to use a computer for their type of work.

3. *Train.* To make sure that the automation implemented is effectively utilized, any workers who use new computers or machinery should be trained.

4. *Evaluate Costs and Benefits over Time.* By assessing the costs and benefits of automation, a firm can decide whether to implement additional automation or revise its existing automation.

Home Depot uses technology to monitor its inventory and its sales of all of its products.

For example, computers can keep track of the daily or weekly volume of each type of product that is purchased at the cash register of a retail store. Therefore, the firm does not need an employee to monitor the inventory of these products. The computer may even be programmed to automatically reorder some products once the inventory is reduced to a specified level. Some hospitals use pharmacy robots that stock and retrieve drugs. This technology increases production without additional labor expenses. Numerous manufacturing firms are using more powerful computers that have increased the speed at which various tasks can be completed.

The Internet Much of the recent improvement in productivity is attributed to the Internet, in particular to its ability to improve the flow of information and communication between a firm's employees, and also between a firm and its customers and suppliers. A recent study by the University of California and the Brookings Institution found that almost half of the productivity improvements in U.S. firms are attributed to the use of Internet business solutions.

Economies of Scale

economies of scale
as the quantity produced increases, the cost per unit decreases

Firms may also be able to reduce costs by achieving **economies of scale,** which reflect a lower average cost incurred from producing a larger volume. To recognize how economies of scale can occur, consider that two types of costs are involved in the production of a product: fixed costs and variable costs. **Fixed costs** are operating expenses that do not change in response to the number of products produced. For example, the cost of renting a specific factory is not affected by the number of products produced there.

fixed costs
operating expenses that do not change in response to the number of products produced

variable costs
operating expenses that vary directly with the number of products produced

Variable costs are operating expenses that vary directly with the number of products produced. As output increases, the variable costs increase, but the fixed costs remain constant. The average cost per unit typically declines as output increases for firms that incur large fixed costs.

Automobile manufacturers incur a large fixed cost because they have to pay for their large facilities (including all the machinery) even if they do not produce many cars. Therefore, they need to produce a large number of cars to reduce the average cost per car produced.

Consider the production of a paperback book that requires some materials (ink and paper) and some manual labor. Assume that a printing company incurs a fixed cost (rent plus machinery) of $40,000 per month. These expenses exist regardless of the number of books printed. Assume that the variable cost of producing each book is $2 per book. The total cost of producing books each month is equal to the fixed cost plus the variable cost. The total cost is estimated for various production levels in Exhibit 9.8.

Exhibit 9.8

Relationship between Production Volume and Costs

Quantity of Books Produced	Fixed Cost	Variable Cost ($2 per Unit)	Total Cost	Average Cost per Unit
1,000	$40,000	$2,000	$42,000	$42.00
3,000	40,000	6,000	46,000	15.33
5,000	40,000	10,000	50,000	10.00
10,000	40,000	20,000	60,000	6.00
15,000	40,000	30,000	70,000	4.67
20,000	40,000	40,000	80,000	4.00
25,000	40,000	50,000	90,000	3.60

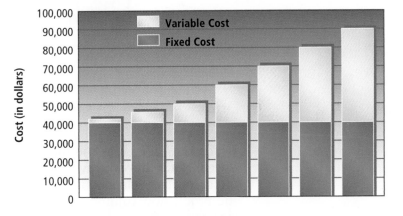

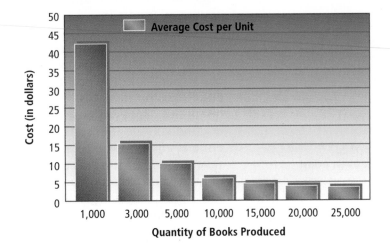

Exhibit 9.9

Relationship between Volume and Profitability

Quantity of Books Produced	Total Revenue (= Quantity × Price)	Total Cost	Profits
1,000	$ 10,000	$42,000	$−32,000
3,000	30,000	46,000	−16,000
5,000	50,000	50,000	0
10,000	100,000	60,000	40,000
15,000	150,000	70,000	80,000
20,000	200,000	80,000	120,000
25,000	250,000	90,000	160,000

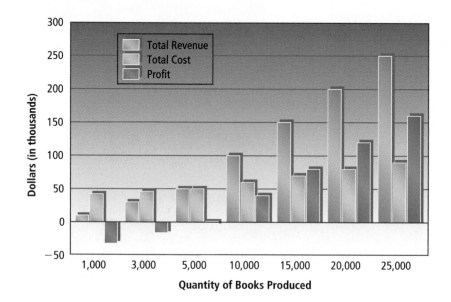

The key measure of production efficiency is the average cost per unit, which is measured as the total cost divided by the number of units produced. Notice how the average cost declines when the production volume increases. This relationship exists because the fixed cost is not affected by the production volume. Therefore, the fixed costs can be spread over a larger production volume. No extra fixed cost is incurred when producing additional products.

Assume that each of the books produced can be sold for $10. Exhibit 9.9 shows the total revenue and total costs for various quantities of books produced. The total revenue is equal to the quantity produced times the price of $10 per book. The profits represent the difference between the total revenue and the total cost. Notice that the firm experiences losses at small quantities. This is because the fixed costs are incurred even though the production volume is low. At the quantity level of 5,000 books, the total revenue is equal to the total cost. The quantity of units sold at which total revenue equals total cost is referred to as the **break-even point.** At any quantity beyond 5,000 books, the firm earns profits. The profits are larger for larger quantities produced. This results from the lower average cost incurred from the production of more books.

Some firms strive to achieve a large market share so that they can achieve economies of scale. For example, Dell typically sets a goal to obtain

break-even point
the quantity of units sold at which total revenue equals total cost

a substantial market share for each of its products. This results in a large production volume so that Dell can achieve economies of scale. One of the largest expenses in the production of computers is the research and development to improve the computers. That expense is incurred whether Dell sells only 20 computers or 50,000 computers. Therefore, the average cost per unit is reduced when Dell produces a large amount of a specific computer.

Restructuring

restructuring
the revision of the production process in an attempt to improve efficiency

reengineering
the redesign of a firm's organizational structure and operations

Restructuring involves the revision of the production process in an attempt to improve efficiency. When restructuring reduces the expense of producing products or services, it can improve the firm's profits and therefore increase the firm's value. Many firms also engage in **reengineering,** which is the redesign of a firm's organizational structure and operations. The reengineering may result in some minor revisions, such as changes in the procedures used to take phone messages or to send packages. Alternatively, the revisions may be much larger, such as a new facility or a new assembly-line operation for production.

downsizing
an attempt by a firm to cut expenses by eliminating job positions

Downsizing   When firms restructure, they also typically engage in **downsizing;** that is, they reduce the number of employees. Firms identify various job positions that can be eliminated without affecting the volume or the quality of products produced. Some downsizing occurs as a result of technology because automated production processes replace human resources (as explained earlier). However, numerous firms downsize even when they have no plans to further automate their production process.

Although downsizing can help a firm achieve cost savings, downsizing also has its disadvantages. First, costs may be associated with the elimination of job positions, such as costs incurred to find other job positions within the firm or outside it for the employees whose jobs were cut. Second, costs may be associated with training some of the remaining employees whose responsibilities were expanded. Third, if the remaining employees believe their own positions may be cut, their morale may decline, reducing their performance. Fourth, downsizing may result in lower quality, as the remaining employees may be assigned more work and may not detect defects in the production process. Some firms become so obsessed with eliminating their inefficient components that they downsize too much. This is referred to as **corporate anorexia.**

corporate anorexia
the problem that occurs when firms become so obsessed with eliminating their inefficient components that they downsize too much

Integration of the Production Tasks

supply chain
the process from the beginning of the production process until the product reaches the customer

The production process described in this chapter consists of related tasks, such that each task can be accomplished only after other tasks have been completed. Thus, if any production task breaks down, the entire production schedule is affected. Furthermore, firms are unable to deliver their products to stores or to customers until all production tasks are completed. Therefore, firms monitor the so-called **supply chain,** or the process from the very beginning of the production process until the product reaches the consumer. Firms that produce products identify a site for production, hire employees, set up work stations, and determine the design and layout that will ensure efficient production. To recognize the integration required, consider the following example:

▶   After an automobile manufacturer identifies a site for production, it hires employees and assigns them to assembly lines.

▶ Machinery and tools (such as special wrenches) are placed along the assembly lines to help the employees assemble the automobiles.

▶ Materials (including steering wheels, seat cushions, engines, and tires) are delivered to different parts of the assembly line so that they can be installed during the production process. The design and layout are structured so that one task is completed before the automobile frame is moved to the next station on the assembly line, and so on. For example, the dashboard may be inserted at one station and the doors and windshield attached at the next station. The dashboard is installed first because inserting a dashboard is more difficult after the doors have been attached.

▶ A sufficient inventory of materials is ordered to accommodate the scheduled production.

▶ Tasks are scheduled so that each person who is assigned a task on the assembly line has enough time to complete it before the automobile frame is moved to the next station. Too much time should not be allocated for a specific task, however, because that would reduce the production volume.

▶ The quality control process takes place at different stations along the assembly line to ensure that each part of the production process is completed according to standards.

How Breakdowns Disrupt the Production Process   When production tasks are integrated, a breakdown in one part of the process may cause the entire production process to be slowed. Consider some examples. First, the machinery used by employees in the production process could break down, disrupting the entire process until the machinery is repaired or replaced. Second, materials needed at different stations along the assembly line may not arrive on time, halting production at those stations and at the stations that follow them on the assembly line. Third, some of the employees who were assigned tasks on the assembly line may become ill or quit, causing production to slow unless replacements are available. Fourth, the quality control process may require that a specific task be redone, disrupting the process because later tasks cannot be completed until the task in question is done properly.

The integration of tasks is not limited to assembly-line production. Firms such as Motorola, Johnson & Johnson, General Dynamics, and AT&T focus on coordinating all their production tasks in a manner that minimizes production cost while maintaining high quality. In fact, these firms frequently restructure their production process, continually searching for more efficient ways to produce their products.

Integration of Tasks at Service Firms   Even service firms use a production process that is integrated and therefore requires that the tasks described in this chapter are completed in a specific order. For example, Amazon.com hires employees to produce the service of fulfilling orders made by customers over a website. The production process for Amazon.com involves forecasting the future demand for books (or other items), ordering a sufficient number of each book to satisfy demand in a future period, storing books at warehouses, receiving orders, fulfilling orders, and ensuring that customers receive quality service (such as quick delivery). If Amazon.com does not order a sufficient amount of books relative to the amount customers order, it will not be able to accommodate all of the demand. Alternatively, if it has a sufficient inventory of the books but does not have enough employees and computer facilities to fulfill the orders, the production process will be disrupted.

Decision Making   Tradeoffs from Production Decisions

Many firms must decide whether to produce all of their products at one manufacturing plant or to have multiple production plants. Consider Cell One Company, which relies on one production plant to produce all of its cell phones. It realizes that if it had plants in several cities, each plant could distribute its cell phones to the retail stores that are near that plant. This would reduce the delivery time and the transportation costs. However, if Cell One had multiple production plants, it would incur higher costs because it would need to rent additional facilities. It would also have to hire more employees for each plant. Overall, Cell One achieves greater economies of scale with a single production plant than if it had additional facilities. The cost savings from having a single plant outweigh the potential cost savings from lower transportation costs if it established additional production plants. In addition, Cell One can also more easily monitor the quality or its production process at a single plant than if it had multiple plants. Therefore, it decides not to establish additional production facilities.

1. Given all the advantages of a single production plant for Cell One Company, why do some companies have multiple production plants?
2. Do you think the costs of maintaining inventory would be higher if Cell One relied on one plant or on many plants for its production? Why?

ANSWERS: 1. For some types of production, economies of scale may be somewhat limited, so the firm does not gain much from producing at a single plant. In addition, some production plants focus on different types of products. For example, a car manufacturer may use one plant to produce trucks and another plant to produce cars. 2. Inventory costs would be lower if Cell One had only one plant. If it had multiple plants, it would need to maintain inventory at every plant.

COLLEGE HEALTH CLUB: AVERAGE COST AT CHC

Sue Kramer wants to ensure that College Health Club is efficiently managed. Since CHC's expenses are mostly fixed, she recognizes the importance of generating economies of scale. She wants to determine the average cost per member served for various possible levels of membership. Since she expects CHC's total expenses over the first year to be $142,000, she estimates the cost per member served as follows:

Impact of Membership Size on CHC's Average Cost per Member

	If 280 Members Join in the First Year	If 300 Members Join in the First Year	If 320 Members Join in the First Year
(1) Total cost	$142,000	$142,000	$142,000
(2) Number of members	280	300	320
(3) Cost per member = (1)/(2)	$507	$473	$444

If 280 members join, the average cost to CHC per member is $507, which exceeds the annual membership fee of $500. The higher the membership, the lower the average cost to CHC per member. This is why it is so important to attract a large membership at CHC.

Summary

1 The key resources used for production are human resources, materials, and other resources (such as the plant, machinery, and equipment).

2 The plant site decision is influenced by

► cost of workplace space,

► cost of labor,

► tax incentives,

► source of demand for the product produced,

► access to transportation, and

► supply of labor.

A site evaluation matrix can be used to assign a rating to each relevant factor and derive a total rating for each possible site.

3 The design and layout of a plant are influenced by the

► site characteristics,

► production process,

► product line, and

► desired production capacity.

4 Production control involves

► purchasing materials, which requires selecting a supplier, negotiating volume discounts, and possibly delegating production to suppliers;

► inventory control, which involves managing various inventories at levels that minimize costs;

► routing, which determines the sequence of tasks necessary to complete production;

► scheduling, which sets time periods for the tasks required within the production process; and

► quality control, which can be used to identify improvements (if any) that need to be made in the production process.

5 The key methods used to improve production efficiency are

► technology, which increases the speed of the production process;

► economies of scale, which reduce the average cost per unit as a result of a higher production volume; and

► restructuring, which is a revision of the production process to reduce production expenses.

How the Chapter Concepts Affect Business Performance

A firm's decisions regarding the production concepts summarized here affect its performance. Its decisions regarding the use of resources and the site to use for production affect the cost of production. Its decisions regarding the control of the production process may ensure that the process remains efficient. In addition, it can monitor quality, which influences revenue because it affects customer satisfaction. The firm's decisions on how to revise the production process to produce more efficiently can reduce production costs.

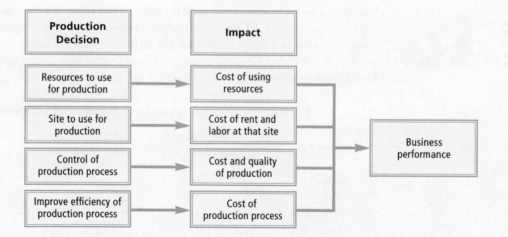

Key Terms

assembly line   317
automated   339
benchmarking   339
break-even point   342
carrying costs   328
corporate anorexia   343
critical path   333
deintegration   327
design   322
downsizing   343
economies of scale   340
fixed costs   340
fixed-position layout   323
flexible manufacturing   323
Gantt chart   331
hotelling   324

inventory control   328
just-in-time (JIT)   328
layout   322
materials requirements
    planning (MRP)   328
order costs   328
outsourcing   326
product layout   323
production control   325
production efficiency   339
production management   316
production process   316
production schedule   330
program evaluation and review
    technique (PERT)   332
quality   333

quality control   333
quality control circle   336
reengineering   343
restructuring   343
routing   330
sampling   336
scheduling   330
stretch targets   339
supply chain   343
total quality management
    (TQM)   333
variable costs   340
work station   317
work-in-process
    inventories   328

Review & Critical Thinking Questions

1. If you were a plant manager, what primary resources would you use for production?

2. Explain the use of work stations and assembly lines.

3. You are moving your plant from the West Coast to the East Coast. What key location factors should be considered?

4. What general factors influence design and layout decisions?

5. What is e-procurement? How can e-procurement benefit a firm?

6. List the five tasks involved in production control.

7. What is outsourcing? What are the advantages and disadvantages of outsourcing?

8. What is deintegration? How can it benefit a manufacturer?

9. Compare just-in-time (JIT) inventory with materials requirements planning (MRP).

10. What is production scheduling? Why is a production schedule so important for a manager?

11. Define PERT. Explain what steps are involved with PERT. Why is it necessary to identify the critical path when working on a project?

12. Define and explain quality control.

13. What is total quality management (TQM)? Briefly summarize the key guidelines for improving quality under TQM.

14. Briefly summarize the methods used by firms to improve production efficiency.

15. Define downsizing and restructuring. How are the two related?

16. What is corporate anorexia? How might corporate anorexia lead to worse business performance than the firm faced prior to downsizing?

17. What are stretch targets, and why would managers set these kinds of efficiency targets if they cannot be achieved under the present conditions?

18. How might labor costs affect site decisions? Will a company always locate where the cost of labor is cheapest?

19. How does the management of inventory lead to better firm performance? If inventory is not managed well, how will the firm be affected?

20. Many communities would like to attract businesses to locate there in order to increase employment. What kinds of incentives can the local government provide to make the location more attractive?

Discussion Questions

1. Would production management apply to a professional basketball team? How?

2. What is hotelling? Can you think of any disadvantages associated with hotelling?

3. Assume that you are a project manager for a large construction company. You have been given an assignment to develop a schedule for the construction of a skyscraper. Discuss how you would develop and implement a schedule.

4. How could a firm use the Internet to provide information on its production management function? How could it use the Internet to provide information on its production control?

5. Assume that your company plans to relocate its plant to a new region and has assigned you to select the new location. What factors would you consider in making the decision?

6. What type of layout is appropriate for each of the following: (a) an aircraft manufacturer, such as Boeing; (b) an automotive plant for a firm such as General Motors; (c) a contractor engaged in new housing construction?

7. You are a manager at a software manufacturer. Describe how the different sources of control may apply to your company.

8. Suppose that a firm has a production location in a small town in the United States, but discovers that it could lower costs substantially by closing the plant in the United States and relocating production to Mexico. What are the ethical issues the firm should consider?

9. Consider the product line of many American car manufacturers. As oil prices rise, how might they alter their product line in response?

10. Assume you are the manager of a firm that is considering outsourcing some of the manufacturing currently being conducted on site. What are the advantages and disadvantages of doing so?

IT'S YOUR DECISION: PRODUCTION DECISIONS AT CHC

1. The cost of land is much higher in the middle of the city than it is on the outskirts of the city where College Health Club (CHC) is located. How does this affect CHC's expenses?

2. What tradeoff is involved in determining the size of the facilities for CHC?

3. CHC can purchase vitamin supplements at a discount if it orders a case of 300 units. It will earn a higher profit per unit when selling the vitamins to its members if it receives that discount. What would be a disadvantage to CHC of buying a large amount of vitamins?

4. Explain why CHC's marketing plan can have an impact on the size of the facilities the club needs.

5. CHC expects total expenses of $142,000 in the first year. It will set the membership fee at $500 and expects to attract 300 members in its first year. It could rent another unit for an extra $12,000 per year. The extra unit may attract additional members because of the added space. Determine CHC's earnings before taxes in the first year if this extra unit is rented and results in:

   a) A total of 314 memberships in the first year.

   b) A total of 320 memberships in the first year.

   c) If the unit will result in 320 memberships in the first year, would you recommend that CHC rent the unit?

6. How can the quality of the service provided by CHC be measured?

7. How should CHC decide what factors to assess when monitoring the quality of the services that it provides?

8. Assume that CHC's members view five key characteristics as important. Can Sue Kramer monitor quality by monitoring the average rating of those five characteristics? Or should she monitor the rating of each individual characteristic? Explain.

9. CHC uses the marketing function to identify health club services that will generate memberships. It then produces the health club services that it believes are desired by

potential members. Explain how CHC's focus on quality is related to production and marketing.

10. Recall that CHC expects total expenses of $142,000 (operating expenses = $138,000 and interest expenses = $4,000) in the first year. It will set its membership fee at $500 and expects to attract 300 members in its first year. Determine the number of memberships at which CHC will break even under the following conditions:

    a) Under prevailing conditions in which the expected total operating expenses are $138,000.

    b) Operating expenses are $146,000 and interest expenses are $4,000.

    c) Operating expenses are $142,000 and interest expenses are $4,000.

    d) Explain the relationship between the total expenses and the break-even level of memberships. How would the break-even level be affected if Sue had rented a smaller facility for her health club? What would be a disadvantage of a smaller facility?

11. A health club differs from manufacturing firms in that it produces a service rather than products. Explain the similarity between the quality control of a service versus a product. Are there any differences between the quality control of a service versus a product?

Investing in a Business

Using the annual report of the firm in which you would like to invest, complete the following:

Questions

1. Describe (in general terms) the firm's production process. What products are produced? Where are the production facilities located? Are the facilities concentrated in one location or scattered?

2. Have the firm's operations been restructured in recent years to improve efficiency? If so, how?

3. Does your firm need to consider labor supply issues when selecting a site?

4. Explain how the business uses technology to promote its production management function. For example, does it use the Internet to provide information about its production management function? Does it provide information regarding the methods used to control production?

5. Does the firm appear to pay attention to customer satisfaction? Explain.

6. Has the firm improved the quality of its products or services in recent years? If so, how?

7. Go to http://hoovers.com and locate the NEWS SEARCH. Type in the name of the firm in the space provided, and review the recent news stories about the firm. Summarize any (at least one) recent news story about the firm that applies to one or more of the key concepts in this chapter.

Case: Selecting the Best Plant Site

Richard Capozzi, an entrepreneur in the high-fashion Italian shoe industry, is planning to relocate his manufacturing operation to the western part of the United States. He is currently considering two different locations. One possible location is outside Los Angeles, and the other is in Oklahoma City.

In analyzing the plant site decision, he is considering several factors. The cost of land is high in Los Angeles. However, local government officials are willing to make tax concessions. This plant location is accessible to transportation; a railroad is adjacent to the plant and an eight-lane interstate is close. Capozzi has identified the

West Coast region as his target market for this type of shoe. An artist by trade, he has developed a unique design that should create mass-market appeal in this geographic area.

The Oklahoma City location has several advantages. Land cost is lower than in Los Angeles. Also, a large supply of trained labor is available in this region.

Another key consideration Capozzi must deal with is raw material availability. The raw material is imported from Italy and is received at the port of entry in Los Angeles. If the operation were located in Oklahoma City, additional ground transportation would be necessary. Transportation costs would, therefore, be lower for the Los Angeles plant, a fact that weighs heavily in Capozzi's decision.

Questions

1. What will influence the plant site decision for Capozzi, and which alternative appears to be optimal?

2. How can each relative factor be rated or evaluated to determine the optimal plant location?

3. How should the decision regarding plant layout and design be determined?

4. What resources will Capozzi need to implement the production plan?

5. Describe the techniques for assessing quality and explain how they might apply to a shoe manufacturer.

6. Do you think this particular type of operation could benefit from economies of scale? Explain.

Video Case: Quality Control at Canondale

Canondale is a bicycle manufacturing firm that makes high-end lightweight road, recreational, and mountain bikes as well as riding apparel. Total quality management (quality control) and rigorous quality standards are essential to Canondale. Quality control takes place through a testing lab, which does frame impact tests and structural and performance testing to meet French, British, and ISO standards and obtains data used to evaluate the strength of the bikes.

Quality control is not limited to the lab, however. Quality is built into the bicycles by the workers rather than through a specific quality control manager inspecting the bikes. Control at the organization is generally decentralized. Employees on the assembly line are empowered to pull bikes off the assembly line if they see a defect. This streamlines operations by building quality control into every bicycle made. To increase quality control and to keep dealers happy, assembly is done in-house. The bikes are assembled in the United States very close to the designers, so that the production managers and designers can share a common culture and communicate effectively. For more information about Canondale, visit its website at http://www.cannondale.com/bikes/index.html.

Questions

1. Why does Canondale's survival depend on its innovation and quality control?

2. Why is it important for Canondale to meet international standards when making its bikes?

3. Why is it an advantage to have assembly done very close to the design center?

Internet Applications

1. http://www.iso.org/iso/en/ISOOnline.frontpage

What are ISO standards? How might a firm benefit from meeting ISO standards? How would a firm go about becoming ISO compliant?

2. http://www.bmpcoe.org

What are best manufacturing processes? Click on "web technologies." What is a Collaborative Work Environment, and how does Internet technology enable it to work?

3. http://manufacturing.stanford.edu

Click on "How Everyday Things Are Made." How do manufacturing processes differ for airplanes, automobiles, clothes, and candy? How are they similar?

Dell's Secret to Success

Go to http://www.reportgallery.com and review Dell's most recent annual report. Also, go to Dell's website (http://www.dell.com) and in the section "about Dell," review the background material about Dell that relates to this chapter.

Questions

1. Describe Dell's goals regarding quality.

2. How does Dell monitor quality?

3. How does customer satisfaction relate to Dell's quality control?

In-Text Study Guide

Answers are in Appendix C at the back of book.

True or False

1. A work station is an area in which one or more employees is assigned a specific task.

2. Design and layout decisions will have an impact on operating expenses.

3. A fixed-position layout is commonly used for assembly-line production.

4. Hotelling represents the sequence of tasks necessary to complete the production of a product.

5. A firm uses outsourcing so that it can hire additional employees.

6. The term "just-in-time" refers to a schedule that illustrates the expected timing for each task within a project.

7. Inventories of partially completed products are called work-in-process.

8. The critical path is the path that takes the shortest time to complete on a PERT diagram.

9. Quality control can be measured by assessing the various characteristics that enhance customer satisfaction.

10. Downsizing has enabled firms to reduce the amount of salary expense required.

Multiple Choice

11. The goal of _____ is to develop an efficient, high-quality process for producing products or services.
    a) conversion management
    b) assembly-line control
    c) flexible manufacturing
    d) production management
    e) routing

12. A _____ represents a series of tasks in which resources are used to produce a product or service.
    a) layout chart
    b) Venn diagram
    c) organization chart
    d) production process
    e) chain of command

13. A sequence of work stations in which each work station is designed to cover specific phases of the production process is called a(n):
    a) assembly line.
    b) hotelling.
    c) deintegration.
    d) product location.
    e) Gantt chart.

14. The factors that affect a site decision include all of the following except:
    a) cost of workplace space.
    b) tax incentives.
    c) source of demand.
    d) access to transportation.
    e) quality assurance.

In-Text Study Guide

Answers are in Appendix C at the back of book.

15. Once a site for the manufacturing plant is chosen, the next step to be determined is:
    a) design and layout.
    b) production control.
    c) hotelling.
    d) deintegration.
    e) inventory control.

16. All of the following characteristics influence design and layout decisions except the:
    a) production process.
    b) desired production capacity.
    c) product line.
    d) purchasing applications.
    e) site.

17. Which of the following production processes is most commonly used for assembly-line production?
    a) flexible manufacturing
    b) fixed-position layout
    c) product layout
    d) capacity layout
    e) cost-benefit layout

18. A production process where employees go to the position of the product, rather than waiting for the product to come to them, is a(n):
    a) assembly line.
    b) batch process.
    c) fixed-position layout.
    d) unit production process.
    e) mass production process.

19. Firms are forced to search for new sites once demand for their product exceeds their:
    a) quality control.
    b) production capacity.
    c) inspection requirements.
    d) routing schedules.
    e) purchase plans.

20. The development of temporary, shared office space for those employees who normally work at home is called:
    a) flexible manufacturing.
    b) deintegration.
    c) production control.
    d) hotelling.
    e) quality control.

21. All of the following are key tasks in production control except:
    a) layout and design.
    b) inventory control.
    c) routing.
    d) scheduling.
    e) quality control.

22. A company that makes use of a(n) _____ can detect the existing level of supplies and automatically reorder when supplies fall to a specific level.
    a) e-procurement system
    b) e-inventory system
    c) e-outsourcing system
    d) e-purchasing system
    e) e-business system

23. A strategy of delegating some production tasks to suppliers is referred to as:
    a) routing.
    b) dispatching.
    c) deintegration.
    d) quality assurance.
    e) hotelling.

24. A system that attempts to reduce material inventories to a bare minimum by frequently ordering small amounts of materials from suppliers is called:
    a) routing.
    b) just-in-time.
    c) scheduling.
    d) quality control.
    e) deintegration.

In-Text Study Guide

Answers are in Appendix C at the back of book.

25. The process of managing inventory at a level that minimizes costs is called:
    a) scheduling.
    b) routing.
    c) dispatching.
    d) production planning.
    e) inventory control.

26. Firms attempt to minimize the amount of inventory they have in order to reduce their:
    a) purchasing costs.
    b) production costs.
    c) carrying costs.
    d) quality control.
    e) human resources.

27. The sequence of tasks necessary to complete the production of a product is:
    a) dispatching.
    b) quality control.
    c) purchasing.
    d) routing.
    e) deintegration.

28. The act of setting time periods for each task in the production process is called:
    a) routing.
    b) scheduling.
    c) inventory control.
    d) dispatching.
    e) quality control.

29. A method of scheduling tasks that illustrates the expected timing for each task within the production process is a(n):
    a) Venn diagram.
    b) Gantt chart.
    c) MRP system.
    d) just-in-time system.
    e) production plan.

30. To minimize delays, the tasks that are part of the _____ are reviewed.
    a) purchasing applications
    b) Gantt chart
    c) critical path
    d) raw material inventory
    e) hotelling

31. Which of the following terms describes the process of monitoring the characteristics of a product to ensure that the firm's standards are met?
    a) expectation downsizing
    b) quality control
    c) critical path management
    d) program evaluation and review technique
    e) work-in-process control

32. A method of evaluating performance by comparison to some specified level, usually a level set by another company, is called:
    a) cost control.
    b) total quality management.
    c) targeting.
    d) benchmarking.
    e) goal setting.

33. Through _____ firms achieve a lower average cost per unit by producing a larger volume.
    a) inventory management
    b) per unit expense control
    c) economies of scale
    d) deintegration
    e) effective marketing

34. At the break-even point:
    a) the number of units produced equals the number of units sold.
    b) economies of scale fail.
    c) the company begins to lose money.
    d) fixed costs equal variable costs.
    e) total revenue equals total cost.

In-Text Study Guide

Answers are in Appendix C at the back of book.

35. The revision of the production process in an attempt to improve efficiency is called:
    a) restructuring.
    b) realignment.
    c) reintegration.
    d) downsizing.
    e) reengineering.

36. The supply chain is:
    a) the flow of inventory from raw materials to finished goods.
    b) the outsourcing process from supplier to firm.
    c) the marketing process from concept to consumption.
    d) the production process from beginning to consumer purchase.
    e) the conversion of resources to a product or service.

Summary/Part III

Management

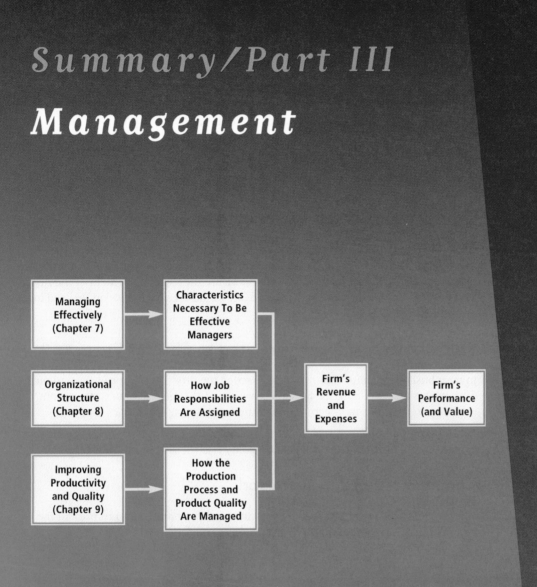

Developing a Management and Production Plan for Campus.com

Strategic and Tactical Plans (related to Chapter 7)

Develop a strategic plan for Campus.com, and explain what tactical plans would be consistent with the strategic plan. Insert these plans into your business plan for Campus.com.

Organizational Structure (related to Chapter 8)

Given the nature of Campus.com's business, what job positions are needed? Include these positions in your business plan for Campus.com. You (or your team) are responsible for overseeing Campus.com and therefore are the top management of the firm. Do not focus on which members of your team would take each position. Instead focus on identifying the positions needed.

Productivity and Quality (related to Chapter 9)

In your business plan for Campus.com, describe the production process used to produce its service. Also, describe how the service will change and how Campus.com might create an efficient system for continued revisions of the service it provides.

How can Campus.com maintain the quality of the service it provides? Include an explanation of how the firm will assure quality control in your business plan.

Communication and Teamwork

You (or your team) may be asked by your instructor to hand in and/or present the part of your business plan that is related to this part of the text.

Integrative Video Case: Quality Control (Ping Golf)

Ping Golf is a manufacturer of golf clubs located in Phoenix. The company has about 900 employees. Ping strives to be the leader in everything in its industry, including service. Ping's employees work for the company because of its commitment to greatness, achieving the best, and finding perfection.

Questions

1 Explain how quality control can be used as a marketing tool in Ping's case.

2 Why might quality control affect the amount of financing that is needed?

3 How do the job responsibilities at Ping Golf relate to the company's efforts to achieve perfection and quality control?

The Stock Market Game

Check the performance of your investment.

Check Your Performance

1. What is the value of your stock investment today?

2. What is your return on your investment? (The website shows the value of the return in dollars and as a percentage of your investment.)

3. How does your return compare to those of other students? (This comparison tells you whether your stock portfolio's performance is relatively high or low.)

Explaining Your Stock Performance

Stock prices are frequently influenced by changes in the firm's management, including changes in the chief executive officer or other high-level managers, the organizational structure, or the production process. A stock's price may rise if such management changes are made and investors expect that the changes will improve the performance of the firm. A stock's price can also decline if the managerial changes are expected to reduce the firm's performance. Review the latest news about your stock.

1. Determine whether specific managerial changes caused the stock price to change.

2. Did your stock's price increase or decrease in response to the announcement of managerial changes?

Running Your Own Business

1. Describe the strategic plan of your business. In this plan, state the business opportunities that exist and the general direction your business will take to capitalize on those opportunities.

2. Explain in detail how your business will operate to achieve your strategic plan.

3. Describe the organizational structure of your business.

4. Provide an organization chart and describe the responsibilities of any employees whom you plan to hire.

5. How might this structure change as the business grows?

6. Describe the production process of your business. That is, describe the tasks that are required to produce your product or service. Indicate the number of employees required and describe other resources (such as machinery) that are needed for production.

7. Describe the facilities needed for production. Will your business require that you rent space in a shopping mall? Describe in general terms the design and layout of the facilities.

8. Estimate the rent expense during the first year for the facilities needed for your business. Also, estimate (if possible) the annual utility expense (such as electricity) for your business facilities.

9. Describe how your business can ensure (a) customer satisfaction, (b) the quality of the product or service you plan to produce, and (c) that customers are treated properly by any employees that you hire.

10 Describe how technology will enable you to improve the quality of the product or service you plan to produce. Explain how your production or customer service may possibly improve over time as a result of technology.

11 Discuss how economies of scale relate to your business.

12 Explain how your business could use the Internet to give customers an opportunity to provide feedback to management.

Your Career in Business: *Pursuing a Major and a Career in Management*

If you are very interested in the topics covered in this section, you may want to consider a major in Management. Some of the courses commonly taken by Management majors are summarized here.

Common Courses For Management Majors

▶ *Organizational Behavior*—Provides a broad overview of key managerial functions, such as organizing, motivating employees, planning, controlling, and teamwork.

▶ *Management Environment*—Focuses on the environment in which managers work and the responsibilities of managers to society and to regulators.

▶ *Human Resource Management*—Focuses on the processes of hiring, training, evaluating performance, and compensating employees.

▶ *Labor Relations*—Examines the labor contract relationships among managers, subordinates, and unions; also covers the process of negotiating.

▶ *Management Strategy*—Focuses on the competitive environment faced by a firm and strategies used by a firm's managers to increase its growth or improve its performance.

▶ *Management Systems*—Focuses on the use of computer software and systems to facilitate decision making.

▶ *Entrepreneurship*—Deals with the creation of business ideas, methods of growing a small business, and the challenges of competing with larger firms.

▶ *Operations Management*—Examines the resources used in the production process, the plant site and layout decisions, alternative production processes, and quality control.

Careers in Management

Information about job positions, salaries, and careers for students who major in Management can be found at the following websites:

▶ Job position websites:

http://jobsearch.monster.com	Administrative and Support Services, Consulting Services, Human Resources, Manufacturing, and Production.
http://careers.yahoo.com	Management Consulting, Management Operations, Retail, Restaurant/ Food Service, Technology, and Transportation.

▶ Salary website:

http://collegejournal.com//salarydata	Consulting, Hotel and Restaurant Management, Human Resources, Logistics, Manufacturing, and Retailing.

Part IV
Managing Employees

Chapter 10
Motivating
Employees

Chapter 11
Hiring, Training,
and Evaluating
Employees

Whereas Part III focused on organizational structure and production, Part IV focuses on human resources (employees), another critical component of management. Part IV contains two chapters that explain how managers can improve the performance of their employees. Chapter 10 describes the methods that can be used to motivate employees. Motivation may be necessary for many employees to perform well. To the extent that managers can effectively motivate employees, they can improve the performance of employees and therefore increase the performance of the firm.

Chapter 11 explains the proper methods for hiring, training, and evaluating the performance of employees. Proper hiring methods ensure that employees have the right background for the types of jobs they may be assigned. Proper training enables employees to apply their skills to perform specific tasks. Proper evaluation methods ensure that employees are rewarded when they perform well and that they are informed of any deficiencies so that they can correct them in the future. If managers can use these methods effectively, they should be able to improve the firm's performance.

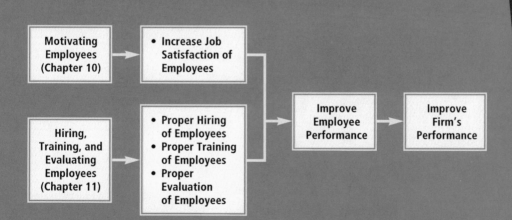

The Learning Goals
of this chapter are to:

Explain how motivating employees
can increase the value of a firm.   *1*

Describe the theories
on motivation.   *2*

Discuss how a firm can motivate
disgruntled employees.   *3*

Describe how a firm can enhance
job satisfaction and thereby
enhance motivation.   *4*

The methods used by Players Company to motivate its employees will influence its performance and therefore its value.

CORBIS, CHICAGO

Motivating Employees

A firm has a strategic plan that identifies opportunities and indicates the future direction of the firm's business. When the firm develops strategies to achieve the strategic plan, it relies on its managers to utilize employees and other resources to make the strategies work. Consider the situation of Players Company, which produces and sells sporting goods. Its performance is highly dependent on the efforts of its employees. Players Company must decide:

▶ What possible methods could it use to motivate its employees.

▶ What type of motivation will be most effective.

▶ How it can ensure that its employees are satisfied with their jobs.

▶ How motivation can improve its value.

If Players Company can successfully motivate its employees, it benefits in two ways. First, if the employees are motivated to work, they will accomplish more tasks, and Players will need fewer employees. Second, if its salespeople are motivated to sell sporting goods, Players, sales volume, and therefore its revenue, will be higher. If Players Company can ensure that its employees are satisfied with their jobs, it will be able to retain employees for a longer period of time and will reduce the expenses associated with training new employees.

The types of decisions described above are necessary for all businesses. This chapter explains how firms can motivate and satisfy employees in a manner that maximizes the firm's value.

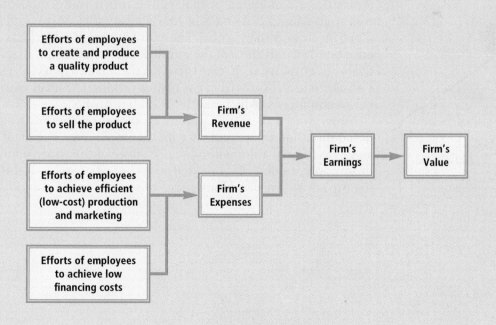

1

Explain how motivating employees can increase the value of a firm.

The Value of Motivation

Many businesses are successful not just because of their business ideas, but also because of their employees. But employees need to be motivated as well as to have the proper skills to do their jobs. Employees at some firms have adequate skills for their jobs, but they lack the motivation to perform well. Consequently, these employees offer only limited help in the production process.

Some firms believe that if they can hire people who are naturally motivated, the employees will perform well in the workplace, but this will not always happen. Although some people naturally make more of an effort to perform well, they will still need a work environment that motivates them.

Consider Anna and Marie, who are equally intelligent and tend to exert the same amount of effort in the workplace. Anna and Marie are hired by two different firms in the same industry for the same type of job. They work the same number of hours and receive the same salary, but their workplaces differ as follows:

	Firm A (which hires Anna)	Firm B (which hires Marie)
Employee work interaction	Frequent	Seldom
Employee social interaction	Frequent	Seldom
Input provided by managers to employees	Frequent	Seldom
Input requested from employees by managers	Frequent	Seldom

Given these conditions, Anna will be much more motivated to perform well than Marie. If Anna and Marie swap jobs, Marie will now be much more motivated than Anna. The point is that the firm has a major influence on the motivation of the employees. To the extent that a firm can motivate its employees, it can increase the productivity of each employee. Consequently, it can achieve a higher production level with a given number of employees, which results in higher profits.

How does a firm motivate its employees? There is no single motivational tool that works perfectly for all employees. The ideal form of motivation may vary among employees. Some of the more popular theories of motivation are described next. These theories can be useful for determining the advantages and limitations of various types of motivation.

Decision Making

Responding to a Lack of Motivation

Players Company (described in the introduction to the chapter) produces and sells sporting goods. Last year it hired eight recent college graduates for various entry-level managerial positions. Each person was a business major with a high grade-point average and very strong letters of recommendation. All of the new hires reported to Joel Kemp. All of them quit their jobs within a year of being hired. Paula Powell, the vice-president of human resources, was shocked that all the new hires quit, so she contacted them to learn their reasons for quitting. They offered different reasons, but all the reasons reflected a lack of motivation. When Paula told Joel Kemp about these responses, he replied, "We paid them well. That should be enough motivation." Paula Powell decides that some changes will be necessary to motivate new employees before Players Company hires any more people.

1. Do you think that the eight entry-level managers would have been more motivated if they had received higher salaries?

2. Joel Kemp suggests that after Players Company hires its next batch of entry-level managers, it should consider hiring a motivational speaker for one day to make a motivational speech. Do you think that this would motivate the entry-level managers?

ANSWERS: 1. No. A higher salary will not substitute for a workplace that motivates employees.   2. No. A motivational speech will not be effective if the workplace does not motivate employees.

2

Describe the theories on motivation.

job satisfaction
the degree to which employees are satisfied with their jobs

Theories on Motivation

The motivation of employees is influenced by **job satisfaction,** or the degree to which employees are satisfied with their jobs. Firms recognize the need to satisfy their employees, as illustrated by the following statements from recent annual reports:

"You will see a greater focus on employee satisfaction . . . which will lead us to higher quality, better growth, and improved profitability."

— Kodak

"Bethlehem's success ultimately depends on the skill, dedication, and support of our employees."

— Bethlehem Steel

Since employees who are satisfied with their jobs are more motivated, managers can motivate employees by ensuring job satisfaction. Some of the more popular theories on motivation are summarized here, followed by some general guidelines that can be used to motivate workers.

Hawthorne Studies

In the late 1920s, researchers studied workers in a Western Electric Plant near Chicago to identify how a variety of conditions affected their level of production. When the lighting was increased, the production level increased. Yet the production level also increased when the lighting was reduced. These workers were then subjected to various break periods; again, the production level increased for both shorter breaks and longer breaks. One interpretation of these results is that workers become more motivated when they feel that they are allowed to participate. Supervisors may be able to motivate workers by giving them more attention and by allowing them to participate. These Hawthorne studies, which ignited further research on motivation, are summarized in Exhibit 10.1 and suggest that human relations can affect a firm's performance.

hierarchy of needs
needs are ranked in five general categories. Once a given category of needs is achieved, people become motivated to reach the next category.

physiological needs
the basic requirements for survival

safety needs
job security and safe working conditions

Maslow's Hierarchy of Needs

In 1943, Abraham Maslow, a psychologist, developed the **hierarchy of needs** theory. This theory suggests that people rank their needs into five general categories. Once they achieve a given category of needs, they become motivated to reach the next category. The categories are identified in Exhibit 10.2, with the most crucial needs on the bottom. **Physiological needs** are the basic requirements for survival, such as food and shelter. Most jobs can help achieve these needs.

Once these needs are fulfilled, **safety needs** (such as job security and safe working conditions) become the most immediate goal. Some jobs sat-

Exhibit 10.1

Summary of the Hawthorne Studies

Exhibit 10.2

Maslow's Hierarchy of Needs

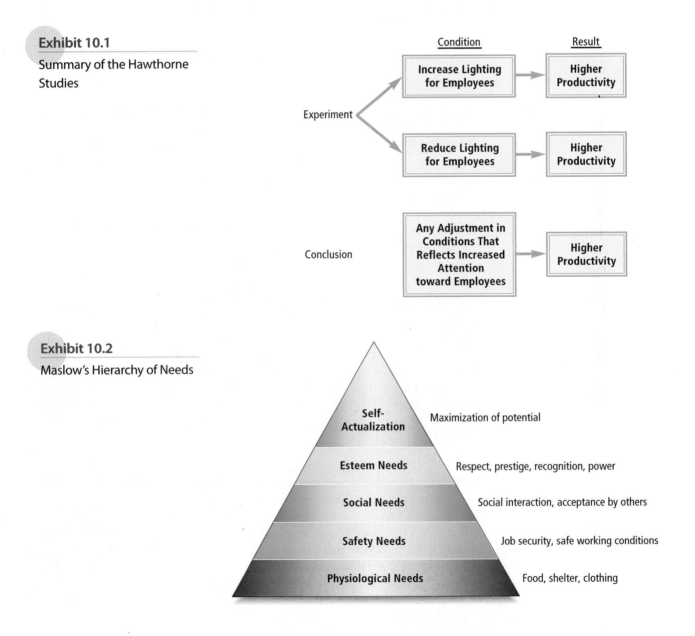

social needs
the need to be part of a group

esteem needs
respect, prestige, and recognition

self-actualization
the need to fully reach one's potential

isfy these needs. People also strive to achieve **social needs,** or the need to be part of a group. Some firms attempt to help employees achieve their social needs, either by grouping workers in teams or by organizing social events after work hours. People may also become motivated to achieve **esteem needs,** such as respect, prestige, and recognition. Some workers may achieve these needs by being promoted within their firms or by receiving special recognition for their work. The final category of needs is **self-actualization,** which represents the need to fully reach one's potential. For example, people may achieve self-actualization by starting and successfully running a specific business that fits their main interests.

The hierarchy of needs theory can be useful for motivating employees because it suggests that different employees may be at different places in the hierarchy. Therefore, their most immediate needs may differ. If managers can identify employees' needs, they will be better able to offer rewards that motivate employees.

Herzberg's Job Satisfaction Study

In the late 1950s, Frederick Herzberg surveyed 200 accountants and engineers about job satisfaction. Herzberg attempted to identify the factors that made them feel dissatisfied with their jobs at a given point in time. He also attempted to identify the factors that made them feel satisfied with their jobs. His study found the following:

Common Factors Identified by Dissatisfied Workers	Common Factors Identified by Satisfied Workers
Working conditions	Achievement
Supervision	Responsibility
Salary	Recognition
Job security	Advancement
Status	Growth

Employee job satisfaction can increase when social interaction is allowed in the workplace.

GETTY IMAGES

hygiene factors

work-related factors that can fulfill basic needs and prevent job dissatisfaction

motivational factors

work-related factors that can lead to job satisfaction and motivate employees

Employees become dissatisfied when they perceive work-related factors in the left column (called **hygiene factors**) as inadequate. Employees are commonly satisfied when the work-related factors in the right column (called **motivational factors**) are offered.

Herzberg's results suggest that factors such as working conditions and salary must be adequate to prevent workers from being dissatisfied. Yet better-than-adequate working conditions and salary will not necessarily lead to a high degree of satisfaction. Instead, a high degree of worker satisfaction is most easily achieved by offering additional benefits, such as responsibility. Thus, if managers assign workers more responsibility, they may increase worker satisfaction and motivate the workers to be more productive. Exhibit 10.3 summarizes Herzberg's job satisfaction study.

Notice how the results of Herzberg's study correspond with the results of Maslow's hierarchy. Herzberg's hygiene factors generally correspond with Maslow's basic needs (such as job security). This suggests that if hygiene factors are adequate, they fulfill some of workers' more basic needs. Fulfillment of these needs can prevent dissatisfaction as employees become motivated to achieve a higher class of needs. Herzberg's motivational factors (such as recognition) generally correspond with Maslow's more ambitious hierarchy needs.

Several U.S. firms, including Ford Motor Company, have implemented workshops to stress teamwork and company loyalty. These workshops build self-esteem by focusing on employees' worth to the company. In this way, the workshops may enable employees to achieve a higher class of needs, thereby increasing job satisfaction.

McGregor's Theory X and Theory Y

Another major contribution to motivation was provided by Douglas McGregor, who developed Theory X and Theory Y. Each of these theories rep-

Exhibit 10.3

Summary of Herzberg's Job Satisfaction Study

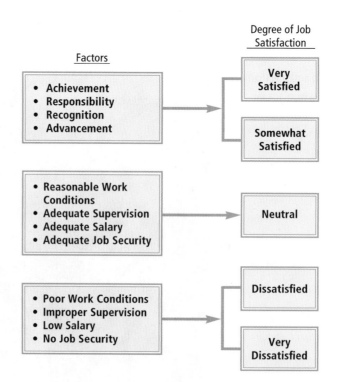

resents supervisors' possible perception of workers. The views of Theories X and Y are summarized as follows:

Theory X	Theory Y
Employees dislike work and job responsibilities and will avoid work if possible.	Employees are willing to work and prefer more responsibility.

The way supervisors view employees can influence the way they treat the employees. Supervisors who believe in Theory X will likely use tight control over workers, with little or no delegation of authority. In addition, employees will be closely monitored to ensure that they perform their tasks. Conversely, supervisors who believe in Theory Y will delegate more authority because they perceive workers as responsible. These supervisors will also allow employees more opportunities to use their creativity. This management approach fulfills employees' needs to be responsible and to achieve respect and recognition. Consequently, these employees are likely to have a higher level of job satisfaction and therefore to be more motivated.

Exhibit 10.4 provides a summary of Theories X and Y. Most employees would prefer that their supervisors follow Theory Y rather than Theory X. Nevertheless, some supervisors may be unable to use Theory Y in specific situations, when they are forced to retain more authority over employees rather than delegate responsibility.

Theory Z

In the 1980s, a new theory on job satisfaction was developed. This theory, called Theory Z, was partially based on the Japanese style of allowing all employees to participate in decision making. Participation can increase job satisfaction because it gives employees responsibility. Job descriptions tend to be less specialized, so employees develop varied skills and have a more flexible career path. To increase job satisfaction, many U.S. firms have begun to allow employees more responsibility.

Expectancy Theory

expectancy theory
holds that an employee's efforts are influenced by the expected outcome (reward) for those efforts

Expectancy theory suggests that an employee's efforts are influenced by the expected outcome (reward) for those efforts. Therefore, employees will be more motivated to achieve goals if they are achievable and offer some reward.

Exhibit 10.4

Summary of McGregor's Theories X and Y

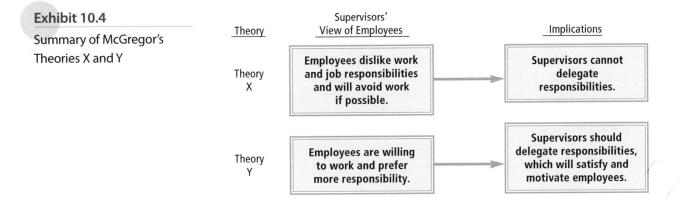

Self-Scoring Exercise

The Frazzle Factor

Read each of the following statements, and rate yourself on a scale of 0 to 3, giving the answer that best describes how you generally feel (3 points for always, 2 points for often, 1 point for sometimes, and 0 points for never). Answer as honestly as you can, and do not spend too much time on any one statement.

Am I Angry?

_____ 1. I feel that people around me make too many irritating mistakes.

_____ 2. I feel annoyed because I do good work or perform well in school, but no one appreciates it.

_____ 3. When people make me angry, I tell them off.

_____ 4. When I am angry, I say things I know will hurt people.

_____ 5. I lose my temper easily.

_____ 6. I feel like striking out at someone who angers me.

_____ 7. When a co-worker or fellow student makes a mistake, I tell him or her about it.

_____ 8. I cannot stand being criticized in public.

Am I Overstressed?

_____ 1. I have to make important snap judgments and decisions.

_____ 2. I am not consulted about what happens on my job or in my classes.

_____ 3. I feel I am underpaid.

_____ 4. I feel that no matter how hard I work, the system will mess it up.

_____ 5. I do not get along with some of my co-workers or fellow students.

_____ 6. I do not trust my superiors at work or my professors at school.

_____ 7. The paperwork burden on my job or at school is getting to me.

_____ 8. I feel people outside the job or the university do not respect what I do.

Scoring

To find your level of anger and potential for aggressive behavior, add your scores from both quiz parts.

40–48: The red flag is waving, and you had better pay attention. You are in the danger zone. You need guidance from a counselor or mental health professional, and you should be getting it now.

30–39: The yellow flag is up. Your stress and anger levels are too high, and you are feeling increasingly hostile. You are still in control, but it would not take much to trigger a violent flare of temper.

10–29: Relax, you are in the broad normal range. Like most people, you get angry occasionally, but usually with some justification. Sometimes you take overt action, but you are not likely to be unreasonably or excessively aggressive.

0–9: Congratulations! You are in great shape. Your stress and anger are well under control, giving you a laid-back personality not prone to violence.

As an example, consider a firm that offers the salesperson who achieves the highest volume of annual sales a one-week vacation in Paris. This type of reward will motivate employees only if two requirements are fulfilled. First, the reward must be desirable to employees. Second, employees must believe they have a chance to earn the reward. If the firm employs 1,000 salespeople, and only one reward is offered, employees may not be motivated because they may perceive that they have little chance of being the top salesperson. Motivation may be absent even in smaller groups if all employees expect that a particular salesperson will generate the highest sales volume.

Motivational rewards are more difficult to offer for jobs where output cannot easily be measured. For example, employees who repair the firm's machinery or respond to customer complaints do not contribute to the firm in a manner that can be easily measured or compared with other employees. Nevertheless, their performance may still be measured by customer satisfaction surveys or by various other performance indicators.

Equity Theory

The **equity theory** of motivation suggests that compensation should be equitable, or in proportion to each employee's contribution. As an example, consider a firm with three employees: Employee 1 contributes 50 percent of the total output, Employee 2 contributes 30 percent, and Employee 3 contributes 20 percent. Assume that the firm plans to allocate $100,000 in bonuses based on the relative contributions of each

equity theory
suggests that compensation should be equitable, or in proportion to each employee's contribution

employee. Using the equity theory, the $100,000 would be allocated as shown in Exhibit 10.5.

If employees believe that they are undercompensated, they may request greater compensation. If their compensation is not increased, employees may reduce their contribution. Equity theory emphasizes that employees can become dissatisfied with their jobs if they believe that they are not equitably compensated.

Supervisors may prevent job dissatisfaction by attempting to provide equitable compensation. A problem, however, is that the supervisor's perception of an employee's contribution may differ from that of the employee. If a firm can define how employee contributions will be measured and compensate accordingly, its employees will be better satisfied and more motivated.

Reinforcement Theory

reinforcement theory
suggests that reinforcement can influence behavior

positive reinforcement
motivates employees by providing rewards for high performance

Reinforcement theory, summarized in Exhibit 10.6, suggests that reinforcement can influence behavior. **Positive reinforcement** motivates employees by providing rewards for high performance. The rewards can

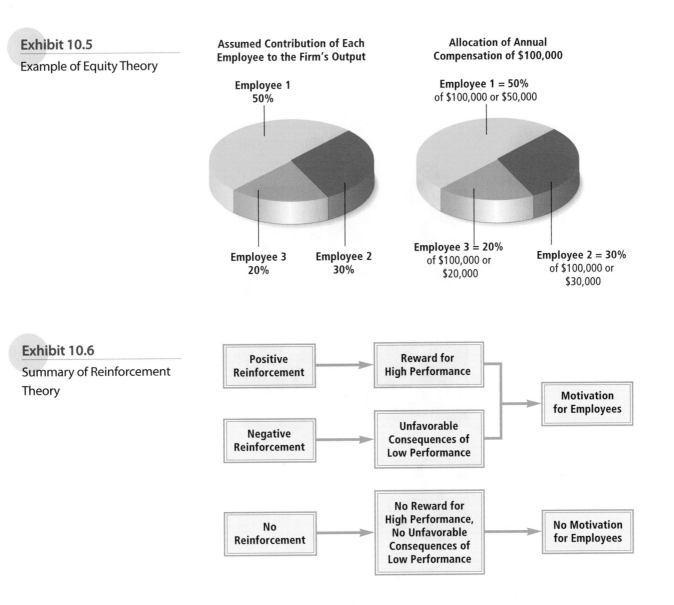

Exhibit 10.5

Example of Equity Theory

Assumed Contribution of Each Employee to the Firm's Output

Employee 1
50%

Employee 3
20%

Employee 2
30%

Allocation of Annual Compensation of $100,000

Employee 1 = 50%
of $100,000 or $50,000

Employee 3 = 20%
of $100,000 or
$20,000

Employee 2 = 30%
of $100,000 or
$30,000

Exhibit 10.6

Summary of Reinforcement Theory

Positive Reinforcement → Reward for High Performance

Negative Reinforcement → Unfavorable Consequences of Low Performance

Reward for High Performance / Unfavorable Consequences of Low Performance → Motivation for Employees

No Reinforcement → No Reward for High Performance, No Unfavorable Consequences of Low Performance → No Motivation for Employees

range from an oral compliment to a promotion or large bonus. Employees may react differently to various forms of positive reinforcement. The more they appreciate the form of reinforcement, the more they will be motivated to continue high performance.

negative reinforcement
motivates employees by encouraging them to behave in a manner that avoids unfavorable consequences

Negative reinforcement motivates employees by encouraging them to behave in a manner that avoids unfavorable consequences. For example, employees may be motivated to complete their assignments today to avoid having to admit the delay in a group meeting or to avoid negative evaluations by their supervisors.

Various forms of negative reinforcement can be used, ranging from a reprimand to job termination. Some supervisors may prefer to consistently offer positive reinforcement for high performance rather than penalize for poor performance. However, offering positive reinforcement for all tasks that are adequately completed may be difficult. Furthermore, if an employee who has performed poorly is not given negative reinforcement, others may think that employee was given preferential treatment, and their general performance may decline as a result.

Motivational Guidelines Offered by Theories

If supervisors can increase employees' job satisfaction, they may motivate employees to be more productive. All of the theories on motivation are briefly summarized in Exhibit 10.7. Based on these theories, some general conclusions can be offered on motivating employees and providing job satisfaction:

1. Employees commonly compare their compensation and perceived contribution with others. To prevent job dissatisfaction, supervisors should ensure that employees are compensated for their contributions.

To increase job satisfaction, managers give employees more responsibility and more opportunity to participate in decision making.

GETTY IMAGES

2. Even if employees are offered high compensation, they will not necessarily be very satisfied. They have other needs as well, such as social needs, responsibility, and self-esteem. Jobs that can fulfill these needs may provide satisfaction and therefore provide motivation.

3. Employees may be motivated if they believe that it is possible to achieve a performance level that will result in a desirable reward.

Exhibit 10.7

Comparison of Motivation Theories

Theory	Implications
Theory developed from Hawthorne studies	Workers can be motivated by attention.
Maslow's hierarchy of needs	Needs of workers vary, and managers can motivate workers to achieve these needs.
Herzberg's job satisfaction study	Compensation, reasonable working conditions, and other factors do not ensure job satisfaction but only prevent job dissatisfaction. Thus, other factors (such as responsibility) may be necessary to motivate workers.
McGregor's Theory X and Theory Y	Based on Theory X, workers will avoid work if possible and cannot accept responsibility. Based on Theory Y, workers are willing to work and prefer more responsibility. If Theory Y exists, managers can motivate workers by delegating responsibility.
Theory Z	Workers are motivated when they are allowed to participate in decision making.
Expectancy theory	Workers are motivated if potential rewards for high performance are desirable and achievable.
Equity theory	Workers are motivated if they are being compensated in accordance with their perceived contribution to the firm.
Reinforcement theory	Good behavior should be positively reinforced and poor behavior should be negatively reinforced to motivate workers in the future.

Decision Making

Determining How to Motivate Employees

Recall that Players Company had problems keeping its new entry-level managers because they were not properly motivated. Paula Powell, the vice-president of human resources, considers the motivation theories and proposes the following changes in the workplace to motivate employees:

▶ An orientation session will be held for new employees so that they can meet other new employees.

▶ All new employees will meet with their respective bosses once a week during the first year. At this meeting, the boss will offer a brief review of the employee's performance. In addition, the employee will have the opportunity to share any concerns about the job with the boss.

▶ The job assignments of the new employees will allow them to have some interaction with different managers and with each other.

Paula expects that these changes will motivate the employees and therefore will help to improve their productivity.

1. Explain how the changes in the workplace environment may allow Players Company to resolve any concerns of the new employees before they become frustrated and quit.

2. What is the benefit of encouraging more interaction among employees?

ANSWERS: 1. The new employees now have the chance to voice their concerns, if any, when they meet with their boss each week. 2. When employees work and interact with others, they feel more involved and believe that their work makes a difference. This motivates them to perform well.

Discuss how a firm can motivate disgruntled employees.

Motivating Disgruntled Employees

A firm may not be able to motivate some employees, regardless of its efforts or the methods used to motivate them. If no form of motivation is effective, the threat of being fired may be used as a last resort to motivate these employees. If firms do not discipline disgruntled employees who are performing poorly, other employees will lose their enthusiasm, especially if they have to cover the work assignments that the disgruntled employees neglect.

If the disgruntled employees are not motivated, they may seek employment elsewhere, which would be beneficial to the firm. However, they may realize that they will be disgruntled wherever they work, and therefore decide not to quit, especially if they can avoid doing their work assignments. Firms should force disgruntled employees to do their jobs and should fire them if they are unwilling to perform, so their bad attitude will not have a negative effect on other employees.

Decision Making

Motivating Disgruntled Employees

Recall that Players Company planned to implement changes in an effort to more effectively motivate new employees. One of the changes instituted by Paula Powell (vice-president of human resources) was that new employees should meet with their boss once a week during the first year to receive a brief review of their progress and discuss any concerns they may have. Joel Kemp, a manager who oversees the work of many entry-level managers, says that he does not have time to meet with the new employees every week.

If Joel is allowed to ignore the rules, other managers will question the rules as well. Paula meets with Joel and explains the importance of motivating the new employees. She then says that while she hopes he will comply rules, he will face disciplinary action if he does not. She takes this step to ensure that the new employees will have an opportunity to interact with their boss so that they will be motivated and will increase their productivity.

1. Is it appropriate for Paula Powell to threaten disciplinary action as a means of motivating Joel Kemp?

2. Explain the problem that may occur if Paula Powell allows Joel to ignore the new rules while all other managers are required to comply.

ANSWERS: 1. Yes, especially if no other form of motivation will be effective. 2. Other managers may quit if they must follow rules that Joel ignores.

Explain how firms can enhance job satisfaction and thereby enhance motivation.

How Firms Can Enhance Job Satisfaction and Motivation

Many of the theories on motivation suggest that firms can motivate employees to perform well by ensuring job satisfaction. In general, the key characteristics that affect job satisfaction are money, security, work schedule, and involvement at work. To motivate employees, firms provide **job enrichment programs,** or programs designed to increase the job satisfac-

job enrichment programs
programs designed to increase the job satisfaction of employees

tion of employees. The following are some of the more popular job enrichment programs:

▶ Adequate compensation program

▶ Job security

▶ Flexible work schedule

▶ Employee involvement programs

To the extent that firms can offer these job enrichment programs to employees, they may be able to motivate employees. Each program is discussed in turn.

Adequate Compensation Program

Firms can attempt to satisfy employees by offering adequate compensation for the work involved. However, adequate compensation will not necessarily motivate employees to make their best effort. Therefore, firms may attempt to ensure that those employees with the highest performance each year receive the highest percentage raises.

merit system
a compensation system that allocates raises according to performance (merit)

A **merit system** allocates raises according to performance (merit). For example, a firm may decide to give its employees an average raise of 5 percent, but poorly performing employees may receive 0 percent while the highest performing employees receive 10 percent. This system provides positive reinforcement for employees who have performed well and punishment for those who have performed poorly. A merit system is normally more effective than the alternative **across-the-board system,** in which all employees receive a similar raise. The across-the-board system provides no motivation because the raise is unrelated to employee performance.

across-the-board system
a compensation system that allocates similar raises to all employees

incentive plans
provide employees with various forms of compensation if they meet specific performance goals

Firms may attempt to reinforce excellent employee performance with other rewards as well as raises. **Incentive plans** provide employees with various forms of compensation if they meet specific performance goals. For example, a firm may offer a weekly or monthly bonus based on the number of components an employee produced or the dollar value of all products an employee sold to customers.

Kodak heavily attempts to tie employee compensation to performance in order to achieve its strategic goals.

Examples of Compensation Programs   The compensation at some firms is composed of base pay and "reward" pay that is tied to specific performance goals. The base pay is set lower than the industry norm for a given job, but the additional reward pay (tied to specific goals) can allow the total compensation to exceed the norm. Employees are more motivated to perform well because they benefit directly from high performance.

Some employees of Enterprise Rent-A-Car Company are compensated according to the firm's profits. Steelworkers at Nucor can earn annual bonuses that exceed their annual base salary. Many salespeople earn bonuses based on their own sales volume.

Kodak uses an incentive plan that allows each executive to earn a bonus based on his or her performance. The performance targets are set by the outside board members who are not employees of Kodak. The bonuses are based on performance measures such as revenue and earnings. Procter & Gamble Company provides bonuses to executives based on some nonfinancial measures, such as integrity and leadership.

The bonuses of chief executive officers (CEOs) at General Electric, IBM, and many other firms are tied to the firm's performance. Performance measures may include revenue, earnings, production efficiency, and customer satisfaction. Firms recognize that tying compensation to performance may increase job satisfaction and motivate employees. The following descriptions of policies from recent annual reports confirm this:

"A company lives or dies by results, and at Campbell, executive pay is linked directly to performance . . . and 100 percent of all incentive bonuses are tied to company performance."

— Campbell's Soup Company

"We are working hard to change the culture of the company by emphasizing and rewarding results, not activity."

— IBM

In addition to linking compensation to performance, some firms also grant stock to their employees as partial compensation for their work. The value of this type of compensation depends on the firm's stock price. To the extent that employees can increase the firm's stock price with hard work, they can enhance their own compensation.

Initially, firms used stock as compensation only for CEOs. In recent years, however, other top managers of firms have been granted stock as well to keep them focused on enhancing the value of the stock. Some firms have extended this concept to all or most of their employees. For example, all employees of Avis receive some shares of Avis stock. This may motivate them to perform well because their performance may enhance the value of the stock they own. One limitation of this approach is that some employees who own only a small amount of stock may believe that their work habits will not have much influence on the firm's profits (and therefore on its stock price). Thus, they will not be motivated because they do not expect that their stock's price will increase as a result of their efforts. Stock options can also lead to conflicts of interest, as discussed in the next chapter.

As an illustration of how a firm's performance and value can improve when its employee compensation is linked to performance, consider the case of Paychex. In January 1998, Paychex announced its intent to tie employee compensation to its performance. Over the next nine months, the

Exhibit 10.8

Impact of New Employee Compensation Policy on the Stock Price of Paychex

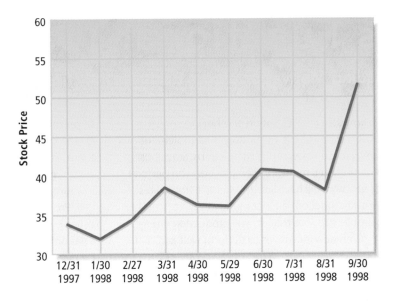

firm's performance and its value (as measured by its stock price) increased substantially, as shown in Exhibit 10.8.

Developing a Proper Compensation Plan   Most compensation plans that tie pay to performance are intended to motivate employees to achieve high performance. The following guidelines can help in designing a compensation plan that motivates employees:

1. **Align the Compensation Plan with Business Goals** Compensation formulas for employees should be set only after the goals of the business are established. This ensures that employees are rewarded in line with their ability to satisfy the business's goals.

2. **Align Compensation with Specific Employee Goals** A compensation plan will motivate employees more successfully if it clearly specifies individual employee goals. Goals for an individual assembly-line employee should focus on specific job responsibilities that the employee can control. Conversely, individual goals that specify high performance for the entire production plant are not under the control of a single employee, and therefore the employee will not be as motivated to perform well.

   Some firms compensate employees according to the performance of a group to which they belong within the firm. The groups are small enough that employees believe they have some control over the performance measurement.

3. **Establish Achievable Goals for Employees** The compensation plan will work better if the goals specified for each employee are achievable. By offering numerous achievable bonuses, managers can increase each employee's perception of the chance to earn a reward. Firms with limited budgets for bonuses can offer rewards that are less extravagant but still desirable.

   Rewards that are desirable and achievable will motivate employees only if they are aware of the bonuses. Offering rewards at the end of the year is too late to motivate employees for that year. Levels of motivation will be higher if employees know about the potential for bonuses at the beginning of the year.

4. **Allow Employee Input on the Compensation Plan** The compensation plan should be developed only after receiving input from employees on how they should be rewarded. Although some employee requests may be unreasonable, allowing employee input can improve job satisfaction.

Cross Functional Teamwork

Spreading Motivation across Business Functions

When a firm uses compensation or other incentives to motivate employees, it must attempt to implement this program across all of its business functions. Since business functions interact, motivating employees who perform one type of function will have limited effects if employees performing other functions are not motivated.

For example, suppose that a firm's production employees are given new incentives to perform well, but marketing employees are not given any new incentives. The quality of the product achieved by the production department is somewhat dependent on the feedback it receives from marketing employees who conduct customer satisfaction surveys. Also, the production department's ability to produce an adequate supply of a product is dependent on the sales forecasts provided by the marketing department. If the sales forecast is too low, the production department may produce an insufficient volume, resulting in shortages.

Production tasks can also affect marketing tasks because effective marketing strategies will result in higher sales only if a sufficient volume of products is produced. Employees assigned to a specific function rely on employees assigned to other functions. Thus, employees who are assigned to a given function and are motivated can achieve high performance only if the other employees they rely on are motivated.

Job Security

Employees who have job security may be more motivated to perform well. They are less likely to be distracted at work because of concern about finding a more secure job.

Although firms recognize that job security can motivate their employees, they may not be able to guarantee job security. When a weakened U.S. economy lowers the demand for the goods and services provided by U.S. firms, these firms cannot afford to retain all of their employees. Even when the economy is strong, some firms are pressured to lay off employees to reduce expenses.

Firms can provide more job security by training employees to handle various tasks so that they can be assigned other duties if their usual assignments are no longer needed. Nevertheless, the firm may not have any job openings to which employees can be reassigned. Further, the job openings may be so different that reassignments are not possible. For example, workers on an assembly line normally would not be qualified to perform accounting or financial analysis jobs for an automobile manufacturer.

Flexible Work Schedule

flextime programs
programs that allow for a more flexible work schedule

compressed workweek
compresses the workload into fewer days per week

Another method of increasing job satisfaction is to implement programs that allow for a more flexible work schedule (called **flextime programs**). Some firms have experimented with a **compressed workweek,** which compresses the workload into fewer days per week. Most commonly, a 5-day, 8-hour-per-day workweek is compressed into four 10-hour days. The main purpose of this schedule is to allow employees to have three-day weekends. When employees are on a schedule that they prefer, they are more motivated to perform well.

GETTY IMAGES

Many employees of firms who are parents can work at home as a result of technology.

job sharing
two or more persons share a particular work schedule

job enlargement
a program to expand (enlarge) the jobs assigned to employees

job rotation
a program that allows a set of employees to periodically rotate their job assignments

Another form of a flexible work schedule is **job sharing,** where two or more persons share a particular work schedule. For example, a firm that needs a 40-hour workweek for deliveries may hire two people to share that position. This allows employees to work part-time and fulfill other obligations such as school or family.

Flexible work schedules are becoming increasingly popular, especially with employees who have specific time commitments involving their children such as attending school or social events. Technology allows many employees to attend these events and still complete their work without being at the workplace. For example, they can access updated data and information regarding their jobs through a special business website that is accessible only to employees. They can have their business e-mail forwarded to their home e-mail address or to some other address that they can access while they are away from the office. They may carry a cell phone for any necessary communication that cannot be handled by e-mail. Technology can also give some employees more time with their families by allowing them to avoid a trip to the office on some days.

Employee Involvement Programs

As the theories summarized earlier indicate, employees are more motivated when they play a bigger role in the firm, either by being more involved in decisions or by being assigned more responsibility. Firms use various methods to allow more employee involvement and responsibility.

Job Enlargement   One method of increasing employee responsibility is to use **job enlargement,** which is a program to expand (enlarge) the jobs assigned to employees. Job enlargement has been implemented at numerous firms such as Motorola and Xerox Corporation that experienced downsizing in the 1990s. The program was implemented not only to motivate employees but also to reduce operating expenses.

Job Rotation   **Job rotation** allows a set of employees to periodically rotate their job assignments. For example, an assembly-line operation may involve five different types of assignments. Each worker may focus on one assignment per week and switch assignments at the beginning of the next week. In this way, a worker performs five different assignments over each five-week period.

Job rotation not only may reduce boredom but also can prepare employees for other jobs if their primary job position is eliminated. In this way, employees can remain employed by the firm. For example, if the demand for a specific type of car declines, the manufacturer of that car may attempt to reassign the employees who worked on that car to work on other cars or trucks.

Empowerment and Participative Management   In recent years, supervisors at many firms have delegated more authority to their employees. This strategy

Self-Scoring Exercise

Are You an Empowered Employee?*

Read each of the following statements carefully. Then, indicate which answer best expresses your level of agreement (5 = strongly agree, 4 = agree, 3 = sometimes agree/sometimes disagree, 2 = disagree, 1 = strongly disagree, and 0 = undecided/do not know). Mark only one answer for each item, and be sure to respond to all items.

_____ 1. I feel free to tell my manager what I think.   5 4 3 2 1 0

_____ 2. My manager is willing to listen to my concerns.   5 4 3 2 1 0

_____ 3. My manager asks for my ideas about things affecting our work.   5 4 3 2 1 0

_____ 4. My manager treats me with respect and dignity.   5 4 3 2 1 0

_____ 5. My manager keeps me informed about things I need to know.   5 4 3 2 1 0

_____ 6. My manager lets me do my job without interfering.   5 4 3 2 1 0

_____ 7. My manager's boss gives us the support we need.   5 4 3 2 1 0

_____ 8. Upper management pays attention to ideas and suggestions from people at my level.   5 4 3 2 1 0

Scoring

To determine if you are an empowered employee, add your scores.

32–40: You are empowered! Managers listen when you speak, respect your ideas, and allow you to do your work.

24–31: You have some power! Your ideas are sometimes considered, and you have some freedom of action.

16–23: You must exercise caution. You cannot speak or act too boldly, and your managers appear to exercise close supervision.

8–15: Your wings are clipped! You work in a powerless, restrictive work environment.

*If you are not employed, discuss these questions with a friend who is employed. Is your friend an empowered employee?

---

empowerment
allowing employees the power to make more decisions

participative management
employees are allowed to participate in various decisions made by their supervisors or others

---

is referred to as **empowerment,** as it allows employees the power to make more decisions. Empowerment is more specific than job enlargement because it focuses on increased authority, whereas job enlargement may not necessarily result in more authority. Empowerment may motivate those employees who are more satisfied when they have more authority. Also, they may be in a better position to make decisions on the tasks they perform than supervisors who are not directly involved in those tasks.

Empowerment is related to **participative management,** in which employees are allowed to participate in various decisions. For example, DaimlerChrysler has a program in which individual workers are asked for suggestions on cost cutting or improving quality. Managers review these suggestions and respond to the workers within a few days.

Empowerment assigns decision-making responsibilities to employees, whereas participative management simply allows for employee input in decisions. In reality, both terms are used to reflect programs that delegate more responsibilities to employees, whether they have complete or partial influence on decisions. The higher level of involvement by employees is supported by Theory Z, as discussed earlier.

A popular form of participative management is **management by objectives (MBO),** in which employees work with their managers to set their goals and determine the manner in which they will complete their tasks. The employees' participation can be beneficial because they are closer to the production process. In addition, if their tasks can be completed in various ways, they may use their own creativity to accomplish the work.

MBO is commonly applied to salespeople by assigning a monthly sales quota (or goal) that is based on historical sales. The actual sales volume may be dependent on the state of the economy, however. Care must be taken to assign a goal that is achievable.

SMALL BUSINESS SURVEY

Do Employees Want More Influence in Business Decisions?

Employees may desire to be involved in business decision making because it increases their influence on the firm's performance. In recent years, the restructuring of firms has resulted in substantially more responsibilities for many employees. A survey of 4,500 workers of various firms was conducted to determine whether workers still wanted to have more influence in business decisions. The results are shown in the following chart:

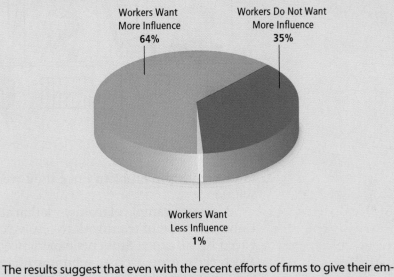

Workers Want
More Influence
64%

Workers Do Not Want
More Influence
35%

Workers Want
Less Influence
1%

The results suggest that even with the recent efforts of firms to give their employees more power and responsibility, employees would generally prefer more responsibility.

---

management by objectives (MBO)
allows employees to participate in setting their goals and determining the manner in which they complete their tasks

teamwork
a group of employees with varied job positions have the responsibility to achieve a specific goal

For production employees, a production volume goal is specified. Some employees may reduce the quality of their work to reach the goal, however, so the objective must specify adequate quality as well as quantity.

Teamwork Another form of employee involvement is **teamwork,** in which a group of employees with varied job positions have the responsibility to achieve a specific goal. Goodyear Tire and Rubber Company uses numerous project teams to achieve its goals. Car manufacturers encourage teamwork to generate new ideas. Employees at Yahoo! are encouraged to share their ideas with others to obtain feedback.

DaimlerChrysler, which was created from Chrysler's merger with Daimler-Benz, designs cars with input from assembly-line workers. Executives establish general guidelines on a type of automobile that will satisfy consumers. The workers are then assembled in teams to work out the design details.

When Jaguar (a subsidiary of Ford Motor Company) desired to improve its customer service, its executives initially attempted to instruct employees on how to provide better service. However, motivating the employees was difficult because they were not satisfied with their jobs. The executives decided to create worker involvement teams to develop a plan for improved customer service. The employees were more willing

Out of Business

to deal with the problem once they were allowed to search for the best solution.

A classic example of teamwork that all students can relate to is Belmont University's use of teamwork to resolve course registration hassles experienced by students. Students experienced difficulties when attempting to add a class, drop a class, submit a financial aid form, or any other task requiring service from the university. In addition, each task had to be completed at a different location on campus. Consequently, the university formed a team of administrators to find a solution that would make the process easier for students. The team proposed the creation of Belmont Central, a one-stop shop where students could accomplish all administrative tasks from registering for courses to applying for financial aid. For Belmont Central to work, its employees would have to be capable of handling all these tasks. Belmont University implemented the plan and trained the employees so that they were capable of handling a wide variety of tasks. As a result, a student now goes to one place and meets with one employee to perform all administrative tasks. The students are much more satisfied with the service than they were in the past, and the university has received an award from *USA Today* for its excellent use of teamwork to resolve its problems.

open-book management
a form of employee involvement that educates employees on their contribution to the firm and enables them to periodically assess their own performance levels

Open-Book Management   Another form of employee involvement is **open-book management,** which educates employees on their contribution to the firm and enables them to periodically assess their own performance levels. Open-book management educates employees on how they affect the key performance measures that are relevant for the firm's owners. In this way, it encourages employees to make decisions and conduct tasks as if they were the firm's owners.

Open-book management has three distinct characteristics:

1. The firm educates all employees on the key performance measurements that affect the firm's profits and value and ensures that these performance measurements are widely available to employees over time (like an "open book" on the firm's performance). For example, various revenue, expense, and production figures may be displayed daily or weekly in the work area.

2. As employees are given the power to make decisions, they are trained to understand how the results of their decisions will affect the firm's overall performance. Thus, salespeople recognize how their efforts affect the firm's total revenue, while engineers recognize how their efforts reduce the cost of producing a product. Many job positions are not tied directly to revenue or total expenses. Therefore, it is helpful to break performance into segments that employees can relate to, such as number of customer complaints, proportion of product defects, or percentage of tasks completed on time. Each of these segments influences the total demand for the firm's product (and therefore the firm's revenue), as well as the expenses incurred.

3. The compensation of employees is typically aligned with their contribution to the firm's overall performance. They may earn some stock so that they are shareholders as well as employees. This reinforces their focus on making decisions that will enhance the firm's value and therefore its stock price. In addition, the firm may provide annual pay raises only to employees who helped improve the firm's performance. Although educating employees on how their work affects the firm's value is useful, a firm may still need to compensate employees for their performance in order to motivate them. Firms may set specific annual performance targets for employees and then continually update the employees on their performance levels throughout the year.

Michael Dell, founder of Dell Corporation, frequently communicates with customers and employees in order to seek ways to improve the performance of the business.

AP/WIDE WORLD PHOTOS

In a recent annual report, Dell, Inc.'s founder Michael Dell stated that it is critical for the company's future success that it recruit, develop, and retain highly skilled people at all levels of the organization. Furthermore, he said that Dell's model of direct customer contact is only as good as the people who apply it to the company's daily business. He also deserves credit for the effective implementation of the customer contact model to the 16,000 Dell employees around the world. Thus, Dell is using a form of open-book management to motivate its employees.

Comparison of Methods Used to Enhance Job Satisfaction

The methods that can enhance job satisfaction and therefore motivate employees are compared in Exhibit 10.9. A combination of methods is especially useful for enhancing job satisfaction. When a firm succeeds in increasing employees' job satisfaction, it will be more effective in motivating the employees to achieve high performance. Therefore, putting emphasis on job satisfaction can improve a firm's profits and value.

Firms That Achieve the Highest Job Satisfaction Level

Many firms use a combination of methods to achieve high job satisfaction. Exhibit 10.10 lists some firms that have been frequently cited as the best firms to work for, along with the methods they use to achieve such high job satisfaction. Notice that each firm has its own way of satisfying employees.

Exhibit 10.9

Methods Used to Enhance Job Satisfaction

Method	Description
1. Adequate compensation program	▶ Align raises with performance.
	▶ Align bonuses with performance.
	▶ Provide stock as partial compensation.
2. Job security	▶ Encourage employees to have a long-term commitment to the firm.
3. Flexible work schedule	▶ Allow employees flexibility on the timing of their work schedules.
4. Employee involvement programs	▶ Implement job enlargement.
	▶ Implement job rotation.
	▶ Implement empowerment and participative management.
	▶ Implement teamwork.
	▶ Implement open-book management.

Exhibit 10.10

Examples of Firms That Have Achieved Very High Job Satisfaction

Firm	Methods Used to Achieve High Job Satisfaction
Southwest Airlines	▶ Treats employees with respect.
	▶ Empowers employees to solve problems.
	▶ Gives awards and recognition to employees.
MBNA	▶ Focuses on hiring employees who get along with other people.
	▶ Provides on-site child care.
Microsoft	▶ Casual work environment.
	▶ Empowers employees to solve problems.
Eddie Bauer	▶ Two-week paid sick leave for new parents.
	▶ Flexible work schedules.

Global Business

Motivating Employees across Countries

The techniques used to motivate employees in the United States may not necessarily be successful in motivating employees in other countries. For example, consider a U.S. firm that has just established a production plant in Eastern Europe. European employees' views on conditions necessary for job satisfaction may differ from those of U.S. production workers. In general, U.S. firms have successfully motivated production workers in the United States by giving them more responsibilities. Assigning additional responsibilities may not motivate production workers in Eastern Europe, however, especially if they have less experience and education. These workers could even be overwhelmed by the extra responsibilities. They might be less capable of striving for efficiency, since their past work experience was in an environment that did not stress efficiency.

In some situations, a U.S. firm may be more capable of motivating foreign workers than U.S. workers. For example, General Motors established a plant in what was then East Germany to produce automobiles. When it trained the workers at this plant, it explained the need for production efficiency to ensure the plant's survival. It asked the workers to provide suggestions on how the plant could increase its production efficiency. These workers offered 10 times as many suggestions as workers at other General Motors plants in Europe. The East German plant could assemble an entire automobile faster than any other General Motors plant. The efficiency of the workers at the East German plant may be attributed to their background. Although these workers did not have many years of experience on automobile assembly lines, they also had not learned any bad habits from working in less efficient assembly systems. Thus, these workers were more capable of learning an efficient production system.

Overall, a firm's ability to motivate workers in a specific country may depend on characteristics that are beyond the firm's control. Workers who will lose their jobs if the firm performs poorly may be more motivated, regardless of the firm's motivation strategies. Workers based in countries with fewer opportunities may be more motivated because they may appreciate their existing jobs more than workers in other countries. Given these differences, a firm may consider using varying motivation strategies for workers in different countries. In general, a firm should attempt to determine what conditions will increase the job satisfaction of workers in a particular country and provide those conditions for workers who perform well.

Decision Making ▶ Increasing Job Satisfaction

Recall that Paula Powell, vice-president of human resources at Players Company, now encourages more interaction among employees as a means of motivating them. However, she also wants to institute strategies that will enhance their job satisfaction. She believes that if employees are very satisfied with their jobs, they will be more motivated. She proposes the following changes, which are approved by the CEO and board of directors:

▶ Employees who have been working from 9 A.M. to 5 P.M. are now allowed to start as early as 7 A.M. as long as they work 8-hour days. They also have the option of working four 10-hour days and taking one day off during the workweek.

▶ Employees are encouraged to offer suggestions to Paula about how Players Company can improve working conditions. Paula promises that she will seriously consider implementing any suggestion if it would enhance job satisfaction and therefore increase productivity.

1. Is there any disadvantage to Players Company from allowing a flexible work schedule?

2. Is there any disadvantage to Players Company from asking employees for suggestions about improving working conditions?

ANSWERS: 1. A flexible work schedule is not always appropriate for jobs that require employees to be in the workplace at specific times. 2. Some suggestions such as a two-day workweek may be inappropriate because they would result in lower productivity. However, Paula Powell can screen out such suggestions.

COLLEGE HEALTH CLUB: MOTIVATING EMPLOYEES AT CHC

One of the decisions that Sue Kramer needs to make as part of her business plan for College Health Club (CHC) is how to hire and motivate employees. Sue plans to hire capable employees who are currently exercise science majors at the college. She wants to ensure that the students are satisfied with their jobs and motivated to perform well. First, she plans to determine the typical compensation level for part-time jobs in the area and will offer wages slightly higher than the norm. Second, she plans to accommodate her employees by allowing them to work fewer hours in a week when they have a major exam or class project. Third, she will welcome employee involvement. As manager of CHC, she plans to interact with employees on a daily basis and ask them for suggestions on improving the club's performance. Fourth, if Sue opens an additional health club in the future, she plans to hire a manager to run that club. She will seriously consider hiring someone who has been an employee at CHC as the manager of the new health club after the person earns a college degree.

Summary

1 If a firm can motivate its employees, it can increase productivity of each employee. Consequently, it can achieve a higher production level with a given number of employees, which results in higher profits. The ideal form of motivation may vary among employees.

2 The main theories on motivation are as follows:

▶ The Hawthorne studies suggest that employees are more motivated when they receive more attention.

▶ Maslow's hierarchy of needs theory suggests that employees are satisfied by different needs, depending on their position within the hierarchy. Firms can satisfy employees at the low end of the hierarchy with job security or safe working conditions. Once basic needs are fulfilled, employees have other needs that must be met. Firms can attempt to satisfy these employees by allowing social interaction or more responsibilities.

▶ Herzberg's job satisfaction study suggests that the factors that prevent job dissatisfaction are different from those that enhance job satisfaction. Adequate salary and working conditions prevent job dissatisfaction, while responsibility and recognition enhance job satisfaction.

▶ McGregor's Theories X and Y suggest that when supervisors believe employees dislike work and responsibilities (Theory X), they do not delegate responsibilities and employees are not motivated; when supervisors believe that employees prefer responsibilities (Theory Y), they delegate more responsibilities, which motivates employees.

▶ Theory Z suggests that employees are more satisfied when they are involved in decision making and therefore may be more motivated.

▶ Expectancy theory suggests that employees are more motivated if compensation is aligned with goals that are achievable and offer some reward.

▶ Equity theory suggests that employees are more motivated if their compensation is aligned with their relative contribution to the firm's total output.

▶ Reinforcement theory suggests that employees are more motivated to perform well if they are rewarded for high performance (positive reinforcement) and penalized for poor performance (negative reinforcement).

3 A firm may not be able to motivate some employees, regardless of its efforts or the methods used to motivate them. If no form of motivation is effective, the threat of being fired may serve as a last resort to motivate these employees.

4 Firms can enhance job satisfaction and therefore motivate employees by providing

▶ an adequate compensation program, which aligns compensation with performance;

▶ job security;

▶ a flexible work schedule; and

▶ employee involvement programs.

How the Chapter Concepts Affect Business Performance

A firm's decisions regarding the motivation concepts summarized here affect its performance. If a firm can motivate its employees, it can improve employee morale and increase productivity. While there are many motivation theories, the proper form of motivation varies with the firm's characteristics and may even vary among employees.

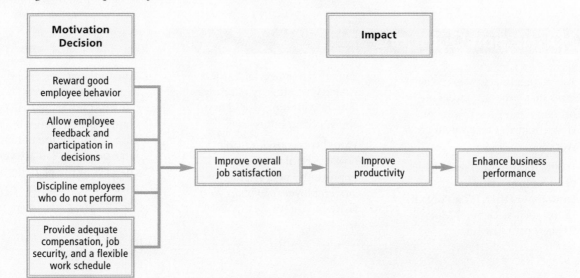

Key Terms

Review & Critical Thinking Questions

1. Identify the categories of Maslow's hierarchy of needs theory.

2. Briefly describe Herzberg's job satisfaction study on worker motivation.

3. Distinguish between McGregor's Theory X and Theory Y perceptions of management.

4. Describe how expectancy theory can motivate behavior.

5. Briefly summarize the equity theory of motivation.

6. Describe the reinforcement theories of motivation and explain how a manager could utilize them.

7. Describe some methods that will enhance job satisfaction and motivate employees.

8. Briefly describe the different forms of flexible work schedules firms use.

9. How can managers utilize strategic planning to motivate their employees and maximize the value of the firm?

10. How are empowerment and participative management related?

11. Discuss the methods used to motivate employees in the United States. Should the same methods be used to motivate employees in other countries?

12. How can a company tie its workers' compensation to the performance of its stock price?

13. How might a merit system provide more motivation to employ-

ees than an across-the-board system?

14. When managers do not align the compensation plan with business goals, what might be the impact on the value of the firm?

15. What are the costs and benefits of job security in motivating employees?

16. How might job sharing lead to a more motivated workforce?

17. Why might job enlargement lead to less motivated workers, rather than more motivated workers?

18. What is management by objectives? Why might it lead to greater employee empowerment?

Discussion Questions

1. You are a manager who recognizes that your employees are primarily motivated by money. How could you motivate them at work?

2. Would motivational techniques be more important for the Atlanta Braves than for an organization such as General Motors? Explain your answer.

3. You are a manager of a video store. Which theory of motivation do you think would best apply to your employees?

4. Would you consider using negative reinforcement to improve the performance of lazy employees? Explain your answer.

5. You and your lazy friend work at a car manufacturer. The company just implemented a new compensation plan with a lower base salary but the potential for large bonuses. You are very excited about the plan, but your friend is not. Explain why this may be so.

6. How could a firm use the Internet and technology to motivate its existing and potential employees?

7. Your company has just begun an open-book management system. You now have the opportunity to evaluate yourself and assess your own performance. How might employees benefit from the system?

8. In a company with many employees, different employees will respond to different kinds of motivation. How can a company work toward satisfying all of its employees, if possible?

9. You are the manager of an employee who complains constantly about the job and is demoralizing the other employees with his complaints. The employee is not performing his duties properly, and productivity in his area has slowed. What can you do to encourage the disgruntled employee?

10. How can you as a manager use knowledge of Maslow's hierarchy of needs to motivate employees without changing the level or structure of employee compensation?

IT'S YOUR DECISION: MOTIVATING EMPLOYEES AT CHC

1. Sue Kramer plans to offer a flexible work schedule, employee involvement, and a free health club membership to employees at College Health Club (CHC). Explain how CHC's performance may increase as a result of these benefits to employees.

2. Which of Maslow's hierarchy of needs are satisfied by employment at CHC? Which of Maslow's hierarchy of needs are not satisfied by employment at CHC?

3. Expectancy theory suggests that employees will perform better if there is a reward for performance. Should CHC have employees compete for an extra reward each year? What is a disadvantage of this strategy?

4. Explain how the job satisfaction of employees at CHC can affect the quality of health club services produced by CHC.

5. A health club differs from manufacturing firms in that it produces a service rather than products. Would a manufacturing firm satisfy Maslow's hierarchy of needs more easily than service firms?

Investing in a Business

Using the annual report of the firm in which you would like to invest, complete the following:

Questions

1. Does the firm appear to recognize that its employees are the key to its success?

2. Does the firm empower its workers? Does it encourage teamwork? Provide details.

3. Explain how the business uses technology to motivate its employees. For example, does it use the Internet to provide information about its compensation programs? Does it use the Internet or e-mail to provide feedback to its employees?

4. Go to http://hoovers.com and locate the NEWS SEARCH. Type in the name of the firm in the space provided, and review the recent news stories about the firm. Summarize any (at least one) recent news story about the firm that applies to one or more of the key concepts in this chapter.

Case: Using Motivation to Enhance Performance

Tom Fry is a plant manager for Ligonier Steel Corporation, located in Ligonier, Pennsylvania. The plant is small, with 250 employees. Its productivity growth rate has stagnated for the past year and a half.

Tom is concerned and decides to meet with employees in various departments. During the meeting, employees disclose that they do not have a chance to interact with one another while on the job. Furthermore, because they do not receive any recognition for their suggestions, their input of ideas for improvement has stopped.

After a week elapses, Tom calls a meeting to announce a new program. He plans to offer rewards for high performance so that employees will be motivated to surpass their quotas. Bonuses will be awarded to employees who exceed their quotas. Tom believes this program will work because of his perception that "money motivates employees."

A few months later, Tom notices that productivity has increased and that employees are enjoying the bonuses they have earned. Tom decides to provide an additional means of motivation. He wants employees to continue to interact with one another to solve work problems and share information. Supervisors now recognize individual accomplishments. They praise employees who make suggestions and identify an employee of the month in the company newsletter to recognize outstanding performance. Tom strongly supports this feature of the program.

The goal is for employees to grow and develop to their fullest potential. Individuals may be retrained or go back to college to permit job growth within the plant. Employees' ideas and contributions are now perceived as a way to enhance their individual career paths. The results have been overwhelming. Tom Fry, supervisors, and employees are all enjoying the benefits that have made Ligonier Steel a satisfying place to work.

Questions

1. Describe the motivation theory that applies to this case.
2. What needs can employees at Ligonier Steel satisfy in performing their jobs?
3. Describe how bonuses motivated the employees at Ligonier Steel.
4. Describe other rewards besides bonuses that can motivate work behavior in this case.
5. Ligonier does not use any negative reinforcement. Does this case illustrate any disadvantages of providing only positive reinforcement?

Video Case: Motivating Employees at Valassis Communications, Inc.

Valassis Communications, Inc., is a leader in the sales promotion industry. It creates promotional newspaper inserts containing coupons from leading consumer companies for 58 million households each Sunday. Employee motivation is very important to Valassis, so it has developed an employee compensation plan that includes base salary, profit sharing, fringe benefits, champion pay, and stock options. In other words, it uses a pay-for-performance system that rewards employees for high performance. The company rewards employees for both individual and team achievements. Team awards are tied to the performance of the firm overall. In this way, employees benefit whenever the shareholders of the firm benefit. Valassis also has an on-site hairdresser, doctor, and fitness center so that employees will enjoy coming to work. On three occasions, it has been included in *Fortune* magazine's list of the 100 best places to work in America. For more information, visit http://www.valassis.com.

Questions

1. Why does Valassis use stock options to compensate employees?
2. Why does Valassis reward people for both teamwork and individual achievement?
3. How does Valassis use champion pay to encourage employees?

Internet Applications

1. http://www.fortune.com/fortune/bestcompanies

Which companies are the top companies to work for? What kinds of benefits do they provide for their employees? Which companies would you like to work for?

2. http://www.nceo.org

Click on "ESOPs." Briefly describe what an employee stock ownership plan is. How might an ESOP encourage employees to be more motivated? How do ESOPS relate to the theories of motivation discussed in the chapter? What is an ownership culture, and how does it create an environment where employees are more empowered?

3. http://www.motivation-tools.com

Click on "Elements of Motivation." What are the three elements of motivation? What are the seven rules of motivation? Do you think motivation results from an individual's own drive, or is it primarily driven by external factors? How can the seven rules of motivation result in better performance for a company?

Dell's Secret to Success

Go to http://www.reportgallery.com and review Dell's most recent annual report. Also, go to Dell's website (http://www.dell.com) and in the section "about Dell," review the background material about Dell that relates to this chapter.

Questions

1. Explain how Dell's treatment of its employees motivates them to perform well.

2. Do you think that training is important to Dell?

3. Dell sometimes promotes some of its employees rather than hiring higher-level employees from other firms. Why is this beneficial?

In-Text Study Guide

Answers are in Appendix C at the back of book.

True or False

1. Maslow's hierarchy of needs identifies superior compensation as the key to employee motivation.

2. According to Frederick Herzberg, hygiene factors are work-related factors that will motivate and please employees.

3. The management strategy of empowerment is favored by Theory X managers.

4. A supervisor who believes in McGregor's Theory Y will likely monitor employees closely to ensure that their work is completed.

5. Equity theory suggests that an employee's efforts are influenced by the expected outcome of those efforts.

6. Negative reinforcement motivates employees by encouraging them to behave in a manner that avoids unfavorable consequences.

7. Most compensation plans that tie pay to performance are intended to motivate employees to achieve high performance.

8. A merit system allocates raises for all employees according to sales of the firm.

9. An across-the-board system is appropriate when all employees deserve the same reward for their work.

10. Open-book management encourages employees to make decisions and conduct tasks as if they were the firm's owners.

11. The techniques of motivation apply across countries.

Multiple Choice

12. By _____ employees to properly perform the tasks they are assigned, management can maximize the firm's value.
    a) motivating
    b) threatening
    c) coercing
    d) manipulating
    e) harassing

13. One implication of the Hawthorne studies is that workers can be motivated by receiving:
    a) attention.
    b) money.
    c) stock.
    d) bonuses.
    e) profit sharing.

14. Maslow's hierarchy of needs theory can be useful for motivating employees because it suggests that:
    a) people are motivated to achieve their work-related hygiene factors.
    b) managers respond to the need for corporate profitability.
    c) employee needs are stable.
    d) employees are motivated by unsatisfied needs.
    e) money is the most important motivating factor.

15. Social interaction and acceptance by others are examples of:
    a) physiological needs.
    b) esteem needs.
    c) safety needs.
    d) social needs.
    e) self-actualization needs.

In-Text Study Guide

Answers are in Appendix C at the back of book.

16. Needs that are satisfied with food, clothing, and shelter are called _____ needs.
    a) safety
    b) social
    c) affiliation
    d) self-esteem
    e) physiological

17. Herzberg's hygiene factors most closely correspond with Maslow's:
    a) physiological needs.
    b) psychological needs.
    c) social needs.
    d) esteem needs.
    e) self-actualization needs.

18. According to Herzberg, employees are commonly most satisfied when offered:
    a) adequate supervision.
    b) adequate salary.
    c) recognition.
    d) job security.
    e) safe working conditions.

19. All of the following are methods used to enhance job satisfaction except:
    a) employee involvement programs.
    b) Theory X management.
    c) job security.
    d) adequate compensation programs.
    e) flexible work schedules.

20. Theory Z suggests that employees are more satisfied when:
    a) they receive above-average pay raises.
    b) their compensation is consistent with their efforts.
    c) managers restrict the delegation of authority.
    d) they are involved in decision making.
    e) appropriate hygiene factors are available.

21. Which of the following theories of management suggests that workers will be motivated if they are compensated in accordance with their perceived contributions to the firm?
    a) expectancy theory
    b) equity theory
    c) need theory
    d) Theory Y
    e) reinforcement theory

22. The reinforcement theory that motivates employees by encouraging them to behave in a manner that avoids unfavorable consequences is _____ reinforcement.
    a) positive
    b) neutral
    c) equity
    d) negative
    e) expectancy

23. In an across-the-board system, all employees receive similar:
    a) raises.
    b) job assignments.
    c) offices.
    d) work schedules.
    e) performance appraisals.

24. Which of the following provides employees with various forms of compensation if specific performance goals are met?
    a) flextime programs
    b) job enlargement
    c) participative management
    d) open-book management
    e) incentive plans

In-Text Study Guide

Answers are in Appendix C at the back of book.

25. Which of the following is not a guideline for designing a motivational compensation system?
    a) align the system with business goals
    b) align the system with specific employee goals
    c) establish systems for rewarding employee seniority
    d) set achievable goals for employees
    e) allow employee input on the compensation system

26. Two or more persons sharing a particular work schedule is called:
    a) job enlargement.
    b) job enrichment.
    c) job sharing.
    d) flextime.
    e) job rotation.

27. Even if the company cannot guarantee continuing employment, it can improve employees' sense of job security by:
    a) empowering employees.
    b) granting stock to employees.
    c) using open-book management.
    d) training employees in various tasks.
    e) instituting compressed workweeks.

28. A program to expand the jobs assigned to employees is called:
    a) hygiene theory.
    b) downsizing.
    c) positive reinforcement.
    d) equity theory of motivation.
    e) job enlargement.

29. An employee involvement program that periodically moves individuals from one job assignment to another is:
    a) job enlargement.
    b) job enrichment.
    c) job rotation.
    d) job sharing.
    e) flextime.

30. _____ can reduce boredom and prepare employees for other jobs if their primary job is eliminated.
    a) Job evaluation
    b) Job rotation
    c) Reengineering
    d) Performance appraisal
    e) Reinforcement

31. Which of the following is an employee involvement program where a group of employees with different job positions are given the responsibility of achieving a specific goal?
    a) management by objectives (MBO)
    b) teamwork
    c) job enlargement
    d) job rotation
    e) job sharing

32. When firms delegate more authority to their employees, this strategy is referred to as:
    a) Theory X management.
    b) empowerment.
    c) the merit system.
    d) McGregor's hygiene theory.
    e) the equity system.

In-Text Study Guide

Answers are in Appendix C at the back of book.

33. Which of the following allows employees to set their own goals and determine the manner in which they accomplish their tasks?
    a) equity theory of motivation
    b) expectancy theory of motivation
    c) management by objectives
    d) Theory X management
    e) Theory Y management

34. In open-book management, the compensation of employees is typically aligned with their contribution to the firm's:
    a) hierarchy of needs.
    b) industry demand.
    c) overall performance.
    d) reinforcement theory.
    e) hygiene theory.

35. Which of the following is an employee involvement program that encourages employees to make decisions and conduct tasks as if they were the firm's owners?
    a) Theory X management
    b) open-book management
    c) Theory Y management
    d) Theory Z management
    e) Theory J management

36. In addition to linking compensation with performance, some firms grant employees _____ for good performance.
    a) internal satisfaction
    b) Theory X involvement
    c) Theory Y involvement
    d) corporate bonds
    e) common stock

GETTY IMAGES

Decisions by Web Czar Company regarding its recruiting and employee compensation will influence its performance and therefore its valuation.

The Learning Goals
of this chapter are to:

Explain human resource planning by firms. *1*

Explain how a firm can ensure equal opportunity and the benefits of doing so. *2*

Differentiate among the types of compensation that firms offer to employees. *3*

Describe the skills of employees that firms develop. *4*

Explain how the performance of employees can be evaluated. *5*

Hiring, Training, and Evaluating Employees

A firm's human resources (employees) are crucial to its performance. Therefore, a firm's performance is dependent on how its human resources are managed. The management of human resources involves recruiting employees, developing their skills, and evaluating their performance. The hiring, training, and evaluation of employees are a key to a firm's success. Consider the situation of the Web Czar Company, which provides website design and related services. Its business has grown substantially in recent years, so it frequently needs to hire additional employees. Web Czar Company must decide:

▶ How should it recruit employees?

▶ How can it ensure equal opportunity for its job positions?

▶ What types of compensation should it provide to employees?

▶ How can it ensure that its employees have the proper skills?

▶ How should the employees be evaluated?

The decision regarding the recruitment of employees is important because it affects the number of qualified candidates the firm will have. The criteria used to make hiring decisions are also important because they will determine which people are hired. If the firm can hire good employees, it will be more successful. The firm's decision regarding compensation affects its expenses. Its decision about evaluating employees is important because the evaluations will determine which employees are promoted over time and become the key decision makers.

The types of decisions described above are necessary for all businesses. This chapter explains how hiring, training, and evaluating can be conducted by Web Czar Company or any other firm in a manner that maximizes its value.

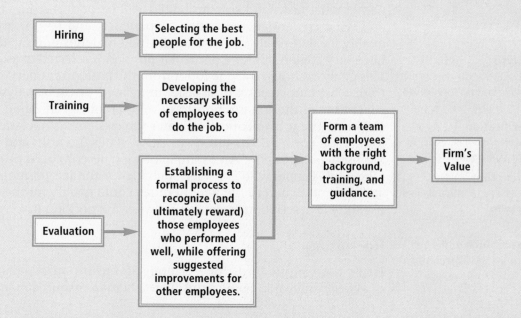

397

Explain human resource planning by firms.

human resource planning
planning to satisfy a firm's needs for employees

Human Resource Planning

Human resource planning involves planning to satisfy a firm's needs for employees. It consists of three tasks:

▶ Forecasting staffing needs
▶ Job analysis
▶ Recruiting

Forecasting Staffing Needs

If staffing needs can be anticipated in advance, the firm has more time to satisfy those needs. Some needs for human resources occur as workers retire or take jobs with other firms. Retirement can be forecasted with some degree of accuracy, but forecasting when an employee will take a job with another firm is difficult.

Additional needs for employees result from expansion. These needs may be determined by assessing the firm's growth trends. For example, if the firm is expected to increase production by 10 percent (in response to increased sales), it may prepare for the creation of new positions to achieve the projected production level. Positions that handle accounting and marketing-related tasks may not be affected by the increased production level.

If the firm foresees a temporary need for higher production, it may avoid hiring new workers, since it would soon have to lay them off. Layoffs not only affect the laid-off workers but also scare those workers who are still employed. In addition, firms that become notorious for layoffs will be less capable of recruiting people for new positions.

If firms avoid hiring during a temporary increase in production, they must achieve their objective in some other way. A common method is to offer overtime to existing workers. An alternative method is to hire temporary workers for part-time or seasonal work.

Once new positions are created, they must be filled. This normally involves job analysis and recruiting, which are discussed in turn.

Job Analysis

job analysis
the analysis used to determine the tasks and the necessary credentials for a particular position

job specification
states the credentials necessary to qualify for a job position

job description
states the tasks and responsibilities of a job position

Before a firm hires a new employee to fill an existing job position, it must decide what tasks and responsibilities will be performed by that position and what credentials (education, experience, and so on) are needed to qualify for that position. The analysis used to determine the tasks and the necessary credentials for a particular position is referred to as **job analysis.** This analysis should include input from the position's supervisor as well as from other employees whose tasks are related. The job analysis allows the supervisor of the job position to develop a job specification and job description. The **job specification** states the credentials necessary to qualify for the job position. The **job description** states the tasks and responsibilities of the job position. An example of a job description is provided in Exhibit 11.1. People who consider applying for the job position use the job specification to determine whether they could qualify for the position and use the job description to determine what the position involves.

human resource manager
helps each specific department recruit candidates for its open positions

Recruiting

Firms use various forms of recruiting to ensure an adequate supply of qualified candidates. Some firms have a **human resource manager** (some-

Exhibit 11.1

Example of a Job Description

Title:	Sales Representative
Department:	Sales
Location:	Southern Division, Atlanta, Georgia

Position Summary

The sales representative meets with prospective customers to sell the firm's products and to ensure that existing customers are satisfied with the products they have purchased.

Relationships

▶ Reports to the regional sales manager for the Southern Division.

▶ Works with five other sales representatives, although each representative has responsibility for his or her own region within the Southern Division.

Main Job Responsibilities

1. Serve existing customers; call on main customers at least once a month to obtain feedback on the performance of products previously sold to them; take any new orders for products.

2. Visit other prospective customers and explain the advantages of each product.

3. Check on customers who are late in paying their bills; provide feedback to the billing department.

4. Meet with the production managers at least once a month to inform them about any product defects cited by customers.

5. Assess the needs of prospective customers; determine whether other related products could be produced to satisfy customers; provide feedback to production managers.

6. Will need to train new sales representatives in the future if growth continues.

7. Overnight travel is necessary for about eight days per month.

8. Sales reports must be completed once a month.

times called the "personnel manager") who helps each specific department recruit candidates for its open positions. To identify potential candidates for the position, the human resource manager may check files of recent applicants who applied before the position was even open. These files are usually created as people submit their applications to the firm over time. In addition, the manager may place an ad in local newspapers. This increases the pool of applicants, as some people are unwilling to submit an application unless they know that a firm has an open position.

Increasingly, companies are also listing positions on their websites. Dell, Inc., uses the Internet extensively in its human resource planning. For example, the company allows potential employees to search for a specific job at its website. Dell also allows applicants to submit their résumés over the Internet. Furthermore, Dell uses its website to provide potential employees with information about benefits and about the areas where its plants and employment sites are located, such as cost-of-living estimates.

Most well-known companies receive a large number of qualified applications for each position. Many firms retain applications for only a few months so that the number of applications does not become excessive.

Internal versus External Recruiting   Recruiting can occur internally or externally. **Internal recruiting** seeks to fill open positions with persons already employed by the firm. Numerous firms post job openings so that existing employees can be informed. Some employees may desire the open positions more than their existing positions.

Internal recruiting can be beneficial because existing employees have already been proven. Their personalities are known, and their potential

internal recruiting
an effort to fill open positions with persons already employed by the firm

Many firms recruit by hosting job fairs, such as this one hosted by Microsoft Corp.

LANDOV LLC

promotion
the assignment of an employee to a higher-level job with more responsibility and compensation

capabilities and limitations can be thoroughly assessed. Internal recruiting also allows existing workers to receive a **promotion** (an assignment of a higher-level job with more responsibility and compensation) or to switch to more desirable tasks. This potential for advancement can motivate employees to perform well. Such potential also reduces job turnover and therefore reduces the costs of hiring and training new employees. Many of the employees that Walt Disney hires for management positions are recruited internally. Wal-Mart has established a "first-in-line" program that it uses to promote its employees to managers, as explained in a recent annual report:

"The Customer-centered Wal-Mart culture must be embraced by thousands of new Associates if the Company is to keep growing. One way we'll retain that culture is by continuing to recruit nearly 70 percent of our management from the ranks of hourly workers. When room is available, college students who are working for Wal-Mart are the first considered for management jobs."

—Wal-Mart Corporation

Firms can do more internal recruiting if their employees are assigned responsibilities and tasks that train them for advanced positions. This strategy conflicts with job specialization because it exposes employees to more varied tasks. Nevertheless, it is necessary to prepare them for other jobs and to reduce the possibility of boredom. Even when a firm is able to fill a position internally, however, the previous position that the employee held becomes open, and the firm must recruit for that position.

external recruiting
an effort to fill positions with applicants from outside the firm

External recruiting is an effort to fill positions with applicants from outside the firm. Some firms may recruit more qualified candidates when using external recruiting, especially for some specialized job positions. Although external recruiting allows the firm to evaluate applicants' potential capabilities and limitations, human resource managers do not have as much information as they do for internal applicants. The applicant's résumé lists previously performed functions and describes the responsibilities of those positions, but it does not indicate how the applicant responds to orders or interacts with other employees. This type of information is more critical for some jobs than others.

Screening Applicants   The recruiting process used to screen job applicants involves several steps. The first step is to assess each application to screen out unqualified applicants. Although the information provided on an application is limited, it is usually sufficient to determine whether the applicant has the minimum background, education, and experience necessary to qualify for the position.

Recruitment software programs eliminate the need for individuals to read and categorize every résumé received. In the past, human resource employees had to sift through numerous résumés to find potential matches for open positions. Résumés that were not an appropriate match were thrown out after a specified amount of time. Recruitment software has reduced costs by creating a more efficient system. Résumés are either received electronically or scanned into the computer and keywords are used to sort them. Human resource departments or the hiring manager can use the software's searching capabilities to identify specific skill or experience requirements. The system also allows for the creation of a database of applicants. This technology allows human resource professionals to spend more time conducting interviews and other important tasks rather than sorting, categorizing, and filing résumés.

The second step in screening applicants is the interview process. Some firms conduct initial interviews of college students at placement centers on college campuses. Other firms conduct initial interviews at their location. The human resource manager uses the personal interview to assess the personality of an applicant, as well as to obtain additional information that

Wal-Mart typically attempts to promote employees within its business as a way of retaining its best employees and reducing turnover.

GETTY IMAGES

was not included on the application. Specifically, an interview can indicate an applicant's punctuality, communication skills, and attitude. Furthermore, an interview allows the firm to obtain more detailed information about the applicant's past experience.

If the first two screening steps can substantially reduce the number of candidates, the human resource manager can allocate more time to assess each remaining applicant during the interview process. Even when these steps have effectively reduced the number of candidates, however, the first interview with each remaining candidate will not necessarily lead to a selection. A second and even third interview may be necessary. These interviews may involve other employees of the firm who have some interaction with the position of concern. The input of these employees can often influence the hiring decision. A typical questionnaire for obtaining employee opinions about an applicant is shown in Exhibit 11.2.

A third step in screening applicants is to contact the applicant's references. This screening method offers limited benefits, however, because applicants normally list only those references who are likely to provide strong recommendations. A survey by the Society for Human Resource Management found that more than 50 percent of the human resource managers surveyed sometimes receive inadequate information about a job applicant's personality traits. More than 40 percent of these managers said that they sometimes receive inadequate information about the applicant's skills and work habits.

employment test
a test of a job candidate's abilities

Another possible step in the screening process is an **employment test,** which is a test of the candidate's abilities. Some tests are designed to assess intuition or willingness to work with others. Other tests are designed to assess specific skills, such as computer skills.

Until recently, some firms also requested a physical examination for candidates they planned to hire. Now, however, firms may request a phys-

Exhibit 11.2

Example of Questionnaire to Obtain Employee Opinions about a Job Applicant

	Strongly Agree	Agree	Unsure	Disagree	Strongly Disagree
Applicant's name _____					
Position to be filled _____					
The applicant possesses the necessary skills to perform the tasks required.					
The applicant would work well with others.					
The applicant would be eager to learn new skills.					
The applicant has good communication skills.					
The applicant would accept responsibility.					
Do you detect any deficiencies in the applicant? (If so, describe them.)					
Do you recommend that we hire the applicant? Why, or why not?					
Signature of employee who is assessing applicant: _____					

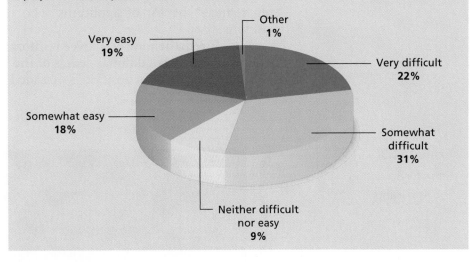

SMALL BUSINESS SURVEY

Recruiting

In a recent National Small Business poll conducted for the NFIB Research Foundation, small businesses were asked how difficult it is to attract and keep good employees. Their responses are shown below:

- Other 1%
- Very easy 19%
- Very difficult 22%
- Somewhat easy 18%
- Somewhat difficult 31%
- Neither difficult nor easy 9%

ical examination only *after* a job offer has been made. This examination can determine whether the individual is physically able to perform the tasks that would be assigned. In addition, the examination can document any medical problems that existed before the individual was employed by the firm. This can protect the firm from being blamed for causing a person's medical problems through unsafe working conditions.

Along with physical examinations, some firms ask new hires to take a drug test. Firms are adversely affected in two ways when their employees take illegal drugs. First, the firm may incur costs for health care and counseling for these employees. Second, the performance of these employees will likely be poor and may even have a negative effect on the performance of their co-workers.

Some firms outsource the task of screening job applicants. For example, Bristol-Myers Squibb Company relies on the company MRI to identify and screen its job applicants. MRI organizes recruiting conferences, where it identifies candidates who may be suitable for the positions that Bristol-Myers Squibb and other firms need to fill.

Make the Hiring Decision   By the time the steps for screening applicants are completed, the application list should have been reduced to a small number of qualified candidates. Some firms take their hiring process very seriously because they recognize that their future performance is highly dependent on the employees that they select, as documented by the following statement:

"The past year's success is the product of a talented, smart, hard-working group, and I take great pride in being a part of this team. Setting the bar high [high standards] in our approach to hiring has been, and will continue to be, the single most important element of Amazon.com's success."

—Amazon.com

Careful screening enables firms to recruit people who turn out to be excellent employees. Consequently, careful recruiting can result in low turnover.

Once the screening is completed, the top candidate can be selected from this list and offered the job; the remaining qualified applicants can be considered if the top candidate does not accept the job offer. Exhibit 11.3 summarizes the steps used to screen job applicants. Notice that each step reduces the list of applicants who would possibly qualify for the position.

Once hired, the new employee is informed about the firm's health and benefits plans and additional details of the job. A summary of the various tasks necessary to fill a position is provided in Exhibit 11.4.

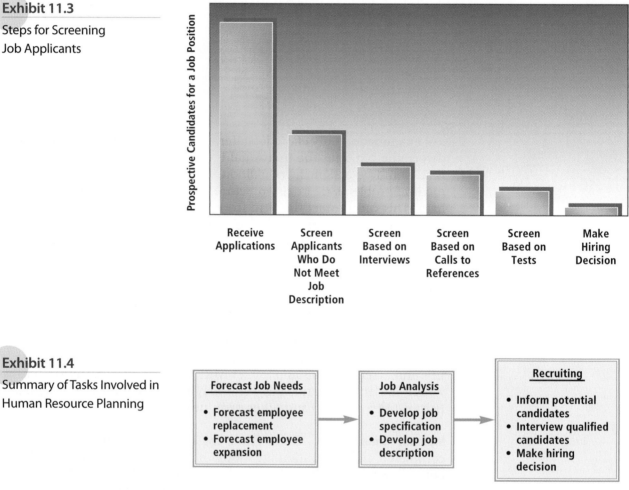

Exhibit 11.3

Steps for Screening Job Applicants

Exhibit 11.4

Summary of Tasks Involved in Human Resource Planning

Decision Making

How to Recruit

The specific manner in which a firm recruits is dependent on its unique characteristics. To illustrate, consider Web Czar Company (introduced at the beginning of the chapter), which develops websites for businesses. The firm recently received many orders from businesses that either want new websites or want to revise their existing websites. Brent Barber, the owner, forecasts that he needs to hire at least two more website designers on a full-time basis. Next, he conducts a job analysis. The job specification states the credentials that the designers need; in particular, they must have completed specific Web design classes. The job description lists the tasks that the positions involve, such as posting images on a website, using animation, and rearranging Web pages.

The next step is external recruiting. Brent has a file of résumés that he recently received. Hoping to attract more applicants before he makes the hiring decisions, he also runs ads containing the job description in local newspapers and posts a notice about the positions on Web Czar's own website and on several job position websites. By conducting an accurate forecast and creating a clear job specification and a clear job description, Brent is able to hire two qualified website designers. Consequently, he will be able to keep up with the demand for his services, which will increase his firm's revenue and therefore increase its profits.

1. What problem might Web Czar Company encounter if it hired an applicant whose résumé listed proper credentials without interviewing the applicant?

2. If Web Czar has many qualified applicants for its job positions and they all appear to be enthusiastic about working for the company, what criterion should Web Czar use to make its hiring decision?

Answers: 1. Even though the credentials on the résumé are excellent, the applicant may not get along with other workers. 2. Web Czar Company should attempt to determine which applicants will work well with its existing employees.

2

Explain how a firm can ensure equal opportunity and the benefits of doing so.

Providing Equal Opportunity

When recruiting candidates for a job position, managers should not discriminate based on factors that are unrelated to potential job performance. First, such discrimination is illegal. Second, discrimination may reduce the efficiency of the employees in the workplace.

Federal Laws Related to Discrimination

Federal laws prohibit such discrimination. The following are some of the laws enacted to prevent discrimination or improper treatment:

▶ The Equal Pay Act of 1963 states that men and women performing similar work must receive the same pay.

▶ The Civil Rights Act of 1964 prohibits discrimination based on race, gender, religion, or national origin.

▶ The Age Discrimination in Employment Act of 1967, amended in 1978, prohibits employers from discriminating against people who are 40 years old or older.

▶ The Americans with Disabilities Act (ADA) of 1990 prohibits discrimination against people who are disabled.

▶ The Civil Rights Act of 1991 enables women, minorities, and disabled people who believe that they have been subject to discrimination to sue firms. This act protects against discrimination in the hiring process or the employee evaluation process. It also protects against sexual harassment in the workplace.

Overall, the federal laws have helped to encourage firms to make hiring decisions without discriminating.

Diversity Incentives

While the federal laws can penalize firms for discriminating, many firms now recognize the potential benefits of a more diverse workplace. These firms strive for diversity not just to abide by the laws, but because it can enhance their value.

Diversity can benefit firms in three ways. First, studies have shown that employees who work in a diverse workplace tend to be more innovative. Second, employees in a diverse workplace are more likely to understand different points of view and be capable of interacting with a diverse set of customers. The proportion of a firm's customer base that consists of minorities will continue to increase. Third, a larger proportion of eligible employees will be from minority groups in the future.

Data from the U.S. Census Bureau illustrate how the number of minority customers and eligible minority employees has grown and will

Allstate recently received recognition for its efforts to achieve a diverse work force.

GETTY IMAGES

grow in the future. During the period 1990–2000, the white population in the United States increased by 3.4 percent; the African American population increased by 16 percent; the Native American population, by 15 percent; and the Hispanic population, by 50 percent. Thus, U.S. population growth is heavily dominated by minority groups. Together, these three minority groups represent 25 percent of the U.S. population now, and by the year 2050, they are expected to represent 38 percent.

By the year 2025, minority groups will in aggregate represent the majority of the population in some states. The total college-age population in the United States is ex-

Exhibit 11.5

Sampling of Firms That Are Known for Establishing a More Diverse Workplace

Name of Firm	Proportion of New Hires Who Are Minorities	Proportion of Workforce Who Are Minorities	Proportion of Managers Who Are Minorities	Number of Board Members Who Are Minorities
McDonald's	37%	55%	38%	2 out of 16
BellSouth	39	31	26	2 out of 13
Lucent Technologies	44	30	23	1 out of 6
PepsiCo	33	27	16	4 out of 15
Colgate-Palmolive	43	29	27	1 out of 8
Procter & Gamble	17	17	17	2 out of 16
Levi Strauss	47	57	33	1 out of 14
United Parcel Service	52	35	28	3 out of 13
American Express	35	27	20	2 out of 12
Coca-Cola	40	32	19	1 out of 12

pected to grow by 16 percent by the year 2015, and minorities will account for 80 percent of this growth. Hispanics will account for half of the growth in the minority college-age population, while African Americans and Native Americans will make up the remainder. Thus, firms that create a diverse workplace will be able to match the more diverse customer base that will develop over time and will have better access to the pool of eligible employees.

Firms Recognized for Achieving Diversity   Some of the firms that have made much progress in establishing a more diverse workplace are listed in Exhibit 11.5. These firms not only have recently hired minorities, but also have achieved diversity among their managers, and even among their board members. These firms demonstrate that diversity in the workplace can be accomplished and that firms with diverse sets of employees can be successful. Some of the largest firms in the United States, including Merrill Lynch, American Express, and Symantec, now have minorities serving as chief executive officer (CEO).

Firms in the United States have also been making efforts to hire and promote more women. Women now occupy about 46 percent of all managerial and administrative positions in U.S. firms. In addition, they hold about 14 percent of all board member positions. These percentages are much higher than those in most other countries.

A survey of human resource managers conducted by the Society of Human Resource Management found that 85 percent of the managers surveyed expect to see more opportunities for women in the future and 79 percent expect to see more opportunities for minorities.

Decision Making

Decision Making ▸ Ensuring Equal Opportunity in New Job Positions

Recall that Web Czar Company, was planning to hire for two new website designer job positions. Brent Barber, the owner, wants to ensure that the company allows for equal opportunity for women and minorities in those positions. He decides to use the following strategies for this purpose:

▸ Web Czar has implemented a policy of promoting internally when its employees qualify for open job positions; because many women and minority employees already work as technicians for the company's website designers, this policy gives them a chance for advancement into the website designer positions.

▸ Web Czar lists its job openings in local newspapers and on websites that appeal to all races and genders so that it reaches a diverse audience when advertising a job opening.

With these strategies, Web Czar has been able to achieve diversity and a good working environment, which results in efficient production of its website design services.

1. Explain how Web Czar's strategy for allowing for equal opportunity is related to its human resource planning process.

2. Under what conditions might a policy to promote existing employees to open job positions not allow for equal opportunity?

ANSWERS: 1. Web Czar should use a human resource planning (recruiting) process to ensure that it reaches minorities and women who may apply for the job positions. 2. If women and minorities are not already represented within the existing set of employees, then a firm's internal promotion policy will not provide equal opportunity. Since the existing set of employees at Web Czar is diverse, its internal promotion policy should allow equal opportunity for higher-level job positions.

3

Differentiate among the types of compensation that firms offer to employees.

Compensation Packages That Firms Offer

Firms attempt to reward their employees by providing adequate compensation. The level of compensation is usually established by determining what employees at other firms with similar job characteristics earn. Information on compensation levels can be obtained by conducting a salary survey or from various publications that report salary levels for different jobs. The wide differences in compensation among job positions are attributed to differences in the supply of people who have a particular skill and the demand for people with that skill. For example, demand for employees who have extensive experience in business financing decisions is high, but the supply of people with such experience is limited. Therefore, firms offer a high level of compensation to attract these people. Conversely, the supply of people who can qualify as a clerk is large, so firms can offer relatively low compensation to hire clerks.

compensation package
the total monetary compensation and benefits offered to employees

A **compensation package** consists of the total monetary compensation and benefits offered to employees. Some employees think of their compensation only in terms of their salary, but the benefits that some firms offer may be more valuable than the salary. The typical elements of a compensation package are salary, stock options, commissions, bonuses, profit sharing, benefits, and perquisites.

Salary

salary (or wages)
the dollars paid for a job over a specific period

Salary (or wages) is the dollars paid for a job over a specific period. The salary can be expressed per hour, per pay period, or per year and is fixed over a particular time period.

Stock Options

stock options

a form of compensation that allows employees to purchase shares of their employer's stock at a specific price

Stock options allow employees to purchase the firm's stock at a specific price. Consider employees who have been given stock options to buy 100 shares of stock at a price of $20 per share. This means that they can purchase the stock for this price, regardless of the stock's market price. Thus, even if the stock's market price rises to $30 per share, the employees can still buy the stock for $20 per share. They would need $2,000 (computed as 100 shares × $20 per share) to purchase 100 shares. If the firm performs well over time, the stock price will rise, and their 100 shares will be worth even more. Thus, these employees are motivated to perform well because they benefit directly when the firm performs well. As part-owners of the firm, they share in its profits.

Many firms provide stock options to their high-level managers, such as the CEO, vice-presidents, and other managers. Some firms, however, such as Starbucks and Microsoft, provide stock options to all of their employees. This can motivate all employees to perform well. Starbucks grants stock options to its employees in proportion to their salaries. An employee who received a salary of $20,000 in 1991 would have earned more than $50,000 by the year 2000 from owning the stock options.

Microsoft attributes much of its success to its use of stock options. Because of its strong performance (and therefore substantial increase in its stock price) since 1992, its managers who were hired in 1992 or before are now millionaires because their shares are worth more than $1 million.

A recent annual report of Wal-Mart summarized the potential benefits to a firm that uses stock options to compensate employees:

"The ownership of Wal-Mart stock and options by directors and senior management is important because these individuals represent the Shareholders and should act in a manner consistent with the long-term interests of Shareholders. Making equity part of their compensation helps achieve this objective."

Senior management has a great responsibility to represent the interests of all shareholders. Wal-Mart provides stock and options as a means of both recruiting the best and rewarding its senior management.

AP/WIDE WORLD PHOTOS

In order to hire and retain talented employees, Amazon.com uses stock options as a major part of its compensation. By providing stock options, its employees have ownership in the firm, and their business decisions can affect the value of the shares they own. As the following comment indicates, Amazon believes that its success is highly influenced by its ability to motivate its employees:

"We will continue to focus on hiring and retaining versatile and talented employees, and continue to weight their compensation to stock options rather than cash. We know our success will be largely affected by our ability to attract and retain a motivated employee base, each of whom must think like, and therefore must actually be, an owner."

—Amazon.com

How Options Can Cause a Conflict of Interests   Stock options can also lead to problems for a firm's shareholders, however. When the top managers use their stock options to obtain the firm's stock, they want to sell that stock during a period when the stock's price is high. Although owning stock is supposed to encourage managers to improve the firm so that they benefit from a higher stock price, stock ownership may tempt them to manipulate the financial statements to boost the stock price. In some cases, a firm's managers have increased investor demand for the stock by using accounting methods that temporarily boosted the firm's earnings. The high demand caused the stock price to rise, allowing the managers to sell their holdings of stock at a high price. When investors learned that the firm's earnings were exaggerated, they sold their stock, causing the price to decline, but by that time the managers had already sold their shares. During the 2001–2002 period, managers of several firms, including Enron, Global Crossing, and WorldCom, were accused of using accounting to inflate their earnings and mislead investors in this way.

Some firms not only exaggerated their earnings, but failed to disclose financial problems. In several cases, managers knew of problems at a firm but withheld relevant information from the public until after they had sold their holdings of the firm's stock. The managers issued overly optimistic financial reports so that other shareholders would not sell the firm's stock and cause the price to decline until the managers had sold their shares. Thus, the managers were able to benefit at the expense of other investors who purchased the stock from them at a high price without realizing the firm's financial problems.

As an example, Enron manipulated its earnings so that they increased over 20 consecutive quarters leading up to 2001. Enron's stock price rose over time along with the earnings. When investors recognized that Enron was manipulating its earnings, however, they dumped the stock, and the stock price declined abruptly in 2001. In November 2001, Enron filed for bankruptcy. Yet, before Enron's price declined, 29 Enron executives or board members sold their holdings of Enron stock for more than $1 billion. In particular, Enron's CEO sold more than $100 million worth of Enron stock before the financial problems were disclosed. The CEO and other top managers were able to sell their shares at a high price because other shareholders did not know about Enron's problems. Thus, the managers benefited at the expense of the other shareholders. Similar abuses have occurred at other firms, although to a lesser extent.

The lesson of the Enron scandal is that managers who receive stock options as compensation may be tempted to manipulate the firm's stock price so that they can sell their shares at a high price. Although managers cannot control the stock's price directly, they can influence the price indirectly through the information that they release or withhold. Thus, they have an incentive to exaggerate the earnings, issue overly optimistic reports, or withhold bad news; by doing so, they can indirectly push the stock price higher and then sell their stock holdings at a high price.

A firm's board of directors should attempt to prevent such abuses. The board of directors can enact guidelines that allow the managers or board members to sell only a small amount of their stock holdings in any particular quarter or year. In this way, the managers will not have an incentive to create an artificially high stock price in any particular quarter or year because they will not be able to sell all of their stock at that time.

Commissions

commissions
compensation for meeting specific sales objectives

Commissions normally represent compensation for meeting specific sales objectives. For example, salespeople at many firms receive a base salary, plus a percentage of their total sales volume as monetary compensation. Commissions are not used for jobs where employee performance cannot be as easily measured.

Bonuses

bonus
an extra onetime payment at the end of a period in which performance was measured

A **bonus** is an extra onetime payment at the end of a period in which performance was measured. Bonuses are usually paid less frequently than commissions (such as once a year). A bonus may be paid for efforts to increase revenue, reduce expenses, or improve customer satisfaction. In most cases, the bonus is not set by a formula; thus, supervisors have some flexibility in determining the bonus for each employee. The total amount of bonus funds that are available for employees may be dependent on the firm's profits for the year of concern.

At Disney, 70 percent of the bonus compensation for executives is based on specific financial performance measures, such as earnings. The advantage of using these types of measures is that executives are encouraged to focus on specific financial goals that should also satisfy the company's shareholders.

Profit Sharing

profit sharing
a portion of the firm's profits is paid to employees

Some firms, such as Continental Airlines and General Motors, offer employees **profit sharing,** in which a portion of the firm's profits is paid to employees. Boeing, J.P. Morgan Chase, and many other firms also offer profit sharing to some of their employees. This motivates employees to perform in a manner that improves profitability.

Employee Benefits

employee benefits
additional privileges beyond compensation payments, such as paid vacation time; health, life, or dental insurance; and pension programs

Employees may also receive **employee benefits,** which are additional privileges beyond compensation payments, such as paid vacation time; health, life, or dental insurance; and pension programs. Typically, these employee benefits are not taxed. Many firms provide substantial employee benefits to their employees. The cost of providing health insurance has

SMALL BUSINESS SURVEY

Do Firms Reward Employees for Customer Satisfaction?

A survey of 164 CEOs asked whether their nonsales employees (not directly involved with the sale of products) are rewarded for satisfying customers. The results of the survey are summarized in the following chart:

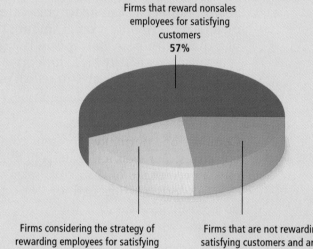

Firms that reward nonsales employees for satisfying customers
57%

Firms considering the strategy of rewarding employees for satisfying customers
23%

Firms that are not rewarding employees for satisfying customers and are not considering such a strategy
20%

The results suggest that most firms now recognize the importance of customer satisfaction and are attempting to reward employees to ensure customer satisfaction.

SMALL BUSINESS SURVEY

Which Employee Benefits Are Most Important to Employees?

A recent survey by Transamerica asked employees of small businesses how important various employee benefits were to them. Their responses are shown here:

	Very Important	Somewhat Important	Not Very Important
Retirement contributions by employer	44%	40%	16%
Retirement contributions by employee allowed	58%	33%	8%
Health insurance coverage	90%	6%	5%
Life insurance coverage	48%	32%	20%
Disability insurance coverage	59%	32%	9%
Stock options	13%	46%	41%

Global Business

Compensating Employees across Countries

The manner in which firms compensate their employees may vary across countries. Salary may be perceived as less important in a country where personal income tax rates are high. If a large portion of the salary is taxed, employees may prefer other forms of compensation. The health benefits that a firm offers may be less important in countries that provide free medical services.

Some U.S. firms, such as Gillette and PepsiCo, offer their employees opportunities to purchase their stock at below-market prices. Most employees in the United States perceive this form of employee compensation as desirable. Employees in other countries, however, perceive it as less desirable. The rules for individuals who purchase stock vary among countries. For example, individuals in Brazil, China, and India are restricted from purchasing or owning stock under some circumstances. The taxes imposed on the profits earned by individuals on their stocks also vary across countries, which makes stock ownership less desirable for employees based in certain countries. Furthermore, individuals in some countries are more comfortable investing in bank deposits rather than in stocks.

Since employees based in different countries may have varying views about compensation, a firm with employees in several countries should consider tailoring its compensation plans to fit the characteristics of each country. The firm may provide higher salaries in one country and more health benefits in another. Before establishing a compensation plan in a given country, the firm should assess the specific tax laws of that country and survey individuals to determine the types of compensation that are most desirable. When a firm designs a compensation plan to fit the country's characteristics, it can improve employee job satisfaction.

---

soared in recent years. Many firms, such as Johnson & Johnson, have responded by offering preventive health-care programs. Some firms now give employees incentives to stay healthy by reducing the insurance premiums charged to employees who receive favorable scores on cholesterol levels, blood pressure, fitness, and body fat.

Perquisites

perquisites
additional privileges beyond compensation payments and employee benefits

Some firms offer **perquisites** (or "perks") to high-level employees; these are additional privileges beyond compensation payments and employee benefits. Common perquisites include free parking, a company car, club memberships, telephone credit cards, and an expense account.

Comparison across Jobs

The forms of compensation allocated to employees vary with their jobs, as shown in Exhibit 11.6. Employees who are directly involved in the production process (such as assembly-line workers) tend to receive most of their compensation in the form of salary. Low-level managers may also receive most of their compensation as salary but may receive a small bonus and profit sharing.

Many salespeople in the computer and technology sectors earn more compensation in the form of commissions than as salary. High-level managers, such as vice-presidents and CEOs, normally have a high salary and the potential for a large bonus. Their employee benefits are also relatively large, and they normally are awarded various perks as well.

Exhibit 11.6

How Forms of Compensation
Can Vary across Job
Descriptions

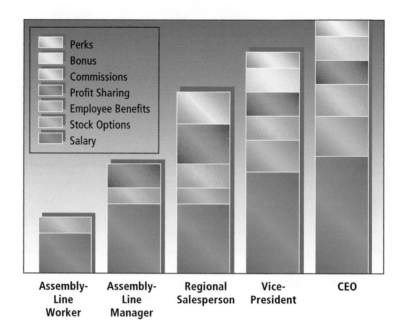

Legend:
- Perks
- Bonus
- Commissions
- Profit Sharing
- Employee Benefits
- Stock Options
- Salary

Categories:
Assembly-Line Worker | Assembly-Line Manager | Regional Salesperson | Vice-President | CEO

Decision Making

Selecting the Proper Compensation Package

The ideal compensation package a firm should offer to its employees is dependent on the specific characteristics of the firm. To illustrate, consider Web Czar Company, which has three types of job positions: (1) Web design specialists (website designers), who are responsible for the development of websites; (2) Web technicians, who provide technical assistance to the Web design specialists; and (3) Customer service representatives, who sell the Web design services to businesses.

The compensation varies with the job position. The technicians are paid a salary and may receive a bonus if they perform well for the Web design specialists. The Web design specialists receive a salary and may receive a bonus if customers are very satisfied with the websites they create. The customer service representatives receive a salary and a commission based on the volume of orders that they solicit from businesses. All employees have an incentive to perform well because their compensation is directly tied to their work performance. Web Czar's compensation package has resulted in a large volume of orders due to the efforts of the customer representatives and high production quality due to the efforts of the Web design specialists and Web technicians.

1. Suppose that Web Czar Company offered salaries that were typically 30 percent lower than those for similar jobs elsewhere and had a program that would allow employees to earn a bonus of up to 50 percent of their salary each year. Would Web Czar be successful in recruiting if it typically performed poorly?

2. Should managers of Web Czar Company who are on the board of directors have a major influence on the compensation paid to the CEO? Why or why not?

ANSWERS: 1. No. The applicants would recognize that the bonus would likely be zero in the future if Web Czar continued to perform poorly. 2. No. The managers might want to provide the CEO with an excessive salary so that the CEO would give them a large raise.

Describe the skills of employees that firms develop.

Developing Skills of Employees

Firms that hire employees provide training to develop various employee skills. Motorola has established its own university where each employee receives at least one week of training per year. A study by the management consulting firm Ernst & Young found that firms that invest in training programs are more profitable. To illustrate the attention that can be given to training, consider the case of The Home Depot Company. Its employees frequently interact with customers and need to have sufficient expertise to explain how various products can be used. The managers interact with the employees and with customers. The Home Depot Company has established an initiative focused on training, as explained in its recent annual report:

"We believe our greatest competitive advantage is our people. That's why we launched human resources initiatives designed to attract, motivate, and retain the best employees in the industry. Through learning programs for associates and leadership development of district and store managers, we will increasingly shift our store management focus from 'operating a box' to 'managing a business.'"

Some of the more common types of training provided to employees are discussed next.

Technical Skills

Employees must be trained to perform the various tasks they engage in daily. Ace Hardware offers courses to train its employees in the use of the products that it sells. As factories owned by firms such as General Motors and Boeing incorporate more advanced technology, employees receive more training. These firms spend millions of dollars every year on training. With new development in computer technology, employees of travel agencies, mail-order clothing firms, retail stores, and large corporations must

Out of Business

SMALL BUSINESS SURVEY

How Do CEOs Allocate Their Time When Managing Employees?

A survey of 280 CEOs of small businesses asked how they allocate their time when managing employees. Results of this survey are summarized in the following chart:

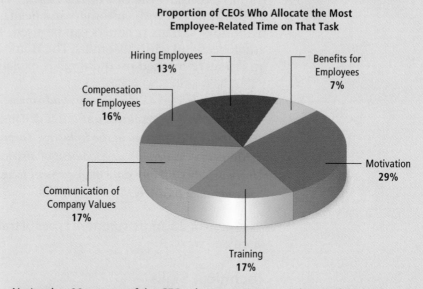

Proportion of CEOs Who Allocate the Most Employee-Related Time on That Task

Hiring Employees 13%

Compensation for Employees 16%

Benefits for Employees 7%

Communication of Company Values 17%

Motivation 29%

Training 17%

Notice that 29 percent of the CEOs chose motivation as the employee-related task that required the most time. The survey also shows that hiring employees required the most time for 13 percent of the CEOs, and training employees required the most time for 17 percent of the CEOs.

receive more training on using computers. In addition, employees who are assigned to new jobs will require extra training. Firms recognize that expenses may be incurred each year to continually develop each employee's skills.

Decision-Making Skills

Firms can benefit from providing their employees with some guidelines to consider when making decisions and generating ideas. For example, Xerox trains all of its employees to follow a six-step process when generating ideas and making decisions. Kodak employees who recently created new products are asked to share their knowledge with other employees who are attempting to develop new products. Motorola trains its employees to apply new technology to develop new products. Ace Hardware offers courses on management skills for its managers.

Customer Service Skills

Employees who frequently deal with customers need to have customer service skills. Many employees in tourism industries such as airlines and hotels are trained to satisfy customers. The hotel chain Marriott International provides training on serving customers, with refresher sessions after the first and second months. The training is intended not only to ensure customer satisfaction but also to provide employees with an orientation that makes them more comfortable (and increases employee satisfaction). Ace Hardware offers courses for its managers to develop customer service skills. Walt Disney provides extensive training to its newly hired employees. Customer service skills are also necessary for employees hired by firms to sell products or deal with customer complaints.

Safety Skills

Firms also educate employees about safety within the work environment. This includes training employees on how to use machinery and equipment in factories owned by large manufacturing firms, such as Caterpillar and Goodyear Tire. United Parcel Service (UPS) implements training programs for its employees on handling hazardous materials. Training programs not only reassure employees but also reduce health-care and legal expenses that could be incurred as a result of work-related injuries.

Human Relations Skills

Some training seminars may be necessary for supervisors who lack skills in managing other employees. In general, this type of training helps supervisors recognize that their employees not only deserve to be treated properly but also will perform better if they are treated well.

Firms commonly provide seminars on diversity to help employees of different races, genders, and religions become more sensitive to other views. Denny's offers employee training on diversity to prevent racial discrimination. Diversity training may enable a firm to create an environment in which people work together more effectively, thereby improving the firm's performance. It may also prevent friction between employees and thus can possibly prevent discrimination or harassment lawsuits against the firm.

Training seminars are also designed to improve relationships among employees across various divisions so that employees can work together in teams. For example, Motorola and Xerox provide seminars on teamwork for employees. Anheuser-Busch organizes regular meetings between employees and executives.

Pfizer provides training to its employees and to various sales representatives about different types of Pfizer products, so that they can more easily sell these products.

CORBIS, CHICAGO

Decision Making

Training Employees

The specific methods used to develop employee skills at a firm are dependent on the characteristics of the firm. Recall that Web Czar Company has three types of employees. The Web technicians are required to periodically take courses that cover the latest technology for website design. The Web design specialists are required to take classes that update them on trends in website design. The customer service representatives also receive training in website design and in communication because they often must explain various website features in nontechnical terms. As a result of the training, the employees at Web Czar Company have improved the quality of the their website design services, which has led to an increased demand and higher revenue. In addition, their training has allowed them to provide the services more efficiently, which has led to a reduction in production expenses. Overall, their training has resulted in higher profits.

1. Explain how Web Czar's need to develop the skills of its employees is related to its hiring process.

2. Explain why some training may be necessary over time, even when the employees are fully qualified.

ANSWERS: 1. If it hires more qualified employees, it may not need to develop their skills. 2. Technology changes over time, so employees may require training to ensure that they understand the latest technology.

Evaluation of Employee Performance

Explain how the performance of employees can be evaluated.

Employees often perceive performance evaluation as only a method for allocating raises. Yet, if supervisors properly conduct the evaluation, it can also provide feedback and direction to employees. An evaluation should indicate an employee's strengths and weaknesses and may influence an employee's chances of being promoted within the firm in the future.

Segmenting the Evaluation into Different Criteria

The overall performance of most employees is normally based on multiple criteria. Therefore, an evaluation can best be conducted by segmenting the evaluation into the criteria that are relevant for each particular job position. For example, consider employees who have excellent technical skills for their jobs, but are not dependable. Since they rate high on one criterion and low on another, their overall performance might be evaluated as about average. An average rating for overall performance, however, does not specifically pinpoint the employees' favorable or unfavorable work habits.

Segmenting performance evaluation into different criteria can help supervisors pinpoint specific strengths and weaknesses. Evaluating each criterion separately provides more specific information to employees about how they may improve. In our example, the employees who receive a low rating on dependability can focus on improving that behavior. Furthermore, these employees can see from their evaluation that their supervisor recognized their strong technical skills. Without a detailed evaluation, employees may not recognize what tasks they do well (in the opinion of supervisors) and what specific weaknesses need to be improved.

Objective versus Subjective Criteria   Some performance criteria are objective, such as parts produced per week, number of days absent, percentage of deadlines missed, and proportion of defective parts caused by employee er-

Exhibit 11.7

Examples of Direct Measures of Performance

Job Position	Direct Measures of Performance
Salesperson	Dollar volume of sales over a specific period Number of new customers Number of delinquent accounts collected Net sales per month in territory
Manager	Number of employee grievances Cost reductions Absenteeism Unit safety record Timeliness in completing appraisals Employee satisfaction with manager Division production Diversity of new hires
Administrative assistant	Number of letters prepared Word processing speed Number of errors in filing Number of tasks returned for reprocessing Number of calls screened

rors. Examples of direct measures of performance are provided for specific job positions in Exhibit 11.7 to illustrate how the measures vary by type of job. Other characteristics not shown in Exhibit 11.7 that are commonly assessed for some job positions include organization, communication, and decision-making skills.

Some criteria are less objective but still important. For example, sometimes the quality of work cannot be measured by part defects because many jobs do not focus on producing a single product. Therefore, quality of work may be subjectively assessed by a supervisor. Also, the willingness of an employee to help other employees is an important criterion that is subjective.

Using a Performance Evaluation Form

Supervisors are typically required to complete a performance evaluation form at the end of each year. An example of such a form is shown in Exhibit 11.8. When supervisors measure the performance of employees, they normally classify the employee in one of several categories such as the following: (1) outstanding, (2) above average, (3) average, (4) below average, and (5) poor. The set of criteria can be more specific for particular jobs within the firm. For example, assembly-line workers may be rated by the total components produced and production quality. A company salesperson may be evaluated by the number of computers sold and the quality of service provided to customers. It is important that supervisors inform employees of the criteria by which they will be rated. Otherwise, they may allocate too much time to tasks that supervisors view as less important.

Assigning Weights to the Criteria

An employee's ratings on all relevant criteria can be combined to determine the employee's overall performance level. Some firms use systems that weight and rate the criteria used to evaluate the employee. For

Exhibit 11.8

Example of Performance Appraisal Form

Employee Name _____ Date _____

Position _____

Behavior Ratings: Check the one characteristic that best applies.

Quality of Work (refers to accuracy and margin of error):

_____ 1. Makes errors frequently and repeatedly

_____ 2. Often makes errors

_____ 3. Is accurate; makes occasional errors

_____ 4. Is accurate; rarely makes errors

_____ 5. Is exacting and precise

Quantity of Work (refers to amount of production or results):

_____ 1. Usually does not complete workload as assigned

_____ 2. Often accomplishes part of a task

_____ 3. Handles workload as assigned

_____ 4. Turns out more work than requested

_____ 5. Handles an unusually large volume of work

Timeliness (refers to completion of task, within time allowed):

_____ 1. Does not complete duties on time

_____ 2. Is often late in completing tasks

_____ 3. Completes tasks on time

_____ 4. Usually completes tasks in advance of deadlines

_____ 5. Always completes all tasks in advance of deadlines

Attendance and Punctuality (refers to adhering to work schedule assigned):

_____ 1. Is usually tardy or absent

_____ 2. Is often tardy or absent

_____ 3. Normally is not tardy or absent

_____ 4. Makes a point of being on the job and on time

_____ 5. Is extremely conscientious about attendance

Responsibility (refers to completing assignments and projects):

_____ 1. Usually does not assume responsibility for completing assignments

_____ 2. Is at times reluctant to accept delegated responsibility

_____ 3. Accepts and discharges delegated duties willingly

_____ 4. Accepts additional responsibility

_____ 5. Is a self-starter who seeks out more effective ways to achieve results or seeks additional responsibilities

Cooperation with Others (refers to working and communicating with supervisors and co-workers):

_____ 1. Has difficulty working with others and often complains when given assignments

_____ 2. Sometimes has difficulty working with others and often complains when given assignments

_____ 3. Usually is agreeable and obliging; generally helps out when requested

_____ 4. Works well with others; welcomes assignments and is quick to offer assistance

_____ 5. Is an outstanding team worker; always assists others and continually encourages cooperation by setting an excellent example

Performance Summary (include strong areas and areas for future emphasis in improving performance or developing additional job skills):

Employee Comments or Concerns:

Signatures:

Human Resource Manager _____ Date _____

Employee _____ Date _____

Supervisor _____ Date _____

example, bank tellers may be rated according to their speed in handling customer transactions, their quality (accuracy) in handling money transactions, and their ability to satisfy customers. The speed may be monitored by supervisors over time, while accuracy is measured by balancing the accounts at the end of each day, and customer satisfaction is measured from customer feedback over time.

The different criteria must also be weighted separately because some of the employee's assignments may be considered more important than others. Using our example, assume that the weights are determined as follows:

Speed in handling customer transactions	30%
Accuracy in handling customer transactions	50%
Satisfying customers	<u>20%</u>
	100%

The sum of the weights of all criteria should be 100 percent. The weighting system should be communicated to employees when they begin a job position so that they understand what characteristics are most important within the evaluation.

To demonstrate how an overall performance measure is derived, assume that in our example the supervisor rated the bank teller as shown in Exhibit 11.9. The overall rating is the weighted average of 4.5; this rating is between "above average" and "outstanding." Other bank tellers could also be periodically rated in this manner. At the end of each year, the ratings may be used to determine the raise for each teller. The ratings may also be reviewed along with other characteristics (such as experience) when the employees are considered for a promotion.

This system of developing an overall rating is more appropriate when a few key criteria can be used to assess an employee throughout a period. When employees have numerous job assignments, however, accounting for all types of assignments within the performance evaluation is more difficult. Nevertheless, some of the assignments may be combined into a single characteristic, such as "customer service" or "ability to complete tasks on time."

Some supervisors may believe that a weighted system is too structured and does not account for some relevant characteristics, such as ability to get along with other employees. Nevertheless, characteristics like these could be included within the weighting system.

Exhibit 11.9

Developing an Overall Rating

Characteristic	Rating	Weight	Weighted Rating
Speed in handling customer transactions	4 (above average)	30%	$4 \times 30\% = 1.2$
Accuracy in handling customer transactions	5 (outstanding)	50%	$5 \times 50\% = 2.5$
Satisfying customers	4 (above average)	20%	$4 \times 20\% = \underline{.8}$

Overall rating = 4.5

Cross Functional Teamwork

How Job Responsibilities across Business Functions Can Complicate Performance Evaluations

Firms have increasingly encouraged employees to perform a variety of business functions to achieve higher levels of job satisfaction and efficiency. Although this form of job enlargement has been successful, it can complicate the evaluation of an employee's performance. Consider an employee of a sporting goods store whose only responsibility is stringing tennis rackets. The performance of this employee is judged by the number of tennis rackets strung and the quality of the stringing (as measured by customer feedback).

The employee's responsibilities are then enlarged to include visiting country clubs and selling tennis rackets to them. Whereas the employee's initial job focused on as-

sembly of tennis rackets, the enlarged responsibilities involve marketing the tennis rackets. Furthermore, other employees are also involved in stringing rackets and making sales calls to country clubs.

The performance evaluation of the employee has become more complicated for two reasons. First, more than one task now must be assessed. Second, other employees are also involved in completing these tasks, which makes it difficult to measure one employee's individual contribution. That is, a firm can easily assess the performance of a team of employees, but it cannot easily assess the performance of each employee within the team.

Steps for Proper Performance Evaluation

Firms can follow specific steps for performance evaluation that demonstrate fairness and recognition of employees' rights and also satisfy legal guidelines:

1. Supervisors should communicate job responsibilities to employees when they are hired. Supervisors should also communicate any changes in employee job responsibilities over time. This communication can be done orally, but it should be backed up with a letter to the employee. The letters are not as personal as oral communication, but they provide documentation in case a disagreement arises in the future about assignments and responsibilities. The letters may not only provide support to defend against employee lawsuits, but they also force supervisors to pinpoint the specific tasks for employees in a particular job position.

2. When supervisors notice that employees have deficiencies, they should inform the employees of those deficiencies. This communication may occur in the form of a standard periodic review. Supervisors may prefer to inform employees of deficiencies immediately, rather than wait for the review period. Employees should be given a chance to respond to the criticism. Supervisors may also allow a short period of time for employees to correct the deficiencies. Supervisors should also communicate with employees who were evaluated favorably so that those employees recognize that their efforts are appreciated.

3. Supervisors should be consistent when conducting performance evaluations. That is, two employees who have a similar deficiency should be treated equally in the evaluation process. Many supervisors find it

easier to communicate deficiencies to employees who are more willing to accept criticism, but it is only fair to treat employees with the same deficiencies similarly.

Action Due to Performance Evaluations

Some performance evaluations require supervisors to take action. Employees who receive a very favorable evaluation may deserve some type of recognition or even a promotion. If supervisors do not acknowledge such outstanding performance, employees may either lose their enthusiasm and reduce their effort or search for a new job at a firm that will reward them for high performance. Supervisors should acknowledge high performance so that the employee will continue to perform well in the future.

Employees who receive unfavorable evaluations must also be given attention. Supervisors must determine the reasons for poor performance. Some reasons (such as a family illness) may have a temporary adverse impact on performance and can be corrected. Other reasons, such as a bad attitude, may not be temporary. When supervisors give employees an unfavorable evaluation, they must decide whether to take any additional actions. If the employees were unaware of their own deficiencies, the unfavorable evaluation can pinpoint the deficiencies that employees must correct. In this case, the supervisor may simply need to monitor the employees closely and ensure that the deficiencies are corrected.

If the employees were already aware of their deficiencies before the evaluation period, however, they may be unable or unwilling to correct them. This situation is more serious, and the supervisor may need to take action. The action should be consistent with the firm's guidelines and may include reassigning the employees to new jobs, suspending them temporarily, or firing them. A supervisor's action toward a poorly performing worker can affect the attitudes of other employees. If no penalty is imposed on an employee for poor performance, other employees may react by reducing their productivity as well.

Firms must follow certain procedures to fire an employee. These procedures are intended to prevent firms from firing employees without reason. Specifically, supervisors should identify deficiencies in employees' evaluations and give them a chance to respond.

Dealing with Lawsuits by Fired Employees

It is not uncommon for employees to sue the firm after being fired. Some lawsuits argue that the plaintiff—the fired employee—did not receive due process. Others argue that the firing occurred because of discrimination based on race, gender, age, religion, or national origin. Many firms with numerous employees have been sued for this reason, even when their supervisors have followed all proper procedures. Complaints of discrimination are first filed with the Equal Employment Opportunity Commission (EEOC), which is responsible for enforcing the discrimination laws. About 20 percent of the complaints filed with the EEOC are judged to state a reasonable cause for the fired employee to take action, while 80 percent of the complaints are considered to have no reasonable basis. Even when the EEOC believes the complaint is not valid, however, the fired employee can still sue the firm. Although the laws that prohibit discrimination have good intentions, the court system has not effectively separated the frivolous cases from the valid ones. Consequently, legal expenses for many firms have risen substantially.

Two other factors have also contributed to the surge of employee lawsuits in recent years. First, as of 1991, plaintiffs have a right to a trial by jury. Juries are commonly perceived to be more sympathetic toward plaintiffs than judges are. Also, juries are perceived as more unpredictable, which can be a concern for firms that are sued by employees. A second reason for the rise in lawsuits is that as a result of the Civil Rights Act of 1991, plaintiffs can be awarded not only compensatory damages (such as back pay) but also punitive damages (to penalize the firm) and legal expenses. Therefore, plaintiffs and their attorneys can now receive much larger amounts of money.

Recognizing that employee lawsuits can be very costly, some firms have attempted to settle lawsuits before trial to reduce their legal expenses and avoid negative publicity. However, settling a lawsuit that has no merit may result in other frivolous lawsuits by employees.

Furthermore, a firm should not ignore an employee's deficiencies out of fear that the employee will sue. Doing so will reduce the motivation of other employees when they notice that one employee is receiving special treatment. Despite the increase in employee lawsuits, firms must still attempt to ensure that their employees are doing the jobs that they are paid to do. While firms cannot necessarily avoid employee lawsuits, they can attempt to establish training and performance evaluation guidelines that will reduce the chances of lawsuits or increase their chances of winning if a suit does occur. The court system has generally sided with firms in cases in which supervisors followed proper procedures in firing employees.

Employee Evaluation of Supervisors

upward appraisals
used to measure the managerial abilities of supervisors

Some firms allow employees to evaluate their supervisors. The evaluations can then be used to measure the managerial abilities of the supervisors. These so-called **upward appraisals** have been used by many firms, including AT&T and Dow Chemical. An upward evaluation is more effective if it is anonymous. Otherwise, workers may automatically submit a very favorable evaluation either in the hope that their supervisor will return the favor or to avoid retaliation. Evaluations of the supervisor may identify deficiencies, which can then be corrected so that the supervisor can more effectively manage employees in the future. The evaluation form should allow each criterion to be evaluated separately so that the supervisor can recognize which characteristics need to be improved.

Decision Making

Evaluating Employees

The manner in which a firm should assess the performance of its employees is dependent on its specific characteristics. To illustrate, consider Web Czar Company. The Web design specialists (website designers) evaluate the technicians who work for them based on the speed at which the technicians complete their assigned tasks and the quality of their work. The Web design specialists are evaluated according to the speed at which they complete website designs and the quality of their work. The quality is measured by a survey of the businesses that hired Web Czar to design their websites. The customer service representatives who sell website design services to businesses are evaluated based on the amount of orders that they generate and how satisfied customers were with their service. All of the employees understand how they are rated and how they are compensated. As a result, they are motivated to perform well.

1. Explain how the process used by Web Czar Company for evaluating employees is related to its compensation system.

2. Explain how the process used by Web Czar Company to evaluate its employees affects the motivation of the employees.

ANSWERS: 1. The evaluations influence the compensation paid. 2. Because the employees understand how they are assessed and realize that they will receive a better evaluation if they exert more effort, they are motivated to work harder.

COLLEGE HEALTH CLUB: DEVELOPING EMPLOYEE SKILLS AND EVALUATING PERFORMANCE AT CHC

Sue Kramer realizes that if her employees are trained properly, they will serve the members better, and the members will be more satisfied with the health club.

Therefore, she plans to focus her employee training on three areas. First, when she hires her part-time employees, she will stress the need for safety. She wants to ensure that each employee understands the potential dangers in using the weight and exercise machines. Sue will provide all of her members with a booklet on safety, but she also wants her employees to understand the safety features so that they can help any members who are not using the machines properly. Second, Sue wants to make sure that her employees understand the importance of customer relations, especially in a service business like a health club. Third, she plans to emphasize human relations skills by explaining the need for the part-time employees to work together.

As Sue tries to decide on a method for evaluating the performance of her employees, she again recognizes that a key role of the employees is to satisfy CHC's members. Therefore, she will rate each employee's customer relations skills. To obtain feedback from members about CHC's services, Sue is asking them to complete survey forms. The survey forms will ask the members if they have any comments about the individual employees. In addition, Sue will rate employees according to how well they work with other employees. Now that she has identified the specific criteria to be used to evaluate the employees, she will communicate these criteria to the employees when she hires them so that they know how they will be evaluated. She will also remind them of these criteria during the training in customer relations and human relations skills.

Summary

1 The main functions involved in human resource planning are

▶ forecasting human resource needs;

▶ job analysis, which determines the tasks the job position involves and the credentials necessary to qualify for the position; and

▶ recruiting, which involves screening applicants and deciding who to hire.

2 When recruiting, managers should ensure that they provide equal opportunity to all applicants. Some very well-known firms have made much progress in achieving diversity in recent years. Diversity can benefit firms because it may encourage innovation, it allows for different points of view, and a larger proportion of eligible employees will be from minority groups in the future.

3 Compensation packages offered by firms can include salary, stock options, commissions, bonuses, profit sharing, employee benefits, and perquisites.

4 After firms hire employees, they commonly provide training to enhance technical skills, decision-making skills, customer service skills, safety skills, and human relations skills.

5 The performance of employees can be evaluated by segmenting the evaluation into different criteria, assigning an evaluation rating to each criterion, and weighting each criterion. The overall performance rating is the weighted average of all criteria that were assigned a rating.

Once supervisors evaluate employees, they should discuss the evaluations with the employees and identify any specific strengths, as well as any specific weaknesses that need to be improved.

How the Chapter Concepts Affect Business Performance

A firm's decisions regarding the human resource concepts summarized here affect its performance. A firm's employees are often its most valuable resource. Effective human resource planning allows the firm to anticipate job needs on time. Providing equal opportunity for job positions allows the most qualified people to attain the job positions. Providing proper forms of compensation can motivate employees. Proper training can ensure that the employees have the skills to perform well. An effective system for evaluating employees and tying compensation to the evaluations can motivate employees to perform well.

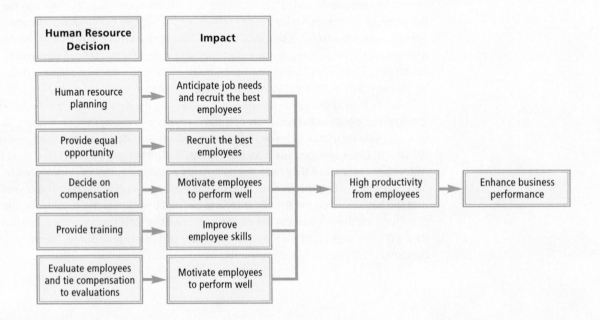

Key Terms

bonus   411
boycott (chap. appendix)   438
commissions   411
compensation package   408
craft unions (chap. appendix)   435
employee benefits   411
employment test   402
external recruiting   400
human resource manager   398
human resource planning   398
industrial unions
   (chap. appendix)   435
injunction (chap. appendix)   439
internal recruiting   399
international unions
   (chap. appendix)   435

job analysis   398
job description   398
job specification   398
labor union (chap. appendix)   435
Landrum-Griffin Act
   (chap. appendix)   436
local unions (chap. appendix)   435
lockout (chap. appendix)   439
national unions
   (chap. appendix)   435
Norris-LaGuardia Act
   (chap. appendix)   436
perquisites   413
picketing (chap. appendix)   438
profit sharing   411
promotion   400

right-to-work
   (chap. appendix)   436
salary   408
stock options   409
strike (chap. appendix)   438
Taft-Hartley Act
   (chap. appendix)   436
upward appraisals   424
Wagner Act (chap. appendix)   436
yellow-dog contract
   (chap. appendix)   436

Review & Critical Thinking Questions

1. Describe the tasks involved in developing a human resource plan.

2. What is the purpose of a job analysis? What two documents can be developed from a job analysis?

3. Distinguish internal recruiting from external recruiting.

4. Describe the steps involved in the recruiting process to screen job applicants.

5. Describe the various types of compensation packages that could be offered to employees.

6. Discuss the types of skills that an employee could develop from a firm's training program.

7. How can segmenting an evaluation into different criteria help a supervisor pinpoint specific strengths and weaknesses of an employee's job performance?

8. Why has the number of employee lawsuits that claim discrimination increased in recent years? How should a firm deal with these lawsuits?

9. How can striving for diversity enhance the value of firms?

10. What is the purpose of an upward appraisal? How should such an appraisal be conducted?

11. How can stock options cause a conflict of interest between shareholders and the firm's managers? What can the board of directors do to minimize such conflicts of interest?

12. How can management reduce employees' need for union representation? (See the chapter appendix.)

13. Despite the drawbacks, why might managers prefer to engage in external recruiting rather than internal recruiting?

14. Why is it important to provide adequate compensation and training to employees?

15. Why should employees be wary of top-level executives who are paid primarily in stock options?

16. Why are employee evaluations of supervisors important?

17. What is the difference between objective and subjective evaluation criteria? Which work better, and why?

Discussion Questions

1. You are a human resource manager and have been assigned to develop a compensation policy with supplemental pay benefits for your employees. What benefit do you think employees most desire today?

2. You are a manager and have an employee with three years' work experience who refuses to be retrained. This employee further refuses to discuss his performance appraisal with you. What should your next step be?

3. How could a firm use the Internet to attract new employees? How could it use the Internet to evaluate existing employees?

4. You have just opened a Jeep Cherokee dealership. Which of your employees would be paid salaries? Which would be paid hourly wages? Which would receive commissions and/or perquisites?

5. You know your firm's chief financial officer (CFO). She just told you that she will sell her shares of the company's stock as soon as possible and advises you to do the same. What do you think this indicates? What do you think you should do?

6. You are a manager in a company where a group of workers have petitioned for union representation. What factors would cause workers to do this? What can managers do to reduce the possibility that workers will vote in favor of union representation? (See the chapter appendix.)

7. You are the manager of a manufacturing plant. What kinds of evaluation criteria would you use to evaluate employees? How would you go about setting up the evaluation process so that all employees know where they stand?

8. What are the tradeoffs inherent in continuous employee training or morale building?

9. You are a board member who is not employed by the firm. You are on the compensation committee and must come up with a compensation plan for the CEO of the company. What criteria would you consider?

10. You have an employee who feels that her manager discriminated against her in not promoting her to a higher position. What could you have done to minimize the risk of a lawsuit?

IT'S YOUR DECISION: HIRING AND EVALUATING EMPLOYEES AT CHC

1. Should Sue Kramer require job applicants at CHC to take drug tests?

2. What criteria can Sue use to measure the performance of an aerobics instructor that she hires?

3. What steps should Sue take if an employee she hires performs poorly?

4. Employees at CHC have various tasks, such as responding to members' requests for help using exercise machines (this is a production task) and showing prospective members around the club (this is a marketing task). If Sue creates a bonus plan that offers a bonus to any employee who signs up new members, why might the production quality decline?

5. A health club differs from manufacturing firms in that it produces a service rather than products. Explain why a bonus plan for high performance may be more difficult to implement in a service firm such as CHC than for a manufacturing firm.

Investing in a Business

Using the annual report of the firm in which you would like to invest, complete the following:

1. Does the firm periodically provide special training to its employees? If so, provide details.

2. Does the firm offer bonuses to its employees as an incentive? If so, are the bonuses tied to employee performance? Provide details.

3. Does the firm offer any other programs that are designed to achieve employee satisfaction, such as a flexible work schedule? If so, provide details.

4. Explain how the business uses technology to hire, train, and evaluate employees. For example, does it use the Internet to provide information about job openings or its compensation programs?

5. Go to http://hoovers.com and locate the NEWS SEARCH. Type in the name of the firm in the space provided, and review the recent news stories about the firm. Summarize any (at least one) recent news story about the firm that applies to one or more of the key concepts in this chapter.

Case: Filling Job Positions

George DeCaro, a human resource manager of Bobcat International, a manufacturer of bobcats, has just received a directive from the president of the company. The directive reads: "We have just completed our strategy for the year. The thrust of this strategy is to increase our market share by 22 percent over the next three years." It continues: "We must be ready for this challenge by increasing production, and the human resource department must staff the organization with 37 new jobs."

George's task is to forecast job requirements each year for the next three years. George recognizes that both internal and external recruiting will have to be undertaken. The firm's philosophy is to promote from within whenever possible. This procedure promotes high morale and contributes to the overall success of the organization. However, most of the 37 jobs will have to be filled externally. He ponders the sources for recruiting potential job candidates for semiskilled plant jobs that pay an hourly rate.

Another consideration for George is diversity. Bobcat is currently not very diversified, and George contem-

plates whether the externally filled positions should be used to increase Bobcat's diversity.

George works well with the firm's president and wants to request a meeting to demonstrate how the human resource department will perform a vital role in helping the firm meet its objectives.

Questions

1. What is the human resource plan in this case? Discuss its major tasks.

2. What is job analysis in general? How should it be used in this case?

3. Discuss George's sources for recruiting potential employees for the plant jobs.

4. What should be on George's agenda for the meeting with the company's president?

5. How could Bobcat benefit from a more diverse workforce?

Video Case: Recruiting and Training at Valassis Communications

Valassis Communications, Inc., a leader in the sales promotion industry, creates promotional inserts for newspapers. Employee selection is vital to Valassis, which attributes much of its success to its employees. It considers hiring the right people to be the most important aspect of management. Its human resource department is very selective when it evaluates job candidates. Because the company wants employees who fit into its organizational culture, the department also tests applicants in various ways to determine whether they would fit into the company environment. Applicants who can be assigned goals and are motivated to meet them are more likely to be satisfied working at Valassis. Once hired,

employees who perform well are rewarded well so that Valassis can retain the best employees. For more information, visit http://www.valassis.com.

Questions

1 What kind of corporate culture does Valassis have?

2 Why does Valassis spend so much time and money on interviewing job applicants?

3 What could go wrong if Valassis did not recruit the right employees?

Internet Applications

1. http://www.careerbuilder.com

How does this website benefit employees seeking jobs? How does it benefit potential employers? Click on "job search." Search for a job category of your choice in your geographic area. Would you post your résumé on this website? Why or why not?

2. http://www.dol.gov

What does this site tell you about labor standards in the United States? How could you use this website to iden-

tify rules that the government has established regarding labor laws?

3. http://www.eeoc.gov

What does this site tell you about equal opportunity hiring practices that encourage diversity? Click on "discriminatory practices." Under which laws and in which aspects of employment are employers prohibited from discriminating?

Dell's Secret to Success

Go to http://www.reportgallery.com and review Dell's most recent annual report. Also, go to Dell's website (http://www.dell.com) and in the section "about Dell," review the background material about Dell that relates to this chapter.

Questions

1 Describe Dell's success in achieving a diverse workplace.

2 How do you think diversity has resulted in higher performance at Dell?

3 Do you think Dell benefits from providing options to buy its stock at a low price as partial compensation to employees?

In-Text Study Guide

Answers are in Appendix C at the back of book.

True or False

1. Job analysis represents the forecasting of a firm's employee needs.

2. One task of human resource planning is recruiting.

3. Firms tend to avoid hiring new full-time workers to meet temporary needs for higher production levels.

4. A job specification states the credentials necessary to qualify for the position.

5. Federal laws make it illegal to discriminate on the basis of factors not related to potential job performance.

6. Employee benefits such as health insurance and dental insurance are taxed.

7. Firms should offer the same compensation package to their workers in foreign countries that they offer to employees in their home country.

8. The overall performance evaluation of most employees is based on multiple criteria.

9. Employees perceive performance evaluation as a method for allocating wage increases.

10. Each of the performance criteria must be weighted equally to avoid unbalancing the performance appraisal.

Multiple Choice

11. The document that specifies credentials necessary to qualify for the job position is a:
    a) job specification.
    b) job description.
    c) job analysis.
    d) job evaluation.
    e) performance evaluation.

12. A major responsibility of a human resource manager is to:
    a) help each specific department recruit candidates for its open positions.
    b) conduct the performance evaluations for all employees.
    c) establish the information system and local area network used by the firm's employees.
    d) help select the members of top management who will serve on the firm's board of directors.
    e) prevent the formation of labor unions.

13. The tasks and responsibilities of a job position are disclosed in a(n):
    a) job specification.
    b) indenture agreement.
    c) job description.
    d) organization chart.
    e) staffing report.

14. The process used to determine the tasks and the necessary credentials for a particular position is referred to as:
    a) job analysis.
    b) job screening.
    c) human resource planning.
    d) human resource forecasting.
    e) recruiting.

15. Human resource planning includes all of the following tasks except:
    a) designing the appropriate compensation package.
    b) performing job analysis.
    c) forecasting employment needs.
    d) recruiting.

In-Text Study Guide

Answers are in Appendix C at the back of book.

16. If firms wish to avoid hiring during a temporary increase in production, they can offer _____ to existing workers.
    a) overtime
    b) vacations
    c) training programs
    d) affirmative action
    e) orientation programs

17. When a firm attempts to fill job openings with persons it already employs, it is engaging in:
    a) intrapreneurship.
    b) internal recruiting.
    c) entrenchment.
    d) precruiting.
    e) focused recruiting.

18. A(n) _____ is an assignment to a higher-level job with more responsibility and greater pay.
    a) transfer
    b) lateral assignment
    c) perquisite
    d) upward appraisal
    e) promotion

19. A firm's human resource manager can obtain detailed information about the applicant's past work experience through a(n):
    a) employment test.
    b) physical exam.
    c) interview.
    d) orientation program.
    e) job analysis.

20. A step in the recruiting process that involves screening applicants is the:
    a) training procedure.
    b) orientation procedure.
    c) upward appraisal.
    d) interview.
    e) probation period.

21. All of the following are advantages of diversity in the workplace except:
    a) increased innovation.
    b) less chance of discrimination lawsuits.
    c) enhanced ability to interact with customers.
    d) better access to the pool of eligible employees.
    e) a change in the production process.

22. A company gives employees the right to purchase its stock at a specified price when it provides them with:
    a) presumptive rights.
    b) an indenture agreement.
    c) stock options.
    d) a stock preference.
    e) a closed-end agreement.

23. The use of stock options as a means of compensation:
    a) legally can be provided only to top executives and members of the board of directors.
    b) is declining in popularity since options reduce the firm's profits.
    c) is opposed by labor unions, since options are available only to nonunion employees.
    d) may tempt managers to manipulate financial statements to boost stock prices.
    e) has allowed workers in many firms to control who serves on the board of directors of their firm.

24. The case of Enron and other corporate scandals shows that managers who receive stock options may be tempted to do all of the following except:
    a) magnify company expenses.
    b) manipulate the stock price.
    c) exaggerate company earnings.
    d) issue overly optimistic reports.
    e) withhold bad news.

In-Text Study Guide

25. An extra onetime payment at the end of a period in which performance was measured is a:
    a) salary.
    b) wage.
    c) stock option.
    d) piece rate.
    e) bonus.

26. _____ normally represent compensation for achieving specific sales objectives and often are part of the compensation received by people working in sales positions.
    a) Pensions
    b) Commissions
    c) Perquisites
    d) Stock options
    e) Dividends

27. Additional privileges given to high-level employees, such as a company car or membership in an exclusive club, are known as:
    a) professional privileges.
    b) commissions.
    c) executive options.
    d) perquisites.
    e) golden parachutes.

28. _____ are additional privileges, such as paid vacation time and health and dental insurance, given to most or all employees.
    a) Employee benefits
    b) Perquisites
    c) Commissions
    d) Implicit compensations
    e) Kickbacks

29. Employees who are directly involved in the production process (such as assembly-line workers) tend to receive most of their compensation in the form of a:
    a) bonus.
    b) commission.
    c) salary.
    d) stock option.
    e) perquisite.

30. If a manager is having difficulties managing his or her subordinates, _____ would be recommended.
    a) human relations training
    b) safety skills training
    c) decision-making skill training
    d) customer service training
    e) technical training

31. A performance evaluation:
    a) should avoid subjective criteria because they are impossible to measure with any accuracy.
    b) is only useful as a means of determining whether employees qualify for pay raises.
    c) is typically based on multiple criteria, some of which are objective while others are subjective.
    d) is only necessary for workers who are likely candidates for higher-level positions.
    e) should be given only to workers who are experiencing job-related problems.

32. The following are objective criteria in performance evaluation except for:
    a) parts produced per week.
    b) number of days absent.
    c) percentage of deadlines missed.
    d) defective parts produced by employee errors.
    e) willingness of an employee to help other employees.

In-Text Study Guide

Answers are in Appendix C at the back of book.

33. If an employee receives a poor performance appraisal, the first action that should be taken is:
    a) communicating the performance criteria to the employee.
    b) terminating the employee.
    c) determining the reasons for poor performance.
    d) suspending the employee.
    e) reassigning the employee.

34. When firms allow employees to evaluate their supervisors, this process is known as a(n):
    a) management audit.
    b) upward appraisal.
    c) forward appraisal.
    d) peer review.
    e) executive evaluation.

35. When employees evaluate their supervisors, the results are likely to be more meaningful if the appraisal is done:
    a) verbally, with nothing put in writing.
    b) without the supervisor's knowledge.
    c) no more than once every two years.
    d) anonymously.
    e) only by employees who have known the supervisor for more than two years.

36. Lawsuits against firms by fired employees:
    a) have become much less common in recent years.
    b) allow the fired employees to collect compensatory damages, but not punitive damages.
    c) are decided by a judge rather than a jury.
    d) usually should be settled out of court as soon as possible to avoid negative publicity.
    e) are usually settled in favor of the firm if supervisors followed proper procedures when firing the employees.

Chapter 11 Appendix
Labor Unions

GETTY IMAGES

A **labor union** is established to represent the views, needs, and concerns of labor. A union can attempt to determine the needs of its workers and then negotiate with the firm's management to satisfy those needs. The needs may include job security, safer working conditions, and higher salaries. The union may be able to negotiate for the workers better than they can themselves, because the workers do not have the time or the expertise for negotiating with management. Furthermore, management would not have the time to deal with each worker's needs separately. The union serves as the representative for all workers.

Background on Unions

Unions can be classified as either craft or industrial. **Craft unions** are organized according to a specific craft (or trade), such as plumbing. **Industrial unions** are organized for a specific industry. Unions can also be classified as either local or national. **Local unions** are composed of members in a specified local area. **National unions** are composed of members throughout the country. Some local unions are part of a national union. **International unions** have members in several countries.

History of Union Activities

The popularity of unions has been affected by various laws, summarized next.

labor union
an association established to represent the views, needs, and concerns of labor

craft unions
unions organized according to a specific craft (or trade), such as plumbing

industrial unions
unions organized for a specific industry

local unions
unions composed of members in a specified local area

national unions
unions composed of members throughout the country

international unions
unions that have members in several countries

The Norris-LaGuardia Act   Before 1932, the courts commonly accommodated employer requests to issue injunctions against unions. In 1932, Congress passed the **Norris-LaGuardia Act,** which restricted the use of injunctions against unions and allowed unions to publicize a labor dispute. It also prohibited employers from forcing workers to sign a **yellow-dog contract,** which was a contract requiring employees to refrain from joining a union as a condition of employment.

The Wagner Act   Even with the Norris-LaGuardia Act, firms were able to discourage employees from joining or organizing unions. The **Wagner Act** (also referred to as the National Labor Relations Act) prohibited firms from interfering with workers' efforts to organize or join unions. Employers could not discriminate against employees who participated in union activities. In addition, the act required employers to negotiate with the union representing employees.

The Taft-Hartley Act   Although the Wagner Act reduced employer discrimination against union participants, it was unable to reduce the number of strikes. The **Taft-Hartley Act,** an amendment to the Wagner Act, prohibited unions from pressuring employees to join. An exception is the union

Norris-LaGuardia Act
restricted the use of injunctions against unions and allowed unions to publicize a labor dispute

yellow-dog contract
a contract requiring employees to refrain from joining a union as a condition of employment

Wagner Act
prohibited firms from interfering with workers' efforts to organize or join unions

Taft-Hartley Act
an amendment to the Wagner Act that prohibited unions from pressuring employees to join

right-to-work
allows states to prohibit union shops

Landrum-Griffin Act
required labor unions to specify in their bylaws the membership eligibility requirements, dues, and collective bargaining procedures

shop, where new employees are required to join the union. The **right-to-work** section of this act allows states to prohibit union shops (several states have used this power).

The Landrum-Griffin Act   In 1959, Congress passed the **Landrum-Griffin Act** (originally called the Labor-Management Reporting and Disclosure Act of 1959). This act required labor unions to specify in their bylaws the membership eligibility requirements, dues, and collective bargaining procedures.

Trends in Union Popularity

Union membership declined slightly in the early 1930s, as firms discouraged workers from participating in labor activities. After the Wagner Act was passed in 1935, union membership increased rapidly. By 1945, more than one-fourth of all workers were union members. During the 1980s and 1990s, however, union membership consistently declined. By 2000, less than 12 percent of all workers were union members. One of the reasons for the decline was the inability of some unionized firms to compete with nonunion firms whose expenses were lower.

Negotiations between Unions and Management

Contracts between unions and management commonly last for two to three years. An attempt is made to agree to a new contract before the existing contract expires. The union obtains feedback from its members on what working conditions need to be improved. The union also obtains data on existing wages and employee benefits provided for jobs similar to those of members. Management assesses existing conditions and determines the types of provisions it may be willing to make.

Before the actual negotiations begin, the union may offer a proposed revision of the existing contract. This proposal often includes very high demands, which management will surely refuse. Management may also offer a proposed revision of the existing contract that the union will surely refuse. Normally, the original gap between the two sides is very large. This establishes the foundation for negotiations.

When the union and management meet to negotiate a new contract, the more critical issues to be discussed include the following:

▶ Salaries

▶ Job security

▶ Management rights

▶ Grievance procedures

Salaries

A general concern of unions is to improve or at least maintain their members' standard of living. Unions are credited for negotiating high wages for their members. Unionized grocery store employees commonly receive at least double the salaries of nonunionized employees in the same job positions. Airline pilot captains of unionized airlines, such as American and

Delta, earn more than $100,000 per year, while pilot captains of non-unionized airlines commonly earn less than $50,000 per year.

Unions attempt to negotiate for salary increases that will at least match expected increases in the cost of living. They also monitor salaries of workers at other firms to determine the salary increases that they will request. For example, the United Auto Workers (UAW) commonly uses the content of its contract with one car manufacturer to negotiate its new contract with another car manufacturer.

If the firm has experienced high profits in recent years, a union may use this as reason to negotiate for large wage increases. Conversely, firms that recently experienced losses will argue that they cannot afford to make pay increases. When pilots at Continental Airlines did not receive a salary increase over several years, poor relations developed between the pilots and management at Continental.

Job Security

Job security is a key issue from the perspective of workers. They want to be assured of a job until retirement. Management may not be willing to guarantee job security but may at least specify the conditions under which workers will be laid off. Workers with less seniority are more likely to be laid off.

Although unions are unable to force management to guarantee lifetime jobs, they are somewhat successful at obtaining supplemental unemployment benefits for workers. Firms that offer these benefits contribute an amount for each hour worked into a fund. The fund is used to compensate workers who are laid off. This compensation is a supplement to the normal unemployment compensation workers receive.

Unions may also attempt to prevent management from replacing workers with machines. Management may agree to such demands if the unions reduce some of their other demands. Unions emphasize this issue in industries such as automobile manufacturing, where some tasks are highly repetitive and therefore workers are more likely to be replaced by machines.

For some workers, job security may be more important than higher wages. Therefore, firms that are willing to provide job security may not have to provide large increases in wages.

Management Rights

Management expects to have various rights as to how it manages its workers. For example, the union-management contract may state a specified number of work hours. Management may also retain the rights to make hiring, promotional, and transferring decisions without influence by unions.

Grievance Procedures

A grievance is a complaint made by an employee or the union. Contracts between a union and management specify procedures for resolving a grievance. The first step normally calls for a meeting between the employee, his or her supervisor, and a union representative. If this meeting does not resolve the grievance, the union normally meets with high-level managers.

Conflicts between Unions and Management

Unions use various methods to bargain for better working conditions or higher compensation. Employees may attempt to pressure management by **picketing,** or walking around near the employer's building with signs complaining of poor working conditions. Employees can also **boycott** the products and services offered by refusing to purchase them.

picketing
walking around near the employer's building with signs complaining of poor working conditions

boycott
refusing to purchase products and services

strike
a discontinuation of employee services

Labor Strikes

A more dramatic method of bargaining is a **strike,** which is a discontinuation of employee services. Two recent well-publicized strikes were those by employees at UPS and at General Motors. The goal of the UPS strike was to achieve better wages. The objective of the General Motors strike was to ensure that some of GM's plants would not be closed.

The impact of a strike on a firm depends on the firm's ability to carry on operations during the strike. For example, if all machinists of a manufacturing firm strike, the firm's production will be severely reduced unless its other workers can substitute. Most firms carry an inventory of finished products that may be used to accommodate orders during the strike. However, even a large inventory will not be sufficient if the strike lasts long enough.

The publicity of a strike can reduce a firm's perceived credibility. Even though a strike is only temporary, it can create permanent damage. Some firms have long-term arrangements with other companies to provide a specified volume of supplies periodically. If these companies fear that their orders will not be satisfied because of a strike, they will search for a firm that is less likely to experience a strike.

To illustrate how the dissatisfaction of employees can affect a firm's value, consider the case of Caterpillar. About 14,000 of Caterpillar's workers went on strike on June 21, 1994. Exhibit 11.A1 shows the stock price of Caterpillar around the time of the strike. Notice how the stock price declined by more than $4 per share in response to the strike. The strike lasted more than 17 months. Caterpillar replaced many of the strikers with temporary workers and experienced record earnings over the strike period. By

Exhibit 11.A1

Example of How a Strike Can Affect a Firm's Value

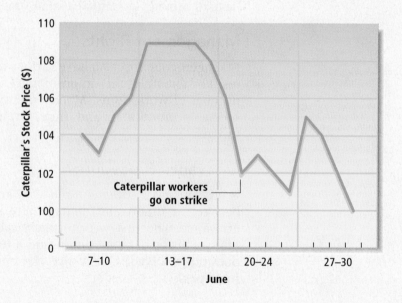

the end of the strike, about one-third of the strikers returned to work without any compromise by Caterpillar.

Management's Response to Strikes

injunction
a court order to prevent a union from a particular activity such as picketing

lockout
prevents employees from working until an agreement between management and labor is reached

Management may respond to union pressure by obtaining an **injunction,** which is a court order to prevent the union from a particular activity such as picketing. Alternatively, it could use a **lockout,** which prevents employees from working until an agreement between management and labor is reached.

Another common response by management is to show how large benefits to workers will possibly result in the firm's failure, which would effectively terminate all jobs. The management of Northwest Airlines and US Air (now US Airways) used this approach in the mid-1990s to prevent excessive demands by the union. In 2005, Delta Airlines and Northwest Airlines used this strategy. Some airlines have recently offered its pilots partial ownership of the firm in place of salary increases.

The amount of bargaining power a union has is partially dependent on whether the firm can easily replace employees who go on strike. For example, an airline cannot easily replace pilots in a short period of time because of the extensive training needed. Other workers with specialized mechanical skills also have some bargaining power. When 33,000 machinists of Boeing (a producer of aircraft) went on strike in 1995, they forced Boeing to provide a larger salary increase as an incentive to end the strike. However, a strike by workers at Bridgestone/Firestone (a producer of tires) was not as successful, as the firm hired replacement workers.

Management's Criticism of Unions

Unions are criticized by management for several reasons, some of which are discussed here.

Higher Prices or Lower Profits If unions achieve high wages for employees, firms may pass the increase on to consumers in the form of higher prices. If firms do not pass the increase on, their profits may be reduced and the shareholders of the firm will be adversely affected. In essence, the disadvantages to the consumers or shareholders offset the benefits to employees.

A related criticism is that high wages resulting from the union can reduce the firm's ability to compete internationally. This was a major criticism during the 1980s, when many foreign competitors increased their market share in the United States.

Adverse Impact on Economic Conditions A decision to strike by some unions can severely damage a given industry. Unions have the power to close large manufacturing plants, shut down an airline's operations, or even halt garbage collection. Some shutdowns can have a severe impact on the local area.

Production Inefficiency Some unions have negotiated for a minimum number of workers to perform a specific task. In some cases, the number of workers has exceeded the number actually needed. A related criticism is that workers are sometimes perceived to be protected from being fired if they are in a union. A firm may be unwilling to fire an unproductive employee if it believes the union will file a grievance. If a firm retains unproductive workers, its efficiency is reduced, and its cost of production increases.

How Firms Reduce Employees' Desire for a Union

The management of some firms has consistently maintained good relations with labor. Consequently, labor has not attempted to organize a union. The following guidelines are some of the more common methods used to maintain good relations with employees:

1. Management should promote employees from within so that employees are satisfied with their career paths.

2. Management should attempt to avoid layoffs so that employees do not feel threatened whenever business slows down. This may be achieved by reassigning job positions to some employees who are no longer needed in their original positions.

3. Management should allow employees responsibility and input into some decisions. Labor contracts between labor and management may require labor-management committees to be created at each plant to develop methods for improving efficiency. This is a classic example of considering input from employees.

4. Management should maintain reasonable working conditions to demonstrate fairness to employees.

5. Management should offer reasonable and competitive wages so that employees feel properly rewarded and are not continually quitting to take other jobs.

The points just listed represent the key provisions for which unions negotiate. If the firm adheres to these guidelines, workers may not need to organize a union.

Summary/Part IV

Managing Employees

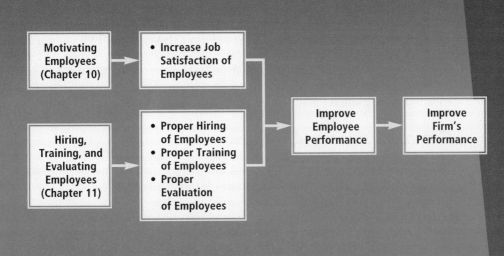

Developing the Human Resource Plan for Campus.com

Motivating Employees (related to Chapter 10)

In your business plan for Campus.com, describe how you can offer favorable working conditions (do not include compensation here) that will motivate the employees whom you may need to hire over time. That is, explain how you will ensure that employees help you achieve high performance and are willing to continue working at this business for several years. Identify any disadvantages of these methods that may limit their effectiveness.

Evaluating Employees (related to Chapter 11)

In your business plan for Campus.com, describe how you will assess the performance of your employees. How can you compensate the employees in a manner that will ensure that they will try to maximize the performance of the firm?

Communication and Teamwork

You (or your team) may be asked by your instructor to hand in and/or present the part of your business plan that relates to this part of the text.

Integrative Video Case: Effective Management (Café Pilon)

Café Pilon is the premier Cuban espresso company in the world. It is run by the third generation of the Soto family, who have been in the coffee roasting business since 1865. Pilon was a national brand of coffee in Cuba, and when the father started the business, he obtained financing from an investor and bought the Pilon name when the founder retired. The current members of the Soto family, who came to the United States from Cuba in 1965, attribute the success of their company to several factors, including hard work and perseverance. They initially went door to door winning business by giving away coffee. Now, 80 percent of the company's customers are grocery stores, and the other 20 percent are restaurants, cafés, and hospitals. Café Pilon also customizes orders for large customers who want a special blend. The company says that buying the right quality is more important than buying at the right price. Café Pilon uses the Internet to sell its coffee and attract new customers.

Questions

1 Explain how effective production of products by Pilon is related to marketing.

2 Explain why the reasons for Café Pilon's success may result in improved employee performance.

3 What does Café Pilon prize in its employees?

4 Why does the Soto family maintain the Pilon name on its coffees rather than using the name Soto?

The Stock Market Game

Check the performance of your investment.

Check Your Performance

1 What is the value of your stock investment today?

2 What is your return on your investment?

3 How does your return compare to those of other students? (This comparison tells you whether your stock's performance is relatively high or low.)

Explaining Your Stock Performance

Stock prices are frequently influenced by changes in the firm's management policies toward its employees, including new policies for awarding bonuses or other compensation. A stock's price may increase if such management policies are changed and investors expect the changes to improve the firm's performance. A stock's price can also decrease if the policy changes are expected to reduce the firm's performance. Review the latest news about your stocks.

1 Determine whether the price of your stock was affected (since you purchased it) as a result of the firm's motivation and personnel policy changes (the main topic in this part of the text).

2 Identify the specific change in managerial policies related to motivation or personnel decisions that caused the stock price to change.

3 Did the stock's price increase or decrease in response to the announcement of new policies related to employee motivation or personnel?

Running Your Own Business

1 How can you empower your employees so that they have an incentive to perform well?

2 Describe how you might encourage your employees to use teamwork.

3 Describe how each of the theories discussed in this part of the text would apply to your employees or yourself.

4 Develop a job description for the employees that you would need to hire for your business. Include the required education and skills within the job description.

5 Describe the training (if any) that you would have to provide to any employees you hire for your business.

6 Describe how you would compensate your employees. Would you offer bonuses as an incentive? If so, describe how you would determine the bonus.

7 Describe the criteria you would use to evaluate the performance of your employees.

8 Describe how you could use the Internet to attract new employees or to motivate existing employees.

Your Career in Business: *Pursuing a Major and a Career in Human Resources*

If you are very interested in the topics covered in this section, you may want to consider a major in Human Resources (sometimes referred to as "Personnel Management"). Some of the courses commonly taken by Human Resource majors are summarized here.

Common Courses for Human Resource Majors

▶ *Organizational Behavior*—Provides a broad overview of key managerial functions, such as organizing, motivating employees, planning, controlling, and teamwork.

▶ *Management Environment*—Focuses on the environment in which managers work and the responsibilities of managers to society and to regulators.

▶ *Human Resource Management*—Focuses on the processes of hiring, training, evaluating performance, and compensating employees.

▶ *Labor Relations*—Examines the labor contract relationships among managers, subordinates, and unions; also covers the process of negotiating.

▶ *Management Strategy*—Focuses on the competitive environment faced by a firm and strategies used by a firm's managers to increase its growth or improve its performance.

▶ *Management Systems*—Explains the application of computer software and systems to facilitate decision making.

▶ *Psychology*—In particular, courses that attempt to explain human behavior and the human response to penalties, rewards, and incentives.

Careers in Human Resources

Information about job positions, salaries, and careers for students who major in Human Resources can be found at the following websites:

▶ Job position websites:

http://jobsearch.monster.com	Administrative and Support Services, Consulting Services, and Human Resources.
http://careers.yahoo.com	Management Consulting.

▶ Salary website:

http://collegejournal.com/salarydata	Consulting, Human Resources, and Logistics.

Some of the job positions described at these websites may require work experience or a graduate degree.

Part V
Marketing

Marketing can be broadly defined as the actions of firms to plan and execute the design, pricing, distribution, and promotion of products. A firm's marketing mix is the combination of the product, pricing, distribution, and promotion strategies used to sell products.

In applying these strategies, a firm begins by using marketing research to define a consumer need. Once a product is developed to satisfy this need, a pricing decision is made. The pricing policy affects the demand for the product and therefore affects the firm's revenue. Then, a method of distributing the product to consumers must be selected. The use of intermediaries tends to make the product more accessible to customers but also results in higher prices. Finally, a promotion strategy must be designed to make consumers aware of the product or to convince them that this product is superior to others.

To recognize how all four strategies are used by a single firm, consider a computer firm that identifies a software package that consumers need. The firm develops the software (product strategy), sets a price for the software (pricing strategy), decides to sell the software through specific computer stores (distribution strategy), and decides to advertise the software in magazines (promotion strategy). These marketing strategies continue to be used as the product follows the typical life cycle. For example, the firm may conduct marketing research to determine whether the product should be revised or targeted toward a different market. The pricing policy could change if the target market is revised or if the production costs change. The decision regarding the channel of distribution will be reviewed periodically to determine whether some alternative channel is more feasible. The promotion strategy may be revised in response to changes in the target market, pricing, phase of the life cycle, or the channel of distribution. Chapter 12 focuses on the creation and pricing of products, Chapter 13 focuses on distributing products, and Chapter 14 focuses on promoting products.

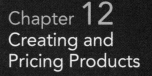

Chapter 12
Creating and Pricing Products

Chapter 13
Distributing Products

Chapter 14
Promoting Products

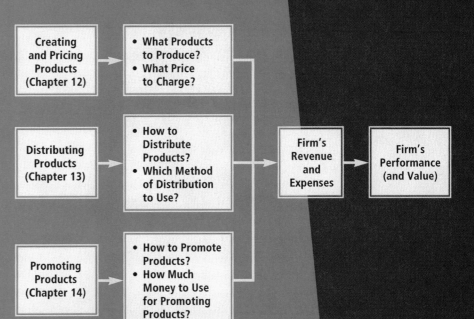

Chapter
12

NightLife Film Company's performance is highly dependent on the products (films) it creates, and the prices that it charges for them.

The Learning Goals of this chapter are to:

Define product line and product mix and identity the phases of the product life cycle. *1*

Identify the main factors that affect a product's target market. *2*

Identify the steps involved in creating a new product. *3*

Explain the common methods used to differentiate a product. *4*

Identify the factors that influence the pricing decision. *5*

Discuss other pricing decisions that a firm may make. *6*

Creating and Pricing Products

Product strategies dictate the types of products that a firm creates to satisfy customers, whereas pricing strategies determine the prices to be charged for those products. Both strategies influence the demand for the products produced by the firm and therefore determine the amount of revenue that the firm will generate over a particular period. Consider the situation of NightLife Film Company, which produces science fiction films that are shown in movie theaters. In the past, most of its films were targeted to moviegoers ranging in age from 14 to 25 years old. When NightLife plans the production of new films, it must decide:

▶ What types of consumers (target market) will pay to see its films?

▶ What steps must it take to create new films (products)?

▶ How can it differentiate its films from the films produced by its competitors?

▶ What is the life cycle of its films?

▶ When it creates DVDs for its films, what price should it charge?

▶ Should it consider price discounts for some customers?

If NightLife can successfully determine the target market that will be interested in its films, it can focus its advertising on those customers. NightLife needs to differentiate its business from others to attract customers. If it can sustain the popularity of its product (and therefore the demand) over a long period of time, it will generate more revenue. Its pricing decisions on the films' DVDs are also important because those prices will affect the amount of revenue generated from selling DVDs.

The types of decisions described here are necessary for all businesses. This chapter explains how the product and pricing decisions by NightLife Film Company or any other firm can be conducted in a manner that maximizes the firm's value.

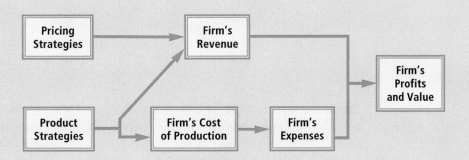

Define product line and product mix and identify the phases of the product life cycle.

product
a physical good or service that can satisfy consumer needs

convenience products
products that are widely available to consumers, are purchased frequently, and are easily accessible

shopping products
products that are not purchased frequently

specialty products
products that specific consumers consider to be special and therefore make a special effort to purchase

product line
a set of related products or services offered by a single firm

product mix
the assortment of products offered by a firm

Background on Products

The term **product** can be broadly defined to include both physical goods and services that can satisfy consumer needs. Firms must continually improve existing products and develop new products to satisfy customers over time. In this way, firms generate high sales growth, which normally increases their value.

Most products produced to serve consumers can be classified as (1) convenience products, (2) shopping products, or (3) specialty products. **Convenience products** are widely available to consumers, are purchased frequently, and are easily accessible. Milk, newspapers, soda, and chewing gum are examples of convenience products.

Shopping products differ from convenience products in that they are not purchased frequently. Before purchasing shopping goods, consumers typically shop around and compare the quality and prices of competing products. Furniture and appliances are examples of shopping products.

Specialty products are products that specific consumers consider to be special and therefore make a special effort to purchase. A Rolex watch and a Jaguar automobile are examples of specialty products. When evaluating specialty products, consumers base their purchasing decision primarily on personal preference, not on comparative pricing.

Product Line

A **product line** is a set of related products or services offered by a single firm. For example, Coke, Diet Coke, Caffeine-Free Diet Coke, and Sprite are all part of a single product line at The Coca-Cola Company. Pepsi, Diet Pepsi, Mountain Dew, and All-Sport are all part of a single product line at PepsiCo.

A product line tends to expand over time as a firm identifies other consumer needs. The Coca-Cola Company recognizes that consumers differ with respect to their desire for a specific taste, caffeine versus no caffeine, and diet versus regular. It has expanded its product line of soft drinks to satisfy various needs. Procter & Gamble has added different versions of its Tide detergent such as Tide with Bleach to its product line over time, while Taco Bell has added various low-fat food items to its menus.

Product Mix

The assortment of products offered by a firm is referred to as the **product mix.** Most firms tend to expand their product mix over time as they identify other consumer needs or preferences. Before firms add more products to their product mix, they should determine whether a demand for new products exists and whether they are capable of efficiently providing those products. A firm may even decide to discontinue one of the products in its product mix.

Examples of a Product Mix   Quaker State originally focused on motor oil but added windshield washer fluid, brake fluid, and many other automobile products to its product mix. Amazon.com originally focused on selling books, but has added electronics, toys, music, kitchen products, drugs, and health and beauty products. The product mix of Liz Claiborne, Inc., includes clothing for women, jewelry, fashion accessories, and clothing for men.

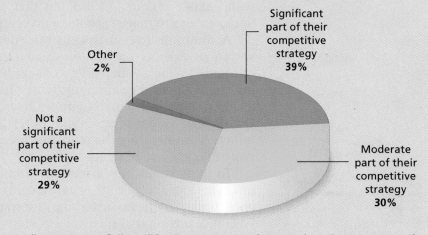

SMALL BUSINESS SURVEY

Product Choices as a Competitive Advantage

In a recent National Small Business poll conducted for the NFIB Research Foundation, small businesses were asked whether they add more choices (variations) of their existing products as part of their strategy to develop a competitive advantage. Their responses are shown here:

Other
2%

Significant
part of their
competitive
strategy
39%

Not a
significant
part of their
competitive
strategy
29%

Moderate
part of their
competitive
strategy
30%

Overall, 69 percent of all small businesses surveyed use product choices as part of their competitive strategy.

Exhibit 12.1

Product Mix of IBM

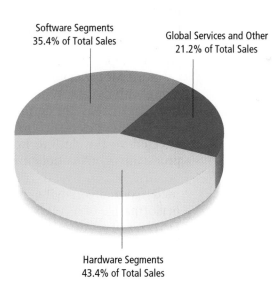

Software Segments
35.4% of Total Sales

Global Services and Other
21.2% of Total Sales

Hardware Segments
43.4% of Total Sales

IBM's product mix includes software, hardware, and global services, as shown in Exhibit 12.1. The hardware segment generates more sales than either of the other segments, but its proportion of total sales is lower than in previous years. Meanwhile, the proportion of total sales generated by IBM's global services segment (which includes information technology) has increased substantially. This change in the relative proportions reflects IBM's shift away from its hardware product line and into other product lines related to information technology.

Service firms also have a product mix. For example, some commercial banks accept deposits, provide checking services, extend loans, and offer insurance products.

Diversifying the Product Mix   When their primary product is subject to wide swings in demand, firms tend to diversify their product mix so that they will not be completely dependent on one market. By diversifying, they are not as reliant on a single product whose performance is uncertain. Firms with flexible production facilities that allow for the production of additional goods are more capable of diversifying their product mix.

A common diversification strategy is for a firm to diversify products within its existing production capabilities. For example, hospital supply companies offer a wide variety of supplies that can be sold to each hospital. The Walt Disney Company, which had focused on producing films for children, now offers many gift products. Clothing manufacturers such as Donna Karan offer several types of clothes that can be sold to each retail outlet. A product mix that contains several related products can allow for more efficient use of salespeople.

To understand how firms can benefit from expanding their product mix, consider the case of Amazon.com, which initially focused on filling book orders requested over the Internet. First, it began to offer CDs as well, recognizing that if customers are willing to order books online, they may also order other products. Second, it had already proved that it could provide reliable service, so customers trusted that the additional services would be reliable as well. Third, it could use its existing technology to fill CD orders, which increased efficiency. Amazon.com also acquired a stake in Drugstore.com because it believed that it could fill drug orders requested over the Internet. The growth of Amazon.com demonstrates how a firm can expand by using the resources that initially made it successful to offer additional products.

Ford Motor Company has diversified by producing a variety of trucks along with its cars. When demand for its cars is stagnant, it may still benefit from an increase in demand for trucks. Seagrams Company traditionally focused on sales of alcoholic beverages, but its performance was adversely affected by the decline in demand for alcoholic drinks. It responded by producing nonalcoholic beverages to reduce its risk of poor performance because of exposure to a single industry. Exxon (now ExxonMobil) benefited from diversifying into the petrochemical businesses because the performance of its oil business was highly exposed to changes in the market price of crude oil. DuPont produces a wide variety of products, including nylon, coatings, pharmaceuticals, polyester, and specialty fibers. Dow Chemical Company has diversified across chemicals, plastics, and energy products. Wal-Mart diversified its retail business by also becoming a retailer of groceries.

The following comments from a recent annual report from Textron (a large diversified firm) confirm the potential benefits of diversification:

"Textron's presence in diverse industries helps achieve balance and stability in a variety of economic environments by providing insulation from business and industry cycles. More specifically, we were able to maintain consistent growth . . . because the growth of our Aircraft, Automotive, Industrial and Finance businesses more than offset the downturns in the Systems and Components segment."

In addition to offering wireless Internet access, some Starbucks Coffee shops allow customers to download music, an expansion of services intended to attract more customers.

GETTY IMAGES

After Starbucks became famous for its coffee, it diversified its product line to offer more flavors. Now it has added a new service of wireless Internet access in its stores for convenience purposes. In doing this, Starbucks established a new theme of providing a "third place" to customers beyond their home and their workplace. By offering Internet access, it not only diversifies its sources of revenue, but its customers tend to stay longer, so it sells more coffee. Some of the stores are being transformed into Hear Music Coffeehouses, where customers can make custom CDs. Thus, Starbucks is expanding its services to the point that it may even be competing with Apple Computer. Most importantly, it is providing other services so that if there is ever a sudden decline in the demand for coffee, it will still attract customers.

Dell historically focused on the production of personal computers (PCs), but recognizing that the growth in PC sales would be limited, it began to produce and sell printers and other related products in 2003. In its first year, it managed to capture 19 percent of the market for low-cost all-in-one inkjet printers. It even changed its name from Dell Computer to Dell, Inc., to reflect its strategy of diversifying its products. Dell's sales of PCs still account for most of its revenue, but that may change over time as it continues to diversify its products.

Bookseller Barnes & Noble created superstores that offer DVDs as well as books. These stores also have an arrangement with Starbucks to serve coffee within the stores. By offering additional products, Barnes & Noble may attract more customers to its stores.

Improving the Convenience of the Product

A firm may also extend its product by making the product more accessible and more convenient to use or acquire. To many consumers, convenience may be just as important as the product itself. Advances in technology have enabled firms to improve the convenience of their products. For example, firms now provide complete information about their products online. Products such as books can be ordered online at any time. Services such as airline tickets and rental cars can also be reserved online at any time. In addition, checking in at the airport has been simplified by the installation of kiosks, where customers can check in by swiping a credit card through the machine and can even change their seat assignment. The kiosks have significantly reduced the time spent standing in line.

While Barnes & Noble has stores located throughout the United States, it recognized that some customers prefer to order their books online. Therefore, it created an online service (http://www.barnesandnoble.com) that offers more than 1 million books that are still in print, along with music and movies.

Product Life Cycle

Most products experience a **product life cycle,** or a typical set of phases over their lifetime. The marketing decisions made about a particular product may be influenced by the prevailing phase of the cycle. The typical product life cycle has four specific phases:

product life cycle
the typical set of phases that a product experiences over its lifetime

▶ Introduction
▶ Growth
▶ Maturity
▶ Decline

introduction phase
the initial period in which consumers are informed about a product

Introduction The **introduction phase** is the initial period in which consumers are informed about a new product. The promotion of the product is intended to introduce the product and make consumers aware of it. In some cases, the product is first tested in particular areas to determine consumer reaction. For example, the concept of direct satellite television was tested in various locations. The initial cost of producing and advertising the product may exceed the revenue received during this phase. The price of the product may initially be set high if no other competing products are in the market yet. This strategy is referred to as **price skimming.**

price skimming
the strategy of initially setting a high price for a product if no other competing products are in the market yet

growth phase
the period in which sales of a product increase rapidly

Growth The **growth phase** is the period in which sales of the product increase rapidly. The marketing of the product is typically intended to reinforce its features. Cellular telephones and direct satellite TVs are in the growth phase. Other firms that are aware of the product's success may attempt to create a similar or superior product. The price of the product may be lowered once competing products enter the market.

maturity phase
the period in which additional competing products have entered the market, and sales of a product level off because of competition

Maturity The **maturity phase** is the period in which additional competing products have entered the market, and sales of the product level off because of the increased competition. At this point, most marketing strategies are used to ensure that customers are still aware that the product exists. Some marketing strategies may offer special discounts to maintain market share. The firm may also revise the design of the existing product (product differentiation) to maintain market share. Standard cable television service is an example of a product at the maturity phase.

decline phase
the period in which sales of a product decline, either because of reduced consumer demand for that type of product or because competitors are gaining market share

Decline The **decline phase** is the period in which sales of the product decline, either because of reduced consumer demand for that type of product or because competitors are gaining market share. If firms do not prepare for a decline phase on some products, they may experience an abrupt decline in business. Some firms begin to prepare two or more years before the anticipated decline phase by planning revisions in their existing products or services.

Exhibit 12.2

Product Life Cycle Phases

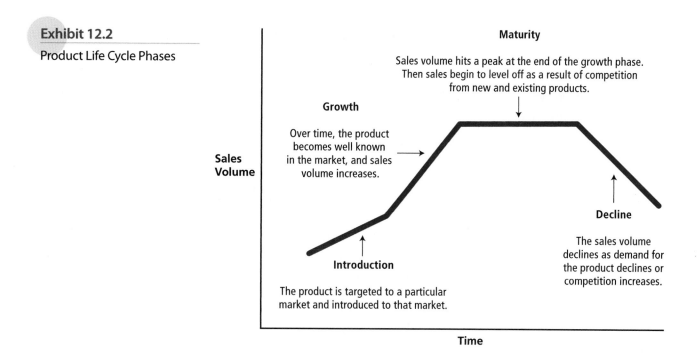

The product life cycle is illustrated in Exhibit 12.2. The length of a cycle tends to vary among types of products. It also varies among the firms that sell a particular type of product because some firms lengthen the cycle by continually differentiating their product to maintain market share.

Decision Making

Deciding the Product Line and Mix

NightLife Film Company must decide how to expand its product offerings. One way it could expand its product line is by offering new types of science fiction films that might appeal to different age groups. Another possibility is to produce comedies or other types of films. NightLife must also decide how to expand its product mix. It currently produces films for theaters and sells DVDs of the films several months after they have been in theaters. It considered producing some short documentaries for television. It also considered creating computer software that could be downloaded to play movies that it could sell online. The company decided to focus its product line on science fiction, but to offer more variety within this theme to reach different age groups. It also decided not to expand its product mix at this time because it does not have the expertise to produce other types of products.

1. What is a disadvantage to NightLife of keeping its product line focused on science fiction?

2. How could NightLife benefit from a more diversified product mix?

ANSWERS: 1. It might benefit from a broader product line because it relies so heavily on science fiction, and the popularity of these types of films may decline someday. 2. Consumers may stop going to movies in the future if they can view all movies on their computer or on television. NightLife should attempt to position itself for alternative ways in which consumers may see new movies in the future.

Identify the main factors that affect a product's target market.

target market
a group of individuals or organizations with similar traits who may purchase a particular product

consumer markets
markets for various consumer products and services (such as cameras, clothes, and household items)

industrial markets
markets for industrial products that are purchased by firms (such as plastic and steel)

Identifying a Target Market

The consumers who purchase a particular product may have specific traits in common and thus also have similar needs. Firms attempt to identify these traits so that they can target their marketing toward people with those traits. Marketing efforts are usually targeted toward a particular **target market,** which is a group of individuals or organizations with similar traits who may purchase a particular product.

Target markets can be broadly classified as consumer markets or industrial markets. **Consumer markets** exist for various consumer products and services (such as cameras, clothes, and household items), while **industrial markets** exist for industrial products that are purchased by firms (such as plastic and steel). Some products (such as tires) can serve consumer markets or industrial markets (such as car manufacturers). Classifying markets as consumer or industrial provides only a broad description of the types of customers who purchase products, however. Consequently, firms attempt to describe their target markets more narrowly.

Common traits used to describe a target market include the consumer's gender, age, and income bracket. For example, the target market for dirt bikes may be males under 30 years of age, while the target market for three-month cruises may be wealthy males or females over 50 years of age. Eddie Bauer produces a line of casual clothes for a target market of customers between 30 and 50 years of age, while Carters produces clothes for babies.

Factors That Affect the Size of a Target Market

As time passes, the demand for products changes. Firms attempt to be in a position to benefit from a possible increase in demand for particular products. For example, some hotels in Los Angeles and New York have antici-

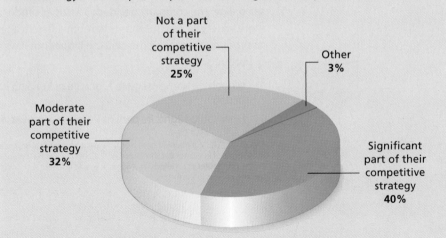

SMALL BUSINESS SURVEY

Identifying the Target Market

In a recent National Small Business poll conducted for the NFIB Research Foundation, small businesses were asked whether they refine their target market as part of their strategy to develop a competitive advantage. Their responses are shown here:

Not a part of their competitive strategy
25%

Other
3%

Moderate part of their competitive strategy
32%

Significant part of their competitive strategy
40%

pated an increase in Japanese guests and have offered new conveniences to capture that portion of the market. Common conveniences offered are Japanese translators, rooms with bamboo screens, and a Japanese-language newspaper for these guests.

As consumer preferences change, the size of a particular target market can change. Firms monitor consumer preferences over time to anticipate how the size of their target market may be affected. The following are key factors that affect consumer preferences and therefore affect the size of the target market:

▶ Demographics

▶ Geography

▶ Economic factors

▶ Social values

demographics

characteristics of the human population or specific segments of the population

Demographics   The total demand for particular products or services is dependent on the **demographics,** or characteristics of the human population or specific segments of the population. As demographic conditions change, so does the demand. For example, demographic statistics show an increase in the number of women who work outside the home. Firms have adjusted their product lines to capitalize on this change. Clothing stores have created more lines of business clothing for women. Food manufacturers have created easy-to-fix frozen foods to accommodate the busy schedules of wage-earning women. The tendency for people to have less free time and more income has resulted in increased demand for more convenience services, such as quick oil changes and tire replacement services.

One of the most relevant demographic characteristics is age because target markets are sometimes defined by age levels. Demographic statistics show that the population is growing older. Consequently, the popularity of sports cars has declined as customers look for cars that are dependable and safe. Automobile manufacturers have adjusted to this demographic change by supplying fewer sports cars. Home Depot created an installation service business to capitalize on the growing number of mature customers who prefer not to do repair or installation work themselves.

Although the population has generally grown older, the number of children in the United States has recently increased. Many of these recently born children have two parents who work outside the home and spend large sums of money on their children. Firms such as OshKosh B' Gosh and The Gap have capitalized on this trend by producing high-quality (and high-priced) children's clothing.

To illustrate how characteristics of the population can change over time, consider the changes over the 20-year period 1985–2005, shown in Exhibit 12.3. In general, the population has grown larger, while both the number of people age 65 or older and the number of households earning

Exhibit 12.3

Changes in Consumer Characteristics in Last 20 Years (from 1985 to 2005)

1. U.S. population has increased
2. Higher proportion of people age 65 or older
3. Higher proportion of households with income over $60,000
4. Higher proportion of minority households with income over $60,000
5. Higher proportion of high school students who enter college
6. Higher proportion of minority high school students who enter college

more than $60,000 annually have increased. Such information is relevant to firms because it suggests that the size of specific target markets may be changing over time.

Geography   The total demand for a product is also influenced by geography. Firms target snow tires to the northern states and surfboards to the east and west coasts of the United States. Tastes are also influenced by geography. The demand for spicy foods is higher in the southwestern states than in other states.

Economic Factors   As economic conditions change, so do consumer preferences. During a recessionary period, the demand for most types of goods declines. Specialty and shopping products are especially sensitive to these conditions. During a recession, firms may promote necessities rather than specialty products. In addition, their pricing may be more competitive. When the economy becomes stronger, firms have more flexibility to raise prices and may also promote specialty products more than necessities.

Interest rates can also have a major impact on consumer demand. When interest rates are low, consumers are more willing to purchase goods with borrowed money. The demand for products such as automobiles, boats, and homes is especially sensitive to interest rate movements because these products are often purchased with borrowed funds.

Social Values   As the social values of consumers change, so do their preferences. For example, the demand for cigarettes and whiskey has declined as consumers have become more aware of the dangers to health from using these products. If a firm producing either of these products anticipates a change in preferences, it can begin to shift its marketing mix. Alternatively, it could modify its product to capitalize on the trend. For example, it could reduce the alcohol content of its whiskey or the tar and nicotine content of its cigarettes. It may also revise its promotion strategy to inform the public of these changes.

Out of Business

Global Business

Targeting Foreign Countries

When firms sell their product mix in foreign countries, they must recognize that consumer characteristics vary across countries. Consider the case of Bestfoods International. This former U.S. firm was acquired by the Dutch firm Unilever in 2000, but it provides an excellent example of international marketing. Bestfoods produced numerous food products, including Skippy peanut butter, Mazola corn oil, and Hellmann's mayonnaise. Its global marketing strategy was to penetrate any foreign markets where there was sufficient demand. It recognized that some of its products would be more successful than others in particular foreign markets. Thus, it considered the characteristics of the foreign country before it decided which products to market in that country.

The following brief summary of just a few of Bestfoods' products illustrates how it targeted its products to specific countries:

1 Bestfoods sold mayonnaise in Argentina, Brazil, and Chile and introduced it in Panama and Venezuela in the late 1990s. It experienced high sales of mayonnaise in the Czech Republic and Slovakia and also marketed mayonnaise in Spain.

2 Bestfoods sold ready-to-eat desserts and dessert mixes in Europe, including Yabon cakes in France and Ambrosia rice puddings in the United Kingdom. It also sold dessert mixes in Latin America under the Kremel, Maizena, and Maravilla brands.

3 Bestfoods sold pasta in Europe under the Napolina and Knorr brands and in Asia under the Royal and Bestfoods brands.

In general, the product mix marketed by Bestfoods in any given country was dependent on the characteristics of the people in that country. It periodically changed the product mix that it marketed in a particular country in response to changes in that country's characteristics.

The Use of E-Marketing to Expand the Target Market

The term *e-marketing* refers to the use of the Internet to execute the design, pricing, distribution, and promotion of products. E-marketing is part of *e-commerce*, which is the use of electronic technology to conduct business transactions, such as selling products and acquiring information about consumers, more efficiently. In a recent survey of 109 executives, 62 percent said that marketing is the most important component of their e-commerce. Amazon.com's use of e-marketing to differentiate itself from other book retailers demonstrates the importance of e-marketing. Amazon uses its website to accept orders and payment online from customers anywhere in the United States and delivers the products directly to the customers. By using the Internet, it offers customers convenience because they can purchase books without going to a store. Thus, Amazon has created a means by which it can reach a much broader target market than if it had simply opened bookstores in various locations, and it is able to offer lower prices by selling direct, without the need for retail outlets. Amazon has also personalized the website for each customer depending on what books the customer recently ordered. Thus, its "store" is structured to highlight the books that will fit the particular customer's interests.

Other retailers have noticed the popularity of ordering books online and have developed their own online systems to complement their "bricks and mortar" stores. In this way, they have also extended their target markets. Many firms that sell clothing, office supplies, travel services, electronic equipment, and many other products are using e-marketing to reach a larger target market. Marriott International has an efficient website that helps match its hotels with travelers' interests. Southwest Airlines has an effective website that accepts online orders. It receives more than 30 percent of its revenue from online orders. UPS has developed a very efficient website that allows customers to track packages. The brokerage firm Charles Schwab has set up a website to receive orders to buy or sell stocks or other securities. More than 80 percent of its orders are conducted online.

The Internet also enables firms to target foreign markets. By establishing a foreign-language website that can accept orders and allow customers to pay by credit card, a firm can sell its products in foreign countries. It does not need to establish an office or hire employees in a foreign country to conduct this type of business. It can rely on its existing facilities to produce the products, use its website to market the product and accept payment, and deliver its product to the foreign customers via mail services.

In addition to allowing firms to receive orders at lower costs and to expand their target markets, e-marketing can enhance a firm's distribution (as described in Chapter 13) and its promotion of products (as described in Chapter 14).

Decision Making

Deciding on the Target Market

Recall that NightLife Film Company, which was introduced at the beginning of this chapter, produces science fiction films. It recently completed a new film called *Lost Planet II,* a sequel to its film *Lost Planet,* which it released a year ago. NightLife plans to advertise its new film to consumers, but it first needs to determine its target market for this film. It expects that the target market will be similar to the target market for *Lost Planet,* which attracted customers in the age range from 14 to 25.

1. Why is it important for NightLife Film Company to decide on its target market before it advertises the film?

2. Why might the target market influence the type of theaters where the film will draw the most customers?

ANSWERS: 1. Its decision of where to advertise is dependent on its target market. If it plans to market the film to people in the 14–25 age group, it will advertise in places where the ads will be seen by that target market. 2. Some theaters tend to attract a specific age bracket, so the film will likely attract more viewers at a theater that is typically attended by people who fit the age range of the target market.

Creating New Products

3

Identify the steps involved in creating a new product.

obsolete

less useful than in the past

In a given year, firms may offer more than 20,000 new products. The vast majority of these products will be discontinued within six months. These statistics suggest how difficult it is to create new products that are successful. Nevertheless, the profits from a single successful product may offset the losses resulting from several failed products.

A new product does not have to represent a famous invention. Most new products are simply improvements of existing products. Existing products become **obsolete,** or less useful than in the past, for two reasons.

fashion obsolescence
no longer being in fashion

They may experience **fashion obsolescence** and no longer be in fashion. For example, the demand for some types of clothes declines over time because of fashion obsolescence.

technological obsolescence
being inferior to new products

Alternatively, products may experience **technological obsolescence** and be inferior to new products that are technologically more advanced. For example, when Hewlett-Packard creates faster printers, the old models are subject to technological obsolescence.

Some products are created as an addition to the existing product line, rather than as a replacement for existing products. For example, Starbucks periodically adds new flavors to its existing coffee list, and Coca-Cola periodically adds new soft drinks to its existing product line.

Many additional products are created in response to customer feedback. For example, when customers frequently order a type of product that a firm does not sell, these requests prompt the firm to add that type of product to its product line. Clothing manufacturers rely heavily on customer requests to determine the types of new clothing that they produce. Many service firms expand their services in response to requests by customers.

Use of Marketing Research to Create New Products

When firms develop products, they assess the market to monitor the marketing strategies of their competitors. However, merely monitoring competitors may cause the firm to be a follower rather than a leader. Many firms prefer to make product decisions that are more innovative than those of their competitors. To obtain more insight on what consumers want, firms use **marketing research,** which is the accumulation and analysis of data in order to make a particular marketing decision.

marketing research
the accumulation and analysis of data in order to make a particular marketing decision

Marketing research is useful for making product decisions. A marketing survey may find that many consumers desire a specific product that is not available. It may also identify deficiencies in the firm's existing products; this information can then be used to correct these deficiencies. The design and quality of a product may be revised to accommodate consumer preferences. For example, computer firms build computers and

The Coca-Cola Company frequently adds new products to its product line, so that it can provide a wide variety of choices to its customers in anticipation that demand for any single product can change over time.

LANDOV LLC

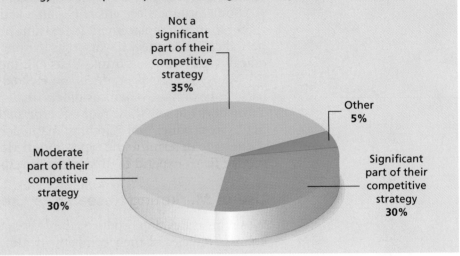
automobile manufacturers design their new cars to accommodate their perception of what consumers want. Firms' perceptions of consumer preferences are more accurate when backed by marketing research.

Both new and revised products may be tested with marketing research. The products are given to prospective customers who are asked to assess various features of the products. This type of research allows firms to make further revisions that will satisfy customers.

To enable a firm to have confidence in the data obtained from marketing research, sample groups of consumers who represent the target market are studied. Many marketing research studies result in a marketing decision that will cost millions of dollars. If the marketing research leads to incorrect conclusions, the decision could result in a large loss for the firm.

One limitation of using marketing research to identify consumer preferences is that tastes change rapidly. Products, such as clothing, that were popular when the marketing research was conducted may be out of style by the time they are designed and distributed to the market.

How E-Marketing Complements Marketing Research   A key to developing or improving new products is to receive feedback on existing or experimental products. Many firms rely on e-marketing to support their product development. The Internet is particularly useful for marketing research because of its speed: companies and customers get the information they want much faster.

Firms can use the Internet for marketing research in several ways. First, by having a customer service e-mail system, a firm can obtain comments from customers about its existing products. Customers are more likely to provide feedback if they can simply send an e-mail than if they must send a letter. Second, because the firm has its customers' e-mail addresses, it can easily contact the customers to request feedback about a particular product or about their preferences. An online survey is a fast way

SMALL BUSINESS SURVEY

What Are the Keys to Creating Successful Products?

A survey asked 550 manufacturers of products to identify the sources of new product ideas. Each possible source listed in the following chart was rated 1 to 5, with 5 indicating that the source was frequently used by a firm for generating new product ideas. The chart shows the average score across the 550 manufacturers for each possible source of new product ideas.

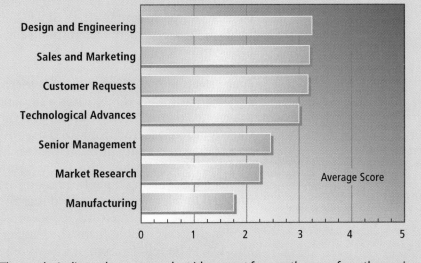

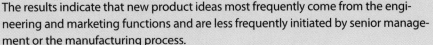

The results indicate that new product ideas most frequently come from the engineering and marketing functions and are less frequently initiated by senior management or the manufacturing process.

of gathering information. Third, a firm may even send out samples of an experimental product to customers who are willing to e-mail their assessment of the product to the firm. Samples have been so popular with many customers that some retailers have begun to offer online order services as well.

Procter & Gamble is well known for its extensive market research. In a recent year, about 50 percent of its huge market research budget was used for online market research. It can usually complete an online survey within 10 days, versus three or four weeks for a personal survey. In addition, an online survey costs substantially less than a personal survey. Another advantage is that some consumers are more open with their opinions online than when they are asked to respond to a survey conducted by a person.

Use of Research and Development to Create Products

Firms invest funds in research and development (R&D) to design new products or to improve the products they already produce. Manufacturing firms tend to invest more money in R&D than service firms because technology can improve manufactured products more easily than services.

Firms that spend money on R&D expect the benefits to exceed the expenses. Procter & Gamble's R&D resulted in its two-in-one shampoo and conditioner technology. It attributes the success of its Pantene Pro-V to its product technology. This product is now the leading shampoo in several countries. Procter & Gamble has improved the technology of Tide detergent more than 70 times. Technological development can also enable a firm to gain an advantage over its competitors. Many large firms typically spend more than $1 billion on R&D per year.

Because R&D can be so expensive, some firms have created alliances to conduct R&D. They share the costs and their technology in attempting to develop products. An alliance not only combines expertise from two or more firms, but it may also reduce the costs to each individual firm.

To expand their product line, many firms have recently increased their investment in R&D. For example, Abbott Laboratories has consistently increased its investment in R&D. Since Abbott Laboratories produces various medical drugs, its future performance is heavily dependent on its ability to create new drugs.

Using Patents to Protect Research and Development   One potential limitation of R&D is that a firm that creates a new product may not always be able to prevent its competitors from copying the idea. The potential to recover all the expenses incurred from R&D may depend on whether the ideas can be protected from competitors. To protect their ideas, firms apply for **patents,** which allow exclusive rights to the production and sale of a specific product. The U.S. Patent Office grants about 3,500 patents per week. Patents are pursued for a wide variety of products, ranging from medical drugs to special sunglasses and microwave popcorn.

Patents can enable firms that engage in extensive R&D, such as IBM and 3M, to benefit from their inventions because the patents prevent competitors from copying the ideas. The 3M Company, which created Post-it Notes, commonly obtains at least 400 patents per year. As an example of the importance of patents, consider the following comments from a recent annual report of Hewlett-Packard:

"HP's R&D budgets and activity continue to ensure our leadership as one of the most productive product development and research institutes in the world. . . . In 2001, HP was awarded nearly 1,000 patents in the United States and filed 5,000 patent applications worldwide. This essentially translates into protecting 20 new inventions every working day."

Patents also have some disadvantages that should be recognized. Patent applications are quite tedious and may require a 20- to 40-page description of the product. Some technical patent applications are even more detailed and may contain more than 100 pages of description. Because of the large backlog of patent applications, the approval process can take several months. Many applications are not approved because the Patent Office decides that the ideas do not represent a new product. Even when a patent application is approved, it is difficult for the inventor to prevent other businesses from copying the idea in some form. Obtaining patents can also be expensive. To obtain a patent internationally, the cost is typically at least $100,000.

Steps Necessary to Create a New Product

The following steps are typically necessary to create a new product:

▶ Develop a product idea.
▶ Assess the feasibility of a product idea.

patents
allow exclusive rights to the production and sale of a specific product

> ▶ Design and test the product.
> ▶ Distribute and promote the product.
> ▶ Post-audit the product.

Develop a Product Idea   The first step in creating a new product is to develop an idea. When the focus is on improving an existing product, the idea already exists, and the firm simply attempts to make it better. When developing an entirely new product, a common method is to identify consumer needs or preferences that are not being satisfied by existing products. The ultimate goal is to develop a product that is superior to existing products in satisfying the consumer.

As firms attempt to improve existing products or create new products, they must determine what will satisfy customers. The commitment of some firms to customer satisfaction is confirmed by the following statements in recent annual reports:

"Kodak's future is in total customer satisfaction."

—Eastman Kodak

"I [the CEO] want everyone in IBM to be obsessed with satisfying our customers."

—IBM

"We aim to redouble our efforts . . . toward one simple goal: meeting the needs of our customers."

—Apple Computer

Identifying consumer preferences so as to improve a product or create a new product may involve monitoring consumer behavior. For example, an airline may monitor flights to determine the most disturbing inconveniences, such as cramped seating. This leads to ideas for an improved product, such as wider seats. To satisfy consumer preferences, rental car

Patents are created for many new products, including snowmobile skis as shown here. Patents can allow a firm to benefit from its innovations and protect it from other competitors who want to copy the innovation.

AP/WIDE WORLD PHOTOS

companies at airports now allow their key customers to go straight from the airplane to their cars (rather than stand in line at the counter).

Technology can be used to monitor consumer behavior. When Amazon .com fills orders, it requests information about the customers. Thus, when Amazon considers expanding its product line, it knows the characteristics of the consumers who are buying its existing products. Based on this information about consumer preferences, it can attempt to identify other products that will sell over the Internet.

An alternative to monitoring consumer behavior is surveying people about their behavior. Surveys may be conducted by employees or consulting firms. Again, the goal is to identify consumer preferences that have not been fulfilled. In recent years, recognition of heightened consumer concern about health has led to many ideas for new products and revisions of existing products. For example, food manufacturers responded by creating more nutritious cereals and frozen dinners.

Each consumer preference that deserves attention results from a lack of or a deficiency in an existing product. The firm must determine how this lack or deficiency can be corrected by creating a new product or improving an existing product. In the mid-1990s, IBM decided that it needed to increase the processing speed of its computers. IBM incurred substantial expenses as a result of this decision to improve its products. However, the demand for these improved products increased, resulting in higher revenue.

Assess the Feasibility of a Product Idea   Any idea for a new or improved product should be assessed by estimating the costs and benefits. The idea should be undertaken only if the benefits outweigh the costs. For example, American Airlines removed some seats to better satisfy customers by providing more leg room. The most obvious cost was the expense of removing the seats, but other costs were incurred as well. The strategy reduced the airline's seating capacity. The cost of this reduction was forgone revenue on those flights that were at full capacity. In addition, an airplane could not be used while the work was being performed. Any forgone revenue during that period also represented a cost of improving the product. Nevertheless, American hoped that the benefit of more leg room would lead to greater consumer satisfaction and thus to greater demand for its service, resulting in more revenue.

Design and Test the Product   If the firm believes the new (or revised) product is feasible, it must determine the design and other characteristics of the product. The new product may be tested before being fully implemented. For example, an airline such as American Airlines may first revise its seating structure in a few planes to determine consumer reaction. If the actual costs exceed the benefits, the proposed changes will not be made on other airplanes. If the change has a favorable impact, however, it may be made throughout the entire fleet.

Distribute and Promote the Product   When firms introduce new products or improve existing products, they typically attempt to inform consumers. New or improved products are introduced to consumers through various marketing techniques. As an example, an airline that widens its seats may advertise this feature in the media. Additional expenses required to promote

Cross Functional Teamwork

Interaction among Product Decisions and Other Business Decisions

When marketing managers create a new product, they must design it in a manner that will attract customers. They must also decide the price at which the product will be sold. These marketing decisions require communication between the marketing managers and the managers who oversee production. Marketing managers explain to the production managers how they would like the product to be designed. The production managers may offer revisions that can improve the design. They also provide estimates on the costs of production. The cost per unit is typically dependent on the volume of products to be produced; therefore, the cost per unit can be estimated only after the marketing managers determine the volume that will need to be produced to satisfy the demand. Since the pricing decision is influenced by the cost of producing the product, the price cannot be determined by the marketing managers until they receive cost estimates from the production managers.

Once the marketing managers have received the necessary input from the production managers and have developed plans for the design and pricing of the product, a financial analysis by the financial managers is necessary to ensure that the proposal is feasible. The financial analysis involves estimating the revenue the firm will generate as a result of creating this product. It also involves estimating production expenses. Using these estimates, the financial managers can determine whether the new product will provide an adequate return to make the firm's investment in the development of this product worthwhile. The marketing managers should attempt to develop the product only if the financial analysis suggests that it will provide an adequate return to the firm. If the marketing managers decide to develop this product, they will inform the production managers, who may need to hire additional production employees. In addition, the financial managers must be informed because they may need to obtain funds to finance production.

Although the marketing managers may be responsible for the creation of new products, they rely on input from the production and financial managers when deciding whether each product is worthwhile and when determining the design and price of the new product.

the revised design should be accounted for when determining whether it is worthwhile to create a new design.

Post-Audit the Product   After the new product has been introduced into the market, the actual costs and benefits should be measured and compared with the costs and benefits that were forecasted earlier. This comparison determines whether the cost-benefit analysis was reasonably accurate. If costs were severely underestimated or benefits were severely overestimated, the firm may need to adjust its method of analysis for evaluating other new products in the future. In addition, the post-audit of costs and benefits can be used for future development of the same product. For example, if the actual costs of improving the airplanes outweigh the benefits, the airline may revert to its original product design when new airplanes are needed.

Summary of Steps Used to Create or Revise a Product   A summary of the steps involved in creating or revising a product is shown in Exhibit 12.4. Notice that the whole process is initiated by attempting to satisfy consumer preferences.

Exhibit 12.4

Steps Involved in Creating or Revising a Product

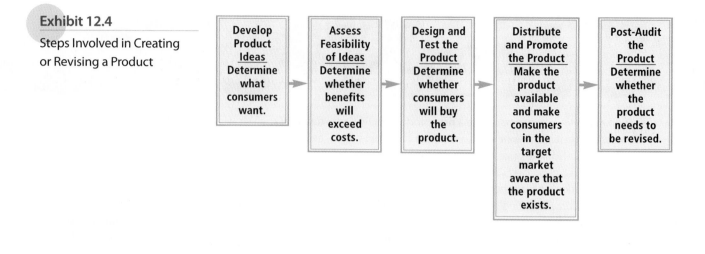

| Develop Product Ideas Determine what consumers want. | → | Assess Feasibility of Ideas Determine whether benefits will exceed costs. | → | Design and Test the Product Determine whether consumers will buy the product. | → | Distribute and Promote the Product Make the product available and make consumers in the target market aware that the product exists. | → | Post-Audit the Product Determine whether the product needs to be revised. |

Decision Making

Creating a New Product

NightLife Film Company is continually in the process of developing science fiction films. It has excellent production and technical employees who create the special effects that have made its films so popular. NightLife has just completed a film and wants to begin the production of a new film. Rather than trying a different type of film, it decides to produce another science fiction film because that will enable it to capitalize on its strengths and experience.

1. NightLife Film Company conducts marketing research by providing an online survey to anyone who wants to review its films. How can it use this information as it produces a new film?

2. If NightLife produces a film too quickly and rushes it into theaters, how will the revenue from the film be affected?

ANSWERS: 1. The marketing research can be used to determine what consumers liked about its previous films, such as the characters, plot, and special effects. Then it can use this information when producing the next film. 2. The revenue will be lower because the film will receive bad reviews and many potential customers will decide not to see the film.

Explain the common methods used to differentiate a product.

product differentiation
a firm's effort to distinguish its product from competitors' products in a manner that makes the product more desirable

Product Differentiation

Product differentiation is the effort of a firm to distinguish its product from competitors' products in a manner that makes the product more desirable. Some products are differentiated from competing products by their quality. For example, Starbucks coffee has become popular around the country because of its quality, even though its price is high. Kay-Bee Toys used a marketing strategy of specializing in a small selection of high-quality toys, rather than competing with Wal-Mart for the entire line of toys.

All firms look for some type of competitive advantage that will distinguish their product from the rest. The following are some of the more common methods used to differentiate the product:

▶ Unique product design

▶ Unique packaging

▶ Unique branding

Unique Product Design

Some products are differentiated by their design. Consider a homebuilder who builds homes and sells them once they are completed. The builder can attempt to build homes that will satisfy buyers by considering the following questions:

1. Would consumers in this neighborhood prefer one- or two-story homes?

2. Is a basement desirable?

3. Is a fireplace desirable?

4. What is a popular size for homes in this neighborhood?

5. What type of architecture is popular in this neighborhood?

Once these and other issues are resolved, the builder can build homes with specifications that will attract buyers.

Various characteristics can make one product better than others, including safety, reliability, and ease of use. Firms such as AT&T, Kodak, and Audi have a reputation for reliability, which helps create a demand for their products. Producers attempt to improve reliability by using high-quality materials, providing service, and offering warranties. However, attempts to improve reliability usually result in higher costs.

Differentiating the Design of a Service   Just as firms that produce products attempt to create unique designs for their products, service firms attempt to develop unique services. For example, Southwest Airlines designed a differentiated service by focusing on many short routes that previously were not available to customers. Some grocery stores allow customers to purchase groceries online and provide a delivery service so that the customers do not have to shop at the store.

Most services can be differentiated by timing and efficiency. A firm that provides the service desired by customers on time and at a reasonable price has a good chance of being successful. Its method of differentiating itself from competitors is to prove that customers can trust it to provide what it promised and to do so on time. Firms that offer services commonly use a strategy of promising to provide service of a certain quality and then keeping their promises. A firm that delivers what it promised may not only receive additional business from those customers, but may also obtain other business from referrals.

Unique Packaging

A packaging strategy can determine the success or failure of a product, especially for products whose quality levels are quite similar. In an attempt to differentiate themselves from the competition, some firms have repackaged various grocery products in unbreakable or easily disposable containers.

Many packaging strategies focus on convenience. Motor oil is now packaged in containers with convenient twist-off caps, and many canned foods have pull-tabs. Tide detergent is packaged in both powder and liquid so that consumers can choose their preferred form.

Packaging can also provide advertising. For example, many food products such as microwave dinners are packaged with the preparation instructions on the outside. These instructions also demonstrate how simple

The packaging of products like these is important because it can influence the buying behavior of consumers.

PHOTOEDIT, INC.

the preparation is. Packaging also informs consumers about the nutrition of foods or the effectiveness of health-care products. The advertising on the package may be the key factor that encourages consumers to purchase one product instead of others.

Unique Branding

branding
a method of identifying products and differentiating them from competing products

trademark
a brand's form of identification that is legally protected from use by other firms

Branding is a method of identifying products and differentiating them from competing products. Brands are typically represented by a name and a symbol. A **trademark** is a brand's form of identification that is legally protected from use by other firms. Some trademarks have become so common that they represent the product itself. For example, "Coke" is often used to refer to any cola drink, and "Kleenex" is frequently used to refer to any facial tissue. Some symbols are more recognizable than the brand name. Levi's jeans, Nike, Pepsi, and Mercedes all have easily recognized symbols.

family branding
branding of all or most products produced by a company

individual branding
the assignment of a unique brand name to different products or groups of products

Family versus Individual Branding   Companies that produce goods assign either a family or an individual brand to their products. **Family branding** is the branding of all or most products produced by a company. The Coca-Cola Company sells Coca-Cola, Diet Coke, Cherry Coke, and other soft drinks. Ford, RCA, IBM, and Intel use family branding to distinguish their products from the competition.

Companies that use **individual branding** assign a unique brand name to different products or groups of products. For example, Procter & Gamble produces Tide, Bold, and Era. General Mills produces numerous brands of cereal. Many clothing manufacturers use different brand names. One product line may be marketed to prestigious clothing shops. A second line may be marketed to retail stores. To preserve the prestige, the top quality brand may not be sold in retail stores.

producer brands
brands that reflect the manufacturer of the products

store brands
brands that reflect the retail store where the products are sold

generic brands
products that are not branded by the producer or the store

Producer versus Store Brands Most products can be classified as either a producer brand, a store brand, or a generic brand. **Producer brands** reflect the manufacturer of the products. Examples of producer brands include Black & Decker, Frito-Lay, and Fisher Price. These brands are usually well known because they are sold to retail stores nationwide. **Store brands** reflect the retail store where the products are sold. For example, Sears and J. C. Penney offer some products with their own label. Even if store brands are produced by firms other than the retailer, the names of the producers are not identified. Store brand products do not have as much prestige as popular producer brands; however, they often have a lower price.

Some products are not branded by either the producer or the store. These products have a so-called **generic brand.** The label on generic products simply describes the product. Generic brands have become increasingly popular over the last decade because their prices are relatively low. They are most popular for products that are likely to be similar among brands, such as napkins and paper plates. Customers are comfortable purchasing generic brands of these products because there is not much risk in buying a cheaper product.

Benefits of Branding Branding continually exposes a company's name to the public. If the company is respected, its new products may be trusted because they carry the company brand name. If they carried a different name, new products introduced by the firm would likely not sell as well.

Many firms with a brand name use their name to enter new markets. The Coca-Cola Company uses its name to promote new soft drinks that it creates. Nabisco can more easily penetrate the market for various specialty foods because of its reputation for quality food products. These firms not only are able to offer new products but also may enter new geographic markets (such as foreign countries) because of their brand name.

A brand is especially useful for differentiating a product when there are only a few major competitors. For example, many consumers select among only two or three brands of some products, such as toothpaste or computers. The importance of branding is emphasized in a recent annual report of Procter & Gamble:

"Consumers have to trust that a brand will meet all their needs all the time. That requires superior product technology. And it also requires sufficient breadth of product choices. We should never give consumers a . . . reason to switch away from one of our brands."

Having an established brand name is also often crucial to obtaining space in a store. For example, Coca-Cola and Pepsi often receive the majority of a store's soft drink shelf space. The same is true for some cereals, detergents, and even dog food. Retail stores normally allocate more space for products with popular brand names.

Branding also applies to services. When Southwest Airlines begins to serve a new route, it uses its brand (reliability, good service, low prices) to attract customers.

co-branding
firms agree to offer a combination of two noncompeting products at a discounted price

A recent trend in branding is **co-branding,** in which firms agree to offer a combination of two noncompeting products at a discounted price. For example, Blockbuster Entertainment Group issues VISA cards. Blockbuster customers can get discounts on DVD rentals by using their VISA cards.

Exhibit 12.5

Methods Used to Differentiate Products

Method	Achieve Superiority by:
Unique design	Higher level of product safety, reliability, or ease of use.
Unique packaging	Packaging to get consumers' attention or to improve convenience.
Unique branding	Using the firm's image to gain credibility, or using a unique brand name to imply prestige.

Summary of Methods Used to Differentiate Products

Exhibit 12.5 summarizes the methods used to achieve product differentiation. Firms sometimes combine several methods to differentiate their products. For example, if Kodak creates a product that is technologically superior to others, it may also differentiate the product by packaging it in a special manner and by using the Kodak family brand name.

To understand how some firms use all three methods to differentiate their products, consider the following comment from an annual report:

"Liz Claiborne, Inc., must work more diligently than ever to truly differentiate its brands, . . . applying product innovation [such as a unique design], canny brand marketing, . . . superb customer service and exceptional in-store presentation [unique packaging] to win over a consumer who has abundant choices."

—Liz Claiborne, Inc.

Decision Making

Differentiating the Product

NightLife Film Company has noticed that many other movie producers are beginning to offer science fiction films. Thus, it will have to make an effort to differentiate its films from those of its competitors so that its films will continue to attract a large number of customers. To do this, NightLife can continue to capitalize on its special effects. It can also produce sequels of its earlier movies so that its potential customers will recognize the themes.

1. Do you think that NightLife's brand name of NightLife Film Company will help it differentiate its next film from those of competitors?

2. Will it be easier for NightLife Film Company to differentiate its films in the science fiction market where there is limited competition than it would be in the comedy market where the competition is more intense?

ANSWERS: 1. NightLife is known for its science fiction movies, so its brand name should help to differentiate its new film from those of competitors. 2. Yes. If there are fewer competitors, it is easier for a firm to differentiate its product.

Pricing Strategies

Identify the factors that influence the pricing decision.

Whether a firm produces industrial steel, textbooks, or haircuts, it needs to determine a price for its product. Managers typically attempt to set a price that will maximize the firm's value. The price charged for a product affects the firm's revenue and therefore its earnings. Recall that the revenue from selling a product is equal to its price times the quantity sold. Although a lower price reduces the revenue received per unit, it typically results in a higher quantity of units sold. A higher price increases the revenue received per unit but results in a lower quantity of units sold. Thus, an obvious trade-off is involved when determining the price for a product.

Firms set the prices of their products by considering the following:

▶ Cost of production

▶ Supply of inventory

▶ Competitors' prices

Pricing According to the Cost of Production

cost-based pricing
estimating the per-unit cost of producing a product and then adding a markup

Some firms set a price for a product by estimating the per-unit cost of producing the product and then adding a markup. This method of pricing products is commonly referred to as **cost-based pricing.** If this method is used, the firm must also account for all production costs that are attributable to the production of that product. Pricing according to cost attempts to ensure that production costs are covered. Virtually all firms consider production costs when setting a price. The difference in price between a Cadillac and a Saturn is partially attributed to the difference in production costs. However, other factors may also influence the pricing decision.

Economies of Scale   The per-unit cost of production may be dependent on production volume. For products subject to economies of scale, the average per-unit cost of production decreases as production volume increases. This is especially true for products or services that have high fixed costs (costs that remain unchanged regardless of the quantity produced), such as automobiles. A pricing strategy must account for economies of scale. If a high price is charged, not only does the sales volume decrease, but also the average cost of producing a small amount increases. For those products or services that are subject to economies of scale, the price should be sufficiently low to achieve a high sales volume (and therefore lower production costs).

Pricing According to the Supply of Inventory

Some pricing decisions are directly related to the supply of inventory. For example, computer firms such as Apple typically reduce prices on existing personal computers to make room for new models that will soon be marketed. Automobile dealerships frequently use this strategy as well. Most manufacturers and retailers tend to reduce prices if they need to reduce their inventory.

Pricing According to Competitors' Prices

Firms commonly consider the prices of competitors when determining the prices of their products. They can use various pricing strategies to compete against other products, as explained next.

penetration pricing
the strategy of setting a lower price than those of competing products to penetrate a market

Penetration Pricing   If a firm wants to be sure that it can sell its product, it may set a lower price than those of competing products to penetrate the market. This pricing strategy is called **penetration pricing** and has been used in various ways by numerous firms, including airlines, automobile manufacturers, and food companies.

Southwest Airlines and Jet Blue Airways are well-known for their effectiveness at using penetration pricing to enter a market.

LANDOV LLC

price-elastic
the demand for a product is highly responsive to price changes

The success of penetration pricing depends on the product's price elasticity, which reflects the responsiveness of consumers to a reduced price. When demand for a product is **price-elastic,** the demand is highly responsive to price changes. Some grocery products such as napkins and paper plates are price-elastic, as price may be the most important criterion that consumers use when deciding which brand to purchase. Many firms, such as Ameritrade, IBM, and Taco Bell have been able to increase their revenue by lowering prices.

When Southwest Airlines entered the airline industry, its average fare was substantially lower than the average fare charged by other airlines for the same routes. Southwest not only pulled customers away from competitors but also created some new customer demand for airline services because of its low prices. Penetration pricing is not always successful, however. Allstate Insurance increased its market share by lowering its insurance prices (premiums), but its profits declined because it lowered its prices too much.

price-inelastic
the demand for a product is not very responsive to price changes

When demand for a product is **price-inelastic,** the demand is not very responsive to price changes. A firm should not use penetration pricing if its product is price-inelastic because most consumers would not switch to the product to take advantage of the lower price. For some products, such as deli products and high-quality automobiles, personalized service and perceived quality may be more important than price. The demand for many services is not responsive to price reductions because consumers may prefer one firm over others. For example, some consumers may be unwilling to switch dentists, hairstylists, or stockbrokers even if a competitor reduces its price.

Defensive Pricing Some pricing decisions are defensive rather than offensive. If a firm recognizes that the price of a competing product has been re-

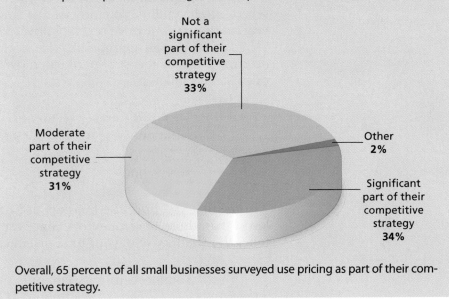

SMALL BUSINESS SURVEY

Pricing as a Competitive Advantage

In a recent National Small Business poll conducted for the NFIB Research Foundation, small businesses were asked whether they use pricing as part of their strategy to develop a competitive advantage. Their responses are shown here:

Not a significant part of their competitive strategy
33%

Other
2%

Moderate part of their competitive strategy
31%

Significant part of their competitive strategy
34%

Overall, 65 percent of all small businesses surveyed use pricing as part of their competitive strategy.

---

defensive pricing
the strategy of reducing a product's price to defend (retain) market share

duced, it may use **defensive pricing,** in which a product's price is reduced to defend (retain) market share. For example, airlines commonly reduce their airfares in response when a competitor lowers its airfares. This response tends to allow all airlines to retain their market share, but their revenue decreases (because of the lower price). Computer firms such as IBM and Dell commonly reduce their prices in response to price reductions by their competitors.

predatory pricing
the strategy of lowering a product's price to drive out new competitors

Some firms lower their price to drive out new competitors that have entered the market. This strategy is called **predatory pricing.**

prestige pricing
the strategy of using a higher price for a product that is intended to have a top-of-the-line image

Prestige Pricing   Firms may use a higher price if their product is intended to have a top-of-the-line image. This pricing strategy is called **prestige pricing.** For example, GapKids sells baby clothing at relatively high prices to create a high-quality image for customers who are not as concerned about price. Microbreweries use prestige pricing in an attempt to create a high-quality image for their beers.

Firms with a diversified product mix may use a penetration pricing strategy for some products and a prestige pricing strategy for others. For example, car manufacturers price some cars as low as possible to increase market share, but use prestige pricing on other models that have a top-of-the-line image.

Example of Setting a Product's Price

To show how a firm may set a product's price, assume that you move to New Orleans and start your own business as a hot dog vendor on the streets of the French Quarter (a tourist district). Assume that you plan to

fixed costs

operating expenses that do not change in response to the number of products produced

variable costs

costs operating expenses that vary directly with the number of products produced that vary with the quantity produced

run this business for one year and that a hot dog cooker can be rented for $4,000 annually. This cost is referred to as a **fixed cost** because the cost of production remains unchanged regardless of how many units are produced. Also assume that your costs for hot dogs, buns, ketchup, and so on are about $.60 per hot dog. These costs are called **variable costs** because they vary with the quantity of hot dogs produced.

Other vendors in the area charge $2.00 per hot dog. After talking with several other vendors, you forecast that you can sell 20,000 hot dogs in one year as long as your price is competitive.

To determine an appropriate price, begin with the cost information and determine the total cost of production over the first year. The total cost is calculated as follows:

$$
\begin{aligned}
\text{Total Cost} &= (\text{Fixed Cost}) + [(\text{Quantity}) \times (\text{Variable Cost per Unit})] \\
&= \$4,000 + [(20,000) \times (\$.60)] \\
&= \$4,000 + \$12,000 \\
&= \$16,000
\end{aligned}
$$

Assume that you price the hot dogs at $1.80 so that your price is slightly lower than those of competitors. Since the total revenue is equal to price times the quantity sold, your total revenue is estimated to be:

$$
\begin{aligned}
\text{Total Revenue} &= (\text{Quantity}) \times (\text{Price per Unit}) \\
&= (20,000) \times (\$1.80) \\
&= \$36,000
\end{aligned}
$$

Thus, your profits would be:

$$
\begin{aligned}
\text{Profits} &= \text{Total Revenue} - \text{Total Cost} \\
&= \$36,000 - \$16,000
\end{aligned}
$$

Your actual revenue over a future period is subject to uncertainty, however. For example, if you sell only 10,000 hot dogs, your revenue would be:

$$
\begin{aligned}
\text{Total Revenue} &= (\text{Quantity}) \times (\text{Price}) \\
&= (10,000) \times (\$1.80) \\
&= \$18,000
\end{aligned}
$$

Your profits would be as follows:

$$
\begin{aligned}
\text{Profits} &= \text{Total Revenue} - \text{Total Cost} \\
&= \$18,000 - \$16,000 \\
&= \$2,000
\end{aligned}
$$

Thus, your profits (revenue minus costs) would be only $2,000. You could attempt to increase your price to make up for the possibility of low sales, but this strategy may conflict with your goal of setting a price that is no higher than the competition. The quantity of hot dogs you sell may decline if you use a higher price.

Exhibit 12.6

Estimation of Costs
and Revenue at Various
Quantities Produced

Quantity (Q)	Fixed Cost	Variable Cost (Q × $.60)	Total Cost	Total Revenue (Q × $1.80)	Profits
1,000	$4,000	$600	$4,600	$1,800	−$2,800
3,000	4,000	1,800	5,800	5,400	−400
4,000	4,000	2,400	6,400	7,200	800
7,000	4,000	4,200	8,200	12,600	4,400
10,000	4,000	6,000	10,000	18,000	8,000
15,000	4,000	9,000	13,000	27,000	14,000
20,000	4,000	12,000	16,000	36,000	20,000
25,000	4,000	15,000	19,000	45,000	26,000
30,000	4,000	18,000	22,000	54,000	32,000

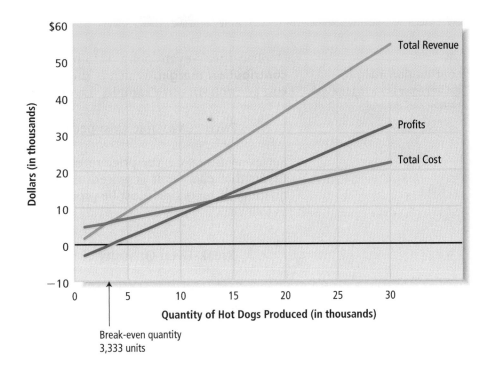

The total cost and total revenue are depicted in Exhibit 12.6 for various quantities of hot dogs produced. Notice that the fixed cost remains unchanged for any quantity produced. The variable cost is equal to the quantity times $.60 per hot dog produced. The total cost is equal to the fixed cost plus the variable cost. The total revenue is equal to the price of $1.80 per hot dog times the quantity of hot dogs produced.

Break-Even Point

break-even point
the quantity of units at which
total revenue equals total cost

The **break-even point** is the quantity of units at which total revenue equals total cost. At any quantity less than the break-even point, total costs exceed total revenue. For any quantity above the break-even point, total revenue exceeds total cost.

Cross Functional Teamwork

Relationship between Pricing and Production Strategies

A firm's plant site, design, and layout decisions are influenced by the pricing of its product (a marketing decision). If the pricing strategy is to price the product high, the sales volume will be smaller. The firm's plant site, design, and layout should allow for sufficient (but not excessive) work space to achieve the relatively low production level needed to accommodate the expected sales volume.

If the firm prices its product more competitively, it will anticipate a much larger sales volume. In this case, it would use a plant site, design, and layout to achieve a much larger level of production. Most firms determine the type of target market they wish to pursue and then implement a pricing strategy before deciding on the plant's site, design, and layout. Thus, the pricing strategy dictates the level of production needed, which influences the plant site, design, and layout.

---

contribution margin

the difference between price and variable cost per unit

The break-even point can be determined by first estimating the **contribution margin,** which is the difference between price and variable cost per unit. In our example, the difference is as follows:

$$\text{Price} - \text{Variable Cost per Unit} = \$1.80 - \$.60 = \$1.20$$

For every unit sold, the price received exceeds the variable cost by $1.20. Given that each unit is priced above the variable cost, the break-even quantity of units that must be produced and sold to cover the fixed cost is as follows:

$$\text{Break-Even Quantity} = \frac{\text{Fixed Cost}}{\text{Price} - \text{Variable Cost per Unit}}$$

In our example, the break-even quantity is as follows:

$$\text{Break-Even Quantity} = \frac{\$4,000}{\$1.80 - \$.60}$$

$$= 3,333$$

If you charge a higher price for hot dogs, your contribution margin is higher, and you will break even at a lower quantity. However, a higher price may result in lower demand and therefore may be less profitable. This example is simplified in that only one product was produced. A hot dog vendor would likely offer other food or beverage products as well. Nevertheless, the example using a single product is sufficient to illustrate the factors that are considered when pricing a product.

Pricing Technology-Based Products

As information technology (IT) is increasingly incorporated into products, manufacturers are having to rethink their traditional pricing strategies. Traditionally, most product costs have come from labor and raw materials. This meant that the variable cost of each unit produced (the costs directly associated with a given unit) was a critical factor in the pricing decision. The IT components of products have a different cost structure, however. Although it may cost millions of dollars to design and test a single chip, once chips are in production, the variable cost of producing additional chips is very small (such as a few dollars or even pennies). The same is true for producing software. As a result, although incorporating IT into a product may dramatically improve product quality, it has little impact on the variable cost of that product. Therefore, variable cost is less useful in deciding on price. Firms with technology-based products need to spread the cost of the technology across their product and ensure that they properly price the product to cover the cost of the technology.

Decision Making

Pricing a Product

Recall that NightLife Film Company produces science fiction movies. After its films are no longer being shown in movie theaters, NightLife produces DVDs of the films and sells them online. It prices the DVDs according to demand. Thus, it sets a high price for DVDs of films that are still popular and a low price for DVDs of films that are no longer in demand.

1. Why doesn't NightLife Film Company use the cost of a film to set the price of a DVD?
2. Other film companies also produce DVDs. Why would NightLife monitor the prices of DVDs sold by other film companies when it sets the price of its DVDs?

ANSWERS:1. Some films that were very costly to produce were not popular, while other films that were inexpensive to produce turned out to be popular. If NightLife set the price of its DVDs based on cost, some DVDs of costly but unpopular films would be priced too high and would not sell at all. 2. NightLife needs to price its DVDs in line with its competitors. If it prices its DVDs too high, the potential customers will avoid its DVDs and purchase those of other film producers instead.

Additional Pricing Decisions

Discuss other pricing decisions that a firm may make.

In addition to setting the price of a product, firms must decide whether to offer special discounts, periodic sales prices, and credit terms for specific customers. Each of these decisions is discussed separately.

Discounting

Since some consumers are willing to pay more for a product than others, a firm may attempt to charge different prices to different customers. For example, restaurants and hotels often offer discounts for senior citizens. Magazines offer student discounts on subscriptions. Airlines tend to charge business travelers at least twice the fares of customers who are paying for the flight themselves. Discounting can enable a firm to attract consumers who are more price conscious, while charging higher prices to other consumers who are less price conscious.

Some firms offer discounted prices to customers who submit orders via the Internet. In this way, the firms encourage more online orders, an advantage because a salesperson is not needed to take these orders. Some airlines and hotels offer special discounts when reservations are made through their websites.

Stores rely on sales specials like those shown here to attract customers.

GETTY IMAGES

Sales Prices

Many firms use sales prices as a means of discounting for those consumers who will make purchases only if the price is reduced. For example, retail stores tend to put some of their products on sale in any given week. This strategy not only attracts customers who may have been unwilling to purchase those products at the full price, but it also encourages them to buy other products while they are at the store.

Stores normally put high prices on many products, such as televisions and shoes, to allow for a major reduction in the prices when the products are on sale. Since most consumers recognize that these products may soon be priced at a 20 to 40 percent discount, they tend to purchase these products only when they are on sale.

Credit Terms

Regardless of the price charged for a product, firms must determine whether they will allow the product to be purchased on credit. Supplier firms commonly allow manufacturing firms to purchase supplies on credit. They would obviously prefer cash sales, since a cash payment avoids the possibility of bad debt and also provides an immediate source of funds. Nevertheless, they may still offer credit to attract some manufacturing firms that do not have cash available. Firms can encourage their customers to pay off their credit by offering a discount. For example, the terms "2/10 net 30" indicate that a 2 percent discount can be taken if the bill is paid within 10 days and that the bill must be paid in full within 30 days.

A change in credit terms can affect a firm's sales. Thus, firms may revise their credit terms as a marketing tool. If a firm desires to increase demand, it may offer an extended period to pay off the credit, such as 2/10 net 60. A disadvantage of this strategy is that many credit balances will be paid off at a slower rate. In addition, the level of bad debt tends to be higher for firms that offer such loose credit terms.

Many retail stores offer credit to customers through MasterCard and VISA credit cards. Retailers pay a percentage of their credit sales (usually around 4 percent) to the sponsor of the card. The advantage of these cards is that the credit balance is paid by a bank, which in turn is responsible for collecting on customer credit.

Many companies, such as Sears, issue their own credit cards to consumers. These companies frequently use the Internet to make customers aware of the benefits associated with owning a credit card issued by the company. Advertising the card on the company's website allows customers to assess the potential benefits of owning the credit card.

Decision Making

Offering Sales Prices

NightLife Film Company has decided to offer a special sales price for one of its popular science fiction DVDs that was created about three months ago. NightLife believes that its regular customers who always buy science fiction DVDs have already purchased this DVD, so it is trying to attract additional customers who may purchase the DVD only if the price is lower. In addition, NightLife hopes that some of these customers will become more interested in its other science fiction DVDs.

1. Why night NightLife offer the special sales price only after the DVD has been on the market for a few months?
2. What is a possible disadvantage to NightLife from offering a DVD at a sales price?

ANSWERS:1. NightLife would prefer to sell the DVD at its normal price to those customers who will definitely purchase the DVD. It can generate more revenue from charging a higher price to its customers. 2. A disadvantage is that NightLife may receive less revenue than if it charged its normal price, assuming that the customers would have purchased the DVD anyway. Also, it is possible that some customers will expect NightLife to offer other DVDs at sales prices in the future and will purchase them only if they are on sale.

COLLEGE HEALTH CLUB: CHC's PRODUCT DIFFERENTIATION, DISCOUNTING, AND CREDIT DECISIONS

Services such as aerobics classes, weight machines, and exercise machines are somewhat similar among health clubs. Nevertheless, Sue Kramer, the president of College Health Club (CHC), thinks that she can differentiate CHC from other health clubs. For college students, CHC offers several advantages. Perhaps the most important advantage is its location. It is located across from the college campus, so students can walk to the club. Since many students do not have cars, this location is a major advantage over other health clubs for the students who live on campus. In addition, CHC's membership fee is lower than that of other health clubs in the area, which is important to college students.

Sue also considers various types of discounting strategies to increase membership at CHC. First, she considered offering a 10 percent discount to any students who signed up in the first week of the fall semester. She decided against that strategy, however, because she was afraid that existing members might become upset that they were not offered the discount.

She also considered increasing the annual membership fee to $525 and offering a student discount so that students could still become members for $500. Nonstudents could more easily afford to pay a slightly higher membership fee. She decided against this policy, however, because she wants to attract more nonstudent members.

Sue also considered offering credit terms to members as a way of increasing memberships. For example, she could allow them to sign up for a membership and then pay three or six months later. She decided against this strategy because some members who receive credit might not ever pay their bill.

Summary

1 A product line is a set a related products or services offered by a single firm. The assortment of products offered by a firm is its product mix. The phases of the product life cycle are

▶ introduction phase, in which consumers are informed about the product;

▶ growth phase, in which the product becomes more popular and increases its share of the market;

▶ maturity phase, in which the sales volume levels off as a result of competition; and

▶ decline phase, in which the sales volume is reduced as a result of competition or reduced consumer demand.

2 The main factors affecting the size of a product's target market are

▶ demographic trends, such as age and income levels;

▶ geography;

▶ economic factors, such as economic growth; and

▶ changes in social values, such as a decline in demand for products perceived to be unhealthy.

3 The main steps involved in creating a new product are

▶ develop a product idea, which may be in response to changes in consumer needs or preferences;

▶ assess the feasibility of the product idea, which entails compar-

ing the expected benefits with the costs of the product;

▶ design the product and test it with some consumers in the target market;

▶ distribute the product so that it is accessible to the target market, and promote the product to ensure that consumers are aware of it; and

▶ post-audit the product to determine whether the product needs to be revised in any way.

4 Some common methods used to differentiate a product are

▶ unique design, in which the product produced is safer, more reliable, easier to use, or has some other advantages;

▶ unique packaging, which can enhance convenience or contain advertising; and

▶ unique branding, which may enhance consumers' perception of the product's quality.

5 The key factors that influence the pricing decision are

▶ cost of production, so the price charged can recover costs incurred;

▶ inventory supply, so the price can be lowered to remove excess inventory; and

▶ prices of competitors, so the price may be set below those of competitors to gain an advantage (penetration pricing) or above those of competitors to create an

image of high quality (prestige pricing).

6 In addition to setting a price for each product, firms need to make these other pricing decisions:

▶ discounting, which involves deciding whether to give discounts to specific customers;

▶ sales prices, which entails deciding whether to put some products on sale for all customers periodically, and what the sales price should be; and

▶ credit terms, which involves deciding whether to provide credit to large customers that buy the product in bulk, and what the credit terms should be.

How the Chapter Concepts Affect Business Performance

A firm's decisions about the product and pricing concepts summarized here affect its performance. Its decisions about products are intended to create products that consumers desire and to identify markets where the products will sell. All product and pricing decisions are intended to affect the demand for the products and therefore the firm's revenue. Since these decisions can influence the demand, they also affect the number of products that need to be produced and therefore affect the firm's expenses.

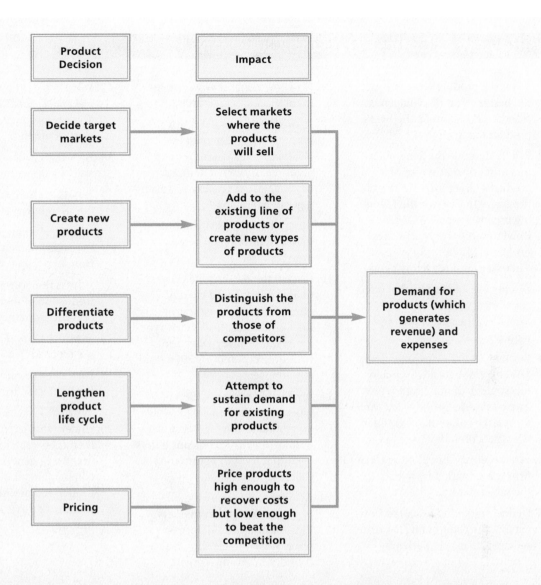

Product Decision	Impact	
Decide target markets	Select markets where the products will sell	
Create new products	Add to the existing line of products or create new types of products	Demand for products (which generates revenue) and expenses
Differentiate products	Distinguish the products from those of competitors	
Lengthen product life cycle	Attempt to sustain demand for existing products	
Pricing	Price products high enough to recover costs but low enough to beat the competition	

Key Terms

branding 470
break-even point 477
co-branding 471
consumer markets 456
contribution margin 478
convenience products 450
cost-based pricing 473
decline phase 454
defensive pricing 475
demographics 457
family branding 470
fashion obsolescence 461
fixed cost 476
generic brands 471

growth phase 454
individual branding 470
industrial markets 456
introduction phase 454
marketing research 461
maturity phase 454
obsolete 460
patents 464
penetration pricing 473
predatory pricing 475
prestige pricing 475
price skimming 454
price-elastic 474
price-inelastic 474

producer brands 471
product 450
product differentiation 468
product life cycle 454
product line 450
product mix 450
shopping products 450
specialty products 450
store brands 471
target market 456
technological obsolescence 461
trademark 470
variable costs 476

Review & Critical Thinking Questions

1. What is a product mix? Is it in the best interest of management to expand or contract the firm's product mix over time?

2. Briefly describe the general factors influencing the size of a product's target market. Identify the target market for the following organizations: (a) Dallas Cowboys, (b) Wal-Mart stores, (c) Midas Muffler, (d) Jeep Cherokee, and (e) Jenny Craig.

3. Discuss the key factors that affect consumer preferences and therefore affect the size of the target market.

4. Discuss the following statement: "We are emphatically global in our strategy of building a few core businesses worldwide." Are most large corporations going in this direction today?

5. What is e-marketing? How can a firm use e-marketing to expand the target market?

6. Define marketing research. How could a firm attempting to create new products use marketing research?

7. How can e-marketing complement marketing research?

8. Assume that you are an inventor who has just created a new product. Will a patent protect your invention in a domestic market? Are there any disadvantages of patents?

9. Describe the steps you should follow in developing a new product.

10. Discuss the product life cycle phases. Identify the current phase for the following products: (a) snowboards, (b) electric typewriters, (c) Harley-Davidson "full-dresser," and (d) 2006 Ford automobile.

11. Briefly describe the different types of pricing strategies. How do you think the type of strategy used by Calvin Klein jeans differs from that used by community colleges?

12. Assume that you are a manager of a retail outlet that markets T-shirts. You must determine a price. What factors should you consider in setting a pricing strategy?

13. What is meant by the term *inelastic demand?* What are some kinds of products that have inelastic demand?

14. How does geography affect the size of a target market?

15. What are three common methods of differentiating a product?

16. What is obsolescence? How can managers prevent their products from becoming obsolete?

17. Why is the post-audit of the introduction of a new product important for managers?

18. How does branding help Nike sell footwear?

19. How does research and development affect a firm's ability to create new products?

20. Under what circumstances might customers prefer a producer brand to a generic brand of a comparable product, even though the producer brand is more expensive than the generic brand?

Discussion Questions

1. Assume that you are a marketing manager for a nationally known pizza chain. You have just read a marketing research article describing the tastes and preferences of consumers throughout the country. You are planning to discuss this subject with your employees at a meeting. Identify the topics that you would discuss with this group.

2. How can a firm use the Internet to differentiate its products from the products of competitors?

How can it use the Internet to identify its target market?

3. You are the marketing manager of a car manufacturer. How could you use e-marketing to expand your target market?

4. What general advice would you give to a retailer when you are very dissatisfied with a service that you have purchased?

5. You are a marketing manager for a restaurant chain. You are aware that the aging population

in this country has become health conscious. What impact do you think these developments will have on the restaurant industry? How could marketing research help in this situation?

6. Although Harley-Davidson "full-dressers" are popular with consumers over 35 years of age, younger motorcycle buyers perceive this vehicle as staid and not sporty enough to suit their tastes. These younger motorcycle

buyers are more likely to buy foreign-made sport motorcycles like the Kawasaki Ninja. Product managers at Harley-Davidson may want to reposition their top-of-the-line "full-dressers" to appeal to younger consumers as well. You are the product manager in charge of developing a plan to achieve this goal. What strategy do you think would be most effective for reaching this market segment?

7. Consider recent purchases you have made. What kinds of convenience products have you bought, and what kind of shopping products have you bought?

Have you bought any specialty products? What aspects of marketing contributed to your economic decision making? For what kinds of products was your demand elastic? For what kinds of products was your demand inelastic?

8. Consider a McDonald's television ad. Who do you think is McDonald's target audience? What kinds of strategies does McDonald's use to market its food to children?

9. You are a manager of a firm that provides credit to its manufacturing clients. How can credit terms be used in marketing?

How can you influence the payment for your products? Is there any risk to extending credit? What are the benefits to your firm from providing a large discount for early payment?

10. You have been hired as a market researcher for a chain of hair salons. How will you go about obtaining information regarding the product mix your firm should offer? How will you identify the demographic characteristics of your target market? What factors would determine the size of your target market?

It's Your Decision: Pricing Decisions at CHC

1. Would prestige pricing be an effective strategy for CHC based on its primary target market?

2. If Sue Kramer, the president of CHC, is considering a pricing strategy of reducing the membership fee, why must she first consider the size of the facilities?

3. Recall that Sue expects total expenses of $142,000 in CHC's first year. Sue will price a membership at $500 and expects to attract 300 members in the first year. Assume that Sue considers lower membership prices than she originally planned. Determine CHC's estimated earnings before taxes based on the following possible pricing scenarios:

If CHC's Membership Price Is:	The Expected Number of Members in the First Year Would Be:	CHC's Earnings before Taxes in the First Year Would Be:
$500 (original plan)	300	_____
$480	310	_____
$460	320	_____
$440	335	_____

Which price should Sue charge? Explain.

4. A health club differs from manufacturing firms in that it produces a service rather than products. Explain how the process of targeting by a service-oriented firm is different than the process of targeting by a manufacturing-oriented firm.

Investing in a Business

Using the annual report of the firm in which you would like to invest, complete the following:

1. Describe the firm's product line or product mix. Does the firm benefit from its brand name?

2. Has the firm developed any new products recently? If so, are these products extensions of the firm's existing product line?

3. Has the firm established any new pricing policies? If so, provide details.

4. Explain how the business uses technology or the Internet to price its products. Explain how the business uses technology or the Internet to identify its target market and to differentiate its product from the products of competitors.

Case: Marketing T-Shirts

Richard Schilo is the owner-operator of Richard's T-Shirts, a manufacturing business. The business has been in operation for two years. Richard has discovered through marketing research that teenagers desire his T-shirts. As a result of this research, Richard introduced a sports line of T-shirts with the endorsements of professional franchises. Richard has had tremendous success with this product line. His business has become highly profitable, having grown 100 percent from the first year's $150,000 in sales to a current level of $300,000 in sales.

Additional marketing research has indicated that the collegiate market offers high growth potential. In the fall, Richard plans to introduce a line of collegiate sweaters at a retail price of $29.95. These sweaters will be sold in college bookstores around the country and will be priced competitively with other comparable sweater lines. The sweaters will be unique in appearance, with embroidered college insignias in school colors and the school mascot on the sweater sleeve. Each sweater will be packaged in a gym bag highlighting the athletic program of the student's choice. An exclusive brand name will be selected for each college and university. The plan is that the brand name will feature that school's athlete of the year.

In the future, Richard plans to introduce his product line to a nationwide network of retail establishments. His pricing strategy will continue during this expansion. His projections show that he will continue to build volume, especially in the retail discount sector, where much growth has taken place in recent years.

Questions

1. Describe the target market for Richard's T-Shirts.

2. Identify and explain some common methods Richard is planning to use to differentiate his sweaters from other competing products.

3. What is the current stage of the product life cycle for these T-shirts?

4. Discuss the pricing strategy that Richard plans to use when he introduces the sweaters.

5. Explain how Richard could use e-marketing to expand his target market.

Video Case: Marketing at Burton Snowboards

Burton Snowboards, which was founded in 1977 by Jeff Burton, an avid snowboarder, is a global leader in the manufacture of snowboards and snowboarding-related gear. In addition to snowboards, Burton's product mix includes a variety of products, such as gloves, boots, hats, and weatherproof clothes. Burton not only produces high-quality products, but it also uses technological advances to improve its products. You can get more information on Burton Snowboards at http://www.Burton.com.

Questions

1. Who is Burton Snowboards' target market? How do you think Burton identified its target market?

2. How does globalization affect Burton's target market and marketing strategy?

3. Are Burton's products convenience, shopping, or specialty products?

4. Do you think demand for Burton's products is elastic or inelastic? How does Burton take this into account when marketing its snowboards?

5. How can Burton Snowboards avoid the obsolescence of its products?

6. How can Burton Snowboards use the Internet to market its products?

7. Is research and development important to Burton? Why?

Internet Applications

1. http://smallbusiness.yahoo.com/marketing

What is e-marketing? What Internet marketing strategies can you identify on this website? How might the managers of a newly established small firm benefit from marketing online? Why might an e-marketing strategy fail?

2. http://www.yum.com

What brands are owned by Yum Brands? Does Yum Brands use family branding or individual branding?

Click on "About" and then on "The Brands." Has Yum Brands been successful in establishing a global marketing strategy?

3. http://www.uspto.gov/index.html

What are patents? What are trademarks? How does the U.S. Patent Office use the Internet to help companies obtain patents and trademarks?

Dell's Secret to Success

Go to http://www.reportgallery.com and review Dell's most recent annual report. Also, go to Dell's website (http://www.dell.com) and in the section "about Dell," review the background material about Dell that relates to this chapter.

Questions

1. Describe Dell's target markets.

2. How has Dell expanded its products?

3. Why do you think Dell benefited from expanding its products to include printers?

In-Text Study Guide

Answers are in Appendix C at the back of book.

True or False

1. Consumers purchasing convenience goods will shop around and compare quality and price of similar products.

2. As new consumer needs are identified, firms tend to expand both their product lines and product mix.

3. Demographics can be used to identify a target market.

4. During a recession, the demand for specialty goods tends to increase.

5. Price skimming is a strategy commonly used in highly competitive markets.

6. A change in interest rates can have a major impact on consumer demand.

7. E-marketing is highly successful in domestic (U.S.) markets, but the high cost of shipping has prevented U.S. companies from using it successfully in foreign markets.

8. A change in credit terms can affect a firm's sales.

9. Warranties can be used to achieve product differentiation.

10. Firms should use penetration pricing if their products are price-inelastic.

Multiple Choice

11. A Rolex watch and a Jaguar automobile are considered:
    a) convenience products.
    b) shopping goods.
    c) industrial products.
    d) specialty products.
    e) priority products.

12. When a hospital supply company offers a wide variety of products to its customers, the firm is:
    a) offering quantity price discounts in order to attract price-conscious customers.
    b) encouraging customers to pay their outstanding debts in order to take advantage of discounts.
    c) practicing product differentiation.
    d) diversifying its product mix.
    e) responding to the needs of a diverse labor force.

13. All of the following are key factors that influence consumer preferences and the size of a target market except:
    a) social values.
    b) anthropology.
    c) economic factors.
    d) geography.
    e) demographics.

14. Cameras, clothes, and household items are examples of products that exist in:
    a) industrial markets.
    b) business markets.
    c) consumer markets.
    d) government markets.
    e) foreign industrial markets.

15. The size of a particular target market is most likely to change in response to a change in:
    a) inflation.
    b) consumer preferences.
    c) interest rates.
    d) the number of competitors.
    e) the size of the largest competitor.

16. When firms develop products, they assess the markets of their competitors to determine their:
    a) financial plans.
    b) marketing strategies.
    c) industrial strategies.
    d) geographic segmentation.
    e) business segmentation.

In-Text Study Guide

Answers are in Appendix C at the back of book.

17. Personal computers are subject to _____ because of the rapid changes in the development of computer hardware components.
    a) product feasibility
    b) penetration pricing
    c) planned obsolescence
    d) the development of generic brands
    e) technological obsolescence

18. E-marketing supports marketing research in all the following ways except:
    a) low cost of personal surveys.
    b) speed of receiving marketing information.
    c) customer openness with opinions.
    d) access to customers of varied income levels.
    e) face-to-face interviews.

19. To develop new ideas for expanding their product line, many firms have recently increased their investment in:
    a) research and development.
    b) production facilities.
    c) distribution facilities.
    d) overseas production and assembly operations.
    e) inventory control.

20. Which of the following can be used by a firm to protect its investments in research and product development?
    a) marketing research
    b) patents
    c) demographics
    d) target market selection
    e) product mix

21. The first step in creating a new product is to:
    a) assess the feasibility of the product.
    b) develop a product idea.
    c) design the product.
    d) test the product.
    e) distribute and promote the product.

22. New and revised products may be tested through:
    a) commercialization.
    b) geographic sales.
    c) product life cycle.
    d) family brands.
    e) marketing research.

23. All of the following are methods commonly used to differentiate products from those of competitors except:
    a) quality.
    b) design.
    c) tax policies.
    d) packaging.
    e) branding.

24. The Coca-Cola Company sells Coca-Cola, Diet Coke, Cherry Coke, and other soft drinks, which is an example of a(n):
    a) family brand.
    b) individual brand.
    c) corporate brand.
    d) trademark.
    e) copyright.

25. Many _____ strategies are focused on convenience.
    a) packaging
    b) economic
    c) partnership
    d) obsolescence
    e) finance

26. Products that are not branded by the producer or retail store are called:
    a) manufacturer brands.
    b) national brands.
    c) store brands.
    d) obsolete brands.
    e) generic brands.

In-Text Study Guide

27. All of the following are benefits of product branding except:
    a) greater company name recognition.
    b) lower prices.
    c) easier to introduce new products.
    d) easier to enter new geographic markets.
    e) easier to obtain retail store shelf space.

28. The process of combining two noncompeting products at a discounted price is called:
    a) complementary advertising.
    b) multiple discounts.
    c) co-branding.
    d) sales promotion double.
    e) quantity pricing.

29. Sales of the product increase rapidly during the _____ phase of the product life cycle.
    a) maturity
    b) introduction
    c) saturation
    d) growth
    e) declining

30. Which of the following pricing strategies would likely be used in a market where no other competitive products are available?
    a) cost-based pricing
    b) penetration pricing
    c) predatory pricing
    d) price skimming
    e) defensive pricing

31. Managers typically attempt to set a price that will maximize a firm's:
    a) value.
    b) cost.
    c) production.
    d) advertising.
    e) promotion.

32. When a firm lowers its price and total revenue increases, it tells us that:
    a) the demand for the product is price-inelastic.
    b) a penetration pricing strategy is being followed.
    c) consumers are not very responsive to price changes.
    d) the demand for the product is price-elastic.
    e) the firm is using a price-skimming strategy.

33. Some pricing decisions are directly related to the supply of:
    a) social values.
    b) social norms.
    c) maintenance operations.
    d) creditors in the marketplace.
    e) inventory.

34. Which of the following pricing strategies adds a profit markup to the per-unit cost of production?
    a) prestige pricing
    b) cost-based pricing
    c) defensive pricing
    d) profit pricing
    e) penetration pricing

35. When a cost of production remains unchanged regardless of how many units are produced, it is referred to as:
    a) variable.
    b) semifinished.
    c) fixed.
    d) in process.
    e) terminal.

36. (Fixed Cost) + (Quantity $\times$ Variable Cost per Unit) describes:
    a) Total Cost.
    b) Total Revenue.
    c) Break-Even Point.
    d) Profits.
    e) Average Cost Per Unit.

In-Text Study Guide

Answers are in Appendix C at the back of book.

37. The break-even point occurs when:
    a) profits are maximized.
    b) sales are at a minimum.
    c) total revenue equals total cost.
    d) contribution margin is highest.
    e) sales discounts are minimized.

38. Discounts:
    a) are considered predatory pricing.
    b) work best in price-inelastic situations.
    c) tend to erode profits.
    d) attract consumers who are price conscious.
    e) are an inefficient means of segmenting the market.

Chapter

13

MASTERFILE CORPORATION

The Learning Goals of this chapter are to:

Explain the advantages and disadvantages of a direct channel of distribution, and identify factors that could determine the optimal channel of distribution. *1*

Differentiate between types of market coverage. *2*

Describe the various forms of transportation used to distribute products. *3*

Explain how the distribution process can be accelerated. *4*

Explain how retailers serve customers. *5*

Explain how wholesalers can serve manufacturers and retailers. *6*

Explain the strategy and potential benefits of vertical channel integration. *7*

The future performance of Italia Company is influenced by decisions about how to distribute its shoes to its customers.

492

Distributing Products

A distribution channel represents the path of a product from the producer to the consumer. The channel often includes marketing intermediaries, or firms that participate in moving the product toward the customer. Consider the case of Italia Company, a U.S. producer of expensive shoes. Italia must make the following decisions:

▶ What should be its optimal form of distribution?

▶ What type of market coverage should it pursue?

▶ How can it accelerate its distribution?

▶ How may retailers improve its distribution?

▶ How may wholesalers improve its distribution?

▶ Should it create its own intermediary to distribute its products?

These types of decisions are necessary for all businesses. This chapter explains how various distribution decisions can be made in a manner that maximizes the firm's value.

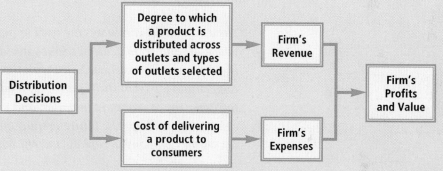

Channels of Distribution

A firm's distribution decision determines the manner by which its products are made accessible to its customers. Firms must develop a strategy to ensure that products are distributed to customers at a place convenient to them. Black & Decker distributes its power tools at various retail stores where customers shop for power tools. Liz Claiborne distributes its clothing at upscale clothing stores where customers shop for quality clothing. Ralston Purina distributes its dog food to grocery stores where customers shop for dog food.

Direct Channel

1

Explain the advantages and disadvantages of a direct channel of distribution, and identify factors that could determine the optimal channel of distribution.

direct channel
the situation when a producer of a product deals directly with customers

When a producer of a product deals directly with customers, marketing intermediaries are not involved; this situation is called a **direct channel.** An example of a direct channel is a firm such as Land's End that produces clothing and sells some clothing directly to customers. Land's End distributes catalogs in the mail to customers, who can call in their orders. It also has a website where consumers can place orders online.

marketing intermediaries
firms that participate in moving
the product from the producer
toward the customer

Advantages of a Direct Channel   The advantage of a direct channel is that the full difference between the manufacturer's cost and the price paid by the consumer goes to the producer. When manufacturers sell directly to customers, they have full control over the price to be charged to the consumer. Conversely, when they sell their products to **marketing intermediaries,** they do not control the prices charged to consumers. Manufacturers also prefer to avoid intermediaries because the prices of their products are increased at each level of the distribution channel, and the manufacturers do not receive any of the markup.

Another advantage of a direct channel is that the producer can easily obtain firsthand feedback on the product. This allows the producer to respond quickly to any customer complaints. Customer feedback also informs the producer about potential problems in the product design and therefore allows for improvement.

Use of a direct channel of distribution is becoming more popular as a result of the Internet. Many manufacturers advertise their products online, take orders on their website, and deliver the products directly to the customers. Dell, Inc., is a good example of a firm that uses the Internet in this way.

Dell justifies its use of a direct channel of distribution in a recent annual report:

"The direct model eliminates the need to support an extensive network of wholesale and retail dealers, thereby avoiding dealer markups; avoids the higher inventory costs associated with the wholesale/retail channel and the competition for retail shelf space. . . . In addition, the direct model allows the Company to maintain, monitor, and update a customer database that can be used to shape the future product offerings. . . . This direct approach allows the Company to rapidly and efficiently deliver relevant technology to its customers."

When Dell sells its computers online, there is no additional markup by intermediaries, so customers get what they want at a lower price, and Dell can still be very profitable. Dell relies heavily on the Internet to facilitate its direct channel of distribution and to receive customer questions. About half of the technical support communication between customers and Dell occurs online. Recently, Dell established some small kiosks where consumers can view and test the computers, but the consumers must still place orders online.

Dell continues the direct relationship with its customers after they purchase their computers. If the customers have complaints, they contact Dell directly. Consequently, Dell can identify any deficiencies and correct them when it designs the next generation of computers. For example, assume that Dell sells a computer model that is popular but would be even more desirable with a redesigned keyboard. Because Dell deals directly with its customers, it will receive frequent feedback from the customers about the keyboard. If instead Dell sold computers to marketing intermediaries, it would not have direct access to customer opinions because the intermediaries would be dealing with the customers.

Disadvantages of a Direct Channel   A direct channel also has some disadvantages. First, manufacturers that use a direct channel need more employees. If a company that produces lumber wants to avoid intermediaries, it has to hire sales and delivery people to sell the lumber directly to consumers. By using intermediaries, the company can specialize in the production of lumber rather than be concerned with selling the lumber directly to consumers. In addition, producers that use a direct channel may have to incur more expenses to promote the product. Intermediaries can promote products through advertisements or even by placing the product in a place where consumers will see it.

Another disadvantage of a direct channel is that the manufacturer may have to sell its products on credit when selling to customers directly. By selling to intermediaries, it may not have to provide credit.

One-Level Channel

one-level channel
one marketing intermediary is between the producer and the customer

merchants
marketing intermediaries that become owners of products and then resell them

In a **one-level channel,** one marketing intermediary is between the producer and the customer, as illustrated in Exhibit 13.1. Some marketing intermediaries (called **merchants**) become owners of the products and then resell them. For example, wholesalers act as merchants by purchasing products in bulk and reselling them to other firms. In addition, retail stores (or "retailers") such as Wal-Mart and Sears act as merchants by purchasing products in bulk and selling them to consumers. GNC (General Nutrition Centers) uses its chain of more than 4,200 retail stores to distribute its vitamins and related products. Foot Locker has more than 2,700 retail outlets that sell athletic shoes produced by Nike, Reebok, and other shoe producers. Other marketing intermediaries, called **agents,** match buyers and sellers of products without becoming owners.

agents
marketing intermediaries that match buyers and sellers of products without becoming owners

Time Warner commonly uses a one-level channel of distribution for its films and records, tapes, and CDs. Its film company distributes films to movie theaters (the retailer), while its record companies distribute records, tapes, and CDs to retail music shops.

Two-Level Channel

two-level channel
two marketing intermediaries are between the producer and the customer

Some products go through a **two-level channel** of distribution, in which two marketing intermediaries are between the producer and the customer. This type of distribution channel is illustrated in Exhibit 13.2. As an example, consider a company that produces lumber and sells it to a wholesaler, who in turn sells the lumber to various retailers. Each piece of lumber goes through two merchants before it reaches the customer.

Exhibit 13.1

Example of a One-Level Channel of Distribution

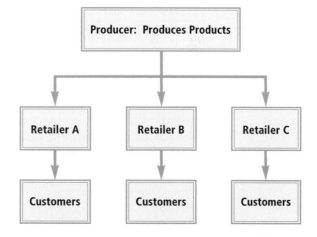

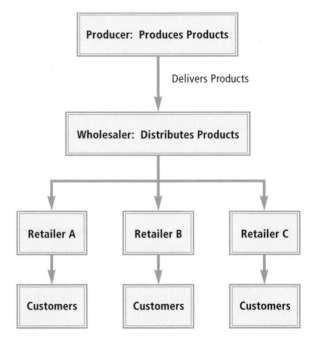

As an alternative, an agent could take orders for lumber from retail stores; then, the agent would contact the lumber company and arrange to have the lumber delivered to the retailers. In this case, the merchant wholesaler is replaced with an agent, but there are still two intermediaries.

Anheuser-Busch typically uses a two-level channel to distribute Budweiser and its other brands of beer. It relies on 900 beer wholesalers to distribute its beer to retail outlets such as grocery and convenience stores.

Benefits for Small Producers   Small businesses that produce one or a few products commonly use a two-level channel of distribution. Because these businesses are not well known, they may not receive orders from retail outlets. Therefore, they rely on agents to sell the products to retailers. Consider all the products that a retailer like Home Depot sells. If an entrepreneur creates a new paint product or other home improvement product, it may use an agent to meet with a representative (called a buyer) of Home Depot who will decide whether Home Depot should carry this product in its stores. A small business that creates only a few products may have a much better chance of succeeding if it can convince a large retailer to carry its products. Thus, an agent can be critical to the success of such a firm.

Summary of Distribution Systems

The most common distribution systems are compared in Exhibit 13.3. Firms can use more than one distribution system. For example, Gillette's shaving products are produced at 32 facilities in 14 countries. They are distributed through wholesalers and retailers through different distribution systems that cover more than 200 countries. Many firms sell products directly to customers through their websites but also sell their products through intermediaries. When firms can avoid a marketing intermediary, they may be able to earn a higher profit per unit on their products, but they will likely sell a smaller quantity unless they use other marketing strategies.

Exhibit 13.3

Comparison of Common
Distribution Systems

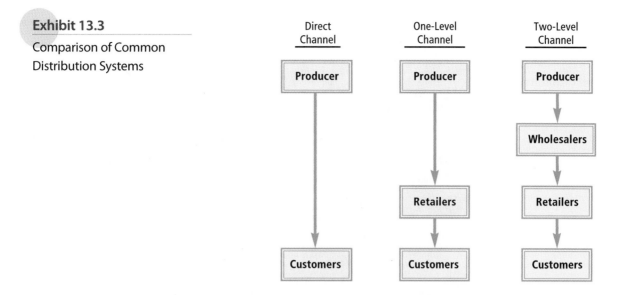

A firm may change its distribution system as circumstances change. For example, Dell, Inc., will soon open an integrated customer center and production facility in Xiamen, China. The facility will give Dell its first major presence in the world's most populous country, where it has marketed computers through distributors for several years. Thus, Dell will convert from a two-level distribution channel in China to a direct distribution channel, which is perfect for a product that may be damaged during transport and is not standardized.

Factors That Determine the Optimal Channel of Distribution

The optimal channel of distribution depends on the product's characteristics, such as its ease of transporting and degree of standardization. The firm's ability to fulfill Internet orders is also a factor. The effects of these characteristics are described next.

Ease of Transporting   If a product can be easily transported, the distribution channel is more likely to involve intermediaries. If the product cannot be transported, the producer may attempt to sell directly to consumers. For example, a manufacturer of built-in swimming pools must deal directly with the consumer, since the product cannot be channeled to the consumer. Conversely, aboveground pools are transportable and are more likely to involve intermediaries.

Degree of Standardization   Products that are standardized are more likely to involve intermediaries. When specifications are unique for each consumer, the producer must deal directly with consumers. For example, specialized office furniture for firms may vary with each firm's preferences. Specialized products cannot be standardized and offered at retail shops.

Internet Orders   Firms that fill orders over the Internet tend to use a direct channel because their website serves as a substitute for a retail store. For example, Amazon.com provides a menu of books and other products that it can deliver to customers so that customers do not need to go to a retail

Gillette has numerous production facilities (like the one shown here) in which it produces and distributes products.

CORBIS, CHICAGO

store to purchase these products. Amazon fills orders by having products delivered directly from its warehouses to customers. In fact, Amazon has recently built new warehouses in additional locations so that it can ensure quick delivery to customers throughout the United States and in many foreign countries.

Gateway sells its computers directly to customers. It states in its annual report that "the direct channel—delivering goods and services directly from manufacturing to customer—is simply the most efficient channel for business." The Gap uses the Internet to sell clothes directly to customers, but it still maintains its retail stores for customers who wish to shop at the mall rather than online.

Decision Making

Selecting the Channels of Distribution

Consider the case of Italia Company (introduced at the beginning of the chapter), which produces expensive shoes. It cannot reach consumers directly from its factory, so it uses a one-level channel in which it distributes its shoes to some retail shoe stores.

1. How could Italia Company use the Internet to create a direct channel of distribution?

2. Should Italia consider a two-level channel of distribution?

ANSWERS: 1. It could create a Web-based business in which it would sell the shoes online and have a delivery service deliver the shoes. 2. It does not need a two-level channel of distribution.

Differentiate between
types of market coverage.

market coverage
the degree of product distribution
among outlets

intensive distribution
the distribution of a product across
most or all possible outlets

selective distribution
the distribution of a product
through selected outlets

exclusive distribution
the distribution of a product
through only one or a few outlets

Selecting the Degree of Market Coverage

Any firm that uses a marketing intermediary must determine a plan for **market coverage,** or the degree of product distribution among outlets. Firms attempt to select the degree of market coverage that can provide consumers with easy access to their products, but they may also need to ensure that the outlets are capable of selling their products. Market coverage can be classified as intensive distribution, selective distribution, or exclusive distribution.

Intensive Distribution

To achieve a high degree of market coverage for all types of consumers, **intensive distribution** is used to distribute a product across most or all possible outlets. Firms that use intensive distribution ensure that consumers will have easy access to the product. Intensive distribution is used for products such as chewing gum and cigarettes that do not take up much space in outlets and do not require any expertise for employees of outlets to sell.

For example, PepsiCo uses intensive distribution to distribute its soft drinks and snacks. PepsiCo's products are sold through retail outlets that focus on food and drinks. The company distributes its soft drinks and snack foods to virtually every supermarket, convenience store, and warehouse club in the United States and in some foreign countries.

Selective Distribution

Selective distribution is used to distribute a product through selected outlets. Some outlets are intentionally avoided. For example, some specialized computer equipment is sold only at outlets that emphasize computer sales because some expertise may be necessary. Some college textbooks are sold only at college bookstores and not at retail bookstores. Liz Claiborne distributes its clothing only to upscale clothing stores.

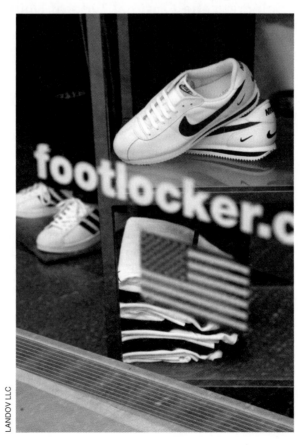

Some of Nike's shoes are sold exclusively to Foot Locker stores.

LANDOV LLC

Exclusive Distribution

With **exclusive distribution,** only one or a few outlets are used. This is an extreme form of selective distribution. For example, some luxury items are distributed exclusively to a few outlets that cater to very wealthy consumers. By limiting the distribution, the firm can create or

	Advantage	Disadvantage
Intensive distribution	Gives consumers easy access.	Many outlets will not accept some products if consumers are unlikely to purchase those products there.
Selective distribution	The distribution is focused on outlets where there will be demand for the products and/or where employees have expertise to sell the products.	Since the distribution is selective, the products are not as accessible as they would be if intensive distribution were used.
Exclusive distribution	Since the distribution is focused on a few outlets, the products are perceived as prestigious. Also the producer can ensure that the outlets where the products are distributed are able to service the product properly.	The product's access to customers is limited.

maintain the prestige of the product. Some Nike brands are sold exclusively to Foot Locker's retail stores.

Some products that have exclusive distribution require specialized service. A firm producing high-quality jewelry may prefer to distribute exclusively to one particular jewelry store in an area where the employees receive extensive training.

Selecting the Optimal Type of Market Coverage

Exhibit 13.4 compares the degrees of market coverage achieved by different distribution systems. The optimal degree of coverage depends on the characteristics of the product.

How Marketing Research Can Influence the Market Coverage Decision   Marketing research can help a firm determine the optimal type of coverage by identifying where consumers desire to purchase products or services. A firm may attempt to get customer feedback before it determines its market coverage. For example, a producer of DVDs could conduct a marketing survey to determine whether consumers would purchase its DVDs at grocery stores and retail stores as well as through video stores. If the survey leads to a decision to distribute through grocery stores, the firm can then use additional marketing research to compare the level of sales at its various outlets. This research will help determine whether the firm should continue distributing DVDs through grocery stores. Nike has used marketing research to determine the types of outlets where it may be able to sell its shoes. When research showed that Foot Locker attracts teenagers who are often willing to spend at least $80 on shoes, Nike decided that Foot Locker was a feasible retail outlet for its shoes.

Decision Making

Selecting the Optimal Market Coverage

The optimal market coverage is dependent on the specific characteristics of the product. Consider the case of Italia Company, which needs to distribute its designer shoes to retailers. It wants to decide on the optimal market coverage for these shoes. Because the shoes have high prices, Italia it uses selective distribution and distributes the shoes through upscale retail stores only.

1. What is a possible disadvantage to Italia Company's decision to focus only on upscale retail stores?
2. How would Italia have to adjust the prices of the shoes if it switched to intensive distribution?

ANSWERS: 1. It can only sell its shoes at a limited number of outlets. 2. It would have to lower the prices so that the shoes might sell at all the retail outlets that are not upscale.

3

Describe the various forms of transportation used to distribute products.

Selecting the Transportation Used to Distribute Products

Any distribution of products from producers to wholesalers or from wholesalers to retailers requires transportation. The cost of transporting some products can exceed the cost of producing them. An inefficient form of transportation can result in higher costs and lower profits for the firm. For each form of transportation, firms should estimate timing, cost, and availability. This assessment allows the firm to choose an optimal method of transportation. The most common forms of transportation used to distribute products are described next.

Truck

Trucks are commonly used for transport because they can reach any destination on land. They can usually transport products quickly and can make several stops. For example, The Coca-Cola Company uses trucks to distribute its soft drinks to retailers in a city.

Rail

Railroads are useful for heavy products, especially when the sender and the receiver are located close to railroad stations. For example, railroads are commonly used to transport coal to electricity-generating plants. If a firm is not adjacent to a station, however, it must reload the product onto a truck. Because the road system allows much more accessibility than railroad tracks, railroads are not useful for short distances. For long distances, however, rail can be a cheaper form of transportation than trucks.

Air

Transportation by air can be quick and relatively inexpensive for light items such as computer chips and jewelry. For a large amount of heavy products such as steel or wood, truck or rail is a better alternative. Even when air is used, trucks are still needed for door-to-door service (to and from the airport).

Toyota has developed a manufacturing plant in Kentucky (shown here) that is used to distribute its cars throughout the United States and to some other countries.

AP/WIDE WORLD PHOTOS

Water

For some coastal or port locations, transportation by water deserves to be considered. Shipping is necessary for the international trade of some goods such as automobiles. Water transportation is often used for transporting bulk products.

Pipeline

For products such as oil and gas, pipelines can be an effective method of transportation. However, the use of pipelines is limited to only a few types of products.

Additional Transportation Decisions

The selection of the proper form of transportation (such as truck, rail, and so on) is only the first step in developing a proper system for transporting products. Consider the transportation decisions faced by Toyota, which sends cars from its factory in Kentucky to various dealerships around the country. It used to let its finished cars sit until it had a large batch to send by rail to a specific city. Now it immediately sends its finished vehicles by rail to a sorting dock, where they are sorted and then delivered to various cities nearby. Consequently the cars no longer sit at the factory. This process has reduced the distribution time by two days.

Also, consider the distribution decisions faced by PepsiCo, which may receive orders for its snack foods and soft drinks from 100 stores in a single city every week. It must determine an efficient way to load the products and then create a route to distribute those products among stores. It must decide the best route and the number of trucks needed to cover the 100 stores. It must also decide whether to distribute snack foods and soft drinks simultaneously or have some trucks distribute snack foods and others distribute soft drinks.

In reality, no formulas are available to determine the ideal distribution system. Most firms attempt to estimate all the expenses associated with each possible way of delivering products that are ordered. Firms compare the total estimated expenses of each method and select the one that is most efficient.

Decision Making

Selecting a Mode of Transportation

Recall that Italia Company produces designer shoes and distributes them to upscale retail shoe stores. Since it is based in San Diego and all of the retailers are based in southern California, it transports its shoes to the retailers by truck. This method is inexpensive because all of the retailers are within an hour's drive of Italia's factory. If Italia decides to distribute its shoes to other markets such as Chicago and New York, delivery by truck would not be efficient. Italia would hire a delivery service to deliver the shoes to some outlets in Chicago and New York. Because it would have to pay a higher cost for this delivery service, it would charge a higher price to the retailers in those cities.

1. Should Italia Company consider transporting its shoes to its existing retailers by rail?
2. Why is Italia's pricing of its shoes partially related to its cost of transporting the shoes?

ANSWERS: 1. No, because trains would not be able to go directly to the retail stores. A truck would still be needed. 2. Italia needs to price the shoes to account for its costs, including the cost of transportation.

4

Explain how the distribution process can be accelerated.

How to Accelerate the Distribution Process

The structure of a firm's distribution system affects its performance. A lengthy distribution process has an adverse effect. First, products will take longer to reach customers, which may allow competitors to supply products to the market sooner. As a result, retail stores or customers may order their products from other firms.

A slow distribution process will also result in a lengthy period from the time the firm invests funds to produce the product until it receives revenue from the sale of the product. In most cases, firms will not receive payment until after customers receive the products. Consequently, firms are forced to invest their funds in the production process for a longer period of time.

To illustrate the importance of speed in the distribution process, consider that the actual time required to distribute a typical cereal box from the producer to the retailer (the grocery store) is about 100 days. Now consider a cereal firm that receives $100 million per year in revenue from the sale of cereal and finds a way to reduce its distribution time from 100 days to 60 days on average. In a typical year, this firm will receive its $100 million of revenue 40 days earlier than before, meaning that it will have 40 extra days to reinvest those funds in other projects. Thus, a reduction in distribution time can enhance a firm's value.

Exhibit 13.5

Example of a Restructured Distribution Process

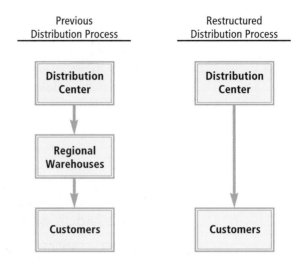

Previous Distribution Process | Restructured Distribution Process

Distribution Center → Regional Warehouses → Customers

Distribution Center → Customers

Streamline the Channels of Distribution

Many firms are attempting to streamline the channels of distribution so that the final product reaches customers more quickly. For example, by eliminating some of its six regional warehouses, National Semiconductor reduced its typical delivery time by 47 percent and its cost of distribution by 2.5 percent. It now sends its microchips directly to customers around the world from its distribution center. This restructuring has removed one level of the distribution process, as shown in Exhibit 13.5.

Restructuring a distribution process commonly results in the elimination of warehouses. When products are light (such as microchips) and can be easily delivered by mail to customers, warehouses may not be needed. Heavy products (such as beverages), however, cannot be easily delivered by mail, so warehouses are necessary.

Use of the Internet for Distribution

Electronic business has streamlined the distribution by providing information on websites so that customers can compare prices and quality of products.

For example, Autobytel.com provides information about new car purchases, offers suggestions about leasing, gives access to dealer invoices, and enables the consumer to find a low-cost car dealer in the area. Paperexchange.com acts as a broker for paper products and equipment. The way consumers make their purchases is gradually changing. The result is more competition among firms and less brand loyalty.

Companies must adapt to this changing business model. Perhaps the most significant change will be the disruption of traditional distribution channels. As the Internet eliminates the distance between producers and consumers, it also eliminates the need for wholesalers, distributors, and retailers. As mentioned earlier, Amazon.com and Dell, Inc., are examples of companies that have prospered without traditional retail outlets.

When firms sell their products directly to customers without using retail stores, they can improve their efficiency. They may be able to sell their product at a lower price as a result. Another significant change occurs in firms' relationships with suppliers and freight haulers. A web of communication allows for increased collaboration and the creation of a partnership in the production chain.

Integrate the Production and Distribution Processes

The distribution process can also be accelerated by improving its interaction with the production process. Notice in Exhibit 13.6 how the production process interacts with the distribution process. As an example, if a firm produces automobiles but does not distribute them quickly, it may have to halt the production process until it has room to store the newly produced automobiles. Alternatively, if an insufficient quantity of automobiles is produced, the manufacturer will not be able to distribute as many automobiles as dealers desire, no matter how efficient its distribution process is.

Saturn ensures that its production and distribution processes interact. Its factories must always have the supplies and parts needed to produce a large volume of automobiles. Then, the automobiles are distributed to numerous dealerships around the country. Local or economic conditions can cause the amount of new automobiles that dealerships periodically need to change abruptly. Thus, Saturn's production and distribution processes must be able to respond quickly to abrupt changes in the demand by dealerships. Since Saturn allows interaction between its production process and its distribution process, it can adjust to satisfy demand.

Compaq Computer (a division of Hewlett-Packard) also used interaction between production and distribution to accelerate its process of distributing computers to more than 30,000 wholesalers and retail stores. It

Exhibit 13.6

Relationship between
Production and Distribution

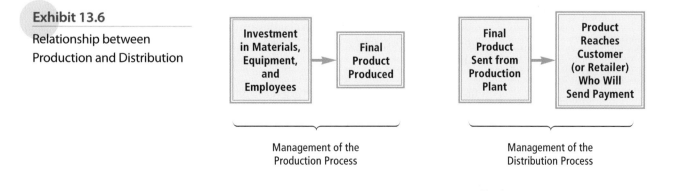

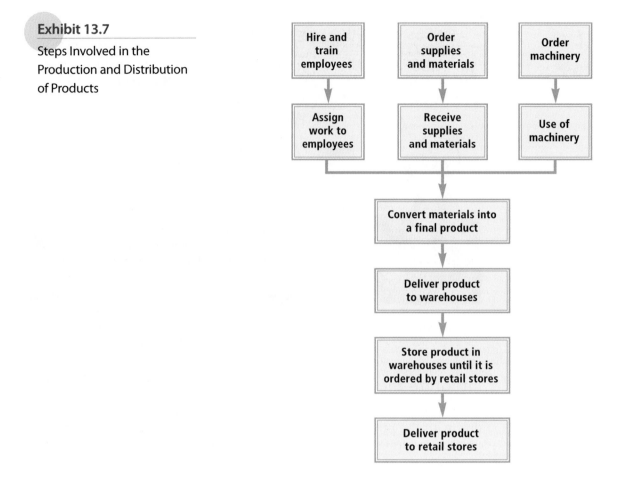

significantly reduced the time from when a final product was produced until it left the production plant. Computer technology was used to indicate which products should be loaded onto specific trucks for delivery purposes.

Exhibit 13.7 provides another perspective on the tasks involved from the time supplies and materials used to produce a product are ordered until the product is delivered to retailers. This exhibit shows how the distribution of products relies on production. If any step in the production process breaks down and lengthens the production period, products will not be distributed on a timely basis.

Assuming that the production process is properly conducted, the firm still needs an efficient distribution system to ensure that products are consistently available for customers. One of the keys to an efficient distribution system is to ensure that any intermediaries used to transfer products from producers to consumers maintain an adequate inventory. The producer must maintain sufficient inventory in anticipation of orders from wholesalers, retailers, or customers. If it does not, it will experience shortages. This task is especially challenging when the firm produces a wide variety of products and sells them to several different intermediaries or customers.

Role of E-Marketing   E-marketing can facilitate the integration between a firm's production and distribution processes. The firm's volume of orders should be updated online and be accessible to both the intermediaries and the production facilities. Consider a manufacturer of video games that has a sales force assigned to sell its games to retail stores. Each salesperson can use the same online ordering service to transmit new orders. The online

Cross Functional Teamwork

Interaction between Distribution Decisions and Other Business Decisions

When marketing managers decide how to distribute a product, they must consider the existing production facilities. Firms that have production facilities scattered around the United States can more easily distribute their products directly from those facilities to the retailer or to the customer. Conversely, firms that use a single manufacturing plant may rely on intermediaries to distribute the product. When a large production facility is needed to achieve production efficiency (as in automobile manufacturing), intermediaries are used to distribute the product.

When a firm creates a new product that will be demanded by customers throughout the United States, it must decide where to produce and how to distribute the product. The two decisions are related. Financial managers of the firm use input provided by production managers on estimated production costs and from marketing managers on estimated distribution costs. If the product is to be produced at a single manufacturing plant, the production cost can be minimized, but the distribution costs are higher. Conversely, if the product is produced at several small manufacturing plants, the production costs are higher, but the distribution costs are relatively low. The financial analysis conducted by financial managers can determine the combination of production and distribution that is most efficient.

Many firms use a single manufacturing plant in the United States and distribute their products throughout the country. If they experience some demand from foreign customers, they may initially attempt to export the products. The cost of distributing products to foreign countries can be very high, however, so U.S. firms often establish a foreign production facility to accommodate the foreign demand. For example, Apple Computer now has three manufacturing plants. Its original plant in California is used to accommodate the demand by U.S. customers. Its plant in Europe produces computer products that are distributed to sales offices throughout Europe. Its plant in Singapore produces computer products that are distributed to sales offices throughout Asia. Apple Computer maintains relatively low distribution expenses by having a manufacturing plant in each region of the world where there is a large demand for its products.

service continuously updates the total orders received by the entire sales force. The firm fills these orders from its existing inventory. Thus, by checking the orders, the firm can determine where future inventory shortages may occur and can increase its production of whatever video games have a low inventory.

Decision Making

Accelerating the Distribution

Recall that Italia Company produces designer shoes. It decides to establish its own e-tail website as a way to allow a faster distribution process to some customers. Although there is a cost to developing the website, Italia will be able to sell its shoes directly to customers targeted for future business. Thus, the price that it will receive from these sales will be higher than the price it receives when it sells its shoes to other retailers who demand a discounted price so that they profit from serving as a retailer.

1. How is Italia's decision to accelerate its distribution process related to its decision regarding its market coverage?

2. Explain how Italia's decision to accelerate the distribution process affects its decision regarding channels of distribution.

ANSWERS: 1. Italia accelerates the distribution process only for a selected group of customers in order to maintain its selective distribution. Generally, accelerating the distribution process results in more intensive market coverage. 2. When Italia accelerates the distribution process by establishing a website, it circumvents some channels of distribution (by avoiding retail stores).

5

Explain how retailers
serve customers.

Background on Retailers

Retailers serve as valuable intermediaries by distributing products directly to customers. One of the most successful retailers in the world is Wal-Mart. It explains that its distribution network is a key to its success in a recent annual report:

"Wal-Mart is in the business of serving customers. In the United States, our operations are centered on operating retail stores and membership warehouse clubs. . . . We have built our business by offering our customers quality merchandise at low prices. We are able to lower the cost of merchandise through our negotiations with suppliers (wholesalers) and by efficiently managing our distribution network."

— Wal-Mart Corporation

Most retailers can be described by the following characteristics:

▶ Number of outlets
▶ Quality of service
▶ Variety of products offered
▶ Store versus nonstore

Number of Outlets

independent retail store
a retailer that has only one outlet

chain
a retailer that has more than one outlet

An **independent retail store** has only one outlet, whereas a **chain** has more than one outlet. Although there are more independent stores than chain stores, the chain stores are larger on average. Chain stores such as Home Depot, Ace Hardware, and Wal-Mart can usually obtain products at a lower cost because they can buy in bulk from the producer (or its intermediaries). Wal-Mart typically deals with the manufacturer so that it can avoid any markup by marketing intermediaries. Chain stores often have a nationwide reputation, which usually provides credibility. This is a major advantage over independent stores.

Quality of Service

full-service retail store
a retailer that generally offers much sales assistance to customers and provides servicing if needed

self-service retail store
a retailer that does not provide sales assistance or service and sells products that do not require much expertise

A **full-service retail store** generally offers much sales assistance to customers and provides servicing if needed. Some products are more appropriate for full service than others. For example, a men's formal wear store offers advice on style and alters the fit for consumers. An electronics store such as Radio Shack provides advice on the use of its products. A **self-service retail store** does not provide sales assistance or service and sells products that do not require much expertise. Examples of self-service stores are Publix Supermarkets and 7-Eleven.

Some retail stores are adapting to the varied preferences of their customers. For example, stores such as Sears and Circuit City offer personalized sales service for customers who need that service. At the same time, they also allow other customers who do not want personalized service to place orders online and pick up the merchandise from the stores. By placing their orders online, the customers avoid time in the store; by picking up the merchandise, they avoid a delivery fee. In addition, they receive the products quicker by picking them up than if they waited for delivery.

Circuit City sells many types of expensive electronic products and provides the personalized service that customers want.

CORBIS, CHICAGO

Variety of Products Offered

specialty retail store
a retailer that specializes in a particular type of product

variety retail store
a retailer that offers numerous types of goods

A **specialty retail store** specializes in a particular type of product, such as sporting goods, furniture, or automobile parts. Kinney's Shoes, which specializes in shoes, is an example of a specialty store. These stores tend to focus on only one or a few types of products but have a wide selection of brands available. A **variety retail store** offers numerous types of goods. For example, KMart, J. C. Penney, and Sears are classified as variety stores because they offer a wide variety of products, including clothes, household appliances, and even furniture.

The advantage of a specialty store is that it may carry a certain degree of prestige. If an upscale clothing store begins to offer other types of products, it may lose its prestige. The disadvantage of a specialty store is that it is not as convenient for consumers who need to purchase a variety of goods. Some consumers may prefer to shop at a store that sells everything they need.

Specialty shops in a shopping mall can retain their specialization and prestige while offering consumers more convenience. Because the mall contains various specialty shops, consumers may perceive it as one large outlet with a variety of products.

Several of these characteristics can be used to describe a single retailer. For example, consider Blockbuster Video. It is a chain, a self-service store, and a specialty store. The Athlete's Foot is a chain, a full-service store, and a specialty store.

Store versus Nonstore

Although most retailers use a store to offer their service, others do not. The three most common types of nonstore retailers are mail-order retailers, websites, and vending machines.

Mail-Order Retailers   A mail-order retailer receives orders through the mail or over the phone. It then sends the products through the mail. Mail-order retailers have become very popular in recent years because many consumers have less leisure time than before and desire shopping convenience. In particular, mail-order clothing retailers have been extremely successful, as consumers find it more convenient to order by phone than to shop in stores. Mail order is more likely to work for products that are light, are somewhat standardized, and do not need to be serviced.

Home shopping networks are a form of mail-order retailing. They have become very popular for specialized items such as jewelry.

Websites   Many firms have established websites where their products can be ordered. One of the main advantages of this method over mail order is that the firm does not have to send out catalogs. In addition, changes can be made easily and frequently.

Most mail-order firms have transformed their business to allow online orders as well. Lands' End is a typical example. It has 16 retail stores and also does substantial business as a catalog retailer, accepting phone orders for clothing and fulfilling the orders by mail. With the emergence of the Internet, Lands' End decided to set up a website and accept online orders. The website can reach customers who do not have a catalog available, and Lands' End can easily change the website at any time, whereas any changes to its catalog will require another distribution to customers by mail. Lands' End's online orders now account for about a third of its total sales.

Vending Machines   Vending machines have also become popular as a result of consumer preferences for convenience. They are often accessible at all hours. Although they were initially used mainly for cigarettes, candy, and soft drinks, some machines are now being used for products such as over-the-counter medications, razors, and travel insurance.

Lands' End has retail outlet stores to complement its catalog service.

GETTY IMAGES

Decision Making

Choosing Retailers

The manner in which a firm should rely on retailers is dependent on the characteristics of the firm. To illustrate, recall that Italia Company produces designer shoes and has restricted its market coverage to some upscale retail shoe stores. Italia wants to reach additional customers without reducing its prestige. It contacts specific upscale clothing stores that have established catalog and website businesses (e-tailing) and accept orders through them. Overall, Italia's plans for using retail stores online are intended to increase its revenue (without hurting its image) and therefore increase its profits.

1. How is Italia's decision to use online retailers related to its decision regarding the degree of market coverage?
2. How is Italia's decision to use online retailers related to its decision about the pricing of products?

ANSWERS: 1. The selection of specific online retailers influences how many customers have access to Italia's product and therefore affects the degree of market coverage. 2. If Italia uses online retailers, it will have to set a price low enough that its shoes will attract demand even after retailers apply a markup to the price that Italia charges the retailers.

Explain how wholesalers can serve manufacturers and retailers.

Background on Wholesalers

Wholesalers are intermediaries that purchase products from manufacturers and sell them to retailers. They are useful to both manufacturers and retailers, as explained next.

How Wholesalers Serve Manufacturers

Wholesalers offer five key services to manufacturers:

▸ Warehousing

▸ Sales expertise

▸ Delivery to retailers

▸ Assumption of credit risk

▸ Information

Warehousing   Wholesalers purchase products from the manufacturer in bulk and maintain these products at their own warehouses. Thus, manufacturers do not need to use their own space to store the products. In addition, manufacturers can maintain a smaller inventory and therefore do not have to invest as much funds in inventory.

To illustrate how manufacturers can benefit from this warehousing, consider Jandy Industries, which produces equipment for swimming pools. Jandy sells its products in bulk to wholesalers that are willing to maintain an inventory of parts. Jandy focuses on maintaining its own inventory of uncommon parts that are not carried by wholesalers.

Sales Expertise   Wholesalers use their sales expertise when selling products to retailers. The retailer's decision to purchase particular products may be primarily due to the wholesaler's persuasion. Once a wholesaler persuades retailers to purchase a product, it will periodically contact the retailers to determine whether they need to purchase more of that product.

This clothing warehouse buys clothing in bulk and then distributes it to retail stores.

GETTY IMAGES

Delivery to Retailers Wholesalers are responsible for delivering products to various retailers. Therefore, manufacturers do not need to be concerned with numerous deliveries. Instead, they can deliver in bulk to wholesalers.

Assumption of Credit Risk When the wholesaler purchases the products from the manufacturer and sells them to retailers on credit, it normally assumes the credit risk (risk that the bill will not be paid). In this case, the manufacturer does not need to worry about the credit risk of the retailers.

Information Wholesalers often receive feedback from retailers and can provide valuable information to manufacturers. For example, they can explain to the manufacturer why sales of the product are lower than expected and can inform the manufacturer about new competing products that are being sold in retail stores.

How Wholesalers Serve Retailers

Wholesalers offer five key services to retailers:

▶ Warehousing
▶ Promotion
▶ Displays
▶ Credit
▶ Information

Warehousing Wholesalers may maintain sufficient inventory so that retailers can order small amounts frequently. Thus, the retailers do not have to maintain a large inventory because the wholesalers have enough inventory to accommodate orders quickly.

Promotion Wholesalers sometimes promote their products, and these efforts may increase the sales of those products by retail stores. The promotional help comes in various forms, including posters or brochures to be displayed in retail stores.

Displays   Some wholesalers set up a display of the products for the retailers. The displays are often designed to attract customers' attention but take up little space. This is important to retailers because they have a limited amount of space.

Credit   Wholesalers sometimes offer products to retailers on credit. This provides a form of financing for retailers, who may have to borrow funds if they are required to make payment when receiving the products.

Information   Wholesalers can inform retailers about policies implemented by other retailers regarding the pricing of products, special sales, or changes in the hours their stores are open. A retailer can use this type of information when it establishes its own related policies.

Decision Making

Whether to Use an Intermediary

The manner in which a firm uses an intermediary is dependent on its specific characteristics. To illustrate, recall that Italia Company produces designer shoes that are sold to specific retailers. Italia is considering using an intermediary to reach additional retail outlets. However, it recognizes that it would have to sell its shoes to the intermediary at a lower price because the intermediary would want profits from selling the shoes to retailers. In addition, Italia is concerned that this form of distribution could lead to more intensive market coverage, which would reduce the appeal of its designer shoes. Italia decides to continue to restrict its distribution so that it can retain its prestige image.

1. Under what conditions could an intermediary benefit Italia?
2. Explain why Italia's decision regarding the use of an intermediary is related to its pricing decision.

ANSWERS: 1. Italia might benefit if the intermediary reaches additional prestige retailers that Italia could not reach on its own. 2. If it uses an intermediary, its prices will have to be low enough to allow the intermediary to apply a markup before selling the shoes to retailers.

Vertical Channel Integration

7

Explain the strategy and potential benefits of vertical channel integration.

vertical channel integration
two or more levels of distribution are managed by a single firm

Some firms use **vertical channel integration,** in which two or more levels of distribution are managed by a single firm. This strategy can be used by manufacturers or retailers, as explained next.

Vertical Channel Integration by Manufacturers

Manufacturers may decide to vertically integrate their operations by establishing retail stores. Consider a producer of clothing that has historically sold its clothes to various retailers. It notices that the retailers' prices are typically about 90 percent above what they paid for the clothes. Consequently, the clothing manufacturer may consider opening its own retail shops if it can achieve higher sales by selling its clothes through these shops.

L. L. Bean has established its own outlet stores that sell the clothing it produces. In this way, the firm serves as the producer and as an intermediary. The intermediaries (outlets) allow the product to be widely distributed. Meanwhile, all earnings generated by the producer or the outlets are beneficial to the owners of L. L. Bean.

Cross Functional Teamwork

Relationship between Pricing and Distribution Strategies

A firm's pricing strategy also influences its distribution strategy. If the pricing strategy is intended to focus only on wealthy customers, the firm's products may be distributed exclusively to upscale outlets. If the prices are set lower to attract a wide variety of customers, however, the products will be distributed across many outlets to achieve broad coverage.

Just as pricing can influence distribution, distribution can influence pricing. When firms began to offer products directly to consumers over the Internet instead of through retail stores, the firms were able to reduce the prices charged because they avoided any intermediaries.

When a producer or wholesaler considers expanding into retailing operations, it must address the following questions:

▶ Can it absorb the cost of leasing store space and employing workers? These costs can be substantial.

▶ Can the firm offer enough product lines to make full use of a store? If the firm specializes in producing pullover shirts, it will not have a sufficient variety to attract consumers.

▶ Will the additional revenue to be earned cover all additional costs incurred?

▶ Will the firm lose the business that it had developed with other retail firms once it begins to compete with those firms on a retail level?

The idea of expansion may become less appealing when the wholesaler addresses these questions.

Vertical Channel Integration by Retailers

Just as a producer may consider establishing retail outlets, a retailer may consider producing its own products. Consider a clothing retailer that has historically purchased its clothes from several different producers. It believes that the producer's cost is about 50 percent less than the price charged to retailers. Consequently, it begins to consider producing the clothes itself. This is the reverse of the previous example. Yet it also involves a firm that is considering vertical integration.

When a retailer considers expanding into production of products, it must address the following questions:

▶ Can it absorb the expenses resulting from production, including the cost of a production plant and new employees?

▶ Does it have the expertise to adjust the production process as consumer tastes change over time? If a clothing manufacturer cannot adjust, it may be stuck with a large inventory of out-of-date clothing.

In general, the firm must decide whether the benefits from producing the clothes itself are greater than the additional costs.

Global Business

Global Distribution

In the United States, the distribution network is well organized. Manufacturers of most products are able to find distributors that have the knowledge and relationships with retailers to distribute the products. In many foreign countries, however, distribution networks are not well organized. Many products have simply not been marketed in some less-developed countries, so a distribution network has never been established for these products. Now that U.S. firms have begun to market numerous products to these countries, they recognize that they cannot necessarily rely on intermediaries to distribute the products. Therefore, the firms may need to distribute their products directly to retail outlets or to the customers who purchase the products.

To illustrate the potential problems associated with distribution in a foreign country, consider the dilemma of Ben & Jerry's Homemade, which has begun to produce and sell ice cream in Russia. In Russia and in some other countries, the distribution of some products is controlled by organized crime. Consequently, distributing products through the existing distribution network may necessitate extra payoffs to the intermediaries. Also, the intermediaries may decide to focus their efforts on selling other products that offer higher payoffs. Rather than search for an intermediary to distribute its ice cream, Ben & Jerry's decided to distribute the ice cream to outlets itself. It identified a reputable firm in Russia to establish a distribution network.

As Ben & Jerry's was distributing ice cream to outlets, it found that they had limited capacity in their freezers to store ice cream. So it provided the outlets with freezers. This allows Ben & Jerry's to distribute more ice cream to each outlet.

Ben & Jerry's also needed to train the outlets' employees about the different flavors of ice cream, which resulted in another type of expense that is not incurred when selling ice cream in the United States. Ben & Jerry's experience in distributing ice cream to outlets in Russia illustrates how the strategy used for distributing a specific product may vary with the country where the product is being sold.

Decision Making

Deciding Whether to Serve as a Retailer

Italia Company has noticed that retail shoe stores commonly charge a very high markup for its shoes. It is considering whether to establish retail shoe stores to distribute its shoes. If it opens its own retail stores, its revenue would be higher because it would receive the retail price when selling shoes rather than selling the shoes to the retail stores at a lower price. However, it would incur the cost of leasing store space and operating the retail stores. This cost would be very large, and Italia Company does not have business experience in the retail shoe business. It decides not to establish retail stores because the expense would be too large.

1. Explain why Italia's distribution would be very limited if it relied solely on the few retail stores that it could create to distribute its shoes.

2. Why can't Italia's website serve as a perfect substitute for a retail store?

ANSWERS: 1. Italia would only attract customers who live near its retail stores. Therefore, its distribution would reach only a small proportion of the customers who may be willing to purchase its shoes. 2. Some customers prefer to shop at stores so that they can try on the shoes and determine whether they are comfortable. These customers tend to buy shoes at retail stores rather than through an online website.

COLLEGE HEALTH CLUB: CHC'S DISTRIBUTION

As Sue Kramer develops her business plan for College Health Club (CHC), she must determine her method of distribution. Her business will provide health club services. Like most services, health club services will be distributed directly to the customer.

Sue also plans to use CHC as a retailer for vitamin supplements. CHC will purchase jars of supplements from a vitamin wholesaler and then sell them to its members. In addition, she considers serving as a retailer of exercise clothing for CHC's members. She met with a wholesaler of exercise clothing to learn what types of clothing she could purchase and at what prices. The retail price charged at CHC would be higher than the wholesale price, resulting in a profit for CHC.

Summary

1 The advantages of a direct channel of distribution are

▶ the full difference between the producer's cost and the price paid by the consumer goes to the producer; and

▶ the producer can easily obtain firsthand feedback on the product, allowing for quick response to customer complaints and the opportunity to quickly correct any deficiencies.

The disadvantages of a direct channel of distribution are

▶ the producer must employ more salespeople;

▶ the producer must provide all product promotions (some intermediaries might be willing to promote the products for producers); and

▶ the producer may have to provide credit to customers and incur the risk of bad debt (some intermediaries might be willing to incur this risk).

The optimal channel of distribution is dependent on the product's ease of transportation: the greater the ease, the more likely that intermediaries could be used. It is also dependent on the product's degree of standardization: the more standardized the product, the more likely that intermediaries could be used.

2 The three types of market coverage are

▶ intensive distribution, which is used to distribute the product across most or all outlets;

▶ selective distribution, which is used to intentionally avoid some outlets; and

▶ exclusive distribution, which uses only one or a few outlets.

3 The most common forms of transportation are truck, rail, air, water, and pipeline. Trucks can reach any destination on land with the ability to make multiple stops. Railroads are useful for heavy products being transported over long distances. Air transportation can be quick and relatively inexpensive for light items. Transportation by water should be considered for coastal or port locations, particularly for bulk products being transported internationally. Pipeline is an effective method of transportation for products such as oil and gas.

4 A quick distribution process not only satisfies customers but also reduces the amount of funds that must be used to support this process. Firms may accelerate their distribution process by reducing the channels of distribution. Alternatively, they may improve the interaction between the distribution and production processes. The distribution process relies on the production process to have products ready when needed.

5 Retailers serve as intermediaries for manufacturers by distributing products directly to customers. Each retailer is distinguished by its characteristics, such as number of outlets (independent versus chain), quality of service (self-service versus full-service), variety of products offered (specialty versus variety), and whether it is a store or a nonstore retailer.

6 Wholesalers serve manufacturers by

▶ maintaining the products purchased at their own warehouse, which allows manufacturers to maintain smaller inventories;

▶ using their sales expertise to sell products to retailers;

▶ delivering the products to retailers;

▶ assuming credit risk in the event that the retailer does not pay its bills; and

▶ providing information to manufacturers about competing products being sold in retail stores.

Wholesalers serve retailers by

▶ maintaining sufficient inventory so that retailers can order small amounts frequently;

▶ sometimes promoting the products they sell to the retailers;

▶ setting up product displays for retailers;

▶ offering products on credit to retailers; and

▶ informing retailers about policies implemented by other retailers regarding the pricing of products, allocation of space, and so on.

7 Vertical channel integration is the managing of more than one level of the distribution system by a single firm. For example, a manufacturer of a product may create an intermediary such as a retail store to distribute the product. Alternatively, an intermediary may decide to produce the product instead of ordering it from manufacturers. In either example, a single firm serves as a manufacturer and an intermediary and would no longer rely on another firm to manufacture or distribute its product.

How the Chapter Concepts Affect Business Performance

A firm's decisions regarding the distribution concepts summarized here affect its performance. The decisions about the channels of distribution, market coverage, and intermediaries determine the number of customers that the firm targets and therefore influence its revenue. Its transportation decision affects its expenses. Its decision to accelerate the distribution process may influence its revenue and its expenses.

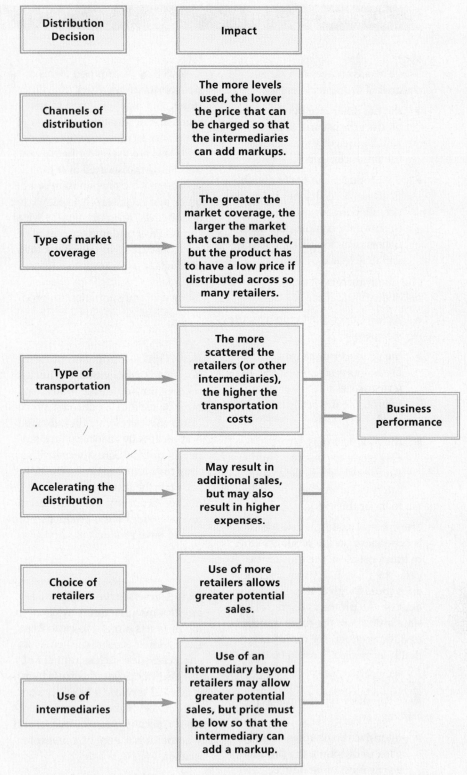

Key Terms

agents   495
chain   508
direct channel   493
exclusive distribution   499
full-service retail store   508
independent retail store   508

intensive distribution   499
market coverage   499
marketing intermediaries   494
merchants   495
one-level channel   495
selective distribution   499

self-service retail store   508
specialty retail store   509
two-level channel   495
variety retail store   509
vertical channel integration   513

Review & Critical Thinking Questions

1. Discuss the advantages and disadvantages of direct channel distribution.

2. Compare and contrast one-level and two-level channels of distribution.

3. Briefly summarize the factors that determine an optimal channel of distribution.

4. What type of distribution system would a manufacturer use for the following products: (a) Calvin Klein jeans, (b) hometown newspapers, (c) Kenmore automatic washers?

5. Explain why Liz Claiborne distributes its clothing at upscale clothing stores as opposed to discount chain stores.

6. How can marketing research determine the optimal type of distribution coverage for a firm?

7. List the various modes of transportation that can be used to distribute a product.

8. What mode of transportation should be considered by an orchid grower in Hawaii who sends orchids to retail stores in other states? Why?

9. A manufacturer who sells staple products to mini-mart service stations would utilize wholesalers and retailers to reach the final customer. Why?

10. What is the relationship between production and distribution in reaching the ultimate consumer?

11. In the United States, the distribution network is well organized. However, in foreign countries, especially developing countries, distribution networks are not well organized. Why is this so?

12. Briefly summarize the characteristics of retailers.

13. List the five key services provided by wholesalers to manufacturers.

14. How do merchants and agents differ?

15. Why might a small producer be part of a two-level channel of distribution rather than a direct channel?

16. Why are Internet businesses likely to involve direct channel distribution?

17. Identify an advantage and a disadvantage of exclusive distribution.

18. How do chains differ from independent retail stores?

19. How do specialty stores differ from variety retail stores?

20. Define vertical channel integration.

Discussion Questions

1. Discuss the likely events resulting from the elimination of intermediaries for the following products: (a) Rolling Rock beer, (b) Levi's jeans, (c) Jeep Grand Cherokee.

2. How can a firm use the Internet to enhance its degree of market coverage? How can it use the Internet to accelerate the distribution process?

3. Recently, community colleges have realized that they must give thought to their distribution systems. What distribution decisions might community colleges have to make?

4. Describe an appropriate channel of distribution for (a) a loaf of bread sold in a local grocery store, (b) a Buick Regal, (c) a door-to-door salesperson.

5. Select the appropriate distribution (intensive, selective, or exclusive) for the following products: (a) Ethan Allen furniture, (b) Marlboro cigarettes, (c) Reebok shoes, (d) *USA Today*.

6. Assume you are a retailer of very expensive jewelry. Would your products be more likely to be sold in a chain or an independent retail outlet? Would your

products be more likely to be sold in a specialty or a variety retail store?

7. Why might a manufacturer prefer to use a wholesaler rather than a direct distribution system in terms of credit risk?

8. How do the services provided by wholesalers to manufacturers differ from those provided by wholesalers to retailers?

9. Why might vertical channel integration benefit a clothes producer? What might be the drawbacks?

10. Why is a quick distribution process beneficial to (a) a retailer of live fish and (b) a swimwear company?

It's Your Decision: Distribution Decisions at CHC

1. A manufacturer of exercise clothing has asked Sue Kramer, the president of CHC, if she wants CHC to serve as a retailer by selling clothes to its members. If Sue agrees to sell exercise clothing produced by the manufacturer, will the distribution system be a direct channel, a one-level channel, or a two-level channel?

2. Sue has considered producing her own line of exercise clothing and selling it at CHC. Would this type of distribution be a direct channel, a one-level channel, or a two-level channel?

3. If Sue decides to produce her own line of clothing to be sold at CHC, does this strategy reflect intensive distribution, selective distribution, or exclusive distribution?

4. A health club differs from manufacturing firms in that it produces a service rather than products. Explain why the distribution strategy of a service firm (such as CHC) is more limited than that of a manufacturing firm.

Investing in a Business

Using the annual report of the firm in which you would like to invest, complete the following:

Questions

1. How does the firm distribute its products to consumers? Does it rely on wholesalers? Does it rely on retail stores?

2. Has the firm revised its distribution methods in recent years? If so, provide details.

3. Explain how the business displays its products and prices over the Internet. Does it distribute products directly to customers who order over the Internet? Does it advertise on the Internet?

4. Go to http://hoovers.com and locate the NEWS SEARCH. Type in the name of the firm in the space provided, and review the recent news stories about the firm. Summarize any (at least one) recent news story about the firm that applies to one or more of the key concepts in this chapter.

Case: Distribution Decisions by Novak, Inc.

Novak, Inc., is a wholesaler in business to sell engine parts for cars. It recently installed a website order system. The system allows a customer (such as a car repair shop) to order inventory parts from anywhere in the United States. Novak can ship directly to the customer.

Larry Novak, president of Novak, Inc., decided to sell more than car engine parts. His plan was to sell technical expertise to provide his customers who own repair shops with information pertaining to car engine parts. With recent technological changes and an increased number of imports entering the United States, repair shops must now handle many different car engine parts. Larry placed his company in a position to be more competitive in the industry by emphasizing information rather than price. His website offers numerous product catalogs and handbooks that provide extensive, detailed descriptions and diagrams of every transmission, as well as specific parts needed to complete the repairs.

With the staggering selection of transmissions in use today, shops cannot begin to keep all the essential parts.

To help alleviate this problem, Novak has organized a national computer network linking its regional offices around the country. It provides information on the status of in-stock inventory, orders expected to come in, and shipping schedules for parts expected to go out. With this information, salespeople can access data on the availability of a product anywhere in the United States and have it shipped to them directly.

Questions

1. Is Novak a wholesaler or a retailer?
2. What is the advantage that Novak is now providing to its customers?
3. Is Novak considered an intermediary? How many levels do Novak's channels of distribution include?
4. Does Novak have a quick distribution process? If so, how?

Video Case: Distribution Strategies at Burton Snowboards

Burton Snowboards, which was founded in 1977 by Jeff Burton, is the world's leading producer of snowboards and snowboarding-related gear. Burton began as a snowboarding manufacturer and has expanded its product line to include weatherproof clothes, boots, and a variety of snowboarding gear, as well as snowboards. Retail stores place orders with manufacturer representatives before the winter snowboarding season. Burton does not maintain a large inventory because it attempts to produce its snowboards on demand. It works closely with retail stores to ensure that the store employees have some knowledge about the snowboards. Burton listens to the feedback that stores receive from customers so that it knows what customers want. Burton also provides advertising signs and promotional bro-

chures to the stores to promote its image. It offers support over the phone if store employees have specific questions about the products it offers. In addition, Burton has a website that provides extensive information to customers and answers their specific questions.

Questions

1. How does globalization affect Burton's target distribution system?
2. How does Burton use the Internet to improve the efficiency of its distribution system?
3. Why is it important for Burton to screen the retail stores that may sell its snowboards?

Internet Applications

1. http://www.walmart.com

Does Wal-Mart use vertical channel integration? How does Wal-Mart use the Internet to improve its distribution system? How does Wal-Mart's website help it to direct customers to its stores?

2. http://www.directchannel.com

What services are provided by this company? How are mailing lists used in distribution? What kind of dis-

tribution system would someone using a mailing list implement?

3. www.mapquest.com

Obtain driving information from your home to a location of your choice. How could a business use a website such as MapQuest to direct its customers to appropriate retailers and service locations? How could a company use this website to expand its degree of market coverage?

Dell's Secret to Success

Go to http://www.reportgallery.com and review Dell's most recent annual report. Also, go to Dell's website (http://www.dell.com) and in the section "about Dell," review the background material about Dell that relates to this chapter.

Questions

1 Review Dell's comments about its distribution. How does it distribute its products to its customers?

2 Describe the advantages that its distribution system offers to Dell. What is a possible disadvantage of Dell's distribution system?

3 Dell's website explains that much of its success is attributed to its website sales. Dell was the first company to generate $1 million in sales from the Internet on a daily basis. Why is Dell's website so important for its particular type of business?

In-Text Study Guide

Answers are in Appendix C at the back of book.

True or False

1. Retailers sell primarily to wholesalers.

2. Manufacturers that use a direct distribution channel need fewer employees than they would need if they used a one-level or two-level channel.

3. Small business firms that produce only a few products typically use a two-level channel of distribution.

4. Products that are standardized are more likely to involve intermediaries.

5. One reason firms may choose an exclusive distribution strategy is to create or maintain prestige for their product.

6. Distribution decisions do not affect the cost of delivering a product.

7. Mathematical formulas are available that determine the ideal distribution system.

8. A lengthy distribution process adversely affects a firm's performance.

9. Wholesalers commonly offer manufacturers sales expertise.

10. Manufacturers can vertically integrate their operations by establishing retail stores.

Multiple Choice

11. The manner by which a firm's products are made accessible to its customers is determined by its:
    a) advertising strategies.
    b) product decisions.
    c) pricing strategies.
    d) distribution decisions.
    e) package designs.

12. A distribution channel represents the path of a product from producer to:
    a) retailer.
    b) wholesaler.
    c) consumer.
    d) manufacturer.
    e) industrial distributor.

13. With a direct channel of distribution, the full difference between the manufacturer's cost and the price paid by the consumer goes to the:
    a) manufacturer.
    b) wholesaler.
    c) retailer.
    d) intermediary.
    e) merchant.

14. Wholesalers are marketing intermediaries who purchase products from manufacturers and sell them to:
    a) final users.
    b) retailers.
    c) other manufacturers.
    d) primary customers.
    e) secondary customers.

15. Marketing intermediaries that match buyers and sellers of products without becoming the owners of the products themselves are known as:
    a) single-service marketers.
    b) agents.
    c) commission-based wholesalers.
    d) stockers.
    e) mediators.

16. Products that are standardized and easily transported are likely to:
    a) be sold at a high markup.
    b) have limited market areas.
    c) use intermediaries in their distribution channels.
    d) be sold at steep discounts.
    e) use a direct channel of distribution.

In-Text Study Guide

Answers are in Appendix C at the back of book.

17. _____ refers to the degree of product distribution among outlets.
    a) The marketing mix
    b) Demographic distribution
    c) Market coverage
    d) Channelization
    e) The retail ratio

18. Firms that fill orders over the Internet tend to use a(n) _____ channel of distribution.
    a) one-level
    b) unidirectional
    c) multimodal
    d) direct
    e) intrinsic

19. _____ distribution is used when a producer distributes its products through certain chosen outlets while intentionally avoiding other possible outlets.
    a) Restrictive
    b) Exclusive
    c) Intensive
    d) Narrow
    e) Selective

20. An advantage of exclusive distribution is that it:
    a) makes the product widely available to consumers at a variety of outlets.
    b) eliminates all market intermediaries.
    c) allows the firm to avoid charging a sales tax on the goods.
    d) may allow the firm to create and maintain an image of prestige.
    e) provides the goods to consumers at the lowest possible cost.

21. Newspaper publishers have their papers available in grocery stores, convenience stores, and vending machines and at many other locations throughout a city. This is an example of a(n) _____ distribution of a product.
    a) nonspecific
    b) specialized
    c) geographically dispersed
    d) intensive
    e) decentralized

22. Exclusive distribution can be viewed as an extreme form of:
    a) intensive distribution.
    b) the one-channel approach.
    c) selective distribution.
    d) price discrimination.
    e) mass merchandising.

23. A(n) _____ is a retailer with only one outlet.
    a) exclusive retailer
    b) independent retail store
    c) wholesaler
    d) franchise retailer
    e) sole proprietorship

24. _____ are usually the best way to ship goods when the goods must be delivered quickly to several different locations in a local area.
    a) Trucks
    b) Barges
    c) The railroads
    d) Pipelines
    e) Containerized modules

25. One way to accelerate the distribution process is to make sure that it is integrated with the _____ process.
    a) marketing
    b) financing
    c) credit approval
    d) advertising
    e) production

In-Text Study Guide

Answers are in Appendix C at the back of book.

26. Restructuring a distribution process commonly results in the elimination of:
    a) production.
    b) warehouses.
    c) manufacturers.
    d) product lines.
    e) product mixes.

27. _____ allows a firm to check orders online, determine where future inventory shortages may occur, and increase its production accordingly.
    a) E-marketing
    b) Integrated production
    c) Source-to-source coordination
    d) Marketing logistics
    e) Inventory management

28. Specialty stores in a shopping mall can offer the customer convenience while retaining their:
    a) selectivity.
    b) prestige.
    c) price advantage.
    d) wide customer appeal.
    e) product variety.

29. A camera shop that has knowledgeable salespeople who can provide advice to purchasers and also offers to service and repair the cameras it sells is an example of a(n):
    a) mass merchandiser.
    b) agent-seller.
    c) one-stop shopping outlet.
    d) distribution chain.
    e) full-service retailer.

30. Stores that tend to focus on only one or a few types of products are:
    a) specialty retailers.
    b) variety department stores.
    c) retail outlets.
    d) discount stores.
    e) cash-and-carry retailers.

31. When the wholesaler purchases the products from the manufacturer and sells them to retailers on credit, it normally assumes the:
    a) package design.
    b) credit risk.
    c) promotional expenses of the manufacturer.
    d) manufacturer's guarantee.
    e) producer's risk.

32. A wholesaler provides all of the following services to manufacturers except:
    a) production.
    b) warehousing.
    c) delivery to retailers.
    d) sales expertise.
    e) feedback from retailers.

33. A situation in which two or more levels of distribution are managed by a single firm is called:
    a) vertical channel integration.
    b) horizontal channel integration.
    c) multilevel marketing.
    d) wheel of retailing.
    e) conglomeration.

34. When a _____ considers vertical integration, it must be concerned about whether it will lose its established business with retail firms.
    a) retailer
    b) producer
    c) service provider
    d) retailer
    e) chain store

35. All of the following are distribution difficulties that firms may encounter when operating internationally except:
    a) poorly organized distribution networks.
    b) organized crime.
    c) payoffs.
    d) lack of potential customers.
    e) lack of intermediaries.

Chapter

14

PHOTOEDIT, INC.

The performance of Karma Coffee House is partially dependent on how it advertises its business to consumers.

The Learning Goals of this chapter are to:

Explain how promotion can benefit firms. *1*

Describe how advertising is used. *2*

Describe the steps involved in personal selling. *3*

Describe the sales promotion methods that are used. *4*

Describe how firms can use public relations to promote products. *5*

Explain how firms select the optimal mix of promotions to use. *6*

Promoting Products

Firms regularly engage in promotion, which is the act of informing or reminding consumers about a specific product or brand. They can use promotion to increase the demand for the product and thereby increase the value of the firm. Consider the situation of Karma Coffee House, which just opened and needs to promote its business to potential customers. Some of its most important promotion decisions are:

▶ What type of advertising should it use?

▶ What other promotion methods should it use?

▶ How it can use public relations to promote its business?

▶ What is the optimal mix of promotions to use?

The decision about the type of advertising is important because it affects the demand by customers. The use of other promotion methods can also affect the demand by customers and therefore affects the firm's revenue. The decision about public relations can also affect the customer demand and therefore the revenue. Karma Coffee House must determine how to allocate its funds to various promotional strategies in a manner that reaches the target market and attracts customers.

The types of decisions described above are necessary for all businesses. This chapter explains how promotion decisions by Karma Coffee House or any other firm can be made in a manner that maximizes its value.

Background on Promotion

1

Explain how promotion can benefit firms.

promotion
the act of informing or reminding consumers about a specific product or brand

Even if a firm's product is properly produced, priced, and distributed, it still needs to be promoted. Firms commonly use **promotion** to supplement the other marketing strategies (product, pricing, and distribution strategies) described in the previous two chapters. For example, an automaker supplements its strategy of improving product quality with promotions that inform consumers about the strategy. An airline typically supplements its strategy to lower prices with promotions that inform consumers about the pricing strategy. A quality product that is reasonably priced may not sell unless it is promoted to make customers aware of it.

To make consumers aware of a new product, promotion can be used when the product is introduced. Promotion can also remind consumers that the product exists. Furthermore, promotion reminds consumers about the product's qualities and the advantages it offers over competing products. Promotion may also include special incentives to induce consumers to purchase a specific product. Promotion may also be used on a long-term basis to protect a product's image and retain its market share.

Effective promotion should increase demand for the product and generate a higher level of sales. To recognize how promotions can enhance product sales, consider the following statement in a recent annual report by Procter & Gamble:

"Our leading brands begin with world-class product technology, but it's advertising that gets consumers' attention and persuades them to use our products again and again. 'Advertising is the lifeblood of our brands.' . . . [A]dvertising is the key driver in all our businesses, but it's especially important for health care products—because consumers want a brand they know and trust. Advertising helps establish the trust."

Promotion Mix

promotion mix
the combination of promotion methods that a firm uses to increase acceptance of its products

The **promotion mix** is the combination of promotion methods that a firm uses to increase acceptance of its products. The four methods of promotion are:

▶ Advertising
▶ Personal selling
▶ Sales promotion
▶ Public relations

Some firms use one of these promotion methods to promote their products, while other firms use two or more. The optimal promotion mix for promoting the product depends on the characteristics of the target market. Each of the four promotion methods is discussed in detail next.

Decision Making

Planning a Promotion Mix

Consider the case of Karma Coffee House (introduced at the beginning of the chapter), which was recently opened in downtown Boston. The owner, Jen Allen, wants to attract many of the people who work in major office complexes nearby. She is hoping that they will stop at Karma for coffee before they start work, after they leave work in the evening, or during breaks or for informal business meetings. Jen decides that the local businesspeople represent her target market.

If Jen does not promote her business, the only people who will know about it will be those who walk by the coffee house. Karma is within a few blocks of large office buildings where thousands of people work, but it is not directly on their path to or from the train station. Thus, those people will not be aware of the coffee house unless Jen uses promotion strategies. However, she cannot afford to spend a lot of money on promotion, so she needs to select promotion strategies that are inexpensive and effective. The future demand for her coffee house services (and therefore the revenue of her business) is highly dependent on the effectiveness of her promotion strategies.

1. Explain why Jen Allen must decide on the target market for Karma Coffee House before she decides what promotion strategies to use.

2. Explain the cost to Karma Coffee House if Jen makes poor decisions about promotion strategies.

ANSWERS: 1. She must decide who Karma's potential customers are so that she can use promotion strategies that reach those customers. 2. If Jen makes poor promotion decisions, Karma Coffee House will incur a cost without generating revenue from its promotion. That is, it may not recapture the amount of money spent on promotion.

Describe how advertising is used.

advertising
a nonpersonal sales presentation communicated through media or nonmedia forms to influence a large number of consumers

brand advertising
a nonpersonal sales presentation about a specific brand

comparative advertising
intended to persuade customers to purchase a specific product by demonstrating a brand's superiority by comparison with other competing brands

reminder advertising
intended to remind consumers of a product's existence

institutional advertising
a nonpersonal sales presentation about a specific institution's product

industry advertising
a nonpersonal sales presentation about a specific industry's product

Advertising

Advertising is a nonpersonal sales presentation communicated through media or nonmedia forms to influence a large number of consumers. It is a common method for promoting products and services. Although advertising is generally more expensive than other methods, it can reach many consumers. Large firms commonly use advertising agencies to develop their promotion strategies for them. Many firms such as Anheuser-Busch, General Motors, and ExxonMobil spend more than $100 million per year on advertising. Procter & Gamble spends more than $3 billion a year on advertising.

Although advertising can be expensive, it can increase a product's market share. One reason for Frito-Lay's increase in market share over time is its heavy use of advertising. Frito-Lay typically spends more than $50 million a year on advertising.

Reasons for Advertising

Advertising is normally intended to enhance the image of a specific brand, institution, or industry. The most common reason is to enhance the image of a specific brand. **Brand advertising** is a nonpersonal sales presentation about a specific brand. Some brands are advertised to inform consumers about changes in the product. GNC (General Nutrition Centers) spends more than $80 million per year on brand advertising. The Gap and The Coca-Cola Company also spend heavily on brand advertising. Amazon.com uses extensive brand advertising on its own website.

Common strategies used to advertise a specific brand are comparative advertising and reminder advertising. **Comparative advertising** is intended to persuade customers to purchase a specific product by demonstrating a brand's superiority by comparison with other competing brands. Some soft drink makers use taste tests to demonstrate the superiority of their respective soft drinks. Volvo advertises its superior safety features, while Saturn advertises that its price is lower than that of its competitors and that its quality is superior.

Reminder advertising is intended to remind consumers of a product's existence. It is commonly used for products that have already proved successful and are at the maturity stage of their life cycle. This type of advertising is frequently used for grocery products such as cereal, peanut butter, and dog food.

A second reason for advertising is to enhance the image of a specific institution. **Institutional advertising** is a nonpersonal sales presentation about a specific institution. For example, firms such as IBM and ExxonMobil sometimes advertise to enhance their overall image, without focusing on a particular product they produce. Utility companies also advertise to enhance their image.

A third reason for advertising is to enhance the image of a specific industry. **Industry advertising** is a nonpersonal sales presentation about a specific industry. Industry associations advertise their respective products (such as orange juice, milk, or beef) to increase demand for these products.

Here is an example of an extreme form of advertising used by Nike to get the attention of its customers.

LANDOV LLC

Forms of Advertising

Firms can advertise their products through various means. The most effective advertising varies with the product and target market of concern. Most types of advertising can be classified as follows:

- ▶ Newspapers
- ▶ Magazines
- ▶ Radio
- ▶ Television
- ▶ Internet
- ▶ E-mail
- ▶ Direct mail
- ▶ Telemarketing
- ▶ Outdoor ads
- ▶ Transportation ads
- ▶ Specialty ads

Newspapers Many small and large businesses use newspaper advertising. It is a convenient way to reach a particular geographic market. Because many stores generate most of their sales from consumers within a 10-mile radius, they use a local newspaper for most of their ads. Newspaper ads can be inserted quickly, allowing firms to advertise only a few days after the idea was created. Best Buy, Publix, and other stores frequently use newspapers as a means of advertising.

Magazines Because most magazines are distributed nationwide, magazine advertising is generally used for products that are distributed nationwide. Some magazines such as *BusinessWeek* have the flexibility to include regional ads that are inserted only in magazines distributed to a certain area.

Radio An advantage of radio advertising is that, unlike magazines and newspapers, it talks to the audience. However, it lacks any visual effect. Because most radio stations serve a local audience, radio ads tend to focus on a particular local area. Furthermore, the particular type of music or other content on each radio station attracts consumers with similar characteristics. Therefore, each station may be perceived to reach a particular target market.

Television   Television ads combine the advantages of print media (such as newspapers and magazines) and radio. They can talk to the audience and provide a visual effect. Ads can be televised locally or nationwide. McDonald's, Sears, Duracell, and AT&T commonly run a commercial more than 20 times in a given week. Although television ads are expensive, they reach a large audience and can be highly effective. Some large firms, such as McDonald's and AT&T, run more than 1,000 television ads per year.

Firms attempt to use television advertising during shows that attract their target market. For example, lipstick and fashion firms may focus on the annual Academy Awards because more than 40 million women are watching. Beer and snack food producers focus on football games, which attract mostly men. A one-minute ad during the Super Bowl costs more than $3 million. The rates are much cheaper for ads that are only televised locally or are run on less-popular shows.

In recent years, many firms (including Procter & Gamble) have created **infomercials,** or commercials that are televised separately rather than within a show. Infomercials typically run for 30 minutes or longer and provide detailed information about a specific product promoted by the firm.

infomercials
commercials that are televised separately rather than within a show

Together, television, radio, magazines, and newspapers account for more than 50 percent of total advertising expenditures. The allocation is shown in Exhibit 14.1.

Internet   The Internet has become a popular way for firms to advertise their products and services. It is a form of nonpersonal communication that can create awareness and persuade the customer.

Initially, firms questioned whether people surfing the Internet would pay attention to ads. There is now much evidence that the Internet can be an effective way to advertise. Consider the case of Bristol-Myers Squibb Company, which experimented with an ad on some financial websites offering a free sample of Excedrin (one of its products) to all viewers who typed in their name and address next to the ad on the website. Bristol-Myers Squibb expected that it would receive 10,000 responses at the very most over a one-month period. Yet, in one month, 30,000 people responded. Thus, the Internet ad experiment was a success. Furthermore,

Exhibit 14.1

Allocation of Advertising Expenditures

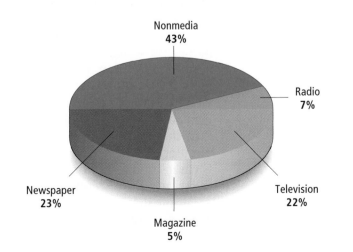

the Internet ads cost less than traditional methods of advertising. Other firms have experienced similar results with ads on the Internet.

Today, Internet advertising can potentially reach a large audience. Yahoo!, AOL, and MSN are viewed by 50 million people a day. In 2004, firms spent about $4 billion for paid advertising on the Internet. Firms such as Microsoft and IBM spend more than $10 million per year on technology-based Internet ads.

Some firms use their own websites to advertise all of their products. When a firm advertises its products on its own website, it attempts to ensure that the website is easily accessible to potential customers, both in the United States and in foreign countries. Some websites are very visible because they are given high priority by search engines, but the number of competing websites is making it difficult for some firms to reach potential customers. For example, more than a million websites are listed in response to a Web search for "clothing," so a firm that wants to sell clothing on the Internet may not receive much attention.

A firm can use various strategies to ensure that its website is noticed. First, a website that sells unusual items may be more visible because it may fit specific searches. For example, a website that is focused on ski clothing would have a better chance of being noticed by customers who do a search for "ski clothing" than a general clothing store, because the website fits that specific search. Second, some firms pay the search engines to receive a higher priority in response to a search term. These sponsored sites appear at the top of the list of all websites that fit a particular search term. The firm may pay the search engine a monthly fee for this priority or pay per click (each time the search engine has led someone to click on the website to visit it). Third, a firm may hire a Web marketing firm to help it receive higher priority from the search engines. The search engines determine the order of the websites provided in response to a search term by using various criteria such as the number of times that the search terms are used on the website's pages. By ensuring that its website meets the criteria, a firm can improve the position of its website on the list. Fourth, a firm can arrange link exchanges from its website to other websites that serve similar types of customers. For example, a website focused on selling skis may be willing to insert a link on its site that will direct viewers to a website focused on selling ski clothing. In return, the website focused on selling ski clothing will insert a link on its site that will direct viewers to the website focused on selling skis.

Firms may also promote their products on other websites that are commonly viewed by people who may purchase their products. One of the most popular types of Internet ads is a "banner ad," which is usually rectangular and placed at the top of a Web page. Toyota, which frequently uses banner ads, found that more than 150,000 Internet users typed in their name and address next to the ad to get more information in a 12-month period. More than 5 percent of those users purchased a Toyota. An alternative type of Internet ad is the "button ad," which takes the viewer to the website of the firm advertised there if the viewer clicks on the ad. When a firm advertises on a website other than its own, it may pay a set fee to the firm that owns the website. Alternatively, the fee may be based on the number of clicks (by viewers) on the ad itself (to learn more about the advertised product) or on the number of orders of the product by viewers (if the ad results in viewers ordering the product).

Some film producers spend millions of dollars on websites dedicated to promote films that they produce. They attract potential customers who visit the websites, and attempt to create interest among people who frequently use the Internet.

E-Mail   Many firms send e-mail messages to their customers to promote products. Some e-mail promotions are general and apply to all customers on the e-mail list. Other e-mail promotions are personalized to fit the customer's interests. For example, Amazon.com sends promotions about specific books to customers who have previously expressed an interest on that topic. Marriott International sends promotions about hotels in specific locations to customers who have previously expressed an interest in those locations.

Direct Mail   Direct-mail advertising is frequently used by local service firms, such as realtors, home repair firms, and lawn service firms. It is also used by cosmetic firms (including Avon Products), as well as numerous clothing firms that send catalogs directly to homes.

If a firm plans to advertise through the mail, it should first obtain a mailing list that fits its target market. For example, Ford Motor Company sends ads to previous Ford customers. Talbots (a clothing firm) sends ads to a mailing list of its previous customers. Another common approach is for a firm to purchase the subscriber list of a magazine that is read by its targeted consumers. Many mailing lists can be separated by state or even zip code. As the price of paper and postage has increased, advertising by direct mail has become more expensive.

telemarketing
the use of the telephone for promoting and selling products

Telemarketing   **Telemarketing** uses the telephone for promoting and selling products. Many local newspaper firms use telemarketing to attract new subscribers. Phone companies and cable companies also use telemarketing to sell their services.

Outdoor Ads   Outdoor ads are shown on billboards and signs. Such ads are normally quite large because consumers are not likely to stop and look at them closely. Vacation-related products and services use outdoor advertising. For example, Disney World ads and Holiday Inn Hotel ads appear on billboards along many highways.

Transportation Ads   Advertisements are often displayed on forms of transportation, such as buses and the roofs of taxi cabs. These ads differ from the outdoor ads just described because they are moving rather than stationary. The ads generally attempt to provide a strong visual effect that can be recognized by consumers while the vehicle is moving.

Specialty Ads   Other forms of nonmedia advertising are also possible, such as T-shirts, hats, and bumper stickers. T-shirts advertise a wide variety of products, from shoes such as Adidas and Nike to soft drinks such as Coca-Cola and Pepsi.

Summary of Forms of Advertising

Exhibit 14.2 summarizes the forms of advertising. It also indicates whether each form targets the national market (nationwide advertising) or a local market.

Exhibit 14.2
Forms of Advertising

Forms of Advertising	Typical Area Targeted
Newspaper	Local
Magazine	National
Radio	Local
Television	National or local
Internet	National
E-mail	National
Direct mail	National or local
Telemarketing	Local
Outdoor	Local
Transportation	Local
Specialty	National or local

Decision Making

Selecting a Form of Advertising

The types of advertising that a firm should use are dependent on its specific characteristics. To illustrate, recall that Karma Coffee House just opened in downtown Boston. Jen Allen (the owner) is considering advertising strategies that may attract the target market. She eliminates magazines, radio, and television because of their high cost. She considers e-mail and direct mail advertising, but she does not think these methods will necessarily reach the specific target market (people who work in the nearby office buildings). Most of these people commute each workday by taking the train into central Boston, and they all use one of three train stations. Jen decides that the best way to inform them of her coffee house is to post ads in these three train stations. She also decides to hire some local college students to stand near the stations and hand out brochures to the commuters in the morning when they are arriving and at about 5 P.M. when they are leaving work. This form of advertising is cheap but effective because it reaches the specific target market that she needs to attract.

1. Some forms of advertising such as local television reach a much larger audience than the advertising strategy chosen by Jen for Karma Coffee House. Why would local television be ineffective for the coffee house?

2. Explain how the decision regarding the location of the business affected the decision of how to advertise.

ANSWERS: 1. The coffee house needs to attract the local businesspeople. Television reaches a much bigger audience, but most of those people are not going to travel downtown just to go to this coffee house. 2. The location dictates the people who are likely to go to the coffee house, as people are not willing to travel far to get coffee. Therefore, its advertising is focused on reaching the people who work nearby and can easily walk to the coffee house.

Personal Selling

Personal selling is a personal sales presentation used to influence one or more consumers. It requires a personal effort to influence a consumer's demand for a product. Salespeople conduct personal selling on a retail basis, on an industrial basis, and on an individual basis. The sales effort on a retail basis is usually less challenging because it is addressed mostly to consumers who have already entered the store with plans to purchase. Many salespeople in retail stores do not earn a commission and thus may be less motivated to make a sale than other salespeople.

Selling on an industrial basis involves selling supplies or products to companies. Salespeople in this capacity are normally paid a salary plus commission. The volume of industrial sales achieved by a salesperson is highly influenced by that person's promotional efforts.

Selling on an individual basis involves selling directly to individual consumers. Some insurance salespeople and financial planners fit this description. Their task is especially challenging if they do not represent a well-known firm, because they must prove their credibility.

Salespeople who sell on an industrial or individual basis generally perform the following steps:

▶ Identify the target market.
▶ Contact potential customers.
▶ Make the sales presentation.
▶ Answer questions.
▶ Close the sale.
▶ Follow up.

Identify the Target Market

An efficient salesperson first determines the type of consumers interested in the product. In this way, less time is wasted on consumers who will not purchase the product, regardless of the sales effort. If previous sales have been made, the previous customers may be an obvious starting point.

Sidebar:

Describe the steps involved in personal selling.

personal selling
a personal sales presentation used to influence one or more consumers

Personal selling is commonly used to sell expensive products, especially when the products require personal service for customers.

CORBIS, CHICAGO

SMALL BUSINESS SURVEY

What Skills Are Needed to Be Successful in Sales?

A survey asked 1,500 sales managers and sales representatives to rank 14 different skills in order of importance for their success. The following table shows the percentage of respondents who ranked each skill as being one of the top four skills in importance:

Skill	Percentage of Respondents
Planning before the sales call	54
Sales approach	48
Assessing the potential customer's needs	47
Managing time	45
Overcoming concerns about the product	42
Closing the sale	36
Initiating sales calls (cold calling)	30
Making presentations	26
Handling problems with the product	20
Negotiating	19
Following up after sales calls	16
Using the telephone to make sales calls	15
Managing paperwork	7
Demonstrating the product	4

Notice that the four activities that were perceived to be most important are conducted before the sales call. This confirms the need for salespeople to plan and organize if they are to be successful.

Industrial salespeople can identify their target market by using library references and the Yellow Pages of a phone book. If they sell safety equipment, they will call almost any manufacturer in their area. If they sell printing presses, their market will be much more limited.

Individual salespeople have more difficulty identifying their market because they are unable to obtain information on each household. Thus, they may send a brochure to the "resident" at each address, asking the recipient to call if interested. The target market initially includes all households but is then reduced to those consumers who call back. Specific subdivisions of households that fit the income profile of typical consumers may be targeted.

Contact Potential Customers

Once potential customers are identified, they should be contacted by phone, e-mail, direct mail, or in person and provided with a brief summary of what the firm can offer them. Interested customers will make an appointment to meet with salespeople. Ideally, the salespeople should schedule appointments so that their time is used efficiently. For example, an industrial salesperson working the state of Florida should not make appointments in Jacksonville (northeast Florida), Miami (southeast), and

Pensacola (northwest) within the same week. Half the week would be devoted to travel alone. The most logical approach is to fill the appointment schedule within a specific area. Individual salespeople should also attempt to schedule appointments on a specific day when they are near the same area.

Make the Sales Presentation

A sales presentation can range from demonstrating how a printing press is used to explaining the benefits of an insurance policy. Industrial salespeople usually bring equipment with them. They also provide free samples of some products to companies. The sales presentation generally describes the use of each product, the price, and the advantages over competing products. The presentation should focus on how a particular product satisfies customer needs.

Answer Questions

Potential customers normally raise questions during the course of the sales presentation. Salespeople should anticipate common questions and prepare responses to them.

Close the Sale

Most salespeople prefer to make (or "close") a sale right after the sales presentation, while the product's advantages are still in the minds of potential customers. For this reason, they may offer some incentive to purchase immediately, such as a discounted price.

Follow Up

A key to long-term selling success is the attention given to purchasers after the sale is made. This effort increases the credibility of salespeople and encourages existing customers to call again when they need additional products. Salespeople should also follow up on potential customers who did not purchase the product after a sales presentation. These potential customers may experience budget changes and become more interested in purchasing the product over time. E-mail facilitates the follow-up communication between the purchasers and the salespeople. Exhibit 14.3 summarizes the steps in personal selling.

Exhibit 14.3

Summary of Tasks Involved in Personal Selling

Task	Description
Identify target market	Focus on types of customers most likely to purchase the product; contact these potential customers by phone or mail.
Contact potential customers	Schedule appointments with potential customers who are located in the same area on the same days.
Make sales presentation	Demonstrate the use and benefits of the product.
Answer questions	Prepare for typical questions and allow potential customers to ask questions.
Close the sale	Close the sale after the presentation, perhaps by offering a discount if a purchase is made immediately.
Follow up	Call customers who recently purchased the product to ensure their satisfaction. Call other potential customers who decided not to purchase the product to determine whether they would like to reconsider.

Managing Salespeople

sales manager
an individual who manages a group of sales representatives

A common goal of many sales representatives is to become a **sales manager** and manage a group of sales representatives. For example, a company with 40 sales representatives around the country may split the geographic markets into four regions. Each region would have 10 sales representatives who are monitored by a sales manager.

Sales managers require some of the same skills as sales representatives. They need to have knowledge of the product and the competition. In addition, they must be able to motivate their representatives to sell. They must also be able to resolve customer complaints on the service provided by representatives and reprimand representatives when necessary. Some people are better suited to selling than managing salespeople. There is a distinct difference between motivating consumers to purchase a product and motivating employees to sell a product.

Since sales managers do not perform the daily tasks of selling the product, they can concentrate on special projects, such as servicing a major customer's massive order of products. They should evaluate the long-term prospects of the product and consider possible plans for expanding the geographic market. Information from their sales representatives may help their assessments.

Decision Making

Personal Selling

To illustrate how personal selling can be used, recall that Jen Allen has just established the Karma Coffee House in downtown Boston and wants to attract local businesspeople. Jen decides to offer a coffee catering service to the nearby office buildings for special events that include coffee and snacks. She obtains a list of the companies based in each building. Then she contacts the person in each company who is responsible for organizing special events and makes a brief sales presentation. Her sales presentations not only generate some catering business for her coffee house, but give her another way to make the local businesspeople aware of her coffee house.

1. What do you think is the major challenge to Jen Allen in making sales presentations to businesses?

2. What is an advantage of personal selling that is not achieved by advertising?

ANSWERS: 1. A major challenge is convincing a contact person in each company to listen to a sales presentation. 2. An advantage of personal selling is that the seller can focus on selling to one person or a small group of people. This format allows for questions from the audience and more interaction than is possible with advertising.

Sales Promotion

Describe the sales promotion methods that are used.

Sales promotion is the set of activities that is intended to influence consumers. It can be an effective means of encouraging consumers to purchase a specific product. The following are the most common sales promotion strategies:

▶ Rebates

▶ Coupons

sales promotion
the set of activities that is intended to influence consumers

▶ Sampling
▶ Displays
▶ Premiums

Rebates

rebate
a potential refund by the manufacturer to the consumer

A **rebate** is a potential refund by the manufacturer to the consumer. When manufacturers desire to increase product demand, they may offer rebates rather than lowering the price charged to the retail store. Lowering the price to the retail store does not guarantee that the store will pass on the discount. Thus, this strategy could result in lower profit per unit without increasing demand. A rebate ensures that consumers receive the manufacturer's discount. Automobile manufacturers frequently offer rebates of $500 or more.

Coupons

coupons
a promotional device used in newspapers, magazines, and ads to encourage the purchase of a product

Coupons are used in newspapers, magazines, and ads to encourage the purchase of a product. They are also commonly packaged with a product so that consumers can use the coupon only if they purchase this same product again. Coupons used in this way can encourage consumers to repeatedly purchase the same brand. Consequently, consumers may become loyal to that brand.

Some coupons are not available until consumers make repeated purchases. For example, airlines offer free flights to frequent fliers, and some hotels offer a free night's stay to frequent customers.

Promoting with coupons may be inefficient for some firms. General Mills had historically used coupons to promote its cereals. However, after learning from marketing research that 98 percent of all cereal coupons are not used, it decided to cut back on this promotion strategy. It reduced annual spending on some promotions by $175 million and focused on improving its product.

Coupons are commonly used as a sales promotion method to sell grocery products.

PHOTOEDIT, INC.

Out of
Business

Sampling

sampling
offering free samples to encourage
consumers to try a new brand or
product

Sampling involves offering free samples to encourage consumers to try a new brand or product. The intent is to lure customers away from competing products. For example, Clinique samples are available in cosmetics departments of retail stores. Food samples are offered in grocery stores. Manufacturing firms also provide samples so that consumers can try out equipment. Samples are even sent through direct mail.

Samples are most commonly used to introduce new products. Firms recognize that once customers become accustomed to a particular brand, they tend to stick with that brand. Thus, the free sample is intended to achieve **brand loyalty,** or the loyalty of consumers to a specific brand over time.

brand loyalty
the loyalty of consumers to a
specific brand over time

Sampling of Services Sampling is used for services as well as products. For example, in 1999 America Online (AOL) provided a limited amount of free online time to potential customers. This strategy allowed customers to experience the service that AOL provides and resulted in a large number of subscriptions to AOL's online service. Subsequently, AOL merged with media giant Time Warner.

Displays

Many stores create special displays to promote particular products. The displays are used to attract consumers who are in the store for other reasons. Products are more likely to get attention if they are located at a point of purchase, such as by the cash registers where consumers are waiting in line. Because there is limited room for displays, companies that want retail stores to display their products are typically willing to set up the display themselves. They may even offer a reduced price to retail stores that allow a display.

Premiums

A **premium** is a gift or prize provided free to consumers who purchase a specific product. For example, *Sports Illustrated* magazine may offer a free sports DVD to new subscribers. A boat manufacturer may offer a free fishing rod to anyone who purchases its boats. Premiums offer an extra incentive to purchase products.

Summary of Sales Promotion Strategies

Exhibit 14.4 provides a summary of sales promotion methods. The ideal strategy is dependent on the features of the product. Sampling and displays are intended to make the consumer aware of the product's qualities, while other sales promotion strategies are intended to make the price of the product appear more reasonable.

Exhibit 14.4

Comparison of Sales Promotion Strategies

Strategy	Description
Rebates	Firm sends refund directly to consumers after product is purchased.
Coupons	Product is sold at a discounted price to consumers with coupons.
Sampling	Free samples of products are distributed to consumers.
Displays	Products are placed in a prominent area in stores.
Premiums	Gifts or prizes are provided free to consumers who purchase a specific product.

Decision Making

Deciding on a Sales Promotion

The ideal sales promotion for a firm is dependent on its specific characteristics. Recall that Karma Coffee House wants to attract businesspeople who commute to downtown Boston. Jen Allen, the owner, decides to provide brochures containing a coupon for a free coffee to all the offices within one mile of the coffee house. She hopes that the coupons will entice people to stop by for a free coffee and that they will come back in the future.

1. What benefit does the sales promotion provide to Karma Coffee House that it would not obtain from advertising?

2. Why is the sales promotion used by Karma Coffee House more expensive than if it just used the brochure for advertising?

ANSWERS: 1. The offer of free coffee in the sales promotion may attract some customers who would ignore advertising that does not include a coupon. 2. The sales promotion is more expensive because it requires the coffee house to provide free coffee to coupon holders. Jen hopes to make up this expense from repeat business in the future from the customers who come for free coffee.

Describe how firms can use public relations to promote products.

public relations
actions taken with the goal of creating or maintaining a favorable public image

Public Relations

The term **public relations** refers to actions taken with the goal of creating or maintaining a favorable public image. Firms attempt to develop good public relations by communicating to the general public, including prospective customers. Public relations can be used to enhance the image of a product or of the firm itself. It may also be used to clarify information in response to adverse publicity. Many firms have a public relations department that provides information about the firm and its products to the public. Public relations departments typically use the media to relay their information to the public.

Firms commonly attempt to be very accessible to the media because they may receive media coverage at no charge. When employees of a firm are quoted by the media, the firm's name is mentioned across a large audience. Some banks assign employees to provide economic forecasts because the media will mention the bank's name when reporting the forecast. Some public relations are not planned but results from a response to circumstances. For example, during the tragedy of September 11, Home Depot offered its support and was recognized by the media for its efforts.

The following are the most common types of public relations strategies:

▶ Special events

▶ News releases

▶ Press conferences

Special Events

Some firms sponsor a special event such as a race. Anheuser-Busch (producer of Budweiser) supports many marathons and festivals where it promotes its name. 7UP promotes local marathons and has even printed the marathon logo and running figures on 7UP cans, which may attract consumers who run or exercise.

The Discovery Channel has promoted its business through Lance Armstrong and bicycle racing. Armstrong won the Tour de France seven times and was retained by the Discovery Channel even after retiring from bicycle racing.

GETTY IMAGES

Global Business

Promoting Products across Countries

When firms promote products, they tend to emphasize the features that give those products an advantage over all others. Yet consumers in different countries may base their purchase decisions on different features. A product may be popular in the United States because it is durable, but it may be popular in another country because of its low price. Therefore, a firm may need to revise its promotional strategy according to the country. In addition, the manner in which a feature is promoted may vary with the country. Television commercials may not reach a large audience in some less-developed countries, where they may be seen by only the relatively wealthy consumers. Some television commercials may still be effective in these countries if the ads are seen by the type of people who would likely purchase the product. U.S. firms must recognize that the typical profile of the people in foreign countries who watch television or read specific newspapers may vary from the profile in the United States.

Furthermore, firms that hire celebrities to promote products must consider the perceptions of the consumers in each country. Cindy Crawford, Donovan McNabb, and Serena Williams may be more effective for promotions of products in the United States than in other countries. Brad Pitt is very popular in Asia because of the distribution of his films. Another reason promotions of a particular product vary across countries is that each country's government has its own rules and restrictions. A commercial that is acceptable in one country may be restricted in another country. The United Kingdom prohibits commercials from directly comparing one product with a competing product. Therefore, commercials that compared Pepsi with Coca-Cola had to be revised to compare Pepsi against Brand X.

Given the different perceptions of products by consumers across countries and different government regulations, a firm may have to create a different promotion for a particular product in each country where the product is sold. Just as firms create products that are tailored to the unique characteristics of consumers in a specific country, they should also promote products in a manner that appeals to specific consumers.

News Releases

news release
a brief written announcement about a firm provided by that firm to the media

A **news release** is a brief written announcement about a firm provided by that firm to the media. It enables the firm to update the public about its products or operations. It may also be used to clarify information in response to false rumors that could adversely affect the firm's reputation. The news release may include the name and phone number of an employee who can provide more details if desired by the media. There is no charge for providing a news release, but the firm incurs an indirect cost for hiring employees to promote news releases. Also, there is no guarantee that a news release will be publicized by the media.

Press Conferences

press conference
an oral announcement about a firm provided by that firm to the media

A **press conference** is an oral announcement about a firm provided by that firm to the media. Like a news release, a press conference may be intended to enhance the firm's image or to eliminate any adverse effects caused by false rumors. A press conference is more personal than a news release because an employee of the firm makes the announcement directly to the media and may even be willing to answer questions from the media. There is no charge for organizing a press conference, but there is an indirect cost of hiring employees to perform the necessary tasks.

Decision Making

Taking Advantage of Public Relations

The manner in which a firm should use public relations is dependent on its specific characteristics. To illustrate, recall that Karma Coffee House wants to attract businesspeople who commute to downtown Boston. Jen Allen, Karma's owner, decides to sponsor a coffee-tasting event that is specifically for the local businesses. She sets up a temporary display near each office building where people can sample a number of new coffee flavors. In this way, she ensures that the workers in each building see that they can sample free coffee before they enter their building. Each person who samples the coffee receives a brochure with information about Karma Coffee House.

1. What benefit does this form of public relations provide to Karma Coffee House that it would not obtain from advertising?

2. Why might the free coffee tasting be a more effective form of public relations for Karma Coffee House than sponsoring a run or some other event?

ANSWERS: 1. The public relations event allows people in the target market to sample coffee made by Karma Coffee House, which is a step beyond just advertising the coffee house. 2. This public relations event is focused on sampling the product that represents Karma Coffee House. It is also focused on the people in the target market.

Explain how firms select the optimal mix of promotions to use.

Determining the Optimal Promotion Mix

Exhibit 14.5 provides a brief summary of the various promotion methods. Each method has its own advantages and disadvantages, so no single method is ideal for all products. Firms must decide whether to use advertising, personal selling, sales promotion, publicity, or some mix of these promotion methods to promote their products. Firms must consider the characteristics of their target market and their promotion budget when determining the optimal promotion mix, as explained next.

Target Market

If a firm's target market is made up of a wide variety of customers throughout a specific region, it may use advertising to promote its product. If a firm produces a surgical device for a target market of hospital surgeons, it may consider using some advertising to make surgeons aware of the device, along with personal selling to explain how the device is used. If the target market is made up of consumers on tight budgets (such as retired people), the firm may use sales promotion methods such as coupons or rebates.

Any of these promotion methods may be complemented with public relations such as sponsoring a special event for consumers who are in the

Exhibit 14.5

Summary of Methods That Make Up the Promotion Mix

Promotion Method	Advantages	Disadvantages
Advertising	Reaches a large number of customers.	Can be expensive; is not personalized.
Personal selling	Provides personalized attention.	Difficult to reach a large number of customers.
Sales promotion	Offers various incentives for consumers to purchase products.	May not reach as many consumers as advertising.
Public relations	Inexpensive method of enhancing the image of the firm or its products.	Provides only a limited amount of promotion because news releases and press conferences may not always be covered by the media.

target market for the product. For example, to promote its female athletic shoes, Reebok sponsored a Sports Training Challenge for female high school athletes.

Firms typically attempt to direct their promotion to the target market. Miller Brewing, Anheuser-Busch, and other beer producers run commercials during sports events and direct the ads at a target market of men. Women's clothing ads are placed in fashion magazines and directed at a target market of women. Procter & Gamble promotes its household products on television shows watched by women because women generally make most of the household purchases.

When firms direct their promotion directly at the target market, they provide information to the consumers who would most likely purchase the products. Consumers become aware of the product without hearing about it from a retailer. They may then request the product from retailers, who in turn request it from wholesalers or producers. This strategy is called a **pull strategy,** because the product is pulled through the distribution channel as a result of consumer demand. For example, suppose that a firm develops a new type of DVD player and advertises it to consumers. As consumers become aware of the product, their demand at retail outlets pulls the product through the distribution channel.

Some producers direct their promotion at wholesalers or retailers instead of their target market. When producers promote their products to wholesalers or retailers, their promotion effort is called a **push strategy.** Wholesalers promote the product to retailers, who in turn promote it to consumers. Thus, the product is pushed through the distribution channel. For example, assume that a manufacturer of a new DVD player has representatives demonstrate its advantages to all wholesalers. The wholesalers then promote the DVD player to retailers so that they can inform consumers. The difference between a push strategy and a pull strategy is illustrated in Exhibit 14.6. Personal selling is commonly used to apply a push strategy.

Surveying the Target Market   Marketing research can enhance a firm's promotion decisions by determining the types of promotions that are favorably received by the target market of concern. For example, a firm that sells

pull strategy
firms direct their promotion directly at the target market, and consumers in turn request the product from wholesalers or producers

push strategy
producers direct their promotion of a product at wholesalers or retailers, who in turn promote it to consumers

Exhibit 14.6

Comparison of Pull and Push Strategies

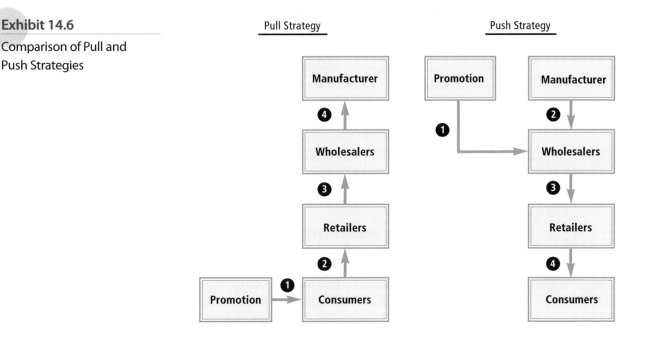

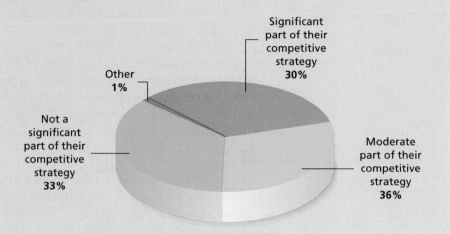

clothing to teenagers may survey a sample of teenagers for feedback on various promotions that it may offer. The firm will implement the promotion strategy that is likely to result in the highest level of sales (assuming each promotion strategy has the same cost), based on the feedback from the teenagers surveyed.

Promotion Budget

promotion budget
the amount of funds that have been set aside to pay for all promotion methods over a specified period

A **promotion budget** is the amount of funds that have been set aside to pay for all promotion methods over a specified period. Firms may establish a promotion budget for each product that they produce. The budget may be large if the firm believes that promotion will have a major effect on sales or is necessary to prevent a substantial decline in sales. If the promotion budget for a specific product is small, advertising on television or in widely distributed magazines may not be possible. The firm may have to rely on inexpensive advertising (such as local newspapers) and inexpensive sales promotion methods (such as displays). Perhaps no single type of promotion will be as effective by itself.

The promotion budget varies substantially across firms and may even vary for each firm's product line over time. The promotion budget for a specific product is influenced by the following characteristics:

▶ Phase of the product life cycle

▶ Competition

▶ Economic conditions

Phase of the Product Life Cycle   Products that are just being introduced to the market will require more promotions to inform customers about the products. Products that are in the growth phase are promoted to inform and remind customers. Products in the maturity or decline phases of the life cycle may not require as much promotion. Nevertheless, they may still need some promotion to remind customers and retain their market share. The amount

Exhibit 14.7

Amount of Promotion Used throughout the Product's Life Cycle

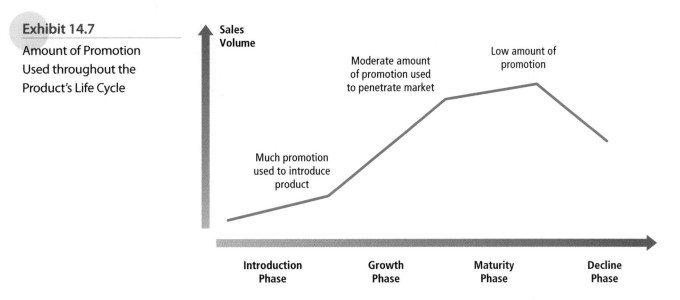

of promotion typically used for different phases of the life cycle is shown in Exhibit 14.7. Firms that revise their products in an effort to extend the life cycle may use a large amount of promotion even in the maturity phase.

Competition   A firm whose competitors frequently advertise may feel compelled to match their advertising with its own promotional campaign. This is a defensive strategy. As this illustrates, firms use advertising not only as an aggressive strategy to increase market share but also as a defensive strategy to retain existing market share.

Economic Conditions   Firms respond in different ways to favorable economic conditions. Some firms may increase their promotion because they can better afford it. Others will cut back, expecting the strong economy to carry their products. In a stagnant economy, firms may attempt to heavily promote their products in an attempt to maintain demand.

Evaluating and Revising a Firm's Promotions

Firms recognize that marketing can have a major impact on sales, but they also want to make sure that their promotion efforts are worth the cost. They view marketing as an investment, not just an expense, and they want to see the results of that investment. Thus, an important part of promotions involves determining whether the promotion strategy was successful. Many companies, including Home Depot, Procter & Gamble, Gillette, and Kraft Foods, are working to make their marketing strategies more accountable. They are attempting to determine the precise impact of their promotions so that they can decide whether to use similar promotions in the future. For example, DaimlerChrysler has shifted some of its promotions to special events so that it can monitor the responses of the potential customers who were targeted during the events. Some websites that allow Internet advertising are capable of determining how many times customers clicked on an ad for more details or ordered products online (when available) in response to an ad.

If a firm establishes measurable objectives at the time of the promotion, it can assess whether the objectives were achieved. For example, consider a strategy that is intended to increase revenue by 10 percent over the next year. Once the year is over, the firm can compare the actual revenue with the revenue goal to determine whether the goal was achieved. This type

Cross Functional Teamwork

Interaction between Promotion Decisions and Other Business Decisions

When marketing managers make promotion decisions, they must interact with other managers of the firm. The amount of promotion that is used for a particular product will influence demand for that product. If marketing managers anticipate a larger demand for the product in response to new promotion strategies, they must inform the production department. The production managers must be aware of the anticipated demand so that they can produce a sufficient volume of products. Promotions that increase demand will increase sales only if the firm produces a larger volume in anticipation of the larger demand. Otherwise, the firm will experience shortages, and customers who are unable to purchase the product may purchase it from a competitor. In some cases, production may already be at full capacity, which means that the promotion may not be worthwhile until the manufacturing process can be revised to increase capacity.

Marketing managers also interact with financial managers about promotion decisions for the following reasons. First, when marketing managers estimate the costs of a specific promotion and the extra revenue that will be generated over time as a result of that promotion, they may rely on financial managers to assess whether the promotion will provide an adequate return to make it worthwhile to the firm. Second, when marketing managers decide to implement large promotions, they may need a substantial amount of funds; they can inform the financial managers, who may determine the best method to obtain those funds. Thus, marketing managers rely on input from both the production managers and the financial managers when making their promotion decisions.

Victoria's Secret relies on models to do promotional tours in which they promote Victoria Secret products.

GETTY IMAGES

of comparison can be useful for determining whether various promotion strategies are successful over time.

If the objectives of the promotion strategy are not accomplished, the firm may revise its strategy. Sometimes a marketing plan fails because the objectives were overly optimistic. In this situation, the firm may need to revise its objectives rather than its strategies. Firms must also recognize that changes in other conditions may affect revenue. For example, poor economic conditions may cause a firm's revenue to be less than the goal established even if the promotion strategy was effective.

Sometimes a firm may need to change its promotion mix. If consumer characteristics or market conditions change, the firm may revise its promotion mix to give more prominence to some strategies and less to others.

Decision Making

Revising the Promotion Mix over Time

To illustrate how the promotion mix may change over time, reconsider the case of Karma Coffee House. The initial goal of Jen Allen, the owner, was simply to make her target market (local businesspeople) aware of Karma's existence. Thus, the promotion mix included advertising brochures, coupons, and public relations events that would create awareness. As time passes, Karma will face other types of challenges, such as making sure that its customer are continually satisfied. Consumer habits and tastes can change over time. In addition, other coffee houses may open nearby, creating more intense competition. Karma Coffee House may still need promotion strategies, but for different reasons than when it opened. If it begins to lose some of its customers, it may need to advertise that it is offering new coffee flavors or new snacks.

1. If the target market of Karma Coffee House changes from young local businesspeople to older local businesspeople, how will this affect its promotion mix?

2. If the target market of Karma Coffee House changes from local businesspeople to local households (people who live nearby), how will this affect its promotion mix?

ANSWERS: 1. Karma will need to determine whether the older businesspeople prefer different flavors of coffee. It will then use promotion to focus on the coffee or services desired by that target market. 2. It will need to determine whether the local households prefer different flavors of coffee. It will then use promotion to focus on the coffee or services desired by that target market.

COLLEGE HEALTH CLUB: PROMOTION AT CHC

As Sue Kramer develops her business plan for College Health Club (CHC), she must decide on the mix of different strategies that she will use to promote CHC. She decides to use a promotion mix consisting of (1) advertising through the Texas College newspaper, (2) coupons for vitamin supplements and a free day pass inserted in the Texas College newspaper, and (3) personal selling through monthly presentations about exercise and health to students on campus. All three parts of her promotion mix are focused on the students at the college, who are CHC's target market.

Sue has decided to advertise in the Texas College newspaper because she needs to reach a large number of potential members without spending too much money. Sue ruled out magazines, local television, radio, and the Internet because they are too expensive. She did not think that telemarketing, outdoor ads, transportation ads, or specialty ads would attract many members. Sue has decided that advertising in the college's newspaper is the easiest way to reach her target market. This weekly newspaper is free to students, and most students read it or at least skim it. Sue has decided on an ad that takes up one-quarter of a page and plans to run it for the next 10 weeks. Then she will determine the impact the ad has had on memberships and decide whether to continue running it.

To determine whether her promotion mix is effective, Sue also plans to monitor how the number of memberships changes after implementing her promotion mix. She realizes, however, that memberships may increase for reasons other than the promotion strategies. Therefore, she has included a question on the membership application asking what caused the applicant to purchase a membership. The choices are (1) referral from a friend, (2) advertising in the student newspaper, (3) coupons in the student newspaper, (4) the exercise and health presentations on campus, or (5) other. She can determine from the membership applications which promotion strategies are attracting the most members. This information can help her decide how to use her promotion budget in the future.

Summary

1 Promotional efforts can increase sales or at least prevent a decrease in sales because the brand name stays in the consumer's mind, consumers are informed about the product's advantages, and the product's perceived credibility may be enhanced.

2 The key forms of advertising are newspapers, magazines, radio, television, the Internet, e-mail, direct mail, telemarketing, outdoor ads, transportation ads, and specialty ads.

3 The main steps involved in personal selling are to

▶ identify the target market,

▶ contact potential customers,

▶ make the sales presentation,

▶ answer questions,

▶ close the sale, and

▶ follow up.

4 The most common sales promotion methods include

▶ rebates, in which firms give refunds directly to consumers after the product is purchased;

▶ coupons, which allow products to be sold to specific consumers at discounted prices;

▶ sampling, in which consumers receive free samples of products;

▶ displays, in which products are placed in prominent areas of stores; and

▶ premiums, in which gifts or prizes are provided free to consumers who purchase a specific product.

5 Firms can use public relations to enhance a product's or a firm's image. The most common types of public relations strategies are

▶ special events, which can be sponsored by a firm to promote a specific product;

▶ news releases, which are brief written announcements about a firm provided by the firm to the media; and

▶ press conferences, which are oral announcements about a firm provided by that firm to the media.

6 When a firm selects the optimal promotion mix to use for promoting a product, it considers the

▶ target market, so that it can use a promotion method that properly reaches that target market; and

▶ promotion budget, since only those promotion methods that are affordable can be considered.

How the Chapter Concepts Affect Business Performance

A firm's decisions regarding the promotion concepts summarized here affect its performance. The firm's decision regarding the promotion mix can have a major effect on the size of the market that it reaches and therefore can influence its revenue. This decision also influences the firm's expenses associated with promotion. The specific types of advertising used by the firm affect the demand for its products and the advertising expenses it incurs. Decisions regarding the firm's personal selling and public relations also affect the demand for its products and therefore its revenue.

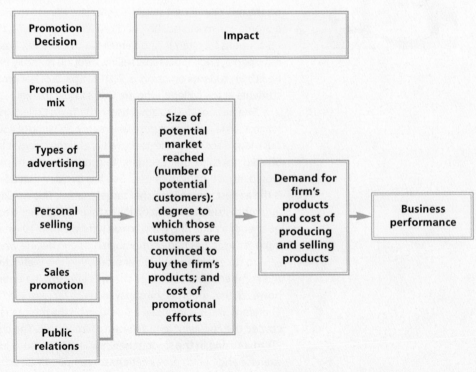

Key Terms

advertising   529
brand advertising   529
brand loyalty   540
comparative advertising   529
coupons   539
industry advertising   529
infomercials   531
institutional advertising   529

news release   543
personal selling   535
premium   541
press conference   543
promotion   527
promotion budget   546
promotion mix   528
public relations   542

pull strategy   545
push strategy   545
rebate   539
reminder advertising   529
sales manager   538
sales promotion   539
sampling   540
telemarketing   533

Review & Critical Thinking Questions

1. How can promotion be used when introducing a new product?

2. What is the promotion mix? List and briefly describe the four methods of promotion.

3. You are planning to start a florist business in your hometown. Would you use media advertising, nonmedia advertising, or both? Why?

4. Why do you think newspaper publishers use telemarketing to develop a customer base?

5. Briefly summarize the steps involved in personal selling.

6. Discuss the types of sales promotion strategies that a donut shop would most likely utilize.

7. Define public relations and explain the role it would play in the law enforcement department of a major city.

8. Compare the pull strategy with the push strategy associated with promotion.

9. Discuss the different types of promotion that would be utilized throughout the product life cycle for a product or service.

10. How do economic conditions affect a firm's promotion budget?

11. What are the skills a good sales manager should possess?

12. Consider a television ad for toothpaste that claims that a particular brand outperforms rival toothpastes in preventing cavities. What kind of advertising is being used?

13. Assume that you are the sales manager of a neighborhood grocery store. What form of advertising would likely work best for your store?

14. Why might an advertising strategy that uses e-mail to reach customers fail?

15. Assume that you are the sales representative for a candy company. How might you use sampling as a promotional strategy?

16. McDonald's provides a free toy for children with every Happy Meal purchase. What kind of sales promotion strategy is McDonald's using?

17. The sales manager of a firm decides to contribute to a walk to raise money for breast cancer research. What kind of public relations effort is the firm using?

18. Why might infomercials be effective? Why might they not be effective?

19. Why might firms review the promotion budget after a particular promotion strategy has been put in place?

20. Why might telemarketing fail as a marketing strategy?

Discussion Questions

1. As a sales manager in a new automobile dealership, what role would you play in the company, and what would your responsibilities be?

2. You are the owner of a minimart convenience store. What processes could you utilize to identify your target market?

3. You are a salesperson in an office supply business. Why is it important to be persistent and utilize follow-up visits with your customers?

4. Identify and explain the different types of promotion methods in the following examples:

   a. Tiger Woods plays golf wearing Nike apparel.

   b. A local supermarket introduces a scratch-and-win ticket.

   c. Assume that you are a college graduate. Your local college calls you, asking you to make a donation for its capital funding program.

5. How can a firm use the Internet to identify its target market? How can it use the Internet to promote its products?

6. Discuss the promotion strategies that would be utilized by a manufacturer in promoting the following brands. Indicate whether the strategy focuses on product positioning or image building.

   a. Corvette convertible

   b. Dove facial soap

   c. Craftsman tools

   d. Mountain Dew soft drink

7. Think of a recent television ad that you recently saw. Which ad comes to mind first? Was the ad effective? Did it make you want to buy the product being advertised?

8. Assume that you are the manager of a company that sells books that can be downloaded from the Internet. Why is it important for your company to have a high ranking in search engines? What impact will higher visibility have on the firm? Would it be difficult to get a high search engine ranking for a company that sells e-books?

9. What are some ways for companies to use public relations to promote their stock to investors? How can firms use the Internet and television ads to reach people who might be potential investors?

10. Assume you are the marketing manager of a chewing gum producer. How can you use marketing research to identify the most effective advertising strategy? How can you use surveys to generate information on customer perception of the product?

IT'S YOUR DECISION: PROMOTION DECISIONS AT CHC

1. How could Sue Kramer, the president of CHC, use direct-mail advertising to focus specifically on CHC's target market?

2. How could Sue use personal selling to promote CHC?

3. How could Sue use premiums to promote CHC?

4. If Sue is planning a major promotion strategy that will attract additional members, why must she first consider the size of CHC's facilities?

5. Recall that Sue expects total expenses of $142,000 in CHC's first year. She will set the membership fee at $500 and expects to attract 300 members in the first year. Sue is considering a promotion involving coupons inserted in the school newspaper. Determine CHC's earnings based on the following coupon strategies over the first year:

If CHC Provides a Discount Coupon of:	The Expected Number of Memberships Would Be:	CHC's Earnings before Taxes in the First Year Would Be:
$5	302	_____
10	303	_____
20	310	_____
30	320	_____

Which discount coupon strategy would you use? Explain.

6. A health club differs from manufacturing firms in that it produces a service rather than products. Explain why the promotion policy of a service firm (such as CHC) is different from that of a manufacturing firm.

Investing in a Business

Using the annual report of the firm in which you would like to invest, complete the following:

Questions

1. How does the firm promote its products? Does it use the media to promote its products? Provide details.

2. Does the firm rely heavily on promotion to sell its products? How much money has it allocated toward its promotion budget this year?

3. In reviewing the key terms in this chapter, which do you think could apply to promoting your company's products?

4. Explain how the business uses technology to promote its products over the Internet. Does it provide rebates to customers using the website to purchase products? What do you find most appealing about the firm's website? What do you find least appealing?

5. Go to http://hoovers.com and locate the NEWS SEARCH. Type in the name of the firm in the space provided, and review the recent news stories about the firm. Summarize any (at least one) recent news story about the firm that applies to one or more of the key concepts in this chapter.

Case: Promoting Products on the Internet

Ken Brabec has created a DVD, "How to Improve Your Tennis Game," by compiling tips on specific aspects of the game from several tennis pros around the country. He would like to sell the DVD to DVD/video stores, but he realizes that these stores normally deal with large broadcasting and movie companies instead of individuals.

Ken decides that he will try to market the DVDs to people directly. He can easily mail a DVD to anyone who orders one, but he needs to decide how to promote the DVD. Since he can easily mail DVDs to customers, he wants to promote his DVD throughout the United States. He first considers advertising in various tennis magazines, but he cannot afford the fee they charge for even a single ad. Ken's funds are limited, and he is not willing to risk all of his money on a few advertisements. Consequently, he decides to advertise his DVD on various websites, where the advertising fees are relatively low. He still needs to decide the best way to advertise over the Internet, however.

Questions

1. What types of websites should Ken use to advertise his tennis DVD?

2. Ken plans to advertise initially on five different websites. He may continue ads on the websites that generate the most sales of his DVDs. How can Ken determine which of his ads on the Internet are receiving the most attention?

3. Ken is trying to decide whether the promotion on the website should provide an order form for customers to send in. This method would be relatively inexpensive. Alternatively, he could allow customers to order the DVD over the Internet. This method is more expensive. Is there any benefit to allowing customers to order the DVD over the Internet using a credit card?

Video Case: Distribution Promotion Decisions at Oxygen

Oxygen is a full-service communications company that does communications, advertising, public relations, and plan-and-buy media for its clients. It also has a TV network with Internet operations. Oxygen has a strategic branding approach for everything it does. Its divisions work together to establish the brand. Its managers argue that a brand is a personality. Brands can create thoughts, feelings, and communications regarding the perception of a product. Oxygen's products in branding are targeted at women.

Television is an important part of Oxygen's marketing mix. It ran a woman-centered ad during the Superbowl that generated a great deal of interest in the company. Oxygen also has a grassroots program that created a mobile demo unit so that people could interface with potential customers. Four pavilions were set up in different markets around the country to raise the company's profile. The company also worked with local universities to find out what women want in their media brands. Finally, Oxygen became involved in com-

munity service geared toward women in local markets. More information about Oxygen can be found at http://www.oxygen.com.

Questions

1. Why does Oxygen's management argue that the company has to make sure it is communicating consistently across divisions?
2. How did Oxygen determine the market of women?
3. How does Oxygen relate to women?
4. How does Oxygen use the Internet to promote its brand?
5. Why did women respond positively to the Superbowl ad campaign?
6. How did Oxygen's strategy to get cable coverage differ from the strategy used by other networks?

Internet Applications

1. http://www.prsa.org

What is public relations? What kinds of information are available at this website? Click on "About PRSA" and "Member Benefits." What kinds of benefits are available from the Public Relations Society of America?

2. http://www.webuildpages.com

What is Internet marketing? What is search engine optimization? How can companies use the Internet to pro-

mote their products? Why is it important to direct traffic to a company's website?

3. http://www.superbowl-ads.com

What kinds of information are available on this website? What is the most recent news on advertising strategies used by U.S. firms? Click on *USA Today*'s "Ad Meter." What does the site say about the effectiveness of recent ads?

Dell's Secret to Success

Go to http://www.reportgallery.com and review Dell's most recent annual report. Also, go to Dell's website (http://www.dell.com) and in the section "about Dell," review the background material about Dell that relates to this chapter.

Questions

1. Search for any comments that Dell makes about the promotion of its products. Describe Dell's marketing.

2. Notice that Dell normally does not focus its annual report on marketing. Dell does not advertise its products excessively. Dell appears to be focused on demonstrating quality rather than promoting itself. Does this strategy make sense?

3. Would Dell's marketing strategy be effective for a new firm?

In-Text Study Guide

Answers are in Appendix C at the back of book.

True or False

1. Comparative advertising is intended to enhance the image of a firm without focusing on a particular product.

2. The promotion mix is the combination of promotion methods that a firm uses to increase the acceptance of its products.

3. The Internet, magazines, direct mail, and television are all forms of advertising.

4. A key to successful selling is the follow-up service to customers provided by salespeople.

5. Television advertising is the most widely used form of personal selling for medium and large businesses.

6. Rebates and coupons are used to offer a price discount from retailers to their customers.

7. A firm using a push strategy will aim its promotional message directly at the target market customers.

8. Public relations is one of the most expensive forms of sales promotion.

9. One factor that will influence the size of the promotion budget for a product is the phase of the product in the product life cycle.

10. Sales managers perform the daily tasks of selling the product.

Multiple Choice

11. Even if a firm's product is properly produced, priced, and distributed, it still needs to be:
    a) manufactured.
    b) inspected.
    c) graded.
    d) promoted.
    e) market tested.

12. All of the following are methods of promotion except:
    a) target marketing.
    b) personal selling.
    c) advertising.
    d) sales promotion.
    e) public relations.

13. The act of informing or reminding consumers about a specific product or brand is referred to as:
    a) personal selling.
    b) production.
    c) finance.
    d) promotion.
    e) research and development.

14. Which of the following promotion strategies is a nonpersonal sales promotion aimed at a large number of consumers?
    a) advertising
    b) public relations
    c) telemarketing
    d) retail selling
    e) mega-marketing

15. A nonpersonal sales presentation about a specific brand is:
    a) institutional advertising.
    b) personal selling.
    c) brand advertising.
    d) comparative advertising.
    e) reminder advertising.

16. The type of advertising that is used for grocery products such as cereal, peanut butter, and dog food is:
    a) institutional advertising.
    b) reminder advertising.
    c) the push strategy.
    d) industry advertising.
    e) public relations advertising.

In-Text Study Guide

Answers are in Appendix C at the back of book.

17. Ads that show consumers choosing between Pepsi and Coca-Cola are examples of _____ advertising.
    a) comparative
    b) institutional
    c) industry
    d) reminder
    e) generic

18. All of the following are forms of advertising except:
    a) direct mail.
    b) outdoor ads.
    c) personal selling.
    d) online banner ads.
    e) transportation ads.

19. Ads that are televised separately rather than within a show are called:
    a) commercials.
    b) specialty ads.
    c) infomercials.
    d) institutional ads.
    e) direct-mail ads.

20. All of the following are advantages of Internet advertising except:
    a) direct, personal contact with the potential consumer.
    b) low cost.
    c) fees can be based on the number of customer orders.
    d) generates high levels of response.
    e) can create product awareness.

21. The use of the telephone for promoting and selling products is known as:
    a) telepromotion.
    b) telemarketing.
    c) online sales promotion.
    d) telecommunication mix.
    e) annoying phone calls.

22. Salespeople generally perform all of the following steps except:
    a) identify the target market.
    b) follow up.
    c) contact potential customers.
    d) make the sales presentation.
    e) advertising.

23. A salesperson who has just completed an effective sales presentation should attempt to:
    a) analyze the market.
    b) win at all costs.
    c) close the sale.
    d) exploit the customer.
    e) maximize sales returns and allowances.

24. A visual method that retail stores use in promoting particular products is a:
    a) display.
    b) rebate.
    c) coupon.
    d) premium.
    e) market.

25. The promotion strategy of sampling is most often used to:
    a) provide customers with a premium as an incentive to purchase more of the product.
    b) introduce new products.
    c) give customers a discount if a larger quantity is purchased.
    d) serve as a reminder for former customers to buy the product again.
    e) unload surplus inventory.

In-Text Study Guide

26. The main, immediate goal of public relations is to:
    a) remind customers of the firm's existence.
    b) compare the firm's brand to a competitor's brand.
    c) identify the firm's target market.
    d) enhance the image of the firm.
    e) increase sales.

27. Which of the following sales promotion strategies provides a gift or prize to consumers who purchase a specific product?
    a) pull
    b) push
    c) sampling
    d) rebates
    e) premiums

28. When firms promote products, they highlight the advantages over all other products. They emphasize the product's:
    a) publicity.
    b) features.
    c) sales promotion.
    d) labeling.
    e) life cycle.

29. Firms that hire _____ to promote products must consider the perceptions of the consumers in each country.
    a) accountants
    b) economists
    c) suppliers
    d) clients
    e) celebrities

30. Which of the following is a public relations strategy in which an organization provides the media with a written announcement?
    a) special events
    b) press conference
    c) concert sponsorship
    d) direct mail
    e) news release

31. If a firm's target market is made up of a wide variety of customers throughout a specific region, it would likely use _____ to promote its product.
    a) personal selling
    b) advertising
    c) door-to-door sales
    d) one-on-one communication
    e) target marketing

32. When producers promote their products to wholesalers or retailers, their promotion effort is called a:
    a) push strategy.
    b) premium price strategy.
    c) sales promotion.
    d) market segmentation.
    e) pull strategy.

33. Which of the following is a strategy where firms focus their promotional messages on the target market customers, who in turn request the product from wholesalers or producers?
    a) push
    b) co-branding
    c) product life cycle
    d) sponsorship
    e) pull

In-Text Study Guide

Answers are in Appendix C at the back of book.

34. The promotion budget varies substantially across firms and may even vary for each firm's product line over time. Its characteristics are influenced by all of the following except:
    a) size of human resource department.
    b) competition.
    c) phase of the product life cycle.
    d) economic conditions.

35. If marketing managers anticipate a larger demand for a product in response to new promotion strategies, they must inform their:
    a) labor union.
    b) stockholders.
    c) creditors.
    d) production department.
    e) appropriate government agency.

Marketing

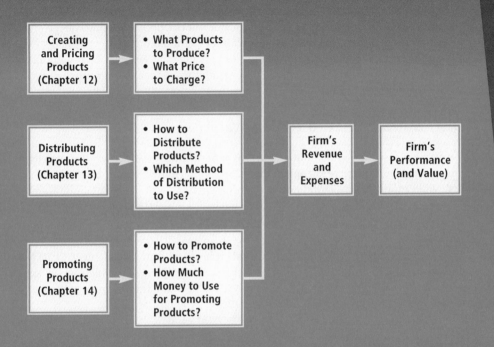

Developing the Marketing Plan for Campus.com

Product Line and Target Market (related to Chapter 12)

In your business plan for Campus.com, suggest how the firm could expand its product line. That is, what other services could it offer to its customers while still continuing its main type of business? How could it expand its target market?

Pricing (related to Chapter 12)

Campus.com will charge a price per standard service offered (information on one college). What factors should be considered when determining the price to be charged? The initial idea was to charge $1 per request (for information about one college provided to one customer). In your business plan for Campus.com, state your plans for pricing the service. You do not need to use the pricing of $1 per request if you think you have a better pricing policy. If you plan to offer some type of quantity discount, specify that within your business plan.

Distribution (related to Chapter 13)

In your business plan, explain how Campus.com distributes its service. If some customers cannot obtain a hard copy of the information (if their printer is not working), how will Campus.com distribute its services to them?

Promotion (related to Chapter 14)

In your business plan for Campus.com, explain how the firm should advertise its services. Should it focus on high school students, on the parents of the high school students, or on both target markets? Explain. Where should Campus.com advertise its services, assuming it wants to limit its advertising expenditures?

Communication and Teamwork

You (or your team) may be asked by your instructor to hand in and/or present the part of your business plan that relates to this part of the text.

Integrative Video Case: Pricing Strategy at World Gym

World Gym is one of America's most reputable fitness organizations. Founded in 1989, World Gym Showcase Square's original strategy was to target a broad market ranging from experienced bodybuilders to novice gym users. The owners established their facilities in high-traffic areas with little competition. When World Gym was founded, there was a strong demand for medium-priced fitness facilities, but only a few existed. World Gym originally set a low price to induce consumers to try its facilities and remain as customers. The strategy was far more successful than the owners anticipated. In fact, the marketing campaign was so successful that World Gym was able to raise its prices and become a price leader. Soon, however, competitors such as Gold's Gym began to enter the market and located their facilities near World Gym. When World Gym's owners recognized that they were losing customers to the new competitors, they decided to lower membership prices in response. Thus, World Gym changes its pricing strategy in response to the changing business environment.

Today, World Gym has expanded across the United States and into several other countries. It uses its website to promote its services by providing information to potential and existing customers. The website includes a store locator as well as information on prices, fitness classes, and equipment. You can find more information on World Gym at http://www.worldgym.com/.

Questions

1. How did World Gym originally market its products to potential gym customers?
2. How has World Gym used its pricing strategy to lure customers from competing fitness facilities?
3. How has World Gym responded to competition and changes in the market environment?
4. How does World Gym use the Internet to promote its services?

The Stock Market Game

Check the performance of your stock.

Check Your Performance

1. What is the value of your stock investment today?
2. What is your return on your investment?
3. How did your return compare to those of other students? (This comparison tells you whether your stock's performance is relatively high or low.)

Explaining Your Stock Performance

Stock prices are frequently influenced by changes in the firm's marketing strategies, including new products, pricing, or promotion strategies. A stock's price may increase if the firm institutes new marketing strategies and investors expect the changes to improve its performance. A stock's price can also decline if the marketing strategies are expected to reduce the firm's performance. Review the latest news about your stock.

1. Determine how your stock's price was affected (since you purchased it) by changes in the firm's marketing strategies (the main topic in this part of the text).
2. Identify the specific type of marketing policies that caused the stock price to change.
3. Did the stock price increase or decrease in response to the announcement of new marketing policies?

Running Your Own Business

1. Describe in detail how the product you plan to produce is different from those offered by competitors. Identify any advantages of your product over those of the competition.
2. Explain how the pricing of your product will be determined. Explain how your product's price will compare with prices of competing products.
3. Can the unique features of your product be protected from competitors?
4. Describe how your business will distribute the product to customers.

5 Explain whether the cost of distributing your product will be affected substantially if there is a large increase in the price of gasoline or in postal rates.

6 Describe how your business will promote its product. Will it use media to advertise? If so, how?

7 Estimate the amount of money that will be allocated for promotion during the first year.

8 Would coupons or rebates be an effective promotion method for your product? Why or why not?

9 How could your firm use public relations to promote your company or product?

10 How could your firm use the Internet (or other technology) to promote your company or product?

Your Career in Business: *Pursuing a Major and a Career in Marketing*

If you are very interested in the topics covered in this section, you may want to consider a major in marketing. Some of the more common courses taken by marketing majors are summarized here.

Common Courses for Marketing Majors

▶ *Advertising*—Focuses on methods of promoting products, alternative types of advertising, the use of the media for advertising, and the role of advertising agencies.

▶ *Marketing Environment*—Discusses the impact of social, technological, and other environmental conditions on marketing decisions and looks at how marketing decisions have changed in response to changes in the marketing environment.

▶ *Distribution Systems*—Examines the role of inventory maintenance for distribution, channels of distribution, and transportation methods used for distribution.

▶ *Promotional Management*—Examines how consumers make purchasing decisions, what factors drive their decisions, and how firms can capitalize on this information.

▶ *Marketing Research*—Focuses on methods of assessing consumer purchases and the effects of marketing strategies; discusses gathering data, analysis, and deriving implications from the analysis.

▶ *Marketing Strategy*—Explains how marketing concepts can be applied to solve marketing problems and make marketing decisions.

▶ *Services Marketing*—Describes the application of marketing strategy to services.

▶ *Marketing Planning*—Focuses on the process of developing a marketing plan, including the creation of a product, the identification of a target market, and the creation of a structure for distribution and promotion.

▶ *Psychology courses*—Specifically, those courses that explain human behavior as related to consumption, preferences, and needs.

Careers in Marketing

Information about job positions, salaries, and careers for students who major in marketing can be found at the following websites:

▶ Job position websites:

http://jobsearch.monster.com   Advertising, marketing, public relations, retail, wholesale, sales, transportation, warehousing

http://careers.yahoo.com   Advertising, public relations, marketing, retail, transportation, logistics

▶ Salary website:

http://collegejournal.com/salarydata   Advertising, marketing, public relations, food processing, retailing, sales

Part VI
Financial Management